WHEN THEORIES TOUCH

CIPS Series on The Boundaries of Psychoanalysis
Series Editor: Meg Beaudoin, PhD, FIPA

CIPS
CONFEDERATION OF INDEPENDENT PSYCHOANALYTIC SOCIETIES
www.cipsusa.org

The Confederation of Independent Psychoanalytic Societies (CIPS) is the national professional association for the independent component societies of the International Psychoanalytical Association (IPA) in the USA. CIPS also hosts the Direct Member Society for psychoanalysts belonging to other IPA societies. Our members represent a wide spectrum of psychoanalytic perspectives as well as a diversity of academic backgrounds. The CIPS Book Series, The Boundaries of Psychoanalysis, represents the intellectual activity of our community. The volumes explore the internal and external boundaries of psychoanalysis, examining the interrelationships between various psychoanalytic theoretical and clinical perspectives as well as between psychoanalysis and other disciplines.

WHEN THEORIES TOUCH
A Historical and Theoretical Integration of Psychoanalytic Thought

Steven J. Ellman

LONDON AND NEW YORK

First published 2010 by Karnac Books Ltd.

Published 2018 by Routledge
2 Park Square, Milton Park, Abingdon, Oxon OX14 4RN
52 Vanderbilt Avenue, New York, NY 10017

Routledge is an imprint of the Taylor & Francis Group, an informa business

Copyright © 2010 Steven J. Ellman

The right of Steven J. Ellman to be identified as the author of this work has been asserted in accordance with §§ 77 and 78 of the Copyright Design and Patents Act 1988.

All rights reserved. No part of this book may be reprinted or reproduced or utilised in any form or by any electronic, mechanical, or other means, now known or hereafter invented, including photocopying and recording, or in any information storage or retrieval system, without permission in writing from the publishers.

Notice:
Product or corporate names may be trademarks or registered trademarks, and are used only for identification and explanation without intent to infringe.

British Library Cataloguing in Publication Data

A C.I.P. for this book is available from the British Library

ISBN 13: 978-1-85575-868-1 (pbk)

Edited, designed and produced by The Studio Publishing Services Ltd

CONTENTS

BRIEF HISTORY AND ACKNOWLEDGEMENTS	ix
ABOUT THE AUTHOR	xi
SERIES EDITOR'S PREFACE	xiii
PREFACE	xvii
PART I: FREUD CHAPTERS	1

CHAPTER ONE
Freud's heroic era: the first ten years   3

CHAPTER TWO
The psychoanalytic era begins: 27
dream theory–psycho-sexuality

CHAPTER THREE
Freud's object relations era: the metapsychological papers   83

CHAPTER FOUR
The structural model   131

PART II: MAJOR POST-FREUDIAN THEORISTS 167

CHAPTER FIVE
The new ego psychology:
Anna Freud and Heinz Hartmann 169

CHAPTER SIX
The Kleinian revolution 215

CHAPTER SEVEN
The controversial discussions 255
Neal Vorus

CHAPTER EIGHT
Klein's "Envy and gratitude" 291

CHAPTER NINE
Fairbairn: a new object relations voice 329

CHAPTER TEN
Winnicott: in search of the real 359

CHAPTER ELEVEN
Sullivan: interpersonal psychoanalysis, relational beginnings 413

CHAPTER TWELVE
Mahler: symbiosis and separation–individuation 427
Anni Bergman and Steven Ellman

CHAPTER THIRTEEN
Kohut: a new self-psychological perspective 457

CHAPTER FOURTEEN
Kernberg: integrating object relations and ego psychology 491
Monica Carsky and Steven Ellman

CHAPTER FIFTEEN
Bion, Klein, and Freud 521
Vicki Stevens

CHAPTER SIXTEEN
From ego psychology to contemporary conflict theory: 541
a historical overview
Arnold D. Richards and Arthur A. Lynch

PART III: CONTEMPORARY ISSUES IN 559
PSYCHOANALYSIS

CHAPTER SEVENTEEN
Structural theory, relational critiques, and integrative 561
attempts

CHAPTER EIGHTEEN
A tentative developmental model 621

EPILOGUE 653

REFERENCES 657

INDEX 691

BRIEF HISTORY AND ACKNOWLEDGEMENTS

I started teaching the object relations course in the Doctoral Program of Clinical Psychology at City University of New York in 1972 or 1973. I had studied Fairbairn, Klein, Winnicott, and others as a result of a chance encounter during my graduate training at New York University. At that time, a fellow student told me about Harry Guntrip, whom he had met in the UK. Guntrip told him about Fairbairn, and a year or two later (Guntrip, 1968) published a book detailing his version of Fairbairn's object relations theory. Although I was studying Freudian theory with George Klein, Bob Holt, Leo Goldberger, and Merton Gill at New York University, I found Fairbairn's work exciting and Guntrip's book equally stimulating. At that time, I saw nothing incompatible between Freud and Guntrip and Fairbairn, despite the latter's statements that their work was an alternative to Freudian theory. In my mind I saw clear connections; after reading Guntrip, I wrote to him and finally had lunch with him when he came to the USA. I tried to tell him about the connections that I envisioned, and his patient and kind response to me was that I should read Winnicott and Klein and Balint and . . . and . . . This was 1971, and at that time I was reading Searles and Kohut, who also seemed to me to be compatible with my version of Freudian theory.

I began to teach a course titled "Disorders of the self", where I included Freud, Kohut, Sullivan, Winnicott, Searles, Guntrip, Fairbairn, Anna Freud, and Hartmann. All of these authors seemed to me to be getting at an aspect of disturbance in the experience of a unified sense of self. Now I realize that this may seem like a strange list, since Hartmann and Anna Freud are ego psychologists not self-psychologists, but in both of their work I saw the beginnings of a theory of self that I felt fitted in with a version of Freudian theory that some friends said was only present in my mind.

Given this long-winded introduction, I want to thank George Klein, Bob Holt, Bernie Kalinkowitz, and Leo Goldberger for being stimulating teachers who allowed their students enough freedom to find their own voice. Certainly, Guntrip was extraordinarily kind to meet with me and offer some guidance and encouragement. My thesis adviser was Harry Fiss, and, though my thesis was an experimental study in sleep research, Harry, George, and Leo continuously engaged me in enough theoretical discussions about the meaning of rapid eye movement (REM) sleep that in various ways they have all influenced the content of this volume.

Of course, my primary and necessary acknowledgement should be to those generations of students who had to bear my different versions of the theorists that I am presenting in this volume. Many of you contributed knowingly and unknowingly to the present volume. My wife has to be mentioned here, since she frequently had to put aside her wonderful expositions (particularly around the topic of envy) to read one or another version of a given theorist. Everyone who is struggling to be an author should have such a wife.

I want to thank my peer group, who kindly read a number of the chapters in this volume. The group consists of Drs Sheldon Bach, Norbert Freedman, Mark Gruness, and Irving Steingart. Since Dr Bach has a house near mine in the country, he unfortunately had to read parts of the last section of the book several times. Thanks to Dr Lew Aron for his incisive comments on my Winnicott chapter. Thanks to Dr David Scharff for reading the Fairbairn chapter and offering advice and useful guidance. Thanks to Michael Moskowitz for being such a good friend and offering such helpful suggestions. Many thanks to Peter Kaufman (my tennis partner) for helping me with all of the relational theorists. He was a true partner in Chapter Seventeen.

ABOUT THE AUTHOR

Steven J. Ellman gained a PhD in Clinical Psychology in 1968 from New York University, and graduated from psychoanalytic training in 1982 from the Institute for Psychoanalytic Training and Research (IPTAR). His postdoctoral training was in the Psychology and Neurophysiology of Sleep and Dreams at Albert Einstein College of Medicine, after which he became a Professor in the Graduate School of City University of New York (CUNY). Throughout most of his career he has been both a clinician and researcher. At CUNY, he was Director of the PhD program in Clinical Psychology and is now, after thirty years as a Professor at CUNY, Professor-Emeritus. He has published more than seventy papers on psychoanalysis, sleep and dreams, and the neurophysiology of motivation. In addition, he has published and co-edited four psychoanalytic volumes and two volumes on sleep and dreams, the best known of which are *Freud's Technique Papers: A Contemporary Perspective* (1991, Jason Aronson), and *The Mind in Sleep*, (with J. S. Antrobus, 1991, Wiley). He has been President of IPTAR twice, Program Chair, and is a training and supervising analyst at IPTAR. He is also Clinical Professor at New York University Post-Doctoral Program in Psychoanalysis and Psychotherapy. Steven Ellman was the first President of the

Confederation of Independent Psychoanalytic Societies (CIPS), which is the national professional organization of the independent International Psychoanalytic Association (IPA) societies of the USA, is a member of the IPA, and was previously on the Executive Council of the IPA. He is a member of the American Psychological Association, and has held many editorial positions on various psychoanalytic journals.

SERIES EDITOR'S PREFACE

We are honoured to have *When Theories Touch*, by Steven J. Ellman, PhD, serve as the inaugural volume for the CIPS Book Series. This series, *The Boundaries of Psychoanalysis*, was founded to examine the interrelationships between a variety of psychoanalytic points of view as well as the interrelationships between psychoanalysis and other disciplines. It is dedicated to the exploration of the various ways in which a multiplicity of perspectives can inform and enrich one another. Clearly, this is a way of looking at things that is at the heart of Dr Ellman's book.

In *When Theories Touch*, one finds this integrative approach on many levels. Steve Ellman leads us through a comprehensive review of the main theoretical contributions of the major psychoanalytic theorists from Freud to the present. The review is deep as well as broad, and sets the groundwork for a meaningful analysis of the divergence and convergence of multiple psychoanalytic perspectives. What emerges out of this examination is a multiple factor model for psychoanalysis that accounts for the intersections and disparities between theories and that makes bridges over posited unbridgeables.

For example, in discussing the relational and classical positions, Dr Ellman argues that what has been posed as the unbridgeable dichotomy of whether we are fundamentally object seeking or pleasure seeking is a "false dichotomy". He suggests that not only is it clear that we are both object and pleasure seeking, but that perhaps neither of these are properly understood as the primary motive cause. Fundamental to Dr Ellman's approach is the recognition that multiple models may be useful in understanding different individuals' development, or, more accurately, different mother–infant pairs' development. One model may have more explanatory power for one dyad and a different model may be more useful in understanding another. This would, of course, be the case for either a parent–infant dyad or an analytic dyad.

The flexibility inherent in a multiple factor model such as Dr Ellman's makes it possible to remain true to the phenomenological experience of particular individuals while, at the same time, recognizing the necessity of a theoretical model for any understanding or organization of such experience. It also opens the way for alternative integrations that might take better account of particular experiential organizations. In Dr Ellman's words,

I am trying to show the convergences and divergences of different theoretical positions; perhaps it may help some clinicians to more accurately identify how they combine different theoretical perspectives. I hope it may encourage new integrations that may provide a better fit for some analytic dyads. [p. xiv]

It is in regard to this very possibility of the development of alternative integrations that we are most indebted to Dr Ellman's detailed account of the models of the major psychoanalytic theorists. The solid foundation that Dr Ellman provides makes it possible for new theoretical integrations that emerge to be coherently based on a nuanced appreciation of how and where alternative models cohere. This greatly enhances the synthetic power and, thus, the explanatory value of such new integrations.

Dr Ellman's own integration makes use of Freud, Fairbairn, Winnicott, and Klein, as well as his own empirical research on REM sleep, to elaborate a psychoanalytic developmental model that takes account of both relational and physiological factors and that is capable of providing a theoretical foundation for the understanding of therapeutic action in the clinical situation. This model is an impressive example of the explanatory power of an integrated multiple factor model that is grounded on a thorough understanding of the various models that have presented themselves throughout the history of psychoanalysis. The reader will find him/herself enriched by both Dr Ellman's model and by the possibility for further syntheses that his analysis opens up for us.

We at CIPS hope that the volumes of this series will promote that very integrative spirit that informs Steve Ellman's *When Theories Touch*. He has provided us with a paradigm for what can emerge when a diversity of viewpoints are allowed to interface with one another. The volumes of the CIPS Book Series, *The Boundaries of Psychoanalysis*, are meant to explore this interaction between multiple viewpoints within psychoanalysis, our internal boundaries, and, in the same spirit, to explore the interaction of psychoanalysis and other areas of study, our external boundaries. We are most grateful to Dr Ellman for providing the series with such a fine beginning.

I would like to take this opportunity to thank a number of other people whose active support of *The Boundaries of Psychoanalysis* has been instrumental in its realization. I am particularly grateful to the members of the CIPS Book Series committee; Christopher Christian, PhD, Steven Ellman, PhD, Jared Russell, MS, Phyllis Sloate, PhD, and Leigh Tobias, PhD. Their sustained and unqualified dedication to our project over the several years it took to bring it to fruition has been invaluable. I would also like to thank Rick Perlman, PhD, President of CIPS, first for having the confidence in me to entrust me with the leadership of this project, and second for providing me with the personal and organizational support that has made my work possible. Finally, I want to express my appreciation to Oliver Rathbone of Karnac Books. We are deeply indebted to him for giving the CIPS Book Series a home, for his enthusiastic responsiveness to our ideas, and his expert guidance so graciously given.

Meg Beaudoin, PhD, FIPA
Series Editor

PREFACE

My desire to write the present volume has a long history that began when I started teaching a course in object relations in the early 1970s. From that time until now, I have varied in the extent that I was protagonist for a particular theoretical point of view. Perhaps it would be more accurate to say that the extent did not vary (I was sure at each point in time), but my preferred theory changed somewhat from era to era. Despite these changes, I have always included a variety of authors from different points of view in my courses. Early on, Sullivan was a featured writer, as was Fromm-Reichmann, Freud, Searles, Guntrip, Winnicott, Kohut, and Anna Freud. This group were important authors in most of my courses. Although, in my early years, I was not truly aware of psychoanalytic politics, as I went into psychoanalytic training I began to learn who were the "good" people and who were those that were not "truly analysts". For those unaware of the sarcasm in the last remark, let me be more explicit; during my years of analytic training the worse thing that one could hear is that you were not really doing analytic work or that you were not, or someone you respected, was not a "real" analyst. At some point in the early 1980s, I wrote a favourable to glowing review of Loewald's *Collected Papers*. I remember (with excruciating detail) how my supervisor wondered how I could write a favourable review, since Loewald was not "truly" an analyst. Of course, I was frightened, and wondered if someone like Loewald was not an analyst then surely I was not an analyst. Fortunately, those times are mostly gone and the type of prejudice that existed has, at the very least, greatly attenuated. In some ways, I am depending on there being a new attitude in today's readers; an attitude that wants to see what is valuable in each position rather than finding what in a position makes it less good than the one that you are espousing.

Perhaps I am being too optimistic, for, in this era of materialism and practicality, it is not surprising that the intellectual underpinnings of psychoanalysis have been, if not forsaken, at least overlooked. I will echo and paraphrase what many before me have said: it is impossible to do psychoanalytic clinical treatment (or probably any treatment) without either an implicit or explicit theory governing one's approach. It is the view in this volume that few clinicians have a consistent theoretical perspective with regard to their clinical work. Rather, they borrow from several orientations, consciously or unconsciously, and construct an implicit theory of their own (Sandler & Sandler, 1994). The best of clinicians do this for each patient, and the theory subtly changes to meet the needs of the analytic dyad. In this volume, I am trying to show the convergences and divergences of different theoretical positions; perhaps it may help some clinicians to more accurately identify how they combine different theoretical perspectives. I hope it may encourage new integrations that may provide a better fit for some analytic dyads.

Although various analysts have written about an era of convergence (Wallerstein, 1988), to some extent one might consider that psychoanalysis has entered into a time that is best thought of as similar to the era of the tower of Babel. (I apologize, since I have used this paragraph before [Ellman, 1996]. However, as it was in a paper that was read by so few people, I have felt entitled to reuse it.) There is however a difference; in the Old Testament G-d created many languages and there was confusion. In the new testament of psychoanalysis, we use the same language and there is confusion. It is unclear for instance whether authors' from different theoretical perspectives when using the same theoretical terms are actually using the same concept. This tower of Babel however can be seen as having different effects; as a factor that makes it difficult or impossible for us to communicate, or as a precursor to developing new theoretical concepts and new ways of describing clinical experiences. In my mind new integrations have already begun, but the tower to some extent hinders our attempts to accomplish this task. In the present volume it is my desire to help deconstruct (literally) the tower, and reconstruct (literally) concepts in psychoanalysis that will be placed in a language that hopefully is readily understood. If possible this language will be English rather than a psychoanalytic language that sometimes obscures rather than clarifies. This of course is not meant to do away with terms that are meaningful but to attempt to clarify terms and concepts and substitute English where possible.

Structure of the book

The book is divided into three sections. In the first section, there are four chapters looking at what I will term Freud's four different theories. Now, these are not four absolutely separate theories, but, in each of the eras described, Freud strongly shifted his emphasis. Here I will repeat what I have said previously (Ellman, 1991) Freud is always interesting, but he is even more interesting in terms of the questions that he poses than the answers he provides. In the second section of the book, there are chapters on what I will call the major theorists after Freud, and before the era of what I will roughly label contemporary psychoanalysis. The authors covered in the second section are Hartmann and Anna Freud (together in one chapter), Melanie Klein, Fairbairn, Winnicott, Sullivan, Mahler, Kohut, Kernberg, Bion, and a chapter on the movement from classical theory to contemporary conflict theory.

In the first two sections, there is an attempt to get inside each theory and to try to give a feeling for what has impelled a given theorist to present a new theoretical perspective. These first two sections begin each chapter with a brief summary and end each chapter with commentary. Part of the reason that commentary is placed at the end of a chapter is to allow me to focus only or mainly on the author's position. There is an attempt to state the author's view as clearly as possible before critiquing this view or comparing it to other points of view. Obviously, I will not always be successful in explicating a position without my bias affecting the presentation. I will do the best that I can, and when I am aware of my bias affecting my presentation, I will try to indicate that this has occurred. In those instances, the commentary will be presented within the chapter rather than in the commentary section. In the second section, there are two chapters that I co-authored and three chapters written by other authors. The chapter on Mahler was written by Anni Bergman and myself. Anni Bergman was a long time collaborator of Mahler's and is a wonderful author and clinician. Monica Carsky and I wrote the Kernberg chapter. Monica worked with Kernberg for many years, she is also one of the most astute theorists and clinicians that I know. Richards and Lynch wrote Chapter Sixteen, on contemporary conflict theory. Both of these authors are well known for their articles and have published widely. Vicki Stevens has written the chapter on Bion. She is from the Psychoanalytic Center of California, an institute that Bion was affiliated with when he came to Los Angeles. She has written on Bion and studies with analysts who were analysed or supervised by Bion.

Neil Vorus wrote the chapter on the controversial discussions. I was Neil's thesis adviser when he began this project, and one of the benefits of sponsoring theses is that you can learn from outstanding students like Dr Vorus.

I have chosen to have other authors collaborate on or write these chapters for various reasons; the chapter on Bion is one that I felt I could write intellectually, but I thought that I have not taught or studied Bion enough times to have him in my bones (Goldman, 1993b). The chapter on contemporary conflict theory covers an area I know quite well, but, for various reasons, I did not think that I could approach this material with enough objectivity. Yes, I know that objectivity is a fantasy of mine, but since it is a fantasy that I prize, I decided to ask for help, and Richards and Lynch are the best people I know in terms of their knowledge in this area. I feel similarly with the chapter on Kernberg: I know the material very well but I needed someone to temper my reactions to some of the issues that Kernberg raises. The chapter on Mahler I wrote with Anni Bergman because I wanted to write something with her. I feel fortunate to be party to the way in which she approaches this material. Based on what I have written, one would be right to conclude that, in all of the other chapters, I felt a strong identification with the author that I was describing. Sullivan may be the exception, but, clearly, in the course of my career I have felt a strong identification with Sullivan. I hope this becomes apparent in the reading of this chapter.

In the last section of the book I depart from the previous format, but, I trust, not from the spirit that I hope is present in the first two thirds of the book. This section of the book will both integrate past positions and present new contemporary positions, including my own. The focus will be on how these theories have led to contemporary theories of psychoanalytic clinical interventions. There will also be a summation of some of my past research and how this research has led me to a theory that has both developmental and clinical implications. In this section I spend a good deal of time talking about the relational position and neo-Kleinian psychoanalysis.

I have not included Lacan in this volume, since my knowledge of Lacan is quite limited. In preparation for my volumes on technique (Ellman, 1991; Ellman & Moskowitz, 1998), I did review Lacan's essays on Freud"s technique papers and some other aspects of his writings. Although I was interested in his views, I did not think that I knew enough about Lacan to feature him in the present volume. As far as I can tell, Lacan's influence on French psychoanalysis is profound, and I did not want to try to systematically present Green or Laplanche's work without showing how this in part evolved from, and in response to, Lacan. Thus, my references to French psychoanalysis are limited. I hope to remedy this lack in the future.

Given today's movement away from Freud, why did I include four chapters on Freud in the present volume? It seems to me that it is still impossible to understand the controversies and oscillating positions in psychoanalysis without understanding Freud. Most of the issues that are being debated started with, and are strongly influenced by, Freud. In any event, to fully understand most positions it is necessary to understand some aspects of Freud. Moreover, Freud tackles many questions that are unresolved to the present time. Despite the dense nature of one or two of the chapters on Freud, it is my hope that one can see how various authors have utilized aspects of Freudian theory or, alternatively, built their theories around the rejection of Freudian theory.

Overview of guiding meta-theoretical views

I am primarily a psychoanalyst who is, in part, responding to the currents present in contemporary psychoanalysis. One of the currents is the stipulation by Greenberg and Mitchell (1983), and later Mitchell (1995), where they argue that there is a basic incompatibility between what they term the drive/structural and the relational/structural models. They have stated that much of the complexity of psychoanalytic thought is clarified if one chooses between these alternatives. Throughout the volume, I will argue that the complexity generated by the tension between these two models (and others) is at the heart of psychoanalytic understanding and that a complete psychoanalytic theory has to blend aspects of both these positions (and other positions as well). At different junctures of the present volume, I argue that the way that Greenberg and Mitchell have stated their position seems as if they are making a logically necessary case. It is my view that there is nothing that is logically necessary about their argument. Rather, they are stating one alternative point of view, and I hope to show that we have moved to a place where different perspectives can be profitably blended, both clinically and theoretically. This, of course, will not abolish some differences between positions, but, rather, try to show the power of a position that attempts to synthesize several points of view. One aspect of this synthesis is a biological perspective that attempts to integrate developmental and clinical phenomena. This perspective does not hold drive theory as the central causative factor, but as one factor in a multiple factor model. The main factor in describing most people is the internalization of relationships (object relations) and conflicts attendant to these internalizations. In looking at most individuals, the biological factors that I will propose play a background role at best, with some other people they are powerful factors. Of course, one can never make this statement in a vacuum, and I will try to describe the environmental conditions that either facilitate or attenuate certain types of conflicts, internalizations, and representations.

I am clearly stating that I will be proposing a multiple factor model that blends aspects of a number of theories. Since it is my view that part of the reason for splits and bifurcations occurring in psychoanalysis have to do with political factors, I will, at the beginning of the last (third) section of this volume try in a general way to elucidate some of these factors. It is my hope that, in providing this brief description, I will abreact my political tendencies and finally the cathartic method will have worked. Of course, I know that this wish will not be realized, but it is an ideal that I hope at least guides the spirit of the present volume.

There is one overriding perspective and two separate but interlocking themes that advance through this volume. The overriding perspective is that each (most) theorist(s) that we will encounter tends to bifurcate the field. Freud's bifurcations occurred in each era of his writings. This was true even if a position he took contradicted a previous position. The strongest contemporary bifurcation is that of Greenberg and Mitchell, but this is a characteristic of most (perhaps all) of the theories that we will experience. The contention in the present volume is that every theorist that we look at (with the exception of ... reader, fill in the blank) has offered something of interest and of importance. For example, one might consider the bifurcation of Greenberg and Mitchell destructive, while I believe it was theoretically cleansing. It set the conditions for various discussions that should have occurred (or I wish had occurred) years before their insightful, moving volume. I believe the era has shifted and a new convergence is possible, and I hope to follow their example and construct a volume that is useful for the present era.

The question now (at least in my view) is how to incorporate what is of value of a given theorist within a new theoretical matrix. I will try to give some examples of this in my own attempts, but my view is that there are a variety of others who will create their own integrations. The hope is that this book will encourage other integrations.

The main theme clinically is that in every theoretical perspective there is an attempt to facilitate a patient's expression of their psychological difficulties, and in each of these perspectives there is, at the same time, a way of safeguarding the analyst from the full expression of a patient's (analysand's) psychological world. In many theories, this exploration is thought to occur via transference. If one accepts transference as a feasible concept, then the guiding assumption is that every (most) analyst(s) need(s) in some way to limit the full expression of transference. To clarify this "need", it assumes that the analyst cannot easily endure the unabated manifestation of transference. There is a similar tension assumed to be present for theories that feature relational assumptions, or interpersonal dynamics, etc. In so far as the patient concentrates on their own internal world, the analyst is prone to truncate this tendency and introduce her/him self into the treatment situation.

In addition, in each theory there is a tension between the effects of the therapeutic relationship and the uncovering of, or insight into, a person's difficulties. For example, in Freud's theory, the powerful emphasis was on the expression of, and then the uncovering or understanding of, the transference. The person of the analyst was considered to be substantially less important. In Sullivan's theoretical matrix, the person of the analyst was emphasized to a much greater extent, and transference was replaced by other concepts. This difference is often expressed in terms of insight *vs.* the therapeutic relationship, or discovering the past *vs.* the creation of the present relationship. I believe that most analysts today believe that both insight (joined with feeling states) and the therapeutic or the real relationship are important aspects of the clinical situation. Towards the end of the book, I will present a theoretical statement which includes both perspectives in what I will call a dynamic theoretical structure.

The overblown phrase, dynamic theoretical structure, simply refers to the idea that, at times, there may be more attention paid to one or another aspect of the clinical situation. Thus, I will maintain that, from the patient's point of view, there are times when the situation calls for a one-person emphasis and, at other points, a two-person emphasis is crucial. Of course, in line with my overall perspective, the bifurcation of one- and two-person characterizations will be seen as artificial. The argument will be made that most of these functions should be viewed in a continuous manner, so that most of the time the situation is neither one or two but somewhere in between (averaging about 1.7). This is a rough approximation of what Ogden (1997b) means when he indicates that, although there is a constant intersubjective presence in analysis, the patient's subjectivity should be privileged. Whether one wants to consider the therapeutic situation as necessarily or continuously an intersubjective event is a question that will be focused on in the last section of the book. Although there are a variety of other clinical dichotomies that will be looked in the present volume, I will turn to another theme that has divided the psychoanalytic community for decades: Freud's concept of instinct or drive.

This concept is frequently amalgamated with his theory of psycho-sexual stages. As a preliminary remark, there is nothing logically necessary that combines instinct theory with psycho-sexual stages. Freud might well have developed one concept without the other. Clearly, Freud was looking for what he considered to be postulates or basic ideas for his clinical–theoretical concepts. The concept of instinct implies, but does not specify, what are the assumed physiological or neurophysiological processes. It does imply bodily sequela, and Freud frequently maintained a stance that he stated in 1923, that even the ego was first and foremost a body ego (Freud, 1923b). In this statement, Freud did not logically need the concept of instinct, since he could have maintained that the infant's/developing child's representational world is formed through a focus on biological functioning (e.g., eating, sleeping, excretions, etc.). Since Freud's cynosure was instinctually driven, a number of divisions (bifurcations) arose. Is psychoanalysis a biological or a psychological theory (Gill, 1976)? Are we referring to meaning or mechanism (Klein, 1976). The question that we will look at is whether there can be a psychological theory that considers the possibility of important biological influences. Going one step further, is it possible to posit a theory of drive without this concept being the major factor of one's theoretical structure? Without attempting to answer this question at this point, it should be restated that the breaking down of bifurcations should be replaced by a dynamic multiple factor model. Thus, factors will vary in terms of their importance, depending on whom you are trying to describe or understand.

My hope in this volume is at least to stir a number of questions and attempts at new theoretical combinations. Moreover, implicitly, I hope to stimulate thoughts about empirical studies that might clarify some of these theoretical questions.

PART I
FREUD CHAPTERS

CHAPTER ONE

Freud's heroic era: the first ten years

Slightly before, slightly beyond

Chapter summary

The title of the chapter is from Walter Stewart's book, *Psychoanalysis: The First Ten Years* (1963). In this chapter we look at the beginning of Freud's career as a therapist and an emerging psychoanalyst. He attempts to formulate a theory where psychological disturbances are caused by a combination of environmental events and physiological conditions. He is strongly influenced by the neurophysiologists of his era, and the familiar Freudian concepts such as fantasy and transference do not play a prominent role in the theory of this era. Rather, in adults there are actual causes that produce neurotic symptoms. The sexual practices of the era are thought by Freud to produce symptoms such as anxiety and neurasthenia. He calls neuroses that are produced by sexual practices, such as excessive masturbation or coitus interruptus, actual neuroses. Neuroses that are caused by conditions in childhood are called psychogenic neuroses, but these disorders are also caused by "real" events, trauma in childhood. The trauma that

Freud finds most often involves sexual abuse (before the child's eighth birthday). This is a real event that causes psychological disturbance, and here Freud uses the concept of undischarged tension or libido to explain both the actual and psychological neuroses. Freud's emerging psychological treatment is one where he is attempting to extirpate pathogenic memories through the cathartic method. In effect, he is attempting to have patients experience strong emotional reaction (abreaction) by bringing memories to consciousness. In this period, Freud has not fully developed the idea of unconscious ideas and his treatment method involves trying to pressure patients into remembering and abreacting. During this era, Freud moves from the use of hypnosis (Breuer's technique) to a psychotherapy that is labelled the pressure technique.

Despite the fact that Freud has not yet developed his psychoanalytic theory, one can see many of his concepts in embryonic form. The concept of defence, resistance, and the beginning of the concept of unconscious motivation all have their roots in this period of Freud's career. There are, of course, many other fragments in his emerging theory, including ideas about dreams and the importance of fantasy. Freud also begins his self-analysis during this period, and this is one factor that will lead Freud to question whether his patient's reports of sexual abuse are real or the product of fantasy developed early in the person's life.

Brief historical introduction

In 1882, a meeting occurred that contributed to changing the history of psychiatry and, indeed, of intellectual life in the Western hemisphere during the twentieth century and perhaps beyond. In this meeting, Josef Breuer told Sigmund Freud about his treatment of Anna O (Bertha Pappenheim). This discussion strongly contributed to Freud's subsequent decision to begin to study hysteria. Freud began to collaborate with Breuer a number of years after this conversation, and in the interim he studied with Charcot and learnt about the views of Janet and Bernheim. He also translated and wrote a preface to Bernheim's (1888) book *Suggestion*. Although various analysts have tried to minimize the effect of Breuer's work and theoretical formulations on Freud, in my view it was the intrigue of the narrative that Breuer was experiencing with Bertha Pappenheim that captured Freud. Breuer, at this point in time, was a sophisticated reader of the scientific literature and his views about cortical tonicity also influenced Freud at various points in his career. However, it was the narrative of Ms Pappenheim and of the patients after her, in what Stewart (1963) calls Freud's heroic period, that truly fascinated the young physician whose literary tendencies in many ways were more prominent than his scientific interests (Steiner, 2001).

It is not the aim of the present chapter(s) to trace the intellectual influences on Freud; rather, we will evaluate his contributions as the most convincing evidence of how the intellectual ferment of his era affected his writings. We begin this chapter at a time (1892–1898) when Freud is starting to revolutionize the world of psychiatry with his theoretical concepts and his new psychotherapeutic technique. At this point in his career, Freud's theoretical attempts are intimately intermingled with his therapeutic venture. (In a previous volume [1991] I expressed the view that, as Freud's career progressed, he became increasingly involved in theoretical issues and that the psychoanalytic situation lost a position of primary importance. This was not a linear progression, for, in the era 1907–1916, he was active in writing about psychoanalytic treatment as well as bringing forth seminal theoretical papers. However, later in his career, when he was putting forth his best known works such as *The Ego and the Id* [1923b] he was no longer intensely involved in the clinical situation. Rather, he had become a world figure who was doing training analyses which were frequently not serious analytic encounters, in my opinion.) We join him when he and Breuer are describing their experiences in treating patients that they have diagnosed as hysterics (Breuer & Freud, 1895d). In fact, the patients that Freud treated in the late 1880s and 1890s presented a wide assortment of symptomatology and complaints, including conversion symptoms (pain in limbs, paresis, aphonia, etc.), depression, impotence, and hallucinations. It does not take a particularly careful reading of Freud's cases to see that he was not only treating hysterics, but also patients who, in modern terms, run the gamut of diagnostic categories (including neurotic, borderline, and psychotic disorders). While Freud heard a wide array of symptoms and complaints in this, his "heroic era", his focus was on the dramatic symptomatology he was encountering. Given this concern, many of the patients Freud saw in these early "heroic days" would today not be diagnosed in the same manner that governed Breuer and Freud's nosological distinctions. Freud's first therapeutic attempts were designed to remove the patient's symptoms as rapidly as possible. He quickly learned that at times patients did not share his goals.

In the *Standard Edition* (Volume 2) the editors state that, "The *Studies on Hysteria* are usually regarded as the starting point of psycho-analysis". They contend that the most important of Freud's achievements recorded in this volume is the "invention of the first instrument for the scientific examination of the human mind" (*S.E.* 2, p. xvi). This comment on the part of the editors reveals their particular bias in understanding Freud's work. The use of the term scientific is difficult to deal with in today's psychoanalytic world. On the one hand, researchers might criticize the term, since Freud in any ordinary sense of the term was not conducting scientific research. Certain clinicians, on the other hand, have criticized Freud for being overly scientific. They maintain that he did not sufficiently emphasize the literary aspects of psychoanalysis. It is fascinating "to trace the early steps of the development" (*S.E.*, 2, p. xvi) of his psychotherapeutic method, but the theoretical concepts that he formulates and comes to accept in this volume can be viewed as equally important in the history of psychoanalysis. He gives graphic clinical examples of how he conceptualizes his new ideas about the nature of defence and defence hysteria. (He does not, at this time, distinguish between resistance and defence, although he uses both terms.) He also gives us a clear indication of how he is conceiving of an idea that is not in consciousness. There is a temptation to say an idea that is unconscious, but, at this point in time, Freud has not yet fully elaborated this theoretical concept. Freud does present one of his first notions of the organization of ideas outside of consciousness (or in what he calls the secondary group of ideas). Freud, at this point, distinguishes between a primary group of ideas or associations, which are conscious, and a secondary split of group of ideas, which are outside of consciousness. Where are they, one might ask? There are two possible answers to this question: it is possible to think of a splitting of consciousness, or one might think of the ideas as unconscious. Freud, at this point, has not fully thought through where his concept of defence is about to take him and psychoanalysis. We will look at this issue more systematically in this and the next chapter.

The attempt to delineate an era is of course highly artificial, and we will, at times, need to make reference to Freud's earlier work (or activities) to gain a clearer vision of his theoretical positions during this period. In a similar vein, while we will not be focusing on biographical material, at times we will look at aspects of Freud's life. For example, it is hard to understand some of Freud's theoretical preoccupations unless one has some inkling of his relationship during this period with Fliess, Freud's confidant, co-conspirator and the recipient of a good deal of Freud's transference. In this brief introduction, we have gone over some of Freud's career prior to this period; here we can begin to look at the new concepts that Freud is beginning to develop.

We will begin by looking at Freud's first publication with Breuer and showing how it presages many of his concepts during this period. Then we will systematically look at the development of each of the ideas that Freud has introduced in his preliminary communication. In this chapter, we will look quote Freud extensively to give the reader more of a first-hand sense of Freud's conceptualizations in this, perhaps most unfamiliar, era of his work.

Studies on hysteria: preliminary communication

Freud tells us "that psycho-analysis started with researches into hysteria" (1913m, p. 207) and that hypnosis was his original therapeutic technique. In his publication with Breuer (Breuer & Freud, 1893a) he is describing his experiences treating patients who are diagnosed as hysterics. Today, many of these patients would not be diagnosed as having hysterical disorders. Rather, many of them would be seen as having conversion symptoms, at times with more severe diagnoses. By and large, these patients are women (Freud had presented a paper on his treatment of a male hysteric, and some members of the audience treated this report with some scepticism) whose complaints have usually not been taken seriously by the physicians of Freud's Vienna or, indeed, by physicians in most of the European continent. Breuer, in 1882, had told Freud of a hysterical patient he had treated and this conversation had what might be considered a deferred influence on Freud. We know that, several years later, Freud travelled to Paris to study with Charcot. Freud told Charcot of Breuer's treatment of Anna O (Bertha Pappenheim); however, Charcot seemed to evince little interest in the case report. Nevertheless, when Freud returned to Vienna, he found a path back to Breuer and Breuer's method of treatment where he utilized hypnosis, called the cathartic method. By the time Breuer and Freud are publishing their preliminary communication (1893a), Freud has already treated several hysterical patients using hypnosis and the cathartic method. He has also begun to experiment with other methods of treatment and, in 1895, he publishes his new method and his new ideas about hysteria.

In 1893, he and Breuer tell us that the aim of his hypnotic technique is to bring about the "reproduction of a memory which was of importance in bringing about the onset of the hysteria . . . the memory [is] either of a single major trauma . . . or of a series of interconnected part-traumas" (Breuer & Freud, 1893a, p. 14). It was Freud's view that "hysterics suffer mainly from reminiscences" (*ibid.*). These memories or reminiscences are the result of psychical trauma "or more precisely the memory of the trauma . . . [which] acts like a foreign body long after its entry must continue to be regarded as an agent that is still at work" (*ibid.*, p. 6). Breuer and Freud reported that, to their surprise,

> Each individual hysterical symptom immediately and permanently disappeared when we had succeeded in bringing clearly to light the memory of the event by which it was provoked and in arousing its accompanying affect, and when the patient had described that event in the greatest possible detail and had put the effect into words. Recollection without affect almost invariably produces no result. [*ibid.*]

Thus, in Freud's early conceptualizations, he is attempting to establish the precipitating cause(s) of hysterical attacks. He has found that usually the patient is unaware of the meaning of these attacks. As a result of his and Breuer's investigations, they have seen that external events determine the pathway of hysterical attacks and that each attack is related to the first attack. This relationship may extend over many years, and they comment on the similarity of hysteria to the traumatic neuroses. There is a clear precipitating event and a clear relationship between the precipitating event and subsequent attacks. They wondered whether all neuroses are formed in the way that they have conceptualized the hysterical neuroses.

Beyond this attempt to describe the course of hysterical symptoms, Freud also points out that the symptoms are related to painful, anxiety-provoking memories that are stored apart from the person's primary or conscious (primary system) ideas about themselves. These thoughts, which are stored as a secondary group (secondary system) of ideas, are not readily accessible to consciousness. Freud contrasts hysterics with normal or "healthy" experiences. In normal circumstances, the affect associated with disturbing events is worn away or discharged. In the following paragraph, we can see Freud's ideas of how memories are normally managed.

> The fading of a memory or the losing of its affect depends on various factors. The most important of these is whether there has been an energetic reaction to the event that provokes an affect. By "reaction" we here understand the whole class of voluntary and involuntary reflexes—from tears to acts of revenge—in which, as experience shows us, the affects are discharged. If this reaction takes place to a sufficient amount a large part of the effect disappears as a result. Linguistic usage bears witness to this fact of daily observation by such phrases as "to cry oneself out", and to "blow off steam" (literally "to rage oneself out"). If the reaction is suppressed, the affect remains attached to the memory. An injury that has been repaid, even if only in words, is recollected quite differently from one that has had to be accepted. [1893a, p. 8]

In this formulation, Freud maintained that under normal or optimal circumstances people are able to deal with, or wear away, distressing affect by fully experiencing or discharging the affect. They may also deal with an affect by being able to counteract an experience in thought or action. If, for instance, a situation stimulated an idea that brought up the affect of shame, the person might be able to nullify this idea by reminding themselves of their positive attributes. They might assure themselves that the event that caused the affect of shame was a singular or infrequent occurrence, and this might allow them to wear away this affect. Alternatively, they might do something in reality to counteract this experience. Thus, normal people are continually discharging affect or putting a memory of a disturbing or humiliating circumstance into appropriate perspective. They are able to this "by considering (one's) own worth" (*ibid.*, p. 9). Put in other terms, a normal person can have either small abreactions (discharges of affect through thought or action) or deal with the personal insult or aversive effect more gradually "through the process of association" (*ibid.*). Forgetting, or, more accurately, the fading of memories, takes place when the affect is "worn away". Freud believed that memories can be fully recaptured when the affect is reunited with the idea or representation. Thus, even normal memories are potentially available if the affect is reunited with the idea. For this to occur in this model, the affect must be stimulated by an external source. This point will become clearer as we progress further into Freud's ideas. Freud has implicitly introduced several of the themes that will continue in his work to the end of his career. The first of these has already begun to surface, that is, the concept of psychic energy. This theoretical assumption is more formally stated in "The neuro-psychoses of defence" (1894a), but here this concept is present as an accompaniment to his ideas about defence. Defence is a concept that is lurking behind and within the phrase, "hysterics suffer from reminiscences". In addition, Freud states that the reminiscences are "experiences . . . completely absent from the patients' (normal or conscious) memory" (1893a, p. 9). This is what Freud is referring to as the secondary group of ideas, or what we might say is the beginning of his theory of unconscious processes. Forgetting takes place when the affect is worn away from the idea, this is true in both normal and neurotic experience. The difference is how the affect is worn away: in normal experience, it is worn away in the primary associational pathway; in neurotic experience, it is dispatched through the process of defence.

Defence in hysteria and the psychoneuroses

Breuer, Janet, and Charcot: alternative concepts

A reader of Breuer and Freud's preliminary communication would have been hard pressed to guess what was in store for the psychiatric world during the next few years. Freud gave little indication of his new theoretical inclinations in his chapter with Breuer. In this chapter, hypnoid states are mentioned as an important factor in the aetiology of hysteria. (*Studies on Hysteria* was published in 1895, but the first chapter in this book (co-authored by Breuer and Freud) had been published previously as a paper in 1893.) In Breuer's theoretical chapter in *Studies on Hysteria*, he presents a sophisticated neurophysiological theory about the genesis of hypnoid states. Breuer saw hypnoid states as a necessary condition for the formation of hysterical or conversion symptoms. It was his view that, during this type of hypnogogic (what I mean here is a state that is close to sleep onset, as hypnogogic imagery is that imagery that one has while falling asleep) state the person was more prone to be overwhelmed (traumatized) by stimuli. His theory stated the conditions for a threshold shift that made the cortex more susceptible to trauma. While Breuer did not stress innate factors, he certainly was influenced by the *zeitgeist* of the times, where innate factors were taken to be the main variable in the causal chain leading to hysterical conditions. Janet had previously maintained that hysteria "is based on an innate weakness of the capacity for psychical synthesis" (Freud, 1894a, p. 46). Although Charcot designated certain types of hysteria as traumatic in origin, the ultimate causal factor for him was also an inherited predisposition. Freud did not, at this time, actively dispute these theoretical accounts and, in fact, as we will see, he had his own hypothesis about the type of physiological factors that predisposed patients to hysteria. However, by 1894, in "The neuro-psychoses of defence", Freud is distancing himself from Janet, and implicitly from Charcot, and, by 1895, from Breuer as well. Let us look at his comments about Janet.

> According to the theory of Janet the splitting of consciousness is a primary feature of the mental change in hysteria. It is based on an innate weakness of the capacity for psychical synthesis, on the narrowness of the field of consciousness (champ de la conscience) which, in the form of a psychical stigma, is evidence of the degeneracy [by this, Janet meant a capacity for neurological degeneracy] of hysterical individuals. In contradistinction to Janet's view, which seems to me to admit of a great variety of objections, there is the view put forward by Breuer in our joint communication (Breuer and Freud, 1893). According to him, "the basis and sine qua non of

hysteria" is the occurrence of peculiar dream-like states of consciousness with a restricted capacity for association, for which he proposes the name "hypnoid states". In that case, the splitting of consciousness is secondary and acquired; it comes about because the ideas which emerge in hypnoid states are cut off from associative communication with the rest of the content of consciousness.

I am now in a position to bring forward evidence of two other extreme forms of hysteria in which it is impossible to regard the splitting of consciousness as primary in Janet's sense. In the first of these [two further] forms I was repeatedly able to show that the splitting of the content of consciousness is the result of an act of will on the part of the patient; that is to say, it is initiated by an act of will whose motive can be specified. By this I do not of course, mean that the patient intends to bring about a splitting of consciousness. His intention is a different one; but, instead of attaining its aim, it produces a splitting of consciousness.

In the third form of hysteria, which we have demonstrated by means of a psychical analysis of intelligent patients, the splitting of consciousness plays an insignificant part, or perhaps none at all. They are those cases in which what has happened is only that the reaction to traumatic stimuli has failed to occur, and which can also, accordingly, be resolved and cured by "abreaction". These are the pure retention hysterias.

As regards the connection with phobias and obsessions, I am only concerned with the second form of hysteria. For reasons which will soon be evident, I shall call this form "defence hysteria", using the name to distinguish it from hypnoid hysteria and retention hysteria. I may also provisionally present my cases of defence hysteria as "acquired" hysteria, since in them there was no question either of a grave hereditary taint or of an individual degenerative atrophy. [Freud, 1894a, pp. 46–47]

In this extract, we see Freud not only naming a new type of disorder (defence hysteria), but also rejecting the idea that hysteria is primarily based on an inherited predisposition. Janet's view of the innate weakness of the hysteric's capacity for psychical synthesis is specifically cast aside, but, implicitly, he is also disagreeing with Charcot's view of hysteria. Charcot divided hysteria into two forms. In the idiopathic or constitutional form, his view was quite similar to Janet's ideas. He distinguished a traumatic hysteria where an event (a train crash, for example) gave rise to the symptoms of hysteria. He thought this type of hysteria admitted of a psychogenic explanation, but still felt that the proclivity for hysteria was an innate tendency. He reasoned that not all passengers in a train crash developed hysterical symptoms and the distinction between those who did and did not rested on their innate tendencies. Although Freud maintains in "The neuro-psychoses of defence" that there are three types of hysteria (defence, retention, and hypnoid), in Chapter Four of *Studies on Hysteria*, written in 1895, he implies that all hysterical disorders can be seen as a form of defence hysteria.

In this paper, we see Freud tactfully rejecting the idea that either retention or hypnoid hysteria is an actual clinical entity. For Freud, defence is at the heart of hysteria and in (1894) he has extended the idea of defence to both phobias and obsessions. Why did Freud need to postulate the concept of defence? He knew from both his experiences with Breuer and Charcot that, in some cases, traumatic circumstances condition various aspects of hysterical symptoms. His clinical observations were that patients were affected by trauma memories for a long period of time after these events took place. Why, perhaps with Breuer's concept, was this not enough of an explanation? Both retention and hypnoid hysteria hypotheses are forms of trauma overwhelming the central nervous system. Again, Breuer thought that the distressing thoughts and feelings occurred during a hypnoid state which was not part of normal consciousness. Given that these thoughts and feelings happened during a hypnoid (or twilight) state, they were not accessible to normal consciousness or the primary associational pathway. The retention hypothesis logic was similar in that, in this view, the person was not able to consciously retain the trauma. The amount of stimulation involved in the trauma, in this formulation, overwhelms the capacity of the primary associational pathways and was, therefore, not retained in consciousness. More frequently, the way these hypotheses (hypnoid and retention) were stated was that there was a split in the person's consciousness. Freud, in abandoning these ideas for the concept of defence, still had to explain the same phenomena. In "The neuropsychoses of defence", Freud is more explicit about the role of defence:

The task which the ego, in its defensive attitude, sets itself of treating the incompatible idea as "nonarrivee" simply cannot be fulfilled by it. Both the memory trace and the affect which is attached to the idea are there once and for all and cannot be eradicated. But it amounts to an approximate fulfilment of the task if the ego succeeds *in turning the powerful idea into a weak one*, in robbing it of the affect—the sum of excitation—with which it is loaded. The weak idea will then have virtually no demands to make on the work of association. But the sum of excitation which has been detached from it must be put to another use. [1894a, pp. 48–49]

Defence is, then, a process that turns a strong idea into a weak one, but in what form is the weak idea stored? Moreover, in Freud's conceptualization, if it was the quota of affect that determined the strength of an idea, we can then ask what happened to the affect associated with an idea that was strong and yet distressing (i.e., an incompatible idea in the primary associational pathway)? Before we answer these questions, let us turn to Freud where he relates his experience with patients and how he deals with "defensive" patients and comes upon the concept of defence.

When, at our first interview, I asked my patients if they remembered what had originally occasioned the symptom concerned, in some cases they said they knew nothing of it, while in others they brought forward something which they described as an obscure recollection and could not pursue further. If, following the example of Bernheim when he awoke in his patients impressions from their somnambulistic state which had ostensibly been forgotten, I now became insistent—if I assured them that they did know it, that it would occur to their minds,—then, in the first cases, something did actually occur to them, and, in the others, their memory went a step further. After this I became still more insistent; I told the patients to lie down and deliberately close their eyes in order to "concentrate"—all of which had at least some resemblance to hypnosis. I then found that without any hypnosis new recollections emerged which went further back and which probably related to our topic. Experiences like this made me think that it would in fact be possible for the pathogenic groups of ideas, that were after all certainly present, to be brought to light by mere insistence; and since this insistence involved effort on my part and so suggested the idea that I had to overcome a resistance, the situation led me at once to the theory that by means of my psychical work I had to overcome a psychical force in the patients which was opposed to the pathogenic ideas becoming conscious (being remembered). A new understanding seemed to open before my eyes when it occurred to me that this must no doubt be the same psychical force that had played a part in the generating of the hysterical symptom and had at that time prevented the pathogenic idea from becoming conscious. . . . From all this there arose, as it were automatically, the thought of defence. [1895d, p. 268]

Defence, hysteria, and the other neuroses

What can we say about defence in Freud's formulation? Defence is a force, but one that can be overcome by an appropriate act of will. If Freud can convince the patient to try hard enough, they will be able to overcome this force by a greater force, or act of will. The physician or analyst is there to help encourage the person to produce the pathogenic ideas or memories. Freud then concludes that a

> psychical force, aversion on the part of the ego,[1] had originally driven the pathogenic idea out of association and was now opposing its return to memory. The patient's "not knowing" was in part a "not wanting to know", a not wanting which might be to a greater or less extent conscious. [*ibid.*, pp. 269–270]

Here, Freud is not only using the term ego, but he is also allowing for gradations of consciousness in terms of a person's awareness of their use of defence. This idea is one that will change when Freud has more clinical experience and feels compelled to use fewer pressure techniques. In any case, here we see Freud characterize defence as an active process, and, in his chapter on psychotherapy, he implicitly states that all hysteria is related to what he is calling defence hysteria. Even though Freud does not explicitly say so, it is clear that he believes all hysteria is related to defensive processes. Later, we will explore the different conceptions of hysteria that were present during this time period.

In the next extract, we see Freud talking about pathogenic memories as ideas that are lurking close to consciousness.

The pathogenic idea which has ostensibly been forgotten is always lying ready close at hand and can be reached by associations that are easily accessible. It is merely a question of getting some obstacle out of the way. This obstacle seems once again to be the subject's will, and different people can learn with different degrees of ease to free themselves from their intentional thinking and to adopt an attitude of completely objective observation towards the psychical processes taking place in them. What emerges under the pressure of my hand is not always a "forgotten" recollection; it is only in the rarest cases that the actual pathogenic recollections lie so easily ... on the surface. It is much more frequent for an idea to emerge which is an intermediate link in the chain of associations between the idea from which we start and the pathogenic idea which we are in search of ... [*ibid.*, p. 271]

The structure of the secondary system

During this period, we have one of Freud's first attempts at describing the relationship of the secondary and primary systems. He tells us that the secondary ideas are

Stratified in at least three different ways. (I hope I shall presently be able to justify this pictorial mode of expression.) To begin with there is a nucleus consisting in memories of events or trains of thought in which the traumatic factor has culminated or the pathogenic idea has found its purest manifestation. [This nucleus, according to Freud, usually contains the original pathogenic memories that cause or made the person susceptible to conflict and neurotic symptoms.] Round this nucleus we find what is often an incredibly profuse amount of other mnemic material [a term that is used for memories] which has to be worked through in the analysis and which is, as we have said, arranged in a threefold order. [*ibid.*, p. 288]

In this description of the secondary system, Freud is searching for a concept that brings together the principles of this system. In a sense, he fails in this attempt. He tries three overlapping possibilities: the temporal stratification, the concentric stratification, and then a certain type of logical organization that he tells us little about, except that it is the most important aspect of the secondary system. (One is tempted to be anachronistic and say that the logical thread that he is searching for is the logic of a concept soon to come, the primary process.) Here, we can see that even the idea of a pathogenic element invading the body is not entirely embraced by Freud. Although he uses the idea of a foreign body invading the organism, he also gives us a picture of normal and pathological blending at the boundaries of conscious experience. At this point, he is struggling to describe his experience when encountering clinical material. Thus, as one goes deeper towards the pathogenic nucleus, lines criss-cross around it and the resistance to remembering the pathogenic memories is greatest as one comes closer to this hypothesized nucleus. Here, clearly, Freud is envisioning memories, although incompatible ideas (defended ideas) need not be memories, but can be any type of psychological form of ideation.

I have quoted this passage from Freud to show how, at this point, he is searching for a principle that will explain the logic of the secondary system. Even though it might be easiest to think of this system as being layered chronologically, Freud already knew from his clinical experience that this did not account for how these "memories" became conscious in the various forms of treatment that he was inventing or utilizing at this point in his career.

Freud's new concepts: looking backwards and forwards

In these few pages that we have gone over, we have seen Freud introduce a number of concepts that remind us of our vision of the more mature psychoanalytic theory. He has begun to develop the ideas about defence, of a secondary (not conscious) and primary (conscious) system, and of psychic energy. He has used the term ego, and, with this term as well as his other theoretical ideas, we will explore how these ideas change and are transformed depending on the overall structure of Freud's theorizing at the time. There are two other premises of Freud's that will continue become crucial parts of psychoanalytic theorizing: childhood sexuality and the concept of transference. Childhood sexuality will become a cornerstone of Freud's theorizing in every era that follows the present time period. The idea of transference is one that certainly shook the therapeutic world of psychoanalysis (Ellman, 1991). Transference is by no means a concept that has utility only in the clinical setting. Others have utilized and developed Freud's thoughts on transference in areas far beyond the paths that Freud envisioned (e.g., Bion, 1959). Freud recognized the power of this idea, but, as with many of his premises, he did not explore the full implications of transference. Of course, at this time he was creating a theory, a technique, and a new profession.

Transference

Although, for Freud, the concept of transference was primarily related to the clinical situation, his clearest statement of the concept might be in his one of his most theoretical works, *The Interpretation of Dreams* (1900a). We are briefly reviewing the issue of transference in this volume, since one can also consider transference a theoretical concept that explains many aspects of fantasy as well as interpersonal relationships. Freud's first use of the term transference occurs in *Studies on Hysteria*, in his psychotherapy chapter (Chapter Four). Here, he tells us about three possible disruptions in the treatment of hysteria, the third of which he labels transference.

> This is a frequent, and indeed in some analyses a regular, occurrence. Transference on to the physician takes place through a false connection. [This is the first appearance of the use of transference in Freud's writings.] It is impossible to carry any analysis to a conclusion unless we know how to meet the resistance arising in these three ways. But we can find a way of doing so if we make up our minds that this new symptom that has been produced on the old model must be treated in the same way as the old symptoms. Our . . . task is to make the obstacle conscious to the patient. [1895d, pp. 302–303).

> [Freud tells us that] To begin with I was greatly annoyed at this increase in my psychological work, till I came to see that the whole process followed a law; and I then noticed, too, that transference of this kind brought about no great addition to what I had to do. For the patient the work remained the same: she had to overcome the distressing affect aroused by having been able to entertain such a wish even for a moment; and it seemed to make no difference to the success of the treatment whether she made this psychical

repudiation the theme of her work in the historical instance or in the recent one connected with me. The patients, too, gradually learnt to realize that in these transferences on to the figure of the physician it was a question of a compulsion and an illusion which melted away with the conclusion of the analysis. [*ibid.*, p. 304]

It is interesting that Freud sees the idea of a disturbance in the patient's relation to the physician as an *external obstacle*, even though it is met with in every serious analysis. The three types of disturbances, including what Freud calls the transference, are not the main arena of the treatment, but, rather, are considered to be material to be mastered and overcome as expeditiously as possible. He tells us that at first he was annoyed by the transference, but now has dealt with his annoyance, since transference does not really add to his work. Even in these few paragraphs, Freud vacillates in his view of transference. At times, he sees transference as an external obstacle, or even as a nuisance, deterring him from his main task of recovering pathogenic memories; at other times, he is surprisingly modern in his view of transference. Still, transference is restricted to distressing ideas arising from the content of the analysis, and they are ideas that are *false connections*. Freud, at this time, considered obsessive symptomatology as essentially false connections. Thus, if a person defended against one idea and obsessed about another substitute (conscious) idea, the conscious idea was a false connection. He theorized that these super-valent conscious ideas were the result of energy transfers. The process of defence was involved with making a strong idea a weak one, when this happened there was now a new, conscious, strong idea which was the false connection. Transference could be seen as just one type of false connection. Put in other terms, all false connections have a transfer of energy. These false connections, while important, are not the central issue for Freud's treatment to achieve success. At this point, he is still striving to help the patient recollect.

Later in his career, Freud had come to conceive of transference as a crucial aspect of the therapeutic process. The realization of the importance of transference was a painful one, given that it was conceived amid clinical difficulties and disappointments. It is noteworthy that Freud's interest in the topic fluctuated throughout his career. As early as his publication of the Dora case (1905e), Freud was on his way towards recognizing the clinical importance of transference. It was not until the era of his technique papers (1910–1915) that Freud seemed at home with the concept of transference. As we will see, his ease with the concept could not be charted in linear or monotonic terms. During the 1920s, Freud retreated somewhat from his revolutionary theory of transference and returned to some of the ideas that we have just explored. More specifically he returns to the idea involved in the capturing of (or remembering) pathogenic memories.

Sexuality and the psychogenic and actual neuroses

Psychogenic neuroses

To this point in the chapter, we have been discussing what Freud termed the psychogenic neuroses. The two neuroses that we have mentioned in this chapter are hysteria and obsessive–compulsive neuroses. Either of these disorders could be linked with phobic symptoms or anxiety. Freud also discussed psychotic disorders (see "The neuro-psychoses of defence, 1894a) as psychogenic in origin. The origin of psychogenic disorders, until 1897, was what has been called the seduction hypothesis. In this hypothesis, Freud maintained that aetiology of psychogenic disorders was always related to sexual abuse in childhood. This abuse was thought to occur before the age of eight and was traumatic in nature. Freud assumed that the child was both abused and excited, and that there was no appropriate outlet for the excitement. The child, in this view, was not capable of sexual discharge, and this led to a situation where the excitement became aversive. The inability to discharge the stimulation led to a defensive process (where a strong idea is turned into a weak one) and is excluded from the primary system and included in the secondary system. Once sexual ideas and memories were in the secondary system, they were secure or quiescent until, or unless, some external event stimulated these memories. Freud, in his case histories, gives a number of instances of young women having sexual or sexualized experiences that reactivate defended-against memories. These memories might be represented directly or symbolically, but inevitably the memories have symptomatic expression. Most of the women that Freud wrote about developed conversion symptoms and were considered to be hysterics. Most of the men were obsessive–compulsives, although Freud did report on a man whom he considered to be a hysteric. In both disorders, the initial cause was sexual abuse. Usually, obsessive–compulsive patients, after being abused, were also themselves abusers of younger children (siblings, relatives, friends, etc.). Freud thinks at this time that these patients attempted to do to others what had been done to them. This early activity led not only to obsessive–compulsive symptoms, but also to obsessive–compulsive and sadistic tendencies.

The manifestation of different symptoms (or choice of symptom, in modern parlance) depended in large part on the patient's ability for conversion. Alternatively, one might say that a symptom is determined by the disposition of affect when defence occurs. We have to remember that defence is a process where a strong idea is turned into a weak one and the affect is split away from the idea. Thus, the disposition of affect is the final pathway in the type of symptom that is produced. Freud assumed that there were innate biological tendencies that produced conversion symptoms. Thus, in conversion symptoms, the affect associated with the original memory is literally converted into a physical symptom. There may be diverse symptoms, such as blindness, or paralysis, or aphonia. To the extent that an affect is converted into a physical symptom, the patient will experience little accompanying affect, hence the term *la belle indifference*. This term means that the woman is indifferent to her plight, although, as one can read from Freud's case material, this indifference is not long lasting. If the patient does not have the capacity for conversion, then a false connection is made with another idea. More specifically, if the affect is not converted, it becomes attached to another idea in the primary (conscious) system and this explains the overvaluation of certain ideas and behaviours. Thus, an obsessive–compulsive who wants constantly to clean is thinking about an activity that may relate to his defended-against idea. However, it is not clear to him why he has an overwhelming desire to clean things that have already been cleaned. Freud already has begun to think that the false connection is not a random event, but is strongly influence by how the secondary system is stratified.

We have talked about two types of symptoms, but Freud has also posited that anxiety, as a symptom, is an affect that is not otherwise discharged or converted. Thus, in a conversion symptom, if not all the affect is converted into a physical symptom, there can be anxiety or, perhaps, even a false connection formed. In a similar fashion, phobias can be false connections that are a result of an accumulation of a great deal of affect. This affect overwhelms the primary system and produces anxiety to the point of fear. We can see from even this brief look at Freud's ideas about affect that affect can be displaced and that quantitative factors are important in his understanding of how the person experiences affect. In the penultimate paragraph of "The neuro-psychoses of defence", Freud states his view of affect:

> I should like, finally to dwell for a moment on the working hypothesis which I have made use of in this exposition of the neuroses of defence. I refer to the concept that in mental functions something is to be distinguished—a quota of affect or sum of excitation—which possesses all the characteristic of a quantity (though we have no means of measuring it), which is capable of increase, diminution, displacement and discharge, and which is spread over the memory —traces of ideas somewhat as an electric charge is spread over the surface of a body. [1894a, p. 60]

If we look at Freud's views on the production of psychogenic disturbance, we can say that a traumatic environmental event (seduction or sexual abuse) early in life produces a tendency for later psychological disturbance. This disturbance is mediated by physiological factors that are related to the appropriate discharge of affect. The physiological and neuro-physiological factors that Freud posited will be remarked on more fully in the commentary section of this chapter.

Actual neuroses

The term "actual neurosis" is a somewhat strange term to the modern reader. It is hard to imagine that Freud thought that there were sexual practices in an adult's life that produced psychological symptoms. However, he thought that if there is not what he termed appropriate sexual discharge, the chances of developing psychological symptoms is greatly enhanced. If a man or women masturbated too much, Freud thought that this resulted in the symptoms of fatigue or neurasthenia. Similarly, if a person practised coitus interruptus, they might develop symptoms of anxiety neurosis. Clearly, the idea of appropriate discharge was important in Freud's conceptualizations of normality. Thus, a person needed to have consistent orgasms during intercourse to maintain normal discharge patterns. States of actual neurosis occurred when these patterns of discharge did not occur or were interrupted without timely discharge. Freud's treatment of adults whom he diagnosed as actual neurotics was to advise them to change their sexual practices. It is a matter of continuing interest that, through at least fifteen years of Freud's career, he continued to conceive of some individuals as suffering from an actual neurosis. During most of the 1890s, Freud had two major classifications of mental disorders: psychogenic and actual disorders.

Freud and the seduction theory

In talking about defended-against or incompatible ideas, Freud asks, "What is the content of these incompatible ideas?" Freud maintains, "In all the cases I have analysed it was the subject's *sexual life* that had given rise to a distressing affect". Here, Freud is talking about psychogenic disorders and sexual life in terms of sexual abuse during a person's childhood. This was written in 1894, and Freud was seemingly convinced of the validity of the seduction theory or hypothesis. In a subsequent publication, Freud, for one of the few times in his career, states statistics and says that nineteen out of twenty of his patients were sexually abused in early childhood. He is convinced of this relationship and his conviction is documented in his letter to his friend, confidant, and co-conspirator, Wilhelm Fliess. One can see that, at this point in time, Freud's "neurotica" is exciting both Freud and probably his audience, Fliess. Freud's view will change shortly, and by 21 September he evinces strong doubts (Masson, 1985, pp. 264–266) and in October 1897 he writes to Fliess about his misgivings and how he thinks that, for both logical and psychological reasons, the seduction hypothesis cannot be the powerful explanatory concept that he once believed it to be.

The reasons stated in this letter, combined with his own self-analysis, now convince Freud that his hypothesis is incorrect, at least in the way that he originally formulated this concept. He cannot imagine that there are that many perverse fathers. He has to include his own father, since he has diagnosed himself as having certain hysterical symptoms. The questions abound about how he is to regard the sexual content that his patients have provided for him? He will answer these questions by the time we get to our next chapter, but for now Freud's self-analysis is providing him with a number of suggestions that he will take quite seriously. Clearly, there are many authors who have interpreted the reasons for Freud's original seduction hypothesis and the reasons that he gave up this theory (Good, 1995; Masson, 1984; Simon, 1992; Sulloway, 1979). Masson provides the most dramatic explanation and Good (1995, 2006) the most complete series of explanations.

It may strike the contemporary reader that the term "seduction" is rather a mild term for what most would call sexual abuse. What Freud was alluding to was a "passive sexual experience in the first years of childhood" (Masson, 1985, p. 52). Good (2006) relates this to Charcot's influence on Freud, where Charcot thought of hysteria as being caused by trauma where the sufferers were passive recipients of the traumatic experience. Hence, Freud was inclined to believe the patient's statements where they "ascribed their symptoms to passive sexual experiences in the first years of childhood— to put it bluntly to seduction" (Freud, 1914d, p. 17).

Freud's self-analysis

Freud's self-analysis takes place in the period from 1896 to 1900 and lasts for the rest of his career. Eissler (1971) enthusiastically calls Freud's self-analysis one of the great accomplishments in the history of Western civilization. This exaggerated view is perhaps better understood if one considers that Freud's insights into his own psyche were a factor that convinced him that the seduction theory was incorrect. Gay correctly writes that Freud's self analysis "has become the centerpiece of psychoanalytic mythology" (1988, p. 96). He points out that Freud himself has said that, "True self-analysis is impossible, else there would be no illness" (1988, p. 96). However, Freud was inconsistent about this, as he was about a number of issues. As late as 1923 he returns to the idea of someone analysing themselves in his dream papers (Freud, 1923c). Since psychoanalysis is always a dialogue, how does Freud reconcile this idea with his self-analysis? Gay states that Fliess was the other person that Freud dialogued with and the dialogue took place mainly through letters and fantasy. I will not attempt to evaluate Freud's self-analysis, except to say that I have previously indicated (Ellman, 1991) that Freud evaded treatment in the same way that many people avoid the treatment situation. Clearly, he was conflicted about many issues, and clearly he was an amazing human being who triumphed over many difficult circumstances. Would he have been better off had he gone into treatment? Obviously, this is an impossible question: better in what way and for whom, one could multiply the questions and no real answer would be satisfactory. One can only say that, in some way, Freud's self-analysis convinced him that his seduction hypothesis was incorrect in the way that he formulated this hypothesis. He had to look for other explanations and, in the following chapters, we will explore the explanations that he put forth.

This era begins Freud's psychoanalytic journey, and, although I have to some extent downplayed Freud's self-analysis, Eissler's volume systematically looks at Freud's psychopathology in a manner that one should not dismiss. Although I believe that Eissler's idealization causes some difficulties in his analysis, his volume is still one that is replete with interesting interpretations. Certainly, the era ends with Freud leaving the seduction hypothesis, which leads to the next era, where he puts forward new concepts that involve very basic ideas about how human beings develop, think, and process relationships.

Note

1. In this translation, it appears that Freud is using the term ego in the modern sense of the term, that is, the ego of the structural theory. This is, however, an anachronistic view, since Freud does not have a structural concept of ego at this point in time. One could say that ego is equated with the person's sense of self, but even this explanation lacks clarity and simply presents a different, imprecise description to the

term. For the time being, we will be content to say that the term ego conforms to the person's conscious or primary views of themselves. Ideas that are incompatible with these views are opposed in one way or another. Defence is a way in which incompatible ideas are kept out of the person's conscious or primary associations about themselves.

CHAPTER TWO

The psychoanalytic era begins: dream theory–psycho-sexuality

In this chapter we go over both *The Interpretation of Dreams* and *Three Essays on the Theory of Sexuality*. I have put the summaries of both at the beginning of the chapter, although these works are discussed separately.

Summary of "the dream book"

Although Freud initially presented a complex model of dreaming, the emphasis of this model was on the wish. The wish, to paraphrase Freud, is the capital needed to fuel the dream, and Freud and those that followed him have focused heavily on the capital in the business of dreaming. Freud maintained that dreams are instigated by unconscious wishes. After making this assertion, Freud, in Chapter Seven of *The Interpretation of Dreams* (1900a), frequently reminds us of Socrates helping his listeners search for the meaning of the good and the beautiful. The sceptic might ask, if all dreams are instigated by a wish, what about anxiety dreams or dreams that feel horrific and typically are called nightmares? Freud answers these queries and his answers lead him to consider a realm of experience that, up to that point in time, had been largely unexplored: the earliest and deepest recesses of human experience. He defines an unconscious wish as a pleasure that has its source in early childhood. It is a pleasure that, if activated, shows the mind in conflict, since what is pleasurable at one level (unconscious) will cause anxiety on another level (pcs-conscious). This conflict is mediated by the censorship (which serves a defensive function), and these two levels of awareness are *primarily* governed by different modes of cognition (primary *vs.* secondary process).

Why does a dream occur? Here, Freud posits that sleep is both a condition for regression and, during sleep, the censorship is weakened. Thus, the emergence (representation) of a wish (which was activated during the previous day) can more easily occur during sleep. The censorship that is still active provides the impetus for a compromise formation. This compromise formation consists of the transformation of the wish into sensory form that is disguised sufficiently to allow the person to dream and stay asleep. Anxiety dreams, in Freud's theory, signal the failure of the dream process and dream-work to adequately disguise and deal with the wish. In the dream book, Freud theorizes about how different systems communicate, and it is this communication that he labels as transference. It is via the dream that Freud gives theoretical definition to this concept that will gradually change the way he conceptualizes the treatment situation. As a last point in this brief summary, Freud attempts to show the similarities between dream formation, symptom formation, and, during the same time period, a variety of other phenomena (momentary forgetting, slips of tongue, etc. [Freud, 1901b]). In short, Chapter Seven is unparalleled in psychoanalytic thought, in that Freud attempts the most general theory that has been put forth probably up to the present time. Despite this heroic attempt, Freud will find various difficulties with his theoretical structure and certainly others will find even greater difficulty.

Summary of Three Essays on the Theory of Sexuality *(three essays)*

In this work we see Freud (mostly) leaving the seduction hypothesis. Childhood interest in sexuality and bodily functions now becomes a universal tendency. In the first essay, Freud points out that what we call perversions are usual occurrences during different points of development, part of the human condition. He maintains that many of our assumptions about sexuality are biased, and a result of either anxiety or defences against certain types of sexuality. He tries to debunk the prejudices of his time against homosexuality. He maintains that homosexuals are not moral degenerates, although he still holds open the possibility of homosexuality being a result of childhood conflict.

In the second essay, he discusses both the new stages of development that he puts forth (autoerotism and object love) and describes the child's interest in various bodily functions. In the third essay, he describes how males and females differentiate in terms of sexual interest and tendencies. Reading these essays in original form brings the realization that Freud's stages of oral, anal, and phallic organization did not appear until later in his career.

Introduction: the unconscious and psycho-sexuality

It is in this period of Freud's writing that he begins the modern era of psychoanalysis. He now embraces the concepts of the unconscious and universal psycho-sexuality. In this chapter we will discuss two of his best known works, *The Interpretation of Dreams* (dream book) (1900a) and *Three Essays on the Theory of Sexuality* (three essays) (1905d). Interestingly, when students read the three essays, they are always somewhat confused. They are searching for what they already know (or believe) to be Freud's theory of psychosexuality, and they have difficulty in finding it in these essays. This is partly because of the fact that Freud continuously revised the essays by adding footnotes and, at times, even whole passages to this work. As we will see, Freud's theory of psychosexual development does not parallel the more finished, unified, and yet somewhat simplified, version of his ideas that are popularly portrayed in beginning psychoanalytic text books (Brenner, 1955). The same might be said for arguably Freud's most cherished work, *The Interpretation of Dreams*. In this work, he puts forth not only a theory of dream formation, but a model of mental organization that continues as a feasible theory for certain aspects of cognitive functioning. In fact, the work is so dense, rich, and comprehensive that it remains without parallel in psychoanalytic theorizing.

It is important to note that we will be concerned throughout this volume with Freud's revisions of his ideas, particularly concepts that are presented in the three essays and in the dream book. We will look at additions to each volume (or any volume) during the era that Freud made the addition. Thus, our first view of the dream book and the three essays will be based on the text that was presented during that time period.

The dream book

Dreams are instigated by unconscious wishes. This sentence seems clear enough to the modern ear, but Freud will take this statement and from it build a model of the mind. He forges this model by utilizing a late nineteenth century version of the Socratic method. Freud gives us a dialogue between the sceptical listener and the theoretician that frequently reminds us of Socrates searching for, or helping his listeners search for, the meaning of the good and the beautiful. The sceptic might ask, if all dreams are instigated by a wish, what about anxiety dreams or dreams that feel horrific and typically are called nightmares? Freud patiently answers these queries and his answers let him consider a realm of experience that, up to that point in time, had been largely unexplored: the earliest and deepest recesses of human experience. He must define what he means by a wish and how wishes originate. He must tell us why wishes occur in disguised form and how this disguise develops. He must also give us a theory that distinguishes waking and sleeping mentation (a word that is used by sleep researchers, or, at least, a word that I encounter primarily in the sleep research literature, which stands for any type of discernible mental activity) and he implicitly begins to articulate a theory of different states of consciousness. It is easy to be anachronistic and forget that Freud had no idea of sleep stages and certainly did not know anything about rapid eye movement (REM) sleep (Ellman & Antrobus, 1991) or state of consciousness research.

Most importantly, in this new theory of wishes Freud needed to distinguish between levels of consciousness, and here he begins to fully develop his ideas about the role of the unconscious in a person's waking as well as sleeping life. How does the unconscious effect dream experience (or the manifest content of the dream)? This question leads Freud into continuing to develop a theory of defence, postulating an agency of censorship, and, most importantly, positing different processes of cognition (primary and secondary process) that will be a powerful theoretical metaphor to help explain a variety of human activities. He notes that dreams are usually sensory in nature and this observation leads him to question why this should be true of the dream. The question takes Freud into the issue of regression, and here he gives us several uses of this term, which again do not fully conform to the modern use of the term regression. In listing the concepts that Freud introduces in the dream book, I have included transference, despite the fact that Freud first mentions transference (see Chapter One) in *Studies on Hysteria* (Breuer & Freud, 1895d). In the dream book, Freud tries to account for the transfer of unconscious wishes to consciousness. In this work, Freud begins his theoretical understanding of the concept of transference and its counterpart, the concept of defence. It is in the dream book that we begin to see theoretical concepts that attempt to explain what Freud has conceptualized in his clinical writings 5–8 years earlier in *Studies on Hysteria*.

Assumptions about levels of consciousness

When Freud undertook the writing of the dream book, he had more fully developed his ideas about levels of consciousness. Most important in his delineations was his understanding of the unconscious. His concept of the unconscious began with his assumptions about the secondary psychical system. Now, however, we see that the idea of a secondary psychical system is substantially altered. For example, in positing unconscious ideation, Freud emphasized that there were some ideas that were totally inaccessible to conscious awareness. Even in treatment these thoughts (in the broadest sense of the term) cannot be made easily available to the person, and we see that Freud, shortly after the publication of this work, gives up the pressure technique. So, we may say that thoughts in the unconscious are thoughts that the person cannot easily become aware of under any immediate conditions; these thoughts may include memories as well as fantasies. They may emanate from any point in life, but are most notably from childhood. The preconscious, in Freud's theory, is where most cognitive processing occurs; memories and thoughts that are preconscious can achieve consciousness. Thus, there may be a variety of preconscious thoughts that we may not be aware of as we process an event, but these thoughts are potentially available to the person's conscious experience. The preconscious is thus presumed to be a state where procedural memory is processed; hence, tying one's shoes or hitting a golf ball are not things that we are conscious of once having learnt these skills, but memories associated with these skills can be made conscious. In addition, there are a variety of memories that are not conscious but can be voluntarily brought to consciousness.

The definition of consciousness in Freud's era was not viewed as a significant problem, since, in that epoch, to paraphrase Freud, psychical meant conscious. Therefore, any significant action was viewed as a result of consciously formed decisions. Freud's view of consciousness is quite different: the conscious state is seen as equivalent to a sense organ with limited capacities. It was certainly not equated with a person's psychical life, and was not even where most cognitive processing took place. Thus, Freud's new theoretical perspective downplays the role of conscious and even rational thought; decision making is often a process that is dominated by factors outside of a person's awareness.

One might say that there are two different ways in which Freud uses the terms conscious (cs.), preconscious (pcs.), and unconscious (ucs.). One might roughly be called a descriptive use of these terms. The descriptive point of view simply attempts to specify whether an idea is unconscious or preconscious, and this will denote whether this thought is potentially available to the person's conscious experience. Another use of the term occurs when Freud assigns functions and properties to what he has previously described as the unconscious. Thus, he might say that a certain type of thought process goes on in the unconscious and a different type of process goes on in the preconscious. Here, he is talking about more than level of awareness, and he frequently utilizes terms like the system unconscious or the conscious–preconscious system (Freud frequently linked the functions of a person's conscious and preconscious states). Freud will continue for a long time to make a distinction between the descriptive and the systematic uses of pcs., cs., and ucs.

The Freudian unconscious can never be a merely descriptive term, for even in the descriptive use of the term he is postulating processes that are inaccessible to any type of observation. The term is, therefore, a theoretical one in either usage. Thus, I assume that Freud knew, when he was forced to know, that any use of the concept of unconscious processes involves theoretical assumptions and not merely descriptions. Nevertheless, despite this knowledge, Freud often wrote as if one could observe unconscious processes. This tendency has led to some theoretical confusions. One can observe hypothesized manifestations of unconscious processes; one cannot observe the unconscious process itself. This simple point has ramifications beyond the concept of unconscious processes. There is a question as to how to view various theoretical ideas, and this question has stayed with psychoanalysis up to the present time. It is a view of mine that analysts have tended to take various psychoanalytic concepts as directly observable, and this tendency has led to the type of conceptual misunderstandings that I alluded to in talking about Freud. This is a theme that will be taken up with various concepts, such as unconscious processes, defence, and transference. In addition, Freud makes a distinction between metapsychology and clinical observation or theory that will also be questioned in the next chapter.

Forgetting of dreams

Chapter Seven in *The Interpretation of Dreams* is by now almost a legendary chapter in psychoanalysis. It is where Freud gives his most complete theoretical rendering of what he calls the "Psychology of the dream-process". As I have stated, he does much more than this in the chapter, but this is the place where he begins his discourse.

In Chapter Seven, Freud starts off his exegesis by solidifying clinical observations that he has previously reported. It is his view that the "forgetting of dreams is to a great extent a product of resistance" (1900a, p. 520). He cites patients who report having a dream and yet are unable to remember the content of the dream. Freud tells us that, as they proceed with the treatment, they come up against a resistance, and then "I . . . explain something to the patient and help him by encouragement and pressure" (1900a, p. 520) and the patient then exclaims that he/she is able to remember what was dreamt. (Freud was still using the pressure technique at this time.) Freud concludes that by overcoming resistance he is able to help the patient to recall a dream. He reasons that at least some dreams are forgotten because of resistance, as opposed to the other explanations that might be proposed. This is stating the argument in its weak form, since it is clear that Freud believed that most, if not all, dreams are forgotten as a result of repression. He is also reluctant to view sleep as a state that is completely alien to wakefulness. Freud sees a continuum between waking and sleep mechanisms and he believes that psychoanalytic experience bolsters this perspective. Sleep, as we will see, is a time where regressive trends normally predominate, but we will have to wait to fully broach this facet of the theory. We can note, however, that, here again, Freud is taking a different view than his contemporary dream and sleep theorists like Morton Prince (White, 1992). He is obviously aware that dreams occur during sleep, but for him their occurrence depends on various conditions of waking experiences.

Perhaps the most interesting aspect of dream formation that forgetting provides for Freud is that even the remembering of a single element of a dream can lead one to a person's unconscious purposive ideas. Freud maintains that

> Psychiatrists have been far too ready . . . to abandon their belief in the connectedness of psychical processes. I know for a fact that trains of thought without purposive ideas no more occur in hysteria and paranoia than they do in the formation or resolution of dreams. [1900a, pp. 528–529]

In treating the neuroses, Freud's instruction to the patient to free associate is guided by the presumption that the patient will not be able to leave the train of purposive ideas and that "what seem to be the most innocent and arbitrary things which he tells me are in fact related to his illness" (*ibid.*, p. 529).

Most of what we have touched upon to this point could be taken up at any point in the circle that Freud is drawing and eventually these points would connect. We could start by asking what Freud means by a purposive idea, and this would take us into the realm of what he means by wish fulfilment, which in turn takes us into the issue of his ideas about early development. We could ask what Freud means by regression, and this would take us in yet another direction that would begin to tell us how he viewed early cognition. Wherever we started the roads would eventually cross, and so let us go directly to Freud's central hypothesis (wish fulfilment) and work our way back to how and why dreams are forgotten.

Wish fulfilment

Freud begins by citing Aristotle that a dream is thinking that continues during sleep. He then reasonably asks if we can think of various things during waking, why should our sleeping thoughts be restricted to wishes? Let us set aside this question and see first the role that Freud sets for wishes in dreams (dream-wishes). We may state a characteristic that all dream-wishes share; they are wishes that are experienced (or potentially experienced) as not having been gratified. A conscious dream-wish may have been stimulated during the day, but, owing to life's exigencies, the person has not been able to satisfy this wish during the day. At night, this wish might be at the conscious or preconscious level of a person's awareness. Freud proposes, as a second idea, that the dream-wish may have arisen during the day but been repudiated; in that case, what is left over is a wish which has not been dealt with but has met with defensive processes. Freud assumes that wishes of the second kind have been driven into (defended against) the person's unconscious. These wishes are thus no longer available to the person's consciousness. The third type of dream-wish is one that has no direct connection with waking activity, but only becomes active at night under some conditions. This is a wish that is unconscious. There are also preconscious dream-wishes that become activated during sleep and can be considered a fourth type of dream-wish.

Now that we have distinguished levels of wishes, it is important to note that, in adults, Freud's supposition is that a conscious wish can only become a dream instigator if it succeeds in awakening an unconscious wish with the same or a similar meaning. He assumes that unconscious wishes are always on the alert to reinforce conscious or preconscious wishes by "transferring their own great intensity on to" the less intense pcs–cs. wishes. These unconscious wishes are from childhood and are, in Freud's words,

> immortal, [they] remind one of the legendary Titans, weighed down since primeval ages by the massive bulk of the mountains which were once hurled upon them by the victorious gods and which are still shaken from time to time by the convulsion of their limbs. [*ibid.*, p. 553]

His encounters with patients have led him to view the core of the onion as invariably comprising wishes from childhood. He tells us that dream-wishes have the same origin, and that we can more clearly see dream-wishes in the manifest dream when we look at children's dreams. In children, the censor between the pcs. and the ucs. is not fully developed, and so dream-wishes are more directly represented in the manifest dream. In adults, there is a firm censorship between the ucs. and the pcs. and, consequently, in adults unconscious wishes are more disguised. Up to this point, Freud's position is easily understood and reconciled with his later positions. However, when he says that, with children, the dream-wish is one that is an unfulfilled, unrepressed wish from waking life, we are left with a position that is not totally consistent with one that he is to take in later works. We will go back to this when we discuss his views on primal repression. For now, we will be content to say that children's wishes are less likely to be censored than is the case with adults. In this model, the censor guards against unconscious ideas entering consciousness.

What about the daytime events (non-wishes) that act as instigators for dreams; what can we say about this class of experience? Freud has already given a list of wishes that can be a stimulus for a dream, and he tells us that the thoughts that we carry over into sleep are not relegated to the category of wishes. As we enter sleep, there may be a variety of realistic problems that we have not attended to or not been able to solve. These are thoughts that we are still concerned with as we enter sleep; they are not, in and of themselves, wishes. Of course, as was said earlier, we may be thinking about what we have (attempted to) "suppress" during the day (an unfulfilled wish). There may also be a group of events that we have not dealt with during the day that we are relatively indifferent to; this class of events may be activated as we are going to sleep. All of these ideas share the quality of being unfinished. Thus, as the person enters sleep, the group of events that will be most likely to serve as an instigator for the dream is a class of experience(s) that in some way or another is incomplete or unfinished from the dreamer's point of view. Freud calls these experiences the day residue, and these experiences all share another feature, that is, during sleep, they will stimulate an ucs. wish from childhood.

How might we sum up the relationship of the day residue (which is usually pcs.) to dream formation? Freud says that

> There is no doubt that they find their way into dreams in great quantity and that they make use of the content of dreams in order to penetrate into consciousness even during the night. Indeed they occasionally dominate the content of a dream and force it to carry on the activity of daytime. It is certain, too, that the day's residues may be of any other character just as easily as wishes; but it is highly instructive in this connection, and of positively decisive importance for the theory of wish-fulfilment, to observe the condition to which they must submit in order to be received into a dream. [*ibid.*, p. 555]

Freud then likens the day residue to the entrepreneur, the person who has "the idea and the initiative" to begin a project. The entrepreneur, however, can do nothing without the capitalist, who "provides the psychical outlay for the dream" (*ibid.*, p. 561). It is possible for the capitalist to also be the entrepreneur, and, in fact, Freud thinks this is often the case. Freud then plays with the analogy and says that the entrepreneur may offer some capital, or, at other times, a variety of capitalists may contribute to the formation of the dream. The essential point is that the day residue may actually be linked to, or be a derivative of, a dream-wish. Often what is stimulated during the day is itself a wish that during sleep can provide the capital for the dream.

Lest we get awash in wishes, it may be useful to look at a dream and see how Freud is able to analyse a dream within his theoretical boundaries. We will look at a dream of Freud's that he presented in the dream book. The dream is the following: "My friend Otto was looking ill. His face was brown and he had protruding eyes . . ." (*ibid.*, p. 269).

Freud's association is that Otto in the dream had signs of Graves disease (in which your thyroid gland is stimulated excessively and the production of thyroid hormones [thyroxin] is abnormally high. This condition can affect the eyes, causing widening of the lids and bulging of the pupils). Otto is his family physician, and "I owe him more than I can ever hope to repay" (*ibid.*). Freud says that one might think that his dream might be construed as showing concern for Otto, since Freud's wife had mentioned that night that Otto had looked "tired and strained" (*ibid.*). Freud dismisses this explanation and asks why, if he were concerned about Otto's health, would he have given Otto Grave's (Basedow's) disease? Freud's analysis took him back to an accident that had occurred six years before the dream. He was riding in a coach with Professor R, and it was only by "a piece of luck that we all escaped injury" (*ibid.*, p. 270). When they spent a night at an inn, a man with "unmistakable signs of Graves disease—incidentally just as in the dream" asked what he could do for the group. Professor R, "in his decisive manner", asked for a night shirt, and the "fine gentleman rejoined: 'I'm sorry but I can't do that' and left the room" (*ibid.*) Freud's associations to this dream are rich and complex and he ends by asking where is the wish-fulfilment in the dream. He says not in "my avenging myself on my friend Otto [Oscar Rie, his children's pediatrician], whose fate it seems to be ill-treated in my dreams" (*ibid.*, p. 271). (Freud is referring to the Irma [Emma] dream. In the treatment of Irma, Freud called in Fliess, who operated on Irma and badly mangled the case. Freud, in the dream, blames the bad results on Otto [Oscar Rie] and Breuer. See Schur [1966] and Gay [1988] for further commentary on this historic dream.) If the dream is not designed to express hostile wishes towards Otto, what is happening according to Freud? It is his identification with Professor R, who "resembled me in having followed an independent path outside the academic world and had only achieved his well-merited title late in life. So once again I was wanting to be a Professor!" (*ibid.*). This is Freud's "egoistic" concern or wish, the wish to be a professor. The obvious question remains, however: where are the childhood roots to this dream?

For this part of the analysis, we would have to leave Freud's writings (not completely) and venture into biographical detail about his life and the meaning(s) of certain childhood events that he alludes to in his descriptions. An accident that Freud suffered when he was three years old would begin this odyssey, but here I will rest content by saying that Freud's associations certainly take him back to childhood events and to obvious oedipal rivalries. These rivalries are paralleled in the dream and there are, in addition, hints about hostility towards his wife. How one might ultimately interpret this dream would obviously depend on many factors, but there are certainly a number of entrepreneurs and capitalists contributing to the formation of this dream. Rivals and love objects abound from this one-line dream. This dreams affords us the possibility to see Freud's understanding of dream formation in several different ways. First, we can see clear day residue (Freud's wife's concern about Otto) that relates back to both an important event in Freud's adult life as well as his childhood. We can see how a manifest element of a dream that seemingly showed concern for a friend was, in fact, hiding what Freud called "egoistic" wishes. He interprets the dream as being a disguise for his ambitious wishes. All dreams disguise wishes, and here we see that Freud means egoistic wishes in the sense of self serving or ambitions. If we accept that his egoistic ambitions relate to childhood sexual wishes, than we have gone as far as we can in exploring Freud's dream in terms of the entrepreneur–capitalist distinction. It is clear, in the dream book, that Freud did not reveal the childhood roots of his dream.

Transference and the origins of the wish

Let us begin with a question that Freud will answer in several ways in the theoretical matrix of Chapter Seven. How does the entrepreneur appropriate capital to form the structure of the dream? More precisely, we might ask where in the dream is the greatest outlay of capital. Freud answers by saying that usually in dreams there is a point of sensory intensity, and, "as a rule", this marks the most direct representation of the dream-wish. If we are able to unravel the meaning of the dream, then we will see that psychical intensity of the dream-wish is replaced by the sensory intensity of the manifest dream. To explain this, Freud comes up with an idea that is similar to one that he has introduced earlier (1894a, 1895), and that is the notion of a false connection. Here, however, he states it in a manner that brings together another concept that he has previously introduced, transference.

> The elements in the *neighbourhood* of the wish-fulfilment often have nothing to do with its meaning . . . owing to their being in what is often an artificially established connection with the central element (wish), they have acquired enough intensity to become capable of being represented in the dream. Thus the wish's . . . power . . . is diffused over a certain sphere surrounding it. In . . . dreams that are actuated by several wishes, it is easy to delimit the spheres of the different wish-fulfilments, and gaps in the dream may often be understood as frontier zones between those spheres. [1900a, p. 562]

Freud maintains that the dream-wish can become attached to an element of the dream that surrounds the main point of representation. How is that point of representation determined? Freud relates that they may be derivatives of distressing thoughts that run contrary to the wish. This is similar to his previous notion of a false connection being established. Now, however, Freud is telling us more about the defensive nature of the false connection; the wish is disguised when represented by distressing thoughts that run contrary to the central aims of the dream-wish. Thus, Otto was seen by Freud as being ill, and this disguised Freud's unconscious egoistic wish. Freud seemingly could have been concerned with Otto's health, but, after analysis, he says that this is not the reason, for, in the dream, the idea of concern for Otto is a false connection that disguises his true wish.

It is not, however, only ideas that run contrary to the wish that are represented in the dream. Sometimes, the most insignificant daytime images are found in the dream. Freud, in explaining this, begins to give us some of his theoretical ideas about transference. Unconscious ideas are incapable of entering the pcs.–cs. system unless they are able to exercise an effect on and "establish a connection with" (*ibid*.) an already existing pcs. idea. The unconscious idea transfers its intensity to this idea (or makes this idea appreciably more important), and thereby is "covered" by the pcs. thought or representation. "Here we have the fact of 'transference' which provides an explanation of so many striking phenomena in the mental life of neurotics" (*ibid*., pp. 562–563). Freud, as we have seen, has taken up the concept of transference in *Studies on Hysteria* (Breuer & Freud, 1895d), but here he is beginning to embrace and acknowledge the importance of the concept. He is extending its significance, for, although he recounts that he first conceived of transference in his clinical work, he now has implicitly extended the theoretical underpinnings of transference to everyday phenomena, including the dream. We can also say that, if transference occurs in the process of dream formation, it may be possible in other aspects of our everyday life. Here, I am referring to a work of Freud, *The Psychopathology of Everyday Life* (1901b), where Freud in many ways uses the model of dream formation and compromise formation to explain ordinary phenomena, such as momentary forgetting or slips of the tongue. Even in the dream book, Freud gives us indication that he is moving in this theoretical direction. If one looks at various letters to Fliess (Masson, 1985), we see that Freud's thoughts had already traversed this theoretical roadblock. To go back to the specifics of transference we might ask why experiences to which a person is relatively indifferent would be the subject of transference.

Freud's answer is twofold: we must first understand that he feels that he has demonstrated that "every analysis of a dream shows some recent impression woven into its texture and that this recent element is often of the most trivial kind" (1900a, p. 562). This is clearly an empirical statement and one that we look at much later in our analysis. He then goes on to tell us that the reason why these recent and indifferent elements so frequently find their way into dreams as substitutes for the oldest of all the dream-thoughts is that they have least to fear from the censorship. Experiences to which we are indifferent do not find resistance from either below or above. The power of an ucs. thought can easily overwhelm these relatively unimportant experiences, and they therefore make a suitable vehicle for transference. Conversely, the pcs. censor does not pay attention to these relatively trivial, recent experiences, even if they have been somewhat transformed and intensified by the transference process. Here, we can see one of the uses of Freud's idea of compromise formation. The indifferent experience cannot be radically transformed by the ucs. derivative, or the disguise or defensive value will be lost. Nevertheless, there must be some representation of the ucs. idea, or the wish is not expressed, even in symbolic form.

Thus, in the dream, there is a compromise between defensive processes (which are weakened during sleep) and the expression of a dream-wish. Why, we might ask, is it so important to the person to express this ucs. wish? What is the point of all this disguise and mental gymnastics to express a wish that is derived from childhood experience? To answer this question, Freud takes us into one realm of his ideas of early development.

Wishes, hallucinations, and fundamental hypotheses

We have talked about wishes in a general way, but Freud is going to be increasingly more specific about the nature and content of a wish in this publication and in *Three Essays on Sexuality* (which we explore later in this chapter). Here, we will encounter some of his fundamental hypotheses about human life and, implicitly, about evolution. A good deal of what we will go over Freud has attempted to conceptualize in letters to Fliess, or what is today called *The Project for a Scientific Psychology* (1895a, see also Pribram & Gill, 1976). He begins by telling us that, in less developed species, an organism's efforts

> were directed towards keeping itself so far as possible free from stimuli; consequently its first structure followed the plan of a reflex apparatus, so that any sensory excitation impinging on it could be promptly discharged along a motor path. But the exigencies of life interfere with this simple function, and it is to them too, that the apparatus owes the impetuous to further development. [1900a, p. 565]

These sentences are described in the *Standard Edition* as the "so called 'Principle of Constancy'" (1900a, p. 565, fn.), which Freud alludes to in several places but explicitly in *Beyond The Pleasure Principle* (1920g). Here, we can describe this principle in two complementary ways; the organism (any organism) attempts to reduce stimulation to its lowest level. Hence, we can say that discharge of stimulation is the prototypic type of gratification for Freud, more specifically, the adult male orgasm is the type of discharge that Freud's theory views as paradigmatic. Thus, to repeat gratification occurs when we reduce stimulation to its lowest level; orgasm is a discharge which accomplishes this in terms of sexual stimulation. What does Freud mean when he says the exigencies of life interfere with the sensory–motor reflex arc pattern? The example he uses involves a human baby in the midst of experiencing a need state, hunger. The hungry infant kicks and screams "helplessly". The internal situation for the infant remains unaltered, since hunger is not a momentary excitation but rather a need that produces a continuous state of internal or endogenous excitation. A change in the state can only come about if the infant is fed, and this can only happen if a care-giver responds to the infant. When this occurs, it gives rise to satisfaction and produces a cessation of endogenous stimulation. The perception of satisfaction is associated in memory with the memory of "the excitation produced by the need". The next time the need arises, Freud posits that the experience of satisfaction will be evoked in the form of the memory of (or, using the terminology of the *Standard Edition*, the mnemic image of) the original satisfaction. This is what Freud calls a wish-fulfilment; the impulse or impetus to have the perception of satisfaction is the wish, the appearance of the satisfaction is a wish fulfilled. Thus, the "reappearance of the perception (of satisfaction) is the satisfaction of the wish". Freud assumes that the infant's first psychical act or activity is a wish fulfilment that "produces a 'perceptual identity', a repetition of the perception which was linked with the satisfaction of the need" (1900a, p. 566). This associative link between the memory traces is one of contiguity. This bond is established by a form of conditioning. The memory of the need is temporally associated with the memory of satisfaction, and the production of the satisfying mnemic image is an attempt to endogenously produce satisfaction. Obviously, the most direct path for fulfilling a wish is to have the entire memory trace (or original perceptual image) reappear (in energic terms, it is recathected). If this is done in complete sensory detail, Freud calls this a hallucination, and he assumes that this first attempt by the infant is experienced in sensory terms.

This hallucination, or reappearance of the experience of satisfaction, obviously does not bring complete satisfaction. The hunger persists and the

> bitter experience of life must have changed this primitive thought-activity into a more expedient secondary one. . . . In order to arrive

at a more efficient expenditure of psychical force, it is necessary to bring a regression to a halt before it becomes complete, so that it does not proceed beyond the mnemic image, and is able to seek out other paths which lead eventually to the desired perceptual identity being established from the direction of the external world. In other words, it becomes evident that there must be a means of reality-testing (i.e., of testing things to see whether they are real or not). [*ibid.*]

(The term reality testing was added in 1919 by Freud.)

Freud is postulating, in this part of his model, that, after the first experience of satisfaction from the outside world, the infant, when it experiences hunger, endogenously reproduces this experience. In his terms, the infant re-cathects the mnemic image and in this way "re-evoke(s) the perception itself" (*ibid.*). When this hallucination does not significantly reduce the experience of hunger, it becomes necessary to try another pathway, that is, to turn towards reality. What does the infant do? It probably cries in a manner that signals to its care-giver that it is hungry (or that a need has arisen). Here, again, we can say that the infant learns to bring its "regression" to a halt and try other behaviours that will bring it in contact with reality. Freud is once more invoking learning mechanisms; the infant learns that a signal it naturally emits (crying when it is in discomfort) will bring satisfaction. It learns to turn away from what Freud calls regressive activities (the wish-fulfilment, or hallucination) towards the external world.

As we have gone over Freud's ideas about early development, we have implicitly introduced some terms that have not as yet been defined. The term regression, in this context, is one that will need to be more fully explicated. Freud also begins to introduce the idea of the wish-fulfilment as the primary or first activity, and the infant's turn towards the external world (or reality) as a secondary response. Here is the beginning of Freud's ideas about primary and secondary process, which will be highlighted in one of our next sections. Before we discuss these topics, Freud has a few more words to say about wish-fulfilment and the importance of wishes to the development of thought processes.

Freud tells us that thought is a substitute for an unconscious wish. We have seen that the primary wish gives way to secondary activity that deals with reality. Similarly, thoughts that deal with reality begin to take the place of the primary wish. It is his view that the prime mover for the mental apparatus is the wish. This is true in a number of senses of the term "prime mover", and we have seen that he views the wish as appearing first in the infant's development. Freud postulates that the energy for thoughts is derived from the wish, and this is another important sense in which the wish is the prime mover (a term both Aristotle and Augustine utilized). Wishes are prime movers for dream formation and for neurotic symptoms as well. However, in neurotic symptoms, there is always a pcs. wish that is opposing the ucs. wish. (Here, Freud uses the term "wish", but, in modern terms, we might call this a defensive function. However, when Freud puts in terms of "wish", he is giving a picture of the conflict there is between different systems or different areas of the mind.) For a symptom to be formed, the two wishes must be able to merge into a single expression. The pcs. wish in symptom formation has as its function the desire to keep an unconscious idea from attaining consciousness. Typically, the motive for this involves a self-punitive wish or some type of pcs. motive that would act to keep the ucs. wish out of cs. A patient of Freud's had an ucs. wish to be continuously pregnant, and with as many men as possible. "A powerful defensive impulse had sprung up against this unbridled wish. Since the patient (felt) she might lose her figure and her good looks as a result of vomiting" (1900a, p. 570), it was a symptom that expressed her pcs. (defensive) wish to punish herself as well as symbolizing her ucs. wish to become pregnant. The symptom was a compromise formation, in that it expressed tendencies from two different types of motives. We could alternatively say that both the ucs. and pcs. systems were represented in the formation of the symptom.

However, this type of formation is somewhat different in dreams, and Freud says that only occasionally in dream analyses do we come upon reactive creations, as he maintains are found in symptom formation. During sleep, the ucs. wish can usually find expression in the dream after undergoing certain distortions because there is a withdrawal by the pcs.–cs. system into a state of sleep. Freud sees dreams that incorporate ongoing events as examples of the person attempting to maintain the dream narrative in order to remain asleep. Thus, the alarm clock becomes a car alarm in the dream and placed in the context of the dream narrative. During sleep, the strongest wish is to remain sleeping, and, interestingly enough, the dream narrative is designed to continue this state (i.e., the state of sleep). Freud goes so far as to tell us that we have some awareness that we are sleeping during sleep and, correlatively, we are aware that we are dreaming during this activity. Freud cites various people who are even able to direct their dream content while a dream is proceeding (today called lucid dreaming). We will go back to the many interesting questions and fascinating theoretical forays that Freud has introduced, but first the question of Freud's assumptions about the nature of regression beckons, since we have used that term several times and still have not defined this concept.

To modern ears it is a bit confusing to deal with so many systems that have contradictory wishes. The confusion is largely terminological, since we can say that there are different motives that Freud is ascribing to the different systems (Cons.–Pcs. *vs.* Ucs.). We can eliminate the term "wish", and say that if unconscious wishes attain consciousness they would be putting the person in conflict and invoke some type of negative affect. This is what Freud is striving for in describing the wishes of each system. In addition, he is assuming that sleep is a biological and psychological requirement for humans and there is a great need to continue sleep, hence the wish to stay asleep. The manifest dream is then a compromise formation; an unconscious wish is symbolically expressed, but if it is expressed too directly sleep will be disturbed and thus the superordinate wish to stay asleep aids the defensive process. The unconscious wish must not be intense enough to wake the dreamer, but, to be gratifying, it must find expression in the dream. Thus, although the dream is a compromise formation, the compromise is not between competing wishes but, rather, the wish must not become intense enough to wake the dreamer.

Regression

The term regression has several interrelated definitions but it seems likely that the meaning that we will be exploring in this chapter is the least known and least frequently used in psychoanalytic discourse. Most frequently, when the term regression is used, it refers to either psycho-sexual or ego regressions. (For the present, we can say that regression refers to the return to earlier forms of activity or thought processes. It is my view that, most frequently, the term regression is used without precision and the two forms of regression are combined in various ways.) In this context, Freud has designed an aspect of his theoretical model to explain regression. He begins by pointing out that dreams are usually sensory in nature and that the middle voice is normally omitted in the dream. The "perhaps" in the dream is gone, replaced by clear affirmations. If we look at a dream of Freud's (a now famous dream, the Irma dream), Freud wishes to believe that his friend Otto was responsible for a patient's illness. He does not wish to think his friend Dr Wilhelm Fliess was responsible for the patient's condition, even though he knows that various things went wrong when Fliess operated on Irma. Freud tells us in the Irma dream that he replaces the thought of "If only Otto were responsible for Irma's illness" with the thought in the dream, "Yes, Otto is responsible" (1900a, p. 534) for the illness. Freud maintains that typical day-dreams have the same characteristic, that is, the elimination of the middle voice. Day-dreams, however, do not have the intense sensory quality of night dreams. Freud's explanation for this begins with the idea that "the scene of action of dreams is different from that of waking ideational life" (Freud, 1900a, p. 48). He tells Fliess (Letter 83, in Masson, 1985) that this idea of Fechner's is the only intelligent remark he has seen in the dream literature. Freud attempts several analogies to describe the different "scenes" of activity. He pictures the mind as a "compound instrument . . . the components of which we will give the name of 'agencies', or 'systems'" (1900a, p. 537). He names these systems Psi-systems, and gives us a picture of the apparatus. Thus, before we can understand why dreams are typically intense sensory events, we have to understand Freud's model of the mind in terms of reception and retention of images and information (Figure 1).

The large arrow on the left side of the diagram is an indication of a stimulus (endogenous or exogenous) which is received by the sensory end of the apparatus. All psychical activity starts with a stimulus, whether from an internal (endogenous) or external (exogenous) source. Freud states that an activity "ends in

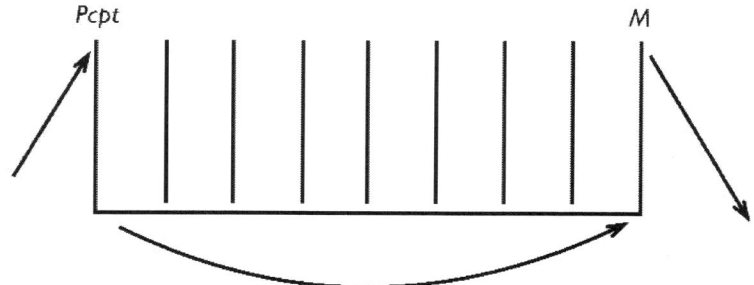

Figure 1. Freud's model of the mind.

innervations". He portrays the system as having both a sensory (receiving) and motor (output) end and to repeat "Psychical processes advance in general from the perceptual end to the motor end" (*ibid.*). The diagram that Freud provides simply shows a stimulus entering in the sensory end and being discharged in the motor end. "Reflex processes (arcs) remain the model of every psychical function" (*ibid.*, p. 538). The lines that are drawn between the ends of the system represent traces that are left in the system from "perceptions which impinge on" the sensory end. These traces are memory traces. They are formed as the sensory end receives perceptions, but they are part of a separate system and they do not alter the sensory end of the system. Freud is postulating a sensory system that receives stimuli, but is not modified by incoming stimuli. This system (the perceptual or Pcpt. system) is in the front and receives impulses "but retains no trace of them"; behind this sensory system lies another system that transforms sensory stimuli into permanent memory traces.

Breuer, in a previous communication, pointed out a logical difficulty that Freud took quite seriously; he stated that in the compound microscope there was no system that both received and retained stimuli. Freud had even more convincing reasons to postulate that the sensory system had limited capacity and functioned to receive, but not to store, stimuli. (We shall see shortly, in this work and throughout Freud's career, that he equated the sensory end with consciousness. Consciousness was not where the major processing or major storage took place in Freud's ideas about cognitive processing.) He begins to tell us that the separate perceptual

(Pcpt.) elements would be obstructed in performing their function if the Pcpt. system retained memory traces. The Pcpt. system optimally handles each new perception in an independent manner. The associative network lies in the mnemic system(s) and there are a number of such systems, according to Freud. Thus, "one and the same excitation leaves a variety of different permanent records" (1900a, p. 538). His idea was that if the Pcpt. system is strongly influenced by memory, then it would be difficult, if not impossible, to obtain a veridical account of reality. This system must, according to Freud, continue to be available to receive incoming stimuli. Freud realizes that at times memories are going to reach Cs., but here he maintains that if memories become conscious they retain few sensory qualities. Thus, usually, it will not be difficult for an individual to discriminate a memory from a sensory stimulus. Freud's position on this point changed somewhat and in 1920g he theorizes "that consciousness actually arises instead of the memory trace" (1900a, p. 540, fn added in 1925).

Freud posits that after the sensory receives a stimulus, it is recorded in several ways (types of memory networks). One memory system will record temporal simultaneity, while other systems will record other types of psychical significance. Here, Freud is talking about the type of psychological significance that he alluded to in *Studies on Hysteria*, that is, symbolic relationships. During sleep, the barrier to the pcs. is lowered (the censorship) and there is less resistance to ucs. mnemic images transferring on to pcs. thoughts. If this occurred during waking, there would be a tendency towards action (in Freud's diagram, the motor end would be activated). During sleep (particularly during dreams), motoric activity is blocked (or made more difficult, as shown by modern sleep research, which has demonstrated that during rapid eye movement [REM] sleep, motor neural activity is actively inhibited [Ellman & Antrobus, 1991]) and the mnemic images are transformed from motoric tendencies to sensory images. This is Freud's concept of regression in this context, the movement from motor tendencies to sensory images. During dreams, the transformation takes place with pcs. thoughts that are strongly influenced by ucs. images.

Freud relates this idea to waking hallucinations, and he tells us that

> My explanation of hallucinations ... is that they are in fact regressions—that is, thought transformed into images, but that the only thoughts that undergo this transformation are those which are intimately linked with memories that have been suppressed or have remained unconscious. [1900a, p. 544]

This the last piece in Freud's idea of regression: regression only takes place with ideas that have been strongly associated with memories or images that have remained unconscious. These memories are wishes from childhood and are, in effect, images of what the person wished would have taken place in childhood. "On this view a dream might be described as a substitute for an infantile scene modified by being transferred on to a recent experience" (*ibid.*, p. 546).

If we look at the ground we have traversed, we can say that dreams are stimulated by wishes and that these wishes are transferred on to receptive pcs. thoughts. These transformed pcs. thoughts are then further transfigured into sensory images. The wishes are always from childhood and are always, at least in part, unconscious. Although we have touched upon this issue, we might again ask the question as to why we do not see these wishes more directly in the dreams of adults. Why are dreams most typically narratives, rather than sensory images that jump from image to image? Why, frequently, do our dreams seem to portray such typical or everyday events?

These questions and others are relevant to Freud's theory of dream formation, and he gives answers to these and a number of other queries that he poses in this Socratic narrative that he is presenting to the world.

The censor, resistance, Cs., and issues of representation

Freud has said that the path from the Ucs. to the Pcs. is barred during the day, but at night the "watchman ... relaxes its activities ... [and] allows the suppressed impulses in the Ucs. to find expression, and makes it possible for hallucinatory regression to occur" (1900a, pp. 567–568). This censor that bars the path between the Ucs. and the Pcs. is equivalent to the idea of a defensive structure, and, in the Freudian language of this era, the censor uses resistance to keep unconscious ideas out of the Pcs.–Cs. system. Freud also conceives of there being a type of censor that can divide the Pcs. from consciousness. To delve into this topic, we must gain a more intensive understanding of Freud's view of the relationship between the Pcs. and consciousness. Here we can learn more about the system Pcs.:

> Pcs. stands like a screen between the system Ucs. and consciousness. The system Pcs. not merely bars access to consciousness, it also controls access to the power of voluntary movement and has at its disposal for distribution a mobile cathectic energy, a part of which is familiar to us in the form of attention . . . But what part is there left to be played in our scheme by consciousness . . . Only that of a sense-organ for the perception of psychical qualities. . . . we can only regard conscious perception as the function proper to a particular system; and for this the abbreviation Cs. seems appropriate . . . we regard this system as resembling the perceptual system Pcpt.: as being susceptible to excitation by qualities but incapable of retaining traces of alterations—that is to say, as having no memory. . . . Excitatory material flows in to the Cs. sense-organ from two directions: from the Pcpt. system, whose excitation . . . is probably submitted to a fresh revision before it becomes a conscious sensation, and from the interior of the apparatus itself, whose quantitative processes are felt qualitatively in the pleasure–unpleasure series when, subject to certain modifications, they make their way to consciousness. [*ibid.*, pp. 615–616]

In this extract we see Freud making reference to assumptions not fully spelled out in the dream book. Rather, in the preceding chapter, we have discussed how quantitative factors can be converted into qualitative perceptions. These ideas, which come from the project, are aspects of Freud's conceptualizations in the dream book. We can see that Freud is placing central importance on the Pcs. system in that it not only controls aspects of consciousness (the mobilization of attention via attention cathexis), but it also controls how an internal signal enters consciousness. The Pcs. is able to transform an excitatory stimulus in terms of how it will be consciously perceived. What is termed an excitatory stimulus is a perception, or memory, or idea that can be transformed in terms of the pleasure or unpleasure that will be consciously perceived. Here, again, is a form of defence that Freud is positing, and what seems like a complete system will, to some extent, unravel when Freud considers the status of the Pcs. censor. Is this censor itself able to attain consciousness? If not, why not particularly the aspect of the censor that is involved in controlling levels of excitation between the Cs. and Pcs. systems? We will wait a number of years before Freud attempts to fully answer these questions, but we can speculate as to why some of these questions were not part of his considerations earlier in his career.

Although we have to wait for some answers we can now consider some of the questions that were introduced at the end of the previous sections. One of Freud's principal theorems is that an idea (memory, experience) may be pleasurable in one system and yet cause unpleasure, or be aversive, in another system. More specifically, an unconscious idea may stand for a certain type of pleasure, but, if perceived in the Pcs.–Cs. system, it would cause anxiety or unpleasure. Thus, if we consider the dream, the ideal compromise is that the dreamer should stay asleep while Ucs. thoughts gain expression in the dream. The necessity for compromise is brought about by the regression that sleep entails, which means the relaxation of the censor. The censor, however, is not completely relaxed, as we have already discussed, and must change or transform Ucs. ideation at least to the extent that the dreamer will not experienced anxiety and thus be able to stay asleep. Following these assumptions, the more common the dream images, the greater the probability of the dreamer staying asleep. This includes providing narratives that will seem like ordinary events to the dreamer. Thus, the censor, with the help of the primary process mechanisms, optimally creates a dream that allows both the expression of Ucs. wishes and the continuation of sleep. What are primary process mechanisms? We have implicitly discussed these concepts, but now, in completing the review of the dream book, we will explicitly discuss some of Freud's best known concepts.

Primary and secondary process

Here, not only can we discuss Freud's distinction between two types of mentation, but we can also review his basic assumptions and apply them to some of the dreams he provides in the dream book. Freud reminds us that dreams, in one sense, are never occupied with minor details, but that there is reason to accept the contrary view that dreams "pick up indifferent refuse left over from the previous day" (1900a, p. 589). We have just discussed that, in order to allow the dreamer to sleep,

> the dream-process finds it easier to get control of recent or indifferent ideational material which has not yet been requisitioned by waking thought-activity; and for reasons of censorship it transfers psychical intensity from what is important but objectionable (in the pcs.–cs.) on to what is indifferent. [*ibid.*]

Freud also reminds us that organic stimuli present during the night (e.g., stomach ache, need to urinate, etc.) are to be regarded as similar to the type of waking indifferent stimuli that we have just discussed. How can we conceive of the system Ucs.? What is the nature of the ideation that is present in this system? How does an idea reach the system Ucs.? What is the nature of the ideation that is present in this system? How does an idea reach the system Ucs.? If we take Freud's ideas about associative trains, or trains of ideas, he says that "a purposive is placed along associative paths with a reasonable amount of 'cathectic energy'". A train of thought that is repudiated is one where the cathectic energy is withdrawn (defence) and is then rendered Ucs. There are trains of thought that, in Freud's words, are "neglected", but remain in the Pcs. This is a train of thought that has not received cathectic energy. Although Freud does not fully deal with this, he is, at this point in time, purposing a quantitative model that determines the level of consciousness of a given train of thought. To be consistent, he would have to maintain that even a neglected Pcs. train of thought has a minimal amount of cathexis to remain in the Pcs. Alternatively, he could maintain that ideas in the Ucs. are forcibly placed in the Ucs. Here, he would be postulating defence as an active inhibitory system. We will have to wait (see Chapters Three, Four, and Five) to talk about these alternative ways of thinking of the process of defence.

Let us go back now to the question of how an idea from the Ucs. enters into the Pcs. and forms an aspect of what we can now call the dream (or the manifest dream, in Freud's terms). Since sleep brings the lowering of the censorship, there is a higher probability of an Ucs. idea entering the Pcs.–Cs. system. It is rare, in adults, for this to happen directly; rather, groups of ideas form within one ideational element. This compression, or "the fact of 'compression'", is called by Freud condensation, and is "responsible for the bewildering impression made on us by dreams, for nothing analogous to it is known to us in mental life that is normal and accessible to consciousness" (*ibid.*, p. 595). Condensation produces a number of effects. Freud is first struck by the fact that it causes an intensification of an idea or image. It also has a defensive aspect, since the condensed image may contain a number of elements with the same theme, but with physically diverse properties. Thus, a patient of mine has a dream about a man who is tall and bald, but much younger, with a goatee. She does not really think that I am included in the dream (I am 6'1" and bald) since the man is young and has a goatee. Here, the reference to me is apparent later in the session, but there is a mild defensive function in that she has combined an element of her brother with elements of her analyst. The elements that symbolize her brother are actually the ones that, in some ways, she wishes to more strenuously defend against in this instance. Freud's examples of condensation are more intricate than the previous example and we will look at some in the postscript to this chapter.

Another aspect of condensations that are of interest to Freud is that sometimes the connections are loose and, in fact, mutually contradictory. Thus, a hated person and elements of a loved person might be included in the same image. Similarly, elements of the present might be combined with images that formed during childhood. Freud, in a summary statement, says that

> It will be seen that the chief characteristic of these processes is that the whole stress is laid upon making the cathecting energy mobile and capable of discharge; the content and the proper meaning of the psychical elements to which the cathexes are attached are treated as of little consequence. [*ibid.*, p. 597]

Freud, in his discussion of primary process, is giving us a picture of a system that is solely interested in discharge or pleasure. The wishes and pleasures of childhood that have been repudiated still exist in the system Ucs. Freud is maintaining that this system operates by different syntactical rules than we normally encounter in ideal Pcs.–Cs. cognitive operations. The Ucs. system takes no account of negatives, or contradictions, or time. Rather, it is a preemptory organization that demands satisfaction in the present. When an element of the Ucs. becomes attached to (or, in Freud's terms, transferred to) a Pcs. representation, the tendency is to make this Pcs. representation operate in terms of Ucs. rules of organization. If we return directly to the extract from Freud, we can say that the object for Ucs. rules is unimportant; what is important is the aim. The aim of the system Ucs. is discharge; it is unimportant with whom or under what circumstances the discharge takes place. Using an obvious example, Freud is picturing a person who wants to have sex but who has no attachment to a given individual; therefore, one partner is as good as the next. In his terminology, this is a person who is operating to a large part in primary process terms and whose cathexes (attachments) can shift from one person to the next as long as he is satisfied.

Freud is also picturing the newborn as being able to receive nourishment from different care-givers as long as the care-giver is able to provide pleasure. (We will see that a modern analyst either has to define pleasure in a way to included maternal attachment or make important modifications in Freud's conceptualizations about early development.) It is later in development (but still quite early) that Freud sees the mother as being represented as permanent figure or object. Here, again, we have to retrace our steps; how does the infant go from an organism that is governed by the system Ucs. and, therefore, the primary process, to one that is not only concerned with discharge and pleasure, but is, in addition, concerned with the object. We have already stated that the infant, after first receiving nourishment, attempts to recreate the situation by a type of perceptual identity; the infant recreates the situation through retrieving memory images of the nourishing situation. Freud calls this a hallucinatory event similar to the motivational conditions necessary for creating a dream. The recreation of the feeding situation is an example of primary process, an endogenously produced image intended to provide gratification. Simply having a sensory image of the feeding situation is, of course, not ultimately gratifying, and so the infant learns both to signal its care-giver in reality and to inhibit the full sensory expression of the gratifying memory. This learning signals the onset of the second system, and Freud, in formally describing this process, says

> that the activity of the first psi-system is directed towards securing the free discharge of the quantities of excitation, while the second system, by means of the cathexes emanating from it, succeeds in inhibiting this discharge and in transforming the cathexis into a quiescent one. [*ibid.*, p. 599]

In this extract, Freud is maintaining that the first system has free or unbound energy that is purely pleasure seeking, and that the second system's task is to both inhibit the primary system and bind the energy from this system so that small amounts of energy can be utilized to direct the person's decision. In this system, objects (persons and things) start to receive stable (relatively) permanent cathexes and, when this occurs, it will matter who feeds the infant. The developmental sequence of how people get represented or internalized will be the subject of a good deal of Freud's subsequent writings. Here, however, he is concerned with conceptualizing what he considers to be these two basic systems. He continues his discussion of the second system, and says that

> under the dominion of the second system the discharge of excitation is governed by quite different mechanical conditions from those in force under the dominion of the first system. When once the second system has concluded its exploratory thought-activity, it releases the inhibition and damming-up of the excitations and allows them to discharge themselves in movement. [*ibid.*, pp. 599–600]

In condensed form, Freud has described the second system. It is a system that can inhibit the first system, veridically perceive reality (through the Cs.–Pcpt. system), expend small quantities of trial energy (thought), and, when appropriate, interact with reality and expend large quantities of energy (motor activity). Thought, in this model, begins as trial action where various alternatives are considered without being fully cathected through motor action. There can be large expenditures of energy by the second system but only if there is a strong investment or commitment to a person (object), or to an activity (work).

We can now summarize the primary and secondary systems, and we are also in a position to summarize Freud's ideas about dream formation. The primary system is primary in two senses of the term: it is the system from which all energy flows, and it is the system that is developmentally primary and which first dominates the life of the infant. The second system comes to inhibit the primary system. The motivation for this inhibition is once again the pleasure principle; if the infant does not begin to deal with reality, it continues to be hungry, and this hunger causes unpleasure. In the infant, the second system inhibits the first system attempts at pleasure and, by doing this, decreases periods of unpleasure, or at least hastens the flow of pleasure or immediate care and nourishment. Thus, the second system also is under the domination of the pleasure principle, but the infant (developing child) optimally comes to learn that dealing with reality is more pleasurable than continuing with, or revelling in, fantasy. The first system is also "totally incapable of bringing anything disagreeable into the context of its thoughts". It remains for the second system to tolerate unpleasurable stimuli. Obviously, an organism that cannot think about unpleasurable issues is one that will not be able to deal with certain aspects of reality. Freud's view is that, in so far as the first system dominates, the person is always attempting to flee aversive situations. In clinical terms, one sees certain types of patients who frequently need to rid their minds of troubling thoughts. One important clue about the type of patient one is seeing has to do with the person's ability to tolerate distressing ideation. Clearly, everyone has to avoid certain types of ideas, but one gets a view of the person by the extent to which the person must rid their mind of distressing ideation. To the extent that this true of an individual, Freud would say to that extent the person is influenced by their primary system (by primary process).

We have focused on the two systems as being in conflict and, to some extent, Freud views this as true for everyone. However, there are times when the two systems work together, and Freud is beginning to see how this is possible in works that we will briefly refer to at the end of the chapter (*Jokes* [1905c], *Psychopathology of Everyday Life* [1901b], etc.). In the dream book, Freud's main focus is to characterize the Ucs. as operating according to primary process principles. In the Ucs., opposites can co-exist, there are no negatives and only the present (no past or future) exists. Discharge is attempted immediately and planning does not go on in this system. In the secondary system (when functioning optimally) there is a past and future and planning is a key element of this system. It is in the Pcs.–Cs. system that reality orientated thinking takes place and where the motor end of the system is controlled. During sleep, when the motor system is quiescent and there are regressive trends brought on by the sleep process, the inhibition of the Ucs. by the Pcs.–Cs. is lessened. The transfers between systems takes place more freely and there is a greater chance for ideation to be intense enough to reach consciousness. When ideation during sleep reaches the Cs.–Pcpt. system, Freud considers this to be a dream. The ideation that reaches Cs. is the manifest dream. The processes that go into developing the ideation that will be intense enough to reach consciousness is called the latent dream.

We have already discussed how the censor helps to inhibit the flow (less than in waking) and, in addition, helps to normally form a narrative that will both allow the expression of Ucs. ideas and allow sleep to continue.

Freud's genius in this work is to be able to bring together the formation of the dream with the development and maintenance of cognitive processes in childhood and adult functioning. In the last section of the book, we will briefly look at the extent to which contemporary research supports Freud's contentions.

Three Essays on Sexuality

It is interesting to go back to Freud's seduction hypothesis and realize that Freud did not completely reject the hypothesis. Gay states that

> Freud insisted that not everything he had written in the mid-1890s on the sexual abuse of children deserved to be rejected: "Seduction has retained a certain significance for etiology." He explicitly noted that two of his early cases, Katharina and a Fraulein Rosalia H, had been assaulted by their fathers. Ceasing to believe everything his patients told him did not require him to fall into the sentimental trap of holding sober black-coated bourgeois incapable of revolting sexual aggression. What Freud repudiated was the seduction theory as a general explanation of how all neuroses originate. [1988, p. 95]

Freud, for a period of time, did not even completely reject the seduction hypothesis as a general theory. After he announced to Fliess that the seduction theory was dead, he still put forth the theory that he ostensibly had rejected (Freud, 1898a; Gay, 1988). Nevertheless, at the same time that he was leaving the seduction theory, he was beginning to take seriously the idea that the sexual thoughts that he began to uncover in his own self-analysis were of a more universal nature. He wrote to Fliess that the Oedipal relationship of the child to its parents was a more general relationship than he had thought, and that it occurred relatively early in childhood (Gay, 1988). This was in 1898, and he began to recognize that things that he called the perverse nature of children might not be pathologically perverse, but, rather, a normal "perversity" that all or most members of the species typically experience. This "perversity" is not the property of neurotics or any other special population, but, rather, at least during different points of development, part of the human condition. This was a startling change in his interest in sexuality, but, as Gay writes, for Freud to believe in the seduction theory he would have to have credited his own father with the role of abuser. No matter what his feelings towards his father, he felt he knew that this was not the case. Thus, we can say that Freud's self analysis was an important factor in leading him to think that sexuality is part of normal childhood experience. There is no doubt that his disappointment in finding that seduction hypothesis was incorrect led him to search for alternative explanations of the clinical phenomena that he was experiencing.

Three crucial essays

Freud begins these essays by maintaining that popular opinion has quite definite ideas about the nature of sexuality. The popular belief is that sexuality is absent in childhood and begins to "set in at the time of puberty"(1905d, p. 135). He will try to demonstrate that sexuality is part of everyone's childhood experience; it is not simply an accidental aspect in the life of a child who is unfortunate enough to have undergone sexual abuse. In his first chapter, he describes what he calls the sexual aberrations. In describing these, he distinguishes the person from whom sexual attraction proceeds (the sexual object), and the act towards which the instinct tends, which is labelled the sexual aim. To fully understand Freud's concepts in these essays, we must go to his ideas about the psycho-neuroses. Neuroses are now viewed as the negative of perversions. In this view, what is defended against by neurotics is a conflict that involves a perverse tendency. Perverse tendencies, however, are perverse not in the sense that the general public might think about these acts, but, rather, they are perverse in that they do not allow for a full developmental sequence.

Freud's view is that perverse tendencies (an unfortunate name) are universally present during childhood. These tendencies (fantasies and/or acts) are part of development, but if one becomes particularly attached to a given tendency, then development for that person cannot proceed in an optimal manner (there is a fixation to this point of development). This attachment can occur because of an over or under stimulation during a given period. Thus, a central concept for Freud that emerges in these essays is the idea of optimal stimulation and optimal frustration. As childhood progresses, the child must be able to endure more and more frustration and, implicitly, it is a parental (maternal) function to be able to help the child endure frustration and turn away from tendencies that were at one time seen by the child as central in its life. Freud's view is that with most people (perhaps everyone), some of these childhood tendencies will be present in adult life. As we shall see, Freud's evaluation of an individual depends on both the extent of these tendencies and the use the person gives to them. Although we might wonder at Freud's use of the popular term "perversions", he deliberately stays with this term to express another central theme of this work: the relationship between childhood and adult sexuality. He not only sees sexual tendencies in children, but how these tendencies are internalized will be crucial in the child's development and adult life.

Essay One: the sexual aberrations

In describing deviations of the sexual object, it is not surprising that Freud starts with a homosexual object choice. Undoubtedly, the choice of homosexuality (or inversion) to begin the discussion of the sexual aberrations is multi-determined. The trial of Oscar Wilde

(Ellmann, 1987) has caused a stir across Europe and homophobia is high in many countries across the continent. Freud maintains that there are no certain conclusions that one can reach about the aetiology of homosexuality, but he is certain about one aspect of how inverts have been characterized. Homosexuality has been characterized both as a type of nervous degeneracy and as a disorder that leads to moral degeneracy. Here, Freud states that

> inversion is found in people who exhibit no other serious deviations from the normal ... and in people whose efficiency is unimpaired, and who are indeed distinguished by specially high intellectual development and ethical culture. [1905d, pp. 138–139].

He also refers to the fact that homosexuality flourished in societies that were of the highest cultural and intellectual accomplishments. Thus, Freud rejects the idea that homosexuality can be characterized as a type of either moral or nervous degeneracy.

Whether homosexuality is innate is a question where Freud is much less certain. He has distinguished levels of homosexuality (absolute, amphigenic, and contingent): thus, one may only choose a same sex partner (absolute), or may equally (or frequently) choose partners from either sex (amphigenic), or may be engaged in homosexual behaviour because of circumstances (incarceration, experimentation, etc.). He views the fact of different levels of homosexuality as arguing against a single genetic theory of homosexuality. In Freud's view, the explanation of homosexual behaviour "is explained neither by the hypothesis that it is innate nor by the alternative hypothesis that it is acquired" (*ibid.*, p. 140). In fact, he questions what one can mean by innate, and rejects what he calls a "crude explanation that everyone is born with his sexual instinct attached to a particular sexual object" (*ibid.*, pp. 140–141).

One might see that Freud, in classifying homosexuality as a perversion, is following the medical precedents of his era; however, his strong voice against viewing homosexuality as a degenerative disorder was a progressive note against a chorus of homophobia sweeping Europe during that era (Ellmann, 1987). Moreover, Freud's view of bisexuality cannot be emphasized strongly enough; although he does not account for homosexuality in terms of "a bi-sexual nature", he does assume that all humans are, to some extent, bisexual.

Freud's view of homosexuality places this tendency as part of normal development, and, in a similar manner, Freud also views a number of sexual practices that were (or are) viewed as perversions as part of normal sexuality in childhood. These perversions can be fetishes or sadomasochistic sexual practices, or common everyday behaviours such as looking at (scopophilia), or wanting to be looked at (exhibitionism). Freud is attempting to show how normal sexuality may contain elements of all or many of these "perverse" tendencies. Thus, wanting a lock of hair of one's beloved (or a scarf or gang jacket) is not peculiar or abnormal unless one's sexual life is either dependent on and/or restricted to these objects. In normal sexuality perverse tendencies may in fact be part of foreplay, or special types of longing for a loved one who is not present. Freud, in ending the first chapter, relates that

> By demonstrating the part played by perverse impulses in the formation of symptoms in the psychoneuroses, we have quite remarkably increased the number of people who might be regarded as perverts. It is not only that neurotics in themselves constitute a very numerous class, but it must also be considered that an unbroken chain bridges the gap between the neuroses in all their manifestations and normality. [1905d, p. 171]

He also concludes by saying that there is something "innate lying behind the perversions but that it is something innate in *everyone*" (*ibid.*), although the environment will play a part in determining the extent to which the perverse tendency manifests itself exclusively or at all in adult life.

Infantile sexuality

In this chapter, Freud fully states his views that the bases for a good deal of adult sexuality (and psychopathology) is formulated in childhood. The experiences that the child undergoes are most frequently subject to infantile amnesia. Thus, the experiences of childhood are not available as conscious memories, even during adolescence. Freud, in this conceptualization, sees the first era of life as an autoerotic period which is then interrupted by what he calls a period of total or partial latency. During this period of latency "mental forces are . . . like dams [and] restrict its [sexuality] flow" (*ibid.*, p. 177). This happens as feelings of shame or disgust help the child turn away from sexuality and towards "aesthetic and moral ideals" (*ibid.*). We might linger and wonder what occurs during the autoerotic period.

Autoerotism. Here, we will have to keep in mind that Freud uses the term autoerotic and the stage of autoerotism in several different ways. In fact, he will gradually change the usage of this term during the next ten years (1905–1915), although he will not stop to systematically align the different uses of the term. In the three essays, Freud is saying that while the aim of sexuality is always for gratification, during autoerotism the object is not clearly defined. Sexuality is autoerotic in the sense that pleasure or satisfaction is found in the person's own body. In this sense, then, everything that occurs before latency is autoerotic. In several years' time, Freud is going to change the meaning of this term, but here autoerotism is defined entirely in terms of the sexual interest of the infant–child.

Although autoerotism is a long period, the parts of the body that the infant–child is interested in varies during this period. The zones, or the parts, of the body that the child is interested in centre around what Freud calls erotogenic zones. Freud writes,

> Our study of thumb-sucking or sensual sucking has already given us the three essential characteristics of an infantile sexual manifestation. At its origin it attaches itself to one of the vital somatic functions. It has as yet no sexual object, and is thus auto-erotic; its sexual aim is dominated by an erotogenic zone. It is to be anticipated that these characteristics will be found to apply equally to most of the other activities of the infantile sexual instincts. [*ibid.*, pp. 182–183]

These erotogenic zones are well known today, and include the anal, oral, and genital zones. It is important to realize that, at this time, Freud is writing about erotogenic zones, not about stages of development. The overriding stage of development is the autoerotic stage. All of these zones will have a sexual meaning and purpose in adult life. For example, the oral zone, through kissing (at least in some cultures), will continue to have an adult sexual meaning. Freud writes that the anal zone "retains a considerable amount of susceptibility to genital stimulation throughout life" (*ibid.*, p. 185).

In the oral zone, a "constitutional intensification" of this zone may induce "perverse kissing or, in males a powerful motive for smoking and drinking" (*ibid.*, p. 182). On the other hand, if the person represses (defends against their oral tendencies) they may experience "disgust at food . . . and hysterical vomiting" (*ibid.*). The child who has strong erotogenic excitement of the anal zone may hold back the contents of their bowels "which act as a stimulating mass upon a sexually sensitive portion of mucous membrane" (*ibid.*, p. 186). In the same way that is true of the oral zone, repressed (defended against) anal tendencies may lead to neurotic organization in adulthood (compulsive rituals, cleaning, etc.). The genital zone is not the earliest component of sexuality but, in Freud's words, "is destined to great things in the future" (*ibid.*, p. 187). The genital area always received stimulation in terms of micturition and in normal bathing and cleaning. Thus, normal pregenital events provide pleasurable stimulation for the infant/developing toddler. Freud tells us it is "Nature's purpose of establishing the future primacy over sexual activity exercised by this erotogenic zone by means of early infantile masturbation, which scarcely a single individual escapes" (*ibid.*, p. 188). Freud then postulates that there are three phases of infantile masturbation: first, early infancy, the second belonging to "the brief efflorescence of sexual activity about the fourth year of life; only the third phase corresponds to pubertal masturbation" (*ibid.*, p. 189).

During this period, Freud finds infantile masturbation a crucial aspect of character formation and of various adult conflicts. It is his view that, while some children may continuously masturbate (from first phase through to adolescence), masturbation typically occurs in more definite form in the second phase of masturbation. This phase of masturbation may "leave behind the deepest (unconscious) impressions in the child's memory" (*ibid.*). Freud does not specify what may occur, since he says that this can only be determined by an analysis of individual cases, but, clearly, during this period of theorizing, masturbatory activity has great significance for Freud. Harkening back to previous ideas, he states that excessive masturbation may be a result of sexual abuse. He admits that he has previously overestimated the frequency of sexual abuse but, nevertheless, it is an important determinant of later conflict. He states that seduction is not required to arouse a child's sexual life, since it can occur spontaneously from internal causes. Thus, while seduction can lead to polymorphous perverse tendencies, normal children show an aptitude that is "innately present in their disposition" (*ibid.*, p. 191).

What are some of the polymorphous perverse tendencies that children can exhibit? Before we can fully answer this question, first we must realize that Freud is placing the object as important in these perverse tendencies. He says,

> It must be admitted that infantile sexual life, in spite of the preponderating dominance of erotogenic zones, exhibits components which from the very first involve other people as sexual objects. Such are the instincts of scopophilia, exhibitionism and cruelty, which appear in a sense independently of erotogenic zones . . . Small children are essentially without shame, and at some periods of their earliest years show an unmistakable satisfaction in exposing their bodies, with especial emphasis on the sexual parts. [*ibid.*, p. 192]

As children get older, they develop a sense of shame in exposing their bodies and, at that time, the scopophilic impulse attains greater importance. Any of these tendencies can be combined and can be manifested in adult life. Cruelty is something of a mystery for Freud, but he does say that it is independent of the sexual instinct and is mastered when the child develops the capacity for pity. To quote Freud's earliest statement on this issue, he says that

> It must be assumed that the impulses of cruelty arise from sources which are in fact independent of sexuality, but may become united with it at an early stage owing to an anastomosis (cross-connection) near their points of origin. [*ibid.*, p. 193 fn]

Freud, in a few pages, is postulating that there are instincts outside of the sexual instinct and that cruelty may have instinctual origins that are closely related to sexuality. Clearly, exhibitionism and scopophilia also can be tied to sexuality, but, like cruelty, they have independent roots. We shall see, in the case of cruelty, that Freud will eventually attempt to provide an elaborate theoretical edifice to explain this universal tendency. However, the other two tendencies will lose their independence in Freud's theory of narcissism. In these essays, not only does cruelty, looking, and being looked at have instinctual roots, but there is also an instinct for knowledge. This instinct reaches its first efflorescence between the ages of three and five. Freud tells us that

> Its activity corresponds on the one hand to a sublimated manner of obtaining mastery, while on the other hand it makes use of the energy of scopophilia. Its relations to sexual life, however, are of particular importance, since we have learnt from psycho-analysis that the instinct for knowledge in children is attracted unexpectedly early and intensively to sexual problems and is in fact possibly first aroused by them. [*ibid.*, p. 194]

In this paragraph, Freud brings forth two interesting ideas that linger in psychoanalysis but never are fully explicated in his theoretical writings. The first is the idea of mastery. Knowledge can be used for mastery over both internal and external (environmental) issues, but Freud never fully develops his ideas about mastery. We will see at various points in his theorizing about drives (or endogenous stimulation) that Freud invokes ideas about mastering one's own internal states. In those contexts, Freud is talking about either transforming the drives or controlling the drives (usually through defence). Here, however, he is implying that there is a separate drive for mastery based on a person's instinct to know and comprehend. This concept will be at the centre of some later theories (e.g., White, 1963).

Freud is, however, clearest and most incisive when he is talking about how the child's natural tendency for research in the world at times receives an injury that may endure well beyond childhood. He tells us that "The fable of the stork is often told to an audience that receives it with deep, though mostly silent, mistrust" (1905d, p. 197). His view is that when the child sees a pregnant woman (particularly its own mother), the child interprets correctly that there is a baby growing inside the woman. His opinion is that, despite the child's curiosity, the child never discovers two elements of sexuality, that is, "the fertilizing role of semen and the existence of the female sexual orifice—the same elements, incidentally, in which the infantile organization is itself undeveloped" (*ibid.*). Thus, the child who carries out its sexual research in "solitude" inevitably is frustrated in the research that he is able to accomplish. The child cannot imagine how the baby can leave the mother through the vaginal opening, nor can the child envision the semen that fertilizes the egg carried by the woman. In Freud's view, the child develops theories of birth that coincide to the types of sexuality that they can accomplish during their childhood. They imagine that "people get babies by eating some particular thing (or) . . . babies are born through the bowel like a discharge of faeces" (*ibid.*, p. 196). Thus, the child sees birth as similar to activities that it is involved in every day.

Children, if they view the sexual act, inevitably regard sex as a type of subjugation. Thus, Freud concludes that they view sex "in a sadistic sense" (*ibid.*). Freud implies that children view the sexual act as sadistic since they cannot imagine any other reason for adults to be in the type of position that the sexual act entails. Moreover, since children are often restricted, they view restrictions as a type of subjugation. It is very difficult to adequately explain to a child why they cannot play with a vase, or run in the street, or through some parts of the house that they are occupying. Thus, any activity that looks a like a subjugation is viewed as a sadistic act.

In the second of the three essays, Freud is clearly laying the groundwork for the importance of fantasy in childhood development. He is beginning to make a distinction that is quite different from the ideas that were present in his previous theoretical attempt, in what we have called the pathogenic memory model. It is not simply the memory, but the child's interpretation of external events that becomes crucial in understanding the child's fantasy life. The basis for the child's fantasy life is dependent on bodily functions that serve as the basis for the child's perceptions of reality. Freud is now placing the child's psychic reality as resting squarely on bodily functions that serve as a way of interpreting the events around the child. Birth, thus, occurs in the same way that other things come out of the body, faeces being a prime example of something being excreted from the body.

Although, clearly, the child's psychic reality cannot be equated with what might be the adult's consensual reality, one can still say that the child's reality has an experiential base, and this experiential base is housed in the child's bodily states and experiences. Fantasy, then, is rooted in experience, although it may be very difficult to tell by behavioural observation what the child is experiencing. Freud assumes that the child's experience (or psychic reality) is based on the interaction between the child's experience with the outside world and the type of bodily experience that the child is encountering. Thus, a child who is centred around the oral zone will have different fantasies than a child who is preoccupied with the anal zone.

Textural interlude

In the previous paragraph, we have used the phrase oral zone, which can be easily be misunderstood as the oral stage of development. Freud, during this era, did not have the concept of psychosexual stages based on erotogenic zones. What is confusing is that on pages 197–199 of the three essays, Freud writes about these stages of development. This section was added to the essays in 1915 and, during subsequent years (up to 1924), the section was rewritten. The oral stage was not introduced until 1915, and it was publicly introduced in the new passages in the three essays. It was not until 1923 that Freud introduces the concept of a phallic stage. In the three essays, although he refers to oral and anal zones, he does not conceptualize these zones in terms of developmental stages. Rather, as we shall see, he thinks of everything that precedes genital primacy (which does not occur until puberty) as part of the autoerotism. Thus, the child's tendency to want oral, anal, or genital stimulation is all considered by Freud to be autoerotic in nature.

A return to text

Freud, in describing fantasy, turns to the anal zone and says that

> The predominance in it of sadism and the cloacal part played by the anal zone give it a quite peculiarly archaic colouring. It is further

characterized by the fact that in it the opposing pairs of instincts are developed to an approximately equal extent, a state of affairs described by Bleuler's happily chosen term "ambivalence. [1905d, p. 199]

Freud, in this essay, is most at home describing anal fantasies, but he also is able to depict how each zone leads to characteristic fantasies. Ambivalence is described in terms of the anal zone, but Freud will extend this concept in later writings. In addition to describing fantasy, Freud also builds intensity factors into his conceptualization of how psychic reality accrues or is internalized. Greater intensity is generally a factor that Freud posits leads to fixation and, thus, causes difficulty for a child to leave libidinal positions. His stance on intensity will be become more complicated as he develops a view of the range of reactions to different internal states.

Freud has spent a good deal of time outlining modes of fantasy, and, towards the end of the second essay, he describes what he calls sources of infantile sexuality. He cites three types of origin of sexual excitation:

[(]A) A reproduction of a satisfaction experienced in connection with other organic processes, (B) Appropriate peripheral stimulation of erotogenic zones, (C) Expression of certain instincts (such as the scopophilic instinct and the instinct of cruelty) of which the origin is not yet completely intelligible. [*ibid.*, pp. 200–201]

Freud cites the skin as prime source of peripheral stimulation, and cites rocking and passive movement, where children are thrown in the air, as other types of sexualized stimulation. Freud then wonders about the "combination of fright and mechanical agitation [which] produces the severe, hysteriform, traumatic neurosis". He goes on to say that

It may at least be assumed that these influences, which, when they are of small intensity, become sources of sexual excitation, [however, they] lead to a profound disorder in the sexual mechanism or chemistry if they operate with exaggerated force. [*ibid.*, p. 202]

Here, we see that Freud uses the idea of intensity to explain how the same type of stimulation can lead to quite different results.

Surprisingly, Freud does not spend a great deal of time in discussing affective or emotive processes. He is interested in understanding how a seeming unpleasurable affect like fright can attach itself to a pleasurable sexual instinct or activity. Essentially, in his explanation, he continues a conditioning notion by saying that if

> erotogenic effect(s) attaches even to intensely painful feelings, especially when the pain is toned down or kept at a distance by some accompanying condition, we should here have one of the main roots of the masochistic–sadistic instinct, into whose numerous complexities we are very gradually gaining some insight. [*ibid.*, p. 204]

Transformations at puberty

Puberty gives infantile sexual life its final shape and also gives the adolescent a chance to revisit some of the issues that were formed during a period where the sexual instinct was largely autoerotic. Now the component instincts combine and are subordinate to the "primacy of the genital zone" (*ibid.*, p. 207). For men, the new sexual aim consists of the discharge of sperm and, with this discharge, the attainment of pleasure. The sexual instinct now, however, is subordinated to the reproductive function; "it becomes, so to say, altruistic" (*ibid.*). Here, we should say a word about the meaning of altruistic. Freud, at this point in his career, is proposing an instinct theory that contrasts the survival of the self with the survival of the species. Pleasure that is simply designed for oneself, that is autoerotic, is under the sway of the former instinct (survival of the self). Thus, the component instincts as they appear in what Freud is now calling the autoerotic phase of development are influenced by survival of the self. In this phase of his theorizing, it is not until puberty that the component instincts join with mature sexuality under the sway of the instinct that is involved with survival of the species. In this sense, sexuality is altruistic in that it gives pleasure to the individual while at the same time it provides a service to the species. Obviously, the service is providing a new member of the species that will help the species survive.

Although, at puberty, the genital zone is the primary zone, the other erotogenic zones during this period play a type of kindling

THE PSYCHOANALYTIC ERA BEGINS 71

function. In Freud's words, they "play an important part in introducing sexual excitement" (*ibid.*, p. 209). Thus, the component instincts in one form or another can serve as forepleasure that stimulates the genital zone to be ready for sexual intercourse. In our society, kissing is perhaps the most popular type of forepleasure that is publicly displayed. Freud assumes that various touching and looking that involve any of the component instincts may serve as forepleasure or foreplay for the sexual act. Freud has no difficulty in conceiving of the sexual act in terms of his theory of drive discharge. Here, we should again look at his words before our analysis of his underlying assumptions. He tells us that

> The part played in this by the erotogenic zones, however, is clear. What is true of one of them is true of all. They are all used to provide a certain amount of pleasure by being stimulated in the way appropriate to them. This pleasure then leads to an increase in tension which in its turn is responsible for producing the necessary motor energy for the conclusion of the sexual act. The penultimate stage of that act is once again the appropriate stimulation of an erotogenic zone (the genital zone itself, the penis) by the appropriate object (the mucous membrane of the vagina); and from the pleasure yielded by this excitation the motor energy is obtained, this time by a reflex path, which brings about the discharge of the sexual substances. This last pleasure is the highest in intensity, and its mechanism differs from that of the earlier pleasure. It is brought about entirely by discharge: it is wholly a pleasure of satisfaction and with it the tension of the libido is for the time being extinguished. [*ibid.*, p. 210]

Freud, here, admits to a difficulty in his theorizing, which will be with him for his entire career. Freud maintains that, despite other opinions, he "must insist that a feeling of tension necessarily involves unpleasure" (*ibid.*, p. 208). This, despite the fact that he also admits that "we are at once brought up against the fact that it is also undoubtedly felt as pleasurable". Clearly, the fact that people report rises in tension as pleasurable is direct evidence against Freud's assumptions about discharge being necessary for pleasure. His answer to this conundrum is to say that everything relating to the problem of pleasure and unpleasure is unanswered and that he will endeavour to "learn as much as possible" about this issue. He does not, however, withdraw his fundamental hypothesis that pleasure is inevitably associated with discharge and unpleasure with a rise in tension. In a footnote to the three essays, Freud says that he has made an attempt at solving this problem "in the first part of my paper on 'The Economic Problem of Masochism'" (*ibid.*, p. 209, fn.). We shall see, in the fourth chapter, our view of Freud's answer, but, at this point in his career, we see him holding on to a theoretical postulate regardless of the evidence that he is confronting and acknowledging.

This theoretical difficulty is not necessarily involved with Freud's central ideas about the relationship of childhood and adult sexuality. It is Freud's view that it is possible to get stuck, or to become fixated, in one of the pregenital zones. This can happen if the pleasure derived from this zone is too great or too small. Thus, Freud has a concept of optimal stimulation, but, in his discussion, he most frequently refers to the possibility of over stimulation leading to a fixation. A fixation with a given zone takes away some of the motivation for proceeding further in sexual development. Thus, the "preparatory act takes the place of the of the normal sexual aim" (*ibid.*, p. 211). This may take the form of sexual preferences (e.g., preferring oral to genital sex), or may result in a perversion. Freud's theoretical ideas about pleasure would, in fact, make the idea of a fixation an impossibility, since one cannot obtain discharge with a component instinct. Freud attempts to deal with this difficulty (*ibid.*, p. 212), but he does not do away with the logical difficulties inherent in his theoretical ideas. The concept of fixation is central to Freudian thought, and yet Freud has not provided the theoretical underpinnings for this concept or how one explains the progression from zone to zone. At this time in his theorizing, he is undoubtedly more focused on his revolutionary ideas about sexuality than the theoretical structure that holds some of these ideas.

Differences between the sexes

Freud states as a matter of fact that "it is not until puberty that the sharp distinction is established between the masculine and feminine characters" (*ibid.*, p. 219). He does say that, while it is true that one can recognize differences in boys and girls in terms of the development of inhibitions, "the auto-erotic activity of the erotogenic zones is, however, the same in both sexes" (*ibid.*) before puberty arises. Girls, in this formulation, tend to develop affects like shame, disgust, and pity earlier than is the case with boys. They also develop stronger tendencies towards repression (i.e., defence), and tend more often to prefer the passive form of the drives. However, "So far as the auto-erotic and masturbatory manifestations of sexuality are concerned, we might lay it down that the sexuality of little girls is of a wholly masculine character" (*ibid.*). Interestingly, even anatomically girls act as little boys, since "the leading erotogenic zone in female children is located at the clitoris, and is thus homologous to the masculine genital zone of the glans penis" (*ibid.*, p. 220). After puberty, the woman transfers her erotogenic zone from the clitoris to the vaginal orifice. The man does not transfer his leading zone, since it remains the penis.

Freud's views on the development of the girl are perhaps his most controversial and most unsatisfactory from a variety of viewpoints. His equation of passive and feminine, he feels, is a cultural assertion. Most commentators feel that Freud's views are clearly manifestations of the prejudices of the culture of that era. He offers little evidence for this assertion and does not realize the extent to which he is codifying society's prejudices. One could continue the recent and past criticisms of Freud's views on women, but we will be content to follow his views since they change to some extent during the course of his career. His most famous quote (made several decades later), that he does not know what women want, may be an admission of the inadequacy of his theory concerning aspects of feminine development. Let us end this chapter with a reminder by Freud that all human beings are a combination of masculine and feminine traits and that these traits are often determined by the culture in which one abides.

Commentary

In various ways, both the revolutionary aspects of *Three Essays on the Theory of Sexuality* and the tentative nature of these essays have been neglected. In these essays, Freud is beginning to look at development in a continuous, integrated manner. He is positing that childhood experiences have an important effect on adult sexuality and on adult character formation. In the next several years, he will give some examples (Freud, 1907b, 1908b) of how early experience is decisive in character development. Since Freud is looking at the continuity of sexual life, he tries to illustrate how early development is formative in determining later sexual tendencies and will strongly influence a person's choice of a love object. In fact, these essays presage Freud's major concern for the next 10–12 years: the development of the capacity for object love. In the three essays, he is concentrating on sexuality and how heterosexuals are able to productively procreate. However, lurking behind this concern is how the species can survive, and Freud is convinced that survival is based on the triumph of object love. We will see that, at times, he is pessimistic about the prospects of the survival of our species. In the next chapter, Freud's views on the development of object love are detailed.

In the three essays, he implicitly gives us the concept of fixation. Thus, pregenital interests and zones are potentially points of fixation or developmental areas that arrest full developmental potential. For Freud, full developmental potential involves genital primacy. It is important to state that, for Freud, genital primacy does not occur until puberty, and so, when we talk about pregenital interests, Freud, in this period, does not have a modern conceptualization of the term pregenital. The contemporary analyst would see pregenital as almost synonymous with the term pre-Oedipal. (There is a period in the genital or phallic stage of development where the Oedipal complex is not yet implicated in the child's development. This is, for example, Brenner's (1976, 1982) view; however, there are clearly other views about the Oedipal stage of development, as we will see in the chapter on Melanie Klein.) During this period, Freud has a literal meaning of the term pregenital: that is, before secondary sexual characteristics have developed. Thus, everything before adolescence is pregenital. Clearly, latency is not here conceived of as a point of fixation, since the zones are relatively quiescent during latency. As we stated in the chapter, Freud does not yet have an idea of stages of development organized in terms of zones. Rather, the zones are points where, during pregenital development, the child is able to have autoerotic pleasures. These pleasures, while momentarily exciting, are, over a period of time, ultimately frustrating, hence the movement from pregenital to genital interest. The genital zone during adolescence (and beyond) is the only one where there can be true satisfaction in terms of tension reduction through orgasm. For Freud, optimal sexual development involves genital primacy, with pregenital zones exciting the way towards genital satisfaction. Thus, in a single sexual encounter, an individual can relive their early sexual life and end the sexual encounter with adult satisfaction through mutual genital orgasm. Implied in this discussion is the definition of Freud's views of psycho-sexual stages at this point in time. He conceptualizes two stages of development: autoerotism and object love. Autoerotism involves all pleasures that occur before the capacity for genital orgasm. Freud assumes genital orgasm occurs for both sexes at puberty. Thus, Freud does not label stages with respect to zone, but, rather, in terms of the child's libidinal relationship to the other (object). What is not well understood in this prior sentence is the term libidinal relationship, or libidinal cathexis. Freud, at this point, is virtually equating the occurrence of a lasting libidinal cathexis as being coincident with the capacity for object love. The capacity of object love is, in turn, related to the development of secondary sexual characteristics necessary for the survival of the species. Even though Freud, at this time, is defining stages in relationship to the development of object love, this view is strongly tied to his view of the biological development of the child and relatively devoid of psychological developmental statements as compared to the statements he will make in the next several years.

Before we look at the logical difficulties of Freud's theory in this era, we must remember that Freud sees ideal development in terms of heterosexual development. However, he spends a good deal of time in the three essays on the question of homosexuality. Freud is writing these essays shortly after Oscar Wilde was on trial (Ellmann, 1987). Freud goes out of his way to maintain that homosexuality is not a form of degeneracy in any sense of the term. It is important to emphasize what has been previously stated: that, while Freud maintains that there are no certain conclusions that one can reach about the aetiology of homosexuality, he is certain about one aspect of how "inverts" have been characterized. Homosexuality has been characterized both as a type of nervous degeneracy and as a disorder that leads to moral degeneracy. Here, Freud is clear that "inversion is found in people who exhibit no other serious deviations from the normal . . . and in people whose efficiency is unimpaired, and who are indeed distinguished by specially high intellectual development and ethical culture" (1905d, pp. 138–139). He also refers to the fact that homosexuality flourished in societies that were of the highest order in cultural and intellectual accomplishments. This revolutionary view is part of his concept that all "perversions" are part of normal development. Moreover, it is also his view that adult perversions are much more common than society would like to admit.

In stating Freud's view, I am not maintaining that homosexuality is a perversion. Rather, I am stating that Freud's view of what has been called perverse behaviour (including thoughts and fantasies) is revolutionary in that he is maintaining that what has been called perverse is experienced by all human beings. Thus, Freud sees intense reactions to homosexuals as indicative of homosexual conflicts. In a similar manner, oral or anal sex viewed in terms of disgust is also seen by Freud as a manifestation of conflict. What society views as perversions, Freud posits is infantile sexuality that is represented in the unconscious, in everyone's unconscious. Affects such as disgust and shame are examples of conflicts that have not been completely defended against or adequately sublimated. (Here, I am being somewhat anachronistic, since Freud has not stated this formulation as clearly as it is being stated above. Nevertheless, Freud has implied such a formulation in the dream book [1900a].) Thus, in adult life, a person is anxious, disgusted, or ashamed because of an earlier fixation caused by conflict at a given point of development. In many ways, this bourgeois Viennese doctor is pointing out that Victorian Europe is hypocritical in many senses of the term.

However, Freud returns to middle-class values when he posits an optimal resolution of sexual preferences. The optimal resolution (or, more accurately, result) of infantile or childhood sexuality is for the male to be active and penetrating and the female to be passive and receptive. This occurs during the period of genital primacy, and both female and male participants should appreciate and be desirous of someone who is different than they are in terms of bodily (genital) development. Thus, homosexuality, while no longer perverse, is now either a genetic disorder, a fixation, and/or, as we shall see later, an element of narcissism. The revolution returns to middle-class values with males asserting and females receiving, while homosexuality is indicative of incomplete development. The theoretical rationale that is provided conceives of human motivation being powered by two drives. Freud imagines that he has derived these two instincts from Darwin, but we shall see in his subsequent publications that these instincts are based at least in part on his conceptualizations of the clinical phenomena he is encountering. They are also based on Freud's misunderstanding of Darwin's revolutionary concepts. Freud's drive, or instinct, theory will be more fully discussed in the next chapter, but here we can at least briefly sketch out some aspects of this aspect of Freudian theory.

Freud's two drives can be roughly translated into survival of the self and survival of the species. In the three essays, Freud is writing about sexuality, and sexuality is in the service of survival of the species. From Freud's point of view, to be in love means, to some extent, to be able and willing to give up self-interest. Freud begins to conceive of the idea of survival of the self as a drive when he begins to think in more detail about the obstacles to developing a love relationship. This leads him to his theory of narcissism, which we shall encounter in the next chapter. Freud will posit that the two drives can potentially be in conflict in early development as well as in adult life. Freud's next bout of theorizing is greatly concerned with the conflicts that he is witnessing clinically and that he is conceptualizing partly in terms of these two drives. It is easy to see that one important way of looking at the three essays is that Freud is attempting or beginning to understand the pathway to true love. In the next decade, he will expand how he views the pathway and point to many obstacles to the development of the capacity for object love.

Earlier in the commentary I mention Freud's logical difficulties in his new theory. For the time being, we will look at two of these difficulties, one which has been the subject of a great deal of literature and the other which is implied by a great deal of this literature. Freud's view of pleasure being restricted to discharge or lowering of tension is questionable at best. His view was based on some of the neurophysiologists of his time, and the idea of the orgasm as the model for pleasurable experiences. It is hard to quarrel with the idea that tension reduction is pleasurable in a variety of circumstances. It seems equally difficult to imagine that this is the only type of experience that provides pleasure to humans (or other species). Numerous studies have shown that a variety of mammalian species (including humans) seek stimulation that raises levels of excitation. This is clearly an argument against the view that pleasure is involved only with lowering levels of excitation. We will encounter some of this research in several chapters of this volume, but, for the present, we will content ourselves with the assertion that the hydraulic model (in Freud's use of this model, he posited that lowering or pumping out excitation down to quiescent levels is the ultimate source of pleasure) as the sole explanation of pleasure is incorrect or not supported by various types of evidence and experience.

We have looked at Freud's psycho-sexual stages at this point in time, and there are only two stages that he names: autoerotism and object love. Autoerotism refers to the time before adolescence, where pleasure is essentially without a libidinal object cathexis. Freud makes it clear that there can be attachments and a type of love before adolescence, but the love, as he will more clearly specify, is based on self-interest. This self-interest pertains to issues of being protected or fed, both issues that relate to survival of the self. However, love of the object as different from the self is, for Freud, not available to the child until the sexual (survival of the species) drive is fully manifested during adolescence. This view will change in the next few years, but the problem of moving from stage to stage will remain. Freud's idea of progression from stage to stage is that while something may be exciting for a time, it is ultimately not pleasurable unless there is tension reduction. Clearly, if there is no tension reduction possible in the pregenital zones, then there can be no lasting pleasure. Passage from autoerotism is then likened to the passage from foreplay to genital sex. One can imagine this passage as happening during a sexual encounter, or even over some finite period of time. It seems quite unlikely that this will occur over a period of years. Thus, the passage from one stage to another implies a capacity to retain tension that seems impossible as a characterization of childhood experience. Let me give an example of the type of questions that can be formulated if one takes this aspect of Freudian theory seriously. How can pregenital fixations be considered pleasurable if they only increase stimulation? If fixations are pregenital and sexual pleasure is not fully possible, how is pleasure represented in the unconscious? It must be represented in terms of excitation rather than discharge, but, for Freud, how can this be considered pleasurable? One could compound this type of question, but, for the time being, we will be content to say that to answer this type of question would require adjustments to Freud's theorizing. This type of attempt will occur in the later sections of this volume.

Commentary: dream book

Although Freud initially presented a complex model of dreaming, the emphasis of this model was on the wish. The wish, to paraphrase Freud, is the capital needed to fuel the dream, and Freud and those that followed him have focused heavily on the capital in the business of dreaming. Freud maintained that dreams are instigated by unconscious wishes. After making this assertion, Freud, in Chapter Seven of *The Interpretation of Dreams* (1900a), frequently reminds us of Socrates helping his listeners search for the meaning of the good and the beautiful. The sceptic might ask, if all dreams are instigated by a wish, what about anxiety dreams, or dreams that feel horrific and typically are called nightmares? Freud answers these queries and his answers lead him to consider a realm of experience that, up to that point in time, had been largely unexplored: the earliest and deepest recesses of human experience. He defines an unconscious wish as a pleasure (to quote Freud, a wish is "a diminution of excitation was felt as pleasure" [*ibid.*, p. 598]) that has its source in early childhood. It is a pleasure that, if activated, shows the mind in conflict, since what is pleasurable at one level (unconscious) will cause anxiety on another level (Pcs–conscious). This conflict is mediated by the censorship (which serves a defensive function), and these two levels of awareness are *primarily* governed by different modes of cognition (primary *vs.* secondary process).

Why does a dream occur? Here, Freud posits that sleep is both a condition for regression and during sleep the censorship is weakened. Thus, the emergence (representation) of a wish (which was activated during the previous day) can more easily occur during sleep. The censorship that is still active provides the impetus for a compromise formation. This compromise formation consists of the transformation of the wish into a sensory form (the movement from motor activity [and thought] to sensory experience is Freud's first definition of regression) that is disguised sufficiently to allow the person to dream and stay asleep. Anxiety dreams, in Freud's theory, signal the failure of the dream process and dream-work to adequately disguise and deal with the wish. In the dream book, Freud theorizes about how different systems communicate, and it is this communication that he labels as transference. Freud says specifically that

> an unconscious idea is as such quite incapable of entering the preconscious and that it can only exercise any effect there by establishing a connection with an idea which already belongs to the preconscious, by transferring its intensity on to it and by getting itself "covered" by it. [*ibid.*, p. 562]

It is via the dream that Freud gives theoretical definition to this concept that will gradually change the way he conceptualizes the treatment situation. As a last point in this brief summary, Freud attempts to show the similarities between dream formation, symptom formation, and, during the same time period, a variety of other phenomena (momentary forgetting, slips of tongue, etc., [Freud, 1901b]). In short, Chapter Seven is unparalleled in psychoanalytic thought, in that Freud attempts the most general theory that has been put forth probably up to the present time. Despite this heroic attempt, Freud will find various difficulties with his theoretical structure and certainly others will find even greater difficulty.

When Freud wrote the dream book, he was just beginning (or about to begin) to develop an instinct or drive theory (I am using these terms synonomously). The first drive theory that he put forth contrasted the drive or tendency towards survival of the self with survival of the species. There were a number of contrasting tendencies that emerged from this conceptualization, ego (self) libido and object (other) libido were translated into issues that involved narcissism and object love, which are primary subject(s) of the next chapter. In the explanation of dreams, Freud posits the idea that in the unconscious there are pleasurable fantasies that would lead to anxiety in the Pcs.–Cs. system. We have just discussed this concept in the commentary of the three essays, but, clearly, Freud's ideas of pleasure are subject to critical scrutiny. We have already discussed the logical and theoretical difficulties, but perhaps what is more important in the psychoanalytic community are the treatment issues that this concept brings forth. On the one hand, the idea of humans as having conflicts about pleasure leads to interpretative comments that seem to be totally absorbed with bodily parts and pleasures. The role of other humans is diminished and the person becomes a solipsistic entity. This, of course, is a caricature of Freud and subsequent analysts, but a tendency that certainly was criticized and caricatured for a good deal of the history of psychoanalysis until the present. On the other hand, Freud's revolutionary insights about the child and how the child sees the world through her/his body can be overlooked easily when concentrating on the patient's relationships. Clearly, when a movement begins in any field, there is a tendency to see the world through the new prism that has been developed. We will see how this prism has been thought to clarify and distort human experience, depending on whose eyes are looking through this new device.

Dream research since Aserinsky and Kleitman's (1953) discovery of rapid eye movement (REM) sleep has produced a vast literature, in part summarized in Ellman and Antrobus (1991). REM sleep is seen by many sleep researchers as the condition for dreaming, or, at least, the condition for producing the type of mentation that most people define as a dream. Solms (1997) have questioned whether REM mechanisms are the necessary condition for dreaming, and their data will be briefly discussed when we go over REM sleep mechanisms and the relationship of REM to pleasure. At this point, it is a task of any dream theory to at least account for the data that has been produced by contemporary sleep and dream researchers.

CHAPTER THREE

Freud's object relations era: the metapsychological papers

Summary

This is the period where Freud is both most prolific and writes a series of papers that are both complex and compelling. Despite this, they are not well integrated into the next period of his theorizing (Chapter Four) where he develops the more familiar structural model (ego, id, and superego). In this epoch, Freud more fully explicates his instinctual theory and uses this theory to reintroduce the concepts of primary and secondary process (see Chapter Two).

During this era, Freud also develops new psycho-sexual stages. These stages are his attempt to explain the difficulties in achieving a fulfilling mutual love relationship. His psycho-sexual stages are somewhat foreign to contemporary psychoanalysts. They are autoerotism, narcissism, object choice (or anal sadism), and object love. These stages are defined in terms of the child's relation to the object (typically, the child parents or fantasized others). Although Freud's theory does not leave his view of the child's powerful interest in her/his body and bodily functions, he puts this interest in terms of how the infant/child internalizes the object. In developing this new theory, Freud posits the concept of narcissism as a developmental stage. He also states a series of fixation points, and only one of these fixation points is in the Oedipal period.

Papers that are labelled his metapsychological papers are his attempt at a more formal theory. His papers "The unconscious" (1915e), "Repression" (1915d), and "Instincts and their vicissitudes" (1915c) are all efforts at systematizing his psychoanalytic theory. These papers, while providing a number of important concepts, did not provide Freud with what he considered to be a systematized theory. There is a long discussion of the papers "Repression" and "The unconscious" at the end of this chapter.

In many ways, this era of Freud's writings is where he is being most influenced by Ferenczi, and, in turn, many of the concepts that he introduces are included and amplified in Melanie Klein's theorizing. This era is perhaps the least well known in terms of the type of theory that Freud was attempting to construct. It is also the period where Freud writes most of his technique papers and it is the time where he is most active as a clinical psychoanalyst.

Introduction

Although this is Freud's most prolific era, it may be the period that is least understood by American psychoanalysts. We have seen that the three essays did not provide us with the Freudian stereotypes to which we have grown accustomed; during the present period (1909–1918) Freud takes us even further away from our convictions about his creation of psychoanalysis. Freud continues to advance the concept of psycho-sexual stages, but here he is mainly concerned with a question that he dealt with more mechanistically in the three essays: the pathway(s) to, object love. Surely, this is a question that can be advanced through the concept of psycho-sexual stages, but Freud's journey is going to take him to places that are normally associated with analysts that today are called object relations theorists.

The path to object love is only one of the themes that we will encounter; during this epoch, Freud attempted to write what he called the metapsychological papers. The editors of the *Standard Edition* write that "The series of 'Papers on Metapsychology' may perhaps be regarded as the most important of all Freud's theoretical writings" (Volume 14, p. 161). Jones (1955) relates that these papers were to consist of a series of twelve essays designed to provide a theoretical foundation for psychoanalytic theory. We know that Freud destroyed (or at least did not publish) seven of the twelve metapsychology papers he wrote. Both the editors of the *Standard Edition* and Jones mourn the loss of these papers. (In fact, one of these papers was found by Ilse Grubrich-Simitis in a trunk belonging to Ferenczi. Ferenczi was one of Freud's closest allies at the time of the writing of the metapsychological papers. This paper has been published, entitled "A phylogenetic fantasy" [1987].) Freud was obviously not completely satisfied with the results of his efforts; nevertheless, we have several important statements of his thinking in the five published papers which are: "Repression" (1915d), "The unconscious" (1915e), "Instincts and their vicissitudes" (1915c), "Mourning and melancholia" (1917e) and "A metapsychological supplement to the theory of dreams" (1917d). In this chapter, we will explore many of the issues that Freud presented in these papers, and we will also look at several other papers from this era (not labelled as metapsychological), including: "Formulations of the two principles of mental functioning" (1911b), the theoretical section (section 3) of *Psycho-analytic Notes on an Autobiographical Account of Paranoia* (1911c) (popularly known as the Schreber case), "The disposition to obsessional neurosis" (1913i), and "On narcissism" (1914c).

The form of our inquiry will change somewhat in this section. In the previous two chapters, we examine each work in chronological order; here, we look at Freud's works in terms of issues rather than in chronological order. Our topics will include a fuller statement of the dual instinct theory, new views on the self and object relations (and object love), fixation points in terms of Freud's views of psychopathology, repression (or defence), the role of the unconscious, and logical difficulties in the new statement of the topographic model. Our emphasis in this chapter will mirror the prominence Freud presents in his concern with the pathways to and regressions from the attainment of object love. In addition, we will start by looking at Freud's definition of metapsychology and his views on epistemological issues of theory construction.

Historical note about metapsychology and theory

Jones writes,

> Freud was now in his sixtieth year and ... he superstitiously believed he had only a few years to live. He was therefore in a mood to attempt something like a synthesis of his most profound psychological conceptions. The mood must been accentuated by the promise of experiences of an indefinitely long war, the hardships of which he might well not survive. Freud's plan was to publish 12 essays in a single volume that might have been titled, "Introduction to Metapsychology" or "Introductory Essays on Metapsychology". [Jones, 1955, p. 207–208]

Freud apparently wrote all of the essays in a relatively short time (between 15 March and 9 August 1915).

The term metapsychology, which Jones credits Freud as coining, is a term that has led to a good deal of confusion in psychoanalytic writing. Freud thought that if psychological processes could be accounted for in terms of dynamic, economic, and topographic assumptions, then he had reached a complete explanation. Metapsychology, then, may be defined as theoretical assumptions that are stated in terms of these three types of viewpoints. He concluded that a psychological explanation is complete if we can ascertain the conflict (or interaction) between levels of consciousness (topographic), the amount and type(s) of energy expended (economic), and the play of forces in the mind which work together or against one another (dynamic) in accounting for a given psychological activity (topographic). There are, however, a number of other definitions that Freud put forth in defining metapsychology (Ellman & Moskowitz, 1980) and, in this context, metapsychology will be designated as theoretical tenets of Freud's that he believed help to explain a range of phenomena. He frequently considered the more basic assumptions to be the ones he stipulated as metapsychological propositions. In a previous publication (*ibid.*), we have stated that Freud's views on metapsychology were conflicted at best, and frequently confused. At times he thought that metapsychology stood apart from clinical psychoanalysis (this is a popular view among contemporary psychoanalysts) and that what Rapaport and Gill (1959) have called the special theory of psychoanalysis was based on findings from the clinical situation. At other times, he saw what he called metapsychology as simply part of psychoanalytic theory.

His attitude towards metapsychology was varied in the same manner as his views concerning the nature or role of theory. At times he indicated that the assumptions that he put forth were tentative and "are not the basis of science, upon which everything rests; that foundation is observation alone" (1914c, p. 77). This view, to some modern ears, seems overly naïve, since Freud seems to be indicating that he believes in the possibility of the pure observer who is able to see reality apart from her/his implicit or explicit theoretical assumptions. Many modern philosophers and psychologists would see this type of pristine observer as an impossibility (Nagel, 1961; Nagel, 1995) and might characterize Freud's statement as mythology at best. Freud, however, only a year later, states,

> The true beginning of scientific activity consists either in describing phenomena and then in proceeding to group, classify and correlate them. Even at the stage of description it is not possible to avoid applying certain abstract ideas to the material in hand, ideas derived from somewhere or other but certainly not from the new observation alone. [1915c, p. 117]

Here, Freud is taking a different position: he is still extolling the scientific observer, but he is clearly acknowledging that, even at the basic stage of description, the observer is guided by, and applies, concepts that are from places other than the observational field. This extract is part of a longer discussion by Freud, where he shows remarkable acuity in discussing the role of theoretical assumptions or postulates in organizing, guiding, and influencing the observations made by an investigator. He also recognizes that to present too precise a theoretical structure would inhibit, rather than facilitate, his theoretical venture. This is frequently the case when a theory is in an early stage of development. He reminds his reader (and presumably himself) that

> The advance of knowledge however, does not tolerate any rigidity even in definitions. Physics furnishes an excellent illustration of the way in which even "basic concepts" that have been established in the form of definitions are constantly being altered in their content. [*ibid.*]

After decrying premature rigidity in definitions, Freud utilizes perhaps the supreme example, where the Einstein revolution in physics demonstrates that even definitions that were considered to be laws of nature can be altered. This more sophisticated statement both acknowledges the importance of theory and indicates that theoretical assumptions can and should be changed at times. In fact, even basic postulates are not safe from intense scrutiny, no matter how cherished they may be. We will see that Freud took the ideas that he presented here very seriously indeed.

Freud's dual instinct theory and the ego: das Ich

Freud, in this era, is continuing a distinction that he began before 1911: the formalization of his instinct theory. When one reads *Three Essays on the Theory of Sexuality* (1905d), it is striking how many times Freud uses the term "instinct". Thus, there is an instinct for knowledge, sexual instincts, component instincts, etc. Bibring has written (1941) that Freud's instinct theory was always a dual instinct theory, but it was not formalized as such until after the writing of the *Three Essays*. In Freud's paper "On narcissism" (1914c), he firmly makes a distinction between the instincts and, for the first time in print, draws a distinction between what he calls ego-libido and object-libido. As we will see, his comments about narcissism require him to develop a theoretical structure that explains (or at least can contain) his new theoretical ideas.

What does he now mean by an instinct? He says, in a paragraph added to the *Three Essays* in 1915,

> "Instinct" is provisionally to be understood the psychical representative of an endosomatic, continuously flowing source of stimulation, as contrasted with a "stimulus", which is set up by single excitations coming from without. The concept of instinct is thus one of those lying on the frontier between the mental and the physical. The simplest and likeliest assumption as to the nature of instincts would seem to be that in itself an instinct is without quality, and, so far as mental life is concerned, is only to be regarded as a measure of the demand made upon the mind for work. [1905d, p. 168]

In his paper "On narcissism", Freud goes further, and talks about the nature of the instincts. The two instincts are survival of the self and survival of the species. These instincts can be in conflict or operate in co-ordination, depending on the object relations of the individual. By and large, survival of the self, which operates mostly through ego-libido, is dominant early in life (Freud, 1911b). At that point, an infant or young child is concerned mostly with satisfying basic needs that are crucial for survival. Thus, the infant may gradually become attached to (and love) the woman who feeds it or the man (or woman) who protects it, and both these forms of love are derived in part from the instinct for survival of the self. This instinct may promote early learning that may help the infant to signal a receptive environment (usually mother) to satisfy its needs and help the infant if it is in distress. When the infant becomes attached to a specific person (using object libido), Freud maintains that the instinct for survival of the species is operative. This later instinct is more commonly known as the sexual instinct, and it is the one that Freud has written about most extensively. This differentiation is, however, not so clear, since Freud writes,

> Just as object-libido at first concealed ego-libido from our observation, so too in connection with the object-choice of infants (and of growing children) what we first noticed was that they derived their sexual objects from their experiences of satisfaction. The first auto-erotic sexual satisfactions are experienced in connection with vital functions which serve the purpose of self-preservation. [1914c, p. 87]

Here, Freud is reminding us that he first studied conflicts that he conceptualized as sexual conflicts or conflicts that involved object libido. Focusing on conflicts around issues of object-libido disguised conflicts involving ego-libido. In a similar manner, he is maintaining that object-libidinal attachments are usually derived from the ego instincts. Clinically, most of Freud's conceptualizations involved hysteria and obsessive–compulsive syndromes, and, in Freud's view, these entities revolved around issues of sexuality (in his present vocabulary, we might say issues that involve object-libido). His consideration of early development was in this era stimulated in part by his wanting to provide a theory that considered more severe disorders, such as paranoia and schizophrenia. (Freud used the word paraphrenia for Bleuler's term schizophrenia. Very few writers followed Freud in using the term paraphrenia. I assume that his reason for developing a new term was partly due to his breaking off relations with Jung and other members of the Swiss analytic community.) These disorders had their origins in early development in Freud's theoretical structure. Given this assumption, it was necessary for Freud to conceptualize early development, and the theory of narcissism was the result. As Freud notes in the above extract, the drives (ego-libido and object-libido) are intertwined even in early development.

Freud's use of the term ego (*das Ich*) is generally, at this point, thought to refer to the self and not to the ego as it is understood in psychoanalytic theory today. The editors of the *Standard Edition* say that

> In this connection it must be pointed out that the meaning which Freud attached to "das Ich" (almost invariably translated by 'the ego' in this edition) underwent a gradual modification. At first he used the term without any great precision, as we might speak of the "the self"; but in his latest writings he gave it a very much more definite and narrow meaning. [1914b, p. 71]

By "latest writings", the editors were referring to Freud's writing after 1920. This view of *das Ich* is undoubtedly the dominant view of contemporary psychoanalysts. However, when we consider Freud's later work, *The Ego and the Id*, we will look at other perspectives on Freud's views of the self *vs.* his views of the ego as a structure.

In this section we have briefly introduced Freud's concept of instinct to be able to discuss some of Freud's other concepts.

New views on the self and the other (object)

An introduction, with some important questions

Up to 1905, Freud thought that there were two stages of development, autoerotism and object love. In this formulation the stage of object love arrives at adolescence and is concomitant with genital primacy. Later (1911c), Freud posits a stage of development between autoerotism and object love, and he calls that stage narcissism. Then (1913i) Freud puts forth a stage of development that the editors of the *Standard Edition* call anal sadism and that I label as object choice. In the present interpretation, Freud (1915c) adds to the theory of narcissism and conceives of the beginning of this stage as coincident with a new concept: the purified pleasure ego. When the stage of narcissism ends, a new stage of development appears that I prefer to call object choice. After object choice, Freud posits that the last stage of childhood development is object love. If we were to summarize Freud's stages, by 1914 there would be autoerotism, narcissism, object choice (anal sadism), and object love. We can now look at each of these stages and see how Freud deals with the seeming contradictions in his conceptualizations.

Freud's object relations stages

The autoerotic stage

The first stage of development is autoeroticism, and during this stage the infant is initially concerned with wished for or hallucinated pleasures. Freud describes this initial response in *The Interpretation of Dreams* (see Chapter Two). Freud states that the infant's pleasure ego operates according to the primary process. However, the pleasure ego rapidly gives way to the reality ego as hallucinated pleasures do not satisfy basic needs such as hunger, thirst, or the alleviation of pain. The infant quickly learns to signal the mother and, when this occurs, Freud posits the existence of secondary process. When the secondary process begins, he assumes a new internal orientation towards reality, and he labels the infant's self or ego the reality ego. In Freud's view of early development, the pleasure ego exists in a pure form for only a short period of time. If the infant has developed a reality ego, what are we to make of Freud's quote when he says that

> ... an organization which ... neglected the reality of the external world could not maintain itself alive for the shortest time ... The employment of a fiction like this is, however, justified when one considers that the infant—provided one includes with it the care it receives from its mother—does almost realize a psychical system of this kind. [1911b, p. 220]

This extract is one where Freud is maintaining that the reality the infant knows is that the mother consistently provides what it needs when it, the infant, signals the mother. Freud assumes that the mother is a consistent enough provider during autoerotism that the infant is not particularly concerned with the mother but, rather, in what she provides in terms of pleasure (nourishment and comfort). Thus, the infant is not concerned with an adult version of reality, but is concerned with reality in the sense that it can behave in particular ways and receive what it wants and needs. The mother, during this stage, is part of the infant's system. As such, she is remembered and is part of the infant's reality, but the infant does not libidinally cathect the maternal representation. The infant experiences the world through states of pleasure and unpleasure.

However one evaluates this conceptualization, there is no contradiction in Freud's theoretical statements. Freud posits that the infant's concerns are with adequately signalling the environment; in this sense, the infant has gone, during the stage of autoerotism, from the pleasure to the reality ego. If things proceed optimally (during this stage), the infant is interested in the environment as a place that will reliably meet its needs. A frequent misconception of Freud's concept of autoerotism is that infant is incapable of learning at this point in time. This is not Freudian theory; rather, the infant learns what it needs to ensure its survival. Freud's concept of what the infant must do to survive is rather circumspect compared to contemporary evolutionary biologists (see Chapter Eighteen).

To comment briefly on this, if one takes Freud's statements in an absolute sense, then this position is an extreme position and it seems unlikely that an infant will not develop any libidinal investment in the mother, even during this stage of development. Freud, however, is trying to give a picture of an infant that is primarily concerned with biological needs. In Jacobson's terms (1964), the infant is concerned with homeostatic balance and its psychophysiological self more than it is with the object (mother) as an independent entity.

Narcissism

Freud begins section 3 of *Psycho-analytic Notes on an Autobiographical Account of a Case of Paranoia* (1911c) by saying that

> We have hitherto been dealing with the father-complex, which was the dominant element in Schreber's case and with the wishful

fantasy round which the illness centred. But in all of this there is nothing characteristic of the form of disease known as paranoia, nothing that might not be found (and that has not in fact been found) in other kinds of neuroses. The distinctive character of paranoia (or of dementia paranoides) must be sought for elsewhere. [1911c, p. 59]

In making this statement, Freud is introducing a topic that he has alluded to in footnotes in *Three Essays* and in more depth in his paper on Leonardo da Vinci (1910c). He has already discussed his new theory with his colleagues (Nunberg & Federn, 1909), but it is in the Schreber case where he begins to talk more definitively about narcissism as a new stage of libidinal development. Freud relates,

Recent investigations have directed our attention to a stage in the development of the libido which it passes through on the way from auto-erotism to object-love. That stage has been given the name of narcissism. During the stage of narcissism the sexual instincts are unified and this unification is one factor which leads to and allows for the choice of a love-object. The first love object is the person themselves, their own body is cathected and this choice is one step along the way to the choice of another person other than himself as his object. [1911c, pp. 61–62]

It takes Freud several years to conceptualize how the shift from autoerotism to narcissism takes place.

The purified pleasure ego

Freud introduces the concept of the purified pleasure ego in "Instincts and their vicissitudes" (1915c). In the following extract, Freud reviews some of what we have just sketched out in the preceding section. He says,

In so far as the ego is auto-erotic, it has no need of the external world, but, in consequence of experiences undergone by the instincts of self-preservation, it acquires objects from that world, and, in spite of everything, it cannot avoid feeling internal instinctual stimuli for a time as unpleasurable. Under the dominance of the pleasure principle a further development now takes place in the ego. In so far as the objects which are presented to it are sources of pleasure, it takes them into itself, "introjects" them (to use Ferenczi's term) and, on the other hand, it expels whatever within itself becomes a cause of unpleasure,

Thus the original "reality-ego", which distinguished internal and external by means of a sound objective criterion, changes into a purified "pleasure-ego" . . . For the (purified) pleasure-ego the external world is divided into a part that is pleasurable, which it has incorporated into itself, and a remainder that is extraneous to it. It has separated off a part of its own self, which it projects into the external world and feels as hostile. [1915c, p. 136]

The purified pleasure ego is a different concept from the pleasure ego and a further refinement of his concept of narcissism. The editors of the *Standard Edition* note that the "reality-ego and the pleasure ego had already been introduced in the paper on the two principles of mental functioning" p. 136). However, Freud is not introducing the term pleasure ego in this essay; rather, he is introducing a new term, "the purified pleasure ego". Freud is maintaining that first there is a pleasure ego, which is quickly replaced by a reality ego. Both of these states (I would call them self states) are occurring during the stage of autoerotism. The reality ego can exist during autoerotism, according to Freud, because the infant is using what it has learnt to signal the mother and the mother (or primary parent) is part of the infant's system that provides the infant with pleasure and satisfaction. From Freud's perspective, the reliability of the mother does not occasion the infant to make a libidinal investment in her person. A libidinal investment occurs only when the infant begins to perceive that the system in some ways has broken down, or is discriminably less reliable than in the past. Thus, in Freud's view, the child does not take the mother in as libidinal object (as opposed to a memory) until the infant is more fully cognizant that the mother can leave or be absent for significant periods of time; in short, until the infant experiences a meaningful and anxiety-producing separation. Before this point, the infant acquires objects primarily on the basis of experiences influenced by "the instincts of self-preservation" (1915c, p. 135).

It is when the infant is forced to perceive and confront its dependence on the mother that Freud sees the infant making a libidinal investment in the mother. This is the point where the stage of narcissism begins. This might seem like an odd statement, since Freud has maintained in previous extracts that the first libidinal investment is towards the person's own self, their own body, and their own early sense of self. One might well ask, what this has to do with internalizing the image of the mother? Here, we must return to the concept of the purified pleasure ego. The purified pleasure ego occurs when the infant no longer can completely rely on the mother as part of its system. The infant experiences frustration that activates a wish that the mother always be present when a need arises. The wish is a cleansing wish that divides the world in a new way. All that is pleasurable is now taken inside the self, all that is unpleasurable is in the environment. The world has been purified and the pleasure-giving aspects of the mother are now represented as part of the self. All that is frustrating is in the environment; this includes aspects of the mother and of the self. In this formulation, the libidinal investment is in the infant's early representation of itself and this representation is combined with an aspect of its mother. This new internal world now reorientates the infant in relationship to the external world.

Freud is here postulating a new type of activity by the infant; that is, the ability of the infant to split its view of its world. Thus, the mother is, from the infant's point of view, not always the same mother. The representation of the mother is split, and the way the self is represented is also split. The purified pleasure ego, then, is the beginning of narcissism, where the infant cathects (invests in a relatively permanent way) itself, but now itself is a combination of the pleasurable parts of itself and its environment (the environment is primarily its mother). Not only is the infant splitting its object world, but it is aided by other mechanisms that Freud is now positing. Freud is hypothesizing that the infant can take in the mother (in fantasy) by the process of introjection and that the infant can expel aspects of the mother and aspects of itself by a process of projection. Freud (1915c) is joining Ferenczi in positing the infant's early representations as being shaped by the processes of introjection and projection.

Most of the remaining part of the narcissistic stage of development is devoted to bringing the infant/developing child to learn to join split images together and develop trusting representations of the external world. This, of course, entails that the child begins to be able to tolerate unpleasurable states for relatively long periods of time. The final part of the narcissistic stage (1911c) is interesting in that Freud calls this the homosexual aspect of narcissism. Here, the child loves those objects that are like itself and, at times, this may entail liking those objects or people that the child perceives are like it in terms of body parts (usually genitals).

Object choice (anal sadism)

Here, during this period, according to the editors of the *Standard Edition*, we have Freud's first attempt to delineate a psycho-sexual stage in terms of a zone of mucous membrane. Freud, during the previous era, has written papers on anality (1907b, 1908b), but he did not conceptualize this as a stage of development. These papers detailed some personality traits that were associated with anal tendencies. Freud made no attempt to specify that this was a universal stage. However, now, in 1912–1913, according to the editors of the *Standard Edition*, Freud posits the first psycho-sexual stage where "one or other of the component instincts dominates the whole picture" (1913i, p. 316). This component instinct is "the anal-sadistic one" (*ibid.*). Freud, in this paper, is attempting to specify the question of choice of neurosis or, in other terms, the fixation points for different disorders (a term I have some difficulty with, clinically). In this paper, he is focusing on obsessive compulsives and he traces their point of fixation to a point where anal sadistic issues are at their height.

Freud's position in this paper is that in normal development the child has to give up a pleasure to keep the love of its mother. More specifically Freud describes the child as enjoying anal activities and then at some point the child's parents are urging the child to give up anal pleasures and be toilet trained. In his developmental schema the child optimally gives up anal pleasures because maintaining the love from its parents is more important than anal pleasures. This is the child's first significant object choice, and this choice moves the mother from a narcissistic object to one that is partially represented as a external love object. The mother is now seen as an external object at this point in time, since the child recognizes that its wishes are distinctly different than its mother's wishes. Although Freud focuses on the body, the child at this age has to begin to listen to various regulations that are designed for the child's safety (and the parents sanity). Clearly, a parent is not able to explain to the child many of the regulations that are gradually being imposed on the increasingly mobile child.

Since it is not always possible to rationally reason with the child, at times the parent might be seen as an aggressive or sadistic object to the child. Freud maintains that if the child is able to make a choice to give up certain pleasures because the loved object is more important than bodily pleasures, this is optimal. If, however, the child obeys primarily because of threats from the parents (one of the most severe threats being the withdrawal of love or even of attention from the parent), Freud posits that this will lend this stage a strong overlay of sadism. To be sure, Freud is maintaining that, from the child's perspective, there is bound to be a certain amount of perceived sadism, but if the child is able to make choices primarily based on love for, or affectionate ties to, the mother, this is optimal, and the child will progress relatively unfettered to the next stage of development. It is important not to minimize the idea that, during this stage, there are always some sadistic elements. However, what is frequently lost in discussing this paper is the importance of object choice in Freud's theoretical ideas. If wanting to please the mother and maintain her love is the prime motivation, there are then fewer sadistic elements in this stage of development. This is a point along the way to the child's final stage of loving and being loved in return (object love). The final stage of object love, where the child loves and wishes to be loved in return, is coincident with Oedipal dynamics. Oedipal dynamics imply a period where the child must tolerate another form of love; that is, a love between two other people that is apart from their love for the child. We will come to the Oedipal stage, but we have to retrace our steps once again to make other distinctions that Freud introduced.

Autoerotism, narcissism, and the different forms of love

It is important to note that Freud's introduction of the concept of the purified pleasure ego occurs in his paper "Instincts and their vicissitudes" (1915c). In this paper, he seems to be writing about instincts, yet, in the middle of the paper, he introduces a number of ideas that are related to our present topic. He relates the different paths that an instinct may follow and talks about the mind in terms of three polarities: self–object, activity–passivity, and pleasure–unpleasure. Each manifestation of instinct has an opposing tendency (active and passive tendency) and is an instinctual manifestation from a certain point of development (fixation). As an illustration, sadism (active) is the opposite of masochism (passive) and is a manifestation of anality. Adult behaviour that is derived from, and primarily determined by, a component instinct is indicative of a fixation. Behaviours from component instincts are only considered part of normal behaviour if, as foreplay, they are combined with a mature process (normally love or mature sexual excitement, see Chapter Two).

The point of the essay, however, lies not just in the explication of the concept of instinct, but, rather, in how the development of love is a manifestation of both instincts and something beyond the instincts. Love, then, is not simply the manifestation of an instinct at a particular point in development. The type of love a person exhibits is a manifestation of their entire psychological make-up, and Freud relates that "we are naturally unwilling to think of love as being some kind of special component instinct" (*ibid.*, p. 133). Loving, in Freud's lexicon, admits of not one, but of three opposites, loving–indifference, loving–hating, and loving–being loved. Freud looks at each of these pairs of opposites and maintains that each pair is indicative of a given developmental era. If Freud were to be entirely consistent, love would admit of four opposites, but we can follow Freud's opposites and then put in one more for the purposes of consistency.

We can now restate that Freud says that during the earliest phase of development the infant is autoerotic and has no experienced need of the external world. The infant is active when it experiences needs and quickly learns to signal for gratification of its needs. At this point in time, if development is optimal, the infant is indifferent to the external world and is concerned with pleasure or need gratification. The objects that the infant acquires during this period of time are internalized (or remembered) "in consequence of experiences undergone by the instincts of self preservation" (*ibid.*, p. 135). Freud concludes that, during this first phase of development, the infant loves what is pleasurable and is indifferent to the external world.

During the next phase of development, beginning with the purified pleasure ego, the infant splits the world, and the aspects of the world that the infant takes as part of itself are loved, while everything that is external is hated. Thus, at the beginning of narcissism, the infant loves what is inside and hates what it perceives as outside of itself. Most of the narcissistic stage of development is devoted to the infant/developing child learning to bring split images together and develop trusting representations of the external world. This, of course, entails that the child begins to be able to tolerate unpleasurable states for relatively long periods of time. The final part of the narcissistic stage (1911c) is interesting in that Freud calls this the homosexual stage or aspect of narcissism. Here, the child loves those objects that are like itself and, at times, this may entail liking those objects or people that the child perceives are like it in terms of body parts (usually genitals). More generally, the child loves those people who want what it wants and hates those people who have different desires.

To briefly summarize again, we can say that during autoerotism there is loving–indifference, and during narcissism there is love and hating (the external environment). During the next stage, object choice, there is loving and the fear of losing maternal love. Perhaps, in an optimal developmental setting, rather than losing the love of the mother, one might say the child wants to maintain the mother's love and have his mother proud of his accomplishments. The opposite then might, more ordinarily, be loving *vs.* hating to lose maternal approval. The mother, during this stage of development, is being represented as more of an external object, but the mother is probably never fully an external object. In Freud's terminology, the mother is always imbued to some extent with narcissistic libido.

In the final stage of infantile development, Freud postulates that object love is now possible and that there is a primacy of the genital zones. This presents a quandary for Freud at this point in his theorizing: in what stage does he place Oedipal dynamics? Full Oedipal dynamics presuppose the primacy of the genital zone and, in the *Three Essays*, Freud maintained that this did not occur until puberty. However, since 1897, he has maintained that there are Oedipal conflicts during childhood (in a letter to Fliess, Masson, 1985, pp. 272, 304). Freud is not going to resolve this logical conflict until *The Ego and the Id* (1923b), but we can say that, during the period we are discussing, it is clear that he is beginning to think that the capacity for object love and the occurrence of Oedipal dynamics coincide and occur during childhood and well before adolescence. Here, the opposites are loving and being loved in return. This dialectic occurs in the midst of Oedipal dynamics. Here we can look at Freud's views of the Oedipus complex, and in the next chapter we will again look at Freud's views when Oedipal dynamics are even more central to his theory.

Some of Freud's writings are in response to criticisms of him by Jung. In answering Jung, he makes it clear that, for him, Oedipal dynamics are quite real in childhood. The boy wants sole possession of his mother and wants to destroy his father. The Oedipus myth is relived in every childhood. The girl is the mirror image and wants sole possession of her father and wishes to destroy her mother. In the language that Freud will use later in *The Ego and the Id* (1923b), this would be termed the positive Oedipal complex for either the boy or the girl. If the boy is predominantly tied to his father, or the girl to her mother, this is termed the negative Oedipal complex. This is one of Freud's explanations for homosexuality, although Freud thought there were several pathways to homosexuality. Given the fact that Oedipal dynamics and the Oedipus myth has occupied Freud's attention since at least 1897, we will do a retrospective of his thoughts on this topic in the next chapter. In the era covered in the next chapter, he definitively makes the Oedipus complex the centre of his developmental and clinical theories.

Although Freud, during the present period, answers Jung by asserting the reality of the Oedipus complex, he responds to Adler by maintaining that Adler has overestimated the importance of the Oedipus complex (particularly in males). Freud's words are of interest here, since later he does not seem to remember this passage. Freud maintains that

> Psycho-analytic research has from the very beginning recognized the existence and importance of the "masculine protest", but it has regarded it, in opposition to Adler, as narcissistic in nature and derived from the castration complex. The "masculine protest" is concerned in the formation of character, into the genesis of which it enters along with many other factors, but it is completely unsuited for explaining the problems of the neuroses, with regard

to which Adler takes account of nothing but the manner in which they serve the ego-instincts, I find it quite impossible to place the genesis of neurosis upon the narrow basis of the castration complex, however powerfully it may come to the fore in men among their resistances to the cure of a neurosis. Incidentally, I know of cases of neurosis in which the "masculine protest", or, as we regard it, the castration complex, plays no pathogenic part, and even fails to appear at all. [1914c, pp. 92–93]

Here, we see Freud expressing an interesting and complex statement. We can first focus on the clearest aspects of Freud's answer to Adler. Freud does not want to place the neuroses or the formation of character formation on only the ego-instincts. Neuroses are, at least in some conditions, a product of conflict between the instincts (ego or self and sexual or object instincts). The castration complex is clearly a sexual issue in two senses of the concept of sexuality. Freud interestingly brings forth only one of these senses, that is, the narcissistic investment of the child in his or her own genitals. In Freudian terms, this narcissistic investment is sexual in nature, since the child has libidinally cathected its own self and its own genitals. In addition, the castration complex implies the threat of castration for desiring another's (one's father) wife. When Freud says at the end of this statement that he knows of cases of neurosis in which the castration complex plays no pathogenic part, he is maintaining that not all disorders have Oedipal dynamics. He seems to be saying that this is not an unusual event and that in any case placing the neuroses "on the narrow basis of the castration complex" is obviously, from his perspective, a mistake. As we will see, this view will change but it is important to remember that when Freud is writing the paper that we are quoting from ("On narcissism", 1914c), he is also in the midst of writing his papers on analytic technique. He is writing the papers on technique in part because this is the period of time when he is most active as a psychoanalytic clinician.

If we are to integrate Freud's disparate statements, we can say that, while Freud certainly considered Oedipal dynamics important, he had a more complex view of fixation points at this point in his career than would be the case in his subsequent theorizing in *The Ego and the Id* (1923b). We can now restate the stages of development, autoerotism, narcissism, object choice (anal sadism), and object love and find a fixation point in and around each stage of development. In discussing psychopathology, Freud developed fixation points for various diagnostic entities that he had encountered in the clinical situation. Freud saw the fixation point for schizophrenia as at the nexus of autoerotism and narcissism. Schizophrenia is the disorder that has the earliest fixation point and involves the least developed capacity for object love. It is Freud's view that, at the beginning of the schizophrenic process, there is a change from object libido into ego libido. This theoretical formulation is an attempt to describe an experience that is noted by megalomania and world destruction fantasies. (As a contemporary example, a patient of mine, during the onset of a schizophrenic episode, became mute for fear that if she spoke her voice would destroy the Bronx [where she was hospitalized] and the West Side of Manhattan [where I live]. This destructive idea was part of her retreat from other people and in her mind, if enacted, would cause the world around her to perish. Thus, in Freud's theoretical lexicon, her representations of other people [object libido] was partially destroyed and converted to a centring of representations on her own powers, horrifying to her as that might have been. Her catatonia was a manifestation of this retreat.) In this conceptualization, megalomania is due to a heightened cathexis of the self: all powers now reside in the self. World destruction fantasies are a result of the movement away from other objects. Freud goes on to say that, as a schizophrenic process continues, the symptoms of the disorder are a partial reversal of the process. Thus, in the second stage, ego libido turns back to object libido, albeit in distorted form. Symptoms like thought disorder, delusion, and hallucinations are seen as an attempt to restore some semblance of object relations. Although Freud uses the metaphor of psychic energy, his description is not dependent on this metaphor. He is talking about an oscillation in schizophrenia as first a movement away from the object world and then a movement back towards the object world, but in a manner that keeps the world disguised from certain types of reality testing.

While Freud saw schizophrenia as having a fixation at the nexus of autoerotism and narcissism, paranoia and various narcissistic disorders have their fixation points during narcissism. Freud opined that, in so far as one had narcissistic difficulties, they were not available to be treated by psychoanalysis. Melancholia or depression had a narcissistic fixation point as well. Freud attempted to restrict psychoanalysis to the two neurotic categories, hysteria and obsessive–compulsive neurosis. Obsessive–compulsive disorders, in Freud's view, had a fixation in the stage that we have called object choice (anal sadism). It is only hysteria (during this stage of theorizing) that has its fixation point during object love. Although Freud made this statement about treatment and narcissism, the patients that he treated were frequently narcissistic and had borderline disorders, in today's psychoanalytic parlance. It is certainly possible to see the "Wolf Man" (Freud, 1918b) as psychotic.

If one looks at Freud's view of fixation points, he sees continuities and recognizes that people's conflicts are admixtures that have their sources in various early experiences. Despite this realization, Freud, at different points, dichotomizes disorders and views any disorder that relates to narcissism as being difficult to treat in a psychoanalytic situation. This view was to change late in his career and will be discussed in the commentary to this chapter. Despite his views on narcissism, it is important to repeat that Freud treated severely disturbed patients who certainly did not adhere to the restrictions that he mentioned. Late in his career, he became convinced by various German analysts that psychoanalysis was of benefit to severely disturbed patients (Freud, 1937d).

Narcissism and melancholia

The search for the lost object is, from Freud's perspective, present whenever there is a significant conflict. Thus, neurotic symptoms are a search for the lost object as part of the formation of neurotic symptoms. In "Mourning and melancholia" (1917e), Freud continues this line of thought and begins to relate melancholia, a "pathological" state, to mourning a normal occurrence. Freud, in describing mourning, says that "We rely on [mourning] being overcome after a certain lapse of time, and we look upon any interference with it as useless or even harmful" (*ibid.*, p. 244). However,

> The distinguishing mental features of melancholia are a profoundly painful dejection, cessation of interest in the outside world, loss of the capacity to love, inhibition of all activity, and a lowering of the

self-regarding feelings to a degree that finds utterance in self-reproaches and self-revilings, and culminates in a delusional expectation of punishment. [*ibid.*]

Although the disturbance of self-regard is "absent in mourning", the other traits are similar to melancholia. In mourning, "Reality-testing has shown that the loved object no longer exists, and it (reality-testing) proceeds to demand that all libido shall be withdrawn from its attachments to that object" (*ibid.*). Since Freud posits "people never willingly abandon a libidinal position", there is a clinging to the lost object in a manner that is intense enough that it might be characterized as an "hallucinatory wishful psychosis" (*ibid.*). However, gradually the object is given up, and the ego becomes free and uninhibited again. In melancholia, the loss might be real or imagined, and frequently the patient might know "whom he has lost but not what he has lost" (*ibid.*, p. 245). Freud concludes that, in melancholia, there is loss of the object that is withdrawn from consciousness. In mourning, on the other hand, there is "nothing about the loss that is unconscious" (*ibid.*). Frequently, in melancholia, the loss is puzzling to the world because "we cannot see what it that is absorbing him so entirely" (*ibid.*, p. 246). Freud then puts forward his well-known aphorism: "In mourning it is the world that has become poor and empty, in melancholia it is the ego itself" (*ibid.*). For Freud, the cardinal element of melancholia is the "extraordinary diminution in (the person's) self-regard". However, there is a caveat in Freud's description: the melancholic complaints, while voiced loudly, "with insignificant modifications . . . fit someone else who the patient loves or has loved" (*ibid.*, p. 248). In short, he says, "We perceive that the self-reproaches are reproaches against a loved object which have been shifted away from it on to the patient's own ego" (*ibid.*). Freud not only compares the melancholic and the mourner, but the melancholic and the neurotic. He compares the operation of defence in the melancholic to repression, the main defence he sees as operative in the neurotic. In the neurotic, when an object choice is defended against, the conscious representation of that object is denied access to the conscious–preconscious system. In Freud's terms, this means that the libido that is attached to this representation is withdrawn and, therefore, either the representation or the meaning of the representation is forced into the unconscious system. The representation symbolically achieves consciousness at times through transference. Thus, there is a withdrawal of libido and then a displacement on to a new object. This new object retains enough disguise so that the defensive operation is not totally disrupted. This is the type of explanation that Freud puts forth in explaining transference in the analytic situation.

In the melancholic, the object cathexis is also withdrawn, but

> the free libido was not placed on to another object; it was withdrawn into the ego. Once in the ego it was not employed in any unspecified way, but served to establish an identification of the ego with the abandoned object. Thus the shadow of the object fell upon the ego. [*ibid.*]

Here, Freud is maintaining that the object is no longer represented as an external object, but as part of the self. However, it is a part of the self that is

> judged by a special agency, as though it were an object, the forsaken object. In this way an object-loss is transformed into an ego-loss and the conflict between the ego and the loved person is transformed into a cleavage between the critical activity of the ego and the ego as altered by identification. [*ibid.*, p. 249]

This now classic passage is one that is replete with ambiguity. What does Freud mean by identification? To what extent does the shadow of the object cover the ego? Perhaps these two questions are really identical in content. It is clear that the object, even as part of the self, has not formed a complete identity with the person's sense of self. As Freud has stated, there is a cleavage in the person's ego or sense of self. Freud, in this passage, is presenting two relatively new and not completely formed concepts, identification and a critical agency in the ego, or what he will come to call the superego. We will have occasion to talk about concepts of interiority. Here, I am referring to concepts that attempt to depict how a person represents her/his world in a stable manner. These concepts include terms like object representation, introjects, as well as identification or internalized representations, but, at this point, let us dwell on other aspects of both of these concepts.

Freud, in writing on how the shadow of the object falls on the ego, is attempting to describe how a narcissistic relationship is represented. In this description, Freud is talking about a narcissistic development secondary to some type of perceived insult or loss. However, as he progresses, he provides a developmental idea when he maintains that identification is a preliminary stage of object-choice. He states, "The ego wants to incorporate this object into itself, and, in accordance with the oral[1] or cannibalistic phase of libidinal development in which it is, it wants to do so by devouring it". In this regard, Freud writes, "Abraham is undoubtedly right in attributing to this connection the refusal of nourishment met with in severe forms of melancholia" (*ibid.*, pp. 249–250). Again, in this essay, Freud writes that the ego progresses from narcissism to narcissistic object-choice to object-cathexis (choice). (If we were to remind him of his other writings [and a later point he will make], we would say that there is a further stage of object-love.) The disposition for melancholia lies in the "predominance of the narcissistic type of object-choice" (*ibid.*, p. 250). Here, Freud includes in the narcissistic object-choice the type of identification that is made.

We have looked at Freud's views about the different types of narcissistic objects that are possible, and we have traced narcissistic development from the purified pleasure ego through homosexuality at the end of narcissism. When Freud writes about incorporation (here, I am following Freud and writing about incorporation as a one early type of identification), he is referring to an early phase of narcissism. The person incorporates another and makes this person a part of his/her self. This type of mechanism is present where the infant/child is keeping those objects that are pleasurable part of herself. Towards the end of narcissism, the child loves those objects that are like herself. This later phase could include persons (objects) that want the same things as the child. We can make sense of Freud's statements at the end of the second section of "On narcissism"; here, he states that as one form of narcissistic love, the person loves someone who was once part of himself (1914c, p. 90). In melancholia, the object is incorporated and is now part of oneself. The loving relationship has shifted to one of ambivalence.

In addition to positing the mechanism of incorporation in the melancholic, Freud writes about the melancholic's ambivalence. Here, it is important to remember that what Freud is referring to is opposing feelings of love and hate. He is not positing (at this time) that ambivalence necessitates object constancy. Here, object constancy is meant to imply having differing attitudes (feelings) towards the same object and being able consciously to feel these different attitudes at the same time. Obsessional patients frequently experience this type of ambivalence. Thus there may be contradictory attitudes towards a given object representation. Freud states,

> If the love for the object—a love which cannot be given up though the object itself is given up—takes refuge in narcissistic identification, then the hate comes into operation on this substitutive object, abusing it, debasing it, making it suffer and deriving sadistic satisfaction from its suffering. [1917e, p. 251]

How is it that a representation that is close to the ego and part of a narcissistic constellation can be hated? Freud's previous conceptualizations of narcissism involved a progression of initially loving what is inside and hating what is outside to loving those objects that are like oneself (or want the same things) and disliking those objects (people) that are seen as different than the self. Now, however, there is an object that is internalized as a result of a narcissistic identification that is hated. How does Freud account for this new type of representation or internal object?

For Freud, the answer lies in the ego treating itself as an object and "if it is able to direct against itself the hostility which relates to an object and which represents the ego's original reaction to objects in the external world" (*ibid.*, p. 252). Thus, an original state of narcissism is returned, but the split that existed between loving those objects that are inside and hating those that are outside now takes place as a completely internal conflict. The narcissistic retreat is one where the object is given up in reality but completely controlled in fantasy. The person is treating an aspect of themselves as they originally (in early development) treated a hated object in the external world.

In these last few pages that we have reviewed, Freud introduces several new concepts, none better known than the cannibalistic phase of development. The oral, or cannibalistic, stage is one of Freud's first discussions of orality as a stage of development. He links the oral stage with the early aspects of narcissism. Thus, during the oral stage, there is a particular type of identification (incorporation) where the infant incorporates those objects that it takes inside of itself. (Freud does not use the term introject in this essay as he did in "Instincts and their vicissitudes" (1915c) and will again later.) The objects that the infant takes in are those that it finds pleasurable, and represents these objects as part of itself. Objects that are aversive are projected to the external world and, in this way, the infant divides the world into good and bad (internal–external). Not surprisingly, the infant/child loves the good and hates the bad. This version of narcissistic development is replayed for Freud in various narcissistic disorders and, specifically, as we have seen, in melancholia. The difference is that the adult melancholic incorporates both the good and bad in terms of internal representations. This is done because, at this point, it is this internalization that allows the melancholic to retain control of the once loved person (object). The loved person then is represented as attached to the self and now is hated. It is both a form of self-hatred and a way of gaining control over a person who was perceived to act in a manner that did not provide adequate love. Freud maintains that, in hearing the melancholic's self-complaints, one can hear the overtones of a complaint against another. Thus, the shadow of the object falls on the ego, but the ego is not completely covered. The other person is a part of the self, but there is a cleavage in terms of the self-representation or a cleavage that is, in Freud's terms, a cleavage in the ego (self).

The first cleavage we have just described is a cleavage in the way that the self is represented. The second is one where Freud is positing that there is an agency of conscience that is separate from the self-representation and that agency oversees, and can be brutally critical of, the self. Freud does not here tell us how this agency develops. In his paper "On narcissism", he did relate that the person often judges himself harshly in terms of what he called a person's ego-ideals. In this paper, he relates that ego-ideals progress from the era of homosexuality. In other terms, a person loves one whom he idealizes, and this idealization is part of a narcissistic identification. Thus, even at this point in his theorizing, Freud views this critical agency as an outgrowth of the processes of identification.

What are we to make of Freud's ideas on identification, particularly identification as incorporation? Here, Freud comments briefly that identifications occur in the transference neuroses as well as in melancholia. The difference is that, in the transference neuroses, the identification is more selective and indicates something in common between the two people. In addition, in the transference neuroses, the object cathexis is not completely given up; rather, the object love maintains its influence in specific conflicts and actions. This forms the possibility of the type of transference that Freud writes about most frequently: transference through the displacement of love from object (person) to object (another person). If this is the prototype of transference, one can see that Freud might be reluctant to treat patients with narcissistic conflicts, since the type of displacement that is possible in transference neurotics is not possible, or barely possible, in people who have central narcissistic conflicts. Freud's ideas about analysability involve a series of contradictions that we will discuss in the commentary section, but, as is true of a number of Freud's injunctions, he frequently violated his own strictures that involve analysability.

In "Mourning and melancholia", Freud not only elaborates his ideas on narcissism, he furthers his attempts to form a diagnostic schema. His diagnostic ideas include disorders from schizophrenia to the transference neuroses. In "Mourning and melancholia", he extends his ideas on narcissism and shows how everyday slights might be the cause of withdrawal of object cathexis. This withdrawal of object cathexis results in the type of identification (incorporative) that is characteristic of melancholics. Freud's diagnostic schema is extended, since he now includes melancholics as having their fixation point during the earlier phase of narcissism. In fact, Freud's paper "Mourning and melancholia" can be viewed more as a paper about narcissistic vulnerability than a paper about depression. Thus, through this paper, we have reviewed Freud's new concepts on narcissism and the development of the self in relation to the other person (object).

Here, I should perhaps point out that the next section in this chapter on the topographic model, while of theoretical and historical interest, is quite dense, particularly when repression and the unconscious are described. I have been advised to warn readers to skip this section (if they so wish) and go to the commentary. I was going to put this section in an addendum, but this advice seems sufficient. I would read the section on the topographic model and a few pages in the section on repression (up to the point of the description of primal repression and/or secondary repression). If still awake at that point read on, if not, take some (legal) stimulant and go to the commentary.

Topographic model, repression, and the unconscious

Topographic model

At this time, Freud's theory of repression is embedded in his topographic model. Before we explore the conceptualizations of repression and the unconscious, we will briefly state the outlines of the topographic model. The topographic model was not elaborated in the dream book, but it certainly has its roots in that seminal publication. The topographic model divides consciousness into three overlapping segments. The distinction between conscious and unconscious states seems to be relatively simple and subject to reports of a person's experience. Consciousness is any representation (a term I have used to refer to any experience, whether purely cognitive or purely affective, or some blend of the two) that a person is immediately aware of and can report to themselves or others. The unconscious is any representation that is not represented at a given point in time in consciousness and is not potentially available for direct representation in consciousness. The assumption for most unconscious representations is that they are actively barred (through defence) from consciousness. The question that Freud poses centres on how an unconscious representation becomes conscious.

Here, the simple division becomes more complex. As an idea enters consciousness, there is always a testing by the censorship (see Chapter Two) that serves a gatekeeper function in terms of what is allowed to enter consciousness. If the idea that is being evaluated is rejected by the censorship, then the idea stays unconscious. The gatekeeper, or censorship, in this case is performing a defensive function. If the idea is not rejected, then it is accessible to consciousness. Not all ideas that are accessible to consciousness are conscious at any moment in time. Freud assumes that there are many memories and thoughts that are accessible to consciousness that are not necessarily conscious. Consciousness is considered by Freud to be a limited capacity, and most of what we consider to be thought or cognition occurs outside of consciousness. Ideas that are not actively barred from consciousness (and therefore are accessible to consciousness), and are not at a given point in time in consciousness, are considered by Freud to be preconscious. Secondary process thought primarily proceeds in the preconscious, while primary process thought occurs in the unconscious system. Freud asks a related question of what happens to the representational properties of an idea when it moves from the unconscious to the conscious (e.g., during analysis or defensive failure). More specifically, does the idea continue to be represented in the unconscious, or is it simply transferred to the conscious, ceasing to be represented in the unconscious? Freud's answer is that an idea can have a double registration and that it can continue to exist in the unconscious even if it attains consciousness. He relates, "If we communicate to a patient some idea which he has at one time repressed but which we have discovered in him, our telling him makes at first no change in his mental condition" (1915e, p. 175). Thus, a patient may hear something about themselves and consciously remember the words, but, unless something else occurs, this will not alter the unconscious representation. Here, Freud is arguing against premature interpretations and providing a theoretical model for why, under some conditions, an interpretation (or cognitive recognition alone) will be ineffective in the clinical situation. He says, "To have heard something and to have experienced something are in their psychological nature two quite different things, even though the content of both is the same" (*ibid.*, p. 176). In the ongoing commentary, we will try to relate these thoughts to Freud's ongoing theory of transference.

To quickly review, at this point in his theorizing Freud is hypothesizing three levels of consciousness: consciousness itself, a preconscious level, and the unconscious. He is assuming that each level communicates with the contiguous level and that the preconscious serves a gate-keeping function for those thoughts and feelings that enter consciousness. Clearly, this censorship function that is part of the preconscious has its roots in Freud's concepts of defence, which began in his description of the formation of the dream (see Chapter Two, "Interpretation of dreams").

Repression

Freud, in writing "On the history of the psycho-analytic movement" (1914d), stated, "the theory of repression is the cornerstone on which the whole structure of psycho-analysis rests" (*ibid.*, p. 16). The theory of repression in this era becomes related to Freud's conceptualization of the unconscious. He assumes that there is a first or primal repression:

> Which consists in the ideational representative of the instinct being denied entrance into the conscious. With this a fixation is established; the representative in question persists unaltered from then onwards and the instinct remains attached to it . . . The second stage of repression, repression proper, affects mental derivatives of the repressed representative, or such trains of thought as, originating elsewhere, have come into associative connection with it. On account of this association, these ideas experience the same fate as what was primally repressed. Repression proper, therefore, is actually an after-pressure. Moreover, it is a mistake to emphasize only the repulsion which operates from the direction of the conscious upon what is to be repressed; quite as important is the attraction exercised by what was primally repressed upon everything with which it can establish a connection. Probably the trend towards repression would fail in its purpose if these two forces did not cooperate, if there were not something previously repressed ready to receive what is repelled by the conscious. [1915d, p. 148]

Primal repression refers to the first repression; this occurs at the point in time when a conflict is initially strong enough to require defences to be instituted automatically to prevent overwhelming anxiety. Thus, a child defends against an impulse to soil or attack if this impulse would be in conflict with either reality (usually in the form of actual parental prohibitions), or something that is powerfully represented in the child's mind (usually parental representations). In the context of the latter, it is important to remember that parental representations are not bound to consensual reality; rather, they are usually a combination of fantasy and reality. When experiences occur after the initial repression, linked directly or symbolically to the repressed material, defence(s) again will be instituted. This is after-repression. The concept of after-repression invokes Freud's push–pull model: ideational elements are pushed out of consciousness and pulled into the unconscious. Thus, an idea is pulled into the unconscious by content that is formed at the point of primal repression. When similar situations occur, there is a tendency again to rid the mind of this material. Freud is saying that this tendency is bolstered by conscious–preconscious tendencies to push the material out of consciousness and by unconscious tendencies that attract material of similar content. As a teenager, there may be a tendency to want to dirty one's room or to attack a parent for some reason; either of these later tendencies might undergo after or secondary repression in this schematic illustration. Although after-repression occurs, this defence does not necessarily successfully keep material out of consciousness. Conflictual unconscious material is always seeking to be expressed in consciousness or, alternatively, through motoric action. This idea is embedded in the phrase "the return of the repressed". The repressed is always seeking to attain conscious expression.

We have so far talked only about ideas that are defended against, but Freud again reminds us that an idea "or group of ideas . . . is cathected with a definite quota of psychical energy . . . coming from an instinct" (1915d, p. 152). Freud, at this point, considers again the transformation of the instincts, and states that the instincts can be transformed into affects "and especially into anxiety" from the "psychical energies of instincts" (*ibid.*, p. 153). Since repression arises to avoid unpleasure,

> the vicissitude of the quota of affect . . . is far more important than the vicissitude of the idea. If a repression does not succeed in preventing feelings of unpleasure or anxiety from arising, we may say that it has failed, even though it may have achieved its purpose as far as the ideational content is concerned. [*ibid.*, p. 154]

Thus, although Freud's theory of affect is not well spelled out at this time (we will look at his theory in Chapter Four), affect plays a key role in the motivation to activate repression. It is the affect associated with the idea that provides the feeling of unpleasure. At this point in his theorizing, Freud sees either pleasure or unpleasure as resulting only from some type of instinctual transformation. Thus, it is not surprising that affect is viewed as a derivative of the instincts.

Freud, in beginning his essay on the unconscious, posits

> that the essence of the process of repression lies, not in putting an end to, in annihilating the idea which represents an instinct, but in preventing it from becoming conscious. When this happens we say of the idea that it is a state of being unconscious . . . [1915e, p. 166]

He goes on to say that the concept of the unconscious is warranted because it is hard to explain the gaps in our state of consciousness. He thinks that there is clear evidence that all that we process cannot be explained by conscious processing, and so what is left is to posit processes outside of our immediate awareness. If Freud had stayed at this level, it is likely that he would have endured less criticism over the decades, but he then distinguishes two gradations or levels of ideation that are outside of consciousness. However, what is controversial in his theory is the concept that repressed ideas are not simply outside of consciousness, but barred from consciousness by a defensive process. In addition, his positing that there are different forms of mentation that characterize the different systems (conscious, secondary process, unconscious, primary process) is also frequently in dispute. Although we have covered the differences between primary and secondary processes (Chapter Two), the conceptualization in this era has an increased connotative meaning. Primary process continues to imply a tendency towards immediate action or gratification. In the extreme, the object is not important, only gratification or pleasure is of importance. In the present era, primary process is unbound energy, or energy that is not bound or tied to any object or person. Secondary process necessarily implies being bound to a particular object and, as such, is necessary for the development of object love. Obviously, no one encounters an adult (or a child) who operates entirely through primary process mechanisms. In this formulation, the extent to which a person has secondary process capabilities available to them, is related to the capacity for object love. This view of primary and secondary process is now in accord with Freud's theoretical concerns during this era.

Unconscious affect and anti-cathexis

In section 3 of his paper "The unconscious", Freud states, "there are no unconscious affects as there are unconscious ideas . . . there may

... be in the system Unconscious affective structures which, like others, become conscious" (p. 178). However, he says,

> unconscious ideas continue to exist after repression as actual structures in the system Unconscious, whereas all that corresponds in that system to unconscious affects is a potential beginning which is prevented from developing. Strictly speaking, then, there are no unconscious affects as there are unconscious ideas. [1915e, p. 178]

Freud discusses that it is common linguistic usage to talk of unconscious love or hate, but, since in his theory affect is a discharge process, it would be logically untenable to talk of unconscious affect. One can express this idea in another, perhaps less formal, manner. For Freud, affect always involves feeling and the only structure capable of feeling in his theory is consciousness. In the commentary section, we will discuss the implications for psychoanalytic treatment in terms of the topographic statues of affects, or whether affects can be considered to exist as unconscious entities.

To this point in his theory of repression and the unconscious, Freud has talked about repression in terms of withdrawal of cathexis. In the paper on the unconscious, Freud maintains that a withdrawal of libido, if it was the only process in after-repressionm would have to go on endlessly, "but the outcome would not be repression" (*ibid.*, p. 180).

> So, too, when it comes to describing primal repression . . . here we are dealing with an unconscious idea which has as yet received no cathexis from the preconscious and therefore cannot have that cathexis withdrawn from it. [*ibid.*, pp. 180–181]

Here, we are at the point of encountering two new concepts: the idea of primal repression and anti-cathexis. Freud maintains that what is necessary to make repression permanent is a process that he calls anti-cathexis, which operates in the system Preconscious. Defence is no longer simply a withdrawal of cathexis, but here Freud is viewing defence as an active process that occurs at the level of the Preconscious.

Anxiety, as an affect, signals the failure of defence. As an illustration, Freud posits that an Unconscious libidinal impulse is strong enough to enter the Preconscious and, in doing so, there is after-repression (a withdrawal of cathexis plus renewed anti-cathexis). This leaves an impulse that is converted into anxiety, since the ideational representation is pushed back into the Unconscious, leaving the affective component in the Preconscious. If this happens repeatedly, then, at times, the affective component can become attached to a substitute idea that reflects a compromise formation. The compromise is one where the substitute idea is remote from, and yet symbolically connected to, the repressed idea. This compromise is frequently in the form of an aversive idea (a phobia, for example) in the Preconscious. Thus, in failure of repression, there is a detaching of the affective and ideational components of the instinct or the unconscious representation. In hysteria and anxiety disorders, the affect becomes active and the ideational component returns to the Unconscious. In obsessional disorders, the ideational component may become partly conscious, but the affective component is inhibited or blocked. Clearly, failure of repression has different implications in different disorders, and Freud attempts to look at each of the transference neuroses and describes what happens when repressions fails. He assumes that the results of failure of repression (e.g., phobia, negation, etc.) all have both gratifying and defensive functions. Imagine a male child who loves his father intensely, and yet wants to violently replace his father (and is also frightened of him). This child (I am referring to a case of Freud's, Little Hans [1909b]), when he develops an animal phobia, is also fascinated with the largeness of the animal (particularly the animal's genitals). The genital idea that is still present in the child's consciousness is, for Freud, an aspect of gratification. However, Freud assumes that this phobia also helps enhance defences against the original idea relating to the child's father. Instead of a wish to hurt the father, there is now an idea of being hurt by a large animal, and yet a fascination with the animal's large penis. There is always a compromise formation present in Freud's conceptualization of the results of the failure of repression.

Freud, in writing the paper on the unconscious, repeats the views he has previously put forth in *Interpretation of Dreams*. The nucleus of "The unconscious" consists of wishful impulses seeking immediate discharge. To quote,

There are in this system no negation, no doubt, no degrees of certainty: all this is only introduced by the work of the censorship between the Unconscious and the Preconscious . . . In the Unconscious there are only contents, cathected with greater or lesser strength. [1915e, p. 186]

He states that

exemption from mutual contradiction, primary process (mobility of cathexes), timelessness, and replacement of external by psychical reality—these are the characteristics which we may expect to find in processes belonging to the system Unconscious. [*ibid.*, p.187]

In the system Preconscious the secondary process is dominant. The processes of the system Preconscious display—no matter whether they are already conscious or only capable of becoming conscious— an inhibition of the tendency of cathected ideas towards discharge . . . Displacements and condensations such as happen in the primary process are excluded or very much restricted. This circumstance caused Breuer to assume the existence of two different states of cathectic energy in mental life: one in which the energy is tonically "bound" and the other in which it is freely mobile and presses towards discharge. In my opinion this distinction represents the deepest insight we have gained up to the present into the nature of nervous energy, and I do not see how we can avoid making it. [*ibid.*, p.188]

Freud, in positing two systems, one freely mobile and seeking discharge and the other bound and possessing a tendency towards inhibiting discharge, is building on a theoretical idea present in "Instincts and their vicissitudes" (1915c). There, he imagines that the cortex is increasingly complex and a great inhibitory system because of the demands made by instinctual stimuli. Thus, the freer and more plastic the instinctual system, the greater the need for a more complicated set of neuronal structures to inhibit and guide the instincts. He distinguishes the type of neuronal system that is only responsive to external stimuli (e.g., in most birds during imprinting) and says that it is the internal stimuli of the instincts that have led to more complex neuronal systems, as opposed to the response to external stimuli. Thus, while these two systems (bound and unbound) are in opposition, they are distinctly and synergistically related.

Freud ends his treatise "The unconscious" by saying that the study of derivatives of the Unconscious will disappoint "our expectations of a schematically clear-cut distinction between the two psychical systems" (1915e, p. 190). The problem, in Freud's view, in differentiating the two systems is that we are so tied to the equation of intentionality and consciousness. Freud tells us, "The more we seek to win our way to a metapsychological view of mental life, the more we must learn to emancipate ourselves from the importance of the symptom 'being conscious'" (ibid., p. 193). Thus, we find unexpected unconscious derivatives achieving consciousness, while some of the strongest barriers to the unconscious that reside in the preconscious remain alien to consciousness. Freud will offer some solutions to these issues in his later theoretical works but his implied solutions at this point in his career are quite intriguing. (He is referring to defences which, here, he assumed to operate on the preconscious level, but nevertheless were hard to make conscious in the clinical situation. In his later work, he will change his definition of the unconscious and maintain that defences are unconscious and that parts of the ego are unconscious.)

Freud, in attempting to formulate what enters consciousness, says,

> Apart from the fact that the conscious is not always conscious but also at times latent, observation has shown that much that shares the characteristics of the system Preconscious does not become conscious; and we learn in addition that the act of becoming conscious is dependent on the attention of the Preconscious being turned in certain directions. [1915e, p. 192]

In a footnote, the editors of the *Standard Edition* translate this sentence as "Literally: 'we learn in addition that becoming conscious is restricted by certain directions of its attention'" (ibid.). Freud, here, is making two distinctions: one that the Preconscious is a system that determines what an individual focuses on in the Cs. System, and two, that there is a second censorship that is "located between the systems Preconscious and Cs." (ibid., p. 193) that actively bars certain ideas and activities that are part of the preconscious from achieving consciousness. Here, Freud is asserting that intentional acts are in some way determined outside of consciousness. Moreover, that consciousness is directed by what is allowed to be "seen" by the preconscious. In other terms, the state of consciousness is implied to be almost a completely receptive state controlled by the intensity of external stimuli and directed by the preconscious in terms of internal presentations.

The unconscious and schizophrenia and narcissism revisited

At the end of the paper on the unconscious, Freud reminds us of a position that he has taken in *Interpretation of Dreams*. Here, he posits that cathexes that are remote from perception are, in themselves, without quality and unconscious, and that they attain their capacity to become conscious only through being linked with words and the residues of perceptions. Although word representations are necessary for consciousness, they are not sufficient to attain consciousness. However, the capacity to link word presentations with sense presentations can only occur in the preconscious.

Freud is maintaining, in this hypothesis, that sense perceptions cannot retain their sensory qualities in the unconscious. It is when thing presentations are linked with word presentations that the thing presentation is "provided with quality" (*ibid.*, p. 202). Freud then goes on to ask a question that is relevant to his whole line of inquiry during this period: how is it that, in schizophrenia, word presentations receive not a less intense cathexis, as is true of the neuroses, but, "on the contrary, receive a more intense cathexis". In the neuroses, word and thing representations are divided and the thing representation is rendered unconscious (in after-repression). Clearly, in hysteria, as opposed to obsessional neuroses, the fate of affect is quite different, but the after repression aspect is similar. In schizophrenia, phenomena like word salads and the concrete overvaluation of words are common events. Freud's answer to this is that the

> Cathexis of the word-presentation ... represents the first of the attempts at recovery ... which so conspicuously dominate the clinical picture of schizophrenia. These endeavours are directed towards regaining the lost object, and it may well be that to achieve this purpose they set off on a path that leads to the object via the verbal part of it, but then find themselves obliged to be content with words instead of things ... We may ... attempt a characterization

of the schizophrenic's mode of thought by saying that he treats concrete things as though they were abstract. [*ibid.*, pp. 203–204]

To more fully understand Freud's position, we have to go back to his paper "On narcissism" (1914c) and section 3 of the Schreber case (1911c). In both of these works Freud maintains that the first aspect of a schizophrenic reaction is a withdrawal of object cathexes. This withdrawal of object cathexes means that there is a transfer of object cathexes into ego (self) cathexes. This leads, at the least, to a heightened sense of self, and, in more dramatic fashion, to grandiose, power-laden, and terrifying ideation. Freud, in this conceptualization, is attempting to picture the schizophrenic as turning away from internal object representations (which refer partly to external objects) and turning towards the self, as is true during early phases of the stage of narcissism. This is one meaning of Freud's use of the term "secondary narcissism", i.e., a return to a narcissistic state of mind. This return leads to grandiose ideas about the self, but also, as a consequence of psychologically removing aspects of the world, world destruction fantasies. World destruction fantasies, as an aspect of the onset of schizophrenia, is a distorted return to the stage of narcissism. Freud is, therefore, likening the movement away from objects to the destruction of objects. When this movement is complete enough, there is a view that the world has been destroyed. In my work with schizophrenic patients, this has always been a powerful fantasy during the onset of schizophrenia.

We have so far mentioned only the first aspect of schizophrenia, but, in Freud's view, whatever the disorder, there is always the search for the lost object. Freud posits that the dramatic symptoms of schizophrenia are, in effect, a manifestation of the search for the lost object. Characteristically, he offers several types of explanations to account for this search. We will look at two of these hypotheses.

Freud, in his paper "On narcissism" (1914c), maintains that in the first step of schizophrenia there is a withdrawal of libido from objects and a return of the libido to the ego (self). Freud states that this accumulation of libido in the ego is experienced as aversive, and to relieve this accumulation there is an attempt to restore libido to objects. The restoration of libido is performed in a distorted manner and, to quote Freud, the schizophrenic is obliged to be content with words instead of things. Thus, the object is not real, but under the complete control of the person. The thing is now a word-object (a word coined for purposes of this discussion) and the word-object is now treated as a real entity.

Freud's second explanation ends in the same place, but begins with the idea of the world being experienced as an overwhelming blow to the person's narcissism. This blow, experienced as coming from the outside, results in a withdrawal of interest (cathexes) from objects. The recovery of some interest in objects is present in Freud's developmental ideas that hypothesize that conflict in each stage leads to a progression towards object love. The lost object, no matter how distorted or preliminary, is an object that provides some sense of love and some impetus for a progression towards a more complete relationship. In schizophrenia, there is an attempt to secure the lost object in early narcissistic terms. The object is treated as real, inside the person and under the person's control. Since the thing representation is no longer present, the word-object can mean anything that the person needs it to mean. The lost object is regained, but reality is lost. The lost object is regained in a manner that does not allow for still further progression towards true object love. In this formulation, for the progression to continue the thing representation must be restored to the word presentation. Here, we end this era of Freud's theorizing to highlight that Freud is attempting to explain even the severest of disturbances in terms of the object-relations model that he develops in his most clinically active era.

Commentary

The most striking aspect of this era of Freud's writings is how little attention has been paid to a series of papers that Freud intended to provide a stable theoretical foundation for psychoanalysis. Clearly, he did not succeed in providing this foundation, but he did succeed in putting forth several papers that provided the theoretical scaffolding for a number of important psychoanalytic theorists. The most arresting features of these papers have been largely ignored in the USA. One could win a bet with most psychoanalysts by asking them what were Freud's psycho-sexual stages by 1911. The answer, as stated in the *Standard Edition*, is autoerotism, narcissism, and object love. In the present interpretation, by 1913 his stages were autoerotism, narcissism, object choice, and object love. The editors of the *Standard Edition* maintain that Freud, in the paper that I am referring to (Freud, 1913i), presented his first psycho-sexual stage defined by mucous membrane (anal sadism). I have called this stage object choice. Freud is positing that, in optimal development, the child makes a choice that the love object is more important than a bodily pleasure. This is a crucial period of choice for the developing child, since it is the first point where mother and child's will may be tested. I have chosen to name the stage in terms of optimal development, rather than in terms of what occurs if conflict predominates.

That is, in optimal development, the child is not forced to comply to give up certain freedoms and bodily pleasures. Rather, in optimal development, the child chooses to give up pleasure and transform some of its activities to please its parents (mother). If the child experiences this as too strong a demand (mother will never love me if I do not comply), then there will be an anal sadistic fixation. If the child is threatened with other punishments, psychological or physical, then there will also be an anal sadistic fixation. If, however, the love of the child and pride in the child's accomplishments is provided (rather than withheld), and this is important to the child, the child can give up or transform its pleasures into activities that are more socially acceptable. This choice is, in my view, a type of landmark for the child, particularly if the child in part experiences it as a choice and achievement. This is also a point where, optimally, the child begins to give up some of its narcissistic predilections. The editors of the *Standard Edition*, in naming the stage "anal sadism", are gently guiding the reader to look for the type of psycho-sexual stage that is more commonly associated with Freudian theory. Anal sadism may, in fact, frequently be a component of this period for most children, but it is not necessarily optimal development, according to Freud.

One can see that, in virtually every paper of this era, Freud is concerned with the way the object is represented. This is true when he introduces the concept of narcissism (1910c, 1911b, 1914c), or even when he is attempting to characterize the role of the instincts. "Mourning and melancholia" is at least a paper about narcissistic loss, and it is a point where he reintroduces the concept of fixation points. Here, Freud again states that it is hysterical neurotics who have their main conflicts in the period of object love. Obsessive–compulsives are fixated in the period of object-choice, and all the other disorders (paranoia, melancholia, schizophrenia) have their conflictual roots in the period of narcissism. Schizophrenics are at the border of narcissism and autoerotism. Freud's view of these fixation points is strongly influenced by his recognition of the clinical significance of transference.

Although Freud had introduced the concept of transference as early as 1895, his recognition of transference as a central clinical concept occurred gradually as he developed his therapeutic concepts. It is during this period (1911–1915) that Freud writes his most important papers on psychoanalytic technique. These papers include his three major papers on transference (1912b, 1914g, 1915a). I have previously stated (Ellman, 1991) that it is during this era that Freud functioned most completely as an analyst. It is also during this period that he seemed most at home with the concept of transference. Earlier in his career, he was developing the idea, and, although he recognized manifestations of transference (see Chapter One), he thought that it was best to ignore these manifestations. As he became more comfortable as an analyst, he realized that to ignore transference manifestations is to leave out of the treatment situation a good deal of what transpires between patient and analyst. His three transference papers detailed how he gradually not only recognized the importance of transference, but how he also recognized how analysts might find powerful difficulties in dealing with transference manifestations. His paper, "Observations on transference-love" (1915a), is a warning to analysts about the evocative nature of transference at times leading an analyst to believe that it is because of his unusual attractiveness that the patient has come to love him. (At this point, I have written "him" since Freud's paper was primarily intended for male analysts who seemed to have difficulties in containing their reactions to female patients' sexuality.) In addition, he was concerned that the analyst might be tempted to manipulate the patient, as opposed to analysing the transference. In my view, this paper demonstrated the depth of Freud's understanding of the intensity and importance of transference in the analytic situation. It also led him to conceptualize and experience (feel) different types of transference reactions that led him to a more differentiated view of the aetiology of the psychopathology or the psychological conditions that he encountered. It is my view that Freud's ability to come to terms with the importance of transference helped him understand psychopathology at a variety of levels. He writes about the difficulties in treating patients with narcissistic difficulties while, at the same time, he treated this type of patient (Ellman, 1991).

Freud's difficulties in experiencing the transference

Surprisingly, in 1914, in the narcissism paper, Freud reintroduces and extends the concept of the actual neurosis. In this paper, the new addition is the inclusion of hypochondria as the third actual neurosis (alongside anxiety neurosis and neurasthenia, see Chapter One). Why has Freud brought back the idea of the actual neurosis?

Here, Freud states,

> Hypochondria, like organic disease, manifests itself in distressing and painful bodily sensations, and it has the same effect as organic disease on the distribution of libido. The hypochondriac withdraws both interest and libido—the latter specifically markedly—from the objects of the external world and concentrates both of them upon the organ that is engaging his attention. [1914c, p. 83]

Freud, in this context, brings forth the idea that in every organ there is a degree of erogenous potential. I will not dwell on this idea, but, rather, move to the central point of this discussion, where Freud states that hypochondria is to paraphrenia (schizophrenia) what the other two actual neuroses are to hysteria and obsessional neurosis. What Freud is maintaining here is that hypochondria is primarily fuelled by ego-libido and is therefore narcissistic in origin. He maintains that there is an actual cause (in the sense of an actual neurosis) to hypochondria as opposed to schizophrenia, where he maintains that this disorder has its roots in psychological factors. I have previously put forth the idea that Freud established and then re-establishes the idea of actual disorders because of his difficulties in experiencing (perhaps accepting) the transference states of each of these disorders. In each of these disorders, the patient is preoccupied with their internal states and there is little room for a discussion of the relationship between analyst and patient. This is true for many patients with narcissistic difficulties, and Freud was seemingly struggling with some patients who would not comply with his ideas of free association in the therapeutic situation. This might have seemed particularly the case if, following Freud's instructions to free associate, the patient could only talk about their anxiety, lack of energy, or hypochondriacal concerns. Even some psychogenic disorders were thought by Freud to be unanalysable. More accurately, he stated that, in so far as a disorder is deeply rooted in narcissistic conflict, the stronger these roots the more difficult it will be analyse such a person. Despite this, as I mentioned (and will shortly discuss), he undertook the analysis of patients who indeed were mired in early developmental trauma.

Here, we can establish a sequence of Freud's ideas about the origins of each disorder and then return to Freud's reasoning about the question of analysability. To reiterate, schizophrenia, melancholia, and paranoia all have their roots in narcissism. Schizophrenia is on the border between autoerotism and narcissism. Freud places obsessional neurosis at the point of object choice or anal sadism, and it is only hysteria where the conflicts are primarily about issues of object love. Since narcissism is a combination of ego and object libido, with still a predominance of ego or (self) libido, Freud questions a patient's ability to form transference relationships in so far as their main issues result from narcissistic roots (fixations). Freud does not discuss why it would not be possible for a patient to transfer ego libidinal cathexes to an analyst. He assumes that only object libidinal cathexes can be transferred to an analyst. In other terms, he assumes that if a patient at the onset of a treatment cannot tolerate differences with the analyst, the patient is not analysable. This assumption was unwarranted, and masked Freud's impatience with analysands who were not able to comply with his analytic preferences. There is now an extensive literature (from Kohut, 1966, 1977, 1984 to Fosshage, 1994, and Bach, 1985, 1994, 2006) on the treatment of patients with narcissistic disorders. Moreover, Kohut (1966) pointed out that Freud committed a logical error when he stated that narcissistic patients were incapable of transference relationships. Kohut correctly stated that Freud confused the idea of these patients being incapable of mature (object) love, but, since transference is an omnipresent presence in Freud's theory, it makes no logical sense to state that they are not able to form transference relationships. The transference relationships that are formed are narcissistic in nature and may be difficult for the analyst to tolerate.

Thus, the transference of the hypochondriacal patient who is preoccupied with his body and the products of his body was not easily decoded by Freud. He could not easily feel the patient's need (as one possibility) to have a parent scrutinize his body. This need felt too real for Freud, and this patient was a version of the bread and dumplings patient that Freud described (derided) in his paper on transference love (1915a). In other terms, this type of patient saw their transference as a real, as opposed to a symbolic, expression of their needs and conflicts. Freud was always more interested in the patient who could quickly (in treatment) symbolize their conflicts and present him with a problem of decoding interesting symbols. Although he advised against early interpretations (Ellman, 1991), he rarely followed his own sage advice. The hypochondriacal patient (or the narcissistic patient) frequently does not tolerate early interpretations (Bach, 1985).

If we were to do an extensive review of Freud's actual conduct as an analyst (Ellman, 1991; Roazen, 1995), we would see that he violated many of the precepts that he put forth in his ideas about psychoanalytic technique. At least two of his published cases were patients (Wolf Man and Rat Man) who had powerful narcissistic issues and conflicts. Thus, although Freud treated a wide range of patients, he frequently had less tolerance for patients who did not present interesting verbal material early in the treatment. If we look at Freud's career, we see that, during the period that he is writing the papers we have reviewed, he is seeing a wide variety of patients and is developing his ideas about psychoanalytic technique. It is the period where he is seeing patients who are not necessarily interested in becoming psychoanalysts and who have not been extensively exposed to the psychoanalytic revolution. After the First World War, Freud is being pressured to produce hard currency because of the extremely high inflation in Austria. He also has become a world figure, and patients are coming from all over the western hemisphere to be treated by Freud. He is seeing patients for shorter periods of time and doing more of what he called "training analyses". In my view, he is no longer nearly as involved in clinical issues and is more involved in psychoanalytic politics and, gradually, in his own series of tragedies that affect both him and his family. In another publication, I have tried to show how, during his next period (structural theory), his ideas about technique regress, or, more descriptively, begin to hearken back to his earlier thoughts about psychoanalytic treatment. What is indisputable is that it is during the period that we have just reviewed that Freud writes most of his papers concerning psychoanalytic technique.

Why, in a book about theory, am I spending time looking at Freud's views on technique and his experience with patients? (The last section of the book will focus on ideas about treatment and how theory has influenced these ideas.) It seems to me that it is his clinical experience that is leading him in this period to formulate a more differentiated theory that, to some extent, de-emphasizes Oedipal conflicts. This is not to say that the Oedipal drama is not important to Freud during this era. It is always his most cherished dynamic formulation. However, during this period, it is not the only point of fixation. In fact, as we have frequently repeated, during this era he conceptualizes only one disorder (hysteria) in terms of Oedipal dynamics. As we will see, this changes in his next theory, and I hypothesize that part of the reason for this change is his isolation from more involving clinical experiences. It is during the present era that Freud grapples with narcissistic transference states. He is seeing patients for longer periods of time and understands transference in a revolutionary manner that has still not been fully understood and integrated in psychoanalysis. Although he fails to fully comprehend the enormity of his new concepts, it is during this period of clinical immersion that Freud offers his fullest and, in many ways, his most interesting theoretical ideas. During the next period, he will both advance new concepts and, in some manner, pull away from some of his most important contributions. Stated more emphatically, it is only during this period that Freud functions as an analyst who seriously considers transference to be a central part of the therapeutic process. It is this clinical attitude that I believe leads him to his most interesting theoretical concepts.

Commentary on metapsychology

Freud at times assumed that many of his concepts were directly derived from observations in the clinical situation. (See Chapter Three for a longer discussion of Freud's changing views on the nature of observation.) Concepts that involved assumptions about psychic energy or, at times, what he called instinct, were usually deemed to come from that "witch" metapsychology (1937c). Repression, transference, and other concepts that were utilized in Freud's descriptions of the clinical process were labelled clinical concepts. This is true, despite the fact that both transference and repression (for example) are unconscious processes. Neither of these concepts is directly observable, but, when one is with a patient, it is possible to feel that there is something transferred from patient to analyst (as well as from analyst to patient). This experience makes transference feel like an empirical concept, even though the analyst knows (should know) that what she/he is experiencing is guided by her/his theory of the situation. All that the analyst can really say directly is that the patient's anger or idealization seems out of proportion to what the analyst thinks is the appropriate proportion if transference were not palpably present (I am using transference as an example; the same type of example could be constructed with assumptions of social constructivism or intersubjectivity) or, more neutrally, that the analyst is thinking or feeling something that the analyst assumes is generated by the patient. Now, when I used the term "palpably", it seems as if I can feel the transference directly, when, in fact, what I can feel is a patient's response, which, in a certain theory, I label as transference. Thus, it is understandable how transference (or perhaps any theoretical concept) might be experienced as an empirical entity if one's theory led them to observe certain patients' reactions as transference.

Most analysts would consider transference as a clinical concept, while psychic energy or drive are metapsychological concepts. In my analysis, this type of theoretical bifurcation is not warranted. Both terms are theoretical terms and, as such, are not directly observable. What are directly observable are some behaviours that one might label as transference. One might, in a similar manner, label some behaviours as drive or drive derivatives. The question that in the present analysis is important is the extent to which a given concept is explanatory. In other terms, is the concept able to provide an explanation for observable phenomena? In addition, an explanation should be able to be falsified. The explanatory concept should provide explanations and predictions or post-dictions that can be potentially proven to be incorrect. This is a difficult criterion for psychoanalytic explanations, and it may be that this type of explanatory statement is only beginning to be formulated. Let us assume that it is more difficult for concepts such as drive, as opposed to transference, to meet this criteria. This would only mean that this type of theoretical statement is less well formulated and perhaps less useful. To label it as metapsychology is, at one and the same time, denigrating the concept and protecting the concept from being evaluated.

Interestingly, in this chapter, we have followed the editors of the *Standard Edition* and labelled "Mourning and melancholia" as a metapsychological paper and noted that the paper "On narcissism" is not listed as a metapsychological paper. Given the content of these two papers, this characterization is arbitrary; there are only historical grounds for this classification, not theoretical or logical criteria.

Brief commentary

In the past I and a colleague (Ellman & Moskowitz, 1980) have commented on the concept of metapsychology. Essentially, we maintained that there is no logical distinction between some concepts that are called clinical and others that are called metapsychology. In our view, Freud used this conceptual category to describe concepts that were both fundamental for him and yet at the same time he was unsure of and realized were highly speculative. Rapaport and Gill (1959) attempt to salvage the concept of metapsychology and are unsuccessful; however, in their salvage attempt, they accentuate a highly important position, that is, the adaptive perspective.

Note

1. This is considered to be part of Freud's initiation of the concept of orality as a stage of development. There are similar passages in *Totem*

and Taboo (1912–1913) and in an added passage to the *Three Essays*, written also in 1915. Freud also takes up similar issues in the case of the "Wolf Man" (1918c) and, in his next era (Chapter Four), begins this discussion in *Group Psychology and the Analysis of the Ego* (1921c). We will encounter this issue again in *The Ego and the Id* (1923b), in Chapter Four.

CHAPTER FOUR

The structural model

Summary

In this chapter, we go over the most familiar Freudian concepts. Freud's structural model is described, and we look at the meaning of the ego, superego, and id. Freud, at this point, reinforces the centrality of the Oedipus complex and the fixation points that were described in Chapter Three are discarded or, at least, no longer mentioned. His new drive theory is discussed, and he now has a theory where the two drives are Eros and Thanatos. Thanatos is often taken to be equivalent to aggression, but this was not Freud's meaning, and this point is discussed in the chapter. The chapter also allows for a review of previous concepts, since, in each of the major works in this era, there is a review of past papers. The main papers that are discussed are *Beyond the Pleasure Principle* (1920g), *The Ego and the Id* (1923b) and *Inhibitions, Symptoms and Anxiety* (1926d). In addition, we will briefly discuss some of Freud's later papers.

Introduction

Here, in this chapter, we arrive at Freud's best-known writings and the works that have exerted the greatest influence in the USA. The works that we will include in our discussion of this era of Freud's writings are *Beyond the Pleasure Principle* (1920g), *The Ego and the Id* (1923b), "The dissolution of the Oedipus complex" (1924d), and *Inhibitions, Symptoms and Anxiety* (1926d). We will also make reference to an earlier paper that heralds this new era: "A child is being beaten" (1919e). In this paper, Freud begins to change his views on masochism and we know now that the case that this paper is based on is his treatment of his daughter, Anna Freud. Despite the fact that *The Ego and the Id* was written after *Beyond the Pleasure Principle*, we will start by looking at *The Ego and the Id*. The most central ideas of Freud's theorizing are contained in this work, and it will provide a context for the rest of his conceptualizations from this era.

During this era, Freud is going to leave behind a good deal of what he has constructed in his previous theorizing, although, as we shall see, it is rare that he completely abandons his previous structures. In fact, one might say that in several ways Freud returns to issues that he grappled with in the *Project* and *Interpretation of Dreams*. In this chapter, we discuss perhaps Freud's least accepted concepts, Eros and Thanatos. These concepts have loosely been translated as drives that correspond to sexuality and aggression. This translation is far from Freud's meaning, and among the theorists that we will encounter in this volume, it is Melanie Klein that perhaps best captures Freud's intent when he proposes his new drive theory. Despite the fact that Freud is changing his theory, in each of his major essays (*Beyond the Pleasure Principle*, *The Ego and the Id*, and *Inhibitions, Symptoms and Anxiety*) he reviews several of the major concepts that he has previously provided. Thus, this last chapter on Freudian concepts will give us a chance to review a number of Freud's theoretical statements. This section is organized by essay, but at times we will wander among Freud's new conceptualizations.

Before we leave this introduction, it is important to note that, during this period, Freud (again) places the Oedipus complex at the centre of his theory of childhood development. It is only when this complex is resolved (dissolved) that a new structure, the superego, is created. The superego is the concept that will incorporate a previous concept, the ego ideal. Freud also introduces the last of his better-known psycho-sexual stages, the phallic stage. With the conceptualization of the phallic stage, his theory of narcissism somewhat fades into the background. Although Freud, at times, uses the concept of narcissism, he does not integrate his earlier theory with his new psycho-sexual stages. Nor does he fully explicate the psycho-sexual stages that now will occupy centre stage in Freudian theory for at least several decades after Freud's death. However, for the first time, the Oedipal drama is linked to childhood sexuality in terms of fantasies about intercourse. Freud now is clearly putting forth this idea of childhood sexuality as central to his theory. Previously, Freud has thought that this sexual idea appeared at the time of puberty. This fact is often glossed over, and today many people read the *Three Essays* and find all of the psycho-sexual stages present in this work. As we have previously pointed out, none of the modern psycho-sexual stages is conceived of in the *Three Essays on the Theory of Sexuality* (see Chapter Two).

Reasons to leave the topographic model

The Ego and the Id (1923b), no matter how distorted or preliminary, is Freud's major work in this era, and, although the other papers that we will cover are extremely important, we will begin this chapter with the concepts that have dominated psychoanalytic thought for at least several decades. *The Ego and the Id* was at least partially stimulated by Freud's growing clinical sophistication in the previous decade. He began to realize that what he called resistance was largely determined by unconscious defences that could not easily be made conscious. Although I have stressed that in previous theoretical papers Freud has, at times, used the term ego as synonymous with self, at the beginning of *The Ego and the Id* he subtly shifts his emphasis.

> We have formed the idea that in each individual there is a coherent organization of mental processes; and we call this his *ego*. It is to this ego that consciousness is attached; the ego controls the approaches to motility—that is, to the discharge of excitations into the external world; it is the mental agency which supervises all its own constituent processes ... From this ego proceed the repressions, too, by means of which it is sought to exclude certain trends in the mind not merely from consciousness but also from other forms of effectiveness and activity. [1923b, p. 17]

Freud now sees the ego as a structure that controls the rate of discharge of excitations into the external world. This paragraph presages Freud's more explicit view that the ego mediates the other structures' relationship to the external world and "reality". This is a view where he now includes consciousness, not as a system, but as part of the ego. Implicitly, he begins to think of the ego as a structure with a number of functions (really abilities) that help to mediate the control of discharge to the external world. We can translate control of discharge to the external world to mean the extent to which either primary or secondary process dominates the ego. Freud is maintaining that the ego structure allows for the possibility of the operation of secondary process. We will look at this point more fully in several sections of this chapter.

In specifying how he has concluded that resistance is unconscious, Freud describes that, in the past, he exhorted patients to overcome their resistances. He maintains that when the analyst makes this exhortation it is unsuccessful, and the analysand is quite unaware of how "the resistance is now at work in him" (*ibid.*). Since the resistance (defence)

> emanates from his ego we find ourselves in an unforeseen situation. We have come upon something in the ego itself which is also unconscious, which behaves exactly like the repressed—that is, which produces powerful effects without itself being conscious and which requires special work before it can be made conscious. [*ibid.*]

Freud concludes, "that the unconscious does not coincide with the repressed; it is still true that all repressed is unconscious, but not all that is unconscious is repressed" (*ibid.*, p. 18).

We must remember why this passage is significant? Previously, Freud maintained that the unconscious is a system that operated according to the primary process. Thus, the unconscious was considered to be a system that only contained ideas that were governed by the primary process which were constantly pressing for immediate discharge. He also implicitly thought of resistance as emanating from the preconscious, and, thus, more or less something that might be more easily under the conscious control of the patient. Here, in *The Ego and the Id*, Freud is implicitly reviewing his clinical experience. He first attempted to overcome resistance

(1895b), then to influence resistance through transference analysis, (1912b), and now he has come to the realization that some aspects of resistance (defence) are unconscious. This implies that resistance must be accorded all the considerations that were present when Freud began to conceptualize how to interpret unconscious fantasy. More importantly for our purposes, Freud recognized that he could no longer "derive neurosis from a conflict between the conscious and the unconscious" (1923b, p. 17). In fact, his definition of the unconscious had to become what he called a descriptive, rather than a systematic, definition. In other terms, he could no longer think of the unconscious as a system being governed by primary process. Not all of the unconscious can be an idea or unconscious fantasy seeking discharge (through gaining control of approaches to activity or consciousness). If defence is unconscious, then we have an unconscious activity with a reverse, or anti-primary process, aim; that is, an aim to keep unconscious fantasy (or ideas) out of consciousness. This would be a way of barring these tendencies from gaining expression, either in conscious thought or through motoric activity. The realization of unconscious defences placed Freud in the position of either maintaining that there were two types of unconscious organizations, or of reconceptualizing his views of the structural conditions of the mind. As we shall see when we discuss his views on the superego as a structure, he faced a similar logical dilemma when he recognized that guilt and masochistic or self-punitive tendencies could also be unconscious.

The Ego and the Id

In discussing the structure of the ego, Freud begins on seemingly old ground. He relates that sensations of pleasure do not strongly impel us, but unpleasurable sensations "impel (us) towards discharge" (1923b, p. 22). In this context, he wonders how any sensations reach consciousness. His conclusion at this point in time is more complicated than the one he advanced in his papers "Repression" (1915d) and "The unconscious" (1915e). Nevertheless, he follows the same logical pathway. Sensations that are pleasurable can reach consciousness without interference; however, sensations that are barred from consciousness (through defence) may become conscious (failure of defence) and, if they become conscious, they are experienced as unpleasure. Sensations, to become conscious, have to be perceived, and to be perceived have to reach the perceptual aspect of the ego (Pcpt. system). This explanation is, at this point, identical to the one that he puts forward in his papers on the unconscious and repression. However, in the next sentence, he adds a complication that stays with us up to the present time.

> It remains true, therefore, that sensations and feelings, too, only become conscious through reaching the system Pcpt., if the way forward is barred, they do not come into being as sensations, although the "something" that corresponds to them in the course of excitation is the same as if they did. We then come to speak, in a condensed and not entirely correct manner, of "unconscious feelings", keeping up an analogy with unconscious ideas which is not altogether justifiable. Actually the difference is that, whereas with unconscious (Ucs.) ideas connecting links must be created before they can be brought into the Cs., with feelings, which are themselves transmitted directly, this does not occur. In other words: the distinction between conscious (Cs.) and preconscious (Pcs.) has no meaning where feelings are concerned; the Pcs. here drops out—and feelings are either conscious or unconscious. Even when they are attached to word-presentations, their becoming conscious is not due to that circumstance, but they become so directly. [1923b, p. 22]

In this extract, Freud is reaffirming his view that for a repressed unconscious idea (thing representation) to become conscious, it must be attached to a word-presentation (in the Pcs.). This assemblage makes possible the perception of the previously unconscious element. Thus, the way one can perceive and consciously be aware of previously defended against ideas is through interpretative efforts that connect thing and word-presentations. This idea reiterates Freud's conceptualization of the importance of interpretative work in psychoanalysis. However, his ideas about feelings are now more confused (or ambivalent) as compared to his previously stated views in "The unconscious (1915e) and "Repression" (1915d). He is, here, maintaining that there is some process that can be described as unconscious feelings or affect. The difference is that feelings as opposed to ideational representations can directly enter consciousness from the unconscious. In other terms, they can be directly perceived without being attached to word representations. In the model that he is now building, unconscious feelings, when not sufficiently defended, have a direct route to the Pcpt. (therefore conscious) portion of the ego, whereas ideational elements in the unconscious have to be attached to word representations to be perceived. Thus, it is possible to have a conscious feeling or affect state and not understand the origins of this state.

We have dwelt on Freud's conceptualizations about how internal sensations or ideation are perceived because he starts out in discussing the ego in terms of Pcpt.–Cs system. This is clearly illustrated by Freud's attempt to schematically represent parts of his new structural model (Figure 2).

At the bottom of the drawing is the id, which represents the drives and Freud's previous thoughts about the unconscious. The repressed (also part of the old unconscious) is separated from the ego, and this separation represents the process of defence. In this drawing, one can see that the ego touches the id and is therefore in constant communication with the id. As we go higher in the ego, we see the Pcs., which is a descriptive term now for cognitive processing that goes on outside of consciousness. This includes various language functions and, importantly, the laying down of memory traces that are available to the Pcpt.–Cs. aspects of the ego.

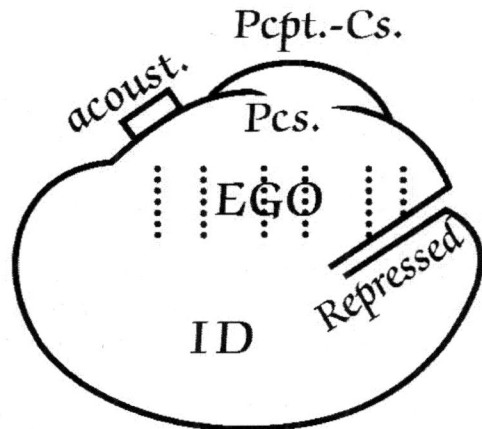

Figure 2. Freud's schematic representation of his structural model.

The ego's surface is the Pcpt. system, which can receive sensations from internal and external sources. Freud takes this diagram seriously and says that

> It is easy to see that the ego is that part of the id which has been modified by the direct influence of the external world through the medium of the Pcpt.–Cs.; in a sense it (the ego) is an extension of the surface-differentiation. [1923b, p. 23]

The ego is, thus, a structure that comes into being through the influence of the external world. The demands of the external world affect the Pcpt.–Cs. system and this system promotes the use of cognitive functions. The Conscious–Pcs. cognitive structures form a structure, the ego. The ego, in this conceptualization, develops out of the id in response to external stimuli that demand a reality response. Only the Pcpt.–Cs. "system" is considered to be an innate structure present from birth.

This structure (Pcpt.–Cs.) is one that is intimately linked to the body and, because of this, is a necessary structure in determining internal and external sources of stimuli. Pain is one way that the ego begins to know its body and, in another crucial quote, Freud tells us that "The ego is first and foremost a bodily ego; it is not merely a surface entity, but is itself the projection of a surface" (*ibid.*, p. 26). Thus, the ego is ultimately derived from bodily sensations, primarily, but not exclusively, from the surface of the body. Thus, one can see that, despite the change in theoretical structure, the role of the body in early development is still considered to be a crucial element in Freud's theorizing.

In one of his memorable statements, Freud likens the ego

> in its relation to the id [as] like a man on horseback, who has to hold in check the superior strength of the horse; with this difference, that the rider tries to do so with his own strength while the ego uses borrowed forces. [1923b, p. 25]

Freud maintains that the ego's energy is gathered from the id, and that often the ego mistakenly feels that it determines its own intentions. Frequently, it is the id that is determining the direction of the action taken. In other terms, Freud is reminding us of his "Copernican" revolution: at times, we incorrectly believe that we

THE STRUCTURAL MODEL   139

are consciously deciding on our actions when, in his view, the id (id aspects of the unconscious) is determining our actions and conscious beliefs. At the end of his description of the relationship of the ego and the id, he reminds us that consciousness is not always present in even our most important problem solving. Of course, he could cite several famous examples of scientists and writers whose discoveries or creations have occurred to them in either altered states or while asleep. However one views these examples, there is no doubt that a good deal of mental processing goes on outside of immediate conscious awareness.

Freud leaves the relationship of the ego and the id and moves to introduce a new concept that will effect both of these agencies. This new, hypothesized structure, the superego, is considered to be stronger than the other two. Freud relates,

> There is another phenomenon, however, which is far stranger. In our analyses we discover that there are people in whom the faculties of self-criticism and conscience—mental activities, that is, that rank as extremely high ones—are unconscious, and unconsciously produce effects of the greatest importance; the example of resistance remaining unconscious during analysis is therefore by no means unique ... This new discovery, which compels us, in spite of our better judgement, to speak of an "unconscious sense of guilt"[1] ... especially when we gradually come to see that in a great number of neuroses an unconscious sense of guilt [is one of] the most powerful obstacles in the way of recovery. [1923b, pp. 26–27]

Freud, in this extract, is telling us not only of his new insight, but also of his difficulties in arriving at this insight. He says this new discovery *compels* us to speak of an unconscious sense of guilt. He also relates that he makes this discovery in spite of his better judgement: one might ask why he is so reluctant to talk about an unconscious sense of guilt. Clearly, the idea of an unconscious sense of guilt is one more step towards the idea of unconscious affect states, and Freud had previously ruled that unconscious affect states are a psychological and logical impossibility. Moreover, in his first conceptualization, the unconscious was a monolithic entity. Now it becomes a complicated state with conflicting motives within this hypothesized topographic area. This new conceptualization is, however, in accord with Freud's previous ideas about technique, although he never fully revisits the issue of psychoanalytic treatment in the light of his new model, the structural model.

Ideals from above and below: superego development

Preliminary considerations

Freud, in discussing a new structure, begins by reminding us that he has already thought of a similar structure, the ego ideal. In his previous conceptualization, the ego ideal is a set of standards that are remnants of narcissistic development. The ego ideal stands for a person or persons or a depersonified set of ideals that serve to guide a person's behaviour and moral standards. (The term depersonified is used to indicate ideals, standards, and values that are no longer represented in terms of something that a particular person [usually mother or father] espouses, but are now represented without reference to a particular person. In other terms, they are now seen as one's own values or standards.) They are, in effect, what a person would like to be in ideal terms. Freud has said previously (1914c) that conflicts will develop if a person's ideals are too far removed from their actual accomplishments and abilities. He has distinguished ideals from sublimation; sublimation implies the ability to carry out tasks. However, in this era, he is extending the idea of ego ideals and using a new term: the superego. He has now realized that part of what he has termed the ego ideal is not conscious and this "is the novelty which calls for explanation" (1923b, p. 28). Why should aspects of an ideal be rendered unconscious? To answer this question, Freud begins to look again at some important aspects of the whole process of internalization. He asks the question of how a child's representational world is developed. The answers he comes up with have influenced generations of psychoanalysts.

He begins by stating that in early development, during the oral phase, "object-cathexis and identification are no doubt indistinguishable from each other" (*ibid.*, p. 29). Object cathexes then proceed from the id, "which *feels* erotic trends as needs. The ego, which to begin with is still feeble, becomes aware of the object-cathexis, and either acquiesces ... or tries to fend them off by the process of repression" (*ibid.*). In either of the alternatives (fending off or accepting), the sexual object is still present, but Freud asks what if the sexual object has to be given up? He answers that a person gives up a sexual object by introjecting (the concept "introjection" has reappeared) the object under the process of identification. The object is then part of the ego, and he states, "this identification [may be] the sole condition under which the id can give up its objects". The character of the ego "is a precipitate of abandoned object-cathexes and . . . it contains the history of those object-choices". (The implications of this statement in terms of psychoanalytic treatment are explored in the discussion section.) Here, Freud is both setting a condition for the process of identification and also reminding us that the id comes before the ego, just as primary process precedes secondary process. Here we see that this line of reasoning has already been stated, and will continue to be one of Freud's conceptualizations about the ego and the id. The ego gains its power from the id by transforming the aims of the id.

Introjection is a process where the person takes an object (or characteristic of an object) as part of their self-representation. However, it is a compromise formation in that when the ego "assumes the features of the object, it is forcing itself, so to speak, upon the id as a love-object and is trying to make good the id's loss by saying: 'Look, you can love me too—I am so like the object'" (*ibid.*, p. 30). This transformation of object love into an identification is, from Freud's perspective, a transformation of object-libido into narcissistic libido. The object is no longer seen in sexual terms, and Freud believes this desexualization is a "a kind of sublimation". He implies that he believes that this is the universal pathway to sublimation, where sublimation takes "place through the mediation of the ego, which begins by changing sexual object-libido into narcissistic libido and then, goes on to give it another aim" (*ibid.*, p. 30). The desexualization of the object is only the beginning of the pathway towards sublimation; changing the libido into another aim or activity is the completed pathway of sublimation.

The Oedipus complex and its renewed centrality

The question of identification is vital to Freud's new concept, the superego. Before we can continue to discuss the superego, it is necessary to look at Freud's ideas about the centrality of the Oedipus complex. During this era, Freud will maintain that Oedipal dynamics are the bedrock of psychoanalysis. This is a change of view from the previous era and it is a change that will be central to one type of contemporary Freudian analyst. Freud is also positing a new stage of development: the phallic stage. In previous essays (1905d) up to this point in time, Freud maintained that it was during adolescence that one saw the efflorescence of sexuality. In several papers written during the present period (Freud, 1923b, 1924d, 1925j, 1926d, 1927e), Freud changes his view and sees the phallic stage child as fantasizing about adult sexuality. The phallic stage is named in terms of the male genital, since Freud now sees the male genital as the primary issue during the Oedipal stage of development. In this conceptualization (castration anxiety), the boy has the genital and is afraid of (anxious about) having it violently damaged or taken from him. The phallic stage girl suffers from penis envy; she realizes that she does not have a male genital and is envious of the male. She is angry with her mother for not providing her with the desired genital equipment. In Freud's terminology, castration anxiety and penis envy are now his bedrock concepts in this Oedipally based theory.

Male development

The boy, from the earliest ages, develops an object-cathexis for his mother "which originally related to the mother's breast" (1923b, p. 31). Even before the onset of the Oedipus complex, the boy is thought to identify with his father. Freud thought that the identification with the father is a primary one that he describes in Chapter Seven in his paper *Group Psychology and the Analysis of the Ego* (1921c). Before the onset of the Oedipus stage, these currents exist simultaneously and are not necessarily in conflict. During the Oedipal phase of development, the boy develops hostility to the father and wishes to gain sole possession of the mother. Obviously, this current implies several new capacities; prominent among them is the ability to see that the mother is interested in another person and that this other person (object) is a rival to the boy's continued desire to keep sole possession of the mother. (In the commentary section, we look at how Freud's current conceptualizations fit in with his previous ideas about the capacity for object-love.) "An ambivalent attitude to his father and an object-relation of a solely affectionate kind to this mother make up the content of the simple positive Oedipus complex in a boy" (1923b, p. 32). With the "demolition" of the Oedipus complex, the boy's object-relation to the mother must be replaced with either an identification with the mother (negative Oedipal) or an increased identification with the father (positive Oedipal). An increased identification with the father is considered "more normal", since it is thought to increase the boy's tendency towards masculinity. In the negative Oedipal outcome, the boy might not only identify with the mother, but also have a strong object-cathexis towards the father (actually or symbolically). If we look at the two different pathways for the boy, we can see that Freud uses the idea of the boy identifying with the mother as one type of explanation for homosexual development in boys. Simply stated, the boy who resolves the Oedipal conflicts primarily with a positive Oedipal tendency leaves the Oedipal stage wanting to be like his father and, to some extent, being willing to give up his exclusive relationship with his mother. In less conflicted development, the boy retains an affectionate stance towards his mother. How he gives up an aspect of his relationship with his mother is a crucial question for his later development. The "negative Oedipal" boy leaves the Oedipal period wanting to be like his mother and having an affectionate and sexualized tie to his father.

Female development

The girl entering the Oedipal stage also wants to have sole possession of her mother. However, with the onset of the phallic stage, she becomes disenchanted with her mother since her mother has not provided her with a penis. She turns towards her father, hoping that he will provide her with what she envies. At the very least, he is the one with the penis that she desires. The girl now wants sole possession of her father and has developed a hostile attitude towards her mother (positive Oedipal). The negative Oedipal is one where the girl still desires her mother and identifies with her father.

The resolution of the Oedipus complex for the girl is one where she identifies with her mother and retains an affectionate tie with her father. As with the boy, optimally she is able to give up the idea of sole possession of her father.

The little girl feels hostility towards, and then identifies with, her mother (perhaps for the first time, according to Freud). This identification, or the strengthening of this identification, leads to an increase in the girl's "femininity" (positive Oedipal). Of course, the girl (like the boy) might identify with the father and continue her object-cathexis towards the mother (negative Oedipal). The girl's positive Oedipal position seems on the surface more confusing, since she first desires sole possession of her mother, then feels hostile towards her, and then identifies with her.

Freud addresses this quandary and other ambiguities by reminding us of his concept of bisexuality and by hypothesizing that most children have a mixture of positive and negative Oedipal dynamics. He maintains that the relative strength of the masculine and feminine dispositions (a genetic trait) is a strong factor in determining whether a positive or negative Oedipal outcome will occur. He states that the mixing of positive and negative Oedipal dynamics is the most common outcome, and that the simplification implied by positive and negative schemas is done for conceptual clarity but rarely met with in that unalloyed fashion in the clinical situation (or other parts of life).

The boy, typically, does not simply identify with the father before the Oedipal period, but also has affectionate ties (object-cathexis) with respect to his father. In a similar manner, the girl does not simply cathect the mother, but also has identified with her before the Oedipal stage. Without spelling out all the combinations and permutations, Freud is clearly saying that whatever event is conceivable does occur at times, and most often positive and negative Oedipal tendencies are mixed and, at least to some extent, in conflict. In this respect, he says that "In my opinion it is advisable in general, and quite especially where neurotics are concerned, to assume the existence of the complete Oedipus complex" (1923b, p. 33). When he uses the term "neurotics", he is referring to anyone who is in a psychoanalytic treatment, regardless of diagnosis.

The superego proper

The identifications during the Oedipus period form a particularly significant modification of the ego (Freud calls it a precipitate of the ego) and in the passing (to some extent, resolution) of the Oedipus complex at least two identifications are united.

> This modification of the ego retains its special position; it confronts the other contents of the ego as an ego ideal or super-ego. The super-ego is, however, not simply a residue of the earliest object-choices of the id; it also represents an energetic reaction-formation against those choices. [*ibid.*, p. 34]

The superego is sibylline in that it looks out in two directions and says, on the one hand, "You ought to be like this" (like your father, for the boy) and, at the same time, contains a prohibition that maintains, "You may not be like your father" (for the boy) (*ibid.*). This two-edged perspective serves the function of both guiding the child in terms of ideals and serving as a motivation to repress certain Oedipal tendencies. The stricter (or harsher) the sense of prohibition of the superego, the greater the likelihood for a stronger sense of unconscious guilt. The superego is always at one and the same time heir to libidinal ties and in touch with the deepest conflicts in the unconscious. Thus, Freud concludes, "Conflicts between the ego and the ideal (super-ego) will . . . ultimately reflect the contrast between what is real and what is psychical, between the external world and the internal world" (*ibid.*, p. 36). Freud goes on to demonstrate the wide range of his theorizing in the next paragraph.

> Religion, morality, and a social sense—the chief elements in the higher side of man—were originally one and the same thing. According to the hypothesis which I put forward in *Totem and Taboo* they were acquired phylogenetically out of the father-complex: religion and moral restraint through the process of mastering the Oedipus complex itself, and social feeling through the necessity for overcoming the rivalry that then remained between the members of the younger generation. The male sex seems to have taken the lead in all these moral acquisitions; and they seem to have then been transmitted to women by cross-inheritance. Even to-day the social feelings arise in the individual as a superstructure built upon impulses of jealous rivalry against his brothers and sisters. Since the hostility

cannot be satisfied, an identification with the former rival develops. The study of mild cases of homosexuality confirms the suspicion that in this instance, too, the identification is a substitute for an affectionate object-choice which has taken the place of the aggressive, hostile attitude. [*ibid.*, p. 37]

We can see, in this section of *The Ego and the Id*, that Freud is basing some of society's strongest elements as developing in response to the Oedipus complex. Moreover, it is the male in this formulation that is the prime instigator and inheritor of the superego. The female achieves this structure by a type of cross-inheritance, by which it seems that Freud means both an actual genetic inheritance and an identification with males. The role of the mother in this formulation is absent, except as a desired possession of the boy and the father and the pre-Oedipal girl. Freud, in relating the superego to these cultural institutions, brings forth both phylogenetic and anthropological considerations. He states that the ego and id are not only structures of humans but of "simpler organisms" as well. Thus, it is not only humans, but also, at least, other mammals, whose instincts have to be tamed and mediated and interfaced with reality. The ego is, after all, according to Freud, the "representative of the external world to the id" (*ibid.*, p. 38). The superego development is similar to experiences that are hypothesized to be involved in totemism. Thus, the ego and superego have their roots either in phylogenetically earlier forms (the ego) or in the earliest forms of groups and the relationship of the group to the leader (the superego).

That Freud finds the root of the ego in other species is not surprising, and nor do the origins of the superego being mirrored in antiquity come as an unsuspected conceptual ancestor. However, Freud, in the next few paragraphs of *The Ego and the Id*, clearly states his Lamarckian roots. (Although Freud's Lamarckian tendencies were apparent from a variety of sources, the publication of *A Phylogenetic Fantasy* (1987, in English) made clear that he, like Jung, believed that acquired characteristics could be inherited.) He tells us,

> The experiences of the ego seem at first to be lost for inheritance; but, when they have been repeated often enough and with sufficient strength in many individuals in successive generations, they

transform themselves, so to say, into experiences of the id, the impressions of which are preserved by heredity. Thus the id, which is capable of receiving inherited tendencies, there are residues of the existences of countless egos; and, when the ego forms its superego out of the id, it may perhaps only be reviving shapes of former egos and be bringing them to resurrection. [*ibid.*]

Here, Freud is saying that not only the ego but the superego as well is influenced, and may well be determined by experiences that have occurred generations, or even millennia, ago. This is a hypothesis that Darwin considered for a long time and realized was not the best (or most accurate) way to formulate evolutionary theory.

Moving away from genetic formulations, Freud maintains that the superego remains in touch with, and reacts against, id dynamics or (unconscious fantasies) that are potentially in conflict with the ego. Freud says, "If the ego has not succeeded in properly mastering the Oedipus complex, the energic cathexis of the latter, springing from the id, will come into operation once more in the reaction-formation of the ego-ideal" (*ibid.*, p. 39). Here, one sees Freud beginning to expand not only the concept of the superego, but also he adds defensive manoeuvres in the ego. The ego is not simply capable of projection and repression, but also reaction-formation, splitting, and defensive identifications. Reaction-formation of the ego-ideal indicates that the person will now be motivated to react against unconscious (id) tendencies. Therefore, someone who might want to be dirty might become scrupulously clean. Freud had, early in his career, given examples (1907b, 1908b) of how anal tendencies might be reacted against, but now he has presented a theoretical structure to house these dynamics.

Beyond the Pleasure Principle: *1920*

Since Freud's work has been tied closely to issues of pleasure and unpleasure, one might wonder what could be beyond the pleasure principle. Before we go to beyond the principle, perhaps we should state the original principle once again. Freud's idea is based on a hydraulic model that posits that pleasure occurs when there is a reduction in the amount of excitation, and unpleasure occurs when there is an increase in excitation. This model is based on the sexual orgasm and on Fechner's principle of constancy. Freud quotes Fechner when he states, "In so far as conscious impulses always have some relation to pleasure or unpleasure, pleasure and unpleasure can be regarded as having a psycho-physical relation to stability and instability" (1920g, p. 8). Freud maintains that the pleasure principle follows from the principle of constancy, and here it seems that the full implications of this statement involve a logical error to be discussed in the commentary section. However, for the present purposes, we can say that what is consistent in this model is that, in so far as there is an increase in conscious excitation, it will be experienced as aversive. It is difficult to relate this aspect of Freud's theory without commentary, but, for the time being, one can only say that Freud's view of pleasure is a restrictive one that does not fit in with either experience or research. Freud has introduced an energic term to account for stability in functioning, "bound energy". In so far as energy is bound, it is tied to either an object (a person, usually) or a function of the ego. Unbound energy is correlated with primary process or the functioning of the id. Thus, if energy is unbound, it is not tied to a particular object or function and is available for rapid discharge. Although there are many meanings of bound and unbound (see Holt [1989] for a full discussion of bound and unbound), we take bound to be correlated with secondary process and unbound to be correlated with primary process. Up to this point, there is nothing that is beyond the pleasure principle in these formulations. Unbound energy is related to tendencies that were pleasurable at one time or as a tendency from one system, the id; if what is unconscious becomes conscious, it would be experienced as aversive. We again come upon the maxim that something that is pleasurable in one system can be unpleasurable in another system.

Freud is able to use these energic hypotheses and keep in place his ideas about the centrality of his version of the pleasure principle. However, when he looks fully at a variety of traumatic conditions and what he labels negative therapeutic reactions, he considers that he needs to revise his ideas about instinctual development. As is true in most of Freud's papers, he does not go directly to the problem at hand, but instead presents several ideas that, in and of themselves, are of interest. In this paper, Freud gives a brief history of the role of transference in psychoanalytic treatment and reminds us of his previous use of the concept of repetition compulsion. Repetition compulsion (1914g) was, in effect, a compromise caused by the failure of repression. A derivative of an unconscious phantasy reached consciousness and resulted in some form of activity, symptom, or continuous mental representation. This failure of repression occurred repeatedly and the continuous consequence was labelled the repetition compulsion. In this formulation, the repetition compulsion is simply a result of the dynamic interplay between conscious, preconscious, and unconscious influences.

In this context, Freud states for the first time that parts of the ego are unconscious and that resistance in the psychoanalytic situation does not come from the unconscious (id, in our new terminology), but, rather, from the unconscious parts of the ego. This change does not cause Freud any difficulty, since he has already gone over the idea (in each era) that what may be pleasurable on one level or in one system (the id/unconscious) may be unpleasurable in another system (ego/conscious). Thus, the compulsion to repeat may be considered an attempt by the id/unconscious to gain control over the mental apparatus while this tendency is resisted (defended against) by the ego/conscious parts of the mind. This conflict is within his ideas of the pleasure principle, but now he is positing

> a new and remarkable fact, namely that the compulsion to repeat also recalls from the past experiences which include no possibility of pleasure, and which can never, even long ago, have brought satisfaction even to instinctual impulses which have since been repressed. [1920g, p. 20]

Thus, Freud is maintaining that the traumatic neuroses are beyond the pleasure principle and calls for a new principle to explain their occurrence. He is also hypothesizing that the negative therapeutic reaction can best be explained by the new concepts that he is putting forth. We might first ask, what is the negative therapeutic reaction (NTR)? Although Freud is influenced by the NTR in *Beyond the Pleasure Principle*, his main discussion is in *The Ego and the Id*. He states,

> There are certain people who behave in a peculiar fashion during the work of analysis. When one speaks hopefully to them or

expresses satisfaction with the progress of the treatment, they show signs of discontent and their condition invariably becomes worse ... later one becomes convinced, not only that such people cannot endure any praise or appreciation, but that they react inversely to the progress of the treatment. ... they get worse during the treatment instead of getting better. They exhibit what is known as a "negative therapeutic reaction". [1920g, p. 49]

Freud goes on to state that the therapeutic difficulties for the patients who prominently display the NTR maintain a resistance "more powerful than the familiar ones of narcissistic inaccessibility, a negative attitude towards the physician and clinging to the gain from illness" (*ibid.*). That Freud talks about NTR as more powerful than narcissistic inaccessibility means he is seeing this "obstacle" as the most powerful of any met in the analytic situation. Previous to this statement, Freud maintained that, to the extent a patient was narcissistic, then to that extent the person was unanalysable (Freud, 1916–1917). Freud and many authors after him see the NTR as strong evidence for the idea of destructive tendencies in human beings. The explanations for NTR are certainly varied, and one can see patients who exhibit these reactions as addicted to pain (Valenstein, 1973), or as having specific difficulties in separation (Akhtar, 1994), or as being in part stimulated by the type of therapeutic interventions used with particular patients. Freud, in seeing this type of reaction, might agree that these patients are addicted to pain, but previously he would need to explain this addiction in terms of the pleasure principle. If this explanation was not available, he would find himself in the quandary that we are now addressing; that is, there are patients who seem to exhibit reactions that are beyond what one would expect based on the pleasure principle.

We have dwelt on the NTR, but the traumatic neuroses were at least as strong a factor in Freud's new theoretical ideas concerning the basic instincts. It was the repetition of traumatic events that was particularly striking for Freud. Even here, Freud wonders if we can see an unalloyed compulsion to repeat that is beyond the pleasure principle. He says,

> We have come across people all of whose human relationships have the same outcome: such as the benefactor who is abandoned in anger after a time by each of his protégés, however much they may

otherwise differ from one another . . . or the man who time after time in the course of his life raises someone else into a position of great private or public authority and replaces him by a new one; or, again, the lover each of whose love affairs with a woman passes through the same phases and reaches the same conclusion. This "perpetual recurrence of the same thing" causes us no astonishment when it relates to *active* behaviour on the part of the person concerned and when we can discern in him an essential character-trait which always remains the same and which is compelled to find expression in a repetition of the same experiences. [1920g, p. 22]

It is when someone endures this type of event in passive form that Freud begins to view them as humans that "override the pleasure principle" (*ibid.*). In particular, it is traumatic dreams that Freud sees most definitely as beyond the pleasure principle. For example, a Holocaust victim continuously re-experiencing in their dream life scenes of death and destruction would be an example for Freud of a dream beyond the pleasure principle. In a similar vein, an African-American who was lynched, but survived the hanging and continuously replays the event in his dreams, presents another example of the type of dream that Freud is attempting to explain. At this point in time, he does not think that a pleasurable unconscious wish has instigated this type of dream. Previously, he had stated that a dream is instigated by a wish, but now either he must change his definition of a wish or conclude that dreams are at times motivated by other factors. Clearly, he concludes the latter, and begins to develop his new drive theory.

Eros and Thanatos

Freud begins section IV of *The Ego and the Id* (I am here switching to *The Ego and the Id*, since Freud covers the same ground as in *Beyond the Pleasure Principle* and adds some ideas about narcissism) by stating that he will give a summary of his "speculative, often far-fetched speculation, which the reader will consider or dismiss according to his predilection" (1923b, p. 24).

He then goes on to present both the rationale and the substance of his new drive theory. He tells us that there are

Two classes of instincts, one of which, the sexual instincts or Eros, is by far the more conspicuous and accessible to study. It comprises not merely the uninhibited sexual instinct proper and the instinctual impulses of an aim-inhibited or sublimated nature derived from it, but also the self-preservative instinct, which must assigned to the ego and which at the beginning of our analytic work we had good reason for contrasting with sexual object-instincts. The second class of instincts was not so easy to point to . . . On the basis of theoretical considerations, supported by biology, we put forward the hypothesis of a death instinct, the task of which is to lead organic life back into the inanimate state. [*ibid.*, p. 40]

The outward manifestation of the death instinct, or Thanatos, is sadism, which previously had been explained in terms of a joining of the sexual and ego-instincts. In this previous formulation, the enjoyment of hurting another person is the combination of excitement (sexuality) and the control over another person (a derivative of the ego-instincts). Sadism, in the new formulation, is Thanatos directed externally. In effect, sadism is an indirect manner of self-preservation. If Thanatos is not directed externally, it may be directed internally. If directed internally, it will lead to self-destructive consequences and, possibly, death. Sadism is, of course, not the only way to preserve life. Freud likens Eros and Thanatos to the physiological processes of anabolism and catabolism. In effect, the building up and breaking down of internal substances. He says that the two classes of instincts are, or may be, "fused, blended and alloyed with each other; [and] that this takes place regularly and very extensively is an assumption indispensable to our conception" (*ibid.*, p. 41). In effect, the blending of the drives (fusion) allows the destructive drive to be tamed and utilized. Since the aim of both drives is to reduce excitation when the infant begins to accumulate tension because of hunger or pain, Eros fuses with Thanatos and says join me and I can reduce this tension. This homunculus description of what Freud terms fusion is an accurate depiction of one aspect of Freud's theoretical ideas about fusion, but the more significant elements of his theorizing involved the ego and his return to the theory of narcissism.

Freud begins by reminding us of a position he has just taken in *The Ego and the Id*:

THE STRUCTURAL MODEL   153

that sublimation may take place regularly through the mediation of the ego. . . . the ego deals with the first object-cathexes of the id (and certainly with later ones too) by taking over the libido from them into itself and binding it to the alteration of the ego by means of identification. The transformation [of erotic libido] into ego-libido of course involves an abandonment of sexual aims, a desexualization. In any case this throws light upon an important function of the ego in its relation to Eros. By thus getting hold of the libido from the object-cathexes, setting itself up as sole love-object, and desexualizing or sublimating the libido of the id, the ego is working in opposition to the purposes of Eros and placing itself at the service of the opposing instinctual impulses. [*ibid.*, pp. 45–46]

Before we expound on these points, let us continue and see where Freud leads us in the next paragraphs.

This would seem to imply an important amplification of the theory of narcissism. At the very beginning, all the libido is accumulated in the id, while the ego is still feeble. The id sends part of this libido out into erotic object-cathexes, whereupon the ego, now grown stronger, tries to get hold of the object-libido and to force itself on the id as a love-object. The narcissism of the ego is thus a secondary one, which has been withdrawn from objects. [*ibid.*, p. 46]

Freud goes on to conclude that the "clamour of life proceeds for the most part from Eros" (*ibid.*). The death instincts are, for the most part, silent, and if one only considered overt activities "we should have difficulties in holding on to our fundamental dualistic point of view" (*ibid.*). Freud then sounds like the metaphysical poets (Donne, Herbert, etc.) when he says that certain animals "die in the act of reproduction because, after Eros has been eliminated through the process of satisfaction, the death instinct has a free hand for accomplishing its purposes" (*ibid.*, p. 47). (And women wonder why men have a difficult time in talking after the sex act . . .)

Freud's extension of narcissism takes into account the new structural theory, and so all libido now exists at the beginning of life in the id. Previously. he declared that all libido began in the ego. However, at that time, ego referred to self, or self in the larger sense of the term. The id begins to cathect objects (become attached to and represent people or objects) in order to satisfy needs and quiet internal stimuli. The ego, in effect, says to the id, "love me since I can deal with reality in a way that is more efficient and leads to more rapid pleasure". In more concrete terms, Freud sees the infant's signalling the mother as an ego function with the energy originally provided by the id. The mother is first cathected by the id and this maternal representation is taken over by the ego. Once this representation is taken over by the ego, the energy becomes ego energy, or ego libido. The ego, more and more, begins to be a structure that quiets tensions and, in effect, becomes a love object for the id. Thus, ego energy almost completely derives from the id and is accrued by the ego in so far as it is effective in reality. Clearly, an infant's effectiveness is largely determined by the way the environment (usually the mother) can read signals emanating from the infant.

Ego libido, then, has a different and yet overlapping meaning with the previous era. On the one hand, ego-libido is the energy provided by the id and transformed into energy for ego activities. On the other hand, ego-libido still refers to narcissistic libido, except now Freud more clearly sees an adaptive function for narcissism. Narcissism now refers to the desexualization of object-cathexes that is transformed into ego-libido. This is narcissistic in two separate ways: it may be that the ego's activities are not necessarily related to the object or relations with objects (solving a maths problem, writing a novel, etc.), the ego energy is designated as narcissistic since it is energy that is not attached to an object and can be used for any given activity. Freud is assuming that various types of work and activities require ego-libido. He is also observing that, during periods of intense work, a person becomes narcissistic in the sense that at times little else matters but their work. He extends this view and says that all creativity depends to some extent on narcissistic conversions or transformations that tend, at least temporarily, to diminish the importance of the object. Thus, Freud is now more fully conceptualizing a point that he mentions in his paper "On narcissism" (1914c, part 3); even in optimal development, a certain amount of narcissism is present and is adaptive.

Freud, in this new conceptualization, is attempting to explain how the ego gains strength and yet, at the same time, is ultimately dependent on the id for its source of energy. He uses a similar explanation for a description of how Eros and Thanatos become fused or blended. The quieting of internal stimulation is best handled with the help of objects that also tend to be life sustaining.

He says,

> The dangerous death instincts are dealt with in the individual in various ways: in part they are rendered harmless by being fused with erotic components, in part they are diverted towards the external world in the form of aggression, while to a large extent they undoubtedly continue their internal work unhindered. How is it then that in melancholia the super-ego can become a kind of gathering-place for the death instincts?
>
> From the point of view of instinctual control, of morality, it may be said of the id that it is totally non-moral, of the ego that it strives to be moral, and of the super-ego that it can be super-moral and then become as cruel as only the id can be. It is remarkable that the more a man checks his aggressiveness towards the exterior the more severe—that is aggressive—he becomes in his ego ideal. [1923b, p. 54]

We have already discussed the fusion of the death and erotic instincts. This discussion took place in the context of the ego and the ego gaining control over tendencies in the id. The fusion of drives occurs in the context of tension reduction, or need satisfaction. It happens in the context of the pleasure principle; Eros says, in effect, join with me and love this object (or ego) and there will be a diminution in tension and therefore an increase in pleasure. Freud is saying that while the death instincts are quieted by fusion, this is not a complete solution for these instinctual tendencies. In addition, they are turned towards external objects, and this saves aspects of the self or ego. Instead of the death instinct causing internal destruction, it is turned outwards towards external objects, thus saving the ego from an internal assault. This, clearly, is not always successful, and Freud posits that, in so far as a man becomes less aggressive, his ego-ideal is unduly strengthened. Freud makes this statement in more emphatic terms when he says that the ego-ideal becomes aggressive, and here he is indicating that the ego-ideal in fact becomes internally punitive and, in the case of melancholics, the superego (ego-ideal) becomes particularly destructive. In summary, we can say that there are four outcomes for the death instincts.

1. They can be fused with Eros and, in effect, bolster and colour erotic and ego activities. Thus, there is frequently a sadistic

component to normal sexuality and an aggressive tinge in many ego activities.
2. The death instincts may also be turned towards external objects and even projected towards external objects. This allows the ego to externalize the destructive drive.
3. The superego, or the ego-ideal, may become infused with the destructive drive, resulting in severe superego recriminations or, in other terms, a punitive internal voice or superego. Freud sees this formation as being influenced by a person's inability to direct destructive tendencies externally in the form of aggression.
4. This is an alternative that Freud does not discuss. That is, what occurs if none of the three previously mentioned outcomes eventuates? This will leave an individual with an unalloyed destructive drive. Freud should predict that this would lead to an individual's death. If this is the prediction, then one has to ask what the conditions are that would produce a destructive drive without mediation by one of the other three possibilities. This question and others will be taken up partly in the commentary to this chapter, and again in our discussion of the work of Melanie Klein.

Concepts from The Ego and the Id and Beyond the Pleasure Principle

In discussing the ego, we have to include two concepts that Freud puts forth in each of the papers that we are considering. Freud, in talking about the role of consciousness, says,

> What consciousness yields consists essentially of perceptions of excitations coming from the external world and of feelings of pleasure and unpleasure which can only arise from within the mental apparatus; it is therefore possible to assign to the system Pcpt.–Cs a position in space. It must lie on the borderline between outside and inside; it must be turned towards the external world and must envelop the other psychical systems. . . . we have merely adopted the views on localization held by cerebral anatomy, which locates the "seat" of consciousness in the cerebral cortex—the outermost, enveloping layer of the central organ. [1920g, p. 24]

Freud goes on to say that consciousness has limited capacity, and that excitations (in the form of sensations and perceptions) do not leave permanent traces in the form of memory. Thus, he conceives of a limited capacity receiving station that is not altered by the reception of new stimuli. It is also the structure that, at birth, has its own energy independent of the id. After receiving stimuli, "the excitation is transmitted to the systems lying next to [it which are] within and that it is in them that its traces are left" (*ibid.*, p. 25). This receiving station then passes along stimuli to other parts of the ego (that are not conscious) that transforms the received stimuli into memory traces. Freud does not think that consciousness is a characteristic of all living matter and presents a phylogenetic hypothesis when he says, "consciousness arises instead of a memory-trace" (*ibid.*). This hypothesis pictures organisms (even most mammals) that do not have the capacity to self-reflect and are governed solely by reactions to past events. Although consciousness has limited capacity, Freud recognizes that the patient must retain "some degree of aloofness, which will enable him, in spite of everything, to recognize that what appears to be reality is in fact only a reflection of a forgotten past" (*ibid.*, p. 19). For the patient to retain this capacity, there must be a conscious system that can observe one's own reactions and behaviours.

We have noted that the Pcpt.–Cs. system is a limited system that is not altered by incoming stimuli; in addition, this system is aligned close to, or next to, that aspect of the cortex that plays a protective role against the intensity of incoming stimuli overwhelming the organism (person). Freud observes that the outermost layer of the cortex has been deadened to some extent, and he reasons that intense stimuli must pass through this layer of cortex, which he likens to a protective shield. He states that the protective function is almost more important than the receptive function of Cs. Thus, Freud presents a cortex with an outer protective layer and a layer right next to the protective layer that is the sensitive receptive layer (Pcpt.–Cs.). The "sensitive cortex" not only receives stimuli from external sources, but also from internal ones. Towards external stimuli there is a shield, but

> Towards the inside there can be no such shield . . . The excitations coming from within are, however, in their intensity and in other,

qualitative, respects—in their amplitude, perhaps—more commensurate with the system's method of working than the stimuli which stream in from the external world. [*ibid.*, p. 29]

Thus, internal stimuli are seen as normally presenting more attenuated or moderate amounts of stimulation that are less likely to be overwhelming.

Affect and stages of anxiety

We have so far looked at Freud's new structural model and his new instinct theory. The structural model places the resolution of the Oedipus complex as the central task in childhood. With this resolution, the superego forms a developmental structure. The ego, in this new theory, gains energy or strength through the fusion of Eros and Thanatos. In this way, the ego sublimates energy from the id to perform reality-orientated tasks. This fusion is aided when the ego gives up object-cathexes and replaces these cathexes with identifications. In both processes, the ego offers itself as a love object to the id. The first process in sublimation (desexualization) is, in other terms, a movement from object libido to narcissistic libido. In ordinary language, the person begins to turn his focus from the object, to tasks that he himself must perform and regulate. This brief review of Freud's theory leaves out the important topic of anxiety and, in fact, all affects or emotions. We have only briefly mentioned the role of affect or emotion in Freud's new theoretical edifice, this despite the fact that the role of anxiety is present in his earliest writings.

Anxiety: new and old concepts

In a letter to Fliess (1894), Freud writes that the cases of anxiety neurosis are always associated with some interference in sexual discharge or orgasm. Freud assumed that this disorder is transformed sexual energy that is discharged as anxiety. This assumption circumvented psychological factors and was a pure physiological hypothesis. Thus, following Fechner, Freud concluded that

THE STRUCTURAL MODEL 159

there was an inherent tendency to reduce excitation to its lowest level and, if one does not do this via sexual channels, then transformed sexuality will be discharged via anxiety. Even the psychogenic neuroses (see Chapter One) followed a similar path to anxiety. It is true that Freud conceptualized a defensive process (that at the time he called repression) as being central in the onset of the psychogenic neuroses. However, once repression occurred, repressed libido was transformed into anxiety (in psychogenic phobias) or transformed or converted into symptoms (in hysteria). The transformation of libido into anxiety was still considered to be a physiological transformation. This is a view that Freud held seemingly into the 1920s (see 1926d, p. 79), and he also continued to present the concept of the actual neuroses, or actual disorders (see Chapter Three), as part of his mature theorizing.

In his paper *Inhibitions, Symptoms and Anxiety* (1926d), Freud (almost entirely) gives up the idea of transformed libido and the concept of actual disorders. One can see by reading *Inhibitions, Symptoms and Anxiety* that he did so reluctantly and in a somewhat confused manner. In a later paper, Freud is clearer and more decisive in stating his new formulations (1933a). Freud had also previously maintained a distinction between internal and externally based anxiety. He saw internally based anxiety as relating to neurotic anxiety (or anxiety based on conflict), and anxiety from exogenous (external) sources as normal. This relates to a distinction that he previously made between fear and anxiety. Fear is based on exogenous stimuli or conditions that a person has doubts about being able to withstand or handle. Anxiety is based on sexual (or instinctual) anxiety from within, where the person (or ego) is fearful of being overwhelmed. Overwhelmed, here, is translated into either feeling compelled to rapidly enact the impulse, or experiencing intense anxiety when the stimulus (fantasy) reaches consciousness and then becoming immobilized by the anxiety and unable to act. (Where I use the word impulse, I would today translate that term into mental representation. Overwhelming mental representations are ones that are experienced in terms of intense affect states.) The ego being overwhelmed can be thought of as one definition of trauma. In his new theory, Freud maintains that there are a series of anxiety situations where the ego is threatened in terms of traumatic consequences. Interestingly, these anxiety situations strongly follow

Freud's previous fixation points (see Chapter Three). One might conceptualize these points in terms of either loss of an object or some form of loss of the object's love. The new anxiety point might be considered to be superego anxiety. It is interesting to point out that, from Freud's new point of view, the intact superego is a precipitate of depersonified identifications.

To look more systematically at points of anxiety, Freud's first anxiety is the anxiety that occurs during birth. Here, of course, is the first separation, and Freud conceptualizes this as one form of anxiety. Rank (1924) had previously posited that birth anxiety is the crucial anxiety in human development. Freud does not follow him in this view, but does include being born as the first anxiety situation. Freud sees the next anxiety as also occurring early in development: that is, anxiety over the loss of the object. For one to understand this as anxiety condition, one has to return to Freud's earlier theorizing (see Chapter Three). Narcissism as a stage of development comes into being in part because the infant notes the loss of the object (mother). This loss is obviously not one that occurs as completely as the phrase "loss of the object" indicates. However, Freud is maintaining that the mother–baby dyad, at some early point, is disrupted, and the baby now perceives that the mother is at times separate or, at least, not available in the way that she had been available earlier in development. The loss is, thus, one of a particular type of mothering that Freud assumes is present in early development. Since Freud does not offer ages, we will discuss the ramifications of this developmental theory later in the volume.

Freud's next point of anxiety is one where the (anal) child (as opposed to the infant) is anxious about the loss of the love of the mother. Here, again, we have to return Freud's earlier writings and realize that Freud is seeing the anal period as a time where narcissistic issues are beginning to be resolved. The child, during the narcissism phase of development, had seen the mother first as part of itself (purified pleasure ego [PPE]), then as like itself (either in terms of attitudes and physiognomy, or like it itself in both these ways). When anxiety occurs from loss of the mother's love, the child now realizes that the mother wants the child to give up some of its pleasures. This demand (from the child's point of view) or request (from the parent's point of view) shows that the mother has a different attitude than the child. She wants the child to do something that is different than the child wishes. Freud assumes that bodily pleasures are most fundamental, and so anal and urethral restrictions are considered to be crucial at this point in develop-ment. Clearly, parental figures at this time of development are restricting and restructuring the child's behaviours and (one hopes) inter-nal world in a variety of ways. Thus, the child is anxious that it will lose the mother's love if it does not give up certain bodily pleasures and various freedoms in terms of its actions and activities.

The next anxiety situation is, in a sense, a new point of anxiety. Castration anxiety and penis envy are now seen as childhood phenomena and, as such, are part of Freud's increased emphasis on childhood sexuality. Castration anxiety is viewed as a loss of an object, but now the object is part of the child's body. For boys, this loss seems like a plausible anxiety situation, but the idea of girls feeling castrated will undergo a great deal of criticism and, gradually, less and less acceptance. I must state that, on rereading this sentence, I have decided to leave it in but to put in a disclaimer here. Obviously, this is a concept that I do not accept in the way that Freud has posited penis envy. I do not have empirical evidence that most analysts do not accept this concept, but it is my sense, based on the analytic literature, that it is not a well accepted concept. Freud's idea is that the boy, during the phallic stage, is both aroused genitally and desirous of sole possession of his mother (positive Oedipal). The talion principle stipulates that the boy's desire to destroy the father (kill the father) will, in the boy's fantasy, be a threat that is seen as also emanating from the father. In other terms, the boy assumes that the father has the same destructive thoughts as he does. Since the boy's gender and his desires are centred on the representation of his penis, destructive fantasies cluster around the idea of being punished by castration. This would destroy the boy's maleness. The girl, in Freud's formulation, is seen as a smaller boy. She values her clitoris and represents the clitoris in phallic terms (a smaller penis). When she realizes that her "penis" is inadequate compared to the boy's, she is envious, desirous of the boy's equipment, and angry with her mother for not providing her with better or, at least, larger equipment. Freud admits to the inadequacy of his understanding and he at times broadcasts that he considers feminine development an unsolved mystery.

Whatever his doubts about his formulations, Freud, at this point, is positing that castration anxiety and penis envy are the end points or bedrock of an analytic process. The idea of castration anxiety as the bedrock of psychoanalytic treatment does not seem consistent with the concept of stages of anxiety. Of course, if one believes that all conflicts coalesce in the Oedipal stage regardless of their point of origin, then the position takes on at least a certain logical consistency. This position is central to the Classical Freudian position (particularly in the USA). Since we have previously detailed the Oedipal triangle, at this point we can simply note that castration anxiety and the Oedipal drama is not integrated with Freud's previous stage, where the development of the capacity for object love is central (Chapter Three). If Freud had stayed completely within his previous paradigm, he would have made the next stage of anxiety loss of parental love. This anxiety would have included castration anxiety and the loss of the love of both parents. This issue is taken up by the next and final stage of anxiety, superego anxiety. Here, the prohibitions that have been internalized act as danger signals if an unconscious impulse is activated that violates whatever prohibitions and ideals the child has assimilated. If a child wants to lie or cheat (assuming these activities violate the parents stated moral standards), in optimal development there are both prohibitions against these behaviours and ideals that contradict these tendencies. An ideal superego is one that is depersonified and is well integrated into the ego functioning. To paraphrase Anna Freud, our knowledge of the superego only occurs if it is in conflict with the ego (A. Freud, 1936). The superego is the residue of parental love and prohibitions and, as such, optimally continues to develop as a structure.

It is important to dwell for a moment on Freud's meaning of a depersonified superego structure. Freud is assuming that there are parental introjects (or representations) that are present in the child's mind before the development of a superego. For example, he assumes that during the anal stage the child has developed what Ferenczi has called "sphincter morality". Thus, the child might picture, imagine, or, in some cases, even hear the parent saying no, or don't do this, etc. Freud does not consider this development (which may indeed occur earlier than the anal stage) to be superego development. Superego development can be said to occur when the values become the child's values, regardless of external praise or punishment. Here, there is a danger of stating a concept in dichotomous terms when it may be much more of a continuous process. Freud sees the idea of an ideal that exists without the person of the parent largely reinforcing this ideal as the basis of the superego structure. Thus, superego development is accomplished in so far as the child has developed her or his own ideals without these ideals depending on the personification of prohibitions or ideals. In addition, Freud sees the superego in optimal development as an open system subject to change through new identifications and the internalization of new values. This will be less possible the greater the degree of personification of the structure. A corollary to this idea is that the greater the degree of personification, the greater the degree of conflict and the higher the probability of repeated behavioural and psychological events. Stated in this way, this can be considered as an illustration of Freud's earlier views of the repetition compulsion.

With Freud's new theory of anxiety, the concept of actual disorders is given up. Anxiety is now a reaction to the characteristic traumas of development, as well as to external events in a person's life. The first time that a child encounters a traumatic situation (e.g., loss of the mother's love), there can be a full and immobilizing anxiety reaction to this situation. After the first new experience of anxiety, at some later point, the child begins to anticipate the occurrence of anxiety, then, instead of a full anxiety reaction, the anxiety is controlled and used as a signal. This signal indicates to the ego that if defences are not employed, there is the danger of anxiety that is traumatic and that threatens to immobilize or, at the very least, be quite disruptive to the child's or adult's functioning. When defensive operations are working effectively, a small signal institutes the employment of a defence, and all of this goes on at, primarily, an unconscious level. To the extent that the anxiety is experienced as a significant event, then to that extent there is a failure of defence. Obviously, a complete failure of defence would be the entire phantasy reaching consciousness. Since this is a rare occurrence, more often a derivative of the phantasy reaches consciousness, and this derivative usually is accompanied by anxiety.

Freud after 1926: summary and critique

Freud, after 1926, writes a number of important papers that are based on the structural theory. His paper that discusses the formation of a fetish is important for a number of reasons, among them that he again edges towards the concept of splitting. The formulation that is presented is heavily dependent on the centrality of castration anxiety. The concept of splitting, in this paper, is less definitive than his earlier view (1915c, see Chapter Three). One could interpret that Freud was positing a perverse state of consciousness. During that state the world is split, and aspects of the world are denied or disavowed. Freud's point is that two currents of thought in the fetishist run in parallel fashion, and one of these currents is based on denial. In this formulation, the male fetishist is thought to deny the absence of a penis in females, even though, in the other current, the absence is acknowledged. Freud posits that "no male human being is spared the fright of castration at the sight of a female genital" (1927e, p. 154). Why most men can overcome this fear and the fetishist is unable to do so is not clear to Freud. He maintains that the fetish is a compromise where the woman does have a penis, except that is "no longer in the same place as it was before" (*ibid.*). Therefore, a foot fetish or a nose fetish (Freud uses a nose fetish as an example in this paper) is always a substitute for the missing penis. Although, in previous papers, Freud mentions this formulation, now, with the renewed importance of castration anxiety, he is much more certain of the formulation. Splitting, as a concept, again reappears in one of his last publications. This paper is, in effect, a continuation of the fetish paper. It was written in 1937 (Jones, 1955, p. 255), but published posthumously in 1940. Here, again, the concept of splitting is tied to disavowal (denial) in response to the threat of castration anxiety.

During this period, Freud writes some of his major culture papers, which were, according to the editors of the *Standard Edition*, as well as Gay (1988), part of his major concern in the last years of his life. *Civilization and its Discontents* (1930a), parts of the *New Introductory Lectures on Psycho-analysis* (1933a), and *Moses and Monotheism* (1939a) are the most significant cultural papers of this era. In addition, Freud writes "Analysis terminable and interminable" (1937a) and a paper on "Constructions in analysis"

(1937d), which are the last "technique" papers that he publishes. In the *New Introductory Lectures*, Freud goes over some of the theoretical revisions of the previous decade. He also reinforces his ideas about castration anxiety and penis envy. Penis envy is a central idea in his concept of feminine development. In *Moses and Monotheism*, he not only states revolutionary ideas about the history of ancient Judaism, but reinforces his Lamarckian genetic concepts. This is a time of disruptions in the world (the depression), in psychoanalytic politics, and in the dangers of the Nazi party gaining control in Germany and then Austria.

After Freud writes *Inhibitions, Symptoms and Anxiety* (1926d), this is perhaps his least productive era. He introduces no revolutionary new concepts and, when he writes the *New Introductory Lectures* (1933a), he attempts to systematize his psychoanalytic theory, but systematization will never be Freud's strong point. For many decades after Freud's death, various writers have tried to show that Freud became a "true" analytic clinician after he proposed the structural theory. It is my view that this is an analytic myth, and that after the First World War Freud effectively stopped practising psychoanalysis. He did training analysis, which he derided in subsequent publications (1937c). I believe he derided training analyses because he knew the ones that he provided were not up to the type of analytic work he had performed before the war. In a previous publication (1991), I discuss this point in more detail.

In my view, while Freud's new theory provides some important insights, it also distances the analyst from the patient. The ego is an impersonal structure organizing cognitive capacities in order to deal with the competing demands of the id, superego, and, most importantly, reality. The self is an experiential concept much closer to a patient's sense of their internal world. While some analysts (Grossman, Van Spruiel) have argued against using the self as a theoretical concept, their arguments are unconvincing unless one assumes that experiential terms have no place in a psychoanalytic theory. I would argue the reverse, and maintain that even the concept of self does not directly get at a patient's experience, and that an analytic language should be as experiential as possible. Freud's structural theory was in part motivated by his observation that some forms of resistance are unconscious. In his theory, this meant that defensive processes are unconscious, and he was in the logical conundrum that was described in the chapter. He had a number of choices, and the one that he made was elegant in a sense, since he put together a number of elements in the model he proposed. He could, alternatively, have described the same processes in terms of how defensive processes affect a person's sense of self, the unity of their experience, what type of experiences become less available to the person as a result of defensive processes, etc. Freud's abstract metaphor (ego) unifies a number of functions, but this abstract metaphor is one that is indicative of Freud's distance from the clinical situation. After the war, he is no longer a true clinician and transference is no longer the reality that it was before the war. He is now a world figure with a world-wide organization (at least in Europe and North America) that he has built. Gradually, as he grows older, he is distanced from the clinical situation, and his new theory is part of this distance. In the last chapters of this volume, we will look at various contemporary interpretations of the Freudian opus. If one goes through Freud's work, it is clear that he proposed a number of concepts that were not always theoretically compatible. It is up to contemporary analysts to determine which of the Freudian views (if any) are to be embraced.

Note

1. The term "unconscious sense of guilt" appeared in Freud's paper "Obsessive actions and religious practices" (1907b). The editors of the *Standard Edition* write that the notion was, however, foreshadowed in Section 2 of "The neuro-psychoses of defence (1894a). While Freud is struggling with the concept of guilt in this paper, one must remember that he did not truly have the concept of the unconscious at this point in time. In that sense, the editors' views are somewhat anachronistic.

PART II
MAJOR POST-FREUDIAN THEORISTS

CHAPTER FIVE

The new ego psychology: Anna Freud and Heinz Hartmann

Summary

This chapter brings together two analysts (Anna Freud and Heinz Hartmann) who were perhaps the two most influential Freudian theorists from 1940–1960 and beyond. Their theoretical efforts were frequently labelled as ego psychology, since the Freudian theory that they promulgated began from Freud's structural theory (Chapter Four). Hartmann and Anna Freud were initially the main explicators of Freud's move to the structural model, and their clarification and development of the structural model help to make it the dominant theoretical influence in the USA. It is hard to understand the import of both Hartmann and Anna Freud without making some attempt to recreate the atmosphere that faced both these theorists in the mid 1930s.

Freud, at this point in time, was quite ill, and was to die in 1939. Melanie Klein was in England and having a substantial impact on the members of the British Psychoanalytic Society. European psychoanalysis was dominated by Freudian theory, but there was unease about considering Thanatos, or the death instinct (see Chapter Four), a central psychoanalytic concept. The idea of a death instinct, while embraced by Klein, was certainly not finding strong acceptance in the Freudian community. Moreover, while Freud had proposed the structural model during the 1920s, few writers (including Freud) had shown the clinical relevance of Freud's newest theory. (Nunberg [1931] extended the idea of ego functions to include the synthetic function. Glover's paper on inexact interpretation in his book on technique [1955] to some extent utilized the new concepts embedded in the structural theory.) It remained for Hartmann and Anna Freud to begin to plumb the implications of the structural model. In 1958, Hartmann published *Ego Psychology and the Problem of Adaptation*, and Anna Freud, in 1936, *The Ego and the Mechanisms of Defence* (the English translation of which was published in 1946). These two works signalled a much fuller acceptance of the structural theory, particularly in the USA. Both of these volumes paid considerably greater attention to the conscious experiences of the patient. While the main focus of Freudian theory was the unconscious, both Anna Freud and Hartmann made the elementary but necessary point that one can only theorize about unconscious tendencies based on certain conscious experiences or actions. In the language of the structural theory, the unconscious is mediated through the ego and known through the preconscious and conscious aspects of the ego. Both Anna Freud and Hartmann also subtly but decisively rejected the idea of Thanatos, much to the disappointment of Freud. Freud, in "Analysis terminable and interminable" (1937c), noted that a number of analysts did not accept his instinct theory and he seemed clearly upset, particularly since some of the revisionists were his closest supporters.

Hartmann was concerned with the problem of adaptation as it related to evolution, and he was determined to move psychoanalysis into a theory that had commerce with the science and social sciences of his time. He did not give up the idea of instinct, but changed it in a manner that he thought fitted in with an organism that had instinctual tendencies that would produce survival of self and species. In this way, he partially returned to the concerns of the earlier Freudian drive theory (see Chapter Three). Neither he nor Anna Freud fully downplay the importance of the drives, but drives are now balanced in a view that tie together, in Hartmann's language, the "rationalism of enlightenment and the irrationalism of the romantics" (1964a, p. 9). Hartmann maintains that analytic conceptions of health "which have developed on the basis of Freud's suggestions often proceed to assign undue prominence to one of these standpoints at the expense of the other" (*ibid*.). He states that when "biological values are acknowledged as supreme, one has approached dangerously near to that malady of the times whose nature it is to worship instinct and pour scorn on reason" (*ibid*.). While Hartmann provides the theoretical and even the meta-theoretical rationale for balancing reason, the environment, and the drives, Anna Freud offers clinical rationale for always beginning with the surface of the mind. Thus, by 1940, ego psychology had begun to achieve a balance that promised a great deal, but the stability of this balance was at least somewhat illusory. Before we approach the illusory elements of this balance, we should first encounter Anna Freud's and Hartmann's attempts to allow the structural theory to encapsulate and describe the normal and "pathological" functions of the human mind.

Anna Freud and the psychoanalytic legacy

I had thought initially of starting this chapter with the work of Heinz Hartmann, but, as I wrote about Hartmann, I began to realize the extent to which some of Hartmann's ideas resonate with, and to some extent depend on, Anna Freud's theorizing. Perhaps my decision is simply based on the historical fact that her volume was published first. At any rate, it is of historical interest that this volume was a present to her father.

Anna Freud, the daughter of Sigmund Freud, obviously holds a unique place in the history of psychoanalysis. She grew up with psychoanalysis and was the subject of one Freud's most famous papers ("A child is being beaten", 1919e), although Freud carefully explained (Ellman, 1991) that one should exercise the greatest caution in analysing friends or family since almost certainly the friendship will be lost. He was able to move around this prohibition when he treated his own daughter (Young-Breuhl, 1988). Anna was one of the analysts who pioneered child analysis and, by the late 1920s, she was in a debate with Melanie Klein that has lasted beyond the lifetime of either protagonist. We know that even after

Klein's death in 1963, the Freudians and Kleinians of Britain and, indeed, around the world, were in quiet and at times not so quiet combat. It is of interest that Coles (1992) begins his biography of Anna Freud by reporting his first view of this famous analyst. He was at Harvard in 1950 as an undergraduate and knew nothing about psychoanalysis. A friend of his told him that Anna Freud was about to give a lecture and that they should go to attend this talk. Coles asked his friend about Anna Freud and all his friend could say was that he could not explain it to Coles, but "She discovered child psychoanalysis" (1992, p. xv). This incident occurred in 1950, but, if Coles had met a Kleinian in Harvard Yard, I feel fairly certain that this hypothetical Kleinian would not have credited Anna Freud with "discovering child psychoanalysis". Coles, from the beginning of his biography to the end, pictures Anna Freud as a modest and yet heroic figure. In Elizabeth Young-Breuhl's moving biography of Anna Freud, one sees a more textured version of this eminent psychoanalyst.

There can be no doubt that Anna Freud led a life devoted to psychoanalysis, the welfare of children, and to her father Sigmund Freud. She was the youngest of his six children, born at a time (1895), when he was creating psychoanalysis. She was his child, patient, confidante, and, in many ways, the protector of her view of Freud's psychoanalysis. Anna Freud began her professional life as a schoolteacher in Vienna, and, after she became a psychoanalyst, she, with her long-time friend and companion, Dorothy Burlingham, "founded a nursery school for the poorest of the poor" (Coles, 1992, p. 16). In March of 1938, finally responding to the threat of the Nazis (to the *anschluss*), she and her father left Vienna for London. In London, she established the Hampstead Clinic, which is primarily a child treatment centre. This centre has also provided intensive clinical training for a large number of mental health workers from around the world. Her work during the Second World War, with Burlingham, afforded help for children who were traumatized or left without parents as a result of the continuous bombing of Britain by the Nazis. After the war, she worked with children from Europe who had been orphaned. For the rest of her life she was devoted to the cause of improving social and educational conditions for children in the UK, the USA, and in many other places in the world. This brief biographical note does not do justice to this rich, complex life of Anna Freud, who, in many ways, holds a unique place in the history of psychoanalysis.

It must seem strange to a reader from this era to hear that Sigmund Freud analysed his own daughter. I have seen no explanation for this occurrence that is fully satisfactory. Coles quotes Dr Grete Bibring, who was certainly a close associate of the Freud family. She relates, "Now—it would never happen. Then—well I am not exaggerating: things were different; psychoanalysis was simply not what is has become today". Bibring goes on to relate that Anna was Sigmund's "treasured and loved companion and heir" (Coles, 1992, p. 12). There were no established analytic institutes during that era, and there were relationships between analyst and patient that today would, at the very least, be highly questionable. For example, Anna Freud maintained both an analysis and a friendship with Eric Erikson. Although I have read many descriptions of this era, it is still hard to justify some of the excesses when these same analysts were critical of others who strayed from what they thought was appropriate analytic practice. We always run the risk of judgements that are anachronistically biased, but, no matter how many descriptions of this era I encounter, this bias remains.

We should note that Anna Freud was friendly with a great number of analysts who migrated to the USA and the UK. Among these analysts was Heinz Hartmann, who, during and after his residency, was something of a teacher and friend to Anna Freud. Interestingly, what I credit as Anna Freud's influence of Hartmann can perhaps more easily be seen as Hartmann influencing Anna Freud before either of them had published their prominent volumes.

In our discussion of Anna Freud's *The Ego and the Mechanisms of Defence*, we will look at her original volume and a volume that reprinted her work (Sandler & Freud, 1983, 1985) some years later. In this reprint, there is an extensive discussion of her work. This discussion is primarily guided by Joseph Sandler, an eminent analyst and theoretician.

The Ego and the Mechanisms of Defence

In a relatively short monograph, Anna Freud is able to translate, redirect, and revise several aspects of Freud's structural theory.

Perhaps more importantly, she creates new concepts, but she modestly cloaks her new concepts within her father's theoretical writings. She begins her treatise by reminding analysts that the predominant view of her time and the previous era (1919–1930) was that the definition of psychoanalysis should be reserved for the new discoveries relating to the unconscious psychic life (A. Freud, 1946). She goes on to say that many analysts confine their "investigations exclusively to infantile phantasies carried on into adult life" (1946, p. 3). This view of psychoanalysis as depth-psychology was counteracted by Freud's essays on the new structural model (Freud, 1920g, 1923b, 1926d). Although she credits her father with this new perspective, before her volume little was done to explicate the implications of the structural model. The ego, in her interpretation of the structural model, is central to the id, the superego, and the external environment. The ego is "so to speak, the medium through which we try to get a picture of the other two (id, superego) institutions (1946, p. 6). When the id, or, more accurately, an unconscious impulse, makes an incursion into the ego, the ego "proceeds to counter-attack and to invade the territory of the id. Its (the ego's) purpose is to put the instincts permanently out of action by means of appropriate defensive manoeuvres" (1946, p. 8). This occurs because this incursion is experienced, for one or another reason, as anxiety provoking. In Freud's structural model, anxiety is a painful affect. Anxiety in controlled amounts acts as a signal to the ego that a potential danger may erupt in the form of unconscious impulses (see Chapter Four). If the ego is not able to defend against the incursion of an unconscious impulse, the ego then may well be inundated by anxiety. Anna Freud concludes that all defensive operations are intended to alleviate or prevent the ego from enduring pain. The analyst's task is to eventually understand the patient's quandary, since this quandary represents a compromise between the structures of the mind. The analyst's task is then to promote the eventual separation of the institutions to facilitate the patient's understanding of how this compromise was formed. The patient must be willing to experience psychic pain as part of the analytic process. This acceptance is a crucial step in the therapeutic process.

It may go undetected that, in this brief review, we see Anna Freud introducing the concept of compromise formation. Although

THE NEW EGO PSYCHOLOGY 175

Freud had implicitly talked about a number of functions being compromise formations, Anna Freud is maintaining that the analytic task is to understand and be able to split apart the compromise formations that inevitably occur when an unconscious impulse gains expression in the ego. Her view of the analytic task is part of her new emphasis on the ego in clinical psychoanalysis. Before exploring her views on technique, it is important to see how she conceptualizes the role of defence and her classification of defence mechanisms.

Mechanisms of defence and the sources of anxiety

Freud first used the term defence in 1894 (Freud, 1894a, see Chapter One) and then later used the term repression instead of defence (Freud, 1915d). Freud subsequently reverted back to the term defence when he developed theoretical concepts that included a number of defensive operations. In *Inhibitions, Symptoms and Anxiety* (Freud, 1926d), he decided to use the term defence as a "general designation for the techniques which the ego makes use of in conflicts" (A. Freud, 1946, p. 46). He retained the word "repression" for that special method of defence which serves the function of protecting the ego from intrusions from the id. The meaning of repression involves a guarding against the word or symbolic or thing representation of the drive. In other terms, repression guards against the ideational components of an unconscious fantasy becoming conscious. More importantly, in this context, repression is an example of a defence where the anxiety is felt by the ego to come from the id. Repression is a defence against the internal danger of an unconscious fantasy achieving consciousness. In her treatise on defence, Anna Freud distinguishes between those defences where the anxiety is perceived to be internal and those defences where the anxiety is perceived to come from the external world. There are several distinctions that she makes, but the main division is between what she describes as those defences that inhibit the ego and those that restrict the ego. Since she elaborately describes ego inhibitive defences, we will begin with her understanding of this type of defence.

Ego inhibitive defences and the danger situations

The distinguishing characteristic for this type of defensive reaction is that the defence is responding to an internal (id or unconscious) impulse. There are three (or four) types of danger situations that involve ego inhibitive defences. The first involves anxiety stimulated by the superego (see Chapter Four). Thus, when there is a danger of the unconscious fantasy (instinct) reaching consciousness, there is typically anxiety stimulated by the superego. Anna Freud describes this process by relating "that some instinctual wish seeks to enter consciousness and with the help of the ego gain gratification . . . but the superego protests. The ego submits to the higher institution" and begins the process of defence. Anna Freud emphasizes that the "ego itself does not regard the impulse with which it is fighting as in the least dangerous" (1946, p. 58). The ego, in this formulation, does not fear the instincts, but, rather, fears the superego. It is the superego structure, which is made up of ideals and prohibitions, which sets the standards as to what can be allowed into consciousness. Anna Freud lists superego anxiety as the most "familiar" type of anxiety encountered in analysis.

As a second form of anxiety, Anna Freud relates that little children defend against their impulses primarily in order not to disobey parental stipulations. Accordingly, she points out that the ego would be receptive to receiving the instincts, but that its defence "against them is motivated by dread of the outside world, i.e., by objective anxiety" (*ibid.*, p. 61). She has stated that the ego will receive instincts unless guided by anxiety directed from the superego or objective anxiety, but, despite this acceptance, the ego does not provide a welcoming atmosphere for the unalloyed gratification of id impulses. It is only when the ego is not well differentiated from the id that it is truly welcoming, as distinguished from tolerant, of the id. Thus, before the superego has been consolidated, objective anxiety motivates the use of inhibitive defences. If objective anxiety has continued to be a strong source of anxiety later in life, then this an indication of a superego that has not been well internalized.

A third type of anxiety that the ego faces comes from what Anna Freud terms the strength of the instincts. She cites Robert Walder, who describes it as the danger that the ego's whole organization may be destroyed or submerged. It is most readily observed during puberty, or at one of the danger points of a developing psychosis. Here, in this source of anxiety, quantitative factors are decisive. The question is, how much incursion of the drives can the ego tolerate before there is a feeling that its structure will be destroyed or submerged? One has to wonder whether a massive incursion of unconscious impulses into the ego is not in some way qualitatively different than the other forms of anxiety.

There is another factor that Anna Freud mentions as a source of anxiety. She mentions it in passing, and clearly she thinks it is of some importance, but not fully a source of anxiety. She posits that, when the synthetic function of the ego is disrupted, this is particularly troublesome, since the ego's ability to compromise opposing tendencies (e.g., homosexuality–heterosexuality, sadism–masochism, etc.) will be disrupted. She states that "which of the two opposing impulses is warded off or admitted . . . is determined . . . by the amount of energy with which each is cathected" (*ibid.*, p. 65). Additional energy on either side of the tendency will be disruptive. In this formulation, the organization that Wälder (1936) posits is held together by what ego psychologists call the synthetic function. Any strong input from an internal or external source will lead to higher probability of this function being disrupted. This, in turn, will negatively affect the organization of the ego We can see from this discussion that hypothesized quantitative factors are as important for Anna Freud as they were for her father.

Naming the defences

We have gone through some of the ways that anxiety will be created in the ego which will lead to the institution of some type of ego inhibitive defence. Anna Freud, in listing defences, ostensibly lists nine, which (at that time) are very "familiar . . . and have been exhaustively described in the theoretical writings of psychoanalysis" (*ibid.*, p. 47). The defences are regression, repression, reaction-formation, isolation, undoing, projection, introjection, turning against the self, and reversal. She adds a tenth defence, which "pertains rather to the study of the normal than to that of neurosis; sublimation, or displacement of instinctual aims". In an interesting discussion many years later with Joseph Sandler (Sandler & Freud, 1983, 1985), she was asked why she did not include identification with the aggressor on this list (since she has a chapter on this topic), and she replied modestly that she did not know if this defence would be accepted. When asked whether there were only ten defences, she replied that she did not know, but speculated there might be as many as twenty. The defences that are listed above are those that are responding to internal impulses where the anxiety is one of the three types of anxiety (superego, objective, strength of drives) that were previously described. There is, however, another type of defence that Anna Freud describes, which is ego restrictive defences.

Here, we can remind ourselves that all defensive operations are intended to alleviate or prevent the ego from enduring pain. The ten listed defences are designed to prevent pain arising from internal sources. Anna Freud, in extending Freud's paper on denial (Freud, 1925h) looks at defensive measures that protect the person (ego) from anxieties that emanate from the environment. In her discussion, she deepens and widens his concept of denial. She does this by looking at the developmental line of the defence. She observes that the young child is in constant contact with her/his parents to provide pleasure and meet its needs. The more one is dependent on the external world the "more opportunity there is to experience pain from that quarter" (1946, p. 74). The young child may not be able to change its environment by physical means or by exerting its will. Thus, at times, there is a need for denial to at least change the child's perception of the environment. Anna Freud sees denial as both a normal developmental occurrence and, in some circumstances, as a pathological defence. Thus, the child may frequently be free "to get rid of unwelcome facts by denying them, while retaining its faculty of reality-testing" (*ibid.*, p. 89) relatively unimpaired (denial in fantasy). This denial in fantasy is a usual and reversible activity that the child indulges in while it grows large enough to deal with the environment that at times is painful, physically or psychologically. When the denial is not reversible in adulthood or later in childhood, this is what Anna Freud calls denial in word and act. Both modalities (language and action) are affected by this type of denial, and the person acts as if there is a reality that is different than the consensual reality. In some circumstances, the person may simply avoid aspects of reality and not be able to come into contact with a part of the environment. Anna Freud emphasizes that denial is not equivalent to a phobia, since, in a phobia, while the anxiety and the defence seem to be in response to the external world, one is "really afraid of his (one's) own inner processes" (*ibid.*, p. 109). In denial, "disagreeable external impressions in the present are warded off, because they might result in the revival of similar impressions from the past" (*ibid.*). The impressions from the past are part of the person's painful environment that the person has to change, or even obliterate. Denial and avoidance are examples of what Anna Freud calls ego restrictive defences, while the other listed defences are ego inhibitive defences.

What is restrictive and what is inhibited in terms of these defences? Here, we have to extrapolate and include Anna Freud's later writings and say that when ego inhibitive defences are used some ego function is inhibited. If we take classic examples, we can say that, in so far as one uses a hysterical style where repression is utilized (repression is hypothesized to be the main defence that people with hysterical styles utilize, whereas isolation is hypothesized to be the main defence that people with obsessive–compulsive styles utilize), then functions like memory and perception will be affected. Hysterics will be less likely to utilize detail when it is necessary, and often memories will be unavailable to them, particularly if repression is used extensively. In looking at obsessive–compulsives, who are hypothesized to use isolation as a main defence, the use of this defence will prevent them from being able to experience various emotions. This will hinder their ability to understand another person's emotional states. One may say this affects their ability to experience the colours and shades of interpersonal interactions.

Ego restrictive defences affect the most important function of the ego, that is, the person's ability to reality test. It may be that the person's sense of reality is affected, and not their reality testing directly; in any case, where ego restrictive defences are utilized, then to that extent an aspect of a person's relationship to reality is in peril. One may wonder about the sharp division between ego inhibitive and restrictive defences, but Anna Freud's dichotomous conceptualization remains throughout her life. In her discussions with Sandler, she wonders why analysts confuse her concept of restriction with the results of a phobia. In phobic reactions, the person may well avoid aspects of reality, but, to repeat her perspective, in phobias, the danger is from within (id impulses). In restrictive defences or responses, the danger is from outside, or, as Sigmund Freud stated, in neurosis, the conflict is between the ego and the id; in psychosis, the conflict is between the ego and reality. Restrictive defences do not necessarily imply psychosis, but are certainly utilized in psychotic states. Clearly, all (or even most) uses of denial do not denote psychosis. This is the case even though Anna Freud maintains that, with restrictive defences, the conflict is between the ego and reality. Although we have focused on denial as an ego restrictive defence, there are certainly more benign forms of ego restriction that involve avoidance of a reality situation.

Some definitions, and questions about defence

Looking at Anna Freud's definitions of defence is both of historical interest and, more importantly, her theorizing about defence has strongly affected the way some analysts (Busch, 1995; Gray, 1994) have thought about the treatment situation. Since defence is a central concept in psychoanalytic theory, we will look at some definitions of defence and ask several questions about how the theory is conceptualized. For example, do defence mechanisms have a singular function, or do they at times act for the purpose of defence and at other points as another type of ego activity? Are all defences unconscious, and, if not, what is a conscious defence? Anna Freud presents ego inhibitive and ego restrictive mechanisms as dichotomous concepts: are there alternative ways of conceiving of these categories, and what are the implications of considering these categories as continuous functions? These questions will guide our entry into Anna Freud's and Sandler's discussion of the concept of defence.

Interestingly, the discussion with Sandler (1985) begins with two defences, projection and introjection. Sigmund Freud posited that these two defences were important neurotic mechanisms. Although Freud did say this at one point, it is interesting to note that he also mentions the mechanism of projection in explaining some of Schreber's symptoms (Freud, 1911c). Few would argue that Schreber was neurotic. In various ways, the discussion of introjection and, particularly, projection gives a good representation of the status of Anna Freud's theorizing about defence and extent to which her views have changed since 1936. Introjection is seen as a mechanism taking in objects, and projection a mechanism where the person rids themselves of painful affects or ideas. She and Sandler conclude that projection is a mechanism where the child (or adult) removes feelings or actions from his own self-representation and represents the unwanted entity in the external world. Sandler, in this context, asks the more general question of whether there are activities that are listed as defences that at times are not used for the purpose of defence. For example, introjection may aid the child (or infant) build their internal world and, thus, may serve a positive non-defensive role in the child's development. Anna Freud agrees that, at times, what she has classified as a defence can be used for other than defensive purposes. Anna Freud is then asked about the difference between introjection and identification. She reported that when she wrote the book, in 1936, there had been a great deal of discussion of the two terms. Anna Freud saw introjection as a taking in of object representations and Sandler suggested that identification enriches the ego as a structure by changing a person's self representation(s). He also suggested that introjection could be seen both as a mechanism important early in life (infancy) and also as a mechanism that provided the five-year-old child with a way to form the superego. He maintained, with Anna Freud's apparent agreement, that identification changes the person's self-representation, while introjection is a process that allows the child to develop object representations. The object representations may occur early in development, or during the process of forming the superego.

Although we have tentatively stated a definition for projection, in addition, Sandler and Freud agree that the term "projection" implies a reflexivity. Thus, if a person has an unconscious thought (e.g., I hate him), the thought is projected to someone where the hatred is directed at the projector; "I hate him" then is returned as "he hates me" (this is the reflexivity). Interestingly, when asked about Freud's (1911c) analysis of Schreber, where Freud utilizes the concept of projection to explain some of Schreber's delusions, Anna Freud maintained that Freud was talking about projection and a reversal. Freud posited that Schreber first projected his homosexual loving feelings to another, but the projection was then reversed from "he loves me" to "he hates me". This reversal occurred because "very little would be accomplished by the mere projection of the homosexual wish . . . there would still be a homosexual relationship" (Sandler & Freud, 1985, p. 141). This explanation seems to run counter to a variety of clinical situations where some individuals who project their homoerotic feelings find homosexual relationships in every corner. Why this could not be true of Schreber is not explained by this comment. Although projection is seen as a main defence to externalize mental contents, Sandler maintains that there are simpler forms of projection where the person believes what they unconsciously or, at times, pre-consciously, wish to believe. For example, if a man wishes that women are attracted to him and want to make advances towards him, projection then allows him to see women as making advances towards him regardless of the actual situation. Sandler would call that a projection. Anna Freud would call that an externalization. Here, again, when pressed for answer as to why this would be an externalization rather than a projection, she answered that this was the convention of the time. Clearly, neither Anna Freud nor Sandler could see a logical reason for this distinction. Thus, what is described as both externalization and projection seems to be related concepts with no clear distinguishing characteristics. In my view, externalization implies an easier access to consciousness.

Looking at introjection and projection as prototypic defences, we can make several conclusions about the status of the theory of defence. If we look at introjection, we can say that it is conceived of as a defence but, under some conditions, may not function as a defence. Thus, introjection may help the developing child to internalize meaningful object relationships, or, at least, object representations. If we look at the concept of projection, it becomes hard, if not impossible, at this point in time to distinguish projection and externalization. Sandler says, after a long discussion, that "people will have to be given license to use projection and externalization interchangeably" (1985, p. 145). Clearly, in the discussion of projection, there is an attempt to look at the conditions where a person attempts to place an idea or affect (that is part of conflict) as part of another person. Anna Freud attempts to hold on to the idea that projection (as opposed to externalization) involves conflicts around aggression, but, after looking at a number of examples, she cannot hold on to this discrimination. What one can say is that humans attempt to evacuate their minds of impulses that cause conflict. At times, what is projected is a wish or desire that the person wishes were true. Thus, the man who sees all women being attracted to him is putting a wish into these women and this activity changes his perception of the women around him. Is this a defence, or under what conditions would one call this a defence? Is the desire to distort reality in some way necessarily a defence? At any rate, it is hard to see the benefit of calling this an externalization as opposed to a projection. In lieu of some other types of experience or data, we might ask whether or not some of the precision attempted in these conceptualizations is purely academic in the pejorative sense of the term academic. In addition, as we look at some other defences, we might ask: are there any ego activities that are seen as purely defensive, or, in other terms, are there ego activities that are used only for the purpose of defence?

Commentary

Let us consider some examples where it is clear that the same activities that are called defensive, at other times are viewed as ego activities, where the main emphasis is not defensive. The examples we will consider are sublimation and identification with the aggressor. Sublimation, defined as "the displacement of the instinctual aim in conformity with higher social values" (*ibid.*, p. 56), clearly can be seen as having other than defensive value and purpose. Although there may be a defensive function to sublimation, the value of sublimation is placed with the transformation of instinctual tendencies towards activities that are under the control of the ego. I have changed Anna Freud's definition, for it seems clear that the term "higher social values" may differ widely in different cultures. The core meaning of the concept is that sublimation is a transformation process that allows the ego (person) to depart from the demands of the drives. It seems possible that this process can occur in a culture that another culture defines as having low social values.

Identification with the aggressor is much more frequently seen as having a purely defensive function. However, any identification may alter the self-representation in a manner that has certain adaptive components. This type of identification may provide the child with an impetus to aggressively or assertively defend their new creations. It may be a useful trait in a competitive society. It seems that this, or any, identification may be utilized in an adaptive manner. The argument may be that this identification is at least motivated by defensive concerns, but even this argument does not take into account the child's (or adult's) possible idealization of the aggressor and a desire to be like the aggressor and have the aggressor's power.

Without continuing this listing of defences, we can say that Anna Freud is correct that many of the defences she has described at times are not utilized purely as defences. However, one may go further and say that the concept of defence has been sorely stretched, and that perhaps most of these mechanisms should be considered as normal tendencies that also have a defensive function. If the concept of compromise formation is an aspect of one's theory (as it is with Anna Freud) then almost every activity has a defensive component. Thus, one may question a good deal of the list Anna Freud has compiled and wonder if one should consider these activities (ego activities, in her terms) as defence mechanisms. This discussion, or question, is more than academic, since, if one has a clear concept of defence, it may be that defence is what is analysed first or, in some ideas about technique, defence is analysed virtually exclusively. If one recognizes that a defensive action serves many functions, then it may be that one might question whether one should necessarily slant one's treatment concepts towards the analysis of defence. If we look at the array of defences that Anna Freud has proposed, it seems that only isolation, repression, and denial are pure defences.

Having stated this, we can note that Anna Freud's distinction between denial in fantasy and denial in word and deed seems to belie the previous statement. During childhood, there is a clear adaptive consequence of denial in fantasy. This type of denial bolsters the child's self esteem and prevents the environment from becoming overwhelming for the child. However, even though there is an adaptive aspect of denial, the function of denial is always the same, to alter a feature of reality. Thus, in the lexicon I am proposing, denial is a pure defence. If we view the concept of repression, we reach the same conclusion. Repression is a defence that features a separation between the ideational and affective component of an unconscious representation. The separation is then followed by a counter (anti-cathexis) against the idea becoming conscious. To put this process in other terms, it is an unconscious activity by the ego to inhibit or block an unwanted idea from becoming conscious. There is no other meaning to repression than this; even if one maintains that, at times, it is adaptive to utilize defensive processes, the purpose is always the same: to prevent an unconscious element from reaching consciousness. In a similar manner, isolation involves a separation between the idea and the affect, but, in the case of isolation, the affect is inhibited while the ideational component is available to the conscious aspects of the ego. It seems that, of all the defences that Anna Freud has listed, only denial, repression, and isolation are used purely for defensive purposes. Denial leads to a restriction of the ego while repression and isolation l ead to an inhibition of the ego. Repression and isolation are unconscious defences and the effects of these defences can only be detected either when the defence fails, or when there is some hypothesized inhibition of an ego function.

If all we are left with are denial, repression, and isolation, then Anna Freud becomes a type of botanist of defensive tendencies and perhaps this is why she considers it possible that there may be as many as twenty (or more) defences. In other terms, if each defensive tendency is called a defence mechanism, then the theoretical rationale is diluted and one has to be content with categorizing defensive tendencies. This focus on defence takes one away from analysing the person, and analysing the person is something that she states is important to her. To gain a fuller appreciation of this, we need to discuss some of her ideas about psychoanalytic treatment.

Psychoanalytic treatment and a brief history of psychoanalysis

Anna Freud, in reviewing the history of psychoanalysis, notes that some views of psychoanalysis held that the "term should be reserved for the new discoveries relating to the unconscious psychic life, i.e. the study of repressed instinctual impulses, affects and phantasies" (1946, p. 3). She counters this assertion by maintaining that "From the beginning analysis, as a therapeutic method, was concerned with the ego and its aberrations" (*ibid.*, p. 4). The aim, in her view, was always the same: "the restoration of the ego to its integrity" (*ibid.*). This is an interesting view, since Freud did not have a full concept of the ego until the 1920s but, nevertheless, before the 1920s used the term to denote the self or the entire person. In this statement, Anna Freud is stipulating that it was always her father's intention to balance the emphasis of unconscious fantasy with the patient's conscious concerns. She typically underestimates that her concerns are a new direction for analysts. She writes as if her emphasis was always her father's emphasis.

Despite her assertion, she briefly reviews the history of psychoanalytic technique and begins with a pre-analytic method, hypnosis. In her view, the hypnotist did not want to engage the ego, but, rather, to bypass ego functions to get at unconscious memories. Her belief was that, with this method, when the patient was away from the physician the ego revolted and reinstated the old symptoms and conflicts. The results of hypnosis were seen as temporary, since the ego of the patient was not recruited as part of the treatment situation. There was a mechanical attempt to extirpate the pathogenic memories.

Interestingly, after stating why analysis moved away from hypnosis, Anna Freud then takes up what some analysts call the fundamental rule of psychoanalysis, free association. In some ways, it has gone unrecognized how Anna Freud has looked at the limitations of free association. She states that the rule of free association was again an attempt to bypass the ego and concentrate only on the id, or id derivatives that appear in the patient's associations. She stipulates that when the analyst tries to impose this rule, he/she asks the patient to be passive in judging what comes to mind and only report (by verbalizing) what appears in consciousness. She cautions the analyst against trying to force the patient to free associate, since, even if the patient complies, this will make a treatment a one-sided affair. Even if were possible to convince the patient to do this, she contends that this would be little better than the technique of hypnosis. She tells us that "Fortunately for analysis such docility in the patient is in practice impossible" (*ibid.*, p.13). At some point, the patient will begin to employ their characteristic defences against the intrusion of unconscious ideas that would be anxiety-provoking. Anna Freud then notes that this is what Freud considered to be resistances to the analytic method. She points out that the "resistances" of the patient are also unconscious, part of the unconscious aspects of the ego. Having noted this, she begins to describe why it is at least as important to analyse the unconscious aspects of the ego as it is to analyse the unconscious impulses of the id.

One of the first tasks of the analyst (perhaps the first from her perspective) is to recognize the type of defence mechanism the patient has employed and to begin to bring this activity firmly into the analysis. When the analyst, for example, can "bring that which has been isolated back into its true context" (*ibid.*, p. 15), then the analyst can re-establish severed connections between the ego and the id. In other terms, the analysis of defence allows the ego to tolerate id derivatives without (one hopes) the derivatives gaining control of the ego. We might pause a moment and discuss what is meant by gaining control of the ego. Both Freud and Anna Freud assumed that when defended against unconscious impulses entered consciousness (or the conscious aspect of the ego) there would be an attempt for these impulses to gain gratification. Gratification occurs in partial form simply by the impulses gaining consciousness, but if the person acts out the impulse in reality, this is a more significant and fuller gratification. If there is a defended against wish to humiliate one's father, the analytic attempt is to keep the wish, once conscious, in the analytic situation. The wish is then enacted or discussed in the analytic situation and is subject to analysis and transformation. If the wish gained control of the ego, this would mean that the patient felt compelled to enact this wish, regardless of the consequences to themselves or their father.

Anna Freud, after discussing the limitations of free association, points out that the dream interpretation, or the exclusive discussion of dreams, is similar conceptually to the concept of free association. Here, too, the patient is in a relatively passive situation, having received a dream during a regressed state (sleep) and reported it back to the analyst. The interpretation of the dream (if one is able to) helps "in the investigation of the id", but is not a full form of the new analysis. Interpreting both symbols and slips of the tongue (parapraxes) is considered to be comparable to free associations. Direct interpretation of parapraxes or symbols bypass the ego and, as such, are like the older forms of treatment (hypnosis and the pressure technique). Clearly, in making these comparisons, Anna Freud is attempting to get the analytic world to concentrate on a fuller version of the patient's productions than she feels has been the case in the past. Thus, she overstates the limitations of each of the activities she discusses, since she wants to put the analyst into a situation where he/she is looking at the patient's transference states. There are obviously many ways that an analyst might approach the discussion of a dream, but Anna Freud is responding to the way analysts of her time approached the issue of dream interpretation. In the same way, she is responding to the way Freud approached free association in a well-known case, the Rat Man (Freud, 1909d).

Although Freud wrote about transference in a number of papers and explicitly in three papers on transference, Anna Freud begins where he left off and assumes that her reader is familiar with Freud's papers on transference. She says that the analysis of libidinal transference states provides information about the patient's past and, thus, helps fill an amnesic gap in the patient's past. This, however, assists us "in the observation of the id only" (1946, p. 19). While this may seem like a minor statement, here, in a few pages, she radically changes the direction of transference analyses. For Freud, transference of erotic impulses was the crucial aspect of analytic treatment. The erotic transference fuelled the repetitions that occurred and filled in the analysis of the past, so that one could reconstruct the patient's past. While this is of some interest, Anna Freud considers this only one factor in analysis, and not, by any means, the most important factor. This is a large shift from her father's emphasis, and this shift is subtly stated so that it will not arouse anxieties among the older analysts.

In Anna Freud's next category, the analysis of transference of defence, she posits that this is the crucial aspect of analysis. The repetition compulsion, she states, does not only extend "to former id-impulses but equally to former defensive measures against the instincts" (*ibid.*, p. 20). She chides analysts not to say that the patients are "pulling the analyst's leg" when the analyst recognizes a defensive stance on the part of the patient. Thus, a patient may say that she/he cannot talk about a given topic and Anna Freud warns against putting pressure upon the patient to be candid, to expose the id-impulse which lies hidden under the defence as manifested in the transference. The patient should be considered to be candid when they are talking about an issue in a way that is available to him/her. In my terminology, she is asking the analyst to trust the patient and to trust the analytic process. If one can analyse the patient's defences we can

> fill in a gap in the patient's memory of his instinctual life [and] ... we acquire information which completes and fills in the gaps in the history of his ego-development or, to put it another way, the history of the transformations through which his instincts have passed. [*ibid.*, p. 21]

Reconstruction is still important to Anna Freud, but it is reconstruction of the ego and the modifications of the ego that have occurred as a result of conflict.

She relates that analysis and reconstruction of the libidinal transference is normally relieving to a patient. The analyst is, in effect, saying, "it is not me that you are in love with, but, rather, you are expressing a past love in the transference". This type of analysis allows the patient to eliminate a potentially embarrassing state. Frequently, the libidinal transference itself is not ego syntonic, and the patient is pleased to be rid of it. This is not the case with defences, since usually they are ego syntonic. Anna Freud tells us that with defence analysis we cannot count on the co-operation of the patient. She states, "Whenever the interpretation touches on the unknown elements of the ego, its activities in the past, that ego is wholly opposed to the work of analysis" (*ibid.*, p. 22). Anna Freud, reluctantly following Reich (1933), calls this analysis "character analysis". (She writes that this type of analysis is "commonly described by the not very felicitous term character analysis" [*ibid.*].) She is willing to use this term because it implies a characteristic response to anxiety that is part of, and accepted by (syntonic to), the ego. We can now substitute Freud's early statement when he tells us that analysing the transference is the most difficult part of the treatment (Freud, 1905e). Character analysis (in the transference) is the most difficult part of the analysis. For Anna Freud, it is also the most important aspect of the analysis.

We leave Anna Freud at this point, but we will return to her work later in the volume when we discuss the issue of defence analysis. Of course, we have only touched on Anna Freud's vast contributions, and at the end of this chapter we will briefly touch on her concept of developmental lines.

Heinz Hartmann

Jacob Arlow wrote,

> The passing of Heinz Hartmann on May 17, 1970 brought to a close one of the most influential and significant careers in the history of psychoanalysis. For more than two decades Hartmann was without question the outstanding theoretician of psychoanalysis and its leading intellectual figure. His work centered on ego psychology. He saw it as the integrating element of psychoanalytic theory and practice, as well as the basis for a theory of general psychology. [1970, p. 620]

Although, clearly, Arlow was presenting a point of view that was based on his own allegiance to the classical position, there is no question that during the time period that he cites Hartmann and Anna Freud were two of the leading figures in psychoanalysis. Interestingly, while Fairbairn is perhaps better known today than in his lifetime, Hartmann's fate can be viewed as the mirror image of Fairbairn's. Hartmann is rarely referred to today, except as a historical figure or to show that his concepts are outdated. Hartmann, like Freud, is often criticized for his use of the concept of psychic energy. Hartmann and his contemporary, David Rapaport, attempted to systematize psychoanalysis. Unfortunately, they took both the concept of psychic energy and the critics of this concept quite seriously. Hartmann felt that Freud had posited several sources of psychic energy, and Hartmann accepted this view and added several other psychic energy concepts. While Hartmann's theories were certainly tied to the concept of psychic energy, the main impetus of his theorizing was an attempt to create both a general psychology and a psychology that tied psychoanalytic theory to environmental interactions.

Hartmann seemed uniquely qualified to integrate psychoanalytic theory and practice into appropriate correlation with each other and with the findings of related disciplines. Hartmann's family on his father's side was a blend of ancestors who were both prominent scientists and social scientists. His father was a well-known academic and historian who later took the post of Austrian ambassador to Germany. The Hartmann household has been described (personal communication) as being an intellectual foundry able to produce the finest of intellects, and, clearly, Heinz Hartmann was a prime product. He was interested in literature, philosophy, and the sciences and social sciences of his time. He was a student of Max Weber, and, through Weber, met with many of the prominent European intellectuals. In the background of this intellectual mixture was the Vienna Circle, whose ideas of verifiability were a continuation of Mach and, later, Bridgeman. Their views on how to operationalize concepts and which concepts were useful would have excluded a large portion of Freudian theory. Hartmann was attempting to answer the Vienna Circle to keep some of the internal language of Freud's theory alive and vibrant. Clearly, he recognized that an American psychiatrist (Sullivan) had been strongly influenced by the logical positivists. He also recognized, as did Anna Freud, that the challenges to Freudian psychoanalytic theory were multiplying rather than abating. Freud had fought back against Adler, Jung, and Rank from 1910 through the 1920s, but now, in the USA, Sullivan, and from Germany (to the USA), Horney and Fromm, were all presenting views in opposition to Freudian drive theory. Moreover, from Hartmann's perspective, the culturalists and Sullivan were leaving or downplaying the centrality of unconscious fantasy. Interestingly, Freudian critics of Hartmann were to see him in a similar light and felt that he and, to lesser extent, Anna Freud were in the process of reducing the theoretical and clinical importance of unconscious fantasy.

Early considerations

Schafer remarks, in assessing Hartmann's contributions (1970, 1976), that it seemed evident that Hartmann was keenly aware of the lack of elegance in psychoanalytic theory as it stood at the end of Freud's life. Schafer describes how Hartmann attempted to systematize a psychoanalytic set of propositions that were in a state of disarray. Freud's postulates were not set in any type of hierarchical order, there were a variety of definitions that were used for the same concept, and these definitions, in turn, were not consistently related to one another. Given the enormous task of coherently arranging these concepts, Schafer finds it striking that Hartmann did not detail his own contributions, nor did he highlight his differences with Freud. Perhaps it is equally striking that Schafer is noting this, for, at that point in time, many psychoanalytic articles (in the USA) would start off with an almost compulsory reference to Freud and would try to show how their contribution was related to a Freudian idea. This, of course, was part of the ritual of showing that indeed one was a *bona fide* psychoanalyst. Schafer was part of a group that sprang from Rapaport and was beginning to critique psychoanalysis in a manner that was as yet unknown in the USA. (Although certainly Sullivan and Fromm were critics of Freudian theory, they were not critics from within the Freudian circle.) In fact, Schafer begins his article (1970) by both noting the open-mindedness of Hartmann's thought and the unfortunate trend to make ego psychology the new orthodoxy.

While considered to be quite orthodox, Hartmann, in some respects, could be considered to be revolutionary, if not in tone, frequently in substance. As early as 1927, Hartmann advocated a scientific approach to psychoanalysis. His concept of scientific approach might be questioned, but certainly he and Kris consistently advocated the study of developmental processes as a method of validating and providing changes in psychoanalytic conceptions. Later, Hartmann stated that all hypotheses, including the hypothesis about instincts, "must be checked . . . as to consistency and conformity with whatever factual knowledge we have in the field with which we are dealing" (1948, p. 370). This is a very different point of view than Freud evinced, since Freud was sceptical about whether other sciences could add to the knowledge accumulated by psychoanalysis. He was particularly sceptical about psychological research adding to, or being capable of verifying, psychoanalytic propositions. Clearly, Hartmann wanted to require psychoanalytic theory to be explanatory (and not merely descriptive), and at some point the theory should produce statements that were capable of being empirically verified. This strong position was never realized.

As Schafer has noted, it may be that the revolutionary aspects of Hartmann's positions were not well noted, since his approach was

THE NEW EGO PSYCHOLOGY   193

always steeped in the history of Freud's writings. Hartmann starts off his 1956 essay on the development of the concept of the ego in Freud's work by assuring the reader that, for the analyst, Freud's thought continues to be very much alive, "indeed an essential element" (1964b, p. 268) in their everyday clinical work. He initially gives the impression that Freudian theory had achieved a substantial degree of systematization and verification. Then, for the rest of the essay, he notes that Freud rarely systematized his thoughts but, rather, went on to new concepts without fully integrating the new with the old. Despite this statement, he continually looks for suggestions in Freud's writings that would contain the elements of, or the precursors to, systematization. Both Hartmann and Kris find that the concept of the ego lays the groundwork for what Kris called "the new environmentalism in psychoanalysis" (Hartmann, 1964b, p. 292). Hartmann also sees Freud's volume on anxiety (*Inhibitions, Symptoms and Anxiety*, 1926d) as the "tracing of internal to external danger situations" (1964b, p. 292). This interaction between the environment and an internal sense of danger is seen as a new development for Freud and a way to differentiate the dependency of the ego on the id and superego and move ego interests towards the external world. In this new formulation, the ego is clearly the seat of anxiety and the seat of all emotions. Hartmann sees Freud as maintaining that "thought processes and ego processes in general are working not with instinctual energy, but with a modified form of energy, called sublimated or desexualized" (*ibid.*, p. 293) Hartmann, having changed Freud's emphasis, then states, "This seems to me a rather radical re-evaluation of the economic role of the ego" (*ibid.*). Similarly, Hartmann sees Freud's new concept of the ego as leading him to conceptualize "the normal as well as the pathological individual" (*ibid.*). Freud's main vector was clearly communicated to the analytic community in that he was interested in describing a patient's mind from his theory of the interior. There is no question that his ideas about the continuity of human experience could be translated into his interest in the normal. It is Hartmann who is trying to redirect the community towards describing the normal as well as the pathological. Hartmann points out that, late in his life, Freud was still modifying his theory of the ego. For example, in 1937c, Freud posited that there are inherited characteristics of the ego and, in 1940a, maintained that there are self-preservative tendencies in the ego but not in the id. Hartmann states that this "clarifies also the difference between the id of the human being and the instincts of the animals" (ibid., p. 295). Again, Hartmann takes a possible suggestion of Freud's and makes it part of a new theory. Hartmann places human self-preservative tendencies as part of adaptive tendencies in the ego. This, then, keeps the id as being a seat of pleasure and of irrational tendencies. This is in line with one view of Freud's theoretical concepts.

Whether one agrees with Hartmann's discussion of Freud or not, it is clear that his explication of these concepts puts Freud in line with Hartmann's emphasis on the biological basis of the ego and the evolutionary role of adaptation in human beings. In emphasis, Hartmann, and Hartmann, Kris, and Lowenstein (Kris and Lowenstein being frequent collaborators of Hartmann), attempted to keep psychoanalysis aligned with a biological approach. While the ego has biological roots, its development is formed by social or environmental conditions as well. From his earliest work, Hartmann thought of the ego as the centre of an individual's functioning. A crucial function of the ego is the synthesizing function, which provides organization and integration for planning, thought, and most cognitive tasks. The synthetic function of the ego allows for smoother adaptation for the individual. The biological basis of the ego is, in Hartmann's view, as firm as the biological basis of the drives was for Freud, and the ego has independent energy from birth onward. The ego may still harness energy derived from the id, but ego functions such as perception and motility are present from birth and have energy that is the independent of the drives (or id). While I have stated that Hartmann's emphasis on reality and survival mechanisms is reminiscent of Freud's first drive theory (see Chapter Three), Hartmann is specifically attempting to correct the views that Freud put forth (Freud, 1939a).

The evolutionary slant of Hartmann's work has been underemphasized, and his views of survival mechanisms are extremely important in how he conceives of early development. He has influenced, and been influenced by, Spitz, whose hospitalism studies powerfully emphasize the role of human contact in early development. It is not well known that Spitz derived his predictions from Freud's later instinct theory. Despite these derivations, Spitz conceived of the results from his New York (1945, 1957) and Denver studies in terms of the ego psychology that Hartmann was developing. For Hartmann, Spitz's studies emphasized the importance of early infant–mother contact in terms of the survival of the infant. Thus, the dependency of the human infant had to meet with a certain type of mothering to survive physically and psychologically.

Some prominent critics

Part of the difficulties in presenting Hartmann's work is that the stereotypes of his work are so ingrained in almost all psychoanalytic theorists that it is difficult to detail his work without wanting to fall back into a characteristic stance put forth by other authors. Authors as divergent as Bergmann (2000) and Greenberg and Mitchell (1983) interestingly overlap in their critiques of Hartmann. Certainly, Bergmann is usually more sympathetic, but, writing at a later time, one might argue that his is the more devastating critique since his volume belatedly announced the end of the Hartmann era. Before going over some of Hartmann's basic concepts, I have decided to feature an essay of Hartmann's where he is using some of his basic concepts to explain aspects of the onset and the underlying causes of schizophrenia. In my view, understanding this essay helps in seeing another side of the Hartmann legacy.

The metapsychology of schizophrenia

Hartmann looks at the role of infant–mother interactions in several of his papers. but it is in "Contributions to the metapsychology of schizophrenia" (1953) that he shows how his theory might be clinically relevant.

Although this paper is about a clinical issue, Hartmann's tone in this paper is similar to the rest of his work. Even the title, which includes the term "metapsychology", might almost warn a reader of the theoretical complexity of the paper. In the course of the paper, Hartmann references numerous figures who have written on schizophrenia, some of whom are psychoanalysts, and many who were not analysts. Piaget and Morris are cited, and some of Piaget's ideas are incorporated into Hartmann's hypothesis about the aetiology of schizophrenia. We can spend a reasonable amount of time on Hartmann's characteristic erudition, but what may be more notable in this essay is that he mentions two of the prominent Kleinians, who were considered by some Freudians as the enemy. Embedded in Klein's theory is a psychotic position (paranoid–schizoid position) and Hartmann mentions her work as part of the increasing number of childhood analysts who are interested in studying childhood psychoses. Rosenfeld and Klein are also mentioned, in terms of the self-destructiveness seen in schizophrenic patients. Both Klein (see Chapters Six and Eight) and Rosenfeld (1952) talk about the splitting of the ego as a result of self-destructive impulses. Hartmann's attempts to be inclusive are more a result of proper academic discipline rather than a powerful desire to integrate other psychoanalytic viewpoints with his ego psychological approach. Despite this, his knowledge of other viewpoints and his intellectual integrity lead him to be more inclusive than he may have fully acknowledged or realized.

Still, in discussing psychosis, Hartmann begins with Freud's distinction that, with neurotic patients, conflicts are seen as occurring intrapsychically between the ego and the id. In psychosis, the conflict is conceived of as occurring between the ego and reality. For Freud, the main factor in psychosis is the strength of the drives, while Hartmann gently but decisively moves the locus of difficulty to the ego as the mediator between the drives and reality. Hartmann particularly focuses on the aspects of the ego that are involved in what Freud called counter-cathexis, or defence. Hartmann, in making this point, reviews Nunberg's statement that loss of object libido destroys repressions and Freud's observation that schizophrenics show a greater reactivity to a variety of stress situations. While Hartmann seemingly accepts these statements, his focus on defence sharpens when he points out that schizophrenics use what he terms primitive defences. The defences that he describes as primitive, both he and Anna Freud posit as being intermittent or not consistently providing a constant counter-cathexis. Put in other terms, repression is a defence that, when working efficiently, is constantly providing a defensive function; primitive defences are utilized intermittently and in response to an external situation that is perceived to be dangerous. For example, projection is a defence that locates an anxiety-provoking idea in another person or situation. A projected idea is too anxiety provoking to be contained internally, and so it is perceived as an external threat or fear. In Freud's first dramatic use of projection, he saw Schreber (Freud, 1911c) as projecting his homosexual ideas on to other figures whom he then feared would rape him and turn him into a woman. What Hartmann terms primitive defences usually alter a person's ability to reality test. This constitutes a severe difficulty, particularly if these defences are a person's primary defences.

For Hartmann, the type of defensive processes employed by schizophrenics is crucial to his understanding of the onset and continuation of the schizophrenic process. His views on defence are intertwined with the concept of neutralization and his stance on the role of aggression in defence. His views on neutralization, while deriving from Freud's view of sublimation, differ in several important ways. Freud thought of Eros, or sexuality, as providing the impetus for sublimation, while Hartmann sees either the sexual or aggressive drives as being able to be neutralized. In Freud's conceptualization of sublimation, the drive was converted and controlled by the ego; the drive is thought of as providing the impetus for a given activity. Thus, although the sexual drive was transformed in sublimation, the activity was thought to be recognizable as a derivative of the drive. In Hartmann's conception of neutralization, the drive is totally converted and can be used by the ego (person) for any ego activity. There is little or no hint of the drive in the neutralized energy. One of the questions Hartmann poses in his view of schizophrenia is the extent to which the drives have been deneutralized during the onset of schizophrenia.

Freud's view stated that during the schizophrenic process there was a movement from object ties to a state of early narcissism. While Hartmann will utilize this view, his conceptualization features the role of aggression in understanding the aetiology of schizophrenia. It is the aggressive drive that fuels the process of defence and it is the breakdown of defensive processes that floods the schizophrenic with aggressive energy. Moreover, it is the early failure to convert the aggressive drive into neutralized energy that renders an individual susceptible to breakdown. Defence, in this hypothesis, is literally seen as a counter-cathexis and the counter aspect is seen as an aggressive or assertive activity by the ego to control or inhibit the expression of unconscious representations. (If one were to look at the logic of Hartmann's concepts, the idea of a counter-cathexis that has aggressive overtones is somewhat at odds with the idea of energy that is truly neutral.) Hartmann, in describing the interactions of people who are susceptible to breakdown, pictures a cycle of recurring aggression. He posits a person who both sees the world as full of aggression and who themselves behave in an aggressive manner (either overtly or covertly). This individual, seeing aggression surrounding him/her, increases his/her own aggressive tendencies and thereby increases the probability of an aggressive response from other individuals. This circular interaction is described by Hartmann on yet another level, as he asserts that this aggressive interaction has the effect of making internal structures (like the superego) harsher and more critical. The individual is then faced not only with external aggression, but internal aggression and self-punitive assaults. The superego in vulnerable individuals is seen as a structure that is inconsistent and harsh and punitive. Given that the person has not a fully developed superego structure, it is personified and replete with voices which are not appropriately de-personified or internalized as gently prohibitive or ideal structures. (When using the term "personified", it is easiest to think of a young child who, to control himself, has to picture his parents saying no in order to stop or inhibit a behaviour. De-personification is the concept of the child internalizing a value that gradually becomes his own without the person of the parent attached to the value.) Whether one wants to call what Hartmann is describing a superego or a precursor to superego development is a terminological question that we will not discuss. However, in describing schizophrenia, Hartmann reminds the reader that "Freud's hypothesis [was] that free aggression increases the proclivity for conflict". In the type of aggressive sequence that Hartmann describes, there is a high probability of aggression becoming de-neutralized, and this aggression "may be interiorized and absorbed by the superego" (1953, p. 198).

Clearly, what Hartmann is describing is not a temporary condition, but a long term tendency. Thus, the onset of schizophrenia depends either on a particular intense interaction or traumatic life event, or factors that he alludes to but does not describe (physiological or neurophysiological changes). The key factor, from Hartmann's perspective, is the de-neutralization of aggression that would occur in a susceptible individual following an incident that stirred aggressive responses. We can break into this cycle at a number of points, but if we start with an incident that stirs an aggressive response in a susceptible individual, we can say that this will lead to some freeing of aggressive energy (de-neutralization) which will increase the probability of an aggressive response from the individual and, in turn, increase the probability of an aggressive response from the environment (people in contact with the susceptible individual). This will, in turn, increase the internal aggressive energy, which may be taken up by the superego and lead to a high probability of the person facing internal and external aggression. Since the de-neutralization that occurs interferes with the more stable defences (repression, for example), the person will be much more likely to utilize or turn more towards what Hartmann terms primitive defences. These defences are what Anna Freud describes as ego restrictive defences (projection, denial, etc.).

Interestingly, some research has looked at Hartmann's hypothesis of the importance of aggression (Silverman, 1967) and shown that the subliminal introduction of an aggressive stimulus increases the severity of symptoms in a schizophrenic population. While this research is by no means definitive, it is an interesting derivation from Hartmann's theoretical views on schizophrenia. Part of the reason to look at this particular essay of Hartmann's is that he shows us how he uses some of his concepts, such as neutralization and the superego, with respect to this clinical entity. Moreover, he tells us about his assumptions about the role of genetic predispositions and neutralization with respect to vulnerability to schizophrenia. He tells us that "these countercarthectic structures, factors like postponement of discharge, but also what Freud called the 'protective barrier against stimuli' are probably among the genetic precursors of later defense mechanisms" (1953, p. 204). He cites Bergman and Escalona's (1949) study and their theoretical concept of a thin protective barrier in an infant who cannot adapt to a constant stimulus. They hypothesized, and eventually presented some data that indicated that a thin protective barrier was a factor in making some young children (and infants) overly sensitive to external stimuli. (Freud's view of the protective barrier involved the idea that the cortex provided a shield against intense stimuli. This prevented very intense stimuli from causing trauma. Escalona, who was a well-known researcher in psychoanalytic circles, used this concept and tried to show that some infants had a thin protective barrier. Her research, while illustrative, was never statistically convincing.) Hartmann assumes that to the extent that one manifests traits such as difficulties in postponing discharge or being extremely sensitive to external stimuli, this will effect the stability of defensive organization. Interestingly, he also provides what he calls an object relations hypothesis with respect to the development of defensive organization.

> I said before that full object relations . . . presuppose, as on contribution from the ego, some degree of neutralization of libidinal as well as aggressive energy which secures constancy of the objects independent of the need situation. [1953, p. 199]

Thus, the mother must be available in a consistent manner across the infant's states and, in particular, must be perceived by the infant as comforting when the infant is not inundated by an extreme state (crying, hunger, pain, etc.). It is his view that the mother will not be easily perceived as a separate object unless the infant can view her in quiet times as well as during times of strong need. The mother, in this formulation, helps the infant begin the neutralization process and helps to make energy available for defence and other ego functions.

Some basic issues and concepts

Before going into concepts that we have not yet covered, it is important to note that, in Hartmann's view of neutralization, he specifically rejects the concept of Thanatos, or the death instinct. Freud thought that the death instinct was brought under control when it fused with Eros (the life, or sexual, instinct). Hartmann rejected the theory of Eros and Thanatos and, instead, substituted sex and aggression in his dual drive theory. He also maintained that fusion of drives was not necessary for the transformation of aggression. Hartmann, Kris, and Lowenstein (1949) assert that not only can the sexual drive be transformed (desexualized), but the aggressive drive can be transformed (deaggressivized). Both of these processes were conceived of as neutralization. Thus, the aggressive drive not only supplanted Thanatos, but it was seen as undergoing transformations that were not present in Freudian theory.

"The average expectable environment" is a phrase from Hartmann that, for a time, was widely quoted and taken as an important condition for normal development. If the average expectable environment is present, one would anticipate normal maturational and developmental growth. In comparing Winnicott's concept of the good enough mother with Hartmann's concept of the average expectable environment, Greenberg and Mitchell state that, for Hartmann, "The emphasis is placed not on a particular quality of responsiveness from the parents, but on characteristics that are innate in man's psychological (and biological) endowment" (1983, p. 249). Winnicott's view of the mother and her providing a "facilitating environment" is specifically "human", while Hartmann's average expectable environment "is a generally biological concept" (*ibid.*, p. 250).

If we compare these quotes with Hartmann's views on the aetiology and onset of schizophrenia, they are somewhat different than one would expect from a biological theorist. One must remember that, in virtually every era (including the present one), schizophrenia has been conceived of as a disorder with strong biological and genetic roots. Hartmann acknowledges this, but, in his essay, his prime concern is, interestingly, an aspect of the experience of the individual. In his view, they are flooded by aggressive ideation (I am for a moment moving away from the energic language of Hartmann). On an interpersonal level, the person is experiencing the world as a dangerous place full of aggression. They have not internalized identifications that are helpful guidelines for the do's and don'ts of the world (in other terms, a stable superego structure). Rather, they have internalized harsh images that are accusatory, punishing, and at times are experienced as threatening the person's existence. This adds to the person's perception of aggression surrounding them, internally and externally. The cycle of aggression that Hartmann posits is one that Kleinians would explain in terms of projective identification. The person projects his aggression into the world and the world returns his aggression, and he then represents the world as an aggressive, life-threatening place. The environment for adult schizophrenics is created by a horrifying internal world that is threatening and terrifying. This world, according to Hartmann, was created by several interdigitating factors. However, before we recount his view of early development, we should note that the onset of schizophrenia is generally noted by either a precipitous shift in environmental conditions or an extreme biological shift, such as the onset of adolescence.

Hartmann's views on the causative factors in schizophrenia blend concepts such as the protective barrier and object relations. If we put this in Winnicottian terms, we can say that it is hard to be a good enough mother to an infant that feels easily threatened, or, at least, disrupted by stimulation that most other infants find acceptable or even pleasurable. Good enough mothering would require an auxiliary ego that provides the infant with more than usual protection. The mother would have to gird herself to the experience that some of what she provides might be felt as aversive by the infant. Her response to this rejection has to be supportive rather than be experienced as a rejection by her infant. Thus, the mother of this type of infant has to be resilient and able withstand what many mothers might experience as an injury (it is hard to feel that what I am providing as a parent is being rejected). Hartmann sees the infant as needing a consistent mother throughout the day, not only at times of need. We need to remember that times of quiet wakefulness are extremely important in this conceptualization. The mother must be perceived during periods where the infant is not besieged by either internal or external stimulation. If this does not happen, then the infant's beginning ability to form internal regulatory channels or controls, defences being one type of internal control, will be impaired. Here, I am maintaining that even in a syndrome like schizophrenia, Hartmann has a strong object relations perspective. Part of the difficulty in reading Hartmann is that he is encased in a language of energies. This is why I have deliberately stated some of his concepts in this paragraph without reference to Freudian, or, rather, Hartmannian psychoanalytic language. To return to Greenberg and Mitchell, they state that Hartmann "holds at birth the most essential part of the new environment is the infant's mother" (1983, p. 251). However, in their view, the mother, for Hartmann, is only important in terms of her controlling "the physical properties of the environment" (*ibid.*). Contrary to this characterization is Hartmann's view that one of the aspects of good enough mothering is how the infant is tended at times when there is no strong need state. I have restated Hartmann's views on schizophrenia to show that his concepts can be utilized with or without reference to biology or the energic language that he uses.

Unfortunately, most of Hartmann's writings have little to do with the type of specificity I have outlined from the "Meta-psychology of schizophrenia". Usually, Hartmann is trying subtly to move the Freudian opus in directions that he thinks will provide psychoanalysis with the concepts that will make it a general psychology. Hartmann, like Greenberg and Mitchell, question Freud's theoretical ideas about the development of the reality principle. They assert that Freud posited that the developing of the reality principle delays immediate pleasures so that more lasting pleasures can be obtained. Greenberg and Mitchell conclude that, for Freud, "Reality remains outside the pleasure sequence ... [and] Object relations a fortiori remain at the periphery of the theory of motivation" (*ibid.*, p. 252). Hartmann is more circumspect, and makes a distinction between ontogenetic and phylogenetic considerations in viewing his version of Freud's concepts.

Freud assumed, as do the ethologists, that in animals there are instincts that ensure that the animal adapts to its environment, or help the animal to do so. Although this assumption was similar, Freud's view of instinct is different than the view of ethologists, who see instincts as either fixed action patterns or derivatives of fixed action patterns. Freud assumed that reality came from the pleasure attendant on dealing with reality. Thus, the shift from the pleasure principle to the reality principle was based on the accrual of pleasure from reality. Hartmann posited that there were no instinctual drives in humans that guarantee adaptation. For Hartmann it is the ego (and principles of regulation) that has survival value. He reasoned that "the reality principle ... would historically precede and hierarchically outrank the pleasure principle" (1958, p. 44). Hartmann's theory changes the Freudian notion of the development of reality testing. In addition the importance of the pleasure–unpleasure sequence is diminished in Hartmann's conceptualizations. Since Hartmann viewed the reality principle as preceding the pleasure principle, logically, Freud's view of primary process would then also have to be altered. At the very least, primary process no longer could be seen as primary in the sense of coming first developmentally. This could, in fact, help with a logical conundrum in what I have called Freud's third psychoanalytic theory (see "Commentary" on Chapter Three). The reality principle preceding the pleasure principle is, for Hartmann, one way of emphasizing the role of adaptation in human development. It is crucial for the survival of the infant to be able to respond in some way to its mothering parent in order to survive. Hartmann, in this way, saw mothering as providing the stimulus conditions that he called the average expectable environment.

A concept seemingly as popular as the average expectable environment was Hartmann's concept of ego autonomy. Ego autonomy might be considered to be a mirror image concept of Freud's view of the ego. Hartmann's ego is initially seen as possessing energy of its own and is the structure that implements the reality principle. Thus, not only is there initial ego autonomy, but the first or overriding principle of the mind (reality principle) is initiated by the ego. Autonomy of the ego is not simply an early development, but, rather, mental health is in part seen as dependent on ego autonomy. Hartmann's ideas were supported and strengthened by Rapaport (1967), who posited that a normal (or ideal) ego is governed by neither the drives nor reality. Bergmann (2000) notes that Sandler adds that a healthy ego gains autonomy from the superego. This view is one that will be contested by a number of analysts, but, for a period of time, it was considered a powerful criterion of mental health. Whether this was merely a conceptual sign of health or one that analysts truly relied on is open to debate. Whatever one's perspective, there is no question that the concept of ego autonomy is a far cry from Freud's ideas in *The Ego and the Id*. Freud's ego is pictured as a rider on a mount that is difficult to control (compromised and controlled by either or both the id and superego). While Freud was hoping for some relief for the weary neurotic, Hartmann and the ego psychologists were looking for much more control over one's internal and external environments. This is most clearly seen in the concept of secondary autonomy. Hartmann assumed that conflicted areas of the ego can become autonomous as a result of good developmental conditions or, alternatively, through psychoanalytic treatment. These factors in the development of secondary autonomy were termed changes in function, and, as such, were not seen as aspects of the ego that had to be or should be analysed. This concept of secondary autonomy was one that, in principle, restricted analytic technique to those areas of the ego that were in conflict. It was thought that these areas of the ego were discernible to the analyst and were not areas that needed analytic intervention.

Brief summary and comparison to Freud

If we briefly review some of the concepts that Hartmann and his colleagues Kris and Lowenstein (1945, 1946, 1949, 1962) have put forth, we can see that Freudian theory is distinctly altered by the new ego psychology. The ego is seen as having a reasonable amount of autonomy that occurs due to both innate factors and later transformations. One of the transformations that can occur is the neutralization of instinctual energy. Hartmann rejects Freud's instinct theory and, instead, substitutes sex and aggression for Eros and Thanatos. Aggression, as well as sex, can be transformed into neutralized energy. This type of energy provides the ego with autonomy in the sense that neutralized energy is no longer tied to its instinctual roots. The new instinct theory also has a new distinct role for aggression. Aggression is converted to provide the ego with energy for defensive functions. Neutralized energy can be utilized by the ego as well as the superego. To the extent that the superego uses neutralized energy, it is less punitive and more well-integrated into ego functioning. The autonomy of the ego is crucial to Hartmann's concern with the concept of adaptation. Adaptation is the crucial concern, since Hartmann attempts to link psychoanalysis with evolutionary biology.

Adaptation is the key concept of ego psychology, and it logically forces Hartmann to implicitly reject Freud's concept of primary process. Hartmann still sees a process such as Freud's primary process as a type of thought that is present in the unconscious and characteristic of one aspect of human thought processes. However, primary process is not primary chronologically, secondary process, or reality testing, is the initial form of thought that human infants begin with in their first interactions with the environment. This shift in Hartmann's theorizing is virtually ignored by both latter-day classical analysts and other critics of Hartmann. Clinically, Anna Freud's emphasis on the ego in the psychoanalytic setting is seconded by Hartmann, who recommends that ego functions be examined as thoroughly as psycho-sexual fixation points. Since adaptation is a key principle of Hartmann's psychoanalytic theory in so far as the ego's autonomy is compromised by conflict, it is the goal of a successful psychoanalysis to restore (or, in some cases, create) this autonomy. Thus, one can judge the severity of conflict by the number and the extent of ego functions that are impaired. This presumes knowledge, or at least a theory, of normal or ideal ego or cognitive functioning. Rapaport (1959) attempted in various ways to provide this type of theorizing. In a less publicized way, he attempted to provide a learning theory for psychoanalysis that, while ingenuous, caught the attention of very few analysts or learning theorists (Schwartz & Schiller, 1970). For Hartmann and other ego psychologists, there is also a hierarchy of ego functions, with the synthetic or integrative ego functions being considered one of the most important. Ego functions are conceived of as interacting with the environment and, since adaptation is a, or even the, key concept of ego psychology, the interaction with the environment takes on new significance in ego psychology.

Freud's emphasis was always on the child's or adult's internal world. He attempted to provide a theoretical diagram of the dynamic interactions among different aspects of a person's mind. At various points, he reminds the reader that he is assuming a certain type of environment, but he rarely tries to describe this environment. Hartmann changes this emphasis and, although he writes in a heavy psychoanalytic accent, Hartmann is almost always concerned with how different environments affect processes of internalization. Even though interactions with the environment are crucial, it is a goal of good development or of analytic treatment for the individual to achieve autonomy from both internal conflict and external conditions. One might see it as Hartmann's compromise with Freud, where he says, in effect, yes we must pay attention to the environment in every circumstance but if we develop well (or are well enough analysed) we can develop autonomy from our environment. Future analysts will sharply criticize the goal of, or the possibility of, this type of ego autonomy.

Superego development, for Hartmann, is similar to Freud's final views on the superego. The superego is the only structure in the tripartite configuration that is a result of development. Both the ego and the id are present at birth, and the ego may develop but it is not a structure that comes into existence as a result of developmental events. The superego comes into being as a result of the passing of the Oedipus complex. It is a product of a resolution of Oedipal conflicts. It is the main agency for initiating defences against incestuous–libidinal or aggressive wishes. Thus, the desire to possess one's mother (or father) and to destroy your Oedipal rival is defended against by the superego motivating ego defences. Living up to one's moral ideals is also a function of the superego, and the development of these ideals allows the person to be independent of the fluctuating standards of the culture. This is not meant to imply that the ideals are immutable, but, rather, ideals, in so far as they are internalized in a coherent superego structure, are relatively impervious to change. One can see that an autonomous ego and a well-integrated superego render the person a good deal of autonomy from both internal and external conflict. This model implies that a well-integrated person is a relatively stable organism with relatively little variation in functioning.

Although autonomous ego functioning was accepted as at least a possibility, there were a number of differentiations that Hartmann era analysts struggled with that have not been well integrated into any contemporary theory. As an example, Hartmann attempted to differentiate the ego from the idea of the self as a structure. Here, there was an attempt to clear up confusions that continued from the different eras of Freudian theory. In what I have termed Freud's third era (Chapter Three), the ego referred to the person and to the person's sense of self. The ego, during this era, was also a self structure that Freud used to describe as one of his polarities, self and object (1915c). Clearly, if the ego is the opposite of an object, the ego in this translation means self. However, is the self considered to be the entire person, an internal structure, a representation of oneself, or is it a momentary feeling state? Freud's rough usage seemed to include aspects of all of the above and, when he began to describe the ego as a structure, he still at times used ego as a term designating self or self-representations. Hartmann, as well as Jacobson (1964), attempted clearly to use the term self as a term meaning a representation which could be in the ego or the id. It could be split and be a representation in both structures, or there could be a double representation (see Chapter Three). Jacobson included in her array of self-concepts grandiose self and idealized self-representations, which were earlier forms of a wished for self-image. These terms all were distinguished from both ego ideal (reserved for moral ideals) and the self-representation. While Jacobson's views are of interest, these distinctions have never been fully explicated.

In a further attempt to clarify Freudian concepts, Hartmann replaced Freud's concept of autoerotism (or primary narcissism, see Chapter Three) with what he termed an early undifferentiated phase of development. This was done to focus on what Jacobson conceptualized as the development of the self as an independent entity. Thus, at the beginning of life, there is an idea of fusion between self and object and the further developmental sequence is, in part, characterized by the differentiation of self and object. Thus, Jacobson's concept of the grandiose self and the idealized self-representations mark developmental steps in the self–object differentiation process. Jacobson's views were developed earlier (in German editions) than 1964, but were fully published in English in that year. Mahler's views of separation and individuation (Mahler, Pine, & Bergmann, 1975) were strongly influenced by both Hartmann and Jacobson. Both Mahler and Jacobson were strongly identified as ego psychologists, but, clearly, Jacobson's views were concurrently influenced by Winnicott and some of the British Independents (see Winnicott, Chapter Ten).

The present chapter on Hartmann was begun by a memorial quote from Arlow, who stated that "For more than two decades Hartmann was without question the outstanding theoretician of psychoanalysis and its leading intellectual figure". Arlow was both part of the Hartmann era and helped to create a new era; he died almost thirty years after Hartmann. One could say that, for a period of time, American psychoanalysis was characterized as being the Arlow and Brenner era. Arlow and Brenner (1964), together and in separate contributions, maintained that almost all mental life has an element of conflict. (In a previous publication [Ellman, 1991], I characterized Brenner's contributions and wrote that he viewed almost all mental phenomena as a product of compromise formation. He wrote back to me, and made only one correction: he crossed out "almost".) Arlow and Brenner, whose influence is still felt, were part of the group that subtly led to the passing of Hartmann's influence. To put this view into a historical perspective, let me take one author's view of three different models "of the genetic relationship between ego and id" (Bergmann, 2000, p. 24).

The first model is Freud's, where Freud saw the ego emerging from the id in order to realistically gain pleasure from and interact with reality (see Chapter Four). The second model is Melanie Klein's, where the ego is present from birth and "operates primarily by use of projection and introjection" (see Chapters Six, Seven, and Eight). Bergmann states that, for Klein, "The main function of the ego is defending against annihilation anxiety" (2000, p. 24). While this is Bergmann's perspective on Klein, see Chapters Six and Eight to explicate what one might mean by annihilation anxiety within Klein's theoretical matrix. Hartmann's model proposes that there are independent ego energies from birth, but the ego as a structure develops out of an undifferentiated matrix. Without a lengthy comparison at this time we can say that Hartmann's model is the only one where conflict is not ubiquitous and where there are areas of functioning that are completely conflict free. Bergmann calls it "the most optimistic of the three", and certainly it is the model that allows for the possibility of development without trauma or near trauma assumed as a normal concomitant of development. Clearly, in Freud's model, there is conflict with the introduction of each new stage of development. This is certainly the case in Kleinian theory, and so, of the three, Hartmann stands alone, although some contemporary models have similar assumptions.

If we try to place Arlow and Brenner on a continuum of optimism or pessimism, clearly they are closer to the Freud–Klein axis. Arlow and Brenner's model(s) (Brenner has put forth several models since Hartmann's death [Brenner, 1994, 1995]) view conflict as a necessary component of all mental life. The concept of a conflict-free zone in the ego (or anywhere) is, at the very least, implicitly rejected and there is a return to an aspect of Freud's conflict model. It is the conflict model from the structural era, and it is based on oedipal dynamics. There is also a return to a muted form of what some people have termed Freud's pessimism, since, in their models, conflict is not abolished or completely transformed during treatment, but, rather, handled in a different, less conflicted manner. Although one may take this as only a minor aspect of Hartmann's theorizing, in fact these changes tilt psychoanalytic concepts away from a theory that focuses on adaptation. The change in this focus also presages the movement away from large theoretical models to an increased interest in developing statements about clinical process. This also rejects the idea of psychoanalysis as a general theory, which was at the centre of Hartmann's ambitions for psychoanalytic theory. One can say that the advent of Arlow and Brenner's structural model signalled the end of the Hartmann era.

Some brief comments about psychoanalytic technique

Hartmann wrote relatively little about psychoanalytic technique and the writing he did do attempted to co-ordinate clinical concepts with his theoretical writing. Since Hartmann, Kris, and Loewenstein were such close collaborators, when Kris or Loewenstein wrote a clinical paper it was implicitly taken as a view of the triumvirate. Both Kris (1951) and Loewenstein (1951) wrote papers on the issue of interpretation in psychoanalytic therapy. In many ways, the two papers were twin examples of how the theory of ego psychology could influence the psychoanalytic situation. Not surprisingly, Kris gives an example from Anna Freud:

> To clarify issues, I cite first a simplified version of an incident in the analysis of a six-year-old boy reported by Anna Freud. The visit to the dentist had been painful. During his analytic interview the little boy displayed a significant set of symptomatic actions related to this experience. He damaged or destroyed various objects belonging to the analyst, and finally repeatedly broke off the points and resharpened a set of pencils. How is this type of behavior to be interpreted?
>
> The interpretation may point to retaliatory castration, may stress the turning of a passive experience into an active one, or may demonstrate that the little boy was identifying himself with the dentist and his aggression. All three interpretations can naturally be related to the anxiety which he had experienced. The choice between the delivery of these or other possible interpretations will clearly depend on the phase of the analysis. The first interpretation, an "id interpretation", is directly aimed at the castration complex. The second and the third aim at mechanisms of defense. The second emphasizes that passivity is difficult to bear and that in assuming an active role, danger is being mastered. The third interpretation

implements the second by pointing out that identification can serve as a mechanism of defense. It might well prove to be a very general mechanism in the little boy's life. It may influence him not only to react aggressively, but to achieve many goals, and may be the motivation of many aspects of his behavior. The interpretation that stresses the mechanism of identification is, therefore, not only the broadest, but it may also open up the largest number of new avenues, and be the one interpretation which the little boy can most easily apply in his self-observation. He might learn to experience certain of his own reactions as "not belonging" (i.e., as symptoms) and thus be led an important step on the way toward readiness for further psychoanalytic work. [Kris, 1951, p. 19]

In this example, Kris clearly states that all three interpretive efforts are important, but the most important, wide reaching, and potentially effective interpretative effort would be the one that interprets the boy's identification. Here, we can see that Kris's goal is to provide an interpretative effort that influences an activity that will probably involve the widest array of ego activities. It can also be tied to unconscious and strictly defensive elements, since most identifications involve both defensive and unconscious fantasy elements. The goal is not simply, or even mostly, to understand unconscious fantasy, but to realign ego functions and free ego functions to provide wider conflict-free sphere(s) in the ego. Although this goal is not explicitly stated in other cases (Kris, 1951) the role of the ego is posited to be decisive and an analysis of unconscious conflict is not sufficient to provide curative elements. Bergmann (2000) states that the Hartmann, Kris, and Loewenstein emphasis on ego functions and on the timing of interpretations should be "read as a polemic against the Kleinians" (p. 27). While, clearly, Kris (1951) and Loewenstein (1951) advocate views that are gradual and require affective attunement, it is hard to see this logically as more of a polemic against Kleinian ideas than Freudian concepts or interpersonalist ideas of the time. Moreover, as we will see, their ideas of treatment are quite different from Brenner's concepts, which are also called ego psychological, or structural. We will return to these ideas later, in the contemporary section of this volume, when we try to include some of these concepts in a contemporary version of psychoanalytic treatment. For now, we will briefly focus on one more element of Kris's views.

A relevant problem in technique consists in establishing the best way of communicating the full set of meanings to the patient. The attempt to restrict the interpretation to the id aspect only represents the older procedure, the one which we believe has on the whole been modified by the change of which we speak. To restrict interpretation to the defense mechanism only may be justifiable by the assumption that the patient is not yet ready—a valuable piece of caution, though it seems that there is a tendency among some analysts to exaggerate such caution at times. [1951, pp. 20–21]

Here, one can see that if Kris is providing an implicit polemic against Kleinian ideas, he is also stipulating an explicit objection to what he considers to be the older, Freudian position. He explicitly argues against interpreting only the id, or unconscious element. He then speaks of the idea of only interpreting the defensive elements, and subtly says that, while caution may be necessary at times, he views analysts who espouse this type of technique as being overly cautious. Here, he is quietly arguing against a view of technique that is derived from Anna Freud. This view is put forth in the contemporary literature by Gray (1994) and Busch (1995, 2006). Interestingly, while Kris and Loewenstein are presenting new versions of psychoanalytic technique, they still emphasize an element that is present in what they have termed the older procedure. Interpretation has a central role in their view of technique, and Loewenstein states, "As a matter of fact, the strengthening of the conflictless sphere of the ego is mainly brought about by interpretation" (1951, p. 2, fn). The centrality of interpretation is one clear link between the technique of Freud and the procedure of the ego psychologists.

Commentary

Both Anna Freud and Hartmann, while certainly part of the classical tradition, should be distinguished from the American classical analysts. Although Hartmann never explicitly differentiated himself from the more contemporary classical analysts, clearly, his emphasis on adaptation should lead to a different type of analytic technique than is normally associated with classical technique. It has led me to advocate that one should not interpret the transference until there is an understanding of the adaptive aspects of a conflict. This means that I wait until I can understand and feel why, for the patient, a particular conflicted pathway was the best alternative available at a certain point in their development. Indeed, it frequently may have been experienced (consciously or unconsciously) as the only alternative available. I specifically focused on Hartmann's essay on schizophrenia to try to show that at times he had early developmental conceptualizations that went beyond the idea of conflicts forming in the Oedipal period. Hartmann, like Anna Freud, took seriously the idea of starting from the surface of the mind, but it is Anna Freud who began the idea of systematic defence analysis.

Paul Gray, a wonderfully kind analyst, followed Anna Freud and conceptualized a different way of attending to the patient's verbalizations. He maintained that often the analyst listens to drive derivatives and does not fully capture the patient's attempts to keep drive elements from consciousness. His systematic attention to the detail of the "functioning ego" enables him to help the patient at another time to voluntarily overcome defensive pressures. Gray has, by and large, limited his work to the analysis of neurotic patients, and so, in his examples, he seems to have naturally engendered trust in his patients. Although he does not attempt to detail what one means by an empathic attitude in the analytic situation, listening to his presentations gives one the feeling that this attitude comes as a natural response by this caring analyst. In many ways, his technique does seem limited to those patients who can develop the capacity for self-observation relatively quickly.

Marianne Goldberger is an analyst who has systematically enlarged and clarified (even further) Gray's concept of close process attention. She is concerned, as was Gray, with how the analyst listens, but she is also quite specific about the role of interpretation in the analytic situation. As was true of Gray, Goldberger attempts, in her interventions, to enlarge the patient's self-observational capacities. She is interested, as are a number of her colleagues (Goldberger, 1995), in developing the analysand's self-analytic abilities. A reasonable inference from Sandell's research is that this type of capacity is important in allowing the results of analysis to continue after the treatment had ended (Sandell et al., 2000). Here, again, we see a continuation of ego psychology applied to the elucidation of psychoanalytic processes and technique.

Fred Busch, however, in his recent work (2006, 2007), is starting to show how defence analysis can have a wider scope and include, or be included in, self-psychological theories and techniques. He is also maintaining that concepts such as transitional space and a certain type of mirroring are not in conflict with the type of defence analysis that Gray has advocated. Busch has suggested that, at times, with at least moderately severe character disorders, some form of mirroring goes on before defence analysis can be fully operative. In the last section of the book, I try to show how this is usually true, even in less disrupted patients. It is simply that trust develops more rapidly with patients with less severe conflicts. I mention Busch and Gray to try to show that the tradition of ego psychology is certainly not moribund; it has simply and naturally been gradually transformed and has begun to meld with other traditions.

CHAPTER SIX

The Kleinian revolution

Summary

This chapter covers Klein's contributions from 1921–1945. From the beginning of her career, fantasy (spelled phantasy by Kleinians) was of extraordinary importance. Tolerating and utilizing phantasy is considered to be a crucial aspect of childhood. It was Klein's view that our educational systems and parental patterns caused children to defend against their phantasy life, which, if appropriately sublimated, would be a main source of creativity. Klein initially felt that she derived this view from Freud. During the period of the present chapter, she begins as an enthusiastic Freudian writer and ends this period as a devoted Kleinian. By 1928, although Klein introduces her new concepts as deriving from Freud, she has already introduced a variety of new thoughts and the beginnings of various extensions, modifications, and new pathways for psychoanalytic theory. She places (Klein, 1928) both Oedipal dynamics and superego development as occurrences within the oral stage. This shift in perspective was in part a result of her analysis of young children. Her new view of development led her to first posit Oedipal dynamics and a superego structure as beginning to appear by the end of the first year of life. In this paper, Klein introduces splitting and projective–introjective sequences as central to her new concepts.

She maintains that superego identifications are often contradictory in nature, and exist side by side without being integrated. She also shifts the centre of development to mother–infant interactions that Freud had implied, but she makes central in her developmental concepts. Each of Freud's Oedipal concepts are mentioned and, at least in some way, reconceptualized. Klein, at this point, introduces the idea of the Oedipal stage and superego occurring during each psycho-sexual stage throughout the developmental cycle. Perhaps her most important papers appear at the end of this period, when she writes two papers on aspects of depression and introduces the concept of the depressive position. During this period and throughout her career, she is one of the analysts who accepts and develops Freud's concepts of Eros and Thanatos.

Biographical note

Melanie Klein grew up in Vienna in an Orthodox Jewish home. Her maiden name was Melanie Reizes and she was the youngest of four children. Her father's original ambition was to become a Rabbi, but, at the age of thirty-seven, he instead began a medical career. He was fifty when Melanie was born, and she, his youngest child, admired him for his scientific bent and his independent spirit (Bion, Rosenfeld, & Segal, 1961). She very much wanted to follow her father's scientific career and become a doctor. Two of Klein's siblings died either in their early childhood (her sister Sidonie at the age of nine) or young adulthood (her brother Emmanuel at the age of twenty-five). Both of these siblings were seemingly talented, and her sister spent some time teaching Melanie rudimentary academic skills. By the time Melanie was twenty-one she was married to Arthur Klein, a chemical engineer. After several years the Kleins settled in Budapest, where Klein read some of Freud's papers and began an analysis with Sandor Ferenczi. Her analysis continued during the First World War, and she claimed to have begun her career in "a Budapest polyclinic under the direction of her former analyst, Ferenczi" (Petot, 1990, p. 3). Petot maintains that this could not have happened in the way that Klein describes, but in any case it is clear that Klein had a close relationship with Ferenczi, who was an analyst devoted to Freud and psychoanalysis. Ferenczi was a creative analyst who strongly influenced Freudian thought. Klein heard Freud speak at the Hungarian Academy of Science and was "certainly enraptured" by psychoanalysis during the psychoanalytic congress where Freud spoke.

In 1919, Klein presented her first paper that was based on the observation of a child's development during a period in which his mother was giving him explanations to satisfy his sexual curiosity. The child had expressed his curiosity through numerous questions and non-verbal enquiries. This child was Erich, Klein's second son, who was five at the time she read the paper. She continued her observations, and gradually the observations transformed into a child analysis. This analysis continued until 1922, and took place in both Hungary and Berlin, where Klein moved in 1921. Her move to Berlin signalled the end of her marriage. Her husband migrated to Sweden during the same time period, and soon after these moves the marriage ended in divorce. In Berlin, Ms Klein came into contact with Karl Abraham, and she entered analysis with Abraham in 1924. Abraham, who is one of the pioneers of psychoanalysis, was elected President of the International Psychoanalytic Association in the same year. More importantly, during this time period, Klein, in her second child analysis, solidified the idea of child analysis, and that with a technique that is used by child practitioners from a variety of orientations (psychoanalytic and non-psychoanalytic). With Rita, her second case (after Erich), she more formally instituted the play technique, which Petot calls "the foundation of all her subsequent discoveries" (1990, p. 10). Whether this is a reasonable assessment is impossible to tell, but it is the case that analysts strongly think that the technique that is used is a powerful determinant of the theory that is developed. Brenner relates that what made the advance of psychoanalysis possible "was the combination of the psychoanalytic method and the psychoanalytic situation" (1982, p. 1). Clearly, Petot and others see the play technique as revolutionizing the treatment of children and providing a new theoretical view of early development. It was initially Klein's views on child analysis that brought her into conflict with Anna Freud. Klein maintained that children were capable of transference reactions and of maintaining a transference neurosis, while Anna Freud's views were quite different concerning the treatment of young children.

After Abraham's untimely death (in 1926), Klein moved to London at the behest of Jones and Strachey, who were both prominent members of the international psychoanalytic movement. The rise of Klein's influence in London brought her into increasing conflict with Anna Freud, and this conflict intensified when Sigmund and Anna Freud left Vienna and moved to London in 1938. When the Freuds arrived in London, Klein was an established and controversial figure in the British Psychoanalytic Association. When Anna Freud became active in London, the now famous controversial discussions began.

These discussions (King & Steiner, 1991) were attempts to delineate the boundaries of psychoanalysis. In the reading of these discussions, they seem to be a combination of exciting intellectual exchanges, political and legalistic disputes, and, at times, a type of inquisition. The Kleinians clearly felt that they were fighting for their psychoanalytic lives. The life of a vibrant organization, the British Psychoanalytic Association, may have hung in the balance. We will not discuss extensively the political aspects of these discussions; however, the content of these discussions will be looked at in some detail (see Chapter Seven), for they are good indicators of how one's interpretation of Freud can be used as a diagnostic test to determine one's theoretical proclivities.

Klein survived the discussions, and a rupture in the British Society developed and was repaired. The repair involved a separate but equal treatment of the theoretical positions. Three groups were established, a Kleinian, Freudian, and a middle, or independent, group. A candidate (student in training) had to choose a group on beginning their training. Although there is cross talk between the groups, one's theoretical and clinical orientation is frequently established by the choice that was made at the beginning of training. Whether these controversies strongly affected Klein's later views will not be discussed, but her most enduring theoretical and clinical contributions were made after the controversies. However, one might say, as Petot does, that it was not until

> after 1932, having finished exploring the early phase of the Oedipus complex, that she shifted her basic intuitions, freed herself from the

influence of Ferenczi and Abraham, and developed her most original conceptions, which for richness and fertility can be compared only with those of Freud. [Petot, 1991, p. ix]

We will look at Klein's concepts in chronological order, and this will allow us to see how these concepts developed and changed. At times we will not note the first use of a term if the term was more fully explicated in later writings.

Introductory or early Kleinian concepts

However one credits the play technique, observations from child analysis were crucial in Klein's ideas about early development. If one were to do an intellectual history of Klein, it would be interesting to know which of Freud's papers were read by her and in what order. Clearly, by 1921, Klein had become an extreme Freudian, wanting to put into place the inferences that she drew from Freud's writings. Her desire was to change the way children were educated, and here the word educated is used in the broadest sense of the term. It was her view that freeing unconscious phantasy material is necessary to allow children access to their creative impulses. She viewed educational practices as stifling and saw rote learning as destroying the child's innate ability for creative ways to view the world. Her comment that "every state of diminished intellectual achievement was a sign of unconscious suffering and the result of repression" (Petot, 1990, p. 45) was a notable statement of how strongly she thought that unconscious conflict was a primary inhibitor of intellectual functioning.

In Klein's first published paper ("The development of a child", 1975), one can see the application of Freudian concepts in the treatment of a child. Initially, the interaction between Klein and Erich was not so much a treatment as an educative experience that was transformed into an early form of child analysis. It was not until the treatment of Rita (in 1923) that Klein's views on interpretation began to take more complete form. She relates,

> My patient Rita, who was two years and nine months old at the beginning of analysis, was a very difficult child to bring up . . . She showed marked obsessional features which had been increasing for

some time, and she insisted on elaborate obsessional ceremonials.
[1945, p. 397]

Klein notes that Rita initially "was particularly afraid of something which I might do to her when I was alone in the room with her" (1955, p. 124). This anxiety or fear is quickly interpreted by Klein. Petot comments that Klein's initial principles of interpretation stipulate that "anxiety which manifests itself in the negative transference" should be quickly interpreted. Klein includes the idea of interpreting both the positive and negative elements of the Oedipus complex, but, in her formulation, "it is the aggressive not the libidinal impulse that gives rise to anxiety" (Petot, 1990, p. 135). It is as if Klein is already beginning to recognize the importance of Thanatos (the death instinct, or destructive drive). Klein, of course, will become the major theorist who embraces Freud's later drive theory. In her early analyses, Petot describes Klein as an extreme Freudian embracing and fully attempting to utilize his concepts (including both Erich and Rita; with Rita, Klein's new concepts are beginning to be conceptualized).

Klein and psycho-sexual stages

It is interesting to dwell on what I would regard as Klein's first major theoretical paper, where she clearly disturbs some of the Freudians of her time. She had already published at least seven papers and given several talks, but, in this paper, "The early stages of the Oedipal conflict" (1928), she reconceptualizes Oedipal and superego development. She writes,

> Ferenczi assumes that, connected with the urethral and anal impulses, there is a "kind of physiological forerunner of the superego", which he terms "sphincter-morality". According to Abraham, anxiety makes its appearance on the cannibalistic level, while the sense of guilt arises in the succeeding early anal–sadistic phase.
> [1928, pp. 186–187]

Her findings lead her to the idea that guilt and anxiety are the direct effect of early Oedipal conflicts. She goes on to say,

It does not seem clear why a child of, say, four years old should set up in his mind an unreal, phantastic image of parents who devour, cut and bite. But it is clear why in a child of about *one year* old the anxiety caused by the beginning of the Oedipus conflict takes the form of a dread of being devoured and destroyed. The superego becomes something which bites, devours and cuts. [*ibid.*, p. 187, original italics]

One of Klein's earliest controversial concepts is her placement of the Oedipal drama during the oral stage. This is certainly controversial, since it was only a few years earlier that Freud had placed the Oedipal stage firmly within the sphere of childhood sexuality. Klein not only places Oedipal dynamics at an earlier point in development, she also states that during each psycho-sexual stage the Oedipal drama reappears. Thus, there is an oral, anal, and phallic (or genital, as Klein renamed the phallic stage) version of Oedipal phenomena. The superego is also seen as being formed and reformed during each of these stages. In optimal development the superego gradually (across stages) becomes less punitive and more integrated into the child's mental life.

It is truly astonishing the number of concepts that are stated and implied in only a few paragraphs of the first two pages of this essay. Klein changes when the Oedipus complex occurs and places the superego as part of the Oedipal drama. She also makes one of the first clinical statements about the nature of splitting as a defence. She tells us that the "analysis of children reveals the structure of the superego as built up of identifications dating from very different periods and contradictory in nature, excessive goodness and excessive severity existing side by side (*ibid.*). Since the superego, from Klein's perspective, arises when oral and anal sadistic tendencies are at their height, the child's sense of guilt about these sadistic tendencies can be overwhelming. She invokes another defence, repression, which must be present early in development to protect the child's "feeble ego". To restate briefly, Klein maintains that both the Oedipal triangle and superego are present by the beginning of the second year of life. Both guilt and anxiety are present, and the child or infant clearly internalizes objects in all of their mental structures (ego, superego, and id). She has already begun to describe the importance of splitting and, at the very least, made

Freudian concepts live in the child's mind in a way that not even the creator of psychoanalysis envisioned.

One might think that, with this introduction, Klein might spend the rest of this paper explicating these concepts. However, after she reminds us that in the oral stages the superego becomes something that bites, she goes on to explain her view of the epistemophilic tendency in children. Due to this impulse, the child wishes to know (Klein does not explain where this impulse comes from or, alternatively, how it is derived), but the "early feeling of not knowing . . . unites with the feeling of being incapable, impotent, which results from the Oedipus situation" (ibid., p. 188). Hate is a derivative of not knowing, and is an important reason for Klein to propose the early analysis of many, perhaps all, children. At this point in her theorizing, hate is an inescapable consequence of early Oedipal dynamics. The child is initially frustrated by the mother in the oral stage (by weaning), and it is during the early anal–sadistic stage that the child "sustains his/her second severe trauma" (ibid., p. 189). Klein assumes that, even in optimal development, weaning is a frustration that the child must at the very least struggle to tolerate. In less than optimal development, she posits that the world is seen as a crueller, more frightening place. During the anal stage (or anal sadism) both the boy and girl go through what Klein labelled the femininity phase of development. It is the mother's body that is seen as the point of action for all sexual activities. Klein, in following and extending a Freudian percept, is thus realizing the full implications of Freud's revolutionary theorizing. According to this percept, the child sees the world through bodily functions and activities and the child's world is dominated by the mother and thoughts of, or, more usually, the actuality of, the mother's body. All that is valuable is inside her body and during this stage of development the world is seen in anal terms. Klein then combines the idea of anality with the reoccurrence of the Oedipal triangle. Babies are inside the mother's body and are anal and urethral babies; the father's penis is also inside the mother's body, making it a dangerous place for the anal stage boy. Thus, the boy and girl both wish to have the mother's valuable possessions (faeces and babies), or, if frustrated, wish to destroy the mother's ability to produce anything of value. Both sexes wished to cut open and rob the mother of her faeces (children). The anal child boy wishes to penetrate the mother and destroy the contents of the mother's body. The boy, simultaneously under the sway of Oedipal tendencies, desires the mother as a love object. He also fears the father in terms of the threat of castration. Under anal–sadistic pressures, his hatred of the mother overwhelms his Oedipal love, while, in addition, castration anxiety brings forth both guilt and anxiety that also tend to blunt his love of his mother. It may be that Klein's most interesting concept (somewhat overlooked today) is that the boy wants to steal (or destroy) the mother's special life-giving organs of receptivity and bounty. In other terms, the boy envies the bountiful mother and this envy has both oral and anal overtones.

Klein assumes that the "dread of the mother is so overwhelming because combined with it is an intense dread of castration by the father" (ibid., p. 190). However, it is also the mother "who takes away the child's (boy's) faeces and that action signifies a mother who dismembers and castrates him" (ibid.). Klein, in this context, is frequently raising quantitative questions in terms of how children will fare in the light of these early conflicts. To the extent that the boy develops excessive sadism in his superego formation, then he will be unable to resolve his aggression towards women. Klein assumes that the boy who intended to rob the mother of her possessions (breast, faeces, babies, and father's penis) fears retaliation from the mother (talion principle). The boy turns towards the father in identification and as a shield from the dreaded mother. The boy's excessive fear and aggression "unites with the pleasure in attack", and, in excess, is a troublesome asocial aspect of the boy's character (ibid., p. 192). Her view is that men will be far more asocial towards women than towards "fellow men". The boy's femininity phase is succeeded by the more "plainly recognizable" Oedipal conflicts during the genital stage (Klein's name for Freud's phallic stage). When the genital stage arises, the boy is even more strongly driven towards identification with the father. The attainment of the genital position, for the boy, is, in large part, decided by the "degree of constitutional genitality" (ibid.). At this point, the genital Oedipal situation, for the boy, occupies a good deal less of her conceptual time then does the femininity phase of development.

The femininity phase of development is also important for the girl and, surprisingly, Klein begins her description with a point of similarity with Helene Deutsch (another noted analyst who was a strong Freudian advocate) (1925): "I entirely agree with Helene Deutsch, who holds that the genital development finds its completion in the successful displacement of the oral libido on to the genital" (1928, p. 192). Klein, however, believes this occurs during the oral stage as opposed to a regression to orality from the genital stage. Klein states that the girl's oral, receptive aim of her genitals "exercises a determining influence in the girl's turning to the father". One again sees here how Klein combines psycho-sexual stages with the occurrence of the Oedipal situation. Klein, for some reason, believes the girl does not obtain as much gratification in masturbation as the boy. She concludes that, as the girl explores her genitals, she has an "intense desire for a new source of gratification", and this, combined with envy of the mother (who possesses the father's penis), is a motive for the girl turning towards the father. She says that the father's caresses have now the effect of a seduction, and are felt as the attraction of the opposite sex. As is the case with the boy, the little girl's femininity phase coincides with anal–sadism and a wish to rob and destroy the mother. If this desire is too strong, the little girl's superego will be excessively cruel and lead to repression and a powerful fixation at this point of development.

The girl's genital development raises a delicate question for Klein: what position does she take on a central Freudian concept, penis envy. Klein maintains that the girl's epistemophilic impulse leads her to discover "her lack of a penis". However, she clearly states, "I regard the deprivation of the breast as the most fundamental cause of the turning to the father". The girl, according to Klein, does not suffer from castration anxiety and so does not resent the mother for allowing her to be castrated, as Freud had posited. Thus, both envy of the breast and frustration at the time of weaning (as well as other normal and abnormal frustrations) lead to a fundamental envy of the mother and her possessions (and abilities). This envy continues into the femininity (anal sadism) phase of development and both the girl and boy leave this stage with a dread of the mother. Both turn towards the father and, while the boy identifies with the father and greatly values (over-values) his penis, the girl is, of necessity, frustrated during the genital Oedipal situation. However,

> Later, when full satisfaction of the love-impulses is obtained, there is joined with this admiration the great gratitude ensuing from the

long-pent-up deprivation. This gratitude finds expression in the greater feminine capacity for complete and lasting surrender to one love-object, especially to the first-love. [1928, p. 194]

Klein also states that the more the little girl's identification with the mother becomes stabilized on a genital level, the greater the chance that the woman's superego will be "characterized by the devoted kindness of a bountiful mother-ideal" (*ibid.*, p. 195). Here, again, is a difference with Freud, for Klein asserts that, while jealousy (or envy) may play a greater part in the lives of women (than men), there is a greater potential capacity to be bountiful and generous in a way that is more rarely found in men. In effect, Klein interprets Freud's conceptualization of a feminine superego as one possibility if ideal development does not take place. What do women want? Klein answers the question that Freud posed by maintaining that it depends on the maternal superego and how it is internalized by the girl.

According to Klein, the dangers for the little girl seem to be greater than for the boy. The boy is "made in the image of his ideal" and his penis is tangible proof of his male identity. The chronic dread of injury for the woman causes her to over-estimate the penis, but Klein does not see this anxiety as the central concern of the Oedipal girl. Klein and Horney both point to the mother and the relationship of the girl with her mother as the prime source of this anxiety. (Karen Horney was another important analyst who started her own school when she came to the USA. Interestingly, Abraham was her analyst as well as Melanie Klein's. Horney was important in moving psychoanalysis away from a phallo-centric theory.) Klein ends her essay by saying that she does not think that her formulations "contradict the statements of Professor Freud" (*ibid.*, p. 197). She states that the early stages of the Oedipus are so strongly affected by pregenital development that, in effect, it is difficult to discriminate Oedipal development until the genital stage occurs. One can state a parallel line of thought with regard to superego development, since the full structure is not in place until the resolution of at least some conflicts in the genital stage of development. Although one might make a reasonable logical case for this type of assertion, the effect on the "Freudian" community was not that of an accepting attitude. In part, the controversy surrounding the idea of early Oedipal development depends on what one wants to label Oedipal. Is all triangulation Oedipal? Does the sexualization of the mother's body necessarily involve Oedipal dynamics? Does the idea or phantasy of the mother possessing all that is valuable inside herself necessarily mean that the penis is inside the mother? One can ask these questions, and even more penetrating questions, about Kleinian concepts. However, whether one wants to see Klein as extending, modifying, or overtly changing Freudian theory frequently depends, at least in part, on one's psychoanalytic politics. Clearly, Klein has changed the concept of the Oedipus complex in this essay. She has also changed a previous view of feminine development as being strongly linked to penis envy. For her, both the boy and the girl suffer anxiety from the projected and then introjected hatred involving the desire to rob and destroy the possessions of the mother's body. This projective–introjective sequence is the forerunner of Klein's concept of projective identification that we will encounter in several of her essays.

In any case, Klein will follow up this remarkable essay with many other essays that rival, and perhaps surpass, the revolutionary nature of this essay. This paper, however, served to firmly establish Klein as an analyst who is putting forth major psychoanalytic concepts.

Kleinian notes

Although there are three more essays we will look at in this phase of Klein's theorizing, it is important in looking at Klein to realize two aspects of her theorizing which frequently are under-valued. Although she does not always state this clearly, Klein has a firm view of what Freud called double representation. (This is my idiosyncratic translation of Freud's use of this concept in his papers "Repression" [1915d] and "The unconscious" [1915e]. See Chapter Three for a discussion of Freud's views on double representation.) Klein's view of the internal object is an object representation that is internalized via phantasy. Phantasy, for Klein, dominates early development and the infant's/child's ability to tolerate frustration is a crucial factor in how phantasy leads to the formation of internal objects. As we have seen in the section titled "Early stages of the

Oedipus conflict", during this phase of Klein's theorizing sadism and hate are crucial elements in determining the child's developmental fate. How well the child can tolerate frustration is, for Klein, a crucial factor in the intensity of the sadistic nature of the child's internal objects. This factor, for Klein, is not the only concept that accounts for the degree of sadism (or terror) associated with internal objects.

Klein assumes that there is not only an internal representation or object, but that there is also a representation, more conscious and more easily influenced by the external world. For ease of communication, this will be labelled the external representation or object. The terrifying aspect of the internal object will then be determined by at least three factors: the strength of the drives, and, more importantly, the child's tolerance for frustration and the behaviour of the mothering parent(s) (in early development). The behaviour of the parent(s) will be a strong determinant of the nature of the external object; that is, how sadistic, how frustrating the parents are in reality will strongly influence the nature of the external representation. This seemingly obvious point has to be seen in terms of how the internal object in the younger child (and infant) will also strongly affect how the external object is represented. In optimal development, parents will be more libidinal than sadistic, and this relatively benign developmental influence will be represented in the child's external object representations. As the child develops, optimally the internal object will be less sadistic and terrifying, and internal and external representations will come to be less divergent and, in ideal development, will be united. One then has to keep in mind that Klein, even in her early writings, does not exclude the environment as an influence in the way the child represents the world. She does have a theory of double representations and the external object is usually a representation that more closely mirrors the reality of the interaction between infant/child and parent. This is not always the case with high intensity children, or children who have a low tolerance for frustration.

Although the point has just been stated, it is important to dwell on two influences in Klein's theorizing: frustration tolerance is, for Klein, an important biological factor in childhood development. As a second point, she is able to place Oedipal dynamics at an early age because she believes that the bodily representations involving sexuality are part of our genetic inheritance. This factor, then, is a second proto-physiological factor, which strongly affects Klein's theoretical offerings. She takes the idea of innate symbols (the raw material of phantasy) much further than Freud did, although one can detect in Freud the same theoretical tendency. Freud's Lamarckian views allowed him, at least covertly, to believe that various types of phantasies were passed from generation to generation. In *Moses and Monotheism* (1939a), one sees this view enunciated clearly, but one can discern Freud's views quite distinctly in a paper he wrote (with Bullitt) as early as 1915. It is my view that one can see Lamarckian ideas in many of Freud's papers. Whether or not one completely accepts this interpretation of Freud, Freud's Lamarckian views are unmistakably presented in at least two publications (Freud, 1939a; Freud & Bullitt, 1967). Klein's ideas of certain symbols as innate are certainly in keeping with a distinct trend in Freudian theory. While Freud implicitly sees Lamarckian genetics as responsible for innate symbols, Klein seemingly takes a more conventional genetic viewpoint. This, of course, is not an argument for the validity of her views; it is simply a point of reference when Freudians consider her views as quite radical and beyond the Freudian opus.

Superego and beyond (before): a note

We have already discussed Klein's concept of the nature of the superego, but, in "The early development of conscience in the child" (1933), Klein adds some clarifications to her early Oedipus paper. In the conscience paper, she clearly states that the superego is formed at the beginning of Oedipal development. This solidifies her departure from Freud's concept of the superego, where he posited that the superego forms after the resolution of Oedipal conflicts. In a prior work (1932), Klein seemed to take a more radical position and maintain that the superego began when the infant first internalizes an object through the process of incorporation. This, of course, would be before Oedipal conflicts even appeared. However, she does not repeat this view. What she does continue is to conceptualize a differentiation between fear and guilt as different states that both emanate from the superego. Fear comes from the earlier superego, which is infused with sadism and terrifying images. Guilt is a product of the later superego that forms in the genital stage. In the early Oedipus paper, Klein's explanation of fear of the object involved her invoking the talion principle. Thus, the infant/child assumed that the object would have identical sadistic wishes to its own sadism. As a result of this equation, the object (person) was to be feared. In the early conscience paper, she shifts (or clarifies) her views and begins to talk about superego objects being projected into the environment. Thus, the parent might become a frightening object because of the infant's/child's projections. (Of course, she could have assumed that the reason that the talion principle exists is because of projected impulses. Freud's assumption of the talion principle has this principle as part of a narcissistic view of the universe, the view that the other has the same thoughts and feelings that one does.) This theoretical movement will find its way to the concept of projective identification, and it is one of Klein's first steps towards this concept.

Klein, in this essay, also repeats the view that it is not that the early superego is weak, but, rather, that it is too strong for the early enfeebled ego. Thus, the superego overwhelms the ego during early points of development. Here, she equates the superego's capacity to cause primitive anxiety states with the concept of a strong superego. Freud's implicit definition of the superego as a strong or firm structure was based on a different definition of strength, which will be discussed at the end of this chapter.

It is important to stress that, in the conscience paper, Klein still sees the early superego as menacing; the early superego is one where there are strong fears of being devoured and torn to bits. Sadism is paramount in the oral phase of development, where cannibalistic phantasies abound. For Klein, there is a stage between the oral and anal stages, and that is the urethral stage. Here, as well as in the anal stage, ejection of urine or faeces "symbolizes a forcible ejection of the incorporated object" alongside active destructive wishes towards the object. More specifically, in this paper Klein reminds us of the femininity phase (although she does not, in this essay, actually use the term), where the child wishes to destroy the inside of the mother's body and "uses its urine and faeces for this purpose" (1933, p. 253). The wish to possess or destroy the content of the mother's body is something that causes fear in the child, and the child projects these impulses on to the object (mother or combined parent).

The idea of emptying one's mind of objects is a topic that is much more fully explored in a 1930 paper where Klein looks at symbolism in early development, or, more accurately, the destruction of symbolism in early development. Here, Klein considers mental processes before the development of the superego. There is an early point before the "formation of a superego [where] the mental apparatus makes use of different methods of defense from those which it employs after it has reached these stages of organization" (1930, p. 220). When Klein talks about "these stages of organization", she means a point where the ego, id, and superego are integrated and form well-developed structures. Klein sees the idea of expulsion of the object as a main defence before these structures are clearly defined and organized. Expulsion of the object, at this early point in development, is a way the infant has of ridding itself of these terrifying objects. Expulsion has, as its corollary, the destruction of the external object. Thus, at an early point of development (certainly before four to six months of age), if the infant is overwhelmed with anxiety it attempts either to expel anxiety-provoking objects from its mind or, alternatively, attempts to destroy anxiety-provoking or (more accurately) terrifying object representations. To the extent that an infant utilizes these defences (or defensive manoeuvres), it is to that extent that the infant harms its ability to symbolize. Here, Klein is following a theme that she has been involved with since she began to analyse Erich. In psychotic children, she sees that the capacity for symbolization has either been destroyed or very badly damaged. For the capacity for symbolization to endure, the infant/child must be able to sufficiently tolerate anxiety. This will permit the child to begin to equate hated objects (internal objects) with new views of the object, and synthesizing these objects allows the child to develop interest in new (object) equations. Great harm to the capacity for symbolization is a death knell for psychological life, from Klein's perspective, and, in the symbolization paper, she tries to show how, when treating children who are psychotic, one can reach and greatly enhance the child's ability for symbolization. The theme, for Klein, in all child analyses is to increase the child's capacity for tolerating and utilizing phantasy. If this can be accomplished, the child's ability to symbolize and be spontaneous will be enhanced. In many ways, Klein equates creativity with being psychologically alive. Klein's ideas about clinical psychoanalysis parallel her ideas about development, in the sense that a main concern for her and subsequent Kleinians is to find ways to keep the psychoanalytic situation alive and vibrant. This may seem like an elementary concern, but Klein and later Kleinians argue that, in many treatments, the life and spontaneity in the treatment situation is sorely lacking. Compliance as a substitute for spontaneity in the psychoanalytic situation is a significant concern in Kleinian concepts about treatment.

In this section ("Superego and beyond") we have seemingly mostly gone beyond Klein's idea about superego development. However, to briefly summarize Klein's views on superego development, we can state that there is a point in early development where the infant is compelled either to empty out or to destroy the contents of their mental life. This point is before the structural development of the superego. When the superego forms, it is early in the Oedipal configuration. The first appearance of the superego during the oral stage is essentially a compilation of oral sadistic images that are terrifying and begin to exert some control (influence) over the infant's oral sadistic wishes to destroy, possess, and dominate the mother's body and bodily products. In this description, it is important to remember that the mother's body is the site of the Oedipal drama. As such, the father's penis is contained in her body and, in that sense, this combined parent is an active part of the Oedipal drama. Klein, during this era, sees the Oedipal drama as being replayed in each psycho-sexual stage. In optimal development, superego development includes fewer sadistic elements, eventuating in a structure that is better integrated with the ego and id and is not subjugated by sadistic elements. Klein is particularly poignant in her descriptions of the bountiful nature of the feminine superego in optimal development. This is in contrast to Freud's view of the weak feminine superego.

Klein's next conceptual step: a preliminary discussion

In discussing Klein's paper on the early development of conscience (1933), Roger Money-Kyrle asks, "How does the change from the early superego, felt as anxiety, and asocial in its effect, to the developed conscience, felt as guilt, and moral in outlook, come about?" (Money-Kyrle, 1975b, p. 431). In Money-Kyrle's view, Klein's theory up to 1933 does not offer an explanation of how this superego transformation occurs. It is his view that Klein's next theoretical concept, the depressive position, provides an adequate theoretical bridge in explaining the transition from the early superego (where fear is the main affect generated) to the superego, which is concerned with morality and produces guilt when superego standards are not met. The concept of position is to become one of the major linchpins in Kleinian theory. She utilizes this theoretical assumption and with it transforms a number of concepts that had already been introduced by other psychoanalytic theorists.

As one example, splitting, as a concept, had already been initiated or at least implied by both Ferenczi and Freud (Chapter Three). Klein, however, actively uses the defence of splitting as an important aspect of her theoretical edifice. She highlights both the developmental and clinical importance of the concept of splitting. The relevance of this concept will, in fact, increase as we go over Klein's later papers. In a similar way, Freud has introduced the idea of a part object, but Klein makes this concept an organic aspect of her new theoretical structure. The distinction between part and whole objects is a crucial feature of the concept of position. As we have seen, Klein has, up to this point in time, focused on the effects of aggression or, more accurately, sadism. In her subsequent papers, she more assiduously considers the implications of Eros and Thanatos, or the life and death instincts. This will, interestingly, lead her to look more closely at what Freud and Abraham called libidinal influences in development. All of these changes are what we will look at in detail in three of Klein's most influential papers. Two of these are "A contribution to the psychogenesis of manic–depressive states" (1935), and "Mourning and its relation to manic–depressive states" (1940). In her third paper, "Love, guilt and reparation" (1937), Klein formalizes her introduction of the concept of repair. Although we are now heralding the forthcoming introduction of the concept of the depressive position, for a moment we might dwell on Money-Kyrle's assertion that Klein's previous concepts could not account for the transformations she describes in superego development.

Money-Kyrle (and analysts who are considered neo-Kleinians) has contended that the concept of position has become the "developmental unit in place of phase of stage" (1975b, p. 433). From their point of view, Klein has moved from a stage developmental theory to one based on position. The question that will be posed in the commentary to this chapter (and implicitly in the chapter) is whether Klein did, in fact, move from a stage to a position theory or whether she combined these two theoretical concepts. Apart from the historical interpretation of Klein's theorizing, the question can be posed as to whether there is anything that is logically incompatible in combining a stage and a position point of view. Perhaps the more relevant consideration is whether there is any explanatory power to be gained by combining these positions.

The paranoid and the depressive positions

During this period (1935–1940), Klein will delineate two forms of anxiety that will change her theorizing for the rest of her career. These two forms of anxiety will define a person's relation to her/his object world. The two forms of anxiety are paranoid and depressive anxiety, and both forms connote several theoretical assumptions. If one is in a position where paranoid anxiety is the dominant theme, then there will be a tendency towards relating to part, rather than whole, objects. In addition, Klein states that in response to paranoid anxiety, the "characteristic defenses are chiefly aimed at annihilating the 'persecutor'". This persecutor can be represented as inside or outside the person's body. Klein relates, "Paranoid anxiety lest the objects [are] sadistically destroyed will themselves be a source of poison and danger inside the subject's body" (1935, p. 264). Thus, unless the person can feel they have destroyed the external object, there will be a chance that the object will be internalized and become an internal persecutor. Why internalize an object that is seen as dangerous and poisonous? Klein assumes that there is a tendency to incorporate objects under the sway of both oral–libidinal (sexual) and oral–sadistic motivations. Thus, in spite of the vehemence of the potential oral–sadistic onslaughts of an introject, there is a tendency at the same time "to be profoundly mistrustful of the objects while yet incorporating them". Here, she is maintaining that, despite the fact that paranoid anxiety leads to the attempt to destroy external objects, there is still a desire to (orally) incorporate these objects. Once internalized, these incorporated objects are perceived as dangerous and, in particular, poisonous. For Klein, if the object is destroyed, then the child's external world can seem horribly impoverished. What are the defences that Klein posits are used against these persecutors? Denial or scotomization is a prime defence, leading to the "restriction of the mechanisms of introjection and projection" (*ibid.*, p. 262). If one denies the existence of the object, in effect it is destroyed, or, in a less extreme case, at least an aspect of the object is eliminated. If the object (more correctly, part-object) is incorporated (taken in), the ego attempts to defend itself by expelling or projecting internal persecutors and this leads to an impoverished internal environment. This impoverished internal environment is one where symbolization is at a minimum and all intellectual capacities are severely inhibited. In addition, in the earliest form of paranoia, there is a "weakening of oral desires" (*ibid.*, p. 264), since, even though incorporation continues, there is a diminished field of possible objects to incorporate (due to denial or scotomization). At this point in her theorizing, the clear division between good and bad objects occurs after the paranoid period of development.

The phrase "after the paranoid period of development" is actually misleading, since, as we shall see, Klein does not see this form of mental organization as ever being left or even fully transformed. Rather, paranoia is gradually replaced by a position that Klein describes as the depressive position. The movement to the depressive position is correlated with the transition of the infant's capacity to synthesize, perceive, and incorporate a whole object. Klein's assumption is that, during paranoia, the infant incorporates partial objects and that these partial objects are frequently destroyed by the infant/child. Although, at this point, Klein stresses the terrifying aspects of early development even during paranoia, "gratifying parts and portions of the real world" (*ibid.*, p. 285) are incorporated.

Before long (after two or three months), the child begins to perceive "more and more of the whole person of the mother". If there is a good relation between mother and infant, the infant is helped to overcome its paranoid anxieties. The child's libidinal fixation to the breast develops into feelings towards the mother as a person. This libidinal shift is occurring at the same time that sadistic tendencies are at their height. Thus, as the child changes its relations to the objects, a dread develops "lest the good object should be expelled along with the bad" (*ibid.*, p. 265). This, in turn, "causes the mechanism of expulsion and projection to lose their value" (*ibid.*). As this happens, the child begins to attempt to introject the good object, becomes anxious about the good object, and desires to keep it intact (in good repair). In viewing this process, one must keep in mind that Klein's picture of the infant/child is one where the subject is characterized as always being in danger of sadistic assault from internal and/or external sources. Nevertheless, during this transition, the infant is able to move from partial to whole objects and is trying to keep these objects safe from sadistic assaults.

What is the depressive aspect of this new situation for the infant? For Klein, the loss of "love" characterizes the depressive position. Virtually as soon as the infant is able to incorporate good whole objects, its depression is caused by the "sense of failure (during weaning and in the periods which proceed [*sic*] and follow it) to secure his good, internalized object, i.e., to possess himself of it" (*ibid.*, p. 267). Thus, having loved, there is an immediate, or at least rapid, sense of loss that follows this initial love. One reason for this immediate loss is the continued presence of the infant's internalized persecutors. This presence is a residue of the initial paranoia during the previous phase of development (really, from the beginning of life). The pining for the loved object characterizes the depressive position. The capacity to pine for a loved object is dependent on the ability to incorporate a whole good object. If the infant fails to secure the good, internalized, whole object, this demonstrates the infant's inability to protect the good object from internalized persecutors.

In Klein's descriptions of early development, one can see internal objects having an active influence in the psychological world of the infant. Clearly, the object-relations dramas that Klein envisions are considerably more complicated than Freud's attempts at viewing the internal world of the infant. Like Freud in his object-relations era, Klein sees the positions she describes as explaining adult psychopathology. Paranoia is viewed in much the same light as Klein's descriptions of early development. The same is true of depressive disorders. In addition, she posits a clear causal link between infantile and adult states:

The first and fundamental external loss of a real loved object, which is experienced through the loss of the breast before and during weaning, will only result in later life in a depressive state if at this early period of development the infant has failed to establish its loved object with its ego. [*ibid.*, p. 287]

A brief aside: comparison of Klein with other analysts

Similarly, Klein sees a close relationship between paranoia and depressive disorders in adult life, and this view is heralded by Kleinians as "a considerable contribution to the general theory of psychosis" (Money-Kyrle, 1975b, p. 434). Before we go on to look at how Klein relates mania to the depressive position and manic–depressive states to depression, let us take a brief look back at Freud, Abraham, Ferenczi, and Glover in terms of some of Klein's new concepts. Glover saw the initial organization of the ego as a loose amalgam of nuclei. The nature of the organization of these nuclei is based on the dominant psycho-sexual stage at any given point in time. Thus, there might be oral or anal ego nuclei, etc. In the oral phase, the ego would be less unified and identifications with external objects would be limited because of this disorganization. Kernberg has called this passive splitting (see Chapter Fourteen on Kernberg) and Schafer (1968) has also seen this organization as a lack of integration rather than as an active motivated state. Thus, in Glover's conceptualization of early development, splitting is a consequence of lack of ego organization. As we will see, this view is diametrically opposed to Klein's view of early development.

Before Glover, Abraham had already written several papers (1921a,b, 1924) where he had talked about infantile depression. His work built on both Freud's papers on infantile sexuality and Freud and Ferenczi's beginning conceptualizations of early development. For Abraham, conflicts around anal sadism were considered to be particularly salient in the formation of infantile depression. While Abraham wrote about infantile depression, Freud's paper "Mourning and melancholia" (1917e) attempted to show the difference between normal mourning and states of depression or melancholia. Klein, during this era, is the first author to feature the universality of the depressive position. Her theory maintains that mourning is pathological to the extent that the person was unable to deal successfully with their sorrow and concern during the childhood depressive positions that they encountered. Klein is introducing a new concept and a new developmental concern: early consideration of the child's ability to deal with sorrow and object loss. Although this has been a concern of other authors, Klein makes this a central position of her new theory.

Mania and the manic–depressive "position"

To start with a brief restatement, Klein maintains that

> There are two sets of fears, feelings and defenses, which, however varied in themselves and however intimately linked together, can, in my view, for purposes of theoretical clearness, be isolated from each other. The first set of feelings and phantasies are the persecutory ones, characterized by fears relating to the destruction of the ego by internal persecutors. The defenses against these fears are predominantly the destruction of the persecutors by violent or secretive and cunning methods ... The second set of feelings which go to make up the depressive position I formerly described without suggesting a term for them. I now propose to use for these feelings of sorrow and concern for the loved objects, the fears of losing them and the longing to regain them, a simple word derived from everyday language—namely the "pining" for the loved object. In short—persecution (by "bad" objects) and the characteristic defenses against it, on the one hand, and pining for the loved ("good") object, on the other, constitute the depressive position. [1940, p. 348]

As the infant fully enters the depressive position, Klein sees a defensive organization arising to deal with the pain of pining. The defences that surface are part of the manic position and form a trio of defensive manoeuvres. Klein considers the development of omnipotent phantasies as a defence designed to control bad objects and restore good objects. Klein relates that omnipotent ideas are very much in line with the type of thought that is present during this early period of development. Thus, bad objects are terrifying and terribly destructive, and good objects are perfect and without fault. The child in the depressive position also utilizes denial and, in this way, eases its sense of loss and attenuates the pining for the lost object. The denial, in effect, questions the loss and allows reality to be less disappointing and more easily moulded to omnipotent phantasies. The third defence is idealization, which allows the infant the phantasy that the all-good object is really available when needed (or, at least, when the infant wants the object to appear). Denial, omnipotence, and idealization, working together, allow the infant/child to ease the pain of pining but also allow the unified object to again be split into good and bad or hated and loved images. These defences, operating together, facilitate the infant in entering a manic state. The infant's manic state wipes away the experience of pining and remorse. Thus, the omnipotence of the manic position allows the infant to move away from depressive affect, but also away from a unified image of the object.

Splitting and reunification as continuous cycles

Klein notes that

> It seems that at this stage of development the unification of external and internal, loved and hated, real and imaginary objects is carried out in such a way that each step in the unification leads again to a renewed splitting of the imagos. [1940, p. 350]

Thus, as with superego development, Klein sees in optimal development an oscillation between paranoia and the depressive position, with a gradual upward movement of the depressive position. Upward movement, in this context, means a continued unification of imagos or representations occurring so that love for the real and internalized objects and trust in them are well established and last for longer periods. When the depressive position is first established in infancy, it is a fragile organization and easily disrupted by manic tendencies and defensive manoeuvres. Although Klein does not mention obsessional defences as part of mania, she does mention that the young child (particularly the infant) does not trust reparative efforts (or thoughts) and may

THE KLEINIAN REVOLUTION 239

feel that his attempts at reparation have not succeeded or will not succeed. This leads in the child—and for that matter to some extent in the adult also—to repeat certain actions obsessionally or—the contrasting method—omnipotence and denial are resorted to. (*ibid.*]

Since Klein sees obsessional defences as operating closely with manic defences, she maintains that there is a sadistic edge in the attempt to control the object. There is often a wish to overcome the object, to rival the object's abilities, and in this way to triumph over the object. Triumphing over the object has several components, but, most importantly, there is an attempt to show that the child is self-sufficient and has no weaknesses or deficiencies.

It is important to again note that Klein does not see these two positions as occurring once in early development, but rather as recurring during each developmental cycle. This is part of the "upward movement"; as the positions recur, there is less and less discrepancy between inner and external representations and loving and hateful representations are gradually brought together in the same object representation. When the child can do this, he/she is truly able to have ambivalent reactions towards another. In early paranoia and the depressive position, Klein sees the infant as undergoing psychotic anxieties. These anxieties are also transformed gradually into more neurotic anxieties, although the potential for psychotic anxieties is always present. Along with the positions recurring, Oedipal triangulations and superego reconfigurations are recurring. Thus, Klein is picturing development as continuing oscillation between positions, with Oedipal and superego developments occurring and recurring throughout the developmental cycle. As previously discussed, Kleinians tend to view this phase of Klein's career as substituting the concept of positions for Freud's theory of psycho-sexual stages. Money-Kyrle, in commenting on this phase of Klein's development, states, "Of central importance is the new idea of position as the developmental unit in place of phase or stage" (1975b, p. 433).

Since Klein places the phenomena of mourning as related to the developmental issues encountered in the depressive position, mourning is encountered in each developmental era. In addition, melancholia and mourning are not seen as disparate phenomena, but as points on a continuum. In her clinical material, she goes over the dangers involved in mourning as well as the dangers of melancholia. During each depressive position, or epoch, there are attempts at reparation, and one might say that the occurrence of each depressive position allows the child to develop fuller love relations and to be less tied to narcissistic vulnerabilities. For example, Klein's view of the need for excessive praise is a projected unconscious view that one is incapable of loving another while at the same time not being able to master one's aggressive impulses towards others. Gradually, as one believes in one's attempts at loving the object and being able to repair the object, or, rather, keep the object in good repair, then, gradually, one does not "need" external praise to nearly the same extent. The need for external praise is then a projected inability to provide self-love and object-love.

Although, during this era, Klein is departing from Freudian theory, she frequently still makes implicit and explicit references to Freudian concepts. She is explicitly utilizing the concept of Oedipal conflicts as being the central focus of her object-relations theory. The idea of psycho-sexual stages is, in my view, also continuously present in her conceptualizations. At various times, she refers to oral and anal phenomena and even to self-preservative needs, a concept that Freud had presented during his object-relations era. However much her descriptions rest on Freudian concepts, her use of these concepts always presents new theoretical pathways. For example, she states that in the early Oedipus, the father's role is in part modelled on the mother, and she terms this modelling "the joint parent". The parents are joint in another, perhaps more basic, sense, since, in the early Oedipus, all sexual activity is seen as occurring in the mother's body. Thus, the father's penis has a continuous presence in the mother's body as the infant/young child is experiencing and re-experiencing Oedipal conflicts. Moreover, the first Oedipal period is brought into existence as a result of the frustration of the ending of breast-feeding (or some equivalent feeding). Thus, in this conceptualization, the Oedipus complex comes into being at the height of sadism (this view will shift). From Klein's perspective, even in happy relationships there is a continued need for reparative tendencies. Thus, the happy wife and mother is still always concerned with her sadistic wishes towards the penis, and continuously has to repair the penis and restore it to good health. One could go on in this section about the new concepts, or at least new angles, on previous concepts that Klein has provided, but, since she will review this material in the next paper we will encounter, let us go on to the cross-roads of Klein's theorizing and look at her next paper, in 1945, "The Oedipus complex in the light of early anxieties". This paper, written after the Freud–Klein controversies, is Klein's definitive statement about the nature of the Oedipus complex.

A brief note on two terminological confusions

In the two papers on the depressive position (Klein, 1935, 1940), Klein uses the term position as frequently as Freud used the term instinct in his early paper on sexuality (Freud, 1905d). We see in these papers an obsessional position and a manic position, etc., but this is an early exuberance in the use of this term. In Klein's later theorizing, there are only two positions: the paranoid–schizoid and the depressive position. The paranoid–schizoid position will be Klein's name for paranoia after her "discussion(s)" with Fairbairn in the mid 1940s. (In the next chapter, we will discuss Klein's 1946 paper where she introduces the term paranoid–schizoid position.) Klein also uses the term ambivalence when she is referring to images or representations that are split and of opposite valence. Freud, at times (e.g., Freud, 1915c), also used the term ambivalence in this manner. Many authors today would distinguish an ambivalent attitude towards a single undivided object from a split object that is represented in two (or more) distinct representations.

The Oedipus complex: a more complete statement

Klein, in presenting her views on the Oedipus complex (1945), is now no longer attempting to minimize her differences with Freud. Klein's clinical material in this essay is primarily from her analysis of Richard, a treatment that she presented in detail in one of her last publications, *Narrative of a Child Analysis* (1961). She also presents clinical material from her analysis of Rita, a case that she has previously presented (1932). Klein, at this point in time, restates many of her previous views: both sexes have early Oedipal development but now early is somewhat earlier than she has previously theorized. Based on her clinical work, she still regards frustration tolerance and the degree of sadism as strong aetiological factors in determining the type and extent of an individual's conflict-laden world of internalized objects. Klein maintains that, from the beginning of life, libido is fused with aggression. This view is a departure from Freud, who saw the fusion of the instincts as a developmental step. (It is my view that, unless we can translate these concepts into concepts with observable consequences, this is largely an academic point. It is the case that Klein, at many points, seems to stress aggression and sadism more than Freud, at least at some points in his theorizing.) More importantly, Klein posits that it is the search for new sources of gratification that produces libidinal progression. Frustration is a factor in all developmental interactions, since, from her point of view, the infant wants "*unlimited* gratification". Inevitably, therefore, whatever the infant's frustration tolerance, he/she will suffer at least some frustration during breast-feeding. Following this frustration, the infant turns towards the penis for oral gratification. "The breast and the penis are, therefore, the primary objects of the infant's oral desires" (1945, p. 408). It comes as no surprise that both Richard and Rita have strong oral–sadistic impulses, and conflicts and excessive anxiety and guilt around the expression of these impulses. This fixation to an early stage of development leads to regression to this stage, and does not allow true genital primacy to be securely established. Klein's view is that psycho-sexual stages are much more fluid than Freud's descriptions had stated or implied. In each era of the child's development, one might see oral, urethral, and anal, as well as genital, impulses arising and active in the child's mind. However, if we look at Klein's statement that the breast and the penis are the primary objects of the infant's oral desires, one can only conclude that within the oral phase (or stage) of development there are characteristic tendencies that dominate each particular epoch of development. It is the present contention that this is the only logically necessary interpretation of Klein's statement. The same point can be maintained when Klein talks about a stage (or phase) of genital primacy. Here, one can only assume that there is a point in development where there is (or should be, in optimal development) genital primacy. By genital primacy, there is an assumption of genital sexual concerns with age-appropriate identifications taking place. During this period, according to Klein, superego development should also be less terrifying and more integrative and significantly less dominated by sadistic introjects. Thus, Oedipal dynamics are, at this point, similar to those described by Freud, although Klein still maintains important differences with Freud. Before we recount those differences, let us consolidate the pregenital differences that divide Freud and Klein.

Klein's later theory: the starting points

Klein, from this point (1945) on, sees object relations beginning from birth onward. Thus, frustration and gratification during (breast) feeding lead immediately to the splitting of the breast and the formation of a loved, good breast and a hated, bad breast. The good is idealized as all good, and, in a mirror image portrait, the bad is terrifying and hated. Frustration at the breast leads both infant boy and girl to the penis, and the penis undergoes a fate similar to the breast. Through a combination of introjection and projection, the good and the bad are both taken in and cast out at different points of environmental interaction. Klein still hypothesizes a double form of representation, with reality images or external images being constantly influenced by internal representations. For example, Klein theorizes that internal images of the breast (mother) and the penis (father) constantly are effecting the realistic representations of mother and father. Klein states, "There is a constant fluctuation between internal and external objects and situations" (1945, p. 409).

In her previous publications, Klein viewed the Oedipus complex as beginning as a result of the frustration of being weaned. Sadism and aggression were seen as the affective and motivational components that initiated the Oedipus complex. Klein now sees Oedipal phenomena coinciding with the onset of the depressive position. The infantile depressive position is the core of her developmental theory, and "the child's fear of the loss of his loved objects, as a consequence of his hatred and aggression, enters into his object relations and Oedipus conflicts from the beginning" (*ibid.*, p. 410). Since, now, object relations are present from birth, the images of the good and bad breast and penis are ones that will shortly be part of an early (the first) superego development. In this interpretation of Klein (with which many psychoanalysts who are identified as Kleinians or neo-Kleinians would disagree, maintaining that Klein had left the concept of psycho-sexual stages and replaced it with the concept of positions), she is seen as loosely holding to the concept of psycho-sexual stages. The stages are identical to Freudian theory (with the inclusion of a urethral stage), but are more fluid, and each psycho-sexual zone makes an appearance in every stage. Thus, in the oral phase of development, there will be urethral, anal, and, certainly, genital phantasies accompanying the oral themes of libidinal incorporation and oral sadism. In this view of Kleinian theory, there is an oscillation of positions within each stage of development. Thus, in the oral stage there is a period of time where paranoid tendencies predominate (soon to be the paranoid–schizoid position). This is followed by the depressive position. The depressive position coincides with the Oedipus complex, while superego fragments precede, and are consolidated during, the depressive position. In pregenital stages there is a splitting of the object during the paranoid position, and then the object is consolidated or formed during the depressive position. Inevitably, during pregenital stages, there is a splitting of the object after the occurrence of the depressive position. This is due to the infant's or developing child's inability to tolerate the intensity of pining for the lost object. With the progression of stages, superego development contains less intense sadistic elements and the superego becomes increasingly influenced by libidinal or loving elements. As the phases progress, there are increasingly successful attempts at reparation, which aid the softening, or libidinization, of the superego. The oscillation of positions occurs throughout development and, as such, Klein sees human beings as always potentially in touch with psychotic elements and anxieties.

Klein's ideas about bisexuality begin from a Freudian base, but here, as well as in most areas, Klein has a good deal to add to Freudian theory. Klein's view of pregenital development is dominated by what she terms the feminine position. The boy's feminine position is arrived at

> Under the dominance of oral, urethral and anal impulses and phantasies and is closely linked with his relation to his mother's breasts.

THE KLEINIAN REVOLUTION   245

If the boy can turn some of his love and libidinal desires from his mother's breast towards his father's penis, while retaining the breast as a good object, then his father's penis will figure in his mind as a good and creative organ which will give libidinal gratification as well as give him children as it does to his mother. These feminine desires are always an inherent feature in the boy's development. They are at the root of his inverted Oedipus complex and constitute the first homosexual position. The reassuring picture of his father's penis as a good and creative organ is also a precondition for the boy's capacity to develop his positive Oedipus desires. For only if the boy has a strong enough belief in the "goodness" of the male genital—his father's as well as his own—can he allow himself to experience his genital desires towards his mother. When his fear of the castrating father is mitigated by trust in the good father, he can face his Oedipus hatred and rivalry. Thus the inverted and positive Oedipus tendencies develop simultaneously, and there is a close interaction between them. [1945, pp. 410–411]

In this passage, Klein maintains that, in pregenital development, the boy is primarily in a negative Oedipal situation. It is only the trust and love of the good father that can help the boy face his rivalrous hatred and come closer to resolving Oedipal conflicts. The interesting aspect of Klein's description is the length of the negative Oedipal phase that she seems to suggest. While, in her theorizing, the boy will encounter Oedipal themes several times during development, it appears that it is not until genital primacy has been achieved that positive Oedipal themes will clearly predominate over negative Oedipal tendencies. This description, of course, places the mother as central in the development of both male and female children. What Klein has done is develop a theory of internalization that takes into account the reality of the primacy of early maternal influence. Freud, in various places, takes note of this fact, but rarely places the maternal influence as central in his formal theorizing.

While Klein sees castration anxiety as a central concern of the boy, unalloyed castration anxiety does not really appear until the genital phase of development, if indeed this anxiety can ever be considered to make an unalloyed appearance. For example, she states,

If various fears are excessive and the urge to repress genital desires is over-strong, difficulties in potency are bound to arise later.

Normally such fears in the boy are counteracted by the picture of his mother's body as the source of all goodness (good milk and babies) as well as by his introjection of loved objects. When his love impulses predominate, the products and content of his body take on the significance of gifts; his penis becomes the means of giving gratification and children to his mother and of making reparation. Also, if the feeling of containing the good breast of his mother and the good penis of his father has the upper hand, the boy derives from this a strengthened trust in himself which allows him to give freer rein to his impulses and desires. In union with his father he feels that his penis acquires reparative and creative qualities. [*ibid.*, p. 412]

In this extract, one can see that at every point of development there is an internal drama of objects moving in conflict with destructive consequences, or in concert towards reparation and creative activities. Thus, all internal objects remain as representations, and are replayed in the oscillation of positions. The oscillation of positions is assumed to be a life-long occurrence. There are, of course, individuals who, for example, are more prone to paranoia, but there will always be some movement of positions in everyone, if only during brief situational occurrences. Clearly, the quality and the nature of internal objects can shift and be transformed. As development progresses, Klein assumes that internal and external, as well as good and bad, representations will be unified. The same can be said for superego representations that derived from internal objects. As the boy is able to identify with the good, loving penis (father), he sees the father as less threatening and the superego of the boy becomes a guide to external action and accomplishment.

Klein, in this paper and in her earlier work (1928), makes note of the fact that both the boy and girl envy the babies and the penis that they phantasize are inside the mother's body. For the boy, this is part of the inverted or negative Oedipal complex. The important aspect of this is that both the boy and the girl go through what Klein has previously called the femininity phase of development. She has previously linked this phase with anality, but the implications of her present theory is that the femininity phase is something that begins with the first Oedipal situation and, in the male, continues as a dominant theme until genital primacy. In the boy, the positive and negative Oedipal themes become blended during the Oedipal themes of the genital phase of development.

The girl, however, begins life with an unconscious knowledge

> that her body contains potential children whom she feels to be her most precious possession. The penis of her father as the giver of children is equated to the production of children and becomes the object of great desire and admiration for the little girl. This relation to the penis as a source of happiness and good gifts is enhanced by the loving and grateful relation to the good breast. Despite this "knowledge" the little girl has grave doubts about her future as a woman who can bear children. The mother is seen as a magical figure able to produce anything and "all goodness springs from her breast". [1945, p. 413]

This magical sense is reinforced by the phantasy that babies and the penis reside in the mother's body. Although the boy shares some of these phantasies, the "desire to receive her father's penis" and her ultimate desire to produce babies is a characteristic end product of the girl's development. Her psychological life is built around her interior world and her "inner objects". Her Oedipal conflicts centre not on castration, as is ultimately the case for the boy, but around the impulse to rob her mother of babies and the penis inside her. The danger in terms of the talion principle is that, in retaliation, the girl's body will be attacked and her good objects will be taken away or spoilt.

Although the boy goes through a phase of envy (part of the inverted or negative Oedipal), for the girl the envy of the mother is a crucial aspect of her positive Oedipal complex. It is part of her motivational stance in terms of her principal identification with her mother. Despite the fact that Klein sees penis envy as a factor in the girl's development, it is an expression of bisexuality and, in this way, is similar to the boy's desire to be a woman (and possess what his mother possesses). Klein further downplays the role of penis envy (as compared to Freud's emphasis) by maintaining that "penis envy covers in some measure the frustrated desire to take her mother's place with the father and to receive children from him" (*ibid.*, p. 414).

We have previously discussed the girl's superego during genital primacy. Here, Klein slightly adds to her theorizing about the girl's superego development. Since the girl's focus is more internal and receptive, she wishes to fill her internal world with good objects.

> In the feminine position she is driven by her sexual desires, and by her longing for a child, to internalize her father's penis . . . while in the male position she wishes to emulate him in all her masculine aspirations and sublimations. [*ibid.*]

This combination of positions allows the girl to be actively receptive and giving (or bountiful) and identify with the mother as the possessor (even if temporarily) of all that is good.

Freud and Klein

If we again compare Freud and Klein's conceptualizations, we have to be aware of from what vantage point we are making this comparison. If one is a cognitive psychologist, Klein and Freud appear quite similar in terms of the majority of their theoretical assumptions. From within the Freudian position, from 1935–1945 Klein was considered to be quite radical in terms of her theoretical suppositions. Klein, in addressing the differences, says that Freud maintains that genital desires begin at about age three and are in ascendance until age five. During this period, the Oedipus complex arises and the genital that is featured is the phallus. Castration anxiety is a core anxiety for boys and penis envy and hatred of the mother takes part in anxiety situations for the girl. Klein's discussion of Freud is a limited one, and so I will wait for the commentary section to try to show that some of the differences between them are illusory and some greater than Klein acknowledges. An indisputable difference is that Klein changes the name of a stage from phallic to genital. She states that Freud's earlier term "genital stage" is more appropriate than phallic. She sees both sexes as experiencing genital sensations from early infancy onwards. Both the positive and negative (inverted) Oedipus complex is first experienced under the influence of "oral libido . . . It is during the stage of genital primacy that the positive Oedipus situation reaches its climax" (*ibid.*, p. 416).

One palpable way of viewing the shift from Freud to Klein is to think about the shift from penis to breast or from father to mother. Clearly, Klein's theorizing is centred on the phantasies that involve the contents of the mother's body. The breast is initially divided into a good and bad object, and these first introjects form the basis of the superego. Just as the father's penis (or a representation of the father) will be important in the course of superego development, the mother (or, initially, the breast) will serve as the foundation for superego development in both the girl and the boy. Both sexes have a task in integrating these images, but the girl will develop the more loving and giving superego in optimal development.

Now we can see that Klein has shifted a good deal in her new psychoanalytic theory. She has retained the idea of instinct, but has utilized this concept much more fully than Freud or any previous Freudian. Love and hate are present at birth as manifestations of the fused drives. There is no initial experience possible without love and hate providing the valence for the experience and the subsequent object that becomes internalized. Objects are internally present from the first moments of life and divided or split on the basis of the affective valence that begins immediately to shape the contents of the infant's mind. The Oedipus complex is present during the first six months of life, and, by that time, there is also superego development. The developmental positions (now primarily the depressive position) are the single most important developmental occurrence and, through the depressive position, Oedipal phenomena are experienced, integrated, and then split apart anew. The oscillations of paranoia and the depressive position continue throughout development, as does the recurrence of Oedipal phenomena and superego development.

The superego is a phantastic internalization of objects filtered through the, as yet, unintegrated affects of love and hate. Integration occurs in several ways: external and internal object representations are gradually brought together, good and bad, or idealized and denigrated, objects are gradually repaired and integrated, and superego representations are integrated as development progresses. One could simplify this statement and maintain that, in optimal development, split structures are gradually integrated into whole objects or structures. Klein's assumption is that when an object is split, there is also a split in the ego, and this tends to make the ego a mass of objects. Certainly, in this respect, she is the first theorist who places the internalization of the object as the centrepiece of her theoretical structure. Since, for Klein, development is not linear, there is constant need to repair the object and to consolidate the splitting that the paranoid position has provided. The sequence of paranoia to depressive position that involves pining and leads to mania requires reparation at each new juncture of the depressive position. In this comparison, I have not bothered to present Freud's views, since these have been presented in some detail. Suffice it to say that, while some aspects of Freudian theory provided the structure for Klein's innovations, from inside psychoanalysis it may feel as if everything has changed; from outside psychoanalysis, while the content of the theory has changed, the architecture looks quite similar.

Perhaps we can end this chapter by saying that, by 1945, Klein is fully ready to be her own theorist. To make a case for a continuous event (the development of Klein's theorizing) occurring at one point in time is, of course, a fiction. One can say that in 1928 (or before), she reconceptualizes the Oedipal situation. By 1935, she establishes the idea of position (depressive position) and links the formation of the depressive position with paranoia, depression, and manic–depressive states. She also, with Joan Riviere, is able to somewhat de-emphasize the role of sadism and destructive tendencies. With Riviere, she gives an account of how the child repairs its internal world from the frequent disruptions and sadistic assaults that she theorizes occur throughout development. By 1945, after the Freud–Klein controversies (or discussions, if you tend to use reaction-formation), Klein clearly declares her differences with Freud. Klein, in her new Oedipal paper, changes developmental ideas and the structuralization of the superego, and acknowledges the fact that she is presenting a theory that takes psychoanalytic thought in new and different directions.

Commentary

It is hard to overestimate the influences of Ferenczi and Abraham on the early development of Klein's theorizing. Ferenczi was not only Klein's initial analyst and teacher, but he is the first analyst to provide concepts of projective–introjective sequences that eventually lead to Klein's concept of projective identification. Ferenczi writes (1909),

To understand better the fundamental character of neurotics one has to compare their behaviour with that of patients suffering from dementia praecox and paranoia. The dementia patient completely detaches his interest from the outer world and becomes autoerotic (Jung, Abraham). The paranoiac, as Freud has pointed out, would like to do the same, but cannot, and so projects on to the outer world the interest that has become a burden to him. The neurosis stands in this respect in a diametrical contrast to paranoia. Whereas the paranoiac expels from his ego the impulses that have become unpleasant, the neurotic helps himself by taking into the ego as large as possible a part of the outer world, making it the object of unconscious phantasies. This is a kind of diluting process, by means of which he tries to mitigate the poignancy of free-floating, unsatisfied, and unsatisfiable, unconscious wish-impulses. One might give to this process, in contrast to projection, the name of introjection. [1909, pp. 41–42]

This is one of Ferenczi's first published statements about projection and introjection, and one where he is using these terms to explain clinical phenomena. Freud uses Ferenczi's ideas to account for his concept of the purified pleasure ego (see Chapter Three). Klein sees the utility of these theories, and develops the concept of projective–introjective sequences (later, projective identification) into a mode of communication in the earliest moments of life. It is also a defence mechanism and at least one of the ways of accounting for transference reactions.

Abraham was really the first and most influential analyst to provide a full developmental theoretical picture for Freud's psycho-sexual stages. When Fairbairn critiques the psycho-sexual stages (see Chapter Nine), he does not go to Freud's writings, but, rather, chooses Abraham's conceptualizations, since they are the richer panoramas of early development. Klein's concepts of early development in many ways spring from Abraham's theoretical/clinical writings. Abraham attempts to develop fixation points for a number of disorders. Klein's concept of the depressive position is reminiscent of Abraham's view of manic–depressive disorders being concomitant with the second half of the oral stage. The first half of the oral stage is a fixation point for schizoid and schizophrenic disorders. It is not too large a leap to think of the paranoid–schizoid position, followed by the depressive position, as in some way harkening back to Abraham's conceptualizations. To be sure, Abraham's views only provided an adumbrated picture of Klein's vibrant concepts. It is also important to note that Abraham's views on envy were different from, and more developed than, the ones that Freud had proposed. Freud mostly discussed the role of envy in terms of penis envy, although he implied a larger role for envious feelings in other writings (1914c, 1915c). Abraham saw envy as appearing much earlier in development and, at first, having nothing to do with penis envy. His concept of envy derived in the oral stage surely was a factor in Klein's later postulates, where envy occupied a crucial role in the paranoid–schizoid position (see Chapter Eight).

Perhaps the two most striking aspects of this Kleinian era is her dating of the Oedipus complex at a much earlier period than Freud, and her concept of the depressive position. Klein's moving the Oedipal period to an earlier time is, in part, based on her analysis of children. She eventually defends her reconstructions (1957) by quoting from Freud's "Constructions in analysis" (1937d) paper. Clearly, Freud developed his theory, in large part, on the basis of reconstructions, or constructions, if one prefers. That Klein used the same method of theory development is here not the question. Here, the question, or, rather, the interpretation of Klein's Oedipal views, is based on her presumed desire to remain within the Freudian tradition. Klein states that she has repeatedly seen that the Oedipal complex comes into operation earlier than had been assumed (Klein, 1928). She could easily have maintained that early triangulation is a forerunner and an important determinant of Oedipal dynamics without positing that Oedipal dynamics appear and reappear right after weaning, then again in the anal stage, and again in what Freud called the phallic stage of development. Later in her theoretical writings, the Oedipal stage is coincident with each appearance of the depressive position. My view is that Klein presented her theory in this manner because Freud had recently said (1923b) that Oedipal dynamics were the bedrock of analytic understanding in the clinical situation. If Oedipal dynamics were the bedrock, how could Klein presume to go beyond the bedrock? One compromise position is that she was not going beyond the bedrock; it was simply that the bedrock occurred earlier than was previously thought to be the case. This was a way to include her new concepts within the Freudian opus despite the fact that Klein's

THE KLEINIAN REVOLUTION   253

early Oedipal manifestations were quite different from Freud's view of the Oedipal complex. Clearly, her view of the Oedipal complex is one that varied depending on when it occurred in development. In Klein's first Oedipal complex, there is a terrifying drama taking place, with a superego structure that is equally terrifying. Although this concept captures some of the drama of Freud's theory, it does not overlap with his picture of the struggle during this period. A main component of the Freudian Oedipal stage is coming to understand that the Oedipal couple may, at times, have different priorities than the Oedipal child. The Oedipal drama features castration anxiety and penis envy, but it also features the growing capacity for love and understanding biological and emotional differences. It is hard to see anything but the barest rudiments of understanding love and emotional differences in Klein's first Oedipal manifestations. At most, there is a unified object that rather quickly is lost in the coming oscillation of stages and in her later theory of positions. Nevertheless, however one defines Oedipal dynamics, the main question is whether the concept of the depressive position is a useful one.

Here, it seems to me that Klein has provided a view that is useful not only for developmental theory, but also for clinical experience with adults. She has taken up an element of Freud's theory and completely transformed his concepts. Freud assumed that with the development of the purified pleasure ego (Chapter Three) there was a movement away from reality and a new structure was formed with the beginning of the stage of narcissism. Klein posits that, during development, with the onset of the depressive position a whole object is formed, and then, in the next stage, the object is split and reformed in the subsequent depressive position. As stages progress, the object is more differentiated, and in the genital (Freud's phallic) stage the depressive position and the Oedipal complex largely coincide with Freud's conceptualization of the Oedipal stage. Thus, whether one wants to call early triangulation Oedipal or not, Klein's contributions, even in the era covered in this chapter, have no rival (excluding Freud) in terms of the originality of her theory. Even in her relatively early to her middle writings, she has transformed psychoanalytic theory.

As a last point in this section, in the body of the chapter it was mentioned that Freud and Klein had different ideas about the strength of the superego. For Freud, a strong superego is a united structure that provides consistent ideals and prohibitions. Freud thought of the male superego as stronger, because the ideals were firmer and ostensibly more consistent. It seems to me that he mistook rigidity for consistency; the more flexible female superego is consistent in the sense of being able to judge different situations and adjust to them as her principles will allow. Klein's idea of the strength of the early superego involved the ferocity of what Anna Freud would consider a punitive superego structure. Thus, Klein's early superego would, in Freudian terms, be considered a primitive fragmentary structure. However, Klein's concept of the later superego of the well-adjusted female (the bountiful female superego) is a strong, unified structure with loving ideals. It is hard to see the male superego as any "stronger" than Klein's description of the mature female superego.

CHAPTER SEVEN

The controversial discussions

> I wish to point out, therefore, that from the beginning of life, on Freud's own hypothesis, the psyche responds to the reality of its experience by interpreting them—or, rather, by misinterpreting them—in a subjective manner that increases it pleasure and preserves it from pain. This act of a subjective interpretation of experience, which it carries out by means of the processes of introjection and projection, is called by Freud hallucination; and it forms the basis of what we mean by phantasy-life
>
> (Riviere, 1936)

> I have always insisted on the necessity of postulating the primary reality function of the primitive ego. Indeed, without such a postulate, there is nothing to prevent us falling into a primitive variety of mysticism
>
> (Glover, quoted in King & Steiner, 1991, p. 399)

Summary

In this chapter, Dr Vorus gives a moving account of the Freud–Klein controversies and some of the historical and political tensions that led up to these fateful discussions. Ellman provides a brief commentary at the end of the chapter. The controversial discussions, in many ways, presaged debates that continued over the next several decades. The divisions that are depicted in this chapter did not allow for meaningful discussions across theoretical lines until the recent past (however one defines recent past).

Introduction

In 1941, the British Psychoanalytic Society entered into what has become known as the Controversial Discussions. These were an institutional response to a schism within the Society that began after Klein presented her paper introducing the depressive position in 1935, and increased dramatically as refugee analysts began arriving from Germany and Austria in the late 1930s. Many social and political factors contributed to the escalating tension within the institute, including anxieties related to the war, the loss by many of a homeland, the recent death of Freud, financial insecurities, disputes over power-sharing within the institute and society, as well as personal rivalries. While undoubtedly important, we will not have time to address these historical factors here in any detail (see Steiner, 1989, and Vorus, 1998, for a more complete discussion of these issues). Instead, we will take up the question posed at the end of the previous chapter: how did the discussions themselves illuminate the relationship between Freudian and Kleinian theory as it existed in the early 1940s? And how might those discussions have shaped the subsequent developments in both lines of thought?

Background of theoretical controversies

Melanie Klein was not always a controversial figure in British psychoanalysis. While her ideas on child analysis had aroused considerable dissent during her early years in Berlin, they found fertile ground when she arrived in London in 1926; by the end of the 1920s, Klein's ideas had assumed some prominence in the British Society. In 1933, this situation began to change, as analysts from Berlin, fleeing Nazism, began filtering into the UK, bringing with them ambivalent attitudes toward Klein's innovations. This ambivalence gave way to overt hostility in 1934, when Klein introduced her concept of the depressive position, which a number of British and continental analysts saw as putting forward views that violated psychoanalysis as they knew it (King, 1991).

While disputes over theoretical differences remained largely civil and subdued through most of the 1930s, the Nazi occupation of Vienna in 1938 set into motion a decisive series of events for both British and Viennese analysts. As it became apparent that the Freuds and their colleagues were in increasing danger, Jones, with the help of Princess Marie Bonaparte, helped secure the safe passage of the Freuds and their colleagues to London, where they were offered not only housing and financial security, but also full membership of the British Psychoanalytic Society (King, 1991). Freud, feeble and ailing with cancer, did not take part in the activities of the British Society, and died less than a year after arriving on British soil. However, Anna Freud quickly became an active participant in the affairs of the society (Young-Bruehl, 1988). This undoubtedly contributed to the polarization of members of the society: both Anna Freud and Melanie Klein were pioneering figures of child psychoanalysis, but they held sharply contrasting opinions on a variety of points regarding child development and the conduct of child treatment, and had been publicly criticizing one another's views since the 1920s (e.g., A. Freud, 1927; Klein, 1927). Now they and their followers occupied the same psychoanalytic institute.

Overt hostilities were delayed by the outbreak of the war, when many of the British analysts (including Klein) fled London in order to avoid air-raids. Those who remained were largely recent immigrants from Germany and Austria (i.e., Anna Freud's group). This led to the interesting situation of recent foreign immigrants, many of whom opposed the ideas of Klein, dominating meetings of the British Psychoanalytic Society for almost two years. In 1941, most of the indigenous members of the British Society, Klein included, returned to London and to active participation (King, 1989).

Tensions, expressed privately and covertly between members prior to this point, reached a peak and began to be openly, at times acrimoniously, expressed in a series of scientific and business meetings, beginning in November 1941. Some of the friction took the form of complaints concerning internal political issues, such as the dominance of the Institute and Society by a few analysts who simultaneously held a number of offices for multiple terms (most notably, Edward Glover). However, one of the primary sources of tension came from the growing sense, among some of the Viennese Freudians, that the Kleinians were a subversive group secretly vying for power whose heretical, distorted ideas threatened to infiltrate the institutions of psychoanalysis and contaminate the Freudian legacy. In response to this sense of imminent danger, the Viennese Freudians began actively contemplating ways to expel the Kleinians, while the latter "circled the wagons" and planned a unified response.

The controversial discussions

These growing tensions reached a watershed in a series of five "Extraordinary Business Meetings" that took place in July 1942. While these were initially taken up with intensely vituperative accusations and countercharges, consensus was eventually reached. It was decided that political differences would be addressed through theoretical debate, and a series of scientific discussions was planned to determine the nature of theoretical differences between the groups in an effort to clarify whether their views were truly incompatible, and, if so, whose were legitimately psychoanalytic.

The Controversial Discussions were these theoretical debates. They consisted of four papers presented by the Kleinians on phantasy, introjection and projection, regression, and the depressive position (authored by Susan Isaacs, Paula Heimann, Isaacs and Heimann, and Klein, respectively). Each paper was distributed ahead of time, then read aloud during a scientific meeting, followed by prepared and spontaneous discussion by members of the society. Much of this discussion centred on the extent to which Klein's views represented a legitimate extension of Freudian theory, or whether they diverged into an incompatible variant (King & Steiner, 1991).

It is important to point out that five of the ten meetings that comprised the discussions themselves were given over to the first paper by Susan Isaacs, entitled "The nature and function of phantasy" (1943). As Steiner (1991) notes, "the notion of unconscious phantasy is probably the major theoretical theme of all the Scientific Discussions" (p. 242), and a close reading of discussions of the three succeeding papers shows them primarily to involve reiterations of fundamental issues raised in the context of phantasy. It is to this paper that we now turn.

The nature and function of phantasy

The First Scientific Meeting in the Series of Discussions on Controversial Issues was held on 27 January 1943, at the British Psychoanalytic Society. The topic was Isaacs' paper, entitled "The nature and function of phantasy", which had been distributed ahead of time. Isaacs' paper discusses the notion of "unconscious phantasy", The spelling of this term, using "ph" to differentiate it from "fantasy", served to distinguish the unconscious character of phantasy from its conscious form, a usage which had its origins when Freud's works were translated from German to English in the 1920s. In an acknowledged extension of Freud's application of the term, Isaacs states in her paper that unconscious phantasies make up the basic content of the mind, and exist from birth onwards. These are seen by her as the psychic representatives of the life and death instincts, and to underlie, on an unconscious level, all mental activities and experiences.

Four general areas of disagreement emerged out of the discussions of this paper. These were: (1) the place of subjective *vs.* objective terminology in describing mental phenomena; (2) phantasy as psychic representation; (3) phantasy and early object relations; and (4) the relation between phantasy and psychic structure. Although most of the discussion about these issues failed to reach satisfactory resolution, it did serve to crystallize the differences. And, as I will demonstrate, each of these areas is tied together by a common philosophical thread, the unravelling of which points the way towards one understanding of the sharp polarization of these psychoanalytic views.

Speaking scientifically: the use of subjective vs. objective terminology to describe mental phenomena

"I wish to state here my opinion that the primary content of all mental processes are unconscious phantasies. Such phantasies are the basis of all unconscious and conscious thought processes" (Isaacs, 1943, p. 272).

This statement by Isaacs introduces the first basic postulate of the Kleinian view of phantasy, which she puts forth after reminding her audience of Freud's emphasis on the psychic *reality* of phantasy productions, not to be diminished in comparison with the reality of material and objective events. She states,

> Again, the word "phantasy" is often used in contrast with "reality", the latter word being taken as identical with "external" or "material" or "objective" facts. But when external reality is called "objective" reality, there is an assumption which denies to psychical reality its own objectivity as a mental fact. [*ibid.*, p. 269]

In postulating parity between psychical and material events, Isaacs seems to be doing two things. The first is emphasizing the reality *for the subject* of his or her unconscious phantasy and the determinative role it plays in shaping his or her psychological world. This is the individual and experiential sense of phantasy as the "primary content of mental life". The second, and more controversial, meaning implied by this definition relates to the language and mode of conceptualization most appropriate to theoretical descriptions of the psyche. For Isaacs, the language of phantasy, rather than that of abstract mechanisms, captures best the actual nature of mental events, because it conveys the meaningfulness inherent in the "psychic character" of those events:

> In particular, the value of the word "phantasy" is that it emphasizes the *psychic character* of the processes we are concerned with. A suggestive way in which this fact is sometimes stated is that the special character of mental as compared with physical processes is that they have *meaning* . . . The word "phantasy" serves to remind us always of this distinctive character of meaning in the mental life. [*ibid.*, p. 272, original italics]

In short, it would seem that Isaacs and the Kleinians assume a categorical distinction between those events of the mind and those

THE CONTROVERSIAL DISCUSSIONS   261

of the body and "material reality": the former follow the symbolic laws of meaningfulness described by Freud, while the latter follow the concrete laws of physical reality. To describe psychic reality in the language of material reality is simply inappropriate, in that it blurs this basic distinction and obscures Freud's discovery that, while distinct, the psychical and the physical have equal claim to the status of "reality", which therefore obviates the need to translate phenomena from the latter realm into the language of the former in order to be "scientific".

In the discussions that follow Isaacs' presentation, this difference in viewpoint regarding objective *vs.* subjective terminology becomes a point of contention between the competing groups. Edward Glover claims Isaacs is "addicted to a sort of psychic anthropomorphism", in which there is a confusion of psychological mechanisms with "concepts of the psychic apparatus" (King & Steiner, 1991, p. 326). Foulkes, an immigrant from Vienna and adherent of Anna Freud, addresses himself to the implications he sees in the Kleinian "confusion" of theoretical and experiential terminology:

> This so-called signicative function of language is precisely the one exclusively to be used in scientific, rational thinking . . . It is this dehydrated, lifeless, skeletal use of words for which we aim, and for good reasons, if we want to compress our clinical experiences, for instance, into scientific terms to be used for a precise and short cut. [Insisting on reducing psychoanalytic concepts to underlying phantasy] would be just the same as to say that somebody who understands the theory of music cannot understand a concert. [Quoted in King & Steiner, 1991, pp. 363–364]

In Foulkes's view, one needs to *abstract from* clinical experience to theoretical concepts in order to make "scientific formulations". To elevate the conscious or unconscious phantasy of internal objects to the same metapsychological status as intrapsychic structure (e.g., ego, superego) is to lose the distinction between clinical data and the theoretical discourse used to order and categorize that data. Foulkes sees a particular problem in this for clinical formulation, in that phantasy concepts (i.e., introjected objects), once elevated to theoretical constructs, would begin to be seen as "primary motors", in the same way as instincts traditionally are. For Foulkes, this is akin to "the religious and spiritual level with an independent soul having energies of its own from another world", and represents a "regression to pre-scientific thinking" (*ibid.*, p. 365).

Ella Sharpe, a member of the independent group, echoes this concern in her contribution to the Third Discussion:

> My query about technique concerns the psychotic belief of actual objects inside, breasts, penises, parents, evil, and good. Sometimes I get the impression that some analysts who deal with these beliefs, interpret to their patients as if they themselves believed not only their patients' beliefs, but in the actuality of the concrete objects inside. [Quoted in King & Steiner, 1991, p. 405]

These views invite responses from Isaacs and her fellow Kleinian, Paula Heimann. To Foulkes, Heimann replies with a clinical discussion (this was a previously presented case, to which Foulkes had referred in his comments), and concludes with the statement that the "devils" that the patient had felt to exist concretely inside "were a creation of her mind, an outcome of her unconscious conflicts, a peculiar blend of love and hate, anxiety and guilt, punishment and reparation" (quoted in King & Steiner, 1991, p. 391). Similarly, in Isaacs' reply to Sharpe, she states:

> Like Miss Sharpe, we believe that the patient believes he has concrete objects and part-objects inside him. And we accept the full weight of his belief, without evasion, we do not, however, ourselves believe that he has, nor give the patient reason to suppose that we believe it. [Quoted in King & Steiner, 1991, p. 459]

It is interesting to note that objections to the loss of distinction between clinical observation and theoretical concepts are uniformly answered from a *clinical* standpoint by the Kleinians; they neither acknowledge nor deny the claim that they have effectively eliminated an important distinction between experiential and theoretical modes of discourse. Their recourse to clinical discussion, while possibly evasive, may also reveal something of the truth of the accusation; to answer the criticism that the theoretical and clinical are insufficiently distinguished with a clinical answer can easily be read as an indirect support of this non-distinction.

However, I would suggest that not addressing the criticisms in the terms they are offered might represent something more fundamental than evasion, something more akin to a *demonstration* of perspective, a response from a different set of ideological co-ordinates. That is, to argue for the distinction between theory and inner experience implies the possibility of an objective vantage point; remember that Foulkes's main worry was that phantasy, rather than instinct, would be seen as a "primary motor" and that, under this delusive belief, mental phenomena would be traced to its unconscious phantasy level and simply left at that. This concern necessarily assumes there is something more absolute—Foulkes puts instinct and the external world in this category—to which phantasy relates as a "significant nodal point" in the clash between these more significant, objective realities. By not explicitly responding to this particular point (and similar ones offered by Brierley, Glover, and Sharpe), Isaacs can be seen as simply responding from a vantage point that sees phenomenal experience itself, whether conscious or unconscious, as the most fundamental level of description of the mind.

This issue is clearly one of fundamental importance; very basic assumptions are involved regarding the place and purpose of theory in psychoanalysis and the proper form of scientific discourse. In a broader sense, basic questions are posed that challenge the dichotomies of objectivity–subjectivity and reality–phantasy. Klein and Isaacs seem to claim that, in the realm of the mind, these dichotomies are inverted; subjectivity and phantasy are the road to truth, and, as such, constitute the only form of reality of the mind that might claim scientific validity: subjectivity takes the place traditionally held by objectivity, as phantasy does that of reality. As I will attempt to show below, this question of the relation between phantasy and reality, and the implicit questioning of the possibility of objectivity with respect to mental phenomena, runs deeply through each area of theoretical controversy between these groups. I will attempt also to demonstrate how the ramifications of this questioning deeply unsettled many of the members of this discussion, and arguably served as an emotional catalyst to the discussions themselves.

Phantasy as psychic representation: arguments over infant subjectivity

In "developing more fully" the postulate that phantasy is the primary content of mental life, Isaacs derives a second postulate from the following statement by Freud: "We suppose that it [the id] is somewhere in direct contact with somatic processes, and takes over from them instinctual needs and gives them mental expression" (Freud, 1933a, p. 98) (Isaacs, 1943, quoted in King & Steiner, 1991, pp. 276–277).

Isaacs states,

> I believe that this "mental expression" is unconscious phantasy. Phantasy is the mental corollary, the psychic representative of instinct. And there is no impulse, no instinctual urge, which is not experienced as (unconscious) phantasy. [Quoted in King & Steiner, 1991, p. 277]

While the first postulate located phantasy as the general constituent of psychic reality, and, by granting that domain conceptual primacy, made phantasy the "primary content", this second postulate articulates the source and substance of phantasy. For Isaacs and Klein, it is the manifestation of instinct in the mental realm. To Klein, instinct may have other manifestations in the physical realm (e.g., physical energy, bodily tension, chemical processes); however, in the mental and, therefore, properly psychoanalytic domain, it will take the form of phantasy.

According to Isaacs, phantasy expresses in action the fulfilment of the particular urge; e.g., an infant's hungry desire to be fed might take the form of an inner experience of sucking at, and perhaps incorporating, the breast. In accord with the characteristics of early mental processes, the infant's wish will be felt as the deed itself, so that "he not only feels 'I want to' but actually 'I am doing' this and that action towards his mother" (*ibid.*).

This model of the early mental equivalence of wish and deed in phantasy provides an important juncture with Freud's writings. Although Isaacs acknowledges that her view of phantasy as the "mental corollary of instinct" goes beyond Freud's written views on the subject, she reads him as coming close to this idea in his thoughts about "hallucinatory wish fulfilment":

> Now I know very well that Freud himself did not say that the "mental expression" of instinctual urges is the same thing as phantasy. But in my view he came very near to this when he postulated the infant's satisfaction of his wishes in *hallucinatory* form . . . in the beginning of mental life, "whatever was thought of (desired) was

simply imagined in a hallucinatory form, as still happens with our dream-thoughts every night. This is an attempt at satisfaction by hallucination" (Freud, 1911[b], p. 219).

Freud does not say that the infant has unconscious phantasies. But the capacity to hallucinate is, in my view, either identical with phantasy or the pre-condition for it. [Quoted in King & Steiner, 1991, p. 278]

Isaacs quotes Freud's statement of the process by which the desired breast is originally "imagined in hallucinatory form" (1911b) before the onset of the reality principle and the subsequent development of other means of attaining satisfaction. It is clear that Freud assumes that this process is a very early attempt at gratification, that it involves conjuring up the wished for satisfaction as an internal reality in a primitive attempt at coping with frustration, via the process of "regression to the sensory end of the psychic apparatus" (Freud, 1900a). Isaacs extends this concept in two important ways. The first extension is to generalize the process of hallucination to all manifestations of instinctual wish. By making phantasy the ubiquitous form of representation of the entire internal world, Isaacs moves beyond the particular situation described by Freud (hallucinated breast as the byproduct of frustrated oral needs). For her, *all* instinctual desires are immediately experienced unconsciously as achieving satisfaction: "And there is no impulse, no instinctual urge, which is not experienced as unconscious phantasy" (Isaacs, quoted in King & Steiner, 1991, p. 277).

Isaacs also extends the relation between instinct and phantasy by making it clear that it is not *only* instinctual wishes that assume their inner representation in phantasy:

Freud refers to "the mental expression of instinctual needs". In my view, this means not only *libidinal* desires, but destructive impulses and anxieties also. Moreover, phantasy soon becomes a means of defence against anxieties, a means of inhibiting and controlling instinctual urges, and expression of reparative wishes. [*ibid.*, original italics]

This seems to move beyond the model explicitly provided by Freud, whereby wishes are experienced as fulfilled only as the most primitive means of coping with frustration. In the above statement,

Isaacs defines phantasy as the representation of all mental impulse, whether it be sexual or aggressive, affect (anxiety), or even an ego mechanism in opposition to impulse (defence).

Further, in early phantasy, "implicit meaning" is given to external sensations through their interaction with wish-fulfilling phantasies; for Isaacs and Klein, sensory experiences are never merely perceived in their brute form, but are always *interpreted* through their interaction with instinctual wishes and frustrations in accord with the pleasure principle. Isaacs quotes Riviere's contribution to the 1936 "Exchange lectures" to this effect:

> I wish especially to point out, therefore, that from the very beginning of life . . . the psyche responds to the reality of its experience by interpreting them—or rather, by *misinterpreting* them—in a subjective manner that increases its pleasure and preserves it from pain . . . The phantasy life of the individual is thus the form in which his real internal and external sensations and perceptions are interpreted and represented to himself in his mind under the influence of the pleasure–pain principle . . . I would draw your attention to the conclusion that phantasy life is never "pure phantasy". It consists of true perceptions and of false interpretations; all phantasies are thus *mixtures* of external and internal reality (Riviere, 1936, p. 399). [Quoted in Isaacs, 1943, p. 282; original italics]

Thus, phantasy is made up of external and internal experiences fused into an individual, subjective rendering of reality. Sensory experience provides many of the ingredients, but the element of *subjectivity* is a function of individual, instinctual experience, and is generated by the hallucinatory mechanism described by Freud. In this way, because we begin life hallucinating instinctual wishes, we are already always subjective beings, and therefore never experience reality in a direct, unmediated fashion.

These expanded views of the relation of instinct and phantasy— that *all* impulses are experienced in hallucinatory form from the beginning of life, including anxiety and defence, and that these hallucinated impulses provide the vehicle for subjective interpretation of experience from the beginning—provoke two different kinds of objections, one narrow, the other global and related to the overall philosophical issue. The narrow objection concerns what is seen as an over-generalization of the early mechanism of "hallucinatory wish-fulfilment" to describe phenomena beyond the meaning originally intended by Freud: the frustration of instinctual needs. In Anna Freud's words:

> With the suggested new use of the term "phantasy" early mental processes are grouped together under a common connotation irrespective of whether they are instinct derivatives or not. Hallucinatory expression is equally ascribed to all these processes, again irrespective of whether they are instinct derivatives or not. The singular nature of all instinctual processes in contrast to others as stressed in the libido theory is thereby obscured. [Quoted in King & Steiner, 1991, p. 329]

In this objection, Anna Freud clearly wants to differentiate those mental processes that are instinctual from the non-instinctual. This position represents a common theme for her throughout these discussions; she is the upholder of *clear distinctions*, whether these lie between libido and non-libido, primary and secondary process, or autoerotism and object-relatedness. Isaacs' response, also characteristic, is to challenge the notion of any such clearly demarcated domains:

> I know of no evidence to show that in the earliest stages we can distinguish between mental processes which are instinct-derivatives and those which are not ... as I have already agreed, the details of the way in which perception and knowledge of external reality become differentiated from phantasy and internal reality await much fuller study. [Isaacs, 1943, pp. 371–372]

Glover articulates the more global critique. His objections are similar to Brierley's, but go beyond the specific issue of instinct and phantasy to a more general criticism of the Kleinian view of the psychic apparatus. He sees the Kleinians as failing to recognize that the human psyche is initially and primarily concerned with adaptation to reality. In his view, far from being the earliest form of thinking, phantasy is a *secondary* development that requires the more highly evolved mind of an older child to attain. Like Anna Freud, Glover's objection begins with references to Isaacs' overgeneralization of "hallucinatory wish fulfilment". However, this serves as a mere entrée to the fundamental objection that the Kleinians misunderstand the nature and function of the psychic apparatus itself. He berates the Kleinians for their neglect of the significance of *reality factors* in the laying down of memory traces of sensory experience . . . They seem to confuse the relations of psychic reality to phantasy and to reality proving respectively. The regression in oral hallucinatory gratification, e.g. activates the memory traces of the *actual experiences* at the sensory end of the apparatus. And reality proving is after all concerned with the relation of gratification or frustration of instincts to the external objects of these instincts, not with snapshots of the Himalaya Mountains. [Quoted in King & Steiner, 1991, p. 327, italics added]

This last statement seems to be a caricature of the Kleinian view that the infant is initially orientated more toward internal phantasy breasts ("snapshots of the Himalaya mountains") than to "real", external gratifications and frustrations. Glover develops this point further in describing the initial formation of (veridical) memory traces as adaptive, mobilized by frustration, and promoting activities that lead to gratification and avoid frustration. Thus, in his view, the basic function of the psychic apparatus is a "reality function", and representations that cohere under this function are realistic images and memories. "Mental representation" and "phantasy" are, therefore, essentially quite distinct. Glover also sees hallucinatory wish fulfilment, which Isaacs describes as the prototype of phantasy, as orientated primarily to reality:

> although the process fails to gratify the instinct it is regulated along reality lines. The hallucinatory regression is an attempt at gratification initiated by frustration but arrested at the imaginal level and so doomed to failure. It is a frustration product characterized by its extreme imaginal intensity, but the imaginal element is in no sense a phantasy. *There is as yet no question of using the term "phantasy" for such psychic events.* Phantasy in the sense in which it is used by Freud is a much later, more complicated, and from the point of view of reality a more revolutionary development. [*ibid.*, p. 397, original italics]

For Glover, phantasy can only take place after some degree of psychic maturation; awareness of the relation between subject, aim, and object is necessary, as is some awareness of the different degrees of frustration. In other words, one must have some modicum of awareness of reality before phantasy is possible; one must be able to relate to reality before a distortion in that relationship (as in phantasy) can take place:

> The divorce of early forms of thought from their original adaptation function can only be achieved through violent strains to the psychic apparatus, as is indeed obvious in the case of regression in the psychoses. [*ibid.*, p. 399]

He makes clear the implication of this view for the question of the early infant's *subjectivity*:

> I repeat, the basic function here is a reality function, i.e. reality in terms of instinct gratification and frustration within an undefined but no doubt short space of time, that is to say as soon as the larval state has passed, the baby has as good (that is to say, adequate and effective) a sense of reality for any given instinct as any of us in this room have for ours, in some respects probably a better (more wholehearted) reality sense. [*ibid.*, p. 397]

Glover clearly sees infancy as beginning with an initial period of "objective" apperception of reality, which underlies the later development of phantasy, exactly the opposite of Isaacs' and Klein's sequence. His objection to the primacy of phantasy is strenuous and categorical, and the sense of danger he feels in this idea is apparent in the following statement:

> I have always insisted on the necessity of postulating the primary reality function of the primitive ego. Indeed, without such a postulate, there is nothing to prevent us falling into a primitive variety of mysticism. [*ibid.*, p. 399]

The feeling of threat here is palpable; it is as if the "primary reality function" stands as a bulwark against the powerful undertow of "mysticism". One senses that Glover fears for the dissolution of his *own* epistemological grounding ("nothing to prevent *us* . . ."), as if the foundation for ideas about certainty and objectivity feel so fragile they might dissolve if Kleinian ideas about phantasy, with their assumption that all mental processes ultimately rest on a ground of phantasy, were accepted.

Characteristically, in Isaacs' response to Glover, the underlying epistemological issues (and anxieties) he raised are simply not addressed. Instead, Isaacs's response to Glover takes up the fight within the context of Freud's views on the subject of phantasy and reality, arguing that her position is more compatible with Freud than is Glover's.

> Dr. Glover asserts that reality-testing and reality-adaptation are quite independent of phantasy and prior to the latter in time of development . . . But this is quite contrary to Freud's own views. There are many passages which show that Freud regarded the reality-principle as the secondary one, coming into operation because the infant finds phantasy unsatisfying. [Isaacs, 1943, p. 465]

Isaacs then cites passages from "Formulations on the two principles of mental functioning" (1911b) and "Negation" (1925h) to support her point. One passage from the latter work seems particularly well chosen to rebut Glover:

> The study of judgment affords us, perhaps for the first time, an insight into the *derivation of an intellectual function from the inter-play of the primary instinctual impulses*. Judging has been systematically developed out of what was in the first instance introduced into the ego or expulsion from the ego carried out according to the pleasure-principle (Freud, 1925h, p. 238). [Quoted in King & Steiner, 1991, p. 467, italics added]

Isaacs concludes:

> *Thus, on Freud's own view, the mechanism of introjection, which arises out of and rests upon the Ucs (unconscious) phantasy of incorporation, underlies not only the retention of memory-traces, but also the function of reality-testing and judgement* . . . On Freud's own teaching, therefore, if we are to understand either phantasy or reality-testing and "intelligence", we must look at mental life as a whole and see the relation between these various functions during the whole process of development. To set them apart and say "that is phantasy but this is perception and intelligence" is to miss the developmental significance of both. [Isaacs, 1943, pp. 467–468; original italics]

This sets the two perspectives in sharp contrast, and also demonstrates the extent to which both sides claim to ground their positions in Freud. To reiterate a point made above, while the opponents of Isaacs and Klein are voicing, mostly indirectly, what might be seen as a kind of epistemological anxiety aroused by Kleinian ideas on phantasy, these seem completely ignored by Isaacs, who speaks from a position in which the differences are simply assumed to constitute different readings from Freud. The notion that there might be something deeply unsettling about the idea that judgement and reality-testing ultimately rest upon phantasies of oral incorporation seems not to have occurred to her. The Kleinians appear to have no difficulty in thinking of phantasy and reality, judgement and imagination, as intrinsically interpenetrating domains.

Phantasy and early object relations: what about "autoerotism"?

The third main aspect of phantasy in Isaacs' presentation concerns the idea that the content of phantasy *always* involves an object relationship, from the very beginning. This is made clear in Isaacs' description of the hallucinated breast, which is simultaneously both the mechanism behind the earliest phantasies and the model of the infant's first object relations:

> What does the infant hallucinate? We may assume, first, the nipple, then the breast, and later, his mother, the whole person . . . hallucination does not stop at the mere picture, but carries him on to what he is, in detail, going to do with the desired object which he imagines (has unconscious phantasies) he has obtained. We know already that it is the oral impulse that is at work, and which conjures up the hallucinated nipple. And the intensity of such a wish and the hate of frustration, will stir up a still stronger desire, viz: to take the whole breast into himself and keep it there, as a source of satisfaction. Thus we must assume that the introjection of the breast is bound up with the earliest forms of the phantasy life. [Isaacs, 1943, p. 278]

Thus, hallucination of the breast as the "earliest form of phantasy life" is both the first appearance of phantasy and the first object relation. It also leads to the first introjection, and, therefore, to the first internal object. In this way, subjective experience, phantasy, and external and internal object relations are inextricably bound up with one another and coterminous in their beginnings; there is no subjective existence without a phantasied object relation, and this object relation is derived from both instinctual experience and actual relations with an external object.

Isaacs supports this view on two bases. First, she finds passages in Freud that she sees as consistent with her view. Interestingly, the first Freudian passage she cites is one that contains an idea about early development—the concept of *autoerotism*—that will be used against her by the Anna Freud group:

> In so far as it is auto-erotic, the ego has no need of the outside world, but . . . it cannot but for a time perceive instinctual stimuli as painful. Under the sway of the pleasure principle there now takes place a further development. The objects presenting themselves, in so far as they are sources of pleasure, are absorbed by the ego into itself, "introjected" . . . while, on the other hand, the ego thrusts forth upon the external world whatever within itself gives rise to pain (v. infra: the mechanism of projection) (Freud, 1915c, pp. 135–136, pp. 138–139). [Quoted in King & Steiner, 1991, pp. 278–279]

This is a passage from "Instincts and their vicissitudes" (1915c), in which Freud is describing the development of the "purified pleasure ego". In Freud's description, as the ego begins to become aware of stimuli, it experiences them as painful and adapts with a new development, whereby pleasurable experiences and objects are absorbed into itself, or "introjected", and painful experiences and objects are expelled from itself, or "projected". Important for Isaacs' argument is the implication that this process takes place extremely early in development, and that Freud seems to see introjection and projection as taking place *in phantasy*. In Isaacs' words:

> I am quite aware that Freud, in describing the primary introjection, nowhere calls it an unconscious phantasy. But, as I have already explained, it is to my mind impossible to see how the process of introjection can otherwise be conceived than as operating through phantasy. I therefore hold that we are entitled to claim Freud's concept of primary introjection as a support for our assumption of the activity of Ucs phantasy in the earliest phases of life. [Isaacs, 1943, p. 279]

It is notable that Isaacs does not address any possible contradiction of this view posed by Freud's idea of an earlier, autoerotic phase ("in so far as it is autoerotic, the ego has no need of the outside world"). The possible contradiction will not be lost on others, however, as I will discuss below.

The second basis of support for early object-related phantasy comes from behavioural observations Isaacs provides in a section of her paper entitled, "Facts of general development". There, Isaacs lists a number of observations (many culled from reports by prominent developmental researchers during the 1930s and 1940s) that she sees as indicating both the presence and quality of phantasied object relations in the first year of life. In particular, she describes an initial predominance of negative over positive expressional signs, evidence of a very early visual orientation towards objects, and manifestations of rapidly progressing perceptual and memory capacity during the first year, culminating in purposeful play and the rudimentary elements of language. From these observations, she argues that the infant is orientated towards objects from the beginning, and has early cognitive capacities and emotional tendencies consistent with the kinds of phantasies described by Klein, particularly in relation to the unfolding of the depressive position in the middle of the first year.

Objections from the Anna Freud group to these views of early object relations also rest on two bases: apparent contradiction with Freud's written views on an initial stage of autoerotism and a more general disagreement over the mental capacities of very young infants. Barbera Lantos, an adherent of Anna Freud, is the first to disagree with Isaacs over the issue of autoerotism, but seems implicitly to agree with her regarding early perceptual abilities and object orientation:

> We estimate the dynamic force of this pleasure so highly that we don't feel the need to look for other explanations. We believe that bodily functions ... and the functioning of the sensory apparatus ... are *pleasurable in themselves*. So is mental development with its gradual acquisition of knowledge and understanding. This pleasure we call *auto-erotic*, referring to the sensory apparatus, organ pleasure, referring to bodily functions and intellectual pleasure—they are all the same in so far as they are pleasures in themselves, that is to say: *pleasures without meaning*. [Quoted in King & Steiner, 1991, p. 349; italics added]

Somewhat later, Lantos adds,

> The actions he performs show in our opinion—his growing intelligence ... The fact that he is able to recognize persons, that he is aware of their coming and going and afraid of their loss, and that he reacts accordingly, is in our opinion bound up with the development of the sensory and mental apparatus without suggesting the existence of phantasies. [*ibid.*, pp. 351–352]

The way in which Lantos uses the concept of autoerotism is important; she is specifically referring here to an absence of conscious phantasies accompanying various forms of play. In Lantos's view, pleasurable behaviour of infants in their first year is autoerotic to the extent that it is enjoyed for immediate sensory pleasure alone, and is not motivated or accompanied by an underlying object-related phantasy. On the other hand, she describes the infant as being aware of, and attached to, objects and exercising its intelligence in relation to objects: thus, autoerotism, in Lantos's usage, does *not* imply a lack of external object relations, i.e., is not equated with an objectless state. Therefore, one can see her objection as directed more towards the issue of early phantasies involving objects than to object relatedness in general.

In contrast to Lantos, Kate Friedlander, another adherent of Anna Freud, views the concept of autoerotism as referring specifically to an object-less state:

> ... it is a basic principle in this analytical conception of the first year of life that the first object relationship to the mother has not been there from the beginning but is the result of a process of development going for months before the high achievement of object relationship of a still primitive kind of course is apparent at all. [Quoted in King & Steiner, 1991, p. 407]

Friedlander emphasizes the immature "brain-anatomy and physiology" of the child in accounting for this prolonged period preceding even very rudimentary object relations.

Interestingly, one can easily see a kind of contradiction emerging in these supposed allied views, both of which invoke the concept of autoerotism in critical responses to Isaacs' interpretation of infant observational data. Lantos explains the capacities described by Isaacs as manifestations of the autoerotic pleasure achieved by the exercise of expanding cognitive capacities in interaction with objects to which the infant has a significant relationship (although one without internal phantasy components), while Friedlander sees the same observed capacities as instances of autoerotic pleasurable activities in an infant largely unrelated to objects due to very primitive cognitive development. Both disagree with Isaacs' view of early object relations on the grounds of autoerotism, but they differ in whether that term simply refers to pleasurable behaviour in the absence of phantasy (Lantos), or a complete absence of object relations (Friedlander).

Anna Freud attempts to reconcile this contradiction in her comments. Referring to the child's earliest relation to the mother, Anna Freud states,

> the infant is at this time exclusively concerned with his own well-being. The mother is important, so far as she serves or disturbs this well-being . . . the infant's object relationship is still an indirect one: changes in the object reach him by way of difference in the satisfaction given. The person of the object remains interchangeable so long as the gratification remains the same. [Quoted in King & Steiner, 1991, pp. 418–419]

The relationship with the object present at the beginning is *indirect*: the mother's actions are extremely important only in so far as they affect experiences of satisfaction and frustration. There is no object relationship "in the proper sense", despite the centrality of the external object in regulating pleasure and pain, because the object is not experienced as an object, but merely as an environmental condition. (This accords with Friedlander's view of autoerotism as devoid of object relations.) In addition, because during this early period the aim of the instinct "is of overwhelming importance" while the object "is only dimly taken into account", sensory experiences exist vividly without a corresponding imaginal component, feelings exist without object phantasies; this is consistent with one aspect of Lantos's view of autoerotism, which assumes some degree of perception and object awareness early in development.

However, this still leaves Lantos's insistence on the child's rapidly expanding intellectual and perceptual abilities, which raises an interesting problem. If the child is acquiring knowledge demonstrably and understanding of the *external* world during the first year, why would we not also assume a parallel level of sophistication in the *internal* world? Why doesn't the child's observable interest in objects from an early age indicate "object-relatedness" in some form? And, how does this observable interest in objects square with Anna Freud's insistence that, for instincts, "the object is only dimly taken into account"?

Anna Freud deals with these issues by drawing a line in the ego, as it were. In essence, she divides the ego's synthetic function in half; part of it functions to synthesize and organize perceptions of the external world, while the other part correlates and orders the instinctual experiences of the internal world. Further, she sees an important differential in the time of onset of each half of the ego's synthesizing activity:

> I consider, in agreement with Mrs. Isaacs, that correlation or synthesis of perception and reality-testing is achieved in degrees from birth onwards . . . [however,] this synthetic function is not exercised on instinctual urges during the first year and, in fact, not until considerably later. Even though correlation of perception grows continually, wishes and impulses continue to be governed by the primary process with its characteristic lack of unification. [Quoted in King & Steiner, 1991, pp. 421–422]

In effect, during the period when perceptions and experiences of the external world are becoming integrated, providing for the kinds of learning observed by developmental researchers, the internal, instinctual realm remains unorganized and diffuse. Because of this, "true object relations", in which a libidinal cathexis is invested in an internal object, cannot yet take place. Instead, we see mere reaction tendencies in response to changed environmental conditions; that is, perceptual maturation and some forms of rudimentary learning take place, but as yet there are no object relations or representations, and certainly no object phantasies.

Isaacs offers replies to each of these points. To Lantos's view of early, autoerotic pleasure as "without phantasy", Isaacs states categorically that "autoerotism cannot be understood without reference to internal objects" (1943, p. 460). While she does not spell out why object phantasies are necessary to understand autoerotism (leaving it for Paula Heimann to take up in her paper on introjection and projection), Isaacs does raise the point that Anna Freud had hoped to adequately address beforehand, which is that

THE CONTROVERSIAL DISCUSSIONS   277

It does not seem reasonable to me to emphasize auto-erotism so strongly whilst at the same time drawing attention, as Dr. Lantos does, to the development of perception and intelligence. Perceptions cannot be developed apart from object relationships, and libidinal and intellectual development are intimately related. [*ibid.*, pp. 460–461]

In reply to Friedlander's view of autoerotism as "object-less", Isaacs responds by quoting directly from Freud:

In the first instance the oral component instinct finds satisfaction anaclitically—on the basis of the satisfaction of the desire for nourishment; and its object is the mother's breast. It then detaches itself, becomes independent and at the same time auto-erotic, that is, it finds an object in the child's own body. [Quoted in King & Steiner, 1991, p. 461]

In this passage, at least, Freud seems clear in describing object relating *prior to* autoerotism. Isaacs acknowledges that, without reading this and similar passages, one could be led to conclude that Freud assumed "a period of unbroken autoerotism from birth onwards" (*ibid.*), but that this did not represent the entirety of Freud's thought. Indeed,

Freud himself nowhere insisted a time period to the duration of unadulterated "primary narcissism". He does not say that it persists unchanged or practically unchanged for several months from birth onwards. For him it is, like "primary process", a limiting concept . . . there is no evidence that it occupies the *whole field* of mental life in the infant beyond the first few hours, or that Freud held that it did. As soon as there is a response to the smell and contact with the breast, as soon as sucking is established, there is some degree . . . of object relationship. [*ibid.*, p. 462; original italics]

Because of the many studies (some of which Isaacs had reviewed in her initial paper) indicating early sensory recognition and response to the mother by the infant, Isaacs "cannot agree that the infant's relation to the breast or to his mother is 'indirect', as Miss Freud puts it. It is direct enough, but in terms different from those of later perception" (*ibid.*, p. 462).

It is clear by now that the term "object relationship" has significantly different meanings for the respective groups. For the Anna

Freud group, it implies a more or less stable libidinal cathexis of an internal representation of an external object, which requires both the perceptual development necessary to begin to relate to external objects and the emotional and cognitive maturation needed to both recognize and care about the object as an independent agent, distinct from "environmental conditions" and the degree of satisfaction of one's own immediate wishes and needs. As Anna Freud begins to make clear, the latter condition requires a longer period of time to achieve than the former, and rests upon the establishment of sufficient internal organization to maintain stable, differentiated representations of objects.

In contrast, Isaacs and the Kleinians see no time delay between awareness of the external object and "object relationship". While the form of object relationship evolves over time (indeed, the form and trajectory of this evolution is arguably Klein's primary theoretical and clinical interest), it is present in some form from the beginning:

> The first object is not the mother, but the nipple–breast. Presently the infant perceives and desires her face, her hands and arms . . . The fact that the infant's early libidinal and perceptual relationships are with part-objects—nipple, breast, face, hands, etc., together with the intensity and depth of his feelings, means that his world is a very different one from our own . . . But it is nonetheless a world of object relationships—*alongside autoerotic satisfactions.* [ibid., p. 463; original italics]

Where the Kleinian view differs most essentially from Anna Freud's perspective is in the assumption of meaning given to object experiences by the very young infant. For Anna Freud, whatever the level of perceptual capacities, there is neither emotional interest in, nor cognitive capacity for, imbuing meaning in objects; pleasures with external objects are autoerotic, both in the sense of being without an internal phantasy corollary as well as being without real interest in, or awareness of, the *source* of the pleasure in and of itself. In short, the Anna Freudian baby is not yet subjective; it responds to the objective sensation without elaboration or additional interest—it is a pure stimulus-response creature. For the Kleinians, while the extreme immaturity of perception is acknowledged and emphasized (at first only part-objects can be registered), subjectivity is present from birth because an inner creation of meaning from the interaction of drive and sensation takes place from the beginning— it is *never* simply a stimulus-response machine, but is always a subjective being, and this is *due to the always present distortion or elaboration of experiences of the object by both instinct and cognitive immaturity*. To set these views in stark relief: the Anna Freudian baby, because it is cognitively and perceptually immature, is *not yet* a subjective creature in the world of objects, and it only becomes so secondary to objective perception of objects. Conversely, the Kleinian baby, *because* it is cognitively and perceptually immature, is *always* a subjective creature in the world of objects, with the degree of objectivity secondary to subjective, instinctual experience. In a word, for the Anna Freudians, objectivity is given, while for the Kleinians, subjectivity is given.

Fighting over Freud: the relation between phantasy and psychic structure

As shown above, the arguments posed by both sides of these debates suggest that differences over the view of early object relationship can, in part, be boiled down to differences over the nature and functioning of the ego in the first year of life. Anna Freud suggests that the ego synthesizes and organizes external reality preferentially, and that the internal world lags behind, remaining diffuse and disorganized throughout the first year, thereby precluding the building up of the object representations required for the infant to relate to an object *qua* object. The ego is viewed as a part of the mind vested with the functions of organizing and synthesizing that which was diffuse and unorganized (the id). Ego and id therefore stand apart, with id (primary process, instincts, pleasure principle) presiding over the internal domain in the first year, and the ego only gradually approaching it to grant it organization. The functional and temporal distinctions between external and internal objects, discussed above, reflect the distinction between ego and id when viewed in this light. It seems that Anna Freud sees the ego and id as antithetical and independent; the id lords over the internal domain, maintaining structureless chaos, while the ego develops in response to the outside world, only bringing itself to the underworld when it has gained sufficient strength and experience from its work above ground. Until the ego can harness the id, and rationality rule over irrationality, true object relationship is impossible. Again, this seems to rest on the notion that object relationship has its beginnings in an objectively perceived experiential world with instinctual elements gradually introduced, but in a way that does not compromise reality testing.

This absolute, polar distinction between the properties of the id and the ego is upheld by Anna Freud in a variety of related contexts. In her first contribution to the Discussions, she objects to Isaacs' statement that primary process underlies all rational thinking on the grounds that this implies a blending of primary and secondary process functioning. Anna Freud's objection places a particular emphasis on the integration of impulses, conflict, and ambivalence implied in many Kleinian formulations of unconscious phantasy:

> There is, in Mrs. Isaacs' description of the unconscious, no free and independent flow of instinctual urges. . . . Impulses enter into *conflict* with each other: the baby cannot feel rage against its mother without feeling its love for her threatened and, consequently, either heightened or diminished. Its *ambivalent* feelings cannot exist side by side but have to be projected outward in part. . . . Unconscious life, according to this paper, thus combines qualities of the primary with important characteristics of the secondary process. [Quoted in King & Steiner, 1991, p. 330]

Anna Freud concludes,

> the new theory, due to the assumption of earlier integration, finds no room for the primary process of functioning in the first year of life. This would cut out the identity of functioning at this stage with functioning in dreams and leave us at a loss where to look for the kind of uncorrelated mental life to which dream-function regresses; or the whole theoretical conception of the primary process is altered so as to include integration with its consequences. This again leaves dream life unaccounted for. [*ibid.*, p. 331]

Essentially, Anna Freud seems to be suggesting that the absolute dichotomy she insists upon is required by the psychoanalytic concept of dreams, because the theory assumes that regression in the temporal and formal senses always occur together. Thus, the formal regression to primary process in dreaming implies a temporal regression to an earlier period to which the dominance of this form of thinking corresponds. This might seem to contradict the position, stated by Glover, that the infant is primarily orientated toward reality and adaptation, were it not for the amended view put forward later by Anna Freud (and discussed above) that the ego is preferentially orientated toward the outer world, leaving inner reality in a state of primary process unintegration during the first year. Taken together, these views present a picture of the mind as cleanly segregated: primary and secondary process, ego and id, impulse and integration are cleaved from the beginning.

Glover elaborates this view further with his objection that "Mrs. Isaacs does nothing to distinguish a cathected memory from a phantasy", and, in fact, that "Mrs. Isaacs' metapsychology implies that thought and phantasy are primarily indistinguishable" (quoted in King & Steiner, 1991, p. 398). Again, the distinction falls along the fault-line established by Anna Freud: memory traces are formed by the "primary reality function of the primitive ego", whereas phantasy, in the form referred to by Klein, would require some sort of admixture of primary process and secondary process, and Glover insists that the capacity for this sort of revolution in mental functioning is a relatively advanced acquisition of the mind. Glover and Anna Freud both insist, in different contexts, on the absolute bifurcation of conscious and unconscious, primary and secondary process, and, implicitly, id and ego in the first year of life. It is important to note how frequently Anna Freud and Glover both invoke concepts from the topographical model in this discussion, leaving the relation of ego to id largely implied. This would seem to give credence to Isaacs' observation that, despite Freud's important (post-1920) revisions, Glover's concepts are largely drawn from Freud's pre-1915 writings, as have been those of the "Vienna group" (cf. p. 454).

For the Kleinians, the relationship between the ego and the id is seen quite differently. Isaacs states,

> Freud himself has repeatedly shown that in his view *the ego is a differentiated part of the id*. He did not put it in those words when he first formulated his views about memory-traces in *The Interpretation of Dreams*, but he has done so since in several of his writings. [1943, p. 463]

Isaacs offers the following quotation from Freud:

> Originally, of course, everything was id; the ego was developed out of the id by the continual influence of the external world. In the course of this slow development certain material in the id was transformed into the preconscious state and was thus taken into the ego. [Quoted in King & Steiner, 1991, p. 463]

Isaacs concludes,

> The ego is not to be thought of as a mere system of marks; a wraith or a shadow of experience. It is a living part of the id which has become modified by experience of the external world, in its search for satisfactions from objects in the external world. (1943, p. 463].

Thus, rather than viewing the ego and id as mutually exclusive, Isaacs sees them as integrally related. The ego develops out of the intersection of id and outside world, and remains tied to both. Learning about external objects is not viewed as distinct from the properties of the id, as assumed by Anna Freud; on the contrary, learning and relating to the world are positively infused by the instincts of the id, beginning with the oral incorporation of aspects of reality very early in development.

> All learning is oral learning, at first. All through the middle of the first year, the infant's hand reaches out to everything he sees in order to put it into his mouth, to feel and explore it. . . . This means that the objects which the child touches and manipulates and looks at and explores are invested with oral libido. He could not be interested in them if this were not so. If he were entirely autoerotic he could not learn. [1943, pp. 463–464]

Again, for Isaacs, the categories drawn by Anna Freud are simply wrong. In her view, one cannot sharply divide ego from id, primary from secondary process, internal from external world, or phantasy from learning; to do so is both artificial and contrary to Freud's own written views. But for Anna Freud, Glover, and their adherents, ignoring these distinctions blurs "Freud's orderly series of concepts". Indeed, looked at from the standpoint of differing views of the ego and its relation to the id, many of the areas of dispute fall into place. If one assumes both that the ego is clearly distinguished from the id (this is implied in nearly every one of Anna Freud's discussions of the concept of phantasy), and that the ego, with its functions of reality testing, secondary process, and synthesis, is the sole agency to deal with reality, then Glover's insistence on the primarily reality-adaptation function of the psyche necessarily follows. Similarly, the view that phantasy does *not* originally underlie activities or relationships in the external world follows from the notion that the ego initially stands apart from the id (and, thus, from wish-fulfilling phantasies), and only begins to relate to it through a belated and gradual domination of the internal domain. In this view, phantasy and object relationship are both developmental accomplishments that signal the ego's appropriation and integration of aspects of the id; in the former case, this takes place through a regressive response to frustration that is only possible after some degree of integration between ego and id has been attained, while in the latter it represents a developmental achievement, an integration of instinctual drive with a representation of the ego.

On the other hand, if one agrees with Freud's statement, quoted above by Isaacs, that the "ego was developed out of the id", it might follow that the various qualities that characterize the ego (secondary process, learning, perception, memory, etc.) similarly evolved out of those that characterize the id (primary process, wish-fulfilment). At the very least, Freud's statement implies no clean demarcation of these processes, and therefore seems inconsistent with the kinds of objections raised by Glover and Anna Freud: for example, that Kleinian conceptualizations violate the "primary reality function of the primitive ego" or find "no room for the primary process of functioning in the first year of life".

It should be noted that one of the most frequent objections raised by Glover and others concerns the selective quotation of Freud by Isaacs. In Glover's words,

> I maintain that Mrs. Isaacs' method of quotation from Freud and other writers does not conform to scientific requirements, in particular that the quotations are given without the necessary context which in many cases would show that they do not support Mrs. Isaacs' contentions. [Quoted in King & Steiner, 1991, p. 325]

These objections are raised at several different points, but not specifically against the above quotations on the relation of ego to id.

Nevertheless, the general objection should be considered, along with the stance taken by each side with respect to the issue of properly interpreting Freudian theory. It is quite clear that, throughout the discussions, the Kleinians quote from Freud's actual text much more frequently than the Anna Freud–Glover group, while the latter is given much more to condensed, authoritative summaries of what they take as the essence of Freudian thought. Both sides accuse the other of misrepresenting Freud. Glover states,

> I don't agree with these contributors who suggest that Freud's basic concepts were mere tentative formulations which he would himself have played about with or modified freely at some later date. The outstanding fact about the theoretical chapter in his *Interpretation of Dreams* and about the formulations contained in his paper "Instincts and their Vicissitudes" is that they have stood the test of time. They are in fact basic. [Quoted in King & Steiner, 1991, p. 396]

Isaacs replies,

> In actual fact, Freud greatly expanded and revised his metapsychology in successive contributions—although he did not always rewrite every part of his earlier work in the new light of his later discoveries and later developments of theory. In Dr. Glover's account of Freud's views he refers only to *The Interpretation of Dreams* (1900[a]) and 'Instincts and their Vicissitudes' (1915[c]). But many other parts of Freud's works have to be considered if we wish to gain an adequate idea of his whole metapsychology. [1943, p. 454]

In a way, these different views of Freud's text can be seen to mirror the perspectives taken on psychic structure, discussed above. In Glover's view, the *facts* are pre-established and "basic" from the beginning, and are, therefore, not subject to interpretation or modification. Just as the ego is in touch with reality from the beginning, and, hence, "realistic" perception could always be envisioned as a return to this pristine early condition, so psychoanalytic theory is clearest in its beginnings, "basic", and the true meaning of later developments is always to be grasped through returning to those founding concepts.

For Isaacs, on the other hand, theory is viewed as organic and growing rather than factual and basic; to get the full meaning of

Freud one needs to follow the interpenetration of ideas and the conceptual launching points leading in various directions, just as the psyche is envisioned as always made up of interpenetrating domains and processes, with no topographical area or period of time segmented off from the rest as enjoying privileged access to truth. Hence, no part of the mind, or theory, is necessarily conceived of as more "basic", but can only be grasped within the context of a much larger and more complicated whole.

Conclusion

Throughout this chapter we have attempted to demonstrate the particular way underlying attitudes about the possibility of objectivity permeated the theoretical discussions of phantasy in the Controversial Discussions. Areas of theoretical disagreement were divided into four: the use of subjective *vs.* objective language in describing mental phenomena; phantasy as psychic representation; phantasy and early object relations; and the relationship between phantasy and psychic structure, and in each area we tried to show how the groups divided over assumptions about whether people are originally, fundamentally, and enduringly in contact with objective reality, or, instead, whether experience is subjective and mutually constructed from internal and external sources from the beginning, with an approach to consensual reality only possible through optimal developmental experiences. These were the foundational ego psychological and Kleinian positions of the 1940s, as viewed in relief through the lens of the Controversial Discussions. As briefly discussed above, the participants' attitudes toward Freudian theory itself were similarly refracted through these particular perspectives.

Having shown this, a number of significant questions emerge. First, to what extent was this division in views a function of the political, social, and identity tensions faced by the various participants of these discussions due to their respective situations in the context of the global warfare, displacement from countries of origin, economic concerns, loss of father and father figure in Freud, etc. In effect, to what extent were these modes of thought expressing more fundamental anxieties originating from individual and group sources? For example, one could argue that the anxiety felt by Anna Freud due to immigration and loss of father, status, and homeland led to a kind of rigidification and need for a more *objective* grounding, just as the threat felt by Glover for his previously near-guaranteed inheritance of leadership of the British Psychoanalytic Society, due to the ascendance of Klein, led him to also want to cling to the "pre-established" facts that used to be "basic", here referring to his own pre-established fact of succession, as well as to issues of theory.

These speculations and others deserve some careful consideration. However, two other questions should probably take priority as we consider the impact of the Controversies on contemporary psychoanalysis. The first question looks back to Freud and asks, does the fact of these divisions around this particular fault-line reflect something of the ultimate origin in the ideas themselves; are these controversies manifesting something underlying in Freudian theory itself? Was Freud split over the question of subjectivity? Does his theory, following some inherent internal division, naturally lead to two contradictory positions regarding the relationship between subjective, individual, constructed experience and objective, veridical perception of reality? If so, this would account for both the mundane observation that the participants of the controversies differed substantially in their reading of Freud, as well as perhaps address the more subtle question of the underlying intellectual source of these sharply polarized stances themselves.

The second question looks to the present and future, and asks, to what extent are current theoretical debates, particularly those between contemporary Freudians and Kleinians, continuing to reflect fundamental epistemological differences? Could it be that an unbridgeable philosophical gulf stymies our attempts at theoretical integration, or even our efforts toward common understanding?

Commentary: S. Ellman

After reading the controversial discussions, one can see the overwhelming importance of Freud at this historical juncture. It is as if the two groups are desperately fighting for Freud's soul, or, less dramatically, at least his belated approval. They are both attempting to prove that they have not strayed from the spirit of his theorizing. Dr Vorus notes that the Freudians (particulary Glover) criticize the Kleinians for taking quotes out of context, while it is rare for the Freudians to directly quote Freud. Neither group fully acknowledges that Freud was, if not unsure at times, certainly liable to sharply change his positions. It is striking that, alongside the occasional brilliant exchange, neither group attempts to fully explicate a version of Freud's theoretical vision. This may be due to the fact that neither group, at this point in time, fully agreed with Freud. Perhaps it is more accurate to state that both groups had substantial disagreements with aspects of Freud's theorizing. It was, therefore, under the guise of Freud worship that the groups engaged in theoretical battle, with neither group as Freudian as they attempted to appear.

If we look at some of Issacs' points it is clear that one even has to grant Glover a hearing. Yes, it is true that in two instances Issacs finds quotes that indicate that Freud stated that the infant was engaged with an object before it becomes autoerotic (King & Steiner, 1991, p. 461); however, what Freud means by "object" in this quote is equivocal and one can find at least twenty quotes which indicate that, during the autoerotic period, the infant is a state of primary narcissism. I have explicated in (Chapters Two and Three) what I think is the main meaning Freud gives this type of statement, but I will briefly reiterate it here and compare Issacs' points to Friedlander's view of autoerotism. Freud states, in a number of contexts, that there are memories of objects (people and parts of people) during autoerotism but, in so far as the stage proceeds "normally", the infant does not make a libidinal investment. That is why the infant loves pleasure and is indifferent to the external world during this stage. It is not that the infant does not learn; it does, but there is a system (mother) who anticipates its needs and responds to its signalling. When the signalling breaks down (crying occurs frequently with no response from the mother), then the infant begins to develop the purified pleasure ego. In relation to the quote that Issacs cites, Freud, a few sentences before, said that "In so far as the ego is auto-erotic, it has no need of the external world, but in consequence of experiences undergone by the instincts of self-preservation, it acquires objects from that world" (1915c, p. 135). When the infant starts to experience unpleasure "the original reality-ego which distinguished internal and external by a sound objective criterion, changes into a purified pleasure-ego" (*ibid.*, p. 136). Unfortunately, the editors of the *Standard Edition* mixed up the purified pleasure-ego with a previous concept of Freud's, the pleasure ego. The pleasure ego from "Two principles of mental functioning" (1911b) was considered by Freud to be the first ego or mental state that hallucinated the breast during the first frustration(s). It was rapidly replaced by the reality ego, and now, in 1915, Freud brings forth a new concept, the purified pleasure ego, which involves the first libidinal cathexis and the beginning of the stage of narcissism. The cathexis is a complicated one: it is of the self, but the self contains, through introjection, the representation of the gratifying object (mother). This sequence could not be a rapid one in development, as Issacs posited, and so she truly either took this quote out of context purposefully, or did not fully understand Freud's intentions.

However, Friedlander's view of autoerotism as object-less is just as far off, since, in the quote that we just looked at, Freud says that during the auto-erotic period, under the sway of the instinct of self-preservation, objects are acquired. Clearly, the infant is not object-less, but, in my interpretation, the objects are not libidinally cathected until they are substantially missed by the infant. This interpretation, I believe, accounts for all the terms that Freud uses and is in line with the majority of his formulations. But, one might ask, so what? Why are we arguing from the authority of Freud? Rather, we should ask: what is he saying that is of use in our theoretical formulations?

I could pick up a number of difficulties in the quoting of Freud, but most notable is Anna Freud's sharp division of the ego and the id. Clearly, this is not Freud's division, and Freud's view of the ego as the horseback rider (see Chapter Four) clearly indicates that the energy of the system in his mind comes from the id. In this respect, phantasy (or fantasy—choose one) is clearly a good part of the infant's early reality. In Freudian terms, this is particularly true if there is not good enough mothering (see Winnicott commentary, Chapter Ten). Anna Freud is presenting her and Hartmann's new view of the ego, which has its own energy from birth onward. In this view, she is strongly influenced by Hartmann and Glover, and is in rough accord with their view. However, it is clearly not Freud's view, even if one can find some quote to quarrel with that assertion. Perhaps most importantly, Anna Freud cannot deal with the idea that Klein is a radical Freudian in a number of ways.

Interestingly, I have quoted Money-Kyrle (1975b) when he says that in 1935 Klein develops "the new idea of position as the developmental unit in place of . . . stage" (p. 433). Issacs, presenting for the Kleinians, maintains that "All learning is oral learning at first" (King & Steiner, 1991, p. 463). Vorus presents an extensive quote about the importance of the mouth, etc. Frequently, during the controversial discussions, Kleinians use the concept of stage, and nowhere do they eschew this concept. As I point out (Chapter Eight), even in "Envy and gratitude" (1957) some of Klein's concepts are hard to understand without the concept of stage. Why would Money-Kyrle not be content with saying that Klein's new concepts in 1935 puts together the idea of part to whole object and shows how the infant/developing child creates whole objects and then splits them up when it cannot bear the mourning involved in being separate from the object (see Chapter Six on pining). In my view, he, at the point he edited Klein's papers in 1975 (1975a,b), was still involved in the controversies, and now, from a position of heightened power (the Kleinians had achieved good positions in the British Psychoanalytic and around the world), tried, in a sense, to overthrow Freud and the Freudians. This somewhat paranoid interpretation of mine might be quite wrong, but, in my view, some of the effects of the controversies are still reverberating to this day. The controversies were, in many ways, brilliant and entertaining to read, but sad in their extreme partisanship.

CHAPTER EIGHT

Klein's "Envy and gratitude"

Summary

This period begins with Klein's paper on schizoid dynamics (1946), which she publishes at the same time that Fairbairn is publishing *his* paper on schizoid dynamics. She now has two named positions, the paranoid–schizoid and the depressive position. The depressive position is thought to occur a good earlier than had been the case in previous publications. Klein, in this era, spells out many of her concepts: projective identification is conceptualized as both an important defence and a mode of communication with both developmental and clinical importance. During this period, Klein writes an important paper on transference, expanding the Freudian concept and using the concept of projective identification to account for transference manifestations. A great deal of the chapter is devoted to her last major work "Envy and gratitude" (1957), where she details the centrality of envy and greed. Dynamics concerning envy and greed account for the most venal of "sins" (or human difficulties), and dynamics concerning envy are an inevitable aspect of early development. Despite her new emphasis on envy, Klein finds some renewed accommodation with

Winnicott. Her new emphasis is a movement to accommodate environmental influences in her theoretical matrix.

The second era of Melanie Klein

By the time we come to the second era of Klein's theorizing, she has passed through the Freud–Klein controversies and survived as a major theorist in the psychoanalytic world. During this period, the discovery, or, perhaps more accurately, the uncovering of R. D. Fairbairn, a Scottish psychoanalyst, was another important, perhaps decisive event, in the history of British (and eventually world wide) psychoanalysis. Fairbairn (see Chapter Nine) was an analyst outside of the mainstream in the UK, who published important papers about schizoid phenomena and presented what he termed an object-relations theory of development. He came to the forefront after the Second World War and, in 1946, Klein and Fairbairn published articles in the *International Journal of Psychoanalysis* describing their positions. Fairbairn's article (1946) was a summary and an extension of four of his previous publications. At the very least, Klein now had someone outside of her circle who joined her as an object-relations theorist. In some interpretations, this was perhaps more important politically than theoretically. This interpretation depends on the theoretical assumptions that one assumed to be present in Klein and Fairbairn's theories. Likierman (2001), in her book on Klein, sees the discovery of Fairbairn as crucial to Klein. This view will be discussed in the commentary section of this chapter.

In this chapter we look mainly at four of Klein's seminal papers. The papers are "Notes on schizoid mechanisms" (1946), "The origins of transference" (1952a), "Some theoretical conclusions regarding the emotional life of the infant" (1952b), and "Envy and gratitude" (1957). We will look at other papers briefly, but primarily in the context of discussing these four central papers.

The first paper,"Notes on schizoid mechanisms" (1946), was written as a type of communication with Fairbairn. This paper demonstrates some of the ways that Klein and Fairbairn agree on some issues of early development and, as importantly, it details areas of distinct disagreement. Although Klein has previously posited ideas that are similar to the ones she describes in this essay, it is a primary essay where she clearly spells out the implications of early splitting. In addition, she agrees with Fairbairn about the importance of schizoid states in early development. She also states unequivocally (again) that the infant is object-related from birth, and that splitting takes place in the earliest phases of development. Thus, the breast (the first object) is split into parts under the sway of the destructive, or death, instinct.

Klein also highlights the adult schizoid's emotional unavailability and detached hostility to the analyst. She relates this unavailability to the defence of splitting, which, in this paper, takes on greater importance and is now unequivocally seen as occurring almost immediately in the infant's developmental sequence. The breast is almost immediately split into a good and bad breast, and loved and hated in accordance with the affective valence assigned to it. This affective valence is largely determined by how the infant's ego structure is able to deal with anxiety states. She is clear that "anxiety arises from the operation of the death instinct within the organism" (1946, p. 4). The death instinct is experienced as a

> Fear of annihilation (death) and takes the form of persecution. Other important sources of primary anxiety are the trauma of birth (separation anxiety) and frustration of bodily needs; and these experiences too are from the beginning felt as being caused by objects. Even if these objects are felt to be external, they become through introjection internal persecutors and thus reinforce the fear of the destructive impulse within. [*ibid.*, pp. 4–5]

The splitting of the object under the threat of the destructive impulse reinforces the idea of the unintegration of the early ego (an acknowledged idea of Winnicott). It also leads to the splitting of the ego; the ego's splits correlate with the extent to which destructive tendencies predominate, or in so far as destructive tendencies cannot be counteracted by libidinal propensities. Klein believes

> that oral–sadistic impulses towards the mother's breast are active from the beginning of life, and . . . in states of frustration and anxiety the oral–sadistic and cannibalistic desires are reinforced, and then the infant feels that he has taken in the nipple and the breast in bits. [*ibid.*, p. 5]

The good breast is taken "in under the dominance of the sucking libido", and, under the sway of libido, the good breast serves as the possible focal point of a cohesive ego development. To preserve the good breast, it is idealized and seen as the bountiful and inexhaustible breast. This, of course, helps to safeguard the good breast and makes it unassailable. Klein, here, views idealization not only in defensive terms, but also as a function of "the power of the instinctual desires which aim at unlimited gratification" (*ibid.*, p. 7). This inexhaustible breast is one that can provide unlimited gratification, and it helps to guard against the sense of destroying or depleting the breast.

Splitting of the object necessarily leads to a split ego, and the ego is weakened to the extent that it is split. A weakened ego is virtually forced to expel hated, bad objects into the environment. In early development, this usually involves part-objects derived from the mother. Klein emphasizes, in distinct terms, that the hated parts of the self, or hated internal objects, are expelled or projected into another, not on to the other. Here, it seems that Klein, in this distinction, is trying both to emphasize her difference with Anna Freud and to give a picture of the actual phantasy that she is positing. The infant unconsciously imagines that it is putting parts of itself into the mother. The infant, in this action, desires not only to rid itself of harmful parts of itself, but also to harm and control the mother. The mother then is reintrojected, and is represented not as a "separate individual but is felt to be the bad self" (*ibid.*, p. 8). This projective–introjective identifcation process is Klein's first description of projective identification. The concept of projective identification will become a central Kleinian concept and has its nascent roots in Klein's frequent depiction of projective–introjective sequences. Projective identification is, for Klein, the prototype of "an aggressive object-relation". It is also the prototype for the baby's communications with the mother; thus, not only bad parts of the self are expelled, but also the good and loving parts of the self undergo projective identification. "The projection of good feelings and good parts of the self . . . is essential for the infant's ability to develop good object-relations" (*ibid.*, p. 9), and is necessary to help the infant to integrate good objects into the ego.

The process of splitting off parts of the self and projecting them into another, and then reintrojecting these parts, is of vital importance for normal development. Although there is a normal tendency to idealize the good object, if the idealization is excessive, the ego (baby or infant) will be impoverished and be (feel) dependent on the idealized object. Klein comments, "With an unassimilated idealized object there goes a feeling that the ego has no life and no value of its own" (*ibid.*). One interpretation of Klein's theorizing is that she is presenting a picture of how the infant and mother communicate through non-verbal affects (actions, and facial and bodily signs). Whether the infant is actually projecting parts of the self into the mother may not be the pivotal point of her essay; rather, she is searching for a theoretical language to show how deeply each participant is affected in the infant–mother interaction. Her view is that there is a balance that must be achieved between projected and introjected elements, and that when this balance is skewed in any direction, the ego can be unduly split, or impoverished. One can say that good enough mothering (a Winnicott phrase) is achieved through appropriate balance of projected and introjected elements. This balance allows for the muting of destructive objects and the enhancing of libidinal elements. The enhanced libidinal elements must also be in balance (i.e., without excessive idealization) and cannot overly dominate the infant's internal life.

It is this last element that bears some relation to the schizoid dynamic in the paranoid–schizoid position. Klein sees the schizoid position leading to either "a compulsive tie to certain objects or— another outcome—to a shrinking from people in order to prevent both a destructive intrusion into them and the danger of retaliation by them" (*ibid.*, p. 11). Thus, the schizoid dynamic is one where one wants excessively close ties or, alternatively, has the extreme desire to move away from other people. Clearly, these are traits that to some extent are found in many individuals, but, to the extent that these traits are central to a person's functioning, in Klein's lexicon they are schizoid. In addition to these traits, "another characteristic of schizoid object-relations is a marked artificiality and lack of spontaneity" (*ibid.*, p. 13). Often, both "psychic reality and the relation to external reality are disturbed" (*ibid.*) when schizoid object-relations dominate a person's interactions. In outlining some of these personality traits, Klein is trying to show that both schizoid and paranoid tendencies arise from the paranoid–schizoid position. During the second quarter of the first year of life, there is an introjection of the complete object. This, of necessity, implies that the good and bad, or loved and hated, aspects of the object are no longer so widely separated and the infant experiences loss in a more intense manner. For Klein, this makes for an "increased understanding of psychic reality and better perception of the external world" (*ibid.*), as well as for a greater synthesis between inner and external situations. Klein stipulates that when the "drive to make reparation . . . comes to the fore" (*ibid.*, p. 14), it allows the child to alleviate guilt and make more realistic responses to the external world. In addition, it adds synthesis and integration of the ego. Even while depressive anxieties are being experienced and worked through, "schizoid mechanisms remain in force", although experienced in modulated form. If schizoid anxieties are too great, there will be a disruption of the depressive position and the ego will be forced "to regress to the paranoid–schizoid position which will reinforce early persecutory and schizoid anxieties" (*ibid.*). Klein, as before, sees the positions oscillating throughout development. As the child progresses, anxieties diminish in intensity, objects become "less idealized and less terrifying, and the ego" becomes more unified (*ibid.*, p. 15). As these unifications occur, reality testing and a sense of reality are less disrupted by unconscious processes.

Fairbairn and Klein

We will have to revisit this question from Fairbairn's point of view, since Klein portrays Fairbairn in a manner that emphasizes only some of his positions. Klein begins by stating that she agrees with Fairbairn that the "occurrence of schizoid and schizophrenic disorders is much wider than has been acknowledged" (*ibid.*, p. 3). She also begins to utilize the term "schizoid" for the infant's initial position. "His term 'schizoid position' would be appropriate if it is understood to cover both persecutory fear and schizoid mechanisms" (*ibid.*). It is her view that, while she concentrates on anxieties and their vicissitudes, Fairbairn largely focuses on ego-development. Klein is able to see the connection between the schizoid position and later schizoid and schizophrenic disorders; she does, however, want to include her previous emphasis on the persecutory aspects of the primary or first position. Her new term, then, is the paranoid–schizoid position. While her agreements with Fairbairn are important, her disagreements are equally important. She has three interrelated points that will remain part of her theory throughout her life.

1. She disagrees with Fairbairn's rejection of Freud's concepts of primary instincts. It is her view that Fairbairn does not "give enough weight to the importance of early anxiety and conflict as well as . . . underrating the role which aggression and hatred play from the beginning of life" (*ibid.*, p. 4).
2. She disagrees with Fairbairn's theory that only bad objects are internalized. She makes it clear that the introjected good breast is a vital part of good ego development.
3. These points lead her to disagree with Fairbairn's revision of Freud's structural ideas as well as his revision of Freud's instinct theory. However, the disagreement is deeper than that, since Klein rejects the dynamics that Fairbairn puts forth for each position. Fairbairn posits that, in the schizoid position, love made hungry (and anxiety about destroying through love) is the key dynamic. In the depressive position, the dynamic is love made angry.

These disagreements with Fairbairn will, on the one hand, continue her ties to the Freudian opus, while her agreements with Fairbairn will allow Klein a new colleague in her efforts to establish psychoanalysis as an object-relations theory. Interestingly, at this point in time, Klein gives various glimpses of how she has become a new Freudian. For example, she maintains that she accepts Freud's idea of the first psychological activity involving the hallucinated breast (see Chapter Two). However, in her view, this leads to a splitting of the object (breast). What happens with this splitting (similarly with idealization) is that the bad breast is denied and omnipotence is reinforced. Thus, the hallucinated breast in Klein's theory leads to an omnipotent denial of frustration and bad circumstances. While one might consider this to be an acceptance of a Freudian tenet, her theorizing goes far enough beyond Freud so that Freud's original idea of hallucinated gratification is somewhat secondary in this description. Klein handles Freud's description of the Schreber case in a similar manner. While Freud, in discussing this case, talks of external splitting by Schreber, Klein interprets this to be a projection of the internal splits in Schreber's ego. Schreber is seen as an example of a schizoid process where Schreber's world destruction phantasies are seen as representing "the annihilation by one part of the self of the other parts—which, as I contend, is a schizoid mechanism" (*ibid.*, p. 23). While this interpretation adds to Freud's ideas, it is in keeping with the general understanding by Freud of Schreber's use of projection. In addition, this interpretation can be integrated into Freud's ideas of world destruction phantasies being part of the onset of schizophrenia. Freud, of course, does not emphasize splitting in the way that Klein has come to do by 1946.

"The emotional life of the infant"

This is one of the papers that serve as a summary for Klein's positions up to 1952. This paper is derived from Klein's writing that began during the period of the controversial discussions. When the controversial discussions were organized to examine Kleinian concepts (1941–1945, see Chapter Seven), Klein wrote a long paper that was subsequently divided into three papers. These three papers were "On the theory of anxiety and guilt" (1948), "Some theoretical conclusions regarding the emotional life of the infant" (1952b), and "On observing the behaviour of young infants" (1952c). (In addition to Klein's paper, three other papers were presented: one by Paula Heimann, one by Susan Issacs, and one by Issacs and Heimann. These papers are contained with Klein's papers in a volume entitled *Developments in Psychoanalysis* [Klein, Heimann, Isaacs, & Riviere, 1952].) Except for her paper on envy (1957), these papers constitute almost all of Klein's final positions on development. Her paper on anxiety and guilt is virtually entirely a restatement of past positions, but does contain a comparison with Freud's and her positions. The new element in this paper that Klein puts forth (restated in her next papers) is that guilt (in fragmentary form) occurs during the paranoid–schizoid position. This view is complementary to her previous view that paranoid–schizoid anxieties occur during the depressive position.

Klein begins by stating that the process of birth (or the loss of intra-uterine life) is felt by the infant "as an attack by hostile forces, i.e., as persecution" (1952b, p. 62). The infant's first experiences of feeding lead to the internalization of an object, the mother's breast. Klein maintains that this "is at first a relation to a part-object, for both oral–libidinal and oral–destructive impulses from the beginning of life are directed towards the mother's breast in particular" (*ibid*.). Since libido and aggression are conceived of as fused, Klein maintains that there is an optimal balance between these two instinctual drives. If there is a state of deprivation (hunger, for example), the balance is upset and this "gives rise to the emotion called greed, which is first and foremost of an oral nature. Any increase in greed strengthens feelings of frustration and in turn the aggressive impulses" (*ibid*.). Klein's mention of greed presages her next major paper and, in this paper, she clearly states that the paranoid–schizoid position first occurs during the first 3–4 months of the infant's life. The split breast is clearly the prototype of all good and bad objects. The good breast represents all helpful and gratifying objects, the bad breast the prototype of all external and internal persecutory objects. These representations are introjected and projected in the way that Klein has described in the paper "Notes on schizoid mechanisms" (1946). Greed now is seen as an important factor, for the "bad breast will devour him in the same greedy way as he desires to devour it" (1952b, p. 64). The idealized breast is seen as the antithesis of the persecuting bad breast. She posits that the stronger the feelings of persecution, the greater the need for an idealized, powerful, good breast to provide protection against persecutory objects. Klein, in this paper, mentions that the early feelings of annihilation lead to extensive splitting, which results in very different types of ego states of consciousness. Powerful persecutory anxiety can lead to a feeling of disintegration and of the ego falling to bits. To the extent that persecutory anxiety is lessened, there is a lessening of splitting. The extent of splitting in this beginning phase of development will be a crucial factor in determining how subsequent defences are developed. Extreme splitting will lead to premature repressive attempts and a tendency to limit communications between various aspects of the mind. The intensity of feelings of persecution strongly influences the degree of splitting of the ego. Klein mentions environmental features as well as frustration tolerance and strength of drive as factors involved in determining the intensity of feelings of persecution. She states that progress in moving from the paranoid–schizoid position is based on libidinal factors predominating over aggressive or destructive tendencies. As was just mentioned, there are vague but significant feelings of guilt during the paranoid–schizoid position. These feelings of guilt are stirred by the greedy impulses, where the infant desire "is to empty the mother's body of everything good and desirable". This attack, which is oral–sadistic in nature, is followed developmentally by attacks

> Predominantly anal—to fill her body with the bad substances and parts of the self which are split off and projected into her. These are mainly represented by excrements which become the means of damaging, destroying or controlling the attacked object. Or the whole self—felt to be the "bad self"—enters the mother's body and takes control of it. In theses various phantasies, the ego takes possession by projection of an external object—first of all the mother—and makes it into an extension of the self. The object becomes to some extent a representative of the ego, and these processes are in my view the basis for identification by projection or "projective identification". Identification by introjection and identification by projection appear to be complementary processes. It seems that the processes underlying projective identification operate already in the earliest relation to the breast. The "vampire-lie" sucking, the scooping out of the breast, develop in the infant's phantasy into making his way into the breast and further into the mother's body. Accordingly, projective identification would start simultaneously with the greedy oral–sadistic introjection of the breast. This hypothesis is in keeping with view often expressed by the writer that introjection and projection interact from the beginning of life. [1952b, pp. 68–69]

Here, Klein is highlighting the importance of the concept of projective identification that had been introduced previously in her 1946 paper. Projective identification occurs from the earliest parts of life and communication between mother and infant is largely determined by the nature of what is projected and reintrojected. Before the integration of the good and bad object takes place, when destructive impulses are at their height, the two aspects of the mother's breast are introjected and form the core of the superego. This early superego gives rise to depressive anxiety in "fleeting experiences". The infant's defences during the paranoid–schizoid position all tend to lead extreme reactions, thus, there are few constant states. However, depressive anxiety during the paranoid–schizoid position is highlighted by Klein as a fleeting experience. Besides projective identification, splitting, omnipotence, idealization, and denial are all defences that are employed during this position. Klein's focus in this paper is on the first 3–4 months of the infant's life, and how, gradually, the infant is able to integrate good and bad elements and develop a more cohesive ego and sense of self. Before we move to Klein's statements about the depressive position, we must remember that, for Klein, all of these developments during the first 3–4 months are infused with phantasy and that the taming and tolerance of phantasy is a key developmental task.

Klein sees the second quarter of the first year of life as a point in development where there are distinct changes in the infant's emotional and intellectual capacities. Although oral trends still predominate, urethral, anal, and genital trends are strengthening and the range of phantasies available to the infant has widened. This leads to changes in the infant's defensive structure. Klein, in this essay, sees the coalescing of the good and bad objects as leading to the infant perceiving the mother not simply as a unified breast (as in past conceptualizations) but, rather, as a "complete object". This tendency towards a whole object is not by any means restricted to the mother, but occurs across the infant's mental life. Thus, divergent trends in the superego are more united and the division between external and internal representations is diminished. Depressive anxiety is now experienced as a dominant source of anxiety and this anxiety is experienced towards the whole object. There is now a greater possibility for true ambivalence (as opposed to splitting), with the infant now sometimes experiencing different affects towards the same object at relatively the same time. The greedy desire to possess the object leads to the infant attempting to inhibit instinctual desires. Greedy impulses are, in part, a response to the fear of irretrievable loss of an indispensable object. The infant identifies with the mother who is injured (or in danger of injury) by internal impulses, and this reinforces "both the drive to make reparation and the ego's attempts to inhibit aggressive impulses" (1952b, p. 73). The infant's ego, unable at this early point in development to deal with the dangers, widening range of impulses and phantasies, affects, and defences, resorts to manic defences to counteract these depressive concerns and anxiety. Klein adds, in emphasis (beyond the previous discussion of manic defences), the idea that "when anxiety is paramount, the ego even denies the fact that it loves the object at all" (*ibid.*). This leads to a regression to the paranoid–schizoid position.

Although Klein's description of the depressive position has not changed appreciably, she does emphasize some elements that will continue to be important in developmental and clinical theories. Although splitting takes place during the depressive position, the division is of the complete object. This splitting leads to an uninjured live object and an injured and endangered one (perhaps dying or dead). Splitting now is a defence against depressive anxiety. This defence is aided by the infant's increasing awareness of a reassuring external world that is now introjected and then projected into a more reassuring object. As the infant's world gradually coalesces, there is an internal union of good and bad and of ego and superego. This puts the infant into contact with his aggression (and bad objects) and under the sway of a more unified ego–superego. This leads to guilt and. in turn. a "drive" towards reparation. There is a strong (or what Klein calls an "over-riding") urge to repair, preserve, or revive the loved injured object. Klein related this drive to states of mourning, and reparation as an attempt to overcome guilt and mourning. Reparation, in the first (or first several) depressive position, is also a denial of the possibility of loss or death of the object. Klein, in her verbalizing for the depressive infant, states, "'My mother is disappearing, she may never return, she is suffering, she is dead. No, this can't be, for I can revive her'" (*ibid.*, p. 75). This is an illustration of Klein's more general point that, in the early stages of development, every aspect of the ego (or of the infant's cognitive capacities) is used at some point as a defence against anxiety. Thus, while reparation is a trend that helps to quiet destructive trends, it is also used as a denial of destructive wishes and tendencies.

We have gone over Klein's views of the Oedipal situation, but here she says that "about the middle of the first year—the infant enters upon the early stages of the direct and inverted Oedipus complex" (*ibid.*, p. 78). While the oral desires are still dominant during this period, Klein sees genital trends "coming strongly to the fore". In previous publications, Klein has emphasized the role of the combined parent (see commentary on Chapter Six), but here, during the depressive position, she states, "a more realistic relation to the parents develops, the infant comes to consider them as separate individuals" (p. 79). In combined form the infant might have seen the mother containing either the father's penis or the complete father. In a similar manner, the infant might have previously seen the father as possessing the mother (or the mother's breasts), or the mother and father joined together in constant intercourse. Klein views the combined parent as an earlier representation; in adulthood, this type of representation is essentially a response to psychotic anxieties. Even though the infant (male or female) views the parents as separate individuals during the depressive position, the primary anxiety is the fear of loss of the mother. In response to this fear, the infant turns to the father, who now is introjected as a complete person "to fulfil this need".

Klein, in this paper, not only mentions greed, but states, "Envy appears to be inherent in oral greed . . . To this primary envy, jealousy is added when the Oedipus situation arises" (*ibid.*, p. 79). Envy and greed thus make their appearance together, and, for the first time in a theoretical article, they are highlighted as important factors in early development. Even these important comments by Klein about envy and greed would not lead one to posit that envy and greed will become central to Klein's theoretical understanding in her next major theoretical paper.

One can see how important early development is to Klein by the fact that the rest of childhood development is described in only 6–7 pages. Essentially, she reminds us that the infantile neurosis begins in the first year of life and ends with the onset of the latency period. Klein's formulations are similar to her previous ideas (1935, 1940), where she sees several episodes of paranoid–schizoid and depressive position oscillation throughout the psycho-sexual stages. She says, "The genital desires towards both parents, which initiate the early stages of the Oedipus complex are at first interwoven with oral, anal and urethral desires and phantasies, both of a libidinal and aggressive nature" (*ibid.*, p. 81). Following Heimann (1952) and Isaacs (1952), if the pregenital Oedipal anxieties are too strongly dominated by destructive tendencies there will be a high probability of "strong fixations to the pre-genital stages" (1952b, p. 81).

Thus, in the oscillation of positions, genital trends should gradually gain dominance. This will lead to a greater capacity for reparation and sublimation. If genital representations are stable and dominated by libidinal (loving) trends, then this will release the "most creative urge of man, the power to give life". Along with this new creativity is the diminution of the terrifying superego. In Klein's newer theory, she begins to downplay the terrifying aspects of the superego and moves these images to the unconscious.

In discussing genital trends, Klein relates these trends to earlier conditions. Thus, the idea of the male giving life is related to restoring the injured or damaged mother. Oral sublimations are essential to reach the genital position, for the capacity of reparation is dependent on the ability to receive goodness, which has its foundations in the oral stage.

As a last point in this essay, one can see how Klein has remained within the shadow of the object (Freud) when she discusses the relationship of obsessional trends and their connection to the second year of life. Obsessional trends can be observed in rituals involving cleanliness and in a general need for repetition. These trends are related to "growing control of bodily functions in the testing of internal dangers by external reality" (*ibid.*, p. 85). It takes little imagination to picture the anal stage child testing boundaries and realities in his struggle to balance the external and internal demands with his anal wishes. In her description, she relates how "Control of the sphincter proves to him that he can control inner dangers and internal objects. Furthermore, the actual excrements serve as evidence against his phantastic fears of their destructive quality" (*ibid.*). In this depiction, Klein comes close to a Freudian description, but her emphasis on internal representations takes her further into the inner world of the child as a result of her object-relations perspective.

"Transference and surrounding issues"

Klein publishes this paper ("The origins of transference", 1952a) fully a decade after the beginning of the controversial discussions. She opens the essay by quoting Freud and devotes a good deal of effort throughout the essay in establishing continuities and comparisons with Freud's positions. The first quote is one where Freud began to understand transference as an important aspect of the psychoanalytic situation (Freud, 1905e). In this essay, Freud asks, what are the transferences? His answer is that transference relationships, as they occur in analysis, "replace some earlier person by the person of the physician [analyst]. [Thus] a whole series of psychological experiences are revived, not as belonging to the past, but as applying to the present" (Klein, 1952a, p. 48). It is not Klein's intent to go over Freud historically, but to build from this idea of transference to the new concept of transference that she is beginning to put forth in this essay. This concept has been implicit in her work for a long while, but here, in this essay, she makes her views more accessible. This is Klein's only paper on transference.

Her view of transference uses as an illustration the earliest object relations where processes of projection and introjection are crucial for the internalization and expulsion of the object. Interestingly, she revisits Freud's use of the terms "auto-erotism" and "narcissism". She maintains that Freud posits that, during these stages, there are no object relations; the infant is, in fact, only auto-erotic or only interested in self-produced pleasures. This, in addition, means that there are no objects that are internalized, and Klein states that "the difference between Freud's views and my own is less wide than appears at first sight, since Freud's statements on this issue are not unequivocal" (*ibid.*, p. 51). Clearly, Klein is right about this, and the view expressed in this volume is quite different than the one that Klein has stated. One must remember that Klein's view is not idiosyncratic and, in fact, her view, at that point in time, is close to the standard view of Freudian thought. Even though this is the case, she tries to show how Freud's ideas at some points are similar to hers. Since I have spent a long time specifying Freud's views (see Chapter Three for commentary on autoerotism and narcissism), let us leave Freud and follow Klein's views on auto-erotism and narcissism.

It will come as no surprise that Klein sees object relations formed in both of these stages, and these relations "include the love for and elation with the internalized good object which in phantasy forms part of the loved body and self" (*ibid.*). Thus, for Klein, during both of these phases of development there is a full range of emotions, phantasies, anxieties, and defences. This view is, of course, in line with all of her previous papers since 1935, and before (she states 1927). However, in this paper she makes a point of trying to show the convergence between her views and Freud's views in *The Ego and the Id*, where he places identifications with the father and parents "'in the prehistory of every person'" (*ibid.*, p. 52).

Given this initial convergence with Freud, Klein goes on to say that, in psychoanalysis, we have to return to transference, which "originates in the earliest stages", or object relations (*ibid.*, p. 53). By doing this, one can look at the relationships between love and hate and the fluctuations of these affects in relation to the objects in the patient's world. The mechanisms that Klein stresses in producing transference are the same ones that are evident in early development, namely, projection and introjection. It is interesting that she uses these terms in this essay instead of her new term "projective identification". Perhaps her attempt to show her continuity with Freud is partly responsible for her use of terms that appear in several of Freud's theoretical papers (see Chapter Three). Thus, she is subtly shifting the mechanism of transference from Freud's view of a displacement from a prior object relationship to the idea of projecting the relationship into the analyst. She does not, in this essay, discount the idea of displacement, but does say that the most meaningful transferences come from the earliest points of development that are characterized by projective–introjective mechanisms. In line with this interpretation, Klein does not use the concept of position in this paper. She tries to show how her theory can be in accord with Freudian thought, yet, at the same time, offer additional explanatory power. An example of this is her view of narcissism and narcissistic states. For Klein, narcissism, as a stage, involves early object relations with the type of projective–introjective mechanisms she has previously described. Narcissistic states, however, are a withdrawal into internal objects and, most frequently, involve a movement away from the external object. Klein, in another paper (Klein, 1952c), describes an infant girl, C, who was left crying for a long period of time because her mother could not hear her cries. When her mother eventually attempted to soothe her by offering her the breast, the child, who normally readily accepted the breast, only took a few sucks and instead turned to sucking her own fingers. Klein comments,

She resorted to sucking her fingers, that is to say to an auto-erotic pleasure (Freud). I would, however, add that in this instance the narcissistic withdrawal was caused by the (temporary) disturbance in the relation to the mother, and that the infant refused to give up sucking her fingers because they were more trust-worthy than the breast. By sucking she re-established the relation to the internal breast and thus regained enough security to renew the good relation to the external breast and mother. [1952c, p. 103]

Klein describes this type of withdrawal as typical of schizoid patients. The movement from this withdrawal would involve the patient (or the infant) projecting into the analyst and introjecting an object or part object in return. This would be an example of transference.

Of particular importance to Klein is the analysis of the negative transference, which had received relatively little attention in psychoanalytic technique. She concludes that this occurred because of the undervaluation of the importance of aggression. Her view of early object relations opens up the possibility of treating more serious disorders through psychoanalysis. In her view, Freud's statement that severe narcissistic disorders could not develop transference relationships is incorrect, and in part is due to Freud's not understanding, or being inconsistent about, the nature of early object relations (see Klein's note in 1952b, pp. 90–91).

"Envy and gratitude": Klein's last contributions

"Envy and gratitude" (1957) was one of Klein's last papers and was certainly her longest theoretical contribution. She had already begun to theorize about envy and greed in previous publications, but in this paper they become her central focus. Even at this late point in her career, Klein is still noting the theoretical similarities between her new concepts and the concepts of both Abraham and Freud. Klein states, "Three decades after Abraham's death, it is a source of great satisfaction to me that my work has contributed to the growing recognition of the full significance of Abraham's discoveries" (1957, p. 177). Klein writes that she and Abraham have "brought out more fully and more deeply the significance of destructive impulses" (*ibid.*, p. 176). She made this statement even though Abraham did not see envy as being present from the beginning of life, but, rather, from the oral–sadistic phase of the oral stage. (Abraham saw orality and anality as occurring in two phases. In both stages he saw the oral–libidinal phase as being followed by the sadistic phase.) Klein assumed that Abraham's early death prevented him from fully integrating Freud's new theory of instincts. However, one might view this as historical speculation: there is no question that Abraham began to conceptualize the importance of envy, and related some of his findings to the strength of the drives. It is clear that Klein wants to underline her relation to Abraham and to Freud. Her relationship to Freud is underscored by her reference to the idea that destructive impulses are operative from the beginning of life. Klein also points out that her inferences are based on reconstructive assumptions, much as was the case with both Freud and Abraham, and she states that this has "become characteristic of the psycho-analytic method" (*ibid.*, p. 177).

Klein, in this essay, begins to describe intra-uterine life when she posits that the "pre-natal state . . . implies a feeling of unity and security . . . We might, therefore, consider the universal longing for the pre-natal state also partly as an expression of the urge for idealization" (*ibid.*, p. 179). Klein states that the first anxiety is involved with birth and if the "birth has been difficult . . . a disturbance in the adaptation to the external world occurs and the relation to the breast starts at a great disadvantage" (*ibid.*). An infant at birth may face three factors that are potentially frustrating and aversive.

1. Birth itself disrupts the infant's sense of security.
2. There is inevitably some frustration by the breast (waiting for the breast, difficulty in the milk flowing, etc.).
3. The inevitable struggle "between life and death instincts" (*ibid.*).

All these factors serve to impede the internalization of the "primal good object, the mother's breast", and, as such, hurt the infant's ability to develop hope, trust, and belief in goodness. Klein now posits that the negative factors that occur have their pathway through envy, which occurs as an affect in the earliest parts of orality. Envy leads to the phantasy that the deprivation the infant experiences is a result of the breast keeping its supplies for itself, thus increasing the infant's sense of frustration.

Klein defines envy as the "angry (destructive) feeling that another person possesses and enjoys something desirable, the envious impulse is to take the good thing away or to spoil it (or destroy it)" (*ibid.*, p. 181). Envious feelings begin from the start of life and are designed to destroy the mother's creativity. Jealousy is a derivative of envy, and occurs later in development. It is a feeling that something valuable (love from a valued other) has been taken away by a third person. Jealousy, therefore, involves a three-person field, while envy is between two people and has it roots in the mother–infant interaction. Greed is the insatiable impulse to possess beyond what one needs and what the other can provide. It originates as the impulse to suck dry and devour the breast. Greed is a destructive introjective phantasy, while envy primarily involves projection. Thus, envy involves the phantasy of putting things into the breast to spoil and destroy it and greed the phantasy of taking from and devouring. Envy, in this sense, is the more destructive affect, although the two affects (envy and greed) frequently go hand in hand (or breast and mouth, to be more accurate). Klein's description of envy is based on the infant's first relationship with its mother, and, although this is the primary envy, she notes that envious feelings occur throughout the development sequence.

Envy is a factor whether or not the breast-feeding experience is satisfactory. If the breast is depriving, there is a phantasy that the bad breast is keeping "the milk, love and care associated with the good breast all to itself" (*ibid.*, p. 183).

> It is perhaps more understandable that the satisfactory breast is also envied. The very ease with which the milk comes—though the infant feels gratified by it—also gives rise to envy because this gift seems something so unattainable. [*ibid.*]

It is readily apparent that Klein sees the newborn present with an active and disturbing phantasy life. Klein also sees envious feelings as a powerful factor in the analytic situation. If the analyst has provided the patient with something that leads to relief, an envious patient may want to destroy the analyst's capacity through destructive criticisms. Just as the baby envies the creativity of the mother, so, too, can the analysand envy the analyst's creativity. Klein maintains that if we trace back the roots of envy we (inevitably) go back to what she terms the "primary one", or the earliest conflict that involves the envy of the breast in one form or another. This is not surprising, since the breast is an important, or, rather, the important, symbol in Kleinian theory. The breast is imbued with qualities going far beyond the actual sustenance it affords. Phantasies about the breast are crucial in the analyses of most, if not all, of Klein's patients.

Since envy, at its core, leads to splitting, it, of necessity, "interferes with the gradual building up of a good object in the transference situation" (*ibid.*, p. 185). No matter how good the mothering, envy will, to some extent, interfere with the development of the good object. Klein, in discussing new methods of feeding, relates that if one attempts to be the perfect mother, there is a danger of indulging the child. Excessive gratification, in her theory, is considered as great a danger as excessive frustration. She states, "A certain amount of frustration followed by gratification might give the infant the feeling that he has been able to cope with his anxiety" (*ibid.*). Thus, she comes to the same position as Freud and Abraham when she states that gratification and frustration are both necessary conditions for optimal development, as long as the infant/child can tolerate the frustration and appreciate the gratification. Frustration and the accompanying conflict is a fundamental element in developing the capacity for creativity. Creativity and the capacity for enjoyment are both factors that militate against destructive elements becoming dominant in an individual's psychological development.

Primary envy and a restatement

Since the breast is the first object and it is the source of gratification and symbolic of all goodness, primary envy involves envy of the mother's breast. There are later forms of envy, "the girl's desire to take her mother's place and the boy's feminine position", but these later forms are no longer focused on the mother's breast but rather on "the mother receiving the father's penis, [or on] babies inside the mother" (*ibid.*, p. 183). In the example of the girl wanting to take the mother's place, envy and jealousy are closely related. Envy, as already mentioned, plays a prominent part in many treatments, and

Klein states that envy is an important aspect of the negative therapeutic reaction. Envy does not allow the gradual building up of a stable positive transference or a good object in the transference situation. Just as the patient wants to be freed from his/her conflicts, the infant wants to be freed from destructive impulses and persecutory anxiety. The feeling that the mother is omnipotent is also mirrored in the transference that the analyst is omnipotent and could free the patient if the analyst chose to do so. To the extent that envy is present, it accentuates the person's greed and, at times, jealousy. The patient who is envious of the analyst's creativity wants more of it and may not want to leave the treatment room, or, alternatively, may feel so guilty that he studiously leaves on time. In either case, Klein sees envy at the heart of many conflicts, particularly with patients who have not built up good objects in their representational world.

The building of good objects is crucial in the person being able to withstand envious affect states. A doubt about the possession of good objects is a contributory factor in greedy and envious responses. The person who is uncertain about maintaining a good object will be uncertain about good feelings and always desirous of obtaining more and more good objects to bolster his supplies. The child or adult who is secure about the good object is able to withstand envious and hateful feelings without these feelings being permanently lodged in the child's attitudes and behaviours. The child's capacity to maintain the good object is strongly related to feelings and expressions of gratitude towards the good object. From Klein's perspective, the relation to the mother remains undisturbed (by envy, frustrations, etc.), partly because of "external circumstances but the internal factors" underlying the capacity for gratitude or the capacity for love "appear[ing] to be innate" (*ibid.*, p. 188). The capacity for enjoyment, for feeling understood, or for experiencing security, are all related to the capacity for gratitude. Klein relates all of these attributes to the introjection of the good breast. "A full gratification at the breast means that the infant feels he has received from his love object a unique gift which he wants to keep" (*ibid.*). Breast-feeding, or, more accurately, early feeding experiences, is, in this theory, the basis of the possibility for a happy life. The ability to appropriately libidinize the breast is the "keep" factor in this developmental sequence. The "recurrent experience makes possible gratitude on the deepest level and plays an important role in the capacity to make reparation" (*ibid.*, p. 189).

Given the importance of the building of the good object, primary envious attacks against the breast are, according to Klein (quoting Chaucer), "the worst sin that is; all other sins are sins only against one virtue, whereas envy is against all virtue and against all goodness" (*ibid.*). One can see how important it is from Klein's vantage point to deal with envious attacks, given that is the most serious sin of even the seven deadly sins. If a person is prone to envious feelings, stressful internal or external conditions will tend to undermine the good object, or whatever elements of a good object are present in the person's internal life. Envy will lead to a high probability of early splitting mechanisms and disintegration. What counteracts the sense of disintegration is an omnipotent phantasy of destroying or spoiling the object. This omnipotent phantasy may prevent disintegration, but it will come at a high cost to the psychic life of the individual. Thus, the person may have omnipotent phantasies of destroying and controlling the envied object, but, at the same time, will cut off any possibility of love or nurturance from the object. Klein's view of the importance of envy leads her into a discussion of the death instinct. This is not surprising, since envy is now considered to be the earliest manifestation of the death instinct.

In the discussion of the death instinct (Thanatos), Klein again goes back to Freud and uses one of his concepts to begin the discussion. Under the influence of the life instinct (Eros), Klein assumes that the ego is able, to some extent, to deflect the death instinct on to external objects. The ego that she posits existing from birth (she notes that her assumption of an ego structure from birth is a concept that is different from Freud's, who assumed that the ego is constructed from instinctual energy) experiences the threat of the first anxiety, annihilation anxiety. The ego, operating under the influence of Eros, then deflects the death instinct outward and in this way reduces internal anxiety. At the same time, this action increases persecutory anxiety, and, through projective identification, the persecuting object becomes part of the infant's internal world. One of the ego's functions is to provide gradual integration of its functions and objects. There is a countervailing tendency on the part of the ego to defend against overwhelming anxiety. This defensive tendency leads to splitting as a means of preserving the ego and reducing the spread of anxiety. Thus, objects are split into good and bad as a means of preserving the ego, even if it is split. This "dispersal" of anxiety, or of the destructive impulses represented in various objects, is a new way in which Klein posits the process of splitting. It is related to her previous ideas, but previously she thought of splitting as a way of separating the good and bad because of the "innate conflict between love and hate" (*ibid.*, p. 190). Now, she is theorizing that the ego splits itself and its objects to disperse destructive tendencies. As we will see, she is thinking of the ego as at times falling to bits, and in this way is probably being influenced by Winnicott and his conceptualization of annihilation anxiety (see Chapter Ten).

The nature of splitting becomes somewhat clearer in Klein's work on envy. Essentially, she uses two factors in explaining the nature of successful splitting in early development. She first reinforces the adaptive aspect of early splitting; it is for the protection of the good object. The early ego cannot withstand unmodified, intense, destructive tendencies, and so splitting is necessary for all infant development. What distinguishes splitting in healthy infants, from splitting in infants who are bound to difficulties in later life (or in relatively nearby childhood)? We must first remember that the task in the depressive position is the integration of the good and the bad objects (as well as other integrations). Klein states first that splitting "only succeeds if there is an adequate capacity for love and a relatively strong ego" (*ibid.*). In the healthy infant, splitting first preserves the good object and, when the infant is ready, the capacity for love makes the good object resilient enough to integrate with the bad object. Here, we see that while Klein will mention environmental factors, she features constitutional factors. She also adds a quantitative factor that could be predictive in determining the child who will successfully heal splits and the child who will suffer products of disintegration during the depressive position.

All good objects are, to some extent, idealized, but Klein maintains that the extent of the idealization is a sign of the depth of the split. If an object is idealized in a more pervasive, intense manner, then this "indicates that it is not the good and the bad that are kept apart, but an idealized and an extremely bad" object that are being kept apart. The split that will keep these two types of objects apart will be very deep, and will make integration during the depressive position more difficult. The depth of the split is an indication of the intensity of destructive impulses and the powerful envious feelings that contributed to this disturbing division. Idealization is a powerful indicator that persecutory anxiety is present in the person's internal world. This line of reasoning is consistent with Klein's previous view of idealization as a defensive product of pining in the depressive position (see Chapter Five). At this point, however, she goes beyond her previous views about idealization and posits that idealization is derived "from an innate feeling that an extremely good breast exists" (*ibid.*, p. 192). Before we briefly enter this new realm, let us summarize Klein's view about splitting, idealization, and persecutory anxiety.

In Klein's present formulation, splitting still occurs as a result of the infant's ego not being able to contain the destructive drive. The split protects the good object and separates it from the bad object. In the present formulation, envy is the embodiment of the destructive drive. It is perhaps more accurate to say that envy and greed embody the destructive drive; however, clearly Klein's focus is on the motivating aspects of envy. Envy spoils the experience of gratification and contributes to the intensification of persecutory anxiety. It does not allow the infant to experience gratitude in a continuous manner, and gratitude is now seen as a forerunner of the experience of reparation and love in the depressive position. To deal with persecutory anxiety, the good object is often idealized and seen as perfect and invulnerable. This formulation is similar to the ideas that Klein has put forth previously, except now both the concept of envy and of splitting have been highlighted in the way that has just been described. This is not a small shift, since envy and, silently, gratitude become the centre of Klein's new theoretical matrix. There is also a shift in her views on idealization, and the innate feeling that a good breast exists is Klein's introduction to the idea that a certain amount of idealization is present even in normal development. Once having stated this, Klein goes on to describe how the idealized object is often part of a love relationship that is unable to last. It is frequently the case with idealized objects that they cannot live up to expectations, and "one love object may frequently have to be exchanged for another" (*ibid.*, p. 193).

Klein, in her description, returns to an earlier position and now sees transient guilt emerging during the paranoid–schizoid position. In cases of excessive envy, guilt may occur as a more prominent factor during the paranoid–schizoid position. This will overwhelm the ego and the guilt will be projected into the environment, and, in this way, increase the infant's persecutory anxiety. It will also be a factor in hurting the chances of integration during the depressive position, since the premature guilt is now confused with guilt arising in the depressive position. This leads to excessive persecutory anxiety during the depressive position. This is but one confusion that arises as a consequence of excessive envy; there are several others, and perhaps the most important of these is the confusion of desires from different psycho-sexual zones. To quote Klein,

> It is my hypothesis that one of the deepest sources of guilt is always linked with the envy of the feeding breast, and with the feeling of having spoilt its goodness by envious attacks. If the primal object has been established with relative stability in early infancy, the guilt aroused by such feelings can be coped with more successfully because then envy is more transient and less liable to endanger the relation to the good object. Excessive envy interferes with adequate oral gratification and so acts as a stimulus towards the intensification of genital desires and trends. This implies that the infant turns too early towards genital gratification, with the consequence that the oral relation becomes genitalized and the genital trends becomes too much colored by oral grievances and anxieties. I have often contended that genital sensations and desires are possibly operative from birth onwards, for instance, it is well known that infant boys have erections at a very early stage. But in speaking of these sensations arising prematurely I mean that genital trends interfere with oral ones at a stage when normally the oral desires are uppermost. Here again we have to consider the effects of early confusion, which expresses itself in a blurring of the oral, anal, and genital impulses and phantasies. [*ibid.*, p. 195]

Here, Klein is looking at a major confusion that arises not only in infants and children, but persists throughout life. This confusion does not allow gratification to occur properly in any sphere and sends the person searching for the idealized object and the idealized gratification. It is an explanation of phenomena that are frequently observed in therapeutic settings and are frequently bewildering to the therapist. Klein is clearly maintaining that, at different phases of development, one zone should appropriately be the dominant one. Thus, in early development, the child's gratification comes primarily from the oral zone. I have quoted Klein extensively here to attempt again to show that her citing the blurring of oral, anal, and genital impulses can logically only be interpreted in terms of the concept of psycho-sexual stage. It is of historical interest that Klein notes erections in infant males. These erections occur almost exclusively in rapid eye movement (REM) sleep. This type of sleep in infants was first noted by Peter Wolff (1966), who, without the aid of electronic devices, noted the occurrence of what he called active sleep, in which male infants would almost inevitably produce erections. Whether this is a sign of genital excitement is, of course, a question that is open to debate.

Envy: the depressive position and the Oedipus complex

Although envy reaches its zenith during the first paranoid–schizoid position it is a factor throughout life. With the onset of the depressive position, the infant/child is able to view the object's badness as in part due to the projection of its aggressive phantasies. Although the split in the object is redressed, the pain of the depressive position is considerable and guilt is a factor that leads the infant to make amends through reparation. This leads to greater trust in the good object, and this trust leads to a less punitive superego structure. Klein's view of the onset of the Oedipus complex remains unchanged in this essay, and, during the first depressive position, Oedipal conflicts emerge. Although, in optimal development, one will see jealousy in the Oedipal stage, Klein states, "There is a direct link between the envy experienced towards the mother's breast and the development of jealousy" (*ibid.*, p. 197). Jealousy is based on the rivalry with the father, since he is suspected of stealing away the mother's breast and attempting to possess the mother. The strength of the envious attacks in the paranoid–schizoid position largely determined the quality and security of the good object for the infant. If the father is seen in paranoid terms (his penis intruding inside the mother's breast), then the jealousy in the depressive–Oedipal stage/position will border on envy. It will then be considerably more difficult to integrate the object, since the object will be infiltrated by the father. The more secure the good object, the greater the possibility of integrating good and bad objects (or representations) and the greater the possibility of the child being willing to acknowledge the mother's relationships with other people. To some extent, the phantasy of the combined parent (father's penis in the mother or mother inside of the father) is a feature of the early Oedipal stage. Even in the earliest Oedipal stage, the quality of the good object will determine the extent to which the phantasy of the combined parent can be dislodged into separate object representations. In more optimal conditions, jealousy is directed towards the rivals (father and siblings or phantasized rivals), and this distributes the destructive tendencies among various people. Thus, the envy towards the mother, or the intense jealous of the combined parents, is lessened when it is distributed among several object representations. Klein also states, "Furthermore, the change from oral desires to genital ones reduces the importance of the mother as a giver of oral enjoyment" (ibid., p. 198). Thus, not only are destructive tendencies distributed among different people, but the interest in different zones leads to a further attenuation.

Klein's views on male and female Oedipal development are largely unchanged from her previous positions, except now envy is a factor in determining the extent and nature of Oedipal jealousy. The boy hates the father "who is envied for the possession of the mother" (ibid., p. 197). The girl's genital desires allow her to find a new love object and now the mother is a rival. The rivalry with the mother is centred around the issue of who will be a recipient of the father's gifts (babies, etc.). To the extent that the girl can control her jealousy and identify with the mother, there is a possibility of a wide range of sublimatory channels. Although Klein does not see penis envy as the primary source of envy in the girl, she does see it as a factor in various analyses that she has conducted. Her view of penis envy, however, is quite different from the Freudian perspective. Penis envy can be traced back to envy of the mother's breast, and "the destructive feelings allied with" the envious attacks on the mother's breast (ibid., p. 198). This envy can lead to a homosexual outcome, or to a type of idealization of the penis. This idealization is unlikely to lead to a satisfactory relationship with a man, and each new male relationship will be seen as a conquest over a real or imagined female rival. If the envy is not "so strong", an idealization of the father (or father's penis) may lead to a loving relationship with a man. The woman "can combine some hatred against the mother and love for the father and later on for other men" (*ibid.*, p.199). The woman's hatred for the mother will exist in a split-off form and still potentially be available to spoil subsequent relationships, particularly those relationships that raise some maternal symbolic equivalents.

Male impotence, compulsive hypersexuality, promiscuity, and homosexuality in men are all traced back to the male's envy of the mother's breast. This occurs when oral gratification is impaired and the hatred of the breast is "transferred to the vagina" (*ibid.*, p. 201). For Klein, in many ways the man is missing the essential component that he envies in his earliest relationship. Obviously, the man is missing breasts, but, as importantly, he is missing the capacity to bear children. Men whose envy is strong not only hate the vagina, but also other feminine traits and characteristics. This extends most notably to the woman's capacity to bear children. If the man's envy is not overpowering, then being a lover and a father allows him to overcome his envy of the maternal figure. Although homosexuality is one pathway taken by a man with excessive maternal envy, a more frequent outcome is the man who uses and denigrates women. This denigration may involve abusing the woman both mentally and physically. Although Klein does not label male envy of the mother as maternal awe, it seems to be an appropriate descriptive label of a feeling that the man cannot internalize except by attempting to debase the idealized object.

Klein states that in both sexes there is a paranoid jealous and rivalry in respect to the inverted (negative) Oedipus complex. In either sex, this paranoid jealousy is related to excessive envy directed towards the primal object. The "good" breast counteracts all these tendencies, and if there is a strong enough good primal internal object, this is representative of the life instinct and creativity. The creativity for both sexes involves the creation of a baby and a sense of well being in this creation. In the man, there is creativity as a father and in his work life. Envy of creativity is a fundamental factor disturbing the creative process. Klein, in this essay, turns to poetry (Milton and Shakespeare) and illustrates how envy plays a crucial role in Satan's attempt to spoil God's creativity. Clearly G-d possesses what Satan can only hope to destroy. In this essay, Klein presents extensive clinical illustrations and they all demonstrate the importance of analysing the patient's destructive envy that is present in the transference.

Primary defences and the depressive position

Klein, from the beginning of her career as an analyst, has maintained that her focus in treatment is the deepest anxiety that is being generated in the analytic situation. In this essay, she reaffirms her view, but subtly shifts her perspective by pointing out that the "first and foremost function of the ego is to deal with anxiety" (*ibid.*, p. 215). This statement shifts the focus of the analyst to defences that are present from the beginning of post-natal life. Here, she again affirms that the capacity to bear anxiety is a constitutional or genetic factor that will determine the type of defence that becomes dominant in a particular phase of development. If there is a low tolerance of anxiety, the ego will be excessively split and persecutory anxiety will dominate the infant's experience. In this paper, splitting is joined by projection (projective identification), omnipotence, and denial as defences that are "reinforced" (stimulated) by envy. However, envy may stimulate any defence, even defences conceptualized as occurring in the depressive position. Of course, the earlier, or more primitive, defences are more usually associated with the dynamics of envy. For example, it is Klein's view that omnipotent idealization of the object is a way of exalting the insecurely fashioned good object and keeping it separated from a "very bad primal object" (*ibid.*, p. 216). In this conceptualization, idealization is a defence against envy as well as a defence against persecutory anxiety. Previously, idealization had been seen as a response to pining in the depressive position (see Chapter Six). In this paper, Klein sees idealization as occurring earlier and as a pernicious defence that reinforces splitting and, in turn, increases persecutory anxiety. Interestingly, it is in this paper that she also maintains that idealization is not simply a pathological process. Idealization may be a residue of the pre-natal state, where there is a "universal longing" for the return of this type of perfect unity (*ibid.*, p. 177). In addition, she states that all infants have some degree of idealization, but that excessive idealization is destructive to the attainment of a secure good object. The idealized object is bound to fall, but is representative of the desire for the good object and is a "a condition for life itself, that is to say, an expression of the life instinct" (*ibid.*, p. 192). Although idealization is seen as a manifestation of a universal longing, it still is viewed mainly as a defensive process, that is, indicative of a split that may temporarily hide the presence of powerful persecutory anxiety and a bad, usually devouring, object.

We have detailed how the presence of a good object is crucial to the movement to the depressive position. This sentence is somewhat misleading, for everyone moves into the depressive position, but, when persecutory anxiety is excessive and (therefore) the good object is not securely represented, the depressive position is strongly infiltrated by paranoid–schizoid anxieties and defences. However,

> Even with people in whom envy is not excessive, the concern for the object, the identification with it, and the fear of its loss and of the harm done to its creativeness, is an important factor in the difficulty of working through the depressive position. [*ibid.*, p. 216]

With the occurrence of the depressive position, there is unification of the object and, under the influence of Oedipal dynamics, there is a natural turning towards other objects (the father, siblings, etc.). This leads both to a dispersal of feeling towards the mother and a sense of loss of the unique first object. The dispersal of loving feelings allows for gratitude to be expressed towards new objects, and normally results in a lowering of interest in the maternal figure. If envy is still a powerful factor during the depressive position, then often there will be strong devaluation of all objects and frequent attempts at spoiling childhood situations that were intended to be pleasurable and/or learning experiences. If the child is more developed in the depressive position, there may be a devaluation of the self rather than a devaluation of the object. This spoiling of the self-representation inhibits the person from creative self-expression, or, at least, from appreciating one's own accomplishments. The guilt about success is powerful in such individuals, and Klein relates this guilt ultimately to the tenuous establishment of the primal good object.

Klein writes about many varieties of what she calls defence, "a frequent method of defense is to stir up in envy in others by one's own success . . . thereby reversing the situation in which envy is experienced" (*ibid.*, p. 217). This defence is based on projective identification, and perceiving envy in others is a defence that increases persecutory anxiety since, in particular, the envious internal object is experienced as the most hostile of persecutors. The affect of indifference is also considered a defence in that feelings of love are stifled, as are corresponding intense (feelings) of hate. This defence is effective "because this (indifference) is less painful than to bear the guilt arising from a combination of love, hate and envy" (*ibid.*, p. 218). Clearly, in the depressive position, when Oedipal strivings arise there is the possibility of reparation and gratitude helping the child through the jealousy and guilt of the Oedipal situation. However, to the extent that envy is still a powerful affect during the depressive position, there is a strong possibility of splitting continuing and paranoid–schizoid defences and anxieties predominating during the depressive position. The repair that should occur during the depressive position will not happen if envy is still intense. The child will then return to the paranoid–schizoid position with little or no improvement over the first occurrence of this position. Here, we should pause and consider what repair is possible during the depressive position.

In "Envy and gratitude", as well as in most of her other theoretical papers, Klein talks about the oscillation of paranoid–schizoid and depressive positions occurring several times during childhood. Let us consider a passage from the paranoid–schizoid position to the depressive position and then a return to the paranoid–schizoid position. After the first depressive position, in optimal development, there should be objects that are less split and more united than was the case in the previous paranoid–schizoid position. There should also be less idealization of the good object and a less punitive or terrifying superego structure. These developments are only possible with a good primal object firmly in place and gratitude having been expressed towards the good and generous primal object. In her new theoretical effort, Klein is maintaining that we can mark the degree of pathology by noting the role and extent of envy as a factor in the person's psychic structure. Envy and, secondarily, greed are direct manifestations of the destructive drive.

Following this line of reasoning, it is hard for the child to receive parental generosity or for the patient to gratefully receive therapeutic help when envious impulses are dominant in a person's psychic economy. Klein notes, in this context, "Distrust and fear of taking in mental food goes back to the distrust of what the envied and spoiled breast offered" (*ibid.*, p. 221). If envious attacks are a powerful part of the depressive position, persecutory anxiety will dominate the picture. Guilt will be of the earliest kind and there will be a strong tendency to want to rid the mind of destructive objects that have been taken in via projective identification. In the extreme, this may lead to a fragmentation of the person's sense of self (or ego structure) and the world will be a confusing *mélange* of idealized and denigrated objects. In a fragmented mind, the valuation of these objects is often rapidly changing. This confusing state is frequently also confusing to both parent and therapist alike. Repair going on in the depressive position allows for objects and self-representations to be unified and more mature gratitude to be expressed towards objects. The reparation will lead to concern for the object and thoughts about the welfare of the object. Obviously, early in development, Klein is talking about concern that is far from adult behaviour, but she is clearly seeing the development of concern via reparation as occurring early in the life cycle.

Klein distinguishes fragmented parts of the ego from coherent, although split, aspects of the ego. If dispersal has led to fragmentation, then it will be much more difficult to make whole coherent representations during either early development or in the therapeutic process. Splitting, as opposed to fragmentation, leads to clear divisions and allows for the greater possibility of unifying the object in early development or in the therapeutic situation. These last ideas may seem confusing, since Klein has also talked about the danger of extreme splitting leading to idealized objects and extremely dangerous persecutory objects.

This confusion is clarified if we realize that she is talking about optimal levels of splitting in early development. Optimal levels are present if the good and bad objects are separated and there is the possibility of experiencing gratitude towards the good object. Moreover, the good object is not overwhelmed by either the danger from the bad object or, more importantly, the danger of frequent, or powerful, envious attacks against the good object. If splitting is too extreme, then it signals strong persecutory anxiety that requires less permeable boundaries. This also is correlated with a good object that further needs to be idealized to keep it relatively invulnerable from attack. If splitting is too permeable, then there is a danger of fragmentation, since there can be both envious attacks against the good object and a confusion between good and bad objects. A firm but permeable boundary allows for easier unification during the subsequent depressive position. As has been frequently mentioned, this is only possible if envy does not destroy the opportunity of unification in the depressive position. Although mourning has not been mentioned in this chapter, Klein has not given up the important concept of the child being able to tolerate the loss of the object during the depressive position. Mourning is extremely important in her ideas of both development and the acceptance of loss in psychoanalytic treatment.

It is important to picture the type of confusional states that Klein is depicting during periods of fragmentation. She is talking about the type of person who cannot discern what to take in, or, once having taken something in, cannot determine whether or not it is of any value. This type of person is frequently spitting out and taking in things in rapid succession, during which processes confusion abounds both internally and in the surrounding environment. Although these states occur frequently in psychosis, they are also typical of impulsive and cyclothymic borderline disorders (among other borderline states). Excessive idealization can be maintained in some individuals, but Klein, here, posits that idealization indicates a split that involves the other aspect of the split containing a persecutory object. Klein points out that the fate of an idealized object is typically to disappoint and fail in some crucial manner. When this happens, the idealized object becomes devalued and there is a rapid and powerful denigration of this person. The rapid fall of the idealized object is evidence to Klein of the persecutory nature of this person's split-off object world. Klein would also maintain that the idealized object fell to the person's uncontrolled envious attacks. These hypothetical illustrations are meant to show that Klein is consistent in her conceptualizations: envy and splitting are present and active in adults as well as in children. Klein uses the same rationale for treatment as she does to explain developmental issues. Thus, the person's internal world demonstrates the same dynamic relationships in adult life as in childhood development.

Review (repeat) of Klein and constitutional factors

Klein considers constitutional factors as even more important than was the case in Freudian theory. It seems clear that, in part, she posits the importance of genetic factors as a link with Freud and the Freudian opus. Klein writes,

> I have previously suggested that greed, hate, and persecutory anxieties in relation to the primal object, the mother's breast, have an innate basis. In this discussion, I have added that envy too, as a powerful expression of oral– and anal–sadistic impulses, is constitutional. The variations in the intensity of these constitutional factors are in my view linked with the preponderance of the one or other instinct in the fusion of the life and death instincts postulated by Freud. [1957, p. 228]

One can see, in this extract, that not only is Klein stating the importance of constitutional factors, but she is also relating this postulate to Freud's instinct theory. Also, in this quote, she implicitly includes Abraham when she talks of the importance of envy in the oral and anal sadistic stages. Previously she had referred to Freud's paper on "Character and anal erotism" (1908b), where he stated that some people's strong anal erotism is constitutional. She also mentions Abraham's emphasis on the strength of oral impulses and its importance in the aetiology of manic–depressive illness. Here, in her last major theoretical paper, she is attempting to forge her links with both Freud and Abraham. In this vein, she also mentions the strength of the ego and the capacity of the ego to tolerate "anxiety, tension and frustration" (*ibid.*). She tells us, "I have had many opportunities in my analytic work to trace the origin of character formation to variations in innate factors" (*ibid.*, p. 229). She details that there are some infants who have had good environments and display excessive envy, and that the opposite also maintains; infants who have experienced great deprivations and yet develop relatively unscathed. While she acknowledges the possible importance of pre-natal (intrauterine) factors, she is firm, nevertheless, in stating the importance of "innate factors". Despite the importance of innate factors, Klein is also firm about how these factors must be dealt with in the transference in a psychoanalytic treatment. Although we will discuss her ideas on treatment in Chapter Seventeen, here we can say that it is clear that she thought that the only way one could establish a good object (if one was not securely present) is to have a full psychoanalytic experience (preferably with a Kleinian analyst). In this treatment, it would be crucial to experience and analyse the patient's envious impulses and envious attacks. At the end of her life, Klein has placed envy at the centre of her theoretical world.

Commentary

In this commentary, one could cite differences with some of Klein's theorizing, or, more appropriately, a sense of appreciation for all of the fruitful concepts that she has developed. While it is true that I doubt that there is an Oedipal stage during the first six months of an infant's life, I find that I do not dwell on the timing of Klein's concepts. I have stated before that I believe (commentary in Chapter Six) that Klein conflates early triangulation with Oedipal dynamics, but this also seems to me of minor moment. Klein's concepts of positions and the manner in which she conceptualizes the movement from part to whole objects are important to revolutionary theoretical statements whenever they occur in development. Klein is providing a picture during childhood of a movement towards symbolization (depressive position), and then, when a new anxiety occurs, a tendency towards fragmentation and an inability for the child to adequately utilize their mental abilities. Her pictures of the way the mind is evacuated during states of anxiety should have (has) changed the way clinicians approach patients who dwell in the paranoid–schizoid position. I find that Bion, who, in my mind, is the exquisite translator of Kleinian concepts (among other talents), is able to show how to utilize her concepts clinically in perhaps a manner that might be somewhat foreign to her. So, in the beginning of this commentary, I want to acknowledge our debt to Klein before I obsess about relatively minor points.

Although in Chapter Six, I frequently refer to Petot's two volumes on the development of Kleinian theory, Meira Likierman has written one of the best recent volumes on Klein. Of particular interest is Likierman's depiction of Ferenczi's influence on Klein. Likierman first notes that Ferenczi, for a long period of time, worked closely with, and strongly influenced, Freud's theorizing. Freud was Ferenczi's analyst for a brief period, and Ferenczi makes a disguised appearance in "Analysis terminable and interminable" (1937c). This is a point I discussed in a previous volume (Ellman, 1991). Certainly, Freud's ideas about the purified pleasure ego (Chapter Three), which included splitting and a projective–introjective sequence, were strongly influenced by Ferenczi, and Freud acknowledged this influence. Likierman maintains that Ferenczi strongly shaped Freud's views on transference; I believe this assertion is incorrect. Freud's views on transference developed slowly and were almost in place before Freud even met Ferenczi. I can only say here what I have stated at length previously (Ellman, 1991, pp. 23–80): Freud's views on transference came almost entirely from his clinical experience and were put in place reluctantly. Freud had difficulty in acknowledging the importance of transference. When he was actively seeing patients no longer (but, rather, doing so-called training analyses, after the First World War), he reverted back to what I have labelled the pathogenic memory model and transference analysis was, in part, left behind.

Klein's views on transference were a combination of Freud's transference papers and her moving to the concept of projective identification. Projective identification was a concept that certainly was influenced by Ferenczi. Perhaps most importantly, Ferenczi's clinical sensibilities allowed Klein to listen to material in a way that freed her imagination and creativity. Therefore, although Freud's views on transference were not particularly affected by Ferenczi, more importantly, Ferenczi had both a direct and indirect impact on Klein's formulations.

Likierman sees Fairbairn's theorizing about schizoid processes as adding depth to Klein's views about the position that preceded the depressive position. Klein, in her 1935 and 1940 papers, saw this period as characterized by the infant experiencing paranoid anxieties. Fairbairn certainly facilitated Klein's thinking about the schizoid dynamics and influenced this position becoming thought of and renamed the paranoid–schizoid position. However, the later centrality of envy in Klein's theorizing far overshadowed any other influence, and this emphasis had little to with Fairbairn. In fact, one can see from Klein's clinical work the concept of envy was implicit in her clinical thinking certainly by 1932 (Klein, 1932). What is more striking, in my view (and for Likierman as well), is Abraham's influence both conceptually and clinically. If one reads Fairbairn (Chapter Nine), he intuitively chooses to compare his views with Abraham's theorizing (as opposed to a comparison with Freud). He summarizes and then departs from Abraham's version of the psycho-sexual stages, but agrees with a number of Abraham's clinical assumptions. Fairbairn chooses to compare his theory to Abraham's version of Freudian theory because Abraham is the author who essentially adds conceptual and clinical depth to Freud's theory of psycho-sexual stages. Of course, Fairbairn differs with most of Freud's and Abraham's theoretical assumptions. Abraham also solidifies the idea of the roots of psychosis and depression as occurring early in the developmental cycle. In addition, envy (before penis envy) is an important aspect of Abraham's theorizing.

I have already mentioned my difference with Money-Kyrle's statement that after 1935 the concept of position has become the "developmental unit in place of phase of stage" (1975b, p. 433). Here is a sentence from Klein (in 1952b), "The infant's first experiences of feeding lead to the internalization of an object, the mother's breast" (p. 62). Klein maintains that this "is at first a relation to a part-object, for both oral–libidinal and oral–destructive impulses from the beginning of life are directed towards the mother's breast in particular" (*ibid.*). In describing the balance between libidinal and destructive tendencies, she says the "emotion called greed, which first and foremost is of an oral nature" *ibid.*, p. 62). Now, one could go on quoting from Klein about anal sadism (in her early and late writings), but I think this quote makes it clear that she is still thinking of positions as oscillating within stages. Certainly, her concept of stage is much more fluid than Freud's and Abraham's, but she is still utilizing the concept of it. Later in this volume (Chapter Eighteen), I suggest that the concept of position be replaced by a more continuous idea that is deduced from the theory of primary and secondary repression (thing and word representations). Perhaps all of these ideas would be clearer if we stated that the concept of stage and position are excellent beginnings in considering a new theory of child development. This theory should include Freud's, Abraham's, and Klein's essential postulate, that in infancy through childhood, the world is viewed through the prism of bodily functions.

If you have read these chapters in order, you have read the controversial discussions. One wonders about the Freudians, who clearly did not believe in Eros and Thanatos, criticizing Klein for not being Freudian enough, or critiquing Klein for her implicit ideas about psychoanalytic technique. If one reads my later chapters it will be clear that I differ with Klein and some neo-Kleinians' ideas about the role of interpretation. Clearly, Klein's idea about interpreting the destructive aspects of a phantasy have been modulated (Spillius, 1988, pp. 8–12), and yet still I will take a different perspective on the role of interpretation. In a later section, I look at criticisms of Kleinian psychoanalytic technique and try to detail some answers from Spillius (see Chapter Eighteen) and others about these criticisms. Nevertheless, there are virtually no clinical conditions where Kleinian concepts have not illuminated my view of the therapeutic situation. I do not think that my view is idiosyncratic, since, in my opinion, many analysts around the world have have been strongly influenced, either implicitly or explicitly, by Kleinian concepts. Frequently, this influence has been modulated by Bion's interpretations and new formulations.

CHAPTER NINE

Fairbairn: a new object relations voice

Summary

W. R. D. Fairbairn was a Scottish psychoanalyst whom in the early 1940s, wrote several vital papers at the same time that the controversial discussions were under way (see Chapter Seven). The controversial discussions between Freudian and Kleinian analysts of the British Psychoanalytic Institute were designed to determine whether Kleinian theory was "truly" psychoanalytic. During this period, Fairbairn developed a theory that was a clear alternative to Freudian psychoanalysis. His focus on early object relationships, while bearing some similarity to Klein's emphasis, came at these issues from a very different perspective. Fairbairn reinterpreted many of Freud's and Abraham's conclusions and, in his interpretation, developed a theory that included a pentagon of structures while eliminating Freud's drive theory. He also rejected a number of aspects of Freud's theorizing that Fairbairn concluded were based on nineteenth century science. In both his developmental theory and his ideas about the psychoanalytic situation, he emphasized schizoid dynamics and proposed that all psychopathology was a response to schizoid dynamics or what he termed "love made hungry". In 1946, he and Klein simultaneously published papers on schizoid dynamics. The publication of Fairbairn's paper, in effect, introduced his ideas to the larger psychoanalytic community. Since that time, the years have been kind to Fairbairn's theorizing; his influence in contemporary psychoanalysis might be greater now than at any point during his lifetime.

W. R. D. Fairbairn

Fairbairn is one of the early psychoanalytic critics of Freudian theory and one of the ancestors of the relational movement. Sutherland, commenting in 1989, states that Fairbairn's theory provided a new paradigm for the twentieth century. He mentions that only a few analysts of his time recognized the enormity of Fairbairn's contributions. Grotstein writes, "W. R. D. Fairbairn is emerging at last from an underserved obscurity into the lime light of current object relations theory . . . His pioneering ideas, prescient in his lifetime, are now enjoying a late and well-deserved full blooming". Grotstein wrote this (on the cover) on the occasion of the publishing of two new volumes that included commentary about Fairbairn and many of his papers (Scharff & Birtles, 1994). They included previously published papers, as well as some of Fairbairn's unpublished papers. These books document Fairbairn's scholarship in general, and his extensive interest in, and study of, Freud's theoretical writings and the psychoanalytic theory of his era. Fairbairn received degrees in both medicine and philosophy at Edinburgh University, where he later taught medical psychology. Scharff and Birtles hypothesize that Fairbairn's philosophic training was one factor that led him to a powerful critique of Freudian theory. He clearly was well versed not only in psychoanalytic theory, but also in the intellectual currents of his time. He was a practising clinician in the suburbs of Edinburgh and saw a wide range of patients. This included a number of psychotic patients, as well as patients who had been sexually abused and some who suffered from trauma produced during the Second World War.

Scharff and Birtles note that Fairbairn's writings "have become an intrinsic, accepted core of the thinking of the independent group of British analysts" (1994, p. xii). His focus on mother–infant interactions, the family and therapist's subjective experience, and countertransference all are topics that are central issues in today's psychoanalytic world. Scharff and Birtles point out that Fairbairn's writings on these topics occurred "fifteen years before Winnicott's and Bowlby's published accounts and expansion of ideas in this realm" (*ibid.*, p. xii). Sutherland (1989) has written that Kohut's ideas show great similarities to Fairbairn's earlier papers. We will not fully explore these contentions in this chapter, but it is clear that Scharff and Birtles (Sutherland, Grotstein, Mitchell, and many others) consider Fairbairn to be one of the seminal psychoanalytic thinkers of the last century.

It is difficult, in writing a book that in part deals with the history of psychoanalysis, not to be anachronistic. It is easy for a contemporary Freudian or Kleinian analyst to maintain that many of the things that Fairbairn put forth are obvious and that of course one deals with the human being and not a compilation of repressed drives or desires. However, Fairbairn is writing his papers for the psychoanalytic audience of the late 1930s through the 1950s. Jones, in a preface to Fairbairn's collected papers, gives a fair indication of the reception to Fairbairn when he writes,

> Dr. Fairbairn's position in the field of psycho-analysis is a special one and one of great interest. Living hundreds of miles from his nearest colleagues, whom he seldom meets, has great advantages, and also some disadvantages. The main advantage is that, being subject to no distraction or interference, he has been able to concentrate entirely on his own ideas as they develop from his daily working experience. This is a situation that conduces to originality, and Dr. Fairbairn's originality is indisputable. On the other hand, it requires very special powers of self-criticism to dispense with the value of discussion with co-workers, who in the nature of things must be able to point out considerations overlooked by a lonely worker or to modify the risk of any one-sided train of thought. It is not for me to forestall the judgment that will be passed on the contents of the book, but I may be allowed to express the firm opinion that it will surely prove extremely stimulating to thought. If it were possible to condense Dr. Fairbairn's new ideas into one sentence, it might run somewhat as follows. Instead of starting, as Freud did, from stimulation of the nervous system proceeding from excitation of various erogenous zones and internal tension arising from gonadic activity, Dr. Fairbairn

starts at the centre of the personality, the ego, and depicts its strivings and difficulties in its endeavour to reach an object where it may find support. [Jones, 1952, p. v]

One can see that Jones, certainly someone near the heart of psychoanalytic currents, saw Fairbairn's ideas as challenging and perhaps revolutionary. In their depiction (that is both Fairbairn's and Jones') of Freudian theory, Fairbairn is seen as contesting Freud's basic ideas in a manner that presented sharp contrasts between the two theoretical approaches. Many of the issues that Fairbairn raises are present in today's psychoanalytic discourse, and in this vein Scharff and Birtles write,

> Like those of Freud, Fairbairn's contributions have been so important that many of them have found their way into our analytic "drinking water", fundamentally nourishing and sustaining without our knowing exactly where they come from. [Scharff & Birtles, 1994, p. xii]

Thus, in many ways, Fairbairn is seen as presenting a new alternative to Freudian theory that has been strongly supported in today's psychoanalytic world. In this chapter, I will not follow Fairbairn's writings in a chronological order, since most of his papers are from one period and are joined in terms of thematic material. Rather, we will follow Fairbairn both in terms of his new concepts and the concepts toward which he levels his criticisms. I will also not include some of the papers he published towards the end of his life, when he seemingly became more of Freudian or, at least, moved towards being an Oedipal theorist. These papers are in some ways a discontinuity from his original contributions and seem to be at least symptomatic of his failing health. Guntrip (1975) writes about Fairbairn's condition at this time, and clearly Guntrip was strongly influenced by Fairbairn's theoretical writings and was also in analysis with Fairbairn.

Basic assumptions: energy, structure, and instinctive behaviour

It is hard to write about Fairbairn without mentioning Freud, since a good deal of his writings begin with and focus on the differences between his views and Freudian theory. Fairbairn maintained that Freud thought of the id as containing directionless energy and of the ego as having energy-less direction. For Fairbairn, dividing the id from the ego and assuming that unified activities can be artificially separated was a myth that was not scientifically or clinically justified. He maintained that the distinction between activity and the energy available to fuel these activities is a false distinction. In addition, he was strongly critical of Freud's tripartite structural theory (the content of Fairbairn's structural views will be more fully discussed later in the chapter). Fairbairn posited that there are energized ego structures that fuel activity that are seen as directed towards objects. He viewed the ego as present from birth and eliminated the concept of the id. Fairbairn saw Freudian metapsychology as a derivative of nineteenth century physics that viewed the world as conglomerates of indivisible particles that were put into motion by energy that is separate from these particles. Thus, in this nineteenth century conceptualization, there is a separation between mass and energy, whereas in Einstein's revolutionary conceptualizations, mass and energy are convertible and inextricably bound together. Of course the division, or splitting, of mass can release immense amounts of energy. As we know too well, this concept served as the basis of atomic energy and the creation of the atomic bomb. One might ask: is the energy produced in atomic explosions separable from mass?

Fairbairn created a theory where he posited that the human being is fundamentally object seeking rather than pleasure seeking (Fairbairn, 1943, p. 60). In making this statement, he concluded that for a human to be primarily pleasure seeking there has to be a deterioration of behaviour (Fairbairn, 1946, p. 139). Since the prime motive is object seeking, if one is primarily focused on pleasure then there is some powerful distortion in the person's ego. Fairbairn's criticisms of Freudian theory were based not primarily on analogies to physics, but on clinical and biological observations. He stated that Freudian psychology rests on

> an unsatisfactory basis ... because it relegates object-relationships to a secondary place. ... It involves the implicit assumption that man by nature is not a social animal ... and that accordingly social behaviour is an acquired characteristic. [Fairbairn, 1956, pp. 131–132]

Here, Fairbairn turned to animal behaviour and states that

> throughout the animal world social (viz. object-seeking) behaviour is in general exhibited from birth; and recent studies of the phenomenon of 'imprinting' in young animals would seem to imply an inherent orientation towards objects" [*ibid.*, p. 132]

The imprinting studies that Fairbairn is referring to were performed by Lorenz and his co-workers. These were studies that showed imprinting in birds (ducks, turkeys, etc.). He went on to say that, in viewing the instinctive behaviour of animals, it appears that they are initially directed by the reality principle rather than by the pleasure principle. He saw a species adaptation to the environment as a "hereditarily transmitted internalization of outer reality" (*ibid.*). Interestingly, Fairbairn was not overly critical of the concept of instinct. He asserts, "it is meaningful to describe basic behaviour as 'instinctive'"; however, "The conception of separate 'instincts' represents no more than a hypostatisation of trends manifesting themselves in instinctive behaviour" (Fairbairn, 1956, p. 133). Thus, while behaviour can be thought of as instinctive, to separate libido and aggression is to make a false separation and this implies that "they exist apart from the structures which they energise" (*ibid.*). It is Freud's "atomism" that Fairbairn is most generally criticizing, not his notion of instinct, or even the idea of libido as energy. While this is true in general of his theorizing, relatively late in his writings Fairbairn (1956) states, "it would seem desirable . . . to regard both libido and aggression as basic 'factors' in behaviour, rather than as 'instinct'" (Fairbairn, 1956, p. 136). While Fairbairn makes this linguistic adjustment in many places, he continued to use the concept of instinct. One might say that he seemed to favour the idea of a libidinal instinct as an endogenous source of energy, but saw aggression as an inborn capacity rather than an instinct. Aggression, in this conceptualization, is an ability (a reactive capacity) rather than a constant pressure on the individual towards action. For Fairbairn, aggression (as an inborn capacity) is not manifested unless stimulated by an environmental source. This, of course, differs from Freud's view of Thanatos, which is a constant pressure on the individual regardless of the environmental source.

Positions and stages of development

Fairbairn begins his discussion of psychopathology with a recounting of Abraham's theory of fixation points. In many ways, Abraham's writings portray the Freudian position in a manner that is more incisive than is present in Freud's theoretical papers. Fairbairn relates that Abraham saw schizoid (and schizophrenic) conditions as related to a "fixation in the earlier oral phase characterized by the dominance of sucking" (Fairbairn, 1941, p. 29). Fairbairn states that there can be no question of the correctness of this formulation. He goes on to say, "Nor, for that matter, can there be any doubt about the correctness of attributing manic–depressive conditions to a fixation in the later oral phase characterized by the emergence of biting" (*ibid.*). Abraham also relates the paranoid state to an early anal fixation, the obsessive compulsive to a later anal fixation, and the hysterical patient to a fixation point in the genital (phallic) stage. These fixation points are virtually identical to the fixation points that Freud posited in his third theory (see Chapter Three). In discussing Abraham's fixation points, Fairbairn acknowledges that the paranoid

> employs a primitive anal technique for the rejection of his objects, [and] the obsessional employs a more developed anal technique for gaining control of his objects, [while] the hysteric attempts to improve his relationship with his objects by a technique involving a renunciation of the genital organs. [*ibid.*, p. 30]

While these "techniques" are employed, they are simply a way to "defend the ego against the effects of an oral origin" (*ibid.*). The schizoid and depressive states (or positions) are the fundamental states "for which an orally based aetiology has been found". Fairbairn is thus maintaining that all psychological disruptions are ultimately causally related to conflicts of an oral origin. (Here, there is a question that Scharff raises, maintaining that Fairbairn spoke of oral tendencies as indicative of mental states. One may ask how else any analyst might speak of oral tendencies.) The states of paranoia, obsessions, and hysteria are to be contrasted with the "schizoid or the depressive state in itself . . . these states have all the character of conditions against which the ego requires to be defended" (*ibid.*). The schizoid and depressive states may have their characteristic defences, but they are the basic states upon which all conflict is based.

In Fairbairn's interpretation, it would seem that Abraham and Freud had somehow stumbled on a correlate of psychopathology but had mistaken this correlate for the primary cause. In implicitly discussing this point, Fairbairn can be construed to look at many such correlates and attempt to place these factors within his new theoretical matrix. For example, Fairbairn points out that, implicitly, both Freud's and Abraham's libido theory requires an object. The libidinal zones are "channels through [which] libido flows . . . The ultimate goal of the libido is the object" (Fairbairn, 1941, p. 31). Fairbairn, then, in a similar manner to early Freud (1895), says, "object libido is determined by similar laws to those which determine the flow of electrical energy" (*ibid.*, p. 32). Libido, in this concept, follows the path of least resistance and "in infancy . . . the path of least resistance . . . happens to lie almost exclusively through the mouth; and the mouth accordingly becomes the dominant libidinal organ" (*ibid.*). Thus, these zones are simply channels that lead to communications with the object. Although Fairbairn accepts the idea of libidinal zones, the oral zone is clearly the one that he sees as having prime importance. This is because it comes into prominence during the period of infantile dependence; this period is, for Fairbairn, the crucial stage in development as well as in the formation of all psychopathology. Although he can understand why Freud and Abraham put forth their concepts of psycho-sexuality, Fairbairn's view is that his theory is the next step in the development of psychoanalysis. His new theory divides development into three broad stages, or three modes of relating: infantile dependence, quasi-independence (transitional) and mature dependence.

Infantile dependence is a period that is divided into two stages, early and late oral. In the early oral, the object is the maternal breast and, during this time, the mother's breast is internalized as a part object. During the late oral stage, the mother is seen as being with the breast and the "whole object is treated characteristically as a part-object" (Fairbairn, 1941, p. 41). Fairbairn states that what is crucial in this stage is that the infant "is genuinely loved as a person by his parents, and that his parents genuinely accept his love" (*ibid.*, p. 39). It is only when this love is present in a form sufficiently convincing for the infant to depend safely upon his real objects that he is able gradually to give up infantile dependence "without misgiving". In the absence of this assurance, the infant/child is unable to truly separate from his internal objects, since this separation would entail overwhelming anxiety and "would be equivalent ... to forfeiting all hope of ever obtaining the satisfaction of his unsatisfied emotional needs" (*ibid.*). Frustration in terms of being loved or having one's love accepted "is the greatest trauma that a child can experience" (*ibid.*, p. 40). All psycho-sexual phenomena that become compulsive are a result of the failure of obtaining satisfactory love relationships with "objects in the outer world".

The next stage, the quasi-independent or transitional stage, is where the other or the whole object is treated "as contents". To understand this stage we must delve a bit deeper into Fairbairn's ideas about infantile dependence. For Fairbairn, this stage of infantile dependence involves a "primary identification with the object" (*ibid.*, p. 42). The task of the stage of quasi-independence is one of differentiating from the object and this tends to resolve "itself into a problem of expelling an incorporated object, i.e., to become a problem of expelling contents" (*ibid.*, p. 43). Here, Fairbairn recognizes Abraham's rationale for the anal stage and the idea of expulsion during this stage. Fairbairn recognizes that expulsion is important, but it is equally important to recognize that the child is not preoccupied with "the disposal of contents at this stage because he is anal, but of his being anal because he is preoccupied at this stage with the disposal of contents" (*ibid.*). The object now is symbolically the contents that the child must expel. This leads to a feeling of independence, but the stage is named quasi-independence since, clearly, the idea of independence is a tenuous fantasy of the child's. Fairbairn characterizes the conflict of the transition stage as a "conflict between a progressive urge to surrender the infantile attitude of identification with the object and a regressive urge to maintain that attitude" (*ibid.*). Fairbairn looks at the progressive urge as being associated with anxiety of being isolated, while the regressive urge is associated with anxieties of being engulfed or imprisoned. Fairbairn describes how the phobic and obsessional techniques are two differing ways of handling the same basic conflict. The phobic method involves either a flight away from, or a return to, the object, while the obsessional technique is involved in either retaining or expelling the object. Since the obsessional technique involves control over the object, Fairbairn sees the obsessional "as predominantly sadistic in nature". Since the phobic technique involves either flight or submission and a return to the object, he views the phobic technique as predominantly masochistic.

The hysterical technique is one that involves an acceptance and an over-idealization of the external object and a rejection of the internal object. Here, Fairbairn states that the acceptance of the object occurs through a love relationship and that the rejection of the object is the rejection of "an internalized object with which there is a considerable measure of identification" (*ibid.*, p. 45). When the hysteric rejects the internalized object, the externalized object is accepted and even over-valued. Although the hysteric may be seen as rejecting their internalized genital representation, this is always "unmasked" as an identification of the rejected genitals with the breast. So, despite the fact that the hysteric is seemingly involved in a new love relationship, the core essential relationship (as is true of all development in the quasi-independent stage) is with the primary or original libidinal object. The hysteric's drama in terms of emotional relationship is seen as over-compensation for the rejection of an internal relationship. Fairbairn explains the hysteric's tendency towards disassociative phenomena as a result of the rejection of internal objects.

In comparing the paranoid and the hysteric Fairbairn states, "the paranoid state must . . . be regarded as representing rejection of the externalized object and acceptance of the internalized object" (*ibid.*) while the reverse is the case for the hysteric. For some readers this may seem like a striking statement, since paranoia and hysterical states are placed on an even footing in terms of severity of disturbance. However, even here, Fairbairn presents an interesting presaging of contemporary trends. The hierarchy of disorders is today either frequently rejected or disorders are combined in such a manner that these combinations bear little relationship to their original meaning. For example, Kernberg's (1975) designation of a borderline hysteric leaves out an essential aspect of Freud's concept of the hysteric as conflicted about object love. Kernberg does this without providing Fairbairn's explanatory concepts. Freud thought of hysteria (see Chapter Three) as a neurosis that indicated that the patient was analysable. He thought that the hysteric was not as disturbed as a paranoid or even an obsessive–compulsive patient.

Fairbairn gives a rationale for why we cannot conceive of one technique as superior or inferior to another. All of the techniques are attempting to defend against either a schizoid or a depressive basic condition. The logical extension of Fairbairn is that a person is designated as more or less conflicted depending on the extent to which their original fixation is manifested. Thus, one might consider the extent to which a hysteric is disassociated or the extent to which the paranoid disturbs (or destroys) their externalized object. We will come back to this issue, but first it is important to state Fairbairn's ideas more fully in terms of his basic positions.

The destructive aspects of love and hate

We have discussed the importance of the stage of infantile dependence, but why is it of such crucial importance in Fairbairn's theory? The answer may seem obvious, since infantile dependence is the first stage of life; however, Fairbairn's ideas about the dynamics of this stage are far from obvious. Fairbairn sees the emotional conflict during the early oral phase of infantile dependence as taking the form of to "suck or not to suck, i.e. to love or not to love" (Fairbairn, 1941, p. 49). This conflict is the main issue that is confronting the schizoid individual. In other terms, the schizoid's dilemma is how to love without destroying the person (object) who is receiving this love. This is a profound and devastating issue, since if one's love is felt as destructive, than it is difficult or impossible to direct love or "libido towards objects in outer reality" (*ibid.*, p. 50). The schizoid individual withdraws from the world (withdraws libido from his objects) and retreats from reality. If the retreat is severe, then a schizophrenic process is at hand. Fairbairn's view of the schizoid is that this type of individual is both introverted and narcissistic. This narcissism, or "sense of superiority", manifests itself with respect to internalized objects, but with respect to external objects there is typically a sense of inferiority. This sense of inferiority is part of the fundamental dilemma of the schizoid individual, which involves a feeling of "utter impotence". The schizoid is unable to move towards another for fear of the destructive power of his love and thus is constantly feeling either empty or useless, and/or having lost his object world. For Fairbairn (and probably most clinicians), this signals the weakening or weakness of an individual's ego. Even in his early papers, Fairbairn emphasizes that splitting is a ubiquitous occurrence, but that the schizoid dilemma can lead to a debilitating process of splitting where the person feels helpless and hopeless. Splitting weakens the ego and there is, at the same time, a renunciation of libidinal attachments, which is a concurrent factor weakening the ego. The danger of loss of the ego is what Fairbairn states is the ultimate psychopathological disaster.

For Fairbairn, if the great problem which confronts the individual in the early oral phase is how to love the object without destroying it by love, the great problem which confronts the individual in the late oral phase is how to love the object without destroying it by hate. Although this is a significant dynamic, it is not the devastating issue of the schizoid dilemma. The schizoid dilemma is that his love will destroy the object he desires and so loving is a futile and destructive act. The depressive's quandary concerns the anxiety of destroying the object through hate. The depressive has advanced to the point where his love seems good and he is able to have relationships with external objects. In Fairbairn's terms, the depressive is inherently ambivalent towards the object. He has not taken the step of directing his hate "predominantly at least, towards the rejected object [for then] he would have been left free to direct [love] towards his accepted object love which was relatively unaccompanied by hate" (*ibid.*, p. 53). The hate towards the object brings up anxiety about loss of the object. The experience or actuality of loss of the object is the essential trauma that provokes the depressive state. These two states during infantile dependence are the fundamental issues that confront all human beings. Fairbairn relates that

> no one ever becomes completely emancipated from the state of infantile dependence, or from some proportionate degree of oral fixation; and there is no one who has completely escaped the necessity of incorporating his early objects. [*ibid.*, p. 56]

In his view, all humans can be classified as either schizoid or depressive in orientation. There may be a hereditary factor in determining the type and strength of fixation that may be related to "the relative strength of the inborn tendencies of sucking and biting" (*ibid.*). Fairbairn relates his ideas to Kretschmer's views, where Kretschmer delineates two basic psychological types, the schizothymic and the cyclothymic. The former type is related to schizophrenia and the second type is related to manic–depressive psychoses. Fairbairn sees striking agreement between his position and Kretschmer's. The main difference, he states, is that Kretschmer regards the temperamental difference between the types as based essentially upon constitutional factors, whereas Fairbairn's view is that psychopathological factors arising during the period of infantile dependence make a considerable contribution to a person's temperamental proclivities. Fairbairn sees Kretschmer's views as providing some independent confirmation of his theory. Interestingly, he tells us that "even the most 'normal' person must be regarded as having potentialities at the deepest levels" (*ibid.*, p. 58). If this is the case with "normal" people, whomever they may be, certainly anyone who wants a complete analysis has to analyse his/her schizoid tendencies and conflicts.

In presenting Fairbairn's theory of psychopathology, up to this point we have extensively reviewed what I regard as his seminal paper on his theory of psychopathology. For most of the present volume I have reserved commentary until the end of the chapter, but the following comment is one that I believe will put Fairbairn in an interesting perspective and also highlight one of the major themes in the present volume. Some relational writers (Greenberg & Mitchell, 1983) have stated that the model just presented preserves ties to what they label the drive/structure model. They see a later Fairbairn model as implicitly replacing the one that I have just discussed. They acknowledge that neither Fairbairn nor Guntrip disavow this model, but it is important to note several additional factors in understanding Fairbairn's (and Guntrip's) theoretical stance. Guntrip was an analytic writer and clinician who was at one time a patient of Fairbairn. He attempted, in various volumes (Guntrip, 1968, 1971), to elucidate Fairbairn's theoretical and clinical views.

For Guntrip, the dynamics discussed in this 1941 paper are central to his (1968, 1971) version of object relations. Guntrip regarded himself as the main advocate of Fairbairn's theory, and it is through Guntrip that, for a long period of time, Fairbairn was known in the USA. Although I would agree with Greenberg and

Mitchell that increasingly Fairbairn emphasized schizoid dynamics, I would maintain that the dynamics he emphasized come directly from his 1941 paper. While he de-emphasized the depressive position in later writings, his emphasis on the destructive aspects of love (as the main schizoid dynamic) did not change. Fairbairn, in 1951, wrote short incisive summaries of all of his theoretical papers. In these summaries, he was not reluctant to change aspects of his theory that he felt needed updating and he did not change this aspect of his theory. Moreover, it is a strange view to maintain that the 1941 paper retains ties to the drive/structural model. My reading of Fairbairn's paper is that he is presenting a new theory that breaks with Freud and Abraham and completely changes the emphasis of psychoanalytic theory. Unless one denies the importance of the mouth in infancy, it is reasonable to observe that the mouth is a gateway to a great deal of interchange during infancy. There is eating and sucking galore. What Fairbairn maintains is that these activities are important in relation to the mother, not mainly as activities in and of themselves. To paraphrase his words, the mouth is a channel to the object because it gives bodily form to the mental style of the infant (by Scharff, personal communication). This is not a tie to the drive/structural model, it is an attempt to make sense out of certain bodily occurrences that Fairbairn thought to be the centre of the Freud/Abraham theory. He rejects this theory even though he can understand why Abraham (and Freud) make it the centre of their theory.

In interpreting Greenberg and Mitchell's stance I can only say that while Fairbairn clearly rejects Freudian drive theory he does provide integrationists with a number of ideas about how to blend Freud's thought with Fairbairn's insights. This is, of course, one of the major themes of the present volume. In their volume, Greenberg and Mitchell deny even the possibility of having an integrated theory and this integration will be a major theme of the final section of this volume.

Bad objects and their return

One of the issues that separated Klein (1946) and Fairbairn (1946) was Klein's rejection of Fairbairn's view that only bad objects are internalized. (Although this is stated as Fairbairn's position, it is my view that Fairbairn sees good objects as being internalized as well.) His emphasis is, however, on the internalization of bad objects. Fairbairn's intent in this theoretical declaration was to establish that what is repressed are not unpleasant or intolerable memories, but rather repression occurs when an object appears, "intolerably bad to the ego" (Fairbairn, 1951, p. 164). In presenting theoretical concepts about the internalization of bad objects, Fairbairn characteristically reminds his reader that psychoanalysis and psychopathology should be the study of the relationships of the ego to its internalized objects. In his view, Freud went from the repression of intolerable memories in his earlier theorizing to his later ideas where the repression of libidinal incestuous impulses were a result of guilt produced by the superego. In rejecting both of these concepts, Fairbairn states, "what are primarily repressed are neither intolerably guilty impulses nor intolerably unpleasant memories, but intolerably bad internalized objects. . . . Impulses become bad when they are directed towards bad objects" (Fairbairn, 1943, p. 62). Bad objects are always intolerably bad and a relationship with a bad object is inevitably shameful. Conversely, "if a child is ashamed of his parents, his parents are (necessarily) bad objects to him" (*ibid.*, p. 64).

All humans internalize bad objects but the influence of the bad object is dependent on the extent of bad objects in the unconscious and their degree of badness. The influence is also dependent on "The extent to which the ego is identified with internalized bad objects and the nature and strength of the defenses which protect the ego from these objects" (*ibid.*, p. 65). Bad objects are so intolerable that a "child would rather be bad himself than have bad objects" (*ibid.*). Thus, the "burden" of badness (being bad) is easier to tolerate than the influence of bad objects. If the child can become bad in a sea of good objects the child achieves some security from the external environment. This defensive manoeuvre, however, leaves the child susceptible to being attacked by internalized bad objects. These manoeuvres, as well as the ego responses by any of the four classic techniques, occurs when repression fails. For Fairbairn there are two kinds of badness; he speaks of conditional and unconditional badness. Thus, an unconditional bad object is one that is an internal persecutor and, in so far as the child identifies with this object, the child experiences badness cognitively and affectively. To alleviate this state, the child internalizes good objects, which then assume a superego role. Once this internalization takes place, Fairbairn posits the occurrence of conditional badness and conditional goodness. In introducing conditional goodness and badness, Fairbairn is able to speak of superego functions without positing a superego structure. If, as a result of internalized good objects, the child is able to be good, he is, in Fairbairn's lexicon, conditionally good. If the child leans towards his internalized bad objects, he is conditionally bad. The conditional situation, then, is one where the child is ruled by a perceived environment that is good, even if the child is conditionally bad. Unconditional badness is a state where not only the person experiences themselves as bad, but the world is also filled with badness. Fairbairn states that "it is better to be a sinner in a world ruled by God (conditional badness) than to live in a world ruled by the Devil (unconditional badness)" (*ibid.*, pp. 66–67).

Fairbairn's view of the internalization of bad objects has direct clinical consequences. The analysis of guilt may disrupt the patient's defensive structure and bring the spontaneous return of bad objects. The superego is seen as providing a defensive function, and if this defensive function is disrupted, then this will lead to an uncovering of bad objects that had been defended against or repressed. In treatment, the return of bad objects is responsible for what Fairbairn terms the transference neurosis. Fairbairn states that the patient quickly recognizes this situation and it is only in "setting of and actual 'good object' relationship with the analyst" (Fairbairn, 1951, p. 166) that the patient can meaningfully utilize this return of bad objects. Here, Fairbairn is one of the first analysts to specifically detail the importance of the actual relationship between analyst and patient. He is not downgrading the importance of transference; rather, he is clearly stating that to withstand the sharp return of bad objects, the therapeutic situation requires a secure relationship between analyst and analysand. The concept of the bad object allows Fairbairn to downgrade Freud's repetition compulsion and Thanatos, or the death instinct. The repetition compulsion is seen as a phenomenon relating to the adhesiveness of the rejecting object to the anti-libidinal ego. He states that it is not that humans compulsively repeat trauma, but, rather, that they are "haunted by bad objects" (*ibid.*). One repeats conflicts when defences are sufficiently impaired, and it is the return of bad objects from which there is no longer any escape (except in death). The inevitability of the bad object is the explanation of the anti-libidinal factor that leads to powerful self-destructive tendencies. The concept of the bad object, in Fairbairn's theory, supplants these Freudian concepts. Fairbairn's object relations concepts could not be contained within Freud's structural theory (see Chapter Four) without a variety of emendations. These revisions led Fairbairn to a structural theory more in accord with the activity of the internalized object in relation to the ego or the self.

Endopsychic structure: good and bad objects

Although Freud had listed the choice of object as one of the main vicissitudes of instinctual development, Fairbairn stated that, while it is true that impulses are necessarily involved with objects, the instincts cannot be "considered apart from ego structures" (Fairbairn, 1951, p. 167) Fairbairn maintains that it is only ego structures that can seek relationships with objects. Instincts, then, are the dynamic constituents of ego structures. By dynamic, Fairbairn means that impulses (instincts) represent the energic movement of ego structures towards objects. Here, Fairbairn returns to his criticisms of Freudian structure and reminds us that he rejects both the concept of the id as the reservoir of the drives and the ego as a structure that develops on the surface of the id. For Fairbairn, the ego is a structure from birth or before, and it is a structure that is "inherently orientated towards objects in outer reality or, in other terms, determined by the reality principle from the beginning" (Fairbairn, 1944, p. 85). The pleasure principle is again a principle that is invoked if conditions for development are unfavourable. The pleasure principle is a sign for Fairbairn of a deteriorative or breakdown process. In addition, Fairbairn maintains that analysis of melancholia provides the cornerstone of Freud's theory of the "mental apparatus". If Freud had stayed with the concept of hysteria as his starting point, Fairbairn maintains that "his conception would have been based upon recognition of the fact that repression implies a splitting of the ego" (Fairbairn, 1951, p. 169). This would have led Melanie Klein (following Freud) to highlight schizoid dynamics rather than the dynamics of the depressive position. (Fairbairn is interpreting Klein and Freud from a particular angle and, in 1944, Klein has not yet named the schizoid position but she has presented material that stresses the importance of the period before the depressive position. This material is similar to some of Fairbairn's ideas about schizoid dynamics [see Chapter Eight].) In making this statement, Fairbairn is now further distancing himself from Klein's object relations theory.

Fairbairn now greatly alters Freud's concept of the ego. The ego is seen not as a single entity, but, rather, Fairbairn posits a "Multiplicity of egos" (Fairbairn, 1944, p. 94). This multiplicity occurs because repression of an object necessarily involves the repression of an ego structure. Fairbairn states "repression is primarily directed against internalized objects which are treated as bad . . . unless it is assumed that internalized objects are structures, the concept of such objects becomes utterly meaningless" (ibid., p. 95). Thus, before the ego undertakes repression, it is split. Once split, one part of the ego can repress another aspect of the ego. This then leads to the establishment of several egos. This multiplicity of egos is, for Fairbairn, part of the explanation of dissociative phenomena found in schizoid states and multiple personalities. Splitting as a defensive manoeuvre has been important for Fairbairn before this point, but now, with his new structural theory, it becomes the central defence mechanism. For Fairbairn, his new conceptualizations help to answer what he sees as another logical difficulty in Freud's structural theory.

Fairbairn states that Freud conceives of the superego as the instigator of repression, but, in his view of Freud, the superego cannot instigate repression until the oedipal stage occurs. Fairbairn sees Klein as attempting to circumvent this problem, but "Melanie Klein's ante-dating the Oedipus situation to infancy provides no real solution, if only because it leaves out the possibility of repression occurring before the super-ego is formed" (Fairbairn, 1951, p. 169). For Fairbairn, the answer to this dilemma is to state that repression is not dependent on the formation of the formation of the superego, but, rather, the superego itself is a later defence against the upsurge of bad objects. Thus, the instigator of repression is not the superego, but the formation of bad objects. As we will shortly see, the formation of bad objects necessarily implies a structural shift in what Fairbairn calls the central ego.

If we briefly review, we can see that, at this point, Fairbairn has done away with the concept of the id and now the superego is no longer a structure, but, rather, the function of the superego is served by a combination of the ideal object and the anti-libidinal ego reacting to conditional badness. Structure now is seen only in terms of the division of the ego into several different sub-structures. We must remember that this is not Freud's version of the ego that gathers its energy from the id. Rather, the ego is now seen as the structural and energic centre. The ego is where impulses emanate from and is initially involved in adaptive pursuits. Fairbairn's theory of psychic structure involves the division of the ego in an effort to control the implications of internalizing bad objects. The internalization of bad objects is, in and of itself, a defensive manoeuvre that, in turn, leads to psychological structure. After Fairbairn takes these decisive theoretical steps, he goes on to specify the fate and contents of the bad object and how the bad object is structuralized.

Although we have mentioned this point, it is worthwhile to remember that, for Fairbairn, the (unconditionally) bad object is internalized to make it at least conditionally bad. In other terms, the bad object is internalized to attenuate its badness; this, in and of itself, is considered a defensive manoeuvre. Once internalized, the bad object has two characteristics, which are split and form the basis of an ego structure. Once internalized, the bad object is split into an "exciting object and a rejecting object". Both objects are repressed by the "original ego". However,

> since this original ego is attached to both objects by a libidinal cathexis involving a high degree of identification, their repression involves a splitting off and repression of parts of the ego which remain closely bound to each object. Repression of the exciting object is thus accompanied by repression of a portion of the ego which I describe as the libidinal ego on the part of the central portion of the ego; and repression of the rejecting object is accompanied by a similar repression of another portion of the ego which I describe as the internal saboteur. [Fairbairn, 1951, pp. 170–171]

It is of mild historic interest to note that the term "internal saboteur" was a term from the cultural influence of the Second World War.

As one can see from this extract, for Fairbairn each internalized object is part of an ego structure that is tied to the central ego. These structures might be compared to the ego (central ego), id (libidinal ego), and internal saboteur (which involves several structures), but, for Fairbairn, each structure is a dynamic ego-structure "assuming a dynamic pattern in relation to one another" (*ibid.*, p. 171). There is first an original ego, which, after repression takes place, is called the central ego. Repression of the bad object leads to the formation of a libidinal ego and an internal saboteur. The libidinal ego contains the exciting object(s) and the internal saboteur contains the rejecting object(s). In Fairbairn's theory, parts of the central ego are conscious, preconscious, and unconscious. The internal saboteur and the libidinal ego are both unconscious.

These structures (the libidinal ego and internal saboteur), while created by repression, are, in effect, an aggressive attack by the central ego against internalized bad objects and the subsidiary egos by which these objects are cathected. Aggression is not the sole province of the central ego, since the "subsidiary egos" also have access to aggression and display aggressive tendencies towards the central ego and each other. In Fairbairn's theory, the internal saboteur seems to more readily express aggression towards the exciting object (libidinal ego), and this would seem to follow in terms of the idea of the internal saboteur helping to defend against excitation and pleasurable experiences. In this vein, Fairbairn reminds us that aggression is not considered to be a drive, but a reactive capacity of the human being when frustrated or provoked. Although aggression cannot be reduced to another state, it is in the service of, or subordinate to, libidinal factors. As we will see later, one of Fairbairn's revisions is to posit a pre-ambivalent object. However, for most of his theoretical career, although ambivalence is not considered to be a preformed state, it occurs quite early in the infant's life.

Ambivalence and aggression both occur as a result of frustration and initially as a result of the trauma of separation, more particularly, separation from one's mother. From the infant's point of view, the mother's separation is a cause of ambivalence, and this ambivalence is intolerable for the infant. "To ameliorate this intolerable situation, he splits the figure of his mother into two objects—a satisfying ('good') object and unsatisfying ('bad') object" (*ibid.*, p.172). The bad object is then split (in the manner previously described) and, thus, the maternal object becomes both an exciting (libidinal ego) and rejecting object (internal saboteur). From this description, it would seem that there is a risk for the infant in expressing either excited or aggressive feelings towards the mother. Fairbairn sees the risk of expressing aggressive ideation as making the maternal object more real as a bad object. This then makes the loss of the object more likely (from the infant's perspective), and this is what Fairbairn has labelled the early affect of depression. The greater danger is expressing libidinal feelings (feelings of love) towards a rejecting object. This involves the schizoid risk of futility, where the infant/child's love is seen as bad and the child experiences itself as impotent and deeply worthless.

Fairbairn is using this description of early development both as a developmental theory and also as a manner in which he explains the schizoid dilemma (throughout life) and the unconscious manifestations of internalized objects. Repression, for Fairbairn, originally emanates from the central ego, but, as development progresses, repression is aided by the internal saboteur. When the internal saboteur aids in repression, Fairbairn calls this secondary or indirect repression. One can see that when Fairbairn talks about dynamic structures he is positing structures that are continuously interacting and have energy of their own, without the need to transform energy from other structures. Moreover, he is assuming that the initial repression (primal in Freud's terminology) occurs as a result of an aggressive thrust by the central ego to tame the bad object. Repression is the first defence against the bad object, but, as the object is repressed, it is split and cathected by one of the two subsidiary egos. This all occurs at an age that is considerably before Freud's Oedipal, and even Klein's version of the Oedipal situation. The view of defences occurring before Oedipal stage dynamics appear reinforces several aspects of Fairbairn's theoretical structure.

Fairbairn states that while Freud made the Oedipal stage the central nexus of conflict, in his theory the crucial period of development is when the child is virtually completely dependent on its mother (infantile dependence). This is the period of time when both direct and indirect repression occur initially. This repression is designed to prevent the infant/child from expressing either libidinal or aggressive impulses toward the mother. These impulses, which have been initially repressed, are further defended against when the child has contact with its mother. While, for Fairbairn, conflicts between infant and mother during infantile dependence are the key conflicts of development, all other manifestations of conflict are derivations of conflicts that occur during the period of infantile dependence. Thus, the Oedipal situation is one place where the derivatives of infantile dependence might be manifested, but the importance of infantile dependence is not diminished by phenomena related to the Oedipal period. In restating this basic point, we can realize that repression is, of necessity, not dependent on either Oedipal dynamics or the development of the superego.

Up to this point, we have stated the basics elements of Fairbairn's theoretical position. In a restatement of his position, he avowed that he found it necessary to introduce a modification of his theoretical position. Fairbairn, in a paper (1940) that we have not included to this point, stated that the first object to be internalized is a "pre-ambivalent object of the early oral phase". He restates this position in a paper published in 1951, and says that when this object is internalized, ambivalence occurs as a result of some "unsatisfying" environmental events. In other terms, the maternal object, in some ways, is then viewed by the infant as both satisfactory and unsatisfactory. This ambivalence is intolerable for the infant, and splitting occurs in a manner that we have described. In review, we can say that the result of splitting is an exciting object and a rejecting object; these objects are cathected respectively by the libidinal ego and the internal saboteur. Fairbairn then maintains,

> It follows ... that, when the exciting and rejecting objects are split off, there remains a nucleus of the original object shorn of its overexciting and over-frustrating elements; and this nucleus then assumes the status of a desexualized and idealized object which is cathected and retained for itself by the central ego. [Fairbairn, 1951, p. 176]

This theoretical change allows Fairbairn to explain how a person can still be aware of an object consciously, and how an aspect of what Freud called the superego functions as part of the central ego. For Fairbairn, the ego-ideal is part of the central ego. What, in Freudian thought, would be the punitive aspects of the superego are contained in the internal saboteur and its relation to the rejecting object. Clinically, these functions often seem quite separate, and, in Fairbairn's model, they are seen as being contained in separate structures. Fairbairn, in making this theoretical shift, also posits an original "unsplit ego which contains the pre-ambivalent object of the early oral phase" (*ibid.*, p. 178). Here, parenthetically, Fairbairn restates his use of the concept of an oral phase of development. His view is that in the earliest part of development there is a unified ego, which accepts the maternal object in an unambivalent manner. He calls this object pre-ambivalent, since its fate is to eventually succumb to ambivalence. Greenberg and Mitchell (1983) have criticized Fairbairn's use of the idea of an unsplit ego, since, as they have stated, other theorists see the unification of the ego as a developmental achievement. However, they wrote this critique at a time before Stern (1985) hypothesized a sense of self that is innate, much as Chomsky's idea of linguistic grammar is innate and pre-wired through genetic transmission. The idea of a unified sense of self (or ego) does not imply an extensive structure, but, rather, a sense of communication with the environment from an organism that has some sense of agency. What the true state of affairs is, of course, a question that one hopes will be settled by further research that will lead to better theoretical integrations.

Commentary

Clearly, Fairbairn is an author who has gained in popularity through the years. Interestingly, Hartmann came close to one position of Fairbairn's when Hartmann declared that the ego has independent energies not related to the id. In my view, Fairbairn has taken the next logical step and eliminated the id as a separate structure. Thus, whether one theorizes that there are instincts in human beings it seems that it would be a break in our phylogenetic heritage to assume that our instincts were not adaptive. I shall present in the last chapter a view of instinct development (or sources of endogenous stimulation), but at this point I would simply state that Fairbairn was closer to contemporary evolution than is the case with Freud's last instinctual model.

In some sense, it is hard to see how Fairbairn could be wrong when he posits that humans are object seeking from birth. A pre-wired communication network between mother and infant, in my view, is a necessity for adaptive development. However, it seems as apparent to me that a good deal of what transpires between mother and infant is mediated through pleasure or pain pathways. I would posit that much of good enough mothering is titrating pleasure–pain states so that the infant is content and not overwhelmed with either internal or external experiences (stimulation). Thus, it seems to be an unfortunate dichotomy to state that the infant is object seeking rather than pleasure seeking. In my view, the object is mediated through pleasure pathways that the infant experiences at various times as crucial to its survival. Therefore, I would not give up Freud's accent on pleasure, but subordinate this accent to the relationship that develops between mother and infant. Here is where theories can intermingle rather than being split apart.

Fairbairn is the author (along with Sullivan), that Mitchell refers to as perhaps most influential in his development of relational psychoanalysis. Fairbairn's emphasis on object relations and his movement away from Freud and Abraham's psycho-sexual theory were strong elements in his becoming a central theorist for relational psychoanalysis. This was true not only in terms of his ideas about early development, but, as importantly, for his emphasis of the significance of the therapeutic relationship. Guntrip quotes Fairbairn as saying, "It's the personal relationship that is therapeutic" (Guntrip, 1975, p. 145) in psychoanalysis. Fairbairn also noted that he had treated a number of schizophrenic patients before writing his pivotal papers and this strongly contributed to his theoretical vision. It is interesting that both Fairbairn and Sullivan had extensive experience in dealing with psychotic patient populations. I believe that these therapeutic experiences led both of these authors to strongly emphasize the real relationship. In the commentary, I will briefly go over this theme and then discuss some of the issues that Harry Guntrip develops as a prime commentator and synthesizer of Fairbairn's contributions.

In treating patients who are seen as severely disturbed, many clinicians stress the idea of supportive rather than exploratory treatment. Even if one believes that there can be exploratory treatments with severely disturbed patients, in my experience it takes a long time for some aspects of the treatment to begin. It may take a long time before some patients will have enough trust to lay aside their delusional or hallucinatory systems and talk about their intense pain. Their anxiety and pain drove them to develop, in Bach's (1985) terms, an anti-world. (By anti-world, I mean a world that takes the person to another area of their mind or experience and seals off the disruptive and disturbing world that surrounds them.) Before one can talk about aspects of the meaning of their hallucinatory states, the patient must trust you and, "the reliability of the analyst is the most important factor . . . because the patient did not experience such reliability in the maternal care of infancy" (Winnicott, 1960a, p. 38). Winnicott describes how the analyst must wait to interpret until the patient experiences the events under their natural omnipotence (see Chapter Ten). In other terms, the analyst waits to a point where the patient does not experience their inner world as being besieged by trauma (felt as coming from outside the self). In this interpretation, both Sullivan and Fairbairn stress the real relationship, because, with the patient population they encountered, this was, at least for many years, the most important aspect of the treatment. It may be that with a number of patients this was not only the most important aspect of the treatment, it was the only aspect of the treatment. In my view, this is not the most complete form of treatment, but certainly, without the appropriate relationship, nothing else can proceed.

Guntrip's view of Fairbairn and Winnicott

Harry Guntrip is both a prominent analytic author in his own right and the first analytic writer who systematically explored Fairbairn's conceptualizations. Guntrip, in 1949, read some of Fairbairn's papers and clearly felt a strong intellectual kinship to Fairbairn. In the 1950s, he decided to go to Fairbairn for an analysis, since "after reading his papers in 1949, I went to him because we stood philosophically on the same ground and no actual intellectual disagreements would interfere with the analysis"(1975, p. 146). Guntrip, after his analysis with Fairbairn, some years later entered into a treatment with Winnicott. In 1975, an article was published comparing his two therapeutic experiences and putting forth some of his ideas about therapeutic efficacy.

After his analysis with Fairbairn, a good deal of Guntrip's writing was to consolidate and explicate Fairbairn's theoretical concepts. In my view, Guntrip elucidated and significantly extended some of Fairbairn's ideas in terms of their clinical consequences. One of the concepts that Guntrip puts forth (1971, 1975) is the idea of a regressed ego that is split off from what Fairbairn calls the libidinal ego. Guntrip describes or explains his own childhood experience in terms of a regressed ego. He pictures this split-off ego as a result of being involved in, and then giving up, a hopeless struggle to get a response from his mother. This structure was, in Guntrip's description, both disassociated and deeply hidden. Guntrip writes that when he published this idea, Winnicott asked, "Is your Regressed ego withdrawn or repressed?" Guntrip replied, "Both. First withdrawn and then kept repressed" (Guntrip, 1975, p.147). Winnicott, in asking this question, might have been referring to his own paper where he differentiates a patient's withdrawal, thereby cutting themselves off from the therapeutic process, as opposed to a regression, where the patient is involved in the treatment, albeit in a manner that expresses and uncovers conflicting tendencies. Guntrip is stating that both these processes occur with the regressed ego. In effect, he is using concepts from two different theoretical perspectives (one that emphasizes disassociation and one that emphasizes what Anna Freud calls ego defence mechanisms).

It might be useful to see how Guntrip uses Fairbairn's ideas to explain certain schizoid conflicts. Guntrip's version of how a schizoid personality attempts the preservation of the ego (self) involves a similar type of compromise formation. Guntrip's conclusion is that preservation of the ego involves the person hating the good object. Why could not someone with strong schizoid tendencies love the good object? Guntrip answers, "the relation to a good object is one of such fear-enforced infantile dependence that it feels smothering . . .Thus claustrophobic anxiety arises" (1968, p. 82). He posits that being around a good object leads to such overwhelming feelings of dependence that even a sense of self (ego) is obliterated. He summarizes the four possibilities of the schizoid personality relationships with other people (objects). If the person attempts to have "No objects [in their life this] involves the fear of ego-loss by depersonalization". If the person attempts to relate to "bad objects [this] involves the fear of ego-loss by disintegration under destructive persecution". If the person attempts to get close to good objects [this] involves the fear of the loss of the active ego by imprisonment in smothering passivity. A compromise remains ... If one hates good objects instead of bad ones, there will not be the same danger of retaliation by the object and also smothering is avoided. [*ibid.*, p. 83]

Guntrip also implies that this compromise (hating the good object) allows the person to stay closer to others, even while hating the people that are near. In this theory, the compromise between good and bad objects allows for object relations to continue and for withdrawal to be less pronounced. Guntrip is describing why some analysts who do not allow the hatred to come forth might not survive, for they will be perceived by the patient as smothering (the patient may report that they seem bored or that nothing is happening). Guntrip, in his writings (and in this illustration), does utilize in more dramatic form what Fairbairn has conceptualized, but he also makes it his by amplifying the clinical ramifications of Fairbairn's thought.

Guntrip's concept of the in and out programme (Guntrip, 1968) is another way of describing the schizoid attempt to stay in contact on the one hand while, on the other, giving expression to the person's constant need to avoid being overwhelmed by relationships that feel too close for psychological comfort. Interestingly, Guntrip's description of Fairbairn as a clinician is that he stayed distant as an analyst and, to his surprise, "I found him gradually falling back on the 'classical analyst' with an 'interpretative technique', when I felt I needed to regress to the level of that severe infancy trauma" (p. 146). Fairbairn, with him, "was more of a technical interpreter than he thought he was, or than I expected" (*ibid.*). Guntrip thought that when he began treatment, Fairbairn was not at the height of his therapeutic or physical powers. I will engage in a bit of wild analysis and wonder whether, with Guntrip, Fairbairn had to prove that he was an analyst. The traditional role of an analyst is to understand and then interpret, and Fairbairn may well have felt that with this psychotherapist, who was travelling to Scotland, he had to show that he was an analyst. In addition, Guntrip relates that by the time he went into analysis with Fairbairn, he "wisely declined to take the strains of severely regressing patients" (1975, p. 146). Unpredictably (at least from his writings), Fairbairn was an Oedipal theory analyst, and, while this did not get to what Guntrip thought were his basic conflicts, it did convince him that he had repressed a traumatic event (having to do with the death of his brother).

One could get lost in Guntrip's fascinating narrative of his traumatic past and his struggle to understand and deal with the repressed trauma that became fully uncovered late in his life. However, I will briefly turn to his account of his treatment with Winnicott. Guntrip's path to Winnicott was similar in one way to his journey to Fairbairn. He began reading Winnicott's papers, and, by 1962, he "had no doubt that he was the only man I could turn to for further help" (1975, p. 152). Winnicott and Guntrip's first contact was through correspondence, and Winnicott initially wrote and said, "I do invite you to look into the matter of your relation to Freud, so that you may have your own relation and not Fairbairn's" (*ibid.*, p. 151). Winnicott was asking Guntrip to find his own Freud, since Winnicott had found his Freud and took from Freud's writings what he needed for his own concepts.

For a moment, I will dwell on some of Winnicott's interventions that set a tone for Guntrip that he felt was extremely useful. Perhaps we should first note that Guntrip describes Fairbairn's manner, his office, and his behaviour in the analytic sessions as appreciably more formal than was the case with Winnicott. Winnicott saw him infrequently (Guntrip states because of travel difficulties), and this might have accounted for Winnicott's informality. This, however, is not Guntrip's construction, but, rather, mine.

Here are some of Guntrip's descriptions of his treatment with Winnicott.

> As I re-read my records I am astonished at the rapidity with which he went to the heart of the matter. At the first session I mentioned the amnesia for the trauma of Percy's [his brother] death. I felt I had had a radical analysis with Fairbairn of the "internalized bad-object defences" I had built up against that, but we had not got down to what I felt was my basic problem, not the actively bad-object mother of later childhood, but the earlier mother who failed to relate at all. Near the end of the session he said: "I've nothing particular to say yet, but if I don't say something, you may begin to feel I'm not here." [*ibid.*, p. 150]

In the second session, Winnicott again made what Guntrip considered to be an interpretation:

> You know about me but I'm not a person to you yet. You may go away feeling alone and that I'm not real. You must have had an earlier illness before Percy was born, and felt mother left you to look after yourself. You accepted Percy as your infant self that needed looking after. When he died, you had nothing and collapsed. [*ibid.*, p. 152]

Guntrip then comments,

> That was a perfect object relations interpretation, but from Winnicott, not Fairbairn. Much later I said that I occasionally felt a "static, unchanging, lifeless state somewhere deep in me, feeling I can't move". Winnicott said: "If 100% of you felt like that, you probably couldn't move and someone would have to wake you. After Percy died, you collapsed bewildered, but managed to salvage enough of yourself to go on living, very energetically, and put the rest in a cocoon, repressed, unconscious." [*ibid.*]

What Guntrip describes as a perfect object relations interpretation, I would say is an example of a transference interpretation. Winnicott interprets that Guntrip will have a reaction that was born in Guntrip's relationship with his mother. He is saying you may feel a similar way with me (Winnicott) that you felt when you were left unattended by your mother. Although Freud did not frequently venture into early maternal relationships, in Winnicott's interpretations the form of the interpretive comment is similar to the form of Freud's transference interpretations. The difference is a combination of the simplicity of delivery and the depth in understanding early relationships that Winnicott evinces. There is another crucial difference in Winnicott's approach, and that is he brings in what I will call the adaptive reasons for Guntrip's repression. Winnicott points out that if Guntrip did not defend against his experiences with his mother, he could not easily "stay awake", or, in other terms, stay alive and energetic. By including Guntrip's desperate need to repress this aspect of his object relations, he demonstrates that he understands that, without this defence, Guntrip's psychological survival would be in jeopardy. These two interpretations, or, more accurately, this interpretative sequence, demonstrate Winnicott's ability to understand the early transference of Guntrip and to portray these transference reactions in a manner that allows Guntrip both to understand the content and to feel that he is present in Winnicott's mind. Moreover, he is present in Winnicott's mind in a way that demonstrates Winnicott's empathic understanding.

Winnicott, in this treatment, is an example of what I would term a contemporary Freudian position. He is able to interpret the transference in a manner that allows Guntrip to include him in his object world. There is an interpenetration of states, and normally it takes a much longer time to achieve this interpenetration. However, Guntrip entered the treatment after years of treatment with Fairbairn, and with an already established positive transference to Winnicott. This transference occurred when Guntrip was impressed by Winnicott's clinical papers. Some analysts would conclude that Guntrip's response to Winnicott was akin to a transference cure. By this, I mean that the content was unimportant, but Guntrip's response to Winnicott was solely coloured by his positive regard of Winnicott. I would argue that Guntrip entered the treatment with Fairbairn in a similar positive transference state, and yet the results were quite different. Winnicott's interpretation allowed him both to enter Guntrip's world and to provide Guntrip with a type of insight that led him to further understanding and trust in his treatment with Winnicott. In Chapter Seventeen, I will propose that the development of trust (analytic trust) allows a patient to tolerate interpretative efforts. If the interpretation proves to be useful, trust is enhanced and leads to further understanding and a deepening of trust. In my view, Winnicott's concern with trust allows him to effectively interpret transference in the analytic situation.

Returning to Fairbairn, he is one of the first (perhaps the first) analyst to bring an object relations perspective to the clinical situation. It is interesting that, despite this theoretical stance, his clinical efforts are still strongly influenced by an older Freudian view. For me, this is an example of Fairbairn holding on to elements in Freudian theory, while at the same time creating a new opus that he gave to the field but could not fully incorporate for himself. Some of Freud's views on the treatment situation bespeak of similar tendencies; that is, he purposes interesting avenues for clinical interventions but cannot follow his own guidelines.

CHAPTER TEN

Winnicott: in search of the real

Summary

We trace Winnicott's writings from his earliest papers to some of his posthumous publications. In his hands, psychoanalytic theory describes human experience in terms of the trials of becoming real or authentic. Each concept of Freud's or Klein's is transformed into his personalized way of understanding the internal life of the baby, and the baby and child present in the adult. In Winnicott, we see the firm beginning (or in parallel with Fairbairn) of the importance of the two person field. Although Winnicott accepts the idea of the infant's instinctual excitement, it is the relationship with the mother that is crucial in the fate of this excitement. In ideal development, the instinctual component is not the important factor, but, rather, it is the overlapping experiences of the two participants that is crucial in terms of what will be internalized in the infant's developing representational world. Winnicott presents a number of concepts that help the infant's/developing child's transition into the world of others, while developing an indwelling sense of self. Perhaps his most familiar concept is that of the transitional object and transitional space. In this space, the child is able to construct the tools to create reality; for Winnicott, the authentic self does not passively receive, but actively creates reality.

Winnicott: brief biographical introduction

It is hard to write a chapter on Donald (D. W.) Winnicott (1896–1971) without becoming involved intensively with Winnicott as a human being. Winnicott (along with Bion and Balint) personifies the idiosyncrasies of the English writer. He rarely enters a field directly, but, rather, from an angle that is both unexpected and somehow refreshing. Klein and Freud, although differing about a number of issues, surveyed developmental processes and the treatment situation through a one-person lens. (Clearly, Klein's concepts imply relational interactions through projective identification; however, her intent is to understand and picture the internal world of the infant and the infant in the adult's mind.) Winnicott is one of the analysts who begins to enlarge the discipline to create a consistent two-person field. This is true of his views of the psychoanalytic situation as well as his conceptualizations of the infant's internal world. At the beginning, for Winnicott, there was first the infant and mother; the infant never existed alone. In this context, it is important to remember that Winnicott was initially a paediatrician and continued to be a paediatrician throughout his psychoanalytic career. His paediatric career left its imprint on all of his psychoanalytic work. He was, of course, a child as well as adult analyst, and, in virtually all of his work, there is a distinct developmental influence. One could fantasize that he could never forget the baby that once existed before there was an adult.

There are two wonderful biographies of Winnicott that document how he traversed the paths between paediatrician and child and adult analyst. These two volumes (Goldman, 1993a,b; Rodman, 2003) show how each aspect of Winnicott's training and life experience enhanced his search for the conditions that would allow the true self meaningfully to emerge. Rodman shows how difficult this path was, particularly how hard it was for Winnicott to differentiate from Klein's overwhelming presence. Despite the trials and travails that he encountered, particularly regarding the strife in the

British Psychoanalytic Society, Winnicott was close to a man for all seasons. Winnicott's authenticity not only captured the attention of generations of psychoanalysts, but his frequent radio appearances made him a national figure in the UK. When Winnicott died, Renatta Gaddini wrote about her witnessing a large group's response to the announcement of his death: "I have never before witnessed such an authentic tribute to a man . . . I felt it to be the natural response to his respect for authenticity and search for the real self" (Rodman, 2003, p. 370). Winnicott's "search" permeates his work and his life. We will relate some of the conditions of this search before we move on to his portrayals of the human condition. (This chapter was written before I read Linda Hopkins's compelling biography on Masud Khan [Hopkins, 2006]. Although Rodman's biography contains many elements of Winnicott's relationship with, and analysis of, Khan, it remained for Hopkins's biography to detail that complex, and, at times, unfortunate relationship.)

A brief foray into the British Psychoanalytic Institute

Rodman begins his biography of Winnicott by describing the conditions that Winnicott encountered when he began his training at the British Psychoanalytic Institute. Melanie Klein (see Chapters Six, Seven, and Eight) had left Berlin and emigrated to the UK in 1926. Rodman sees Klein's entry into the UK as an attempt by the Anglo-Saxon British to better understand the Jewish–European versions of psychoanalysis. If Rodman is correct, then the British had little idea what was in store for them. Klein, of course, was not your typical European analyst. Her views were to revolutionize, or, at least, lead to a potentially strong revision of, European psychoanalysis. However, as we have seen, Klein and Anna Freud, who clashed in 1928, were to meet in the UK almost a decade later. Sigmund and Anna Freud left (fled) Vienna in 1938, and settled in Northern London. Anna Freud began the famous Hampstead Clinic, and she and a number of other European analysts took root in London. Rodman relates, "The primarily Jewish emigrants began to outnumber the original members of the society" (2003, p. 7). The influx of European analysts was a factor that led to the now famous Controversial Discussions. These discussions were a competition for the hearts and minds of analysts in the UK and around the world. Although Anna Freud and her colleagues certainly were part of the impetus for the discussions, the spark that perhaps ignited the controversies was provided by an unlikely source: Melanie Klein's daughter (Melitta Schmideberg) and Dr Schmideberg's analyst, Edward Glover.

Glover was an interesting and controversial figure, and was outspoken in his criticism of a variety of analysts. His attacks on Klein were particularly strong and somewhat surprising, since they appeared to be co-ordinated with his analysand's, Dr Schmideberg's, attacks. As we noted in Chapters Seven and Eight, the controversial discussions resulted in Freudian and Kleinian analysts developing two partially separate training programmes within the British Psychoanalytic Institute. Initially, one programme was led by Melanie Klein and the other by Anna Freud; Winnicott was then placed somewhere between these two groups, and was one of the analysts who helped to develop the middle, or independent, group. This was a group of analysts who did not wish to (or could not) affiliate with either the Kleinian or Freudian group. Although Winnicott was in this middle group, it would be reasonable to consider him a fellow traveller of the Kleinian group. (Although this is my interpretation, I strongly doubt that Kleinians today would share it.) After he graduated from psychoanalytic training in 1934, he rapidly qualified as a child analyst and, from 1935 to 1940, received supervision from Melanie Klein. Rodman reports that she "had selected him to analyze one of her own children" (2003, p. 7). Although Winnicott was not a prime mover in the discussions, his middle group status was annoying to at least some of Klein's followers and also, at different points in time, to Klein. Winnicott's first paper after the war, "Primitive emotional development" (1945), was a sign of his departure from a strict Kleinian orientation and presaged the fuller emergence of Winnicott's true theoretical and clinical self. Winnicott's moving away from a Kleinian position was difficult, and, in fact, he never fully left Klein's orbit. Klein and a colleague of hers, Joan Rievere, who was one of Winnicott's analysts, consistently attempted to convince him that his subjective factors (or personal predilections) did not allow him to be sufficiently objective about Klein's work. Despite, or perhaps because of, these criticisms, Winnicott continued to be associated with Klein throughout the duration of Klein's life. As one factor in this association, Claire

Winnicott, his second wife, was in analysis with Mrs Klein. In parallel fashion, Klein, even late in her life, felt close enough to Winnicott to try to strongly influence some of his views. For example, Winnicott was asked to write a memorial article about Jones (Winnicott, 1958a) and Klein was specific about what she wanted in this memorial. Klein felt indebted to Jones, and was worried that Winnicott (who had conflict with Jones) would not fully enough acknowledge Jones' contributions to psychoanalysis. Winnicott was, then, strongly influenced by Klein in his writing, and clearly Klein felt close enough to Winnicott to "ask" or tell him what to write.

This brief introduction to parts of Winnicott's life does not do justice to any feature of his experience. However, it may give a glimpse of the complex interactions that were present in the British Psychoanalytic Institute as Winnicott was beginning to develop his unique style as an analyst and writer. Analysing Klein's son was particularly difficult, since Klein seemingly wanted to supervise Winnicott in this analysis. This, of course, seems strange to contemporary analysts, but there are, unfortunately, a number of instances of inappropriate or strange analytic behaviour in the early years of analysis (see Anna Freud in Chapter Five). It was difficult for analysts (including Freud) to internalize and live up to some of the ideals Freud clearly stated in his technique papers. Winnicott had great difficulty in keeping Klein away from the treatment he was conducting with Eric, Klein's son. However, through all of the pressure that his ex-supervisor/mentor placed on him, gradually Winnicott was able to turn back some of Klein's requests and begin to leave her powerful influence. During this era (about 1943–1945), in Goldman's terms, he is beginning his quest in search of the real. He is experimenting with ways of conceptualizing what he conceived of as authentic experience.

In search of the real

We might look back and say that the search for the real began early in his career and in some of Winnicott's early publications (1931, 1936, 1941). In these early publications, he tries to characterize mother–infant interactions in situations that are, at one and same time, ordinary and unusual. In terms of ordinary situations,

Winnicott puts forth his observations of infants in circumstances that invoke anxiety and other forms of distress (e.g., difficulties in eating). In one paper, he observes infants in what he calls a set situation. Here, Winnicott sits opposite the mother with a table between them while the mother is holding her baby on her knee. Winnicott then places a shiny spatula on the table and allows the baby to explore it, to handle it, suck on it, drop it, etc. Winnicott notes how the baby behaves and how the mother reacts to the baby. He does not give the mother instructions, but, in a characteristic Winnicottian way, he says that usually "the mother knows what I am about" and, if necessary, he can gradually tell the mother what needs to be done. In fact, what needs to be done is relatively little, except to allow the infant to explore the shiny object and to watch this exploration. In addition, Winnicott is watching the infant–mother interaction and attempting to understand how different types of mothering affect the infant's tendencies to explore in this situation. Already, in this article, one can see Winnicott make psychoanalytic inferences about the infant's internal world and how the infant's mother shapes this world. Here, we can note that Winnicott has started to observe anxiety in young infants and has begun to conceptualize the mother–infant interactions that will be likely to lead to the infant experiencing more intense anxiety, and, conversely, the conditions under which the infant can tolerate anxiety and explore the new situation. Although these early papers are of interest historically, it is Winnicott's paper "Primitive emotional development" (1945) in which he defines his style of writing and his relationship to existing theoretical concepts.

Beginnings of an inner space

Both Klein and Freud attempted to theorize about the infant's/child's internal world, but Winnicott is attempting to write about the infant's personal experience. He starts off his paper "Primitive emotional development" (1945) by relating his personal method of writing a paper.

> It will be clear at once from my title that I have chosen a very wide subject. All I can attempt to do is to make a preliminary personal

statement, as if writing the introductory chapter to a book. I shall not first give a historical survey and show the development of my ideas from the theories of others, because my mind does not work that way. What happens is that I gather this and that, here and there, settle down to clinical experience, form my own theories and then last of all interest myself in looking to see where I stole what. Perhaps this is as good a method as any. [ibid., p. 145]

Winnicott, in describing his method, in effect frees himself from the considerations involved in referencing others and creating a bibliography of work relevant to the topic at hand. This will lead a number of analysts to become annoyed with him, in particular Balint. The two authors that Winnicott frequently referenced were Freud and Klein, and one can consider that he was trying to personalize his views of both of these writers. In this chapter, we will look at a number of Winnicott's papers. In addition, we will draw heavily on *Playing and Reality* (1971) and some of Winnicott's posthumous publications. Before entering into the "modern" era, we will briefly look at one more paper from Winnicott's pre-war writings.

In 1935, Winnicott begins to look at the relationship of fantasy to inner reality in a paper titled "The manic defense". He starts off by restating an important article by Searl (1929), where she views the "flight to reality" as flight from fantasy. Winnicott restates the flight as one from a person's internal reality. In his view, internal reality cannot be stated only in terms of fantasy, but, rather, as an admixture of "the fantasy that is personal and organized, and related historically to the physical experiences, excitements, pleasures and pains of infancy" (1935, p. 130). There is another sense of fantasy in this conceptualization that is "part of the individual's effort to deal with inner reality by fantasizing and moving away from inner reality" (*ibid.*). In this conceptualization, fantasy and daydreams are attempts at omnipotent control of reality and denote an inability to withstand inner reality. It is of interest to look at how Winnicott restates Searl's conclusions;

> Miss Searl writes . . . in danger [the child] wants to keep the ideally loving and loved parents always with it, with no fear of separation; at the same time it wants to destroy in hate the unkind strict parents who leave it exposed to the awful dangers of unsatisfied libidinal tensions. That is, in omnipotent fantasy it eats up both loving and strict parents. [1935, p. 130]

Winnicott answers,

> It would seem that what we meet with is not merely a fantasy of incorporation of good and bad parents; we meet with the fact of which the child is largely unconscious that, for the same reasons that have been operative in the child's relation to the external parents, sadistic attacks are going on inside the child, attacks against the good or mutually loving parents (because by being happy together they frustrate), attacks against the parents made bad by hate, defense against the bad objects that now threaten the ego too, and also attempts to save the good from the bad, and to use the bad to counteract the bad; and so on.
>
> Omnipotent fantasies are not so much the inner reality itself as a defense against the acceptance of it. One finds in this defense a flight to omnipotent fantasy, and flight from some fantasies to other fantasies, and in this sequence a flight to external reality. This is why I think that one cannot compare and contrast fantasy and reality. [*ibid.*]

In this dialogue (created by Winnicott), he both moves away from the Freudian view of Searl and, in moving towards Klein's ideas, actually creates the beginning of a new view or conceptualization of inner reality. Winnicott, in a later footnote to this paper, says that he would "now use the term 'fantasying'" rather than fantasy. He makes this comment since, I believe, he realizes that he is using the term fantasy in two different ways with quite different connotations. In the first sense of the term, fantasy is a personal part of inner reality, related to the experience of pleasure and pain that the child experiences. In the second sense of the term, fantasy is a response to an internal reality that is difficult to deal with or unbearable. It is a flight to a reality where there is an attempt, through the fantasy, to experience omnipotent control over the external reality.

In his first use of the term "fantasy", Winnicott is talking about inner and outer in a manner that is different than Klein, although the point of his paper is an explication and extension of a Kleinian concept. What is implicit in Winnicott's view of the inner is that it is not dominated by the drives in the way that either Freud or Klein had theorized. He is also not distinguishing between an inner and outer set of representations. He is implicitly assuming that inner reality is influenced by pleasure and pain, and he does not mention endogenous factors such as the drives, particularly the destructive drive. His second use of the term fantasy brings him closer to Klein.

The manic defence is an attempt at omnipotent control by a denial of internal reality and a flight to an external reality that moves away from the implications of an inner voice that cannot be tolerated. It is a movement towards the "denial of the sensations of depression—namely the heaviness, the sadness etc. by specifically opposite sensations, lightness, humorousness, etc." (*ibid.*, p. 132). In Winnicott's version of the manic defence, the inner reality is changed by flight to, and control over, the external reality. In her 1935 paper on depression, Klein sees the manic defence playing a similar role.

Here, Klein emphasizes the same type of mechanism and one can see that, although Winnicott has begun subtly to change the idea of inner reality, he is close to Klein in his view of the manic defence. They both maintained that the sense of suspended animation in this state is a way of keeping the "internalized parents" between life and death: neither killing them and fully acknowledging their loss, nor bringing them to life and having to acknowledge their togetherness and the fact of being separate from them. I would imagine that, reading this paper in 1935, one could only conclude that the writer was a true Kleinian. My interpretation about inner reality is one with the benefit of hindsight and a result of my own transference towards Winnicott. In what follows, we will see that Winnicott first states a concept, then restates it and adds a bit to the concept, usually keeping in mind his view of the infant's experience. Thus, it will be our task to look at these concepts several times, and, by the end of the chapter, attempt to integrate his ideas. At times, we will have to be comfortable with a state of unintegration.

Winnicott's true self more fully emerges

In contrast to Winnicott's paper "The manic defence", there is no ambiguity about the fact that, in his paper "Primitive emotional development" (1945), he has moved away from Klein or, more accurately, moved towards his own unique position. In this paper, he takes us back to the infant at birth, and posits that there are three "early processes", integration, personalization, and "following these, the appreciation of time and space and other properties of reality—in short, realization" (1945, p. 149). (These early processes are in Winnicott's view analogous to Freud's use of the concept of primary process, i.e., the earliest or first processes.) In writing this paper, Winnicott is looking at a number of psychotic patients that he has "extensively analysed".

The localization of self in one's own body is often assumed, yet, a psychotic patient in analysis came to recognize that, as a baby, she thought her twin at the other end of the pram was herself. She even felt surprised when her twin was picked up and yet she remained where she was. Her sense of self and other-than-self was undeveloped (1945, p. 149).

Winnicott assumes that integration, as a primary process, is not primary in the sense that Freud used the term (that is, occurring first in development). First, there is unintegration, and he posits this as a primary state (in the sense of it being first). Disintegration as a psychotic process leads regressively to unintegration, and, although unintegration is an end point of psychosis, one can encounter unintegrated portions of many people's psychological lives. Winnicott gives the example of a patient who obsessively gives every detail of a weekend and "feels contented" that he has said all that needs to be said. The analyst, on the other hand, may feel that the analysis has been avoided. Winnicott maintains that perhaps the patient needs to be "known in all his bits and pieces" by the analyst. Winnicott then assumes that this is part of the "ordinary stuff" of infant life, where the mother must gather the bits and pieces of the infant's experience to foster integration. Integration is helped by being kept warm, being handled, bathed, rocked, and named. He also says that integration is helped by the "acute instinctual experiences which tend to gather the personality together from within" (1945, p. 150). Here, he is maintaining that endogenous factors (instinct or drive) at times organize the infant's experience, and Winnicott sees this organization as, under the right conditions, helping to integrate the infant's sense of self.

Infants differ in their paths to integration; some are well on their way in the "first 24 hours of life". For other infants, the process is delayed because of "early inhibitions of greedy attack(s)". Infants can tolerate unintegration if, at times, they come together and feel something integrated. Winnicott does not fully explain at this point what he means by the inhibition of greedy attacks, but it is clear that he thinks that greedy attacks are normal fare and must be tolerated by the mothering parent. Turning away the infant's forays at the breast will lead to the inability of the infant to have full or integrated experiences. Infants can tolerate periods of unintegration if the parent or environment does not pressure them to respond or give up their spontaneous movements. The infant, at this point in time, assumes its environment and only gradually pieces together an object like a mother.

Winnicott links this unintegration and lack of whole object to the transference that psychotic patients display. It demonstrates, for him, "the clearest proof that the psychotic state of unintegration had a natural place at a primitive stage of the emotional development of the individual" (1945, p. 150). Despite his illustration of psychosis and unintegration, Winnicott assumes that every human being is capable of, and occasionally has periods of, unintegration. He states, "we are poor indeed if we are only sane" (*ibid.*, fn). Related to unintegration is the idea of living in one's own body. Personalizing one's experience involves integrating a sense of mind and bodily experiences. These experiences involve what Winnicott calls instinctual experiences, as well as the experience of being cared for and handled. Interestingly, Winnicott focuses on the waking–sleep cycle, and points out that it is a task to integrate these cycles into a person's experience or sense of self. This is opposed to the idea of these experiences being initially disassociated and unintegrated. Since he states (I believe correctly) that nightmares and night terrors are normal occurrences in children, he sees it as a task to integrate these and the dreaming state with waking states. From this perspective, "It is a valuable experience whenever a dream is both dreamed and remembered, precisely because of the breakdown of dissociation that this represents" (*ibid.*, p. 151). In his terms, there is a natural dissociation between wakefulness and sleep. The remembering of a dream breaks down this division or dissociation. From Winnicott's perspective, disassociation is a widespread phenomenon or, as he calls it, a widespread defence mechanism; for example, he states, "urban life is a disassociation, a serious one for civilization" (*ibid.*, p. 152).

Reality and reality adaptation

Winnicott assumes there is a consensual reality, and, in this sense, he is part of the British Empirical tradition. However, his angle in describing reality is, of course, an oblique one. First of all, he talks about the primary relation to reality rather than knowing reality. He also states that the relation to reality is "never fully made and settled" (*ibid.*), implying that there is a continuous dynamic relationship between subject and object (or subject and subject) throughout life. In the following extract, Winnicott says that he will try to give an example of the development of the primary relation to reality, and he will do this in the simplest possible terms. Let us look at this quote and see if we agree that this is the simplest path of describing these experiences.

> I will try to describe in the simplest possible terms this phenomenon as I see it. In terms of baby and mother's breast (I am not claiming that the breast is essential as a vehicle of mother-love) the baby has instinctual urges and predatory ideas. The mother has a breast and the power to produce milk, and the idea that she would like to be attacked by a hungry baby. These two phenomena do not come into relation with each other till the mother and child live an experience together. The mother being mature and physically able has to be the one with tolerance and understanding, so that it is she that produces a situation which may with luck result in the first tie the infant makes with an external object, that is external to self from the infant's point of view.
>
> I think of the process as if two lines came from opposite directions, liable to come near each other. If they overlap there is a moment of illusion—a bit of experience which the infant can take as either his hallucination or a thing belonging to external reality.
>
> In other language, the infant comes to the breast when excited, and ready to hallucinate something fit to be attacked. At that moment the actual nipple appears and he is able to feel it was that nipple that he hallucinated. So his ideas are enriched by actual details of sight, feel, smell, and next time this material is used in the hallucination. In this way he starts to build up a capacity to conjure up what is actually available. [*ibid.*]

In this extract, it is the overlapping of experience that produces the moment of illusion. The moment of illusion is, in effect, a creation of both parties, two lines intersecting and intermingling. It is the creation of reality that is crucial to Winnicott in this primary relation to reality. We will see that the idea of passively receiving experience will, from Winnicott's point of view, lead to distortions in reality. Thus, when the infant is excited and ready to attack, if it receives what it actively hallucinates, then it will build up a capacity to conjure up what is actually available. Thus, it is the receptivity of the mother in terms of the infant's active states that makes the illusion possible. Winnicott maintains that the process is "immensely simplified if the infant is cared for by one person and one technique" (*ibid.*, p. 153). It is the mother's reliability and receptivity that are crucial in providing the infant a simplified world that is possible for the infant to conjure up and comprehend. He states that only on such a foundation can objectivity be built, or a scientific attitude be developed. From this description, we can go back to a previous distinction and say that fantasy is available to the infant to aid in understanding reality (the first hallucinations are examples of this). (It is interesting to note that in the original article [1945], Winnicott uses the word phantasy, following the Kleinian usage. In the reprint of the article, in his collected papers [1958b], the word is changed to fantasy and fantasying instead of phantasy and phantasizing. It is a sign of his moving from the Kleinian realm.) Fantasying, on the other hand, is a defensive stance and a response to frustration. Fantasy, then, is far from frightening even at the beginning of life. The infant's predatory attack on the breast is a normal phenomenon to be received by the mother, and this conjoint experience is the beginning of a healthy relationship to reality. Winnicott accepts the idea of the infant's instinctual excitement, but it is the relationship with the mother that is crucial in the fate of this excitement. In ideal development (just described above), the instinctual component is not the important factor, but, rather, it is the overlapping experiences of the two participants that is crucial in terms of what will be internalized in the infant's developing internal or representational world.

We can approach Winnicott's ideas about external reality from another vantage point, that is, the consideration of frustration and reality. Klein stresses the idea of tolerance for frustration, and Winnicott states that, while we hear about the frustrations imposed by reality, we hear less frequently about the relief and satisfaction it affords. If we again look at the distinction between fantasy and fantasying, fantasy has its borders in a reality experience, while fantasying is limitless; in Winnicott's terms, "there are no brakes on magic". Fantasy offers the possibility of relief from frustration, while fantasying presents limitless possibilities. Thus, at the beginning, there must be a shared reality, with the mother presenting and the infant hallucinating a reality. This joint process leads to "moments of illusion in which the two are taken by him to be identical, which they never in fact are" (1945, p. 154). These moments of illusion lead to fantasy that will bring the infant/child towards reality.

Primitive ruthlessness (stage of pre-concern)

Winnicott posits an early stage of ruthlessness that is defined in terms of how the infant relates to the mother. Here, he means that not only does the infant engage in predatory attacks on the breast, but, importantly, the infant is not concerned with the consequences of these attacks. Even the more mature child, in play with the mother, occasionally displays this type of ruthlessness. Winnicott notes that the mother is the object of these attacks because the infant can expect that she will tolerate this type of ruthless relation. If this type of relationship does not occur, then the individual will be more likely to display ruthless behaviour in later life, particularly in states of disassociation. A half-step or stage before ruthlessness is the point at which the infant lives in its own instinctual environment and, in this environment, a ruthless impulse is not aimed at an object, but, rather, exists as part of the infant's environment. Winnicott's comment on this state is that this situation is "a very poor life". In this earliest of stages, there is no growth, since there is, as of yet, no perceived commerce with the external world. In this early developmental stage, autoerotism and pleasure coincide, but Winnicott is also involved with the idea of seemingly autoerotic activities being performed for consolation and in order to preserve the object. Here, in this relatively early paper, we see Winnicott working out his views on mother–infant interactions that lead to a good enough environment for the infant to develop a tolerable internal world. This tolerable internal world is one that is open to

growth and nurturance from the world surrounding the infant/
developing child.

Although we have not stressed this aspect of the Winnicott's
paper, we should repeat that at this time he was endeavouring to
show how psychotic transference states were similar to the states of
early development. It was his view that, in patients that are (or
were) typically labelled borderline or psychotic, anxiety about
disintegration was a primary concern. The state of disintegration is
a difficult one for most psychoanalysts to contain. This is a different
state than is consistently encountered, in what Winnicott
considered to be the normal conditions of psychoanalysis, in less
severely disrupted people. He maintains, "In psychoanalysis (with
less disrupted patients) as we know it there is no trauma that is
outside the individual's omnipotence. Everything eventually comes
under ego-control, and thus becomes related to secondary processes"
(1960a, p. 37). In Winnicott's view, eventually everything is
interpreted in "terms of love and ambivalence", and the "Analyst is
prepared to wait a long time . . . to do exactly this type of work"
(*ibid.*). Here, Winnicott is maintaining that if, in analysis, the analyst
is prepared to wait to allow the conditions where the patient owns
their feelings, then borderline and psychotic patients can be
analysed. In infancy, however, both good and bad things happen to
the infant that are quite outside the infant's range. The same is true,
Winnicott feels, of most borderline and psychotic conditions in
adulthood. In short, he is saying that in those conditions (and
others) there are traumatic events that occur outside the person's
range or control, or, in fact, even outside of the fantasy of control.
If one is reliable and waits a long time, then it may be possible to
analyse these patients. Later, I will attempt to argue that a concept
that I have introduced, analytic trust (Ellman, 1991, 1998a), is a
derivative of this view of Winnicott's.

A later look at the parent–infant relationship

Although our next look at Winnicott's thinking involves articles
that are published or presented 10–15 years after the 1945 paper, we
will see that these papers are a direct continuation of Winnicott's
earlier views. In these papers, his movement away from Klein is

decisive, and yet, in a Klein retrospective, he makes his debt to her quite clear. While Winnicott does not stress positions in development (as does Klein, see Chapters, Six, Seven, and Eight), he does see the layering of early development as not simply a transformed structure, but as a continuing presence throughout one's life. Although the papers we will now discuss are mostly devoted to concepts of early development, Winnicott cannot avoid drawing a parallel between early development and the psychoanalytic situation. He reiterates that gradually, in borderline conditions, "the patient becomes able to make use of the psycho-analytic interpretations of the original traumata as projections" (1960a, p. 38). The paradox for borderline patients and for infants is that

> what is good and bad in the infant's environment is not in fact a projection, but in spite of this it is necessary, if the individual infant is to develop healthily, that everything shall seem to him to be a projection. [*ibid.*]

Here, Winnicott is restating, in more specific form, that reality testing, or gaining a sense of reality, is not primarily a function of passively receiving "correct" perceptions. Rather, for the infant to be able to process reality, he must actively construct reality. This view is one that has deep developmental implications and also should profoundly affect one's view of the psychoanalytic situation. Clearly, if one sees the importance of the infant actively processing (in fantasy and otherwise cognitively), then it is useful to pay attention to the infant's states and try to engage the infant in mutual activities (play, in the broad sense of the term). Similarly, if one has this view of the treatment situation, then it may indeed be important to have the patient actively process (play, in the broad sense of the term) rather than be only (or mostly) a passive recipient of the analyst's interpretations.

Winnicott, in stating his ideas about early development, indicates that one might view Freud's writings as being greatly involved with early development. However, in the same paper, he goes on to say that Freud might be seen as having "neglected infancy as a state" (*ibid.*, p. 39) Winnicott resolves these seemingly contradictory statements by saying that Freud, "knows that he is taking for granted the very things that are under discussion in this paper." (1960a, p. 38). Freud, in the paper that Winnicott is citing, is discussing the concept of primary process. He is looking at what he is positing to be the cognitive and affective states of the developing infant. In the Freud quote that Winnicott highlights, Freud writes,

> The employment of a fiction like this [about early developmental states] is, however, justified when one considers that the infant—provided one includes with it the care it receives from its mother—does almost realize a psychical system of this kind. [*ibid.*, p. 39]

The fiction that Freud is referring to is the study or view of the infant's internal world without considering the infant's environment. Winnicott notes that the words "provided one includes with it the care it receives from its mother" have great importance in the context of this study. The infant and the maternal care together form a unit. He reminds us that he has already said there is no such thing as an infant, and here it is clarified anew: there is a system that involves mother and infant together. Winnicott, in citing these quotes from Freud, is saying that here "Freud paid full tribute to the function of maternal care, and it must be assumed that he left this subject alone only because he was not ready to discuss its implications" (*ibid.*). This is charitable of Winnicott, but, alternatively, one might say that although Freud gives evidence of understanding the importance of maternal care, it was not a primary interest of his. He was an adult analyst who was interested in understanding the infantile roots of the adult mind. He was not interested in studying mother–infant interactions.

Winnicott, on the other hand, cannot be without the infant–mother dyad, wherever else his theorizing might proceed. He advances his discussion in an interesting way by pausing to define the term "infant". Infancy refers to a phase of development where the organism depends on "maternal empathy rather than on understanding of what is or could be verbally expressed" (*ibid.*, p. 40). Here, implicitly, Winnicott is extending infancy throughout the life span; however, this is not his principal intention. Rather, he is trying to show how infancy is a time of integration and this integration is dependent on maternal care. He writes about this from what he assumes to be the experience of the infant. It is his view that the Freuds (both Sigmund and Anna) see instinctual forces as being a factor early in development. In Winnicott's version of the Freuds' position, anxiety occurs either from instinctual tension or from object loss. He sees this formulation as one that involves a child who is independent, and Winnicott's focus is on a stage of development that comes before independence, or even partial independence. Klein, in Winnicott's opinion, deals extensively with early anxieties and defences. He states that nowhere in her theoretical concepts is the idea of absolute dependence contradicted. Here, one would have to say that Winnicott is not looking fully at the implications of Kleinian thought. However, after this brief historical cleansing, Winnicott returns to his view of the infant. The infant has various potentials but these can only be realized through proper maternal care. Even the instinctual aspect of the infant's development is strongly influenced by maternal care. Winnicott says that, at first, id forces "clamour for attention". As the infant develops, the id becomes "gathered into the service of the ego . . . so that id-satisfactions become ego-strengtheners". If the id remains external to the ego, id satisfactions will remain only physical and will "have the effect of threatening the ego structure" (*ibid.*). In Winnicott's vision, if the mother does not help the infant to mediate instinctual demands, then these demands will not be integrated into the infant's ego structure.

Holding: a primary concept

How does the mother help to mediate instinctual forces or influences? In Winnicott's world, there is a space before instincts are a presence in the infant's world. Holding is the first of stages of parental care where the term holding is used not only in the denotative sense of physically holding, but in the connotative sense of a total environmental presence, or, in Winnicott's terms, living with. Living with does not stop after the phase of holding ends, but, during holding, the mother helps to co-ordinate basic functions (motor and sensory functions, sensation and perception) and begins to help delineate a "limiting membrane, which to some extent (in health) is equated with the surface of the skin. This limiting membrane has a position between inside and an outside, and a body-scheme (schema)" (1960a, p. 45). (See Anzieu [1989] for a

Winnicottian discussion of the importance of the skin as a living membrane.) What does holding provide for the infant? In a moment, we look at a list, but we must remember that, for Winnicott, holding precedes object relationships. During holding, the infant is maximally dependent, but should not be able to experience this state. Thus, holding

> Protects from physiological insult, takes account of the infant's skin sensitivity—touch, temperature, auditory sensitivity, visual sensitivity, sensitivity to falling (action of gravity) and of the infant's lack of knowledge of the existence of anything other than the self. It includes the whole routine of care throughout the day and night, and it is not the same with any two infants because it is part of the infant, and no two infants are alike. Also it follows the minute day-to-day changes belonging to the infant's growth and development, both physical and psychological. [*ibid.*, p. 49]

Holding is a form of loving, and it is a mark of the good enough mother that she can hold her infant. Mothers who cannot hold "produce in the infant a sense of insecurity and distressed crying" (*ibid.*). Holding allows the infant to exist comfortably in an unintegrated state and allows the mother to gradually help towards integration. Anxiety about disintegration is not present until some integration has taken place. The danger of not being held thus is not disintegration, but a sense of annihilation or annihilation anxiety. During the holding phase, while the infant is maximally dependent, the mother acts as an auxiliary (or executive) ego. In mother–infant interactions, the child has the illusion of omnipotence and the true self is thus protected by the maternal ego. Of course, we have just introduced another term: the true self. What is a true self according to Winnicott?

To answer this question, we have to look at not only the theory of the true and false self, but also the concept of annihilation anxiety. The true self, to Winnicott, is the core of the personality (or should be the core in optimal circumstances) and is an inherited potential which is experiencing a continuity of being, and acquires, in its own way and with its own sense of timing, a personal reality and a personal body representation. Good enough mothering allows this potential to emerge at its own speed. Optimally, the mother does not impede or rush development, but takes the cues from her infant as to when the infant is ready to move on or needs to sit still. In extreme circumstances, when the infant suffers impingements that it cannot experience under its own sense of control (or omnipotence, in Winnicott's terms), a psychotic organization may develop. A defence against both impingements and a terrifying world of psychosis is the development of the false self. This is the infant's way of complying with the external world, while, at the same time, avoiding the experience of disintegration. The holding environment should produce continuity of being that leads to increasing integration. The alternative to this continuity is the infant having to react to an impinging environment. In Winnicott's language, reacting interrupts being and annihilates. Being and annihilation are the two alternatives of infant experience during the phase of holding and absolute dependence. Placing holding and absolute dependence together is taking note that while the mother is holding, the infant, initially, is going through the stage of absolute dependence. This is the infant's first stage, and during this period Winnicott assumes that maternal holding allows the infant to develop at its own pace and integrate at its own pace. He also assumes that the mother will support periods of unintegration and allow the infant to proceed through periods of unintegration at its own pace. Holding provides the coverage during the period of absolute dependence. Annihilation anxiety occurs during absolute dependence when holding fails and the environment is experienced as an impingement demanding reactivity. Integration occurs under the influence of a holding environment. Personalization (along with continuity of being) occurs with appropriate handling. Both processes of personalization and integration begin in the phase of absolute dependence. However, object relating begins with object presenting, and this leads into the next phase of development: relative dependence.

Relative dependence to independence

Winnicott notes that impingements are inevitable, but that

> Under favorable conditions the infant establishes a continuity of existence and then begins to develop the sophistications which

makes it possible for impingements to be gathered into the area of omnipotence. At this stage the word death has no possible application, and this makes the term death instinct unacceptable . . . [1960a, p. 47]

From Winnicott's perspective, the idea of death has no meaning until a whole object has been formed and the idea of hate (towards a whole object) is established. (Parenthetically, Winnicott is rejecting Freud and Klein's view of Thanatos, or the death instinct.) Object relationships and instinctual gratification are both dependent on the establishment of ego organization "which is only too easily taken for granted when all goes well" (*ibid.*, p. 49). Thus, before there can be object relationships, there has to be holding and a successful path through absolute dependence. The mother, during absolute dependence, is likened to the pregnant woman undergoing puerperal insanity (due to a "fever" during pregnancy). This fever continues through absolute dependence and gives the mother (through projective identification) a "powerful sense of what the baby needs" (*ibid.*, p. 53). It is difficult for the mother to separate from the infant "at the same speed at which the infant needs to become separate from her" (*ibid.*, p. 54). When this separation begins to occur, the infant moves from the unit (I am and "everything else is not me") (*ibid.*, p. 61) to I am and I exist, and has an introjective–projective interaction with a somewhat recognized not-me. The recognized and important not-me is a crucial signal of the stage of relative dependence. During this new relationship, the child moves from an assumed omnipotence to a state of occasional and defensive omnipotence. This defensive omnipotence is utilized at times to obliterate the movement to relative dependence and to restore absolute dependence and a fantasized holding environment. During this period, disintegration is more of an issue than unintegration, and it is the fear of disintegration that here produces annihilation anxiety. Winnicott's ideas about annihilation involve states of

1. going to pieces;
2. falling for ever;
3. having no relationship to the body;
4. having no orientation.

The first two and the fourth experience are examples of the loss of integration and losing a space–time continuum relationship.

Having no relationship with the body (point 3) is an example of losing a sense of indwelling, which, one hopes, occurs during relative dependence. The baby begins to develop a membrane and a me–not-me experience. A membrane (typically the surface of the skin) delineates this me–not-me experience. Late in this phase, the infant/developing child begins to sense that someone external understands it, and this is an extremely important, ongoing movement towards the last phase, that is, living together. Before reaching this point, the child begins to relate to the world, and this object relating is a function of object presenting. Object presenting is an example of the maternal figure being able to provide gratification, comfort, and avoidance of distress without these states being overtly signalled by the infant. It is the beginning of the infant feeling that it is part of someone's psyche and it is a crucial aspect of the transition from absolute to relative dependence. We will finish this section asking two important and related questions of Winnicott's ideas about early development.

1. How does the infant develop the capacity for aggressive behaviour? Perhaps this question is more accurately phrased in terms of whether or not, in optimal development, the infant/developing child develops aggressive tendencies.
2. How does the developing infant/child obtain the capacity for concern, or when does guilt play a role in the child's development?

The capacity for concern: concern and guilt

Winnicott begins his discussion of concern by saying that concern is the obverse of guilt. Concern is at the heart of all constructive work and play. At the genital level, concern could said to be the basis of the family, where both partners in intercourse take responsibility for the outcome of their actions. The act is not merely involved in pleasure, but in the concern for the development of a family. Even though concern for the other (or for an activity) is invoked in many adult activities, the roots of the capacity for concern occurs "before the period of the classical Oedipus complex" (1963a, p. 73). Winnicott views the development of concern as being dependent on several concurrent factors. First, the infant/child must be able to view the mother as a whole object. He also uses a term that he credits Freud with developing, "the word, 'fusion'" (*ibid.*, p. 74). He states that fusion is the "achievement of emotional development in which the baby experiences erotic and aggressive drives toward the same object at the same time" (*ibid.*). The child has begun to establish a self (sense of self) and has become "a unit that is both physically contained in the body's skin and is psychologically integrated" (*ibid.*, p. 75). The child, in many ways, is independent of the mother's auxiliary ego, and there is now a sense of inside and outside. There is a new psychosomatic life in the child and a richer inner life. In Winnicott's view, the new inner psychic reality that Freud theorized is now becoming a thing to the infant. At this point, Winnicott is positing the child's development of its own psychic reality, and not just about the reality the mother presents to the child. Winnicott talks about this new state as a development of a "simultaneous love–hate experience which implies the achievement of ambivalence, the enrichment and refinement of which leads to the emergence of concern" (*ibid.*). After stating the idea of ambivalence, he introduces a new concept that seemingly explains the type of ambivalence that is present at this point in the child's development. For the immature child, he posits the existence of two maternal representations: the object mother and the environmental mother. These two maternal images must be present before the point of fusion, and it is only when these two representations come together in the child's mind (are fused) that concern is possible.

The object mother is the object of the instincts; this mother is the "object, or owner of the part-object that may satisfy the infant's urgent needs". The environment mother is the source of total management, and is the mother who is part of the infant's total environment. The object mother is used ruthlessly and aggressively and has to experience the full force of the infant's "ruthless" instinctual attacks. The environment mother, although the manager of the total environment, is present in quieter moments where the infant/child is not dominated by "crude instinct-tension" (*ibid.*, p. 76). Winnicott describes the fantasy of "full-blooded id-drives contains attack and destruction" (*ibid.*). The baby wants to devour the object and take possession of the contents of the object. Here, he pictures the object mother as experiencing a Kleinian type attack. The environment mother is protected, and Winnicott states that when the two mothers are fused, the baby, to protect the mother, may wean itself. At the point of fusion, the ruthless usage of the object begins to bring a sense of guilt. Winnicott posits that this sense of guilt is allayed if the infant can repair its relation with the mother by her reliably being present and available. When this becomes a reliable sequence, the infant again is freer in its experience of "id-drives". The repetition of this cycle gradually brings in a possibility of the infant actively giving to the mother. The "Opportunity to contribute . . . [enables] concern to be within the child's capacity" (*ibid.*, p. 77). Winnicott then tries to show how the need to provide is crucial through life, and it is one path through which guilt is allayed and depression and sadness prevented. As an everyday example, Winnicott asks us to "consider a doctor, and his needs. Deprive him of his work and where is he? He needs his patients, and the opportunity to use his skill, as others do" (*ibid.*, p. 78). In addition, Winnicott gives an example where he shows that a girl who was quite "severely ill" began, in therapy sessions, to express the deepest hate of her therapist. During the rest of the day she was making progress and doing constructive things, but in the sessions the "therapist was destroyed utterly, and repeatedly" (*ibid.*, p. 81). One way of looking at the sequence is that the girl could get to constructive aspects of her life because she was encountering her destructive tendencies in the therapeutic situation. Winnicott, however, states that "The constructive and creative experiences were making it possible for the child to get to the experiences of her destructiveness" (*ibid.*). The implications of this statement are profound for Winnicott's ideas about treatment, for he would say that unless the patient can be held and then gradually can give to the therapist, the destructive aspects of the personality will remain too overwhelming for the patient to encounter. We will continue to look at the implications of this type of theorizing in the commentary section on Winnicott.

Guilt and Winnicott's depressive position

Winnicott begins his discussion with Freud's concept of guilt derived from the structural theory (see Chapter Four). He credits

Freud's developing of the concept of superego with clearly underlining the idea that "guilt is a matter of inner reality, or that guilt resides in the intention" (1958b, p. 18). While accepting Freud's meaning of guilt, Winnicott characteristically broadens the concept. He talks about guilt that is tolerated; this manifestation of guilt implies a necessary conflict between love and hate. In talking about the development of the Oedipal child, he says that guilt demonstrates "that the boy could tolerate and hold the conflict, which is in fact an inherent conflict, one that belongs to healthy life" (*ibid.*, p. 17). Here, Winnicott is demonstrating an ability to understand a concept and recognize that there may be different implications than the theorist imagined. Freud, at the end of his life, saw Oedipal conflicts (usually) as the bedrock of psychopathology, Winnicott, in effect going to an earlier Freud, maintains that, in so far as one has conflicts about love, it is a sign of health and solid development. Thus, if the child can tolerate guilt, the child can begin to develop the capacity for love that is not based on narcissistic considerations. The child can love a person towards whom he/she experiences both love and hate; in other terms, the child can love a person who is a unified representation (object) in the child's mind.

Primary maternal preoccupation and me–not-me

The role of aggression

Although this point has certainly been stated and restated in this chapter, Winnicott, in describing primary maternal preoccupation (1956a), relates that this begins at the end of pregnancy and lasts for a few weeks and is not clearly remembered after this period. This state is what allows Winnicott later to mention that one cannot talk about an infant by itself, one always has to consider a mother–infant pair at birth and during absolute dependence. Winnicott, in describing absolute dependence, says that during this period there is an erotic instinct and a potential for aggression. Thus, he implicitly differs with Freud and Klein about the issue of the death instinct and about innate aggression. The potential for aggression is related to motility, and even in the movement of the foetus or the baby's grasp we see the potential for aggression. As was noted earlier, Winnicott uses Freud's term "fusion" to indicate that, during absolute dependence, the infant's potential for aggression is fused with its erotic activities. Thus, the infant's biting or hard sucking is not aggressive *per se*, but, rather, a result of this fusion. If this fusion does not take place, Winnicott posits the possibility of unmitigated destructive tendencies (1956b). During absolute dependence, there is unconcern for the fate of the object, since the object is present as an object that is ruthlessly loved and is an assumed aspect of the infant's world. As the infant becomes aware of an inside and an outside, the infant can begin to experience its intentions towards the object. The infant, as it moves into relative dependence, begins to develop what Klein described as the depressive position, and Winnicott labels as concern. Relative dependence shifts ruthlessness into ruth and unconcern to concern; concomitantly, the infant can experience both guilt and anger. This is possible because the object is now perceived as external. Winnicott relates that

> this important phase of development is composed of innumerable repetitions spread over a period of time. There is a benign circle of (i) instinctual experience, (ii) acceptance of responsibility . . . guilt, (iii) a working through, and (iv) a true restitutive gesture. [1958b, p. 24]

For Winnicott, during the period of relative dependence, maternal representations are first split and then united. Similarly, the aggressive potential is differentiated from erotic tendencies and the infant/toddler/child (Winnicott sees no need to be exact) begins to push back with aggression. This push back helps the me–not-me differentiation and leads to attacks against the object mother. The mother's annihilation and subsequent survival (perhaps better phrased as resurrection) allows the child to experience both guilt and restitutive emotions.

The behaviour of the mother is crucial in Winnicott's version of relative dependence and his stage of concern (which, at times, he alluded to as the depressive position). There are similarities with Klein's depressive position, but the differences are more striking and the role of the mother is far more pronounced in Winnicott's version of the development of concern. Although he spends a reasonable amount of time talking about the development of aggression (from motility to pushing back), there is still not a firm theory of aggression in Winnicott's theorizing.

Winnicott's Klein

In addition, in discussing the concept of the superego, Winnicott says that while the concept was an important advance, the idea of introjection of the father-figure "has turned out to be too simple" (1958b, p. 19). Here, Winnicott is clearly moving towards Klein's ideas about guilt occurring during the depressive position. In preceding chapters (see Chapters Six and Eight), we have looked at how Klein pushed the depressive position earlier and earlier, until it occurs within the first six months of the child's life. Along with the depressive position, the occurrence of the Oedipal stage is seen to occur during this same time period. Interestingly, Winnicott only glancingly discusses the early occurrence of the Oedipal period, but focuses on Klein's contribution in putting forth the concept of the depressive position.

Winnicott discusses Klein's depressive position in various articles, but most specifically in his presentation of the depressive position (1954) his discussion of guilt (1958b), and in a short paper assessing Klein's contributions (1962b). In this last paper, he places Klein's concept of the depressive position as ranking with "Freud's concept of the Oedipus complex" (p. 176). He also discounts the division in the British Psychoanalytic Society (between Anna Freud and Klein), saying that it did not matter to him since he claims to have known little about its origins at the time of the beginning of the controversy. Rather, Winnicott shows how he is able to understand both Freud and Klein within his vision of human development. Before we discuss the depressive position, it is instructive to see how Winnicott integrates these theorists into his vision of the baby. He first credits Klein with making Freud's concept of psychic reality "very real".

Winnicott, in discussing Klein, relates how his then analyst, Strachey, realized that Winnicott's interests took him beyond the "Oedipus complex as the point of origin of (all) individual conflicts". Strachey said to Winnicott,

If you are applying psycho-analytic theory to children you should meet Melanie Klein. She has been enticed over to England by Jones saying some things that may or may not be true, and you must find out for yourself for you will not get what Melanie Klein teaches in my analysis of you. [1962b, p. 173]

Winnicott did meet Mrs Klein, and relates how he felt he had been a pioneer before meeting her and then changed into "being a student with a pioneer teacher". Using Klein's play technique, Winnicott experienced

glimpses into the child's inner world, and one saw that psychic reality can be referred to as "inner" because it does belong to the child's concept of himself as having an inside that is part of the self and an outside that is not-me. [*ibid.*, p. 174]

Winnicott takes this distinction between inner and outer and relates it to projection and introjection. Introjection can be considered a form of taking in and related to eating and the oral stage, projection to ejecting out and related to spitting, excreting faeces, urine, or to screaming. Thus, Winnicott sees a real physical meaning to the psychological pre-history of the terms projection and introjection. The term pre-history is used in this context, since Winnicott views Klein's ideas about object relations as spoiling her contributions, given her tendency to push the age at which complex representations and relationships to appear earlier and earlier in her theory of development. However, Winnicott credits Klein with placing the concepts of projection and introjection, developed "as mental mechanisms in relation to the child's experience of the bodily functions of incorporation and excretion" (*ibid.*, p. 178). He credits Klein with developing a number of other concepts and, interestingly, he credits her with developing a theory of the individual's attainment of a capacity for concern during the depressive position.

This is of interest in understanding Winnicott's translation of Klein. There is no question that she emphasized the role of fantasy (phantasy) and the importance of persecutory anxiety in development. Unquestionably, she also emphasized the "importance of destructive elements in object relationships, i.e., apart from anger" (*ibid.*) caused by frustration. However, although Klein's theory can be understood as developing a theory of the capacity for concern, few would highlight this aspect of her theory. Winnicott, I think, however, correctly shows how Klein's concepts of reparation highlight a pathway for the development of concern. Thus, in this one essay, Winnicott talks about how infants enrich themselves during the oral stage through the mechanisms of projection and introjection and how the depressive position is a pathway towards the capacity for concern. While both the interpretation of Freud and of Klein are correct, the emphasis that Winnicott places on these concepts is neither Freud's nor Klein's emphasis. Despite this, the implications that Winnicott draws are present in both of their theoretical visions. Klein talks about reparation and a split object becoming whole during the depressive position, and Freud talks about the infant's creating a reality through the mechanisms of projection and introjection. Certainly, Abraham is more specific about these issues than Freud, but Freud, Abraham, and Klein all emphasize the anxieties that occur during these states. Winnicott, however, emphasizes the process by which the infant develops the capacity for concern, thus enriching its sense of self. Although he mentions denial of depression, which he labels a manic defence, he does not feature the Kleinian triumvirate of manic defences: denial, omnipotence, and idealization. This is not because Winnicott disputes the existence of these mechanisms, but, rather, because he does not see the necessary splitting of the self as is the case in Klein's conceptualization of at least the first depressive position (see Chapter Six). For Klein, in the first occurrence of the depressive position, the infant/child cannot tolerate the pining for the lost object and, in a manic response, denies the loss and resumes an idealization of the object to attempt to preserve the object. As a further step in the denial of the loss, the infant/child phantasizes omnipotent control over the object. Winnicott does not see this as a necessary occurrence in the depressive position, but, rather, as a pathological response in the depressive position. He would see it as most probably a failure in maternal responsiveness, and here we can see one of the strong differences of emphasis between Klein and Winnicott.

Although Klein has stated that she is sensitive to environmental factors, Winnicott states, "in early works she paid lip-service to environmental" factors but she would never truly understand that, in early dependency, it is not possible to describe an infant without a mother. He goes on to state that "Klein claimed to have paid full attention to the environmental factor, but it is my opinion that she was temperamentally incapable of this" (*ibid.*, p. 177). This is a strong statement by Winnicott, and one that neo-Kleinians would contest. It is not surprising that in this same essay he mentions that he found that Klein did not include him as a Kleinian. Is it a negation when he states that it did not matter to him, for he has not been able to follow anyone, "not even Freud"? He goes on to say that, for example, he never has found any value in Freud's idea of a death instinct. Of course, Klein has featured the death instinct even more prominently than Freud, and so Winnicott is here distinguishing his position from Klein and Freud. In addition, the discussion of the death instinct is strongly tied to Klein's concept of the paranoid–schizoid position.

Here, as we have seen, Klein features the idea of splitting of the object into a good and bad object. This occurs because of the infant's inability to protect the whole object from internal attack. Klein relates this to the presence of the death instinct. She also emphasizes the idea of talion response, or, as Winnicott puts it, talion dread. Winnicott accepts and values both of these concepts, but doubts that the infant starts life in this way, given that there is good enough mothering. Good enough mothering is a concept that clearly separates Winnicott from Klein, since she conceptualizes the occurrence of the paranoid–schizoid position as a universal occurrence after birth. It is the infant's first overall state, and here Winnicott strongly disagrees with Klein. Moreover, it is his view that there are no firm internal objects during absolute dependency, if there is good enough mothering. Here, Winnicott has taken a position that is easily reconciled with Freud's ideas about autoerotism and primary narcissism. It is my view that Winnicott realizes this, and this is the reason he consistently is able to tolerate Freudian concepts. Interestingly, Winnicott does not like the names of either position; he relates that "the term paranoid–schizoid is certainly a bad one" in that it puts the beginning of life as a struggle between the forces of life and death. In Winnicott's view, the mother's maternal preoccupation prevents the infant from experiencing this type of struggle. Good enough mothering is the mother's ability to provide the infant with enough ego coverage so that, during absolute dependency, the infant is naturally omnipotent. This is perhaps a bad term for expressing the view that in good enough development the infant is protected from suffering too many impingements. In addition, the infant can reliably expect to get what it wants approximately when it wants it. This presenting of the appropriate experience (object presenting) is part of the mother's preoccupation with the infant during absolute dependency. The depressive position comes later during relative dependency, and, if things are going well, Winnicott might name this stage the capacity for concern.

Here, we can conclude this discussion by pointing out that Winnicott also thinks the depressive position is a bad name. Despite the poor name, Winnicott credits Klein for making it clear to him "how the capacity for concern and to feel guilty is an achievement, and it this rather than depression that characterizes arrival at the depressive position in the case of the growing baby and child" (1962b, p. 176). Winnicott does acknowledge that when adult patients arrive at this point during analysis, they do get depressed. However, he still emphasizes, even in an adult analysis, that "being depressed is an achievement and implies . . . an acceptance of responsibility for all the destructiveness that is bound up with living, with the instinctual life, and with anger at frustration" (*ibid.*, p. 177). Thus, even though the patient is depressed, Winnicott focuses on the patient's accomplishment in being able to now integrate these previous split parts of the self. He realizes that his attempt to change the name of the depressive position to a name that included the stage of concern is not a serious attempt. Despite his different emphasis, Winnicott appreciates that he would never have reached his position (slight pun), never formulated his theoretical concepts, without coming into contact with Kleinian theory.

Another look at dependence through independence

We have already mentioned that Winnicott viewed the earliest parts of infancy through childhood in terms of three stages: absolute dependence, relative dependence, and a movement towards independence. We have looked at absolute dependence most thoroughly, since, up to 1963, it is the stage that Winnicott emphasizes. During absolute dependence, the parents provide a facilitating environment to enable the infant's genetic endowment to effloresce.

Winnicott notes that adapting to the "infant's maturational processes is a highly complex" (1963b, p. 85) endeavour. The great demands on the parents are met by the mother's "primary maternal preoccupation", which, optimally, is supported by the mother's immediate environment (spouse, significant other, parents, etc.). During this period of time, the mother is also dependent on the infant in the sense that she cannot be without it, at least in terms of thought and frequently in terms of action. Winnicott describes this as holding, and says that the mother's holding meets the infant's ego needs as well as satisfying its instinctual tensions. "No one can hold a baby unless able to identify with the baby." Balint (a major theorist in the UK during Winnicott's lifetime who was also part of the independent, or middle, group in the British Psychoanalytic Society) has referred to the mother metaphorically providing the oxygen in the air (1958c, 1968), of which the infant knows nothing. Balint, here, is making the same point as Winnicott in that the mother literally provides the conditions for the infant's life and well being. Winnicott, in a similar vein, relates, "I could remind you of the bathwater, tested by the mother's elbow . . ." (1963b, p. 86). This, of course, is a simple way that the mother is able to provide a safe environment for the infant. Balint and Winnicott are trying to show that the mother affords the infant this type of safe environment continuously during the early stages of the infant's life.

Holding, during absolute dependence, allows the infant to "go on being", but breaks in holding cause this process to be interrupted. Winnicott calls these interruptions, impingements. Impingements are aversive interruptions in the infant's experience and, if there are enough impingements, there is a danger of the emergence of a false self structure. This would occur as a defensive manoeuvre to protect genetic tendencies (true self) from further assault. Essentially, a false self development is an attempt by the infant to adapt to what it experiences as a hostile environment. Although, in adults, there are natural false self developments, in early development extensive manifestation of a false self indicates a pathological defensive manoeuvre of great importance. In optimal development, gradually the infant is able to tolerate the impingements (gather them into its sense of omnipotence) and, in other terms, gradually begin to tolerate minor failures in adaptation, or, more accurately, tolerate the mother's "failure" to respond in the manner she did during absolute dependence. Concurrently, during relative dependence, the infant's mother begins to resume her own independence, or gives up her (almost) total absorption in the infant. This gradual failing of the mother (or resumption of independence) is timed to coincide with the infant's new cognitive and affective capabilities. In absolute dependence, the infant–mother dyad was a unit, and in that unit the infant's dependence, in Winnicott's words, is a "dependence that is quite beyond the infant's ken" (*ibid.*, p. 87). In relative dependence, the infant's new capacities allow it to tolerate this new inattention while, at the same time, beginning to recognize its dependence on its environment. The infant now "knows in his mind that mother is necessary" (*ibid.*, p. 88). Relative dependence is the time that the infant begins to fuse the different maternal representations. If things have gone well in absolute dependence, relative dependence is the point in development where the infant experiences the drives within the ego as opposed to the drives as an external "clap of thunder". The membrane of self-delineation is being formed, and the infant is making steps towards independence. The steps towards independence are many, but, in this state, the child can accept losses and gradually meet the world and all its complexities because of seeing to a greater extent what is already present in his or her own self. These steps towards independence involve a transition that we have not mentioned in this chapter, and this transition is explicated in some of Winnicott's best known concepts. In the next section, we will try to cover Winnicott's ideas of transitional space and transitional objects, and how these concepts relate to the infant's/developing child's steps towards independence.

Playing and Reality: the transition towards independence and culture

Playing and Reality was first published in 1971, and in this publication Winnicott reproduces concepts that he first presented in 1951 and subsequently published (Winnicott, 1953). Winnicott is somewhat apologetic when he tells his audience that he has to review his previous publication on transitional phenomena. He begins both publications in the same words, by saying that "It is well known that infants as soon as they are born tend to use fist, fingers, thumbs in stimulation of the oral erotogenic zone, in satisfaction of the instincts at that zone". He continues, and states,

> It is also well known that after a few months infants of either sex become fond of playing with dolls, and that most mothers allow their infants some special object and expect them to become, as it were, addicted to such objects. [1971, p. 1]

Winnicott's interest is in understanding these first not-me objects and the role that they play in the infant's development. He almost says that the possession and interest in these not-me objects is separate from oral excitement, but he stops short of saying this and admits the possibility that oral excitement "may be the basis of everything else" (*ibid.*, p. 2). Whether this is the case or not, it is unimportant unless one has to adhere to a doctrinaire approach to theoretical positions. What Winnicott is observing has importance, and he wants to understand the nature of objects that will be utilized as the infant develops (or utilizes) the capacity to recognize the object as not-me. Most importantly, Winnicott wants to approximate the place of the object; is it perceived by the infant as an internal object, an external object, or as somewhere in between? Clearly, Winnicott is looking at this in-between space as a transition between inner and outer and as a space with its own properties. It is an intermediate area, where the infant's experience is somewhere

> between the thumb and the teddy bear, between the oral erotism and [the] true object relationship, between primary creative activity and projection of what has already been introjected, between primary unawareness of indebtedness and the acknowledgement of indebtedness. [*ibid.*]

These intermediate areas are frequently populated by objects that are called transitional objects. Winnicott will see transitional space as an area of creativity for both the infant and adult. It is a place to house and produce objects. It is also a transitional point towards the initiation of an affectionate version of an object relationship.

In a typical manner, Winnicott dates the beginning of transitional phenomena from 4–12 months. Winnicott, in looking at transitional space, says, "I am concerned with the first possession, and with the intermediate area between the subjective and that which is objectively perceived" (1953, p. 89). In terms that we have been using, transitional phenomena begins during the stage of relative dependency. During this period, the infant assumes "rights" over the object and the environment (parents, siblings, etc.) agree to this assumption. Despite the infant's rights, Winnicott sees the appearance of a transitional object as an abrogation of omnipotence. The infant passes from magical omnipotent control to control by manipulation, involving muscle erotism or pleasure from motor co-ordination. The infant is not reality testing in the normal sense of the term; it is building space so that it can create reality. Winnicott, here, is talking about the beginning of the capacity for illusion, which he relates in adult life to the creation and reception of art and religion. He does mention that illusion "becomes the hallmark of madness when an adult puts too powerful a claim on the credulity of others, forcing them to acknowledge a sharing of illusion that is not their own" (1971, p. 3). In this context, the availability of transitional space is necessary for the creation of illusion. Illusion is the creation of a state that is neither a reproduction of reality nor a hallucination.

> It is an area which is not challenged, because no claim is made on its behalf except that it shall exist as a resting-place for the individual engaged in the perpetual human task of keeping inner and outer reality separate yet inter-related. [1953, p. 89]

It is the creation of this relationship that is Winnicott's concern. If these areas are not connected, then reality cannot really be truly believed. Typically, an object exists in transitional space, and this object has particular features.

Although the object may vary (at times it may be the mother, but not in optimal development), it has to be available to be affectionately cuddled as well as excitedly loved and mutilated. Winnicott lists a number of features that are typically present in the transitional object (not all are reproduced here):

I. It must never change unless changed by the infant.
II. It must survive instinctual loving, and also hating and, if it be a feature, pure aggression.
III. Yet it must seem to the infant to give warmth, or to move or have texture, or to do something that seems to show it has vitality or reality of its own.

IV. It comes from without from our point of view, but not so from the point of view of the baby. Neither does it come from within; it is not a hallucination.

V. Its fate is to gradually allowed to be decathected ... so that ... it becomes not so much forgotten as relegated to limbo. The transitional object ... does not 'go inside' ... and it therefore is not forgotten and it is not mourned.

VI. The importance of transitional object is not in symbolism but in its actuality. [*ibid.*, p. 90]

Here, we see that Winnicott is moving to try to describe the conditions that allow the infant to develop a world of its own while gradually moving to understand the world around it. He states that the importance of the object is not in its symbolism, but in its actuality; here, it seems that Winnicott is trying to establish the reality of the transitional object and emphasize that it is a thing in itself. In making this point, Winnicott is saying that the object does not, in reality, stand as a denotative sign for, as an example, oral pleasures. Rather, the infant is creating a world of illusion. Given that this is true, it is hard to believe that there is no symbolic value of the transitional object. Its symbolic value is not that it is part of instinctual development, but that it is a symbol that is important connective tissue for the infant. This connective tissue must be able to tolerate intense affects. For example, the object not only must survive instinctual loving, it must also survive the infant's hate and the infant's aggression. This, in part, is why the object must have some vitality of its own to demonstrate its continuous survival. Interestingly, it is gradually decathected or gradually the child loses a feeling of attachment to the object. The child does not miss the object, because it is replaced in the child's life by a more permanent state of transitional space. Thus, the child now can utilize transitional space without the transitional object.

If we return to the infant, Winnicott tells us that the internal object dies if the external one dies or does not stay vital for the infant. At first, the infant is allowed by its mother to have the illusion that the breast is part of the infant. The mother is essential for the infant to have this illusion, for the mother must place her breast just where it is needed and just when the infant is ready to create the breast. Gradually, when this is repeated, this object presenting helps to create a transitional area between subjective creation and objective perception. The mother helps to create the illusion and helps the infant to accept gradual disillusionment. During this period of disillusionment depression is possible, but it is during this period of time when transitional space begins and illusions come via the transitional object. In the transitional area, controls can be exercised by the child. Omnipotence is gradually replaced by actual control, particularly by motoric control. This actual control comes via the activities of play, where the child gradually encounters reality through what Winnicott calls the subjective objective.

Play allows the child to utilize transitional space and be in a state of "near-withdrawal". This is a state that often characterizes adult play and creativity, and the child and adult "inhabit an area that cannot be easily left, nor can it easily admit intrusions" (1971, p. 50). The child or adult may gather aspects of external reality into the area of play, and this an area that Winnicott likens to dream potential. He says, "the child manipulates external phenomena in the service of the dream and invests chosen external phenomena with dream meaning and feeling" (*ibid.*). Interestingly, Winnicott talks about REM (often called dreaming sleep) and NREM sleep, and tentatively sees these states as being analogous to play and free association (REM), whereas NREM is likened to more ordered thinking and associative processes. Early playing (and, at times, playing in older children and adults) involves bodily actions. The bodily excitement attendant to a playing situation can lead to stimulation of the instincts in a way that threatens the child's sense of autonomy and sense of secure self. Here, Winnicott brings in a quantitative factor, and relates that "instinctual arousal beyond a certain point must lead to climax" (*ibid.*, p. 51). Thus, instinctual excitement is seen as a clap of thunder that the child's sense of self (or ego) cannot contain, and, because of this excitement, the play will be disrupted and possibly destroyed. One might say that instinctual arousal brings with it a reality that the child cannot transform and must attend to almost as if it was an external stimulus that was too intense to either discard or include in the ongoing play. In Winnicott's view, instinctual arousal makes play overly exciting, and this is done relatively easily since play is "inherently exciting and precarious" (*ibid.*).

It is only in play that an individual can be creative, and this creativity takes place in the space between inner reality and the external world. Psychotherapy (or psychoanalysis) should be performed in the space between the two playing areas. "If the patient cannot play then something needs to be done to enable the patient to become able to play . . . If the therapist cannot play, then he is not suitable for the work" (*ibid.*, p. 53). This is a strong and definitive statement by Winnicott. He maintains that it is in the intersection of the playing areas that transference, culture, and the patient seeing the analyst's creativity all take place. More importantly, it is the only way the patient can use her/his creativity and become aligned with their true self. This is the point of the treatment, to help the person in their search for the self. Interestingly, even if a person is able to produce valuable things (artwork, a business, etc.), their search may not be satisfied. It is not the product of the search, but the ability to become aligned with one's products of disintegration. In Winnicott's treatment world, the experience is one of a non-purposive state, as he says it is a sort of ticking over of the unintegrated personality. He refers to this as formlessness. He has changed the idea of free association to one of the patient being able to experience a form of "non-purposive being", which, in Balint's terms, is a form of benign (as opposed to malignant) regression. The patient must be allowed to communicate a succession of thoughts that may be "unrelated thought sequences", which indicates that the patient is relaxed and trusts the therapeutic setting. In effect, these unrelated sequences demonstrate that, during the patient's state of relaxation, they are not associating or thinking to please the analyst. This state may be thought of as a similar idea to Bion's idea of the analyst being without memory or desire. It is only during these states of relaxation that the patient can come together and feel a true sense of self and realize that "I am myself".

Winnicott notes that the most important aspect of the treatment situation is one where the therapist provides an environment of trust, where the patient's play will not be interrupted. As such, there are long periods of time where Winnicott is silent and may take notes, in part to help inhibit his tendency to interpret. He reports that he will write down interpretations rather than saying them to the patient. His "reward for withholding interpretation comes when the patient makes the interpretation herself, perhaps an hour or two later" (*ibid.*, p. 56). Here, Winnicott stresses what many contemporary analysts (e.g., Steingart, 1983, 1995) are beginning to emphasize: the importance of facilitating the patient's capacity for play and creative activity. In this conceptualization, the patient gradually becomes their own analyst in the therapeutic situation.

In many ways, *Playing and Reality* is a recapitulation of various of Winnicott's earlier papers. Obviously, transitional space and transitional objects are concepts that he has introduced in an earlier presentation and paper (1953). In addition, one can look at the capacity to play as a parallel to the capacity to be alone. The paradox of the capacity to be alone is that this capacity is dependent on the existence of a good internalized object. Here, Winnicott credits Klein with the idea that "The capacity to be alone depends on the existence in the psychic reality of the individual of a good object" (1958c, pp. 31–32). Interestingly, the capacity to be alone is dependent on what Winnicott calls ego-relatedness. Ego-relatedness is another name for what he has described: the relation of the capacity of the ego to exist alone in the presence of another. Again, this is possible if the person has internalized a good object. Here, there is an interesting twist in the further development of the capacity to be alone. He reminds us that he said that an id impulse "disrupts a weak ego and strengthens a strong one" (*ibid.*, p. 34). The capacity to receive and process endogenous stimulation is, thus, extremely important, since, if one can process this stimulation (or id impulses), it is one of the powerful situations of being alone. It is a way of recognizing in a striking way one's internal life; it is a recognition that not all stimulation comes from the outside. If one cannot process endogenous stimulation without being disrupted, then Winnicott sees the infant as, in effect, desperately dependent on the external world. It is, in effect, the path to a pathological false self. This type of conceptualization is part of the way that Winnicott blends the concept of endogenous stimulation with object relations. Ego relatedness is, thus, related to both the internalization of a good object and then, when the infant is ready, the processing of the drives (endogenous stimulation). Play, on the other hand, requires the capacity to be alone, but can be disrupted by the intensity of endogenous stimulation. Winnicott retains the concept of endogenous stimulation and blends this idea while featuring an object relations perspective.

Winnicott acknowledges in an interesting way that some of his ideas have a utopian flavour. His focus on creativity and the search for the self may not be possible for large segments of even a contemporary society. In referring to Foucault (1994, which is not the publication date that Winnicott uses, but contains the material he refers to), he hypothesizes that in a different era (perhaps 1,000 years earlier), it was rare that a person could "achieve unit status in personal development" (1971, p. 70). The historical picture that he implies is that humans were a type of herd animal and, after their childhood, lost their sense of individuality. He sees this as also stated in Freud's *Moses and Monotheism* (1939a), where Freud gives a picture of how the Jewish tribes rallied around a leader (Moses). Although Winnicott does not discuss *Moses and Monotheism* he does relate Breasted's view that Freud was the "first individual in human history". In Winnicott's view, humans need science before "men and women could become units integrated in time and space" (1971, p. 69). If Freud and science are harbingers of humans achieving unit status, then clearly this is a new step in at least Western societies. Winnicott sees Klein's contributions as crucial in the development of true creativity. Her dating destructive fantasies as occurring early in life, Winnicott says, "gives it the proper emphasis". Moreover, her idea of "the fusion of erotic and destructive impulses as a sign of health" is an important signpost of development that leads to her concepts of reparation and restitution. Winnicott, despite these kudos to Klein, still states that her "important work does not reach to the subject of creativity itself and therefore it could easily have the effect of further obscuring the main issue" (*ibid.*, p. 70). The main issue is the difference in Winnicott and Klein's versions of how the good object is internalized. Despite Winnicott's debt to Klein, there is an essential cleavage that does not, as yet, allow these two theories to converge.

Despite this cleavage, Winnicott maintains that we need Klein's work on the importance of guilt in determining the establishment of the conditions for reparation. For him, behind Klein's conceptualization, "is Freud's basic concept of ambivalence as an aspect of individual maturity" (*ibid.*). Although this is a reasonable inference from Freud's writings, it is clearly not the emphasis that Freud places on ambivalence. In one sense, Freud was more idealistic than Winnicott, in that he assumed that in "normal" development a person resolved oedipal conflicts. Ambivalence, for Freud, is a fixation point that indicates that oedipal conflicts have not been resolved. Winnicott sees the adaptive aspects of ambivalence and uses the concept as a sign that a person can tolerate two different perspectives at the same time. While this is an achievement, even within Freud's lexicon, it is not the achievement that Freud accents. Goldman puts it well in his comparison between Freud and Winnicott: he states, "Because Freud's theory provided a powerful way of exploring what makes an individual's life unbearable, it could now be extended to examine what it is that makes life feel real and worth living" (1993a, p. 140); "What Freud implies, Winnicott amplifies; what Freud mentions in passing, Winnicott elaborates" (*ibid.*, p. 151); "It is the developing person's relationship to the instinct rather than the development of the instinct within the person that most concerns Winnicott" (*ibid.*, p. 152); "Unlike Freud, Winnicott emphasized that a child can be overwhelmed not only by what a parent does, but by what a parent fails to do" (*ibid.*, p. 155); "Where Freud frequently pictured the ego as emerging from an undifferentiated id–ego matrix, Winnicott reverses the order and asserts that id experiences depend on prior ego development" (*ibid.*, p.166). These quotes from Goldman, in my view, give a good summary of Winnicott's new direction in psychoanalytic theory. It is not a rejection of Freud or Klein, but a new utilization of these theories. It is important to realize that it is not that Winnicott denies that id impulses are present at birth, but, rather, with the appropriate maternal cover, id impulses are not experienced as strong demands. It is the experience of endogenous stimulation that Winnicott emphasizes, and without appropriate maternal cover the infant experiences id impulses (endogenous stimulation) as a clap of thunder. In Winnicott's view of development, the question of priority of drives or ego is besides the point; the main issue is how drives are mediated and how the ego is supported by the mother's auxiliary ego. It is maternal timing, the content of object presenting, and the mother's ability to be utilized by the infant that are the crucial aspects of early development. It is through these early interactions that space can eventually be created for the infant to create its own environment. It is only through the creation of one's perception of the environment that one can truly "objectively perceive" the world. Therefore, the world can only be subjectively–objectively perceived. The ability to be alone to utilize transitional space is dependent on the internalization of a good object. The presence of this internal object allows one to truly be alone and yet never feel alone in the sense of being isolated. Winnicott's seemingly paradoxical statements are only seen in this light if one stays on the surface of human experience. The paradoxes are resolved when one follows Winnicott's path from early experience through the transition to helping to create a perceptual world and helping to create a world that facilitates their own and others' creative expression.

As a final point, we have not frequently mentioned Winnicott's views about Oedipal development, since this was not a major feature of his theorizing. We can end this chapter by saying that Winnicott sees masturbatory activity during the primal scene (real or fantasized) as an expression of the child's individuality. Thus, the Oedipal situation is an important piece of reinforcing the child's ability to be alone while, at the same time, allowing others to have aims that are different from the child's wishes. When the child can excite itself, it can stand apart from the primal couple. Here, again, Winnicott emphasizes the child's ability to make life bearable and exciting while containing its wishes to destroy the other. Some may criticize Winnicott for not presenting a full theory, but it would seem hard to deny that Winnicott makes Freudian and Kleinian theory much fuller and more real.

Commentary

Emanuel Berman (1996), an outstanding Israeli analyst, noted that when I was a psychoanalytic candidate in New York City, I attended a lecture by Winnicott, and during this lecture Winnicott was cruelly treated by the three discussants. While I did attend this lecture, I was not at that time a candidate at the institute (although I later became one) that sponsored the lecture. I did hear Winnicott say that he could understand why America was (at war) in Vietnam. He, of course, was referring to the aggression that was directed at him by American analysts (both the discussants and in the audience). Clearly, Winnicott upset members of an Institute that was (and is) largely a classical psychoanalytic institute. Winnicott spoke in metaphorical terms as opposed to the idea of mechanisms, and he was, from this perspective, imprecise. Berman wrote that a previous publication of mine (1991) was strongly influenced by Winnicott. While this probably is true, it was not my conscious intention to include Winnicott in a prominent position in that volume. However, I think I was simply part of the *zeitgeist* of the time, and did not fully recognize Winnicott's influence. In my view, and the view of many others, Winnicott has been one of the most important analysts in the past thirty years. His work has been claimed by various theoretical orientations, and there are several versions of Winnicott that one can turn to. In the present version, Winnicott stands alone, but can be blended with other theorists. This blend is not Winnicott's, it is another's attempt to create an object in their own transitional space. Although I will try to point out theoretical similarities and convergences, it is not my view that this was Winnicott's intention, but, rather, an attempt that is my own.

Commentary: Winnicott and Freud

The authors whom Winnicott most frequently cited were Freud and Klein. Winnicott was able to reach deeply into the Freudian opus and utilize what he needed for this own theoretical contributions. Greenberg and Mitchell write that "Winnicott preserves (Freudian) tradition in a curious fashion, largely by distorting it" (1983, p. 193). In my view, they make this statement to create a dichotomy between a drive/structural and relational model. Rodman, a biographer of Winnicott, maintains that Freud's theory

> gave rise to two branches, one with an emphasis on the dark and demonic "unreal" elements, the other taking into account the influence of other people, beginning with the mother and progressing to the analyst . . . Winnicott, known generally as a member who is part of the second group, in fact combines the two. . . . He represents the reinstatement of the balance between the real and unreal, much as Freud himself had maintained throughout his career. [2003, p. 130]

Rodman's detailed and illuminating biography demonstrates the real influence of Freud on Winnicott, as well as Winnicott's contributions that extended, amplified, and greatly personalized Freudian thought and psychoanalysis in general.

In the present interpretation, Winnicott's writings help to make sense of what I have called Freud's object relations era (see Chapter Three). Winnicott is one of the writers who has seen and deeply mined the implications of this era of Freud's writings. In my view, there are many points of convergence between these two conceptualizations of early development.

Although Winnicott maintained that he had not read enough Freud, he frequently displayed brilliant insights into either what Freud really meant or what could be created out of Freudian theory. It depends on your transference to Winnicott and Freud as to which interpretation you prefer. I will first compare Freud and Winnicott's views on early development, and then move to their ideas about the treatment situation. To begin, I will posit that Winnicott's concept of absolute dependence is compatible with Freud's idea of autoerotism. In Freud's conceptualization (see Chapter Three), the infant first is concerned with pleasure and assumes that pleasurable events or the removable of unpleasurable stimuli occurs as a result of its actions. To the adult, the infant's actions are signals that the infant's environment (or mother) usually responds to in an appropriate, timely, and satisfying manner. Freud posits that the infant's reality ego during autoerotism is based on the idea that its activities bring pleasure or the removal of unpleasure. As Winnicott pointed out, Freud, in a long footnote (1911b), talked about how this fiction would not be possible unless one assumed that the mother and infant formed a type of system, or unit. There was a similar footnote of Freud's in a later publication (1915c); however, Freud was usually talking about the infant and his theory was concerned with the infant's internal world. He rarely mentioned infant–mother interactions. That he alluded to the mother is not surprising, since Freud obviously knew the basic facts of child development. However, what Freud describes in a footnote is Winnicott's preoccupation for his entire career. Freud's interest was in trying to describe the infant's internal world, not in describing mother–infant interactions.

There are several misunderstandings of Freud's conceptualizations of early development (Stern, 1985). Freud, in describing autoerotism, does not state that the infant is without objects, but that during this stage the infant does not form a libidinal attachment or cathexis. Winnicott makes the same point in a manner that is more alive and less subject to misunderstandings. Winnicott says that the mother forms a unit with the infant, and that the mother places her breast in a position so that, at first, the infant is allowed by its mother to have the illusion that the breast is part of the infant's world. Thus, in Freud's terms, the infant does not libidinally cathect an external object, but, rather, the mother presents her breast and the infant assumes the breast is there whenever it needs or wants the breast. In Winnicott's good enough mothering, the infant can call the breast whenever it wants, and this is what Winnicott calls natural omnipotence. We can say, for the purposes of this comparison, that Winnicott provides an explanation for Freud's view that the infant does not form a libidinal attachment during absolute dependence (or, in Freud's terms, autoerotism). In Winnicott's understanding, if there is a strong libidinal attachment, this most probably is a major impingement for the infant. Thus, for the infant to be well attached to its mother, it interacts with her, but object presenting and the mother's ability to allow herself to be utilized is crucial during absolute dependence (or autoerotism). In Edith Jacobson's theory of early development, the infant's main concern during the first month is the establishment of the psychophysiological self (Jacobson, 1954a).

Greenberg and Mitchell state that Winnicott is "proposing an *alternative* to Freud's approach. He is offering a framework for understanding psychopathology which, firmly rooted in the relational model, is at odds with classical formulations based on drive and defense" (1983, p. 209, original italics). They strongly imply that Winnicott tries to hide the fact that he is no longer an adherent of Freudian positions. One can only make this statement if one ignores a large component of both Freud's and Winnicott's writings. While there is no question that Winnicott changes the direction of Freudian thought, there is also no question that he uses Freud's conceptualizations to create his theory. Since the term "relational model" is one that has several different meanings, I will only say at this point that Winnicott shows how the object relations aspect of Freudian thought can come alive. In addition, we can see how Winnicott's concepts can form a complementary component of a mature Freudian theory. Before we venture into the therapeutic aspect of Winnicott's theory, let us go further into the comparison of Freud and Winnicott's ideas about early development. Freud posits that there is a point at which the infant divides the world and self-organization in terms of pleasure and unpleasure. At this point, the purified pleasure ego indicates the beginning of the phase of narcissism. There is a libidinal cathexis of the object, and the object is seen as part of the self. The mother of unpleasure, who has deserted the infant (from the infant's new perspective), is seen as a bad object separated from the good, pleasure-giving mother. Thus, through splitting, the mother is seen in two distinct representations. This occurs because the mother has gradually (in optimal development) allowed the infant more and more frustration, which the developing infant can now tolerate. The withdrawal of the mother's preoccupation with the infant's needs is a crucial aspect of Freud's conceptualization of the purified pleasure ego. Winnicott, during the phase of relative dependence, also sees the maternal image as split. His view is that there is an object mother and an environmental mother. Winnicott makes a similar point to Freud, using the grammar that is unique to his theory: he states that the mother's primary maternal preoccupation has diminished and she has begun to resume her self interests. The object mother is the object of the instincts; this mother is the object, or owner of the part-object, that may satisfy the infant's urgent needs. The environment mother is the source of total management and is the mother who is part of the infant's total environment. The object mother is used ruthlessly and aggressively and has to experience the full force of the infant's "ruthless" instinctual attacks. The environmental mother, although the manager of the total environment, is present in many more quiet moments, where the infant/child is not dominated by "crude instinct-tension" (1963a, p. 76). Winnicott describes the fantasy of "full-blooded id-drives as containing attack and destruction" (*ibid.*, p. 76). The baby wants to devour the object and take possession of the contents of the object. Here, he pictures the object mother as experiencing a Kleinian type attack.

The first obvious similarity between these two conceptualizations is the fact that the maternal representations are split because of diminished maternal care. As a second point, both authors see the infant's increasing ability to tolerate frustration as an important marker for the mother's naturally diminished involvement. Obviously, most mothers are still extremely involved with the infant's care, but not in the same systematic (Winnicott does not like the term symbiotic) manner. Freud, at this point in his theorizing (1908–1915), does not have an emphasized view of aggression. Interestingly, Winnicott is much clearer in his view of the importance of ruthless aggression. Freud's ideas are directed towards the nature of libidinal investments as development progresses. If aggression is present in Freud's concepts, it is towards the objects that represent frustration and unpleasure. In both Freud's and Winnicott's conceptualizations, it is a developmental task to integrate these split maternal images. Clearly, Winnicott's version is influenced by Klein, and he sees the appearance of guilt as this split begins to be unified in a single maternal representation. His view of early development is far more elaborate than Freud's sketchy outline of a theory. Interestingly, Winnicott is not only more specific about the role of aggressive attacks, he is also more specific about the role of drive, or the instincts. Before we address this point, let us remember why Freud is featuring early development in his theorizing.

He is looking at the development of object love and what he terms the vicissitudes of loving. At first, the infant loves what is pleasurable and is indifferent to the external world. During the purified pleasure ego, the infant loves what is pleasure and part of itself and hates the external world. It is wary of, and distrusts, strangers, since they are part of the external world. Gradually (relatively quickly), as the infant/toddler's intellectual capacity develops, the infant integrates its maternal representations. The infant/toddler then, during the remainder of narcissism, sees the mother as liking what it likes and wanting what it wants. The toddler stills dislikes those things that inhibit or prevent it from doing what it desires. All of these developments, in Freud's theory, are before the point of object choice (anal sadism) and could be stated without the concept of the instincts. Autoerotism and narcissism can be stated purely in terms of pleasure, and Freud's object relations theory can be stated in terms of pleasure and the infant/toddler's relation to its mother or its parental environment. It is true that Freud assumes that, during autoerotism, the instinct for survival of the self is dominant, and that during narcissism the sexual instinct becomes active and there is then a libidinal investment. Logically, however, Freud could have stated these stages of development without mentioning these instincts. Winnicott, on the other hand, specifically talks about the implications of the instincts or endogenous stimulation on the infant's development.

Winnicott's version includes endogenous stimulation as an important aspect of the infant developing its own sense of interiority. Interiority is a term that I am using to describe Winnicott's idea that endogenous stimulation allows the infant to have an experience of its own that is not dependent on the external world. Although instincts are always present, it is the presence of maternal preoccupation that does not allow the infant to be preoccupied with the instincts during absolute dependence. In Winnicott's concept of absolute dependence, the infant should not be preoccupied with either external or internal (endogenous) sources of stimulation. Preoccupation with either is an impingement in his theoretical formulation. Winnicott assumes that it is the mother's sensitivity that allows oral pleasures to be present without the infant experiencing orality as a distinct instinctual experience. The infant assumes, at the beginning of life, that oral pleasures are a part of the self. Thus, if we take Freud's ideas about zones and combine these concepts with Winnicott's theory of maternal preoccupation, we have a more complete picture of infant development. Orality is a means of pleasure, but also the mode of communication in the mother–infant pair. The pleasure should not be independent of the interaction with the mother, but, if the interaction is not pleasurable, it will lead to impingements. Thus, for Winnicott, the object and pleasure are intimately intertwined. One could say that this is true for Freud as well, since the object is an important part of the instinct in his conceptualization. It remains for Winnicott, however, to talk about how the infant can endure and develop during absolute dependence and begin to internalize maternal images.

Freud has put forth a theory of narcissism where he portrays the child as loving those things that are like itself. The child's mother is seen as needing to reflect the child's wishes and only gradually to restrict and redirect the child. Although Freud mentions the concept of sublimation, where the child transforms narcissistic activities into more creative actions, he does not talk about the conditions that would truly facilitate sublimation. Winnicott's ideas about transitional phenomena during and after the period of relative dependence speak clearly to the issue of sublimation. Winnicott is concerned with the creative potential of human beings and how the child gradually is able to take in reality without reality impinging on the child's sense of self. For Winnicott, reality has to be discovered subjectively; for Freud, reality is there to be discovered objectively. If the drives can be tamed, then the person can perceive reality, in Freud's rendition of the development of reality testing. For Winnicott, if reality is impressed on the child, then the child's false self will be utilized in a defensive manner. In a similar way, if the drives are not "covered" by the mother, the infant will have to defensively struggle to deal with endogenous events that it is not prepared to handle. Once the child is able to form transitional space, there may still be narcissistic perceptions, but they will be perceptions that, optimally, are actively formed by the child. Thus, transitional space is neither a relational nor drive concept, but a concept that speaks to the formation of illusion and how illusion, when under control, allows a person to be comfortable with reality. Even in the concept of transitional phenomena, Winnicott states that there is an optimal use of illusion; if illusion is created solely out of subjective elements then the person runs the risk of psychosis or borderline conditions. If transitional space is tilted towards the environment, then there is a danger of illusion being destroyed and the environment experienced as an impingement. One can say that there is nothing incompatible with the idea of transitional space and the concepts of Freudian stages. However, Freud's view of reality testing is quite different from Winnicott's. Freud assumed that reality was out there in the environment, waiting to be discovered; Winnicott conceives of the optimal processing of reality as a subjective–objective discovery process. Winnicott's theorizing is more detailed, consistent, and in line with current developmental theories and research. To avoid being totally anachronistic, one must remember that Freud's main concerns were how conflicts affected and limited cognitive functioning, not how reality was optimally processed.

If we look at this brief comparison, we can construct a developmental model that combines the complimentary views of Winnicott and Freud. During the earliest phase of development, the most important factor is for the infant to feel that its needs are being met in a timely manner. Good enough mothering anticipates the infant's needs and presents to the infant nourishments (or relief) that is approximately what the infant wants. The infant, for a while, assumes that its needs will be met either slightly before or shortly after it signals its mother. The infant can perceive reality in terms of its interaction with the environment, but an intense libidinal cathexis does not occur during this period of development. The infant and mother form a system that allows the infant to experience the world without the drives or the environment intruding as distinct entities. Thus, the infant loves its pleasures or experiences with its mother, and is indifferent to the rest of the environment. Given these statements, one must realize that we are stating development in dichotomous terms when, in reality, it must be more accurately reflected as continuous experiences (or variables). It seems unlikely that there is no libidinal investment or that there is no interest in the environment. Rather, this is not the major vector during this phase of development. Freud's, and even Winnicott's, tendency to occasionally state things in universal terms may lead to an exaggerated view of the infant's experience. It seems unlikely that a perceiving organism such as a human infant would be totally indifferent to the environment. The assumption that the mother's ego protects the infant can be assumed without the idea that this protection is absolute. Good enough protection still may allow the infant to be interested in other parts of its environment. It may also mean that, while the mother is seen as part of its world, there may be the beginnings of what Freud called a libidinal investment or cathexis. Thus, while the infant may not distinctly cathect the mother, the conditions for a strong cathexis should be formed during absolute dependence.

It is more difficult to compare Freud and Winnicott's next stage of development. We have already stated some two of the similarities. Both analysts see the next phase of development occurring as a result of optimal frustration (or gratification), and both see the image of the mother as split during this stage of development. Freud's emphasis is on the infant's holding on to the representation of the mother as continuing to provide pleasure in the same way that occurred in the earlier phase. In this way, the infant refuses to accept the change in mothering that has taken place in normal development. When pleasure does not occur in the way that it had previously happened, this is a result of the hated mother, not the pleasure-giving mother. Thus, frustration is seen as coming from the environment, and the frustrating mother is part of this hated environment. Winnicott's emphasis is on the ruthless instinctual use of the object mother as opposed to the overall management and quiet interactions with the environment mother. For Winnicott, Freud's purified pleasure ego is a result of fantasizing rather than fantasy. For both authors, it is a task to synthesize the different maternal images, but here Freud has a more gradual period of development than is true of Winnicott.

Freud sees the maternal representations as coming together as a result of cognitive development, but the mother is still seen as being an affective part of the toddler/child until object choice occurs. Thus, the child sees the mother in terms of its own desires during the phase of narcissism. One might say that, while this is not a cognitive split, it remains an affective split until the end of narcissism. For Winnicott, the split is repaired more in the mode that Klein describes in her conceptualization of the depressive position. There is guilt and repair, and this now occurs in transitional space. If we jump to the Oedipal stage, we have described Winnicott's view of this stage, and here, again, one can say that Winnicott's description is the mirror image of Freud's. Where Freud emphasizes the threat of the Oedipus complex, Winnicott emphasizes the acceptance of the primal couple and the capacity to be alone during masturbatory episodes. Here, one might say that both Freud and Winnicott are talking about the Oedipal child, Winnicott with the optimal parenting, and Freud where the Oedipal threat is more tangible in the child's environment. While this is one way of combining the two positions, this amalgamation does not fully do justice to the differences between the authors. Freud clearly emphasizes the threatening nature of the Oedipal situation even in optimal development, whereas this is somewhat absent in this aspect of Winnicott's writings. While this is a distinct difference. it is still the case that Freud maintains that for a child to pass through any stage successfully, without a significant fixation, libidinal factors must predominate over aggressive tendencies in the child's representational world. Just as the child chooses the mother's love over pleasures in the stage of object choice (see Chapter Three), the Oedipal child's libidinal attachment to both parents is optimally stronger than its aggressive, envious, Oedipal wishes. Thus, while Freud's emphasis is on the threat during the Oedipal stage, one might say that Winnicott's description is appropriate in a child who can tolerate being separate from the parental (primal) couple.

The comparison of Freud and Winnicott is valid only if one recognizes that Freud's later drive theory (Eros and Thanatos) is not being considered in this comparison. Winnicott rejects the idea of the death instinct, and it is the rejection of this concept that separates Winnicott from Freud (Chapter 4) and Klein. It is Klein who utilizes the death instinct in an even more complete manner than Freud. In her theorizing, she shows the logical, clinical, and developmental implications of the concept of Thanatos. Although Winnicott rejects this concept, his use of the depressive position and his ideas about the ruthless use of the object are derivatives of Kleinian thought. While Winnicott departs from a Kleinian position, his use of Kleinian concepts helps him to fashion his theoretical description of the infant's/child's movement towards creativity and self-cohesion. Despite the fact that Winnicott talks about the ruthless use of the object early in development, it is hard to see how he conceptualizes aggression throughout the developmental cycle. Rodman states that aggression is of crucial importance to Winnicott, but it is not clear how he uses this concept in his ideas of development. As importantly, it is not clear how Winnicott sees aggression (or destructive impulses) as an important aspect of the psychoanalytic situation.

Freud, Winnicott, and a brief note about the analytic situation

Winnicott's ideas about treatment clearly talk about the importance of the relationship in the treatment situation. Freud cites the importance of analytic tact, particularly, before the analyst is able to usefully interpret unconscious fantasy. Interestingly, he also said that, ultimately, psychoanalysis was a treatment of love. What he fully meant by this comment is subject to interpretation. Is it a treatment of love because the patient gradually comes to love the analyst in the transference? Or is it a treatment of love where both analyst and analysand develop a reciprocal love relationship? Freud, in his paper "Observations on transference-love" (1915a), warns the analyst that he may be seduced by the patient's love. Freud states that this is the love of transference, and should be understood as not involving the analyst in reality, but in the transference. In the same paper, he wonders about the nature of love and asks whether all love can be understood in terms of transference love. Freud never fully answers the questions that he poses; rather, most Freudian analysts have interpreted his position to indicate that it is the analysand who provides the love in the analytic situation. It is the analysand's conflicts about love that have produced her/his neurosis. The analyst, in this formulation, receives the love and helps the patient understand her/his unconscious fantasies that are central to their conflicts and are interfering with their capacity to love.

Freud's paper "Observations on transference-love" was not only an exploration of love in the analytic situation, it was also a warning to analysts about enacting (putting into action) feelings of love in the analytic situation. Jung had just had an affair with Spelrich, and, according to Reich (Eissler, 1985), a number of analysts were sexually involved with their patients. Freud was warning analysts literally to be abstinent in the analytic situation. Winnicott is writing 5–30 years after Freud's death, and thirty years after the paper on transference love. It is my assumption that the sexual dangers of analysis had somewhat subsided during this interval (although, after reading Hopkins's biography of Masud Khan [2006], I might want to reconsider that assumption). In any case, the dangers seem to have subsided for Winnicott, since his ideas about holding and some of his practices put him in close contact psychologically and physically with patients whom he felt needed this type of contact.

Holding is a central concept for Winnicott, both in terms of his ideas about development and psychoanalytic treatment. He frequently states that in cases that are not well suited for standard analysis, the reliability of the analyst is more important than the analyst's interpretative abilities. Here, clearly, Winnicott is talking about more than the actual reliability of the analyst, but, rather, the analyst's capacity to provide a stable, safe environment despite the patient's tendencies to destroy such an environment. Winnicott frequently provided more than this for his patients, and there are several accounts of his providing physical contact for them. It is my view that Winnicott's prime motive was to provide a type of holding and allow the patient to use him in a way that they had not been able to use others. Winnicott's association with Masud Khan, a man more troubled and destructive than had been recognized during Winnicott's lifetime, has to some extent sullied Winnicott's reputation (Hopkins, 2006). I believe that Khan's devotion to Winnicott was, in part, due to his wish to gather some of Winnicott's goodness to himself. This, I admit, is a primitive interpretation, but mine nevertheless. This interpretation was put forth before I read Hopkins's biography of Khan. It is hard to reconcile Winnicott's views on treatment with his treatment of Khan. In this analysis, he uses Khan in a manner that, in my mind, is unethical. I find it difficult to say this about an analyst that I admire, but I believe that this has to be stated. Nevertheless, I greatly value Winnicott's contributions and still believe that he was mostly a sincere, caring, and brilliant analyst.

Winnicott's views on holding can be contrasted with his views on destructiveness. He sees the object as being destroyed once it is seen to be outside the infant's (or patient's) omnipotent control. From Winnicott's point of view, this must occur in analysis and in development, lest the infant or patient only commune with internal voices or objects. Thus, for Winnicott, once the object is seen as outside the patient's control, the object must be destroyed in fantasy. The survival of this destruction is, for him, the crucial aspect of an analysis. It is only when the analytic pair can survive this destructive movement that the patient can truly use the other person or object. This conceptualization, then, can be formulated that holding must occur, and then the patient has to feel the analyst in their omnipotent control. This may last for a long period of time, but, at some point when the analyst is beyond this control, the patient experiences him/herself as destroying the analyst and the analytic relationship. It is the survival of this ruthless fantasy that allows for the analytic pair to continue and for new object usage to occur. Winnicott's concentration on the patient in this formulation has its parallel in Winnicott's wondering at some points in his career whether or not he could survive these ruthless attacks. He did for a long time, although many wish he could have survived for a bit longer.

CHAPTER ELEVEN

Sullivan: interpersonal psychoanalysis, relational beginnings

Summary

Harry Stack Sullivan is truly an American original and, although this chapter does not do justice to his enormous influence, I hope the reader can glimpse some of his originality and authenticity. His career is traced from his beginnings in Chicago as a medical resident to his mature years, where he pioneered both a theoretical perspective and treatment modalities for psychotic patients. He, along with Fairbairn and Ferenczi, was perhaps the strongest historical influence in forging relational theory.

Brief personal note

I first encountered Harry Stack Sullivan (1892–1949) in graduate school, since he was a featured author for a segment of the faculty in our clinical psychology programme (NYU Clinical). Sullivan was a major influence for the Director of our programme, Bernie Kalinkowitz. Bernie's version of a Sullivan quote was that schizophrenic patients (people) were more human than otherwise. It was a quote that was oft repeated. Although I read a bit of Sullivan in graduate school, it was not until I began to treat schizophrenic patients that I became interested in Sullivan, partly through the influence of Harold Searles (1965). My interest in schizophrenia has continued to this day. Early in my career, the first course I taught when I was a faculty member at the clinical programme at City University was "Theories of schizophrenia". Sullivan was an author that I featured. This course contained Sullivan, Searles, and Fromm-Reichmann, as well as Freud, Hartmann, and Anna Freud. Winnicott, Kohut, and Guntrip were also authors who were part of this course syllabus. When I started psychoanalytic training at a Freudian institute, Sullivan's presence in my courses became greatly attenuated and eventually disappeared entirely. I have finally returned to a state of *naïveté*, where I believe that each position has a great deal to offer and can provide complimentary viewpoints and, at times, integratable perspectives.

Sullivan, in my era of graduate training, was in part known for his treatment of schizophrenic patients and his directorship of Sheppard and Enoch Pratt Hospital in Maryland. Sullivan was a leading member of a group of psychoanalysts that included Erich Fromm, Frieda Fromm-Reichmann, Clara Thompson, and later, after Sullivan's death, Harold Searles. (Greenberg and Mitchell [1983] also include Karen Horney in this group.) Fromm-Reichmann's patient, Joanne Greenberg, wrote a fictionalized autobiography of her time at Chestnut Lodge, entitled *I Never Promised You a Rose Garden* (1964), which was a best seller. Searles (1965, 1986), during the late 1960s and 1970s, was a noted clinician whose papers on the treatment of schizophrenic and, later, borderline patients were inspirational to many psychiatry residents and psychology interns during this period. The approach put forth by Fromm-Reichmann and Searles might seem foreign, or even quaint, to a contemporary reader, since they, through the influence of Sullivan, offered psychological treatment to schizophrenic patients. Today, the treatment of patients who are diagnosed as schizophrenic is dominated by psycho–pharmacological interventions. The treatment that Sullivan, Fromm-Reichmann, and Searles offered occurred in a therapeutic community, and this type of community arrangement is one that was pioneered by Sullivan and his colleagues. In addition to the therapeutic community, there was also intense individual psychotherapeutic treatment that occurred. It is still my view that this treatment approach has a great deal to offer.

Intellectual beginnings and assumptions

Sullivan was trained as a physician and received his MD in 1919. He was in Chicago at a time when Pierce, Sapir, and Mead, among others, were leading intellectual lights in Chicago and in the USA generally. It is hard to overestimate the influence of the philosophy of pragmatism on Sullivan. Pragmatism was an American answer to speculative European philosophy. It was straightforward (Dewey, not Pierce) and empirical in a non-dogmatic manner. Pragmatism did not have the arrogant fervour that was true of the logical positivist movement. Positivism was begun in Vienna and strongly supported and broadened in the UK. Interestingly, Sullivan saw himself as employing the philosophic principle of operationalism that was a rallying cry of the positivists and a term coined by Percy Bridgeman (1927), a physicist. It is unclear to me the extent to which Sullivan understood the philosophic and theoretical implications of operationalism, but the use of the principle attempted to ban all terms that were in themselves potentially unobservable. From Carnap and Ayer's point of view, this would certainly include a term like the unconscious. Although Bridgeman is credited with the term operationalism, the full philosophic implications of the term was to be spelled out by the Vienna Circle (Carnap, 1952) and the British positivists (Ayer, 1956, 1972). Although certainly Sullivan was closer to the positivist ideal than Freud, he was still a far cry from their stringent criteria.

If we were to find a philosopher who is closer to Sullivan's style, it might be G. E. Moore (1905), whose focus was on doing away with pretentious academic language and substituting, where possible, everyday language that communicated more directly, with less surplus meaning. Sullivan was continuously suspicious of psychiatric and psychoanalytic language. His strong sense was that a good deal of these languages obscured, rather than communicated, important messages. Sullivan could be considered part of the *zeitgeist* of his time that focused on communicating as directly as possible while realizing and appreciating the limitations of linguistic expression. He emphasized relying on "data" that are clearly observable, and he maintained that "a useful theory . . . is one whose terms are clearly understood and whose data consist of that which is publicly available" (Greenberg & Mitchell, 1983, p. 88). Greenberg and Mitchell maintain that this does not make Sullivan a behaviourist, since he includes the patient's verbal report of subjective experiences as well as wishes, fantasies . . . "as long as they can be expressed in language or conveyed nonverbally" (*ibid.*). Here, of course, Freud's meaning of the term "wish" is decisively changed, since a wish, for Freud, is frequently considered to be unconscious and only indirectly observable. Sullivan is very concerned about not overly interpreting what an observer deems to be behaviour that is motivated by unconscious processes. Freud's concept of the unconscious quite clearly refers to events that cannot be experienced directly, and, in Freud's view, unconscious ideation fills many of the gaps present in conscious mental life. This view of the unconscious allowed Freud and Freudian analysts to interpret aspects of patient's behaviour and their conscious mental life. Sullivan tells us,

> The unconscious, from the way I have actually presented the thing, is quite clearly that which cannot be experienced directly, which fills all the gaps in mental life. In that rather broad sense, the postulate of the unconscious has, so far as I know, nothing in the world the matter with it. As soon as you begin to arrange the furniture in something that cannot be directly experienced, you are engaged in a work that requires more than parlor magic and you are apt to be embarrassed by some skeptic. [1950, p. 204]

Clearly, in at least one sense, Sullivan is wrong, since there are few Freudian analysts that report embarrassment as a result of "arranging the furniture". However, Sullivan undoubtedly felt that these analysts should have experienced embarrassment. Although he allows for the idea of the unconscious, he sees little place for this concept in therapeutic interactions. Interpretations that are based on assumptions of unconscious motivation seem to be either futile exercises or, worse, therapeutically foolish. If this is a good representation of Sullivan's perspective, then Greenberg and Mitchell's defence of him as not a behaviourist is somewhat misleading. They tell us that Sullivan "is arguing that we can only meaningfully study what we can observe, and that we can only observe what we can see and hear" (Greenberg & Mitchell, 1983, p. 88). The idea that we can only meaningfully study what we can see and hear is almost an irrelevant point, since we can interpret what we can see and hear in many ways. Parenthetically, I am sure that Greenberg and Mitchell would include feeling states in terms of an experiential array, but it is interesting that in explaining Sullivan's observational stance, they left out feelings and included only seeing and hearing. A good deal of what some clinicians observe are feeling states that are neither seen nor heard, but sometimes, suddenly and for a period of time, are ineffably present. Some analysts (Bach, 2006; Ogden, 1982; Racker, 1968) maintain that these feeling states are the important experiences for the analyst to contemplate.

The main point, then, is how we restrict ourselves to what we see and hear, not whether we do. I would state that only a strict behaviourist can truly limit themselves to what they see and hear. For most others, what they see and hear is interpreted through feeling states and through the lens of their theories, both personal and professional. (Sandler and Sandler [1994] have distinguished three types of theories, personal [conscious], professional, and unconscious, and they maintain that all three theories guide analysts' and therapists' interactions.) In this critique, I am responding to the strong form of Sullivan's statement and, in the strong form of his stated position, he is clearly a behaviourist. In the weak form, he presents a cautionary note that says to therapists, before you interpret beyond what you have directly experienced, think hard about it since you are going into waters that are not well charted. In my idiosyncratic reading of Sullivan, he meant both things: in one sense he was, or wanted to be, a strict behaviourist, and in another, paradoxical sense, he had an uncanny sense of feeling states and unconscious fantasy. To be sure, I do not think that he would have labelled what I am mentioning as unconscious fantasy. In my view, he had a natural feeling for unconscious fantasy and regarded it as part of the patient's experience. He could also express things in an experience-near manner, so that the patient could more readily consider what Sullivan was proposing. A focus of his was, importantly, on the patient's self-esteem, and he was one of the revolutionary clinicians who saw schizophrenia as "constituting a disaster to (one's) self esteem" (Greenberg & Mitchell, 1983, p. 85). From his clinical experience with severely disturbed patients, he concluded that the most important factor in a treatment situation is the personal relationship between therapist and patient.

Sullivan as the quintessential respectful clinician

Interestingly, for a period of time, Sullivan was a defender of Freudian thought. This was the case probably because Freud was one of the few theorists that attempted to make sense of what other theorists might call word salads, or unintelligible verbiage. Freud was an ally in that he assumed there is meaning in symptoms, jokes, slips of the tongue, etc., which others might have thought of as meaningless. Similarly, Sullivan did not consider patients' verbiage as meaningless, but as some form of important communication. When Sullivan did begin to criticize Freudian thought, it was both about the assumptions involved in Freud's theory of the unconscious and, as importantly, that he thought that Freudians under-emphasized social and cultural factors in the development of individuals and communities.

Sullivan was, in the finest sense, an individual who spoke out and spoke up about a variety of issues. His individuality is mirrored in his respect for the individuality of all people, and particularly of patients that he saw in treatment. He, like Winnicott, saw the limitations of his knowledge, and was wary of clinicians who seemed too sure of themselves with patients. He stated that no one can "fully understand another", and, as such, one is fortunate even in understanding oneself. Sullivan strongly suggested that psychiatrists should seek treatment. He was wary of the untreated psychiatrist. He saw the newly analysed and the unanalysed as not the best candidates to see the more severely disturbed patients. He was suspicious of the zealot as well as the psychiatrist who was unaware of their own difficulties or tendencies.

Sullivan's theoretical concepts

The title of interpersonalist is not a misnomer for Sullivan, since he thought that "A personality can never be isolated from the complex of interpersonal relations in which the person lives and has his being" (1940, p. 10). It seems to me that Greenberg and Mitchell highlight this statement by remarking that it "contains important epistemological, metaphysical and methodological implications" (1983, p. 90). They conclude that the analyst is, in effect, a data gatherer and is best thought of as a participant observer. Participant observer, a key Sullivanian concept, is very much in keeping with the famous physicist Heisenberg's (1979) ideas that stipulate that the experimenter effects the experiment, and the experimenter's presence must be taken into account when explaining experimental results. If this is true in experiments in the physical sciences, it must be even more relevant in the social sciences, and particularly in psychoanalysis.

In Sullivan's ideas about energy, we are reminded to some extent of Fairbairn's criticism of Freudian theory. Sullivan, however, is more extreme, and maintains "that the ultimate reality in the universe is energy" (1953, p. 102). It is interesting that Sullivan can present suppositions about the ultimate reality of the universe, but the unconscious is somehow too speculative a concept. On the basis of this assumption, he argues that structures like the ego, superego, mental representations, etc., are mythical, "there are no structures only patterns of energy transformations" (*ibid.*, p. 91). Personality, then, can be conceived of as patterns of energy and not concrete entities, but, rather, processes and patterns in interaction with other persons. If we liken psychoanalysis to modern physics, Sullivan sees himself as a field theorist (like Einstein), whereas Freudian thought is seen as Newtonian in origin. Here, again, this is similar to Fairbairn's critique of Freudian thought. Gill (1983) has seen Sullivan as a precursor to Bowlby (1969, 1973, 1980), although there was a good deal of temporal overlap in their careers. In this view, Sullivan sees the prime human motivation as involving contact with others. Here, Bowlby, Fairbairn, and Sullivan all coalesce in their view of the importance of human contact as the prime mover in human motivation.

Interestingly, Sullivan's views on tenderness have some similarity to Klein's views on projective identification. At least in the early moments of life, Sullivan sees the infant's need for nourishment as calling out to the mother in terms of a complementary need to nurse. Sullivan sees this type of complementary affect as being aroused when needs arise. These needs operate as tendencies towards integration and occur in what Sullivan labels zones of interaction. The oral zone is an early zone of interaction and experience. These zones are crucial in bringing about "durable change", and there are, of course, different meanings, depending on the zone of interaction or zone where the activity is experienced. The zone of interaction acts as not only a filter of experience, but as the "end station in the necessary varieties of communal existence" (Sullivan, 1953, p. 64). Although there are a number of primary zones in the infant (oral, retinal, auditory, tactile and vestibular, kinaesthetic, genital, and anal), these zones can be modified by the educator (an interesting way of talking about the central and peripheral nervous system in human interaction). Sullivan cites Helen Keller as someone whose zones had suffered destruction, but says that she found alternative means of interaction through the educator.

Sullivan specifies periods of development where needs states can be differentiated. Throughout development, there is a need for tenderness and contact with other humans. Infants have a strong need for personal intimacy, tenderness, and for "protective care delicately adjusted to immediate situations" (*ibid.*, p. 290). The need for tenderness and protective care continues into childhood, but "in childhood (1–4) a need for adult participation is added—that is, a need for the interest and participation of significant adults in the child's play" (*ibid.*, p. 291). The juvenile era, which extends into the secondary school years, is marked by a need for an intimate relation with another person of comparable status (4–8). Here, we see the child dealing with other children in co-operative and competitive situations. The end of this era ushers in the era that Sullivan calls preadolescence. Here, Sullivan uses one of his more famous terms: the need for chumship or the need for a chum, a pal who is a member of the same sex. Then adolescence rears its ominous head (one view of adolescence), which, in this culture (it varies, however, from culture to culture), continues until one has patterned some type of performance which satisfies one's lust, one's genital drives. During late adolescence there is further personality development leading to adulthood. During each of the stages there are new forms of relating, all to prevent the "most painful of all human experiences" (Greenberg & Mitchell, 1983, p. 93), loneliness.

Understandably, it is not only the child's needs that are reciprocally experienced but also the mother's anxiety. Anxiety is communicated by an interesting type of empathy where the infant is linked and vulnerable to the "mother's" anxiety states. Whatever the caregiver's intentions, if they are anxious the anxiety is communicated and a reciprocal feedback system is set up with the infant returning the anxiety to the care-giver. This returned anxiety will increase the care-giver's anxiety and this leads to what has been described as "cataclysmic snowballing of distress" (ibid., p. 94). Sullivan's concept of the infant's first true discrimination is the experience of non-anxious states and discriminating these states from anxious states. Good and bad are virtually synonymous with the presence or absence of anxiety. Greenberg and Mitchell translate good and bad states into the idea of good and bad mother, and gradually these states are teased apart and the person is seen somewhat separately. Sullivan sees the character of the child's parents as clearly being the influence that determines the child's personality. To quote, "The infant in Sullivan's system has no psychological existence prior to his or her embeddedness in interactions with the caretakers and discovers him- or herself as well as the 'object' through a complex developmental process" (ibid., p. 95). Early images of the infant are not seen as perceptions, but as "prehensions". Thus, an infant filled with anxiety has a primary need for security from fear and anxiety. At a later age, when the mother is seen as a single person (good mother and bad mother combined) the infant/developing toddler begins to develop behaviours to reduce maternal anxiety. This is an aspect of empathic linkage that is bi-directional.

As an additional note, seeing the infant/child as developing images of good and bad mother or developmentally combining these images into a single unit speaks, in my view, to necessitating some concept of structure. Enduring images, in my view, imply a slowly changing representational field which, in some theories, is what is meant by structure. This note is included to emphasize that some of Sullivan's concepts imply structure at least in terms of some interpersonal interpreters of Sullivanian thought.

Gradually, in development through empathic linkage, there are images of good me and bad me that correspond to some extent with the anxiety states of the parents. There is, in Sullivan's terms, a "much more rudimentary personification, [the] not-me" (1953,

p. 168). This, in Greenberg and Mitchell's view, evolves because of extremely intense anxiety, and these areas of the personality remain unintegrated and unknown. In Sullivan's view,

> The origin of the self-system can be said to rest on the irrational character of culture or more specifically, society. Were it not for the fact that a great many prescribed ways of doing things have to be lived up to, in order that one shall maintain workable, profitable, satisfactory relations with his fellows; or, where the prescriptions for the types of behavior, in carrying on relations with one's fellows perfectly rational—then, for all I know, there would not be evolved, in the course of becoming a person, anything like the sort of self-system that we always encounter. [*ibid.*]

Here, we see Sullivan's clear statement about how society not only influences the type of mental content present, but also the way the mind works (the structure of the mind). Now, Sullivan would not call it structure; in fact, he would decry the term, saying structure is for terms like ego, superego, or id. In terms of this extract, it is hard to see how one conceptualizes an enduring tendency without labelling it as something synonymous to structure. Leaving this issue aside, clearly society is present, and, as the child matures, it develops more complex security operations and gradually develops an overarching structure which is labelled the superior formulation of the self. This overarching structure moves to keep the child away from experiences that arouse anxiety. Various experiences occur to the child that cause anxiety, and the child, in turn, makes parataxic integrations which allow for the experience to be momentary and described as unconnected states of being. (A parataxic distortion would be where the infant, in what Singer [1993] calls an egocentric manner, thinks it had caused the mother's anxiety.)

This type of thought is not a step by step process, but is designed to keep the child from experiencing intense anxiety. Thus, a basic motivational tenet is the avoidance of anxiety to provide the child with security. Security and the satisfaction of needs form a dialectical relationship which the child balances in terms of operations of the self. The need for satisfaction is not a state that requires self-organization, but, if anxiety threatens the occurrence of need satisfaction, there is a need for self-organization and security operations. The self comes to be cherished and contradictory behaviours and feelings are not taken into account to protect the power of the I (a representation of the self). This false power allows for "narcissistic" gratification (a term used by Greenberg and Mitchell [1983]), which can obviate the person's enjoyment of true satisfactions. Security operations prevent the enjoyment of needs and "warp" interpersonal situations and gratifications. It disturbs the person's ability for syntaxic thought. The child gradually learns the "consensually validated" meaning of language—in the widest sense of language. These meanings have been acquired from group activities, interpersonal activities, and social experience. Consensually validated symbol activity involves an appeal to principles which are accepted as true by the hearer. When this happens, the youngster has acquired or learned the syntaxic mode of experience.

Although we have gone over some of Sullivan's basic tenets and looked at his sparse theoretical concepts, it feels that we have not really touched on his unique humanity. Now, perhaps, he would object to my describing him as unique, but, in my view, he was one of a kind; he was a hard-headed humanist and this allowed him relate to a variety of patients in an manner that I can only idealize as authentic. I have not ploughed through my extensive notes on Sullivan, since I did not want to write a long chapter on his theoretical views, but I have to mention him as a pioneer in the treatment of psychotic patients. For me, Sullivan is most interesting in terms of his openness to new experiences. I interpret his disdain for terms such as incorporation and introjection as his resistance to what he regarded as many clinicians' pseudo-explanatory attempts at describing a patient. Frequently, he seems to say (in his biographers' view) that there are many magicians out there (in psychoanalysis, psychotherapy, and psychiatry) who are trying to pull the wool over the eyes of patients and their colleagues. If one reads his early reviews (1931, 1934) one sees how straightforward and incisive he can be, although, clearly, he did not seem to enjoy writing.

I have already made clear that Sullivan's reliance on operationalism as a concept is naïve in today's vernacular, but it was part of the spirit of his time. Anyone who has read Mead and the pragmatists should realize that there was a strong movement to look at social sciences as scientifically as possible. Of course, it was in the USA that the behaviourists flourished, and a good deal of advertising lore was based on John B. Watson's ideas. (See http://en.wikipedia.org/wiki/John_B_Watson for information on his behaviourism, which included the objective study of behaviour; no mental life was considered, nor were internal states, and thought was seen as covert speech.) For many years in the USA, behaviourism was the dominant "theory" in psychology. Certainly, Skinner (1953) and other behaviourists still have a large influence, even in the clinical situation. Given the *zeitgeist* of the times, it is not surprising that Sullivan was sceptical of this new psychoanalytic language that was being flourished in a variety of ways.

There is, of course, another aspect to Sullivan's cautions, which is, it seems to me, that Sullivan's ideas have led directly to some of the questions that relational analysts are posing for classical analysts. Sullivan may have been too extreme in resting his criticisms on the theorem of operationalism, but the content of his scepticism is mirrored in many of the relational critiques that are present in contemporary psychoanalysis. Moreover, although we are not dwelling on this aspect of his writings, his views on adolescent adjustment and some of the differences in gender development are quite contemporary in terms of views of gender development. In addition, Sullivan's emphasis on the issue of self-esteem and the development of the sense of self predates a number of analysts' interest in the concept of self. His emphasis on anxiety in early development in some ways reminds one of Fairbairn and Klein's view of early life in terms of their concept of the paranoid–schizoid position, although what, for Sullivan, is prehension is, for Klein and Fairbairn, an infant with a complex representational world.

Commentary

For the reader who has read other chapters, it must be clear that I believe that Sullivan does not realize the importance of unconscious processes in human interactions. I would dare to venture that with the patient population that Sullivan encountered, there was not a well-differentiated line between conscious and unconscious thought processes. Since there are clear theoretical differences in our perspectives, I prefer in the commentary to write about what

Sullivan has offered me, rather than what, in my view, he undervalues.

Sullivan's views on treatment come from a clinician who, I believe, experienced transference in concrete rather than symbolic terms. His theorizing brings me back to the treatment of a schizophrenic patient who had been hospitalized four times before our treatment began. She was someone who could always home in on my most basic anxieties. This included anxieties and concerns about my body narcissism as well as anxieties about experiencing and responding to her implicit (and, at times, explicit) thoughts of world destruction. Close to the beginning of the treatment, she developed catatonic symptoms where she was either mute or when she spoke echolalically. (Echolalia and echopraxia are catatonic symptoms where the person either echoes the spoken word or mimics body movements. In contemporary treatment facilities, one is less likely to see these symptoms because medication that inhibits the expression of the symptoms is usually applied rapidly and in large quantities.) When she emerged from that state, she knowingly told me that I preferred her silence since I knew what her thunderous voice could do to me and, indeed, to all of New York. Without trying to recapture her full thoughts, she believed that if she spoke with a full voice, the buildings in New York would be destroyed. It was clear to me that before I could say anything to her I would have to listen to what she called her rumblings. I found that if I listened and tried to feel the terror that both emanated from her and was horribly disrupting her, I could gradually be included in her world, first as a spy, and several years later, in a dream, as a man with breasts who was feeding her.

Through Bernie Kalinkowitz and others, I found Sullivan to be an inspiration in treating psychotic patients. I hope, as a clinician, I was able to resist "becoming the analytic zealot [who] knows so many things that are not so that the patient never makes a beginning" (Greenberg & Mitchell, 1983, p. 87). Yes, the quote is correct, and Sullivan, in his inimitable language, is warning that if you think you know so many things in approaching this type of patient, the treatment will never get off the ground, never begin. Sullivan's writings are difficult in that he never really wrote a full volume; rather, his books are compilations of his lectures or taken from his notes. However, in my view, what is most valuable about Sullivan is his authenticity with patients that, at various junctures, unexpectedly jumps off the page. He might be talking about energy, but somehow you can discern that the energy he is referring to is a universal energy that makes all people more human than otherwise.

CHAPTER TWELVE

Mahler: symbiosis and separation–individuation[1]

Freud in relation to Mahler's concerns

Freud was frequently concerned with how the infant began to learn about the external world. In *The Interpretation of Dreams* (1900a), he presents his well-known views of the infant, at first primarily or only concerned with pleasure and, later, through deprivation, coming to know about the external world. This conception of how the infant turns from its primary concern (pleasure or tension reduction) to secondary concerns (the outside world) is based heavily on a tension-regulation model. Freud's later views, which are contained in large part in his papers on narcissism and his metapsychological papers (1914c, 1915c), are less centred on a tension-regulation or reduction model. In these and other papers, Freud put forth the guidelines of an interesting theory of early development, but, in this chapter, we can only sketch out some of his ideas (see Chapters Two and Three). Freud sees the early mental development of the infant and child as taking place along three polarities: pleasure–pain, subject–object, and active–passive, an idea that has a developmental unfolding. In early life, pleasure and pain predominate, and Freud maintains that for the infant or child (we do not know the age range to which Freud referred), the external world is at first primarily a matter of indifference. This corresponds to Freud's notion of primary narcissism, in which satisfaction or pleasure, from the infant's perspective, is autoerotic. At this time, the external world is not cathected with interest (in a general sense) and is indifferent for purposes of satisfaction (Freud, 1914g). Interestingly, although Mahler uses different terminology, her autistic phase bears striking resemblance to this Freudian phase.

At Freud's next step in development, we run into something of a paradox. Freud (1915c) postulates that, as the infant continues to experience the external world, "it acquires objects from the external world, and, in spite of everything, it cannot avoid feeling internal instinctual stimuli for a time as unpleasurable" (1915c, p. 135). As the infant builds up perceptions of (primarily internal) stimuli as unpleasurable and (primarily external) stimuli as pleasurable, it takes into itself (or introjects) the pleasurable stimuli and casts out (or projects) the unpleasurable stimuli. At this point, Freud (1915c) maintains that "the *original* 'reality-ego' which distinguished internal and external by means of sound object criterion changes into a purified pleasure-ego" (*ibid*., p. 136). This pleasure ego has divided the world into all that is pleasurable, which is equated with itself ("ego subject", in Freud's terms), and all that is unpleasurable, which is equated with the external world. One can attempt to equate this idea of the purified pleasure ego with some of Mahler's findings and formulations, but, for the purposes of this chapter, we wish to make several related points about the concepts Freud puts forth.

First, Freud pointed out that development of certain reality-ego functions may be non-monotic (by which I mean that the curve goes up and then goes down, or oscillates in direction). Thus, the infant, at an age prior to the purified pleasure ego, is considered by Freud to be, in some ways, in better contact with reality than when the pleasure ego is formed. We believe this line of reasoning is consistent with several of Freud's concepts at this time (Freud, 1915a,c,e), but the main point we wish to dwell on is that at a time when the infant, according to Freud, is indifferent to the external world, it can still develop a rudimentary reality ego. Thus, Freud saw nothing incompatible with postulating a stage of primary narcissism in which pleasure is seen as passive, internal, and autoerotic, and yet, at the same time, certain types of "learning" can take place. The question, for Freud, was not whether the infant could correctly perceive certain aspects of reality, but, rather, whether or how the object was viewed in terms of the infant's pleasurable and unpleasurable experiences. This is quite a different question from whether the infant can learn to respond during its first weeks or days of life.

As a second general point, Freud (1914c, 1915a) begins at about this time to make use of what today are frequently called projective–introjective mechanisms. These concepts are, of course, used frequently by Mahler, as well as many others, but it is of interest to see the way she has both expanded and particularized the use of these concepts.

As a third related point, we wish to emphasize how, during this era, Freud stresses both the gradual nature of being able to know the pleasure-giving object as a separate entity and, even more important, the very gradual nature of the development of object love. Freud (1915a, 1917e) discusses aspects of the development of object love, but, of course, Mahler is able to delineate with much greater precision concepts such as libidinal object constancy on the pathway to object love. As we will see, Mahler's concepts and observations in many ways begin to fulfil the promissory notes that Freud left us in his many brilliant papers.

In this brief introduction, we have touched on a few of the concepts that Freud introduced that bear some relationship to Mahler's work. We could, of course, make a much fuller comparison, but our intention is only to point out the relationship and set the stage to show how Mahler has built on, and yet gone beyond, what Freud could have even anticipated. In a chapter devoted to a historical recounting of the theorists who bear some important relation to Mahler's work, one would also have to include at least aspects of the work of Hartmann, Kris, and Lowenstein and large parts of Jacobson's work. Both Mahler (1979) and Kernberg (1980a,b) have emphasized in different ways the importance of Jacobson's developmental concepts. Many other influential authors could be named, of course, but, in our opinion, Spitz and Anna Freud's pioneering empirical studies were, in general, an inspiration to psychoanalytic researchers in many ways, particularly in demonstrating that theoretical concepts could be shown to have important empirical consequences.

Although all the authors mentioned have a variety of similarities (and differences) with respect to Mahler's work, in Loewald's words,

> Her clear emphasis on the fundamental importance in early development and continuing throughout life, of differentiation and separation from an encompassing psychical matrix . . . have had a remarkable impact on current analytic understanding of children and adults. [1984, p. 172]

Although Freud implied the "dual unit" or dyad, Mahler makes it the beginning and most important part of her observational and theoretical field.

We shall discuss the work of Margaret Mahler in three parts: (a) her early papers, including her work on infantile psychosis; (b) her research project on separation–individuation and her theory of subphases resulting in beginning self and object constancy; and (c) applications of separation–individuation theory to psychoanalytic theory and treatment.

Early papers

Mahler began her career as a paediatrician and director of a well baby clinic in Vienna. The interests she developed at the outset of her professional life have remained important throughout her career. Probably the most important of these has been her interest in the mother and baby as a dyad, or, as she later referred to it, as a dual unity within one common boundary, a symbiotic pair. Beginning with her first paper delivered in the USA, entitled "Pseudoimbecility: a magic cap of invisibility" (Mahler, 1942) and presented in 1940 to the Psychoanalytic Institute of New York, she demonstrated her interest in the pre-Oedipal era, in motility, and in the affecto–motor communication between mother and child.

> Between child and mother there exists from the beginning a close phylogenetic bond which is unique and much more exclusive than communication by words or thoughts; it is an interrelationship

through the medium of affective expressions ... The interrelation between the unconscious of the mother and the reception of stimulation of the sense organs of the baby is the prototype for a way of communication between child and adult which is not confined within the limited sphere of language. [*ibid.*, p. 4]

In her psychoanalytic work, Mahler began to treat several children suffering from childhood psychosis. This culminated in her eventual formulation of the autistic and symbiotic types of childhood psychosis (Mahler, 1952). She also became interested in determining how normal infants attain a sense of separate identity in the care-giving presence of their mothers. Examination of Mahler's papers of that period (those that preceded the beginning of observational research) reveals how closely connected in her thinking were the phases of early normal development and the consideration of extreme pathology. Mahler is essentially a psychoanalyst and a clinician, and her early papers are filled with clinical vignettes from the many severely disturbed children whom she treated as a child analyst. Yet, her thinking about pathology never overshadowed her interest in normal mental life and her conviction about the importance of the early mother–child relationship.

In an early paper (Mahler, Ross, & DeFries, 1949), Mahler was already dealing with the child's problem around the waning of omnipotence. The child gradually realizes that its power is waning. It has not only to renounce essential gratification, but must in addition lose its sense of omnipotence.

> The language of violent affect is rendered useless as a means of communication with the parents, and the child has to renounce them in favor of speech ... It seems as if these affective outbursts at the age of 2 to 3 years are struggling attempts in the child to maintain the archaic common ground so familiar to it: the intensely pleasurable affective rapport with the parents in the child's affective domination of them. This attempt is destined, like the Oedipal strivings, to fail from the danger of loss of love and fear of castration.
>
> Direct affective attacks failing, the child searches for other means to re-gain entrance to the Garden of Eden. This coincides in time with beginning to walk and the process of taking in impressions of the outside world with all the senses, acquiring knowledge and testing reality. The child utilizes these newly gained discoveries, to share

them with mother and father, and thus restore a common ground with them. The expressions of enchantment and affection, which the parents give so abundantly at the first presentations of such fact finding, bring the child a temporary restoration of the old affective and a new intellectual co-experience with the parents. [*ibid.*, pp. 301–302]

This extract already contains descriptions of behaviours that later, during the observational study of separation and individuation, become incorporated into the careful delineation of the subphases. Mahler's papers on child psychosis contain many references to her view on normal development. In 1952, she stated,

The intrauterine, parasite–host relationship within the mother organism must be replaced in the postnatal period by the infant's being enveloped, as it were, in the extra uterine matrix of the mother's nursing care, a kind of social symbiosis . . . The turning from predominantly proprioceptive awareness to increased sensory awareness of the outer world occurs through the medium of affective rapport with the mother. The baby's libido position thus proceeds from the stage of fetal narcissism to primary body narcissism, a stage in which representation of the mother's body plays a large part . . .

To understand the dynamics in infantile psychosis, observation and study of the most important transitory step in the adaptation to reality is necessary; namely, that step in the development of the sense of reality in which the mother is gradually left outside the omnipotent orbit of the self. This step is preliminary to, and perhaps alternates with, the process of endowing the mother with object-libidinal cathexis. The toddler gradually delimits his own individual entity from the primal mother–infant symbiotic unit. He separates his own self (and his mental representation) from that of the mother. This stage in ego development is a very vulnerable one, particularly in children in whose early life the somatopsychic symbiosis has been pathological. [1952, pp. 132–134]

Mahler's interest in and views on childhood psychosis and normal development were still closely intertwined at this point in her work. These remarks on early development occur in the same paper in which she outlines her views of autistic and symbiotic childhood psychosis. She describes primary autistic psychosis as a syndrome in which the mother, as representative of the outside world, seems never to have been perceived emotionally by the infant. The mother, therefore, remains a part object, seemingly devoid of specific cathexis and not distinguished from inanimate objects. These, according to Mahler, are infants with an inherently defective tension-regulating apparatus, which probably cannot be adequately complemented by even the most competent mothers. The inherent ego deficiency of these infants predisposes them from the very beginning to remain alienated from reality. Mahler (1952) states,

> It would seem that autism is the basic defense attitude of these infants, for whom the beacon of emotional orientation in the outer world—the mother as primary love object—is nonexistent. Early infantile autism develops, I believe, because the infantile personality, devoid of emotional ties to the person of the mother, is unable to cope with external stimuli and inner ex-citations, which threaten from both sides his very existence as an entity. [*ibid.*, p. 145]

Mahler contrasts the autistic psychosis with the symbiotic infantile psychosis. Symbiotic psychosis often goes unnoticed during the first two or three years of the child's life. It becomes evident at a point in development when the phase-specific demands include realization of separateness.

> The mechanisms which are characteristic in the *symbiotic* infantile psychosis are the introjective, projective mechanisms and their psychotic elaboration ... These mechanisms aim at a restoration of the symbiotic parasitic delusion of oneness with the mother and thus are the diametric opposites of the function of autism. ... It seems that the symbiotic psychosis candidates are characterized by an abnormally low tolerance for frustration, and later by a more or less evident lack of emotional separation or differentiation from the mother. Reactions set in ... at those points of the physiological and psychological maturation process at which separateness from the mother must be perceived and faced ... agitated, catatonic like temper tantrums and panic-stricken behavior dominate the picture; these are followed by bizarrely distorted reality testing and hallucinatory attempts at restitution. The aim is restoration and perpetuation of the delusional omnipotence phase of the mother–infant fusion of earliest times—a period at which the mother was

an ever-ready extension of the self, at the service and command of "His Majesty, the Baby". [*ibid.*, pp. 145–146]

The separation–individuation process

Mahler's observational research study of normal mother–child pairs began in 1959, the findings of which have been described in the second volume of *The Selected Papers of Margaret S. Mahler* (1979) and in *The Psychological Birth of the Human Infant* (Mahler, Pine, & Bergman, 1975). This research was prompted by the following questions. How do normal infants, during the first three years of life attain intrapsychic self and object representations? How do they move out of the state of dual unity or symbiosis, during which they are not aware of themselves as separate, and achieve awareness of self as separate from other? How do they attain *a* measure of libidinal self and object constancy? The hypothesis of the study was that the human infant begins life in a state of complete dependence on the mothering one and in a state of non-differentiation, or dual unity. The infant then undergoes a gradual process of differentiation or hatching out, which results in intrapsychic structures of self and object. The goal of the study was to learn about the process by which the first level of identity is achieved.

A setting was created in which mothers could interact freely with their infants. This was a large playroom with many appropriate toys, divided by a low, fencelike partition from the mothers' section. There mothers could sit comfortably and chat while watching their children, who were in a stimulating and safe environment. Participant observers were present at all times, mingling freely with mothers and children while maintaining a friendly, yet neutral, atmosphere. The participant observers later wrote down their observations in detail, and discussions took place in staff and research meetings where observers and investigators met at least once, but more often twice, a week. The research thus created did not take place in an experimental artificial setting, but in a very natural one—an indoor playground, as Mahler called it, where mothers were in charge of their children.

The observations of the participant observers were checked by regular non-participant observations conducted through a one-way mirror. Non-participant observers wrote down what they saw at the time, and thus could obtain greater objectivity and detail than participant observers. Participant observers, however, knew the mothers and children; their observations were more impressionistic and subjective, but, it was thought, more in tune with the affective tone of the mother–child pairs. The mother–child pairs were observed three to four times a week for twenty-one hour-long sessions over a period of 2½ years. The frequency and length of sessions provided a large data base from which it was possible to obtain an intimate and detailed knowledge of each mother–child pair and the development of their relationship.

In addition to participant and non-participant observations, mother–child pairs were regularly filmed. All mothers were interviewed by senior staff members once a week. These clinical interviews provided information about the family's life at home. They also gave the mothers the opportunity to talk about any aspect of themselves or their children that they chose to discuss. Fathers were interviewed several times a year, and home visits were conducted regularly, especially during holiday periods.

Several aspects of the study were of special importance. One, as noted, was the frequency with which observations were undertaken. This provided for a measure of objectivity, since a judgement made one day could be corrected the next. Another essential aspect of the research design was that it combined data from longitudinal and cross-sectional perspectives. Each mother–child pair was observed from the time the child was about six months old to three years of age. At the same time, there were always several mother–child pairs being observed simultaneously. Thus, children of any given age could be compared both with each other and with himself or herself over a time period.

Another essential aspect of the study was that, although observational in method, it was guided by psychoanalytic concepts. We believe that there was a good deal of carry-over from the way psychoanalysts make inferences in the psychoanalytic setting to the way the observers used inferences in these observational studies. As Mahler has put it, in these studies the psychoanalytic eye was guided by the observations themselves, as in the psychoanalytic situation the psychoanalytic ear is led by the analysand's free associations. Thus, this research study relied heavily on the psychoanalytic acumen and empathy of the observers and investigators, who were psychoanalysts. It rested on the meaning and coherence that emerged out of many multi-faceted daily observations. In the psychoanalytic situation, analyst and analysand together create the psychoanalytic life history. In the study of separation–individuation, the observers created the life history of the unfolding mother–child relationship and the unfolding sense of self of the infant.

The subphases

It was the comparative nature of the cross-sectional aspect of the study that eventually led to the delineation of the subphases of the separation–individuation process. For example, in the first group of children observed, a one-year-old girl was seen to explore the room freely, climbing a lot. At first, it seemed surprising that her mother sat calmly, staying in contact with the girl over a distance and directing her to avoid dangerous situations. It was thought, at first, that perhaps this mother–child pair did not like physical contact. However, over time, after observing more mother–child pairs with infants around one year of age, it became clear that this kind of exploration with relatively limited physical contact between mother and child was characteristic of this particular age. This eventually came to be termed the "practising subphase." In another example, a sixteen-month-old boy seemed to be anxiously clinging to his mother. It was not difficult to understand this in terms of the particular mother–child relationship, since the mother had shown considerable ambivalence about her baby after he was born. But, again, after watching more mother–child pairs with children of that age, it became clear that greater concern about mother's whereabouts was a typical phenomenon of the toddler.

The subphases were delineated quite early in the study. However, the intensive study of each mother–child pair made it possible to observe and study the individual variations within the regularity of subphase specificity. Such variations involved the timing, intensity, quality, and mood that characterized each particular mother–child pair. The subphases will be described in the following pages. This description takes into account some of the more recent findings of infant researchers which have contributed to and enriched Mahler's original conceptualizations.

From 0–6 months

Since Mahler undertook her research project on the normal separation–individuation process, a great deal of research has been done with infants and their care-givers, for example, that of Brazelton (1974, 1981); Sander (1976); and Stern (1971, 1974, 1982). This research has shown that neonates are more active and discriminating, more responsive to outside stimuli, than had ever been thought. It has even been shown that they are capable of performing complex tasks. In other words, our view of the infant has been revolutionized. Mahler (personal communication) has reconsidered and rethought her earlier formulations and has agreed that the word "autistic" does not well describe what we now know about the neonate.

A more recent formulation of what Mahler originally called the autistic phase is that it is the time during which newborns have the task of adjusting to extra-uterine existence, of finding their own niche in the external world. They have to achieve physiological homeostasis, that is, adequate inner regulation in synchrony with the vocal and gestural rhythms of their care-giver. Each infant elicits his or her own mother's care-giving, and the mother responds with coenesthetic empathy to the needs of a particular infant. She is enabled to do so by reaching the state described by Winnicott (1956a) as primary maternal preoccupation. Bergman (1982) has attempted to show from the mother's side how this particular empathic state is at times reached easily and smoothly, and at other times with great difficulty.

The symbiotic phase, which is reached at around two months of age, is of great importance for separation–individuation theory, since on it rests the idea of a gradual hatching out, a psychological birth. The findings of contemporary infant research here pointed to the importance of distinguishing the regressed merger experience of pathology from the attunement and reciprocity of the normal symbiotic phase. Pine (1981) has hypothesized that what could be referred to as normal merging occurs during certain brief periods of high drive arousal. Bergman and Chernack (1982), in a paper dealing with preverbal communication, have shown how, during the symbiotic phase, differentiation and merging go hand in hand.

Observers agree that attunement, mutual empathy, or communion between mother and infant are at their height in the period from 2–5 months of age. Empathy is not possible without the ability to freely evoke states of loss of self, while maintaining the ability to regain a state of full awareness. The same happens in the creative process. Where does such ability come from? We believe that the blissfulness of the symbiotic stage, which is still longed for in later life, provides us with a reservoir of self–other experiences, which in normal development are pleasurable and creative.

McDevitt (1979) has elucidated the symbiotic phase from a more cognitive perspective. He states that by age two to three months, the infant (1) both anticipates and initiates the pleasure provided by interaction with the mother; (2) develops a sense of confidence and basic trust in the care-giver and in his or her own initiative; and (3) responds by smiling and direct eye contact. The work of infant researchers has made us more aware of the capacity of the infant not only to initiate contact, but also to control it through gaze and gaze aversion. Thus, the infant's sense of self during the symbiotic phase is fed by experiences that, even at that early period, may be experienced as "his or her own", especially if the care-giving environment is responsive to the infant's more subtle signals and signs. The sense of self also receives important nutrients from the pleasure and attunement the infant experiences with the mother. Thus, from early on, there may be two strands to the infant's experience of self: self-alone and self-with-other. These should, then, be the forerunners or beginnings of separation–individuation. To separate, there must first be self–other and separate-self experiences. Sander (1976) has described these early experiences of self as being alone in the presence of someone, in Winnicott's sense. Thus, the symbiotic phase is the bedrock of libidinal attachment and intimacy on the one hand, and beginnings of self-alone experiences on the other. Even during the early months, for example, infants show individual preferences for colour, for certain tunes, and for varying amounts of stimulation.

Subphase I: differentiation

The subphase of differentiation begins at the height of symbiosis, when the baby begins more active and persistent visual and tactile exploration of the surroundings. The baby begins to perceive things at a greater distance and typically scans the environment, checking back to the mother regularly. This eminently important process of shifting attention cathexis to the outside is what has also been called the hatching process. The fully hatched baby, around the age of 9–10 months, is alert, can easily grasp what he or she wants, sits up freely (Resch, 1979), and is characterized by a general brightening of mood. The differentiation subphase is also the time when unpleasure at the stranger and even anxiety can begin (Emde, Gaensbauer, & Harmon, 1976). The baby also shows unpleasure and sometimes cries when left by the mother, but is usually comforted fairly easily by a non-intrusive mother substitute.

Pushing away from mother and exploration of the environment are quite characteristic of the differentiation subphase. During this time, the child explores, both visually and tactilely, the faces of individuals other than the mother. The infant is also particularly attracted by appendages that can be removed, such as spectacles, beads, or a pencil in the pocket. All these explorations of both the animate and the inanimate, of that which can be removed and held by the infant and that which clearly is part of the other, are important ingredients of the ongoing process of self–object differentiation.

The practising subphase

The practising subphase begins when the now hatched baby begins to be capable of independent locomotion. The early practising period comprises the time of crawling, standing up, and coasting, whereas the practising period proper begins with the mastery of upright locomotion. If we can think of symbiosis as the first blissful stage in human development, the stage of pleasure in mutuality and recognition and exploration of the mother, we can think of the practising subphase as the second blissful period. The mastery of locomotion, at first crawling and then walking, brings with it an enormous increment of energy and pleasure. The ability to go after and get what one wants by one's own efforts, is an immense source of pleasure and satisfaction. Whereas, during differentiation, babies often cry when their mother or even others walk away from them, beginning locomotion counteracts the sense of helplessness. This is a period of rapid development, especially of locomotor and manipulative abilities. The narcissistic investment in the body and in mastery and exploration brings about a temporary lessening in the investment in the mother, who can now be taken for granted. This slight lessening of investment in the mother also protects the baby from a full realization of his or her separateness. The mother is simply assumed to be there unless she is absent for any length of time. More protracted separation changes the practising infant's mood of elation to one of low-keyedness, a temporary lowering of mood which is understood to be caused by the need to hold on to the image of the mother.

Toddlers' expanding locomotor capacities widen their world; there is more to see, more to hear, and more to touch. Along with increasing awareness of the outside world goes the more highly integrated and differentiated knowledge of the body self, as the infant gains increasing mastery over body functions which become more and more intentional and goal directed. Finally, standing, and eventually walking, provide a whole new perspective of the world and add further to the small toddler's sense of elation and exuberance. Another important characteristic of this period is the relative hardiness of the infant, who is quite oblivious to the knocks and falls that are, of course, daily occurrences.

The rapprochement subphase

The expansiveness and omnipotence characteristic of the practising subphase wane as the toddler increasingly comes face to face with the feeling of separateness caused by frustrations that occur as explorations are curtailed by obstacles in the real world. The child also has to face the fact that mother is not always automatically at hand to smooth the way for his explorations. Indeed, there are times when she curtails them in the interest of protecting the child's safety. The infant's former relative obliviousness of the mother is now replaced by active approaches to her.

This rapprochement subphase is again conceptualized in two parts: early rapprochement and the rapprochement crisis. During early rapprochement, the generally good mood of the practising period still prevails as the toddlers attempt to bridge the gap that they are now beginning to perceive between themselves and their mother. Toddlers begin to want to share everything with their mother; most characteristically, they will bring things and put them in their mother's lap, but they will also seek out her active participation in their activities. The availability of the mother during this particular period is of great importance, but, even under the most optimal conditions, the maturational spurt of toddlers' cognitive development makes them realize their separateness and relative helplessness. Toddlers, during rapprochement, wish to be autonomous and find all hindrances to their autonomy extremely disturbing, whether emanating from their own activities, from curtailment by adults, or from their inability to do what they would like.

The child's recognition of his or her separateness and limitation threatens his or her sense of omnipotence, which is still very closely connected with the child's self-esteem. In addition, toddlers have to come to terms with the fact that their mother's wishes and their own by no means always coincide. Toddlers still believe in the omnipotence of their parents and become very angry and sometimes desperate if the parents cannot do for them what they want. "He thinks we can do everything," a mother of a rapprochement-age toddler said recently. Some weeks later, the same mother said, with great relief, "He's beginning to accept that somebody or something can be gone and that I cannot do anything about it." For example, that morning, when the cereal he had wanted was gone, her son agreed to eat a piece of bread and butter rather than insisting or crying for cereal.

While wanting to be independent and autonomous, rapprochement toddlers also often want to control the whereabouts of their mother and want her to partake in all their activities. Anxious clinging or daring darting away, hoping to be caught up and brought back by the mother, are typical behaviours. The toddler at this age does not easily tolerate the mother's attention being elsewhere and is typically quite demanding.

In the course of the rapprochement subphase, the child begins to have a separate mental self. Beginning language and symbolic functioning are very important in bringing a resolution of the rapprochement crisis. Being able to know and name others, and eventually being able to know and name oneself, are important indicators of internal processes that take place at that time. The child begins to know "mine" (Bergman, 1980), but "mine" at that time can express a wish or demand as well as a fact. "Mine" is a precursor to naming oneself or using the personal pronoun.

If development goes reasonably well and the mother is reasonably available to the toddler, the rapproachement crisis is eventually resolved by way of identification and internalization. Successful resolution of the rapprochement crisis by no means always takes place, however. A badly resolved rapprochement crisis leads to intense ambivalence and splitting of the object world into good and bad. The maternal representation may be internalized as an unassimilated bad introject. McDevitt and Mahler (1980) cite four conditions that would lead to poor resolution of the rapproachement crisis: (1) the love object is disappointing and unavailable or excessively unreliable and intrusive; (2) the child experiences the realization of his or her helplessness too abruptly and too painfully, resulting in a too sudden deflation of the child's sense of omnipotence; (3) there has been an excess of trauma; and (4) the child experiences to an unusual degree the narcissistic hurt of the preoedipal castration reaction which accompanies the discovery of the anatomical difference. Under such conditions, rapprochement-type behaviours persist rather than giving way. Such behaviours include excessive separation anxiety, depressive mood, passivity or demandingness, coercivenesss, possessiveness, envy, and temper tantrums.

On the way to object constancy

The fourth and final subphase of separation–individuation is called "on the way to self and object constancy" and is recognized as being open-ended. In the context of separation–individuation theory, self and libidinal object constancy (the achievement of this final subphase) is not seen as a fixed fact, but rather as an ongoing, lifelong process. Nevertheless, a child who has successfully resolved the rapprochement crisis has made an important qualitative change that is quite unmistakable to observers.

Self-constancy develops along with object constancy. In the fourth subphase, the toddler's sense of self includes actions as well as perceptions and feelings. The toddler begins to like to be admired for what he or she can do. Earlier, doing and achieving mastery were enough. Now, the participation of the "other" is an important ingredient in the pleasure of mastery. The qualitative change that comes with the resolution of the rapprochement crisis is comparable to the qualitative change that comes when hatching is accomplished.

Hatching, which means living in the outside world while taking the mother for granted, resolves the crisis of differentiation when the infant, for the first time, becomes exceedingly sensitive to separation from the mother. The infant needs to take the mother for granted, that is, to stay omnipotently at one with her, while, at the same time, turning to the outside world with curiosity, pleasure, and eagerness. The rapprochement crisis is the second crisis of separation. To bring it to a satisfactory resolution, the child has to achieve a degree of internalization, which allows the lessening and eventual relinquishment of omnipotent control. The development of the symbolic function is intimately connected with the lessening of omnipotent control, as it allows the senior toddler to live out and practise in play some of the wishes and fears that arise from the conflict over autonomy and the need or wish to still be "at one" with the powerful, good mother.

Summary

The delineation of the subphases of the separation–individuation process describes the psychological birth of the human infant. Out of the union or attunement of symbiosis with the mother, the infant grows to an increasing awareness of separateness and develops his or her own unique characteristics, in part inborn, in part the result of the intimate interaction between the infant and his or her love objects, the parents. The infant also grows from a stage in which the object is only dimly perceived as outside and separate toward the attainment of a unique attachment to the love object; the infant grows further, toward the stage of loving in which a positive image can be maintained even in the face of anger and frustration and in which the capacity for concern for the other takes the place of the demand for omnipotent control.

Each overlapping stage paves the way for the next. Thus, the solid and pleasurable period of symbiosis means that the child will be more prepared for the stage of differentiation to follow and will meet the stranger or strangeness of the outside world with greater confidence and less anxiety. Similarly, a rich practising subphase, which affords ample opportunity for exploring the outside world while remaining in contact over distance with a supportive and admiring care-giver, will provide the child with a reservoir of resources with which to withstand the onslaughts of the crisis of rapprochement.

The task for the parent changes as the separation–individuation process progresses. During practising, the parent has to be able to follow the cue of the child, who now requires more space in which to try out his or her burgeoning abilities. It is during the period of rapprochement that it becomes more difficult for the mother to remain emotionally available, as the child who has appeared more autonomous during practising now returns to the mother, often with conflicting and unfulfillable demands. Nevertheless, parents who can be playful and patient during the rapprochement period will help the child toward more favourable resolutions during the period on the way to object constancy.

While each subphase paves the way for the next, each subphase also contains a potential for repair if optimal conditions have not prevailed in the preceding period. Each subphase is also separate and discrete (Mahler, Pine, & Bergman, 1975), with its own rewards as well as its own tasks. The little child's personality is pliable and patterns are not fixed, leaving a great deal of room for adaptation. For example, a particular child, whose symbiotic phase had been coloured by his mother's depression during that period, seemed to differentiate rather late. It seemed at first like a possible danger signal. It later seemed, however, that this child had found a way of making up for what he had missed by remaining in the symbiotic orbit for a longer time by emerging into the outside world only slowly, as he became ready to do so. Since this particular mother could respond much better to the active child of separation–individuation, he began to catch up and developed well as time went on.

The theory of separation–individuation is a dynamic developmental theory. It leaves room for progression and regression as well as for the back-and-forth movement between needs for closeness and attachment and needs for exploration and disengagement.

An important result of the study of separation–individuation is the enrichment of knowledge on several topics, which, although already familiar to psychoanalysts and developmentalists, were further illuminated during the years of the research. We would like to mention a few contributions that have dealt with psychoanalytic concepts from a developmental perspective. In an important paper on the development of basic moods, Mahler (1966) considers the tendency to depressive moods in women and ties it to conflicts arising during the rapprochement sub-phase. Furer (1967) writes about developmental aspects of the superego. He considers "identification with the comforter" as a forerunner of the superego and feels that this identification with the active mother "increases the child's capacity to bind its aggression and thus helps bring about the required reaction formation" (1967, p. 279). In an examination of the relationship between adaptation and defence, Mahler and McDevitt (1968) say,

> The child's experiences over the course of time, on the basis of his drive and ego endowment, lead to more or less successful adaptation. His adaptive style contributes to his character traits, as do his defense behaviors. We have observed in our research the process by which these behaviors gradually become internalized as more or less successful defense mechanisms. [*ibid.*, p. 1]

McDevitt (1983) traces the emergence of hostile aggression in the course of the separation–individuation process. Bergman (1982) describes the development of the girl during separation–individuation, with implications for later development.

We would like to mention some other important issues that have been elucidated by the developmental point of view and by the detailed scrutiny of our day-to-day observations in the study of separation–individuation. The first of these is stranger anxiety.

It was Spitz (1957) who first drew attention to stranger anxiety and considered it the second organizer at the age of seven months. This phenomenon has attracted a great deal of attention since Spitz first described it, and the separation–individuation study has contributed to a more detailed understanding of a variety of phenomena subsumed under the concept of stranger reactions. Stranger anxiety is the most visible of a large array of phenomena with which an infant indicates increasing recognition of mother as unique as well as interest and curiosity in the world beyond mother. Thus, we prefer the term "stranger reactions" rather than "stranger anxiety". Stranger reactions can include a variety of affects, ranging from interest and curiosity to wariness and, finally, anxiety and distress. Stranger reactions can even be directed, at a certain age, to the mother or father if they look different from the way they usually do. Early in the study, we heard about a little boy who, at the age of four months, cried when he saw his mother wearing a shower cap. We recently heard of a little girl, aged five months, who was quite concerned when she saw her father after he had shaved his beard and moustache. These are early indications that the child is beginning to form an inner image, which is disturbed if what the child sees is suddenly *very* different from what she or he expects. It seems to us that the timing, the kind, and intensity of the stranger reaction is intimately connected with the mother–child relationship. For example, we recently saw a little girl who showed a marked stranger reaction, even anxiety, at the unusually early age of 3–4 months. She was the daughter of a young mother from a foreign country who had not yet learnt the language very well. This young woman had been quite depressed after she married an American man and went to live in the USA. After the birth of her daughter, her mood improved, and she developed an extremely close symbiotic relationship with the girl. Mother and daughter seemed rather insulated from the rest of the world in which they lived. Thus, it seemed very interesting that this particular little girl showed such early stranger reaction and reacted to outsiders not with curiosity or interest, but with displeasure. When she was seen again at the age of six months, she was still rather wary, but willing to engage in play with a stranger as long as her mother stayed close by.

"Customs inspection" is a term that was coined during the separation–individuation study to describe another type of stranger reaction. This is the way in which the child, in the period of differentiation, around 7–10 months, will examine the faces of strangers, both visually and tactilely, with great interest and absorption. Not all children feel free to engage in this activity with the same amount of intensity and interest, but most will show some interest in the stranger and wish to touch and explore parts of the stranger's face, or, at least, such appendages as beads or spectacles.

Yet another kind of stranger reaction was recently observed in a little boy during the differentiation subphase. This little boy seemed to enjoy attracting the interest of strangers, and he had learnt that when he shouted, most people would look around and smile at him. Thus, in strange places, he would often shout at strangers and then show great pleasure when they paid attention to him. Separation–individuation studies have shown us that the outside world is not just a threat to the unique mother–child relationship; it is also often a source of great excitement and pleasure.

It has long been known that separation from their mother is often painful to children during the first 2–3 years of life. Once again, the study of separation–individuation has given us a developmental view of such separation reactions. It has shown us that sensitivity to separation is very different during the different subphases of the separation–individuation process. Of course, each child's sensitivity to separations will also be determined by the mother–child relationship and by the way the mother handles such separations. Regardless of these individual differences, however, we were able to see a developmental line of separation reactions (McDevitt, 1979). The period of the differentiation sub-phase is a time when most infants first show active protest or distress at separation. This seems to be when they are on the verge of being able to move independently themselves and are trying to do so, but cannot do so yet. It is at this time that they seem to perceive their mother walking away from them and often cry. Most infants at that time accept substitutes without too much difficulty, but the period of differentiation is a sensitive one. It is as if the infant's capacities of discrimination are ahead of his or her capacity to act. The infant is acutely aware that when mother walks away, he or she is not yet able to follow her or call to her. However, the infant has a beginning image of the mother and begins to look at the door through which she might have left. It is also often comforting to the infant to be taken to a window. The child seems, at this time, to have a vague feeling that mother is out there. Thus, going to the window and observing the world in which she is somehow known to be seems to ameliorate the feeling of helplessness or entrapment that might otherwise be present. One mother who was especially sensitive observed that her little boy, at a somewhat older age, would wait by the door in the late afternoon, thereby indicating to her that he was waiting for his father to come home.

By the time they reach the practising period, from about 8–16 months, children are quite aware that their mother might leave and may protest her leaving as soon as she prepares to do so. On the other hand, their newly found ability to crawl, and later to walk, seems to compensate to some extent. No longer are they so dependent on a mother substitute for comfort. Children are now more able to do things for and by themselves that are enjoyable and exciting. They can also attempt to follow the mother. They can go to the door through which she left. They can be more actively engaged with substitute care-givers in the mother's absence.

Nevertheless, during the early practising period, from about 8–13 months, it was observed that infants tended to become much less active when their mother was out of the room. Pleasure and cathexis in the outside world was definitely reduced, and infants began to withdraw into a state called "low-keyedness" (Mahler & McDevitt, 1968). Low-keyedness was conceptualized as a state of holding on to the image of the absent mother by reducing activity and stimulation from the outside. This withdrawal and low-keyedness can be quite dramatic. Equally dramatic is the way in which the child at this age will immediately come back to life as soon as he or she is reunited with mother.

It is during the period of practising that the invisible bond with mother is at its height, and the infant seems to feel as if she were at one with him or her, even while at a distance. Infants at this age characteristically will play at a distance from their mother, but periodically look at her and check back, apparently receiving sustenance from the visual contact. Absence of the mother at this age, if it is too prolonged, and if no adequate substitute care-giver is available, disrupts too suddenly the illusion of oneness with the mother and thus disrupts the elation that is so characteristic of the practising subphase. It may also lead the child to become restless and search for the mother, or to get into dangerous or precipitous situations, probably with the hope of being rescued by her.

The increased sense of separateness during the period of rapprochement brings with it a sense of vulnerability, loneliness, and, often, helplessness. Thus, most children become much more sensitive to separation. Toddlers of the rapprochement subphase are often constantly preoccupied with their mother's whereabouts. They insist on following her through the door and will protest vigorously when separated. Phenomena such as shadowing and darting away have been described as characteristic of toddlers during this period. They can be quite insistent on their mother's exclusive attention and, if it is not easily available, attempt to get this attention by clinging and coercion. Substitutes are no longer as easily accepted, and often familiar substitute care-givers, even fathers, are angrily rejected when the mother is desired. A kind of splitting often occurs in which the absent mother is longed for and the present care-giver is rejected. Beginning feelings of ambivalence are directed toward the mother, who is often seen as interfering with the child's budding autonomy. Thus, the mother is split into the good absent mother who is longed for, and the bad present one who is rejected. At the time of reunion, the mother who returns is no longer necessarily experienced as the pleasurable, life-giving force that she was during practising. Instead, when she returns, she is sometimes avoided. The child veers away and seems angry instead of smiling at the mother's return, and it takes considerable time for a pleasurable reunion to be effected.

The beginning abilities for symbolic play and language help the toddler to withstand separation from the mother. It is only with the advent of the fourth subphase, however, on the way to object constancy, that mother's absence can truly be accepted and the child can be content for longer periods of time without her. By then, the child can understand quite well where mother or father is when they are not with him or her, and can pleasurably anticipate their return. Symbolic play and imitation are important tools for the mastery of separations. These can be played out endlessly by children of different ages, beginning with the simple peek-a-boo of the young infant.

It is important to remember that Mahler's study of separation–individuation was designed to study the emergence of separateness, not the reaction to separation. Children were studied in the care-giving presence of their mothers. Yet, even in this setting, mothers would leave the room for brief periods for their interviews, providing some insight into the developmental reactions to separation from mother.

Applications

In the beginning of this chapter, we briefly mentioned some of Freud's ideas about early development. His ideas about introjective and projective mechanisms were an early attempt to conceptualize how the infant starts to distinguish self and non-self on the basis of other than "reality-ego" considerations. We have attempted to convey a number of the pathways that Mahler and her co-workers have taken to elucidate this and many other related issues. Clearly, Mahler agrees with Freud's contention that the infant and child can normally develop structures on the basis of factors other than those that Freud referred to as reality-ego related. Mahler's conceptualization of libidinal object constancy and the phases of development that lead up to libidinal object constancy are clearly instances of factors that are not simply based on the reality ego.

We deliberately have not used the term "cognitive" in contrast to "emotional" factors, since we believe this type of dichotomy is, for the most part, not a useful one in early development. One might say, for example, that Mahler and Piaget both refer to a series of cognitive structures developed by the infant or child, but, to some extent, they are talking about different types of cognitive structures. Moreover, for Mahler, the intermesh of the infant's and mother's affective states is often a reliable indicator or predictor of how the infant's structures will develop. Thus, Mahler maintains (as did Freud) that cognitive structures that develop in relation to the self (selves) and important object representations follow different developmental lines than other cognitive structures such as those described by Piaget. If this is the case, it raises questions about the relationship between observations and theoretical concepts from a psychoanalytic perspective, on the one hand, and infant experiments, observations, and theoretical concepts of researchers from other perspectives (such as those of cognitive and learning theorists), on the other.

To be more concrete, let us take the example, cited earlier, in which Mahler recently altered her concept of the autistic phase because of current infant research. Clearly, contemporary studies have been striking in pointing out the early perceptual and response capabilities of the infant. Moreover, a number of psychoanalysts, such as Stern, have pointed out that these studies contradict aspects of Mahler's and Freud's thought. Even though the autistic phase is not a central concept to Freud (nor, for that matter, is primary narcissism), the examination of this issue might elucidate some of the difficulties in comparing findings that are couched in psychoanalytic terms with findings from other theoretical points of view. This examination might also touch on some of the difficulties of formulating psychoanalytic concepts.

Freud's notion of primary narcissism can be interpreted in several ways, but one narrow interpretation of Freud (or Mahler) is that he was referring primarily to the building of rudimentary representations of self and object by the infant. During primary narcissism, the infant is not concerned with the object as object, not because the infant cannot discriminate the object, but, rather, because no accumulation of experience (in normal development) has occurred that leads the infant to anticipate a consistent or long period of frustration of primary gratification. If such an accumulation of experience occurs very early, Freud implicitly predicts traumatic results. Freud (1915c) states that even though

> the ego is autoerotic [and] it has no need of the external world, in consequences of experience . . . it acquires objects from that world and, in spite of everything, it cannot avoid feeling internal instinctual stimuli . . . as unpleasurable. [*ibid.*, p. 135]

The purified pleasure ego, then, develops as a response to unpleasurable stimuli, and, although it brings the infant closer to the object, it also causes some distortion in the infant's rudimentary sense of reality.

Freud is here making a unique type of prediction, a prediction that should differentiate to some extent his theoretical position from other positions. There are, of course, difficulties in testing these ideas. We have little idea of the time periods that Freud is postulating. It may be difficult to find ways to measure the infant's postulated split of the world into all good (inside) and all bad (outside). Freud is silent about factors that might influence (retard or advance) the development of the purified pleasure ego, nor does he tell us in detail about factors that might continue the purified pleasure ego longer than developmentally appropriate, or that might lead to the dissipation of the structure earlier than might be desirable. In short, Freud tells us very little that would enable us to develop a testable theory from his writings. It is obviously difficult, therefore, to compare his account of development with other accounts. We believe, however, that even in Freud's sparse writings on early development, there are ideas rich enough that if one rigorously applied his assumptions and tried several time sequences, it might be possible to empirically test his conceptualizations.

Why, one might ask, have we, in our summary of Mahler's contributions, reviewed some relatively obscure sections of Freud's writings? We have done so in part because Freud's writings are finalized and, in some ways, are a simpler version of an early developmental schema than are other psychoanalytic theories. In the main, however, we wish to give a brief illustration of both the difficulties and the potential of even such a seemingly "discarded" (Lichtenberg, 1982) part of Freud's writings as his metapsychological papers. In our opinion, Mahler's pioneering work has some of the same difficulties, but clearly much more potential because of the richness of the observations and concepts of her work.

Let us go, therefore, to Mahler's conceptualization of the autistic phase, which we roughly equated with Freud's ideas of primary narcissism and autoeroticism. This concept is one of the few aspects of Mahler's writings that has been actively disputed. In addition, it is clearly not a central concept for her (her research has not included this phase of development), and therefore might prove useful as an illustration of the richness of her ideas.

In our opinion, the concept of the autistic phase has been translated as a phase without stable representations, or an "objectless" period. This, of course, is one possible translation, but one not necessarily in keeping with Mahler's ideas or with Jacobson's notion of the psychophysiological self, which Mahler has utilized. The key to this notion is the definition of an "objectless" period. If one means a period where no stable perceptions or memories are retained, then the first month of life is probably not an objectless state. However, Mahler, Freud, and Jacobson all describe the state of the infant in this period with respect to gratifying and aversive experiences. They maintain that the infant is interested not in the object, but in the gratification or maintenance of homeostasis, or in something other than the object itself. The fact that the infant possesses aspects of the rudimentary ego does not alter this concept. What, then, is the contradiction with other research? For, if one means by "objectless" state an infant whose main interest is in gratification and who is not motivated or interested in the object (we are of course simplifying), then there is no contradiction.

Part of the difficulty, then, may lie in the manner in which the concepts are stated. Or perhaps it is more accurate to say that the difficulty lies in the fact that the concepts are incompletely stated. Here, Mahler has not gone beyond Freud, and all the questions we previously asked about Freud's ideas can be appropriately applied to Mahler. We believe, however, that all the conditions are present for separation–individuation concepts to be put in the form of a theory that can both do justice to the richness of psychoanalytic concepts and, at the same time, be empirically rigorous.

The line of thought and research that Mahler has pursued in her separation–individuation research is probably the outstanding example in psychoanalysis of how concepts have guided research and, in turn, have themselves been enriched and expanded by the research. Given the outstanding quality and amount of this work, however, we might briefly summarize what we believe are some of the difficulties in this conceptual field. Difficulty in knowing how to conceptually co-ordinate separation–individuation and other aspects of psychoanalysis may, in part, be an empirical question. At this point, however, it is hard to know how to co-ordinate concepts such as psycho-sexual stages, drives, or other aspects of psychological structure in ego psychology. For example, one might ask if drive is a concept that is compatible with the separation–individuation theoretical framework and, if so, does a concept like drive add to this framework? How does one think of psycho-sexual factors in relationship to processes of differentiation or individuation? Many questions such as these can be asked, and it is not a criticism, but, rather, a comment about psychoanalytic thought that there are few substantive attempts to logically order and co-ordinate these concepts. Only if this is done can firm empirical consequences be derived from a theoretical position.

A similar point can be made about separation–individuation concepts even outside the context of the more general psychoanalytic concepts. It is difficult to know the logical status of certain concepts. That is, it is hard to know which concepts are absolutely essential and which are more peripheral. It is also difficult to know how to translate certain concepts into ideas that have firm empirical consequences. For example, there are many instances in the research of children who deviated from what would seem to be expected theoretical norms, but the delimiting conditions were not often given in generalizable statements. A substantial elucidation of these difficulties is beyond the scope of this chapter, however.

We have attempted to give one example of how some of Mahler's and Freud's less-developed ideas and psychoanalytic explanations may be powerful if stated in more specific terms. When that occurs, we may see that even the concept of the autistic phase has a good deal of explanatory power.

Commentary

Since the time of the first writing of this chapter, the popularity of Mahler's writings have waned a great deal. It may be that the autistic stage or phase was poorly named, as is the case with the autorerotic stage or paranoid–schizoid position. Each name denotes unavoidable pathological conditions that all human beings must encounter. Although autoerotism does not necessarily connote pathology, it does suggest that relationships are unimportant during this era of development, while just the reverse is true. Mahler's concept of symbiosis is one that still seems important and is very much in line with Winnicott's concept of absolute dependence. Mahler's concepts suffered from some of the same confusion that were present in critiques of Freudian ideas. The concepts were criticized as if there were no object relationships present in early development, as opposed to stressing a different type of object relationship; the type of relationship that Jacobson detailed as stabilizing the infant's psychophysiological sense of self.

I have included the chapter on Mahler, however, because many of the concepts and observations that Mahler, and later Bergman, have put forth are, in my view, lasting contributions that await a developmental integration with more recent findings. In Chapter Eighteen, I offer the beginnings of a possible integration and I include some of Bergman's ideas that are derived from a more general position than Mahler has put forth. Unfortunately, in psychology and psychoanalysis, it is rare that concepts based on observations survive more than a decade or two, so it may be that we will have to rediscover these concepts again in a different context.

Note

1. This chapter was co-authored by Anni Bergman and Steven Ellman. Anni Bergmann was a collaborator of Mahler's and subsequently an important contributor to the developmental literature (Bergman, 1999). The first few pages of this chapter are a summary of some of the points covered in more detail in Chapters Two and Three. These points have been left in this chapter to give the reader a comparison between Mahler and Freud's theorizing about early development.

CHAPTER THIRTEEN

Kohut: a new self-psychological perspective

Summary

In this chapter, we follow Kohut's work from 1959 to 1984 (his last published volume). Kohut starts by expanding Freudian concepts of narcissism in terms of both a developmental and clinical perspective. By 1972 (at least in retrospect), Kohut's paper on narcissistic rage was a pivotal point in his moving away from Freudian theory and towards a new self-psychological perspective. By 1977, Kohut has moved towards defining a self-psychological perspective where he distinguishes his theory from Freudian, or at least classical, psychoanalytic concepts. His emphasis on the empathic analyst in the analytic situation, has proved a strong influence with analytic clinicians across a number of theoretical orientations.

Heinz Kohut: brief biographical sketch

Heinz Kohut is the founder of the self-psychological movement in the USA. He was born in Vienna (1913–1981) and fled to the USA after the Nazis took power in Austria. Kohut's psychoanalytic career was in Chicago, and during his life he became the central figure at the Chicago Psychoanalytic Institute. (In this context we must remember that before Kohut, Chicago was the home of Franz Alexander, an analyst who attempted to provide "real" gratifications in the psychoanalytic situation. Given recent analyses of psychoanalytic treatment, there are always real gratifications; perhaps Alexander should be described as providing palpable gratifications. Whether one wants to talk about real issues in terms of gratifications depends on your theoretical perspective.) Kohut's early papers were largely involved with music and literature, and demonstrated a sensitivity to artistic and creative efforts. One of his biographers describes Kohut as a Jewish émigré who obscured his Judaism. This same biographer (Strozier, 2001) maintained that in his psychoanalytic approach he became distinctly American, and was strangely secretive about his health and other matters. Whether Kohut was secretive will not be an issue that I will discuss, but, clearly, as an analyst (for his era), he was open to discussing issues that silenced much of the analytic community. One would have to say that Kohut was a complex personality who, at the very least, opened discussions about the treatment of patients who were, to some extent, overlooked by the analytic community.

Kohut's work can be viewed as purely an extension of Freud's theory of narcissism or, alternatively, as an important shift in the way he conceptualized psychoanalytic technique and early development. To appreciate Kohut's theoretical odyssey, we will look at three of his articles between 1966–1972 (much of the content of which is in a book that Kohut wrote in 1971), his 1977 volume, and his posthumously published book (1984). His theory emphasizes affects of shame and embarrassment and makes the regulation of self-esteem a central component of his conceptual concerns. His gradual shift to a theory of the self (as opposed to the ego) allows for more direct clinical statements and a psychoanalytic position that focuses on patient's conscious experiences. Interestingly, at his Institute, Kohut was known as a Freud scholar, and during parts of his career taught many of the Freud courses.

Narcissism as a Freudian

In the first paper we encounter, one can see strong manifestations of his Freud scholarship. Kohut, in this paper, both restates and elaborates Freud's theory of narcissism and, in addition, elucidates an internal contradiction in Freud's statements about narcissism and analysability. One can see the tenor of the times in the way Kohut demonstrates a logical difficulty in Freud's conceptualizations. In effect, he is stating that his views are similar to Freud's and, to the extent that they are different, it is because Freud did not fully understand the implications of his own theory. He is slightly apologetic when he states that he may be extending Freudian concepts. Kohut's criticism involves Freud's assertion that, in so far as a patient is narcissistic, they are unanalysable (Freud, 1916a). Freud's reasoning involved an incorrect derivation from his distinction between narcissistic (ego) and object libido. Freud deduced that if a person's representational world was primarily a narcissistic one, then this type of person could not develop transference reactions in analytic treatment. Freud reasoned that since narcissism is the libidinal cathexis of the self, to the extent that the self is cathected, this depleted the remaining libido available for object cathexes. Thus the more narcissistic libido, the less object libido left for transference displacements. Here we have two of Freud's assumptions. One is that there is a fixed amount of psychic energy in a closed system. Two, that transference is a displacement from one object to another.

However, Freud also pointed out how objects are taken in during the phase of narcissism and cathected with narcissistic libido. Thus, it is not that narcissists do not cathect (become attached to) other people (objects), but, rather, that the attachment is made in a narcissistic form. Kohut, in looking at Freud's conceptualizations, succinctly concludes that "The antithesis to narcissism is not the object relation but object lov." (1966, p. 245). Kohut, here, is stating that, even within Freud's formulations, transference is possible, since objects are cathected during the narcissistic phase of development. Thus, someone who is primarily narcissistic is capable of transference, but not capable of object love. The logical conclusion from Kohut's critique is that, in so far as a person is narcissistic, they will develop narcissistic transference states. Kohut, in his first paper on narcissism (1966) and in his next several manuscripts (1968, 1971, 1972), is going to describe the nature of narcissistic transference(s) and how to handle more effectively these transference states in psychoanalytic treatment.

1966: two developmental pathways

In a 1959 article, Kohut presaged his emphasis on empathic attunement when he put forward the idea that empathy allows us to observe the meaning of the psychological world that surrounds us. "We speak of physical phenomena when the essential ingredient of our observational methods includes our senses, we speak of psychological phenomena when the essential ingredient of our observation is introspection and empathy" (1959, p. 459). As we will see, it is hard to overestimate the role of empathy in Kohut's ideas for developmental issues or questions about the psychoanalytic situation.

In Kohut's first paper on narcissism (1966), he is heavily steeped in the psychoanalytic language of his era. Despite his use of the traditional language, he points out various difficulties in the way that the analytic community has been considering questions that involve the manifestation of narcissistic tendencies. He distinguishes these general difficulties from the more specific aspects of Freudian theory. He maintains that, while narcissism ("the libidinal investment of the self") is neither "pathological nor obnoxious", there is nevertheless a strong prejudice in the psychoanalytic community that decries the appearance of narcissistic phenomena. Kohut, in effect, asks why there is an inconsistency between how the theory describes narcissism and the attitude of analysts towards narcissistic issues (e.g., pride, exhibitionism shame, grandiosity, etc.). Kohut explains this inconsistency as in part due to an "improper intrusion of (our) altruistic value system" (1966, pp. 243–244). This "intrusion" is viewed as a residue of Western puritanical values, which look down on even the expression of useful (healthy) narcissism. More importantly, "these value judgments exert a narrowing effect on clinical practice ... they tend to lead [the analyst] to replace the patient's narcissistic position with object love" (*ibid.*, p. 244). Kohut is pointing to the "fact" that analysts have difficulties in tolerating narcissistic issues in the treatment situation, in part due to their puritanical attitudes. In his view, the analyst attempts to encourage the patient to give up narcissistic concerns in favour of what the analyst feels is a less primitive, more socially acceptable form of relating. Thus, Kohut both points to the analyst's puritanical values and to Freud's conceptualization of analysability as impediments in the treatment of narcissistically vulnerable patients. When Kohut began to write about narcissism (Kohut was part of a *zeitgeist* and perhaps the major force in this movement, although other analysts such as Stone [1954, 1961], Loewald [1960, 1980], and Jacobson [1964] were pointing in the same direction as Kohut), there was a strong prejudice in the United States that indicated that people with narcissistic character traits tended to be unanalysable.

Kohut begins his formulations on narcissistic development by pointing out that during primary narcissism, the I–you differentiation has not yet been firmly established. He is using the term "primary narcissism" to indicate what, in Chapter Three, is called the stage of autoerotism. At some point in development, primary narcissism "is disturbed by maturational pressures and painful psychic tensions which occur because the mother's ministrations are of necessity imperfect" (Kohut, 1966, p. 245). When primary narcissism is disturbed, a new structure is developed, the purified pleasure ego (see Chapter Three: in Freud's theory, this is the beginning point of narcissistic development). The purified pleasure ego (ppe) is a stage in "which everything pleasant, good and perfect is considered as part of a rudimentary self, while everything unpleasant, bad, and imperfect is considered as 'outside'" (*ibid.*). Kohut, in considering the implications of the ppe, then introduces a new concept, the idealized parent imago (image or representation). In his elaboration of the ppe, the infant, emerging from the ppe (and beginning to differentiate from the mother), imbues the object with perfection and power. This idealized parent is, in his view, neither completely subsumed under the heading of narcissism nor of object love. He maintains there is an "intimate" relation between the idealized parent and narcissism, and he retains Freud's concept of homosexual libido. Thus, the idealized object is cathected with homosexual libido whether the object is a same sex or opposite sex person. What does homosexual libido mean in this context? That the infant/developing child sees the world through its own preoccupations and needs, thus, at some point in normal development, there is not a truly separate (realistically perceived) object. In both normal and conflicted (pathological) development, the idealized object may be taken back into the self through the process of identification. Kohut states that, despite the close relationship of the idealized object to narcissistic development, the object is "partly invested with object-libidinal cathexes and the idealized qualities are loved as a source of gratifications to which the child clings tenaciously" (ibid., p. 246). If the idealized object does not provide for the child what the child desires or expects (in line with the idealization), this will be experienced as a loss of the object. Object loss, in this formulation (and in Freud's), leads to the internalization of "drive-regulating psychic structure(s)" (ibid., p. 247). Object loss is seen as occurring gradually and smoothly in the normal course of development, or in traumatic form when there is an actual loss of a parent. Kohut sees optimal loss occurring in small doses during pre-Oedipal development and in more dramatic form during the Oedipal period. The gradual loss pre-Oedipally is seen as contributing to the drive-regulating matrix of the ego, while the more dramatic Oedipal loss leads to the formation of the superego.

If one has read Chapters Three and Four, these formulations must seem quite familiar. Kohut is enlivening and detailing Freud's concepts and formulating how, even in narcissistic development, the love of the object, albeit in rudimentary form, is extremely important. He is extending the idea of object loss in a meaningful way, and trying to show that "Every shortcoming detected in the idealized parent leads to a corresponding internal preservation of the externally lost quality of the object" (ibid.). He gives an example where, when a young child's lie goes undetected, it is an example of losing one aspect of the all-knowing or omniscient idealized object. He illustrates how the loss of this form of the object will be internalized when he says that the omniscience of the object is eventually introjected as a significant aspect of the all-seeing eye, the omniscience of the superego. The original narcissistic investment in the idealized object lends this internalization particular significance, since these idealized qualities are always internalized. This is Kohut's explanation of how the parent's values and ideals, embedded in the idealization, are gradually transmitted to the child.

The ego ideal, in this formulation, is an early representation of the object and is an outgrowth of the ppe. The ego ideal is strongly related to drive control, and is eventually a statement of values and standards resulting in a psychic structure, the superego. The movement from the ppe has two separate (but related) developmental tracks: the ego ideal, and the narcissistic self. This sibylline formation is expressed by Kohut when he states, " I am tempted to say that the ego experiences the influence of the ego ideal as coming from above and that of the narcissistic self as coming from below" (*ibid.*, p. 249). The narcissistic self is viewed as close to the drives and manifests stage-appropriate grandiosity and exhibitionism. Optimally, the narcissistic self is internalized to channel the drives towards activities that fulfil ideals and values. Premature interference with either structure (the narcissistic self or the idealized object) leads to later narcissistic vulnerability. Kohut sees idealization and grandiosity as phase appropriate, and the interference with the development of either state will lead to arrested development and a condition where these fantasies will be "repressed and inaccessible to modifying influences" (*ibid.*). Here, Kohut is maintaining that good enough parenting accepts the child's grandiosity and the child's idealizations. If the parent has difficulty in accepting either aspect of the child's narcissistic development, then structuralization will be affected and some type of defensive process will be instituted. Whether Kohut wants to call this a fixation point will be discussed later, but, clearly, something analogous to fixation is occurring when the parent is unable to allow the child to gradually work through its experience of grandiosity and idealization.

The adult manifestations of narcissistic conflicts are discussed by Kohut and he states that

> If the ego's instinctual investment of the superego remains insufficiently desexualized (or becomes resexualized), moral masochism is the result, a condition in which the ego may wallow in a state of humiliation when it fails to live up to its ideals. In general, however, the ego does not specifically experience a feeling of being narcissistically wounded when it cannot reach the ideals; rather it experiences an emotion akin to longing. [ibid., p. 250]

Kohut, in describing a superego structure that has remained personified (sexualized), posits a state of humiliation for the person if the personified ideals are not realized. This personification occurs if the parent is unable to help the child tolerate the loss of the idealized object. Obviously, conditions can occur that are outside of parental control: death, war, or general societal turmoil that makes an optimal process of idealization difficult to maintain for the child and the parent. Kohut gives an example of a family escaping the Nazis and the difficulties inherent in the parent accepting the child's idealization. One might apply Kohut's ideas to African-American parents who have endured generations of overt and subtle indications of their "inferiority". When the society is constantly broadcasting your inferiority and lack of intelligence, it may be difficult to accept your child's idealization of your omniscience. Kohut's ideas about the difficulties in superego development have a parallel in his conceptualization of the narcissistic self. He states,

> If the grandiosity of the narcissistic self . . . has been insufficiently modified because traumatic onslaughts on the child's self esteem have driven the grandiose fantasies into repression, then the adult ego will tend to vacillate between an irrational overestimation of the self and feelings of inferiority and will react with narcissistic mortification to the thwarting of its ambitions. [*ibid.*, p. 251]

Parental acceptance of the child's grandiosity is phase appropriate, and if it does not occur, then repression of the narcissistic self will be the result. One might state that a longing for an idealized object or a searching for an idealized object, and an inability to tolerate frustration of one's own ambitions, are hallmarks of a person who has not optimally passed through narcissistic development. Although Kohut has largely stayed within a Freudian overlay, he has already extended and clarified the theory and put it more firmly along an object relations pathway. Thus, the idea of superego development is now firmly tied to narcissistic issues that continue from pre-Oedipal stages to the Oedipal stage. In Kohut's next significant paper, he uses his new theoretical concepts to put forth his ideas about the treatment of narcissistic personality disorders.

Treatment implications

In his previous paper, Kohut has already stated that narcissistic character disorders display transference reactions that can be activated in psychoanalysis. In this paper, he leaves the term "narcissistic self", labelling it tautological, and instead substitutes the phrase "grandiose self". There are still two interrelated developmental tracks, which involve a grandiose and exhibitionistic image of the self (formerly narcissistic self) and the idealized parental image. At the beginning of the essay, Kohut, in elaborate form, sets the conditions under which he believes an analysis can take place. He states,

> Severe regressions, whether occurring spontaneously or during therapy, may lead to the activation of unstable, prepsychological fragments of the mind–body–self and its functions which belong to the stage of autoerotism (cf. Nagera, 1964). The pathognomonically specific, transferencelike, therapeutically salutary conditions, however, on which I am focusing, are based on the activation of psychologically elaborated, cohesive configurations which enter into stable amalgamations with the narcissistically perceived psychic representation of the analyst. The relative stability of this narcissistic transference-amalgamation, however, is the prerequisite for the performance of the analytic task in the pathogenic narcissistic areas of the personality. [1968, p. 86]

(This long extract is included to give the reader a sense of the traditional language that was still part of Kohut's psychoanalytic writing style.)

Kohut, here, is setting a boundary where he maintains that if a patient is not able to maintain a stable transference-amalgamation towards the analyst, then an analysis is not possible. He admits that it is difficult to predict whether narcissistic patients will be able to maintain this condition, but, nevertheless, he is willing to put forth a view as to the most effective way to achieve a feasible analytic result. In contemporary terms, Kohut is maintaining that some borderline and psychotic patients are not amenable to the type of treatment that he is advocating. In order to avoid the possibility of becoming anachronistic, I have to repeat that the type of patient that Kohut is describing was frequently considered unanalysable in the USA's psychoanalytic institutes.

In his initial conceptualization, Kohut maintains that there are two main types of narcissistic transference states: idealizing and mirroring transferences. Idealizing transferences are considered those reactions where there is an activation of the idealized parent. Mirroring transferences involved the activation of the grandiose self. Kohut describes the progression in idealizing transferences and in mirroring transferences. The aim of the idealizing transference is to be reunited with an object that can protect and provide supplies for the person who feels powerless and empty without the idealized object (similar underlying dynamic for either transference state). There is a developmental period of vulnerability where the internalization (and transmutation) of the parental representation can be disrupted. This period extends from early infancy through at least the beginning of latency. In this formulation, the successful internalization of the superego allows the child to become independent of the idealized object. The superego subsumes some of the idealization that was reserved for parental figures. The beginning of latency may be considered as still belonging to the Oedipal phase, and so the era of narcissistic vulnerability extends from early infancy to the beginning aspects of latency. This, of course, is, in a sense, a probabilistic statement, since trauma at any stage of development can render the child, adolescent, or adult vulnerable.

If a patient is prone to an idealizing transference, Kohut asserts that little need be said about the beginning of the treatment as long as "the analyst does not interfere by premature transference interpretations" (1968, p. 94). Although he states that the pathognomic regression will establish itself spontaneously, he also declares that there may be severe resistances, given the patient's fear of losing their sense of self or individuality. Kohut does not see these statements as contradictory and, rather, discusses the course of an idealizing transference. When the transference is more fully developed the "patient feels powerful, good and capable" (*ibid.*, p. 93). It is when there is a disruption in the transference through ordinary events, long weekends, vacations, illness, etc., or countertransference induced disruptions, that what Kohut calls the working through phase of the analysis can begin. When the patient experiences a break in the analyst's perfection (empathy) they simultaneously experience the analysis as creating a disturbance in their self-esteem. At this point, they have to be aided by the analyst's interpretive efforts. Kohut describes issues involved in interpretative efforts as occurring in two separate stages. Initially, the major experience of the analysand is one of turning away from the idealized object (the analyst) and exhibiting aspects of the grandiose self. If, however, the analyst is able to interpret the meaning of separations from the analyst on the appropriate level, the transference can resume. The analyst must interpret to the idealizing or narcissistic "libido" and the interpretations should be given with "correct empathy for the analysand's feelings— . . . then there will gradually emerge a host of meaningful memories which concern the dynamic prototypes of the present experience" (*ibid.*, p. 95). Although Kohut mentions, but does not stress, the analyst's countertransference difficulties, he implies that there is substantial strain and some difficulty in the analyst remaining empathic when the patient becomes cold, aloof, and grandiose. This grandiose reaction frequently occurs in response to separations, but more frequent and less dramatic examples include the patient's perceiving a break in the analyst's empathy. However, if the analyst can empathically interpret the patient's disrupted experience, then there will be a host of meaningful memories. For example,

> The patient will recall lonely hours during his childhood in which he attempted to overcome a feeling of fragmentation, hypochondria, and deadness which was due to the separation from the idealized parent. And he will remember, and gratefully understand, how he tried to substitute for the idealized parent imago and its functions by creating erotized replacements and through the frantic hypercathexis of the grandiose self: how he rubbed his face against the rough floor in the basement, looked at the mother's photograph, went through her drawers and smelled her underwear; and how he turned to the performance of grandiose athletic feats in which flying fantasies were being enacted by the child, in order to reassure himself. Adult analogues in the analysis (during the weekend, for example) are intense voyeuristic preoccupations, the impulse to shoplift, and recklessly speedy drives in the car. Childhood memories and deepening understanding of the analogous transference experiences converge in giving assistance to the patient's ego, and the formerly automatic reactions become gradually more aim-inhibited. [*ibid.*, p. 94]

Gradually, the patient will be able to tolerate these shifts in the idealizing transference and be able to maintain a more continuous transference state. Thus, the patient will tolerate disruptions even when the analyst is experienced as, or is actually, separate from the analysand. This gradually developed ability is a sign of structure building. Structure building is concomitantly a sign of the patient completing (moving towards completion of) a line of narcissistic development during analysis. In this discussion, the idealizing transference is eventually transmuted into a healthy structure involving relatively depersonified ideals without strong sadistic and masochistic implications.

Later (1977), Kohut puts forth the idea of the bipolar self thus joining the grandiose self and the idealized object in one structure. During this era, however (1968, 1971), activation of the grandiose self is seen as a separate type of transference state. When the grandiose self is activated in the transference, Kohut labels this a mirroring transference. There are three types of mirroring transference: the earliest (developmentally) is the merger transference, then the twinship, and then what he calls the mirroring transference proper, or what we might label the "gleam in the eye" transference. The merger transference is a state where the person incorporates or includes the analyst in their sense of self. The analyst then is seen as part of themselves. A later form of transference, the twinship or alter-ego transference, is one where the person perceives the other as similar to or just like themselves. What I have called the gleam in the eye transference is one which, in Kohut's terms, mirrors the child's exhibitionistic display where the child is enriched and strengthened by the mother's (parents') attention and acceptance of their play and accomplishments. Through the gleam in the eye, the mother is able to direct or influence the child's activities and sense of appropriate play. As one can see, these transference states are viewed as being virtually direct analogues of childhood experiences.

The key element in the mirror transference is allowing the patient's childhood exhibitionistic fantasies to effloresce. Although this is the key element, Kohut writes that this may be quite difficult; the analyst may be disappointed at the relatively mundane associations that the patient provides. Kohut explains that shame, embarrassment, and a sense of humiliation prevents the analysand from easily being able to transmit their fantasy material. Thus, childhood fantasies of running the world through thought control may be difficult to activate, but, once activated, Kohut warns against attempting to provide a realistic view when these fantasies appear in the treatment situation. If there is a break in the idealizing or mirroring transference, Kohut says that

> Analogous to the therapeutically invaluable, controlled, temporary swings toward the disintegration of the idealizing parent imago

when the idealizing transference is disturbed, we may encounter as a consequence of a disturbance of the mirror transference the temporary fragmentation of the narcissistically cathected, cohesive (body–mind) self and a temporary concentration of the narcissistic cathexes on isolated body parts, isolated mental functions, and isolated actions, which are then experienced as dangerously disconnected from a crumbling self. [1968, p. 98]

The temporary fragmentation of the patient's sense of self, if properly interpreted, leads to an understanding of the role of the analyst's gaze (presence) in establishing the patient's sense of completeness. Gradually, as the grandiose self is revealed, it will lead to the "integration of the grandiose self into the realistic structure of the ego" (*ibid.*, p. 99). The goal of this integration is to first establish, then free from inhibitions, the person's potential for action through ego controlled ambitions and a sense of realistic, positive self-esteem.

Analytic dangers

Kohut, in effect, warns against Alexander's ideas about the corrective emotional experience (Alexander et al., 1946) in that it is usually a mistake to encourage or attempt to stimulate an idealizing or mirroring transference. One might imagine that Kohut would be particularly sensitive to this possibility, since members of the analytic community were already maintaining that his form of treatment bordered on Alexander's ideas of corrective emotional experience. In this vein, Kohut relates that when the analyst does not theoretically understand the analytic process, they "tend to supplement their interpretations with suggestive pressure and the weight of the personality of the therapist becomes of greater importance" (1968, p. 101). However, as our understanding of the issues surrounding narcissism increases, the analytic work becomes "the work of rational success: interpretations and reconstructions" (*ibid.*, p. 102). Thus, the analyst who needed to beguile the patient or dazzle the patient will be replaced by the analyst who can steadfastly apply "solid" analytic principles.

Kohut states that there several analytic "pitfalls" that the analyst may fall into in the treatment of narcissistic patients. He posits a "triad of value judgments, moralizing and therapeutic activism" where the analyst leaves the "basic analytic attitude to become the patient's leader and teacher" (*ibid.*). In addition, there is a possibility of a tendency towards abstract interpretations. Of course, other analysts might state that these dangers are present in all analyses. The question should be, are they more likely to occur in the treatment of narcissistic patients and, if so, why is this the case? Kohut suggests an answer in an example that I have cited several times (Ellman, 1991, 1998a). A Catholic patient had dreams of an inspired, idealistic priest that were assumed to be transference dreams about the analyst. The analyst did not interpret these dreams, but, early in the treatment (when the dreams occurred), related to the patient that he was not a Catholic. He rationalized that he informed the patient of this "reality" because her "hold on reality was tenuous" (*ibid.*, p. 104). Kohut notes that the analyst's behaviour was a rejection of the patient's attempt to forge a mirroring (twinship) transference. Kohut's conclusion is a statement about the countertransference tendencies inherent in treating narcissistic patients:

> An analytically unwarranted rejection of a patient's idealizing attitudes is usually motivated by a defensive fending off of narcissistic tensions, experienced as embarrassment and leading even to hypochondriacal preoccupations, which are generated in the analyst when repressed fantasies of his grandiose self become stimulated by the patient's idealization. [*ibid.*]

Kohut states that the rejections may be small or large, subtle or obvious, but when the analyst in one way or another rejects the patient's transference, the analysis is stifled. Interestingly, in this context, Kohut quotes Freud when he says, "To give someone too little because one loves him too much is being unjust to the patient and a technical error" (*ibid.*, Freud, 1913). Here, Kohut is looking at a countertransference reaction that, in a sense, is counter-intuitive. It is relatively easy to see and relate to the dangers of overtly influencing the patient, attempting to become the charismatic analyst or quasi religious figure. However, Kohut is also positing (and offering case illustrations to bolster his assumptions) that it is quite difficult to accept idealizations. It is also difficult to accept a grandiose patient's transference, but this seems more in line with one's prejudices. It is not easy to relate to a person who is gradually becoming unrealistically enraptured with their own accomplishments, emotional life, and thought processes. However, an idealization is frequently a sought after experience. Why this should be difficult for the analyst is answered by Kohut when he says that in the twinship transference, "the analyst is deprived of even the minimum of narcissistic gratification: the patient's acknowledgement of his separate existence" (1968, p. 107). In this context, I would suggest that Kohut is providing an implicit explanation of the difficulties involved in receiving all transference, not only certain types of narcissistic transference states.

A note on beginning the treatment

Kohut, in this essay, focuses on narcissistic transferences, but, at the end of his essay (and in his 1971 book), he puts forth some of his experience in beginning the treatment with narcissistic patients. He cites a case where he gradually learnt that the patient would be calmed if he only summarized or repeated what she had, in essence, already said. He found that if he ventured beyond what the patient had discovered or thought that she would feel, he was ruining the analysis. (Interestingly, a neo-Kleinian analyst made the same discovery many years later, without mentioning Kohut [see Britton, 1997]. This, of course, is not surprising, since Kohut mentions few other analysts and only at the end of various publications tells us that would have been interesting to compare his work to Jacobson, Klein, and Hartmann to mention just a few names [Kohut, 1968, p. 111].) Clearly, at this point in time, Kohut felt that this example might be considered by some to be non-analytic. Therefore, Kohut again returns to the implicit analytic criticism that he is indulging the patient in order to provide a corrective emotional experience. He is almost vehement when he states that this is only a beginning point in terms of the manifestation of the patient's grandiose self. Later, when the demand could be relaxed, "It was followed by the recall of clusters of analogous memories concerning her mother's entering a phase of depressive self-preoccupation during later periods of the patient's life" (1968, p. 110). Kohut provides more about this patient, but I wish to dwell on how, at this point in time, he is frequently concerned about leaving the classical analytic mode. He needs to demonstrate that he is not gratifying the patient or moving away from the primary analytic instrument, the interpretation. However, even a casual reading of Kohut at this point in his career would lead one to believe that of course he is moving away from the classical tradition. In many ways, he is setting the groundwork for questioning a number of assumptions that were shibboleths of the classical tradition. The question that one might ask here is whether Kohut's ideas can be integrated within a Freudian tradition, but this question will be taken up in Chapter Seventeen of this volume.

Kohut ends this section of his writings by saying that the role of aggression had to be bypassed, and, in his next essay, he gives his version of the role of aggression in the treatment of narcissistic patients.

Narcissistic rage and a further theoretical movement

Kohut's essay on narcissistic rage (1972) is both poetic and evocative, and it gives a version of Kohut's ideas about both rage and aggression. He will write about rage primarily as a response to narcissistic slights or, more accurately, psychological "blows" that cause humiliation and shame. Rage is, in this formulation, a manifestation of an attempt to restore the grandiose self and the idealized object. Before Kohut gets to rage and aggression, he takes a step on a journey that distances him from his Freudian, or, more accurately, his classical, colleagues. He states this point in an interesting way.

> My comments up to this point may be regarded as my attempt to tidy up the house before going on a trip. The house is the work on the libidinal aspects of narcissism—work which is already done but where I wish to straighten out odds and ends before I can leave it. The trip should lead into the rugged terrain of narcissistic rage and, later, into the far-off region of group psychology. [1972, p. 372]

His tidying up took up a good portion of the paper and obviously was quite important to him. It also demonstrated his new directions that, in hindsight, seem inevitable.

Bits and pieces towards the new self-psychology

He begins this cleansing by solidifying a point implied by his previous publications (Kohut, 1966, 1968, 1971). He states that the most important point about narcissistic development is the idea that it is an "independent line of development, from the primitive to the most mature, adaptive, and culturally valuable" (1972, p. 361). Not only is narcissistic development a separate line, it is a line primarily determined by parental responsiveness. "At times parents will relate to the child in empathic narcissistic merger and (at other times) look upon the child as to an independent center of his own initiative, i.e., they invest him with object libido" (*ibid.*, p. 362). Here, Kohut is clearly moving away from the drives as the main determinant of childhood development and, instead, primarily talking about the interaction between parent and child as the decisive factor in both narcissistic and object libidinal development. He also returns to the analyst's attitude towards narcissism, and this time criticizes what he and others have called the U-tube theory.

Freud's model in his paper "On narcissism" (1914c) implied that, in as far as one had narcissistic concerns, concerns about other people (objects) would diminish. Thus, if one invested libido in one's self, libido would shift in the tube away from the other person. An ill person, in this model, does not think about other people, but concentrates on their pain or discomfort. Conversely, if one is in love, then it is possible to endure various kinds of pain (the lover waiting in the cold and rain) to reach the loved one. While Kohut acknowledges that the U-tube can explain these phenomena, he states that the phenomena can just as easily be explained in terms of a deployment of attention (attention cathexes). Thus, when someone is filled with love or pain they can attend to little else.

Kohut finds a difficulty in another area when he concludes that "The sense of heightened self-esteem, for example, which accompanies object love demonstrates a relationship between the two forms of libidinal cathexis which does not correspond to that of the oscillations in a U-tube system" (1972, p. 363). In contradistinction to Kohut's assertion, one should note that Freud's concept was that a lover's self-esteem would increase if they were loved in return, but if their love was unrequited, then self-esteem would suffer. Freud was maintaining that self-esteem was dependent on the interaction between lovers or potential lovers. While I believe this explanation is not incompatible with the U-tube model, it is not Freud's main point. Freud's thesis here is that in love there is a necessary relationship between people (objects) and that the only way one can gain ultimate satisfaction is through personal intimacy (object relations). Freud could have logically dispensed with the metaphor of the U-tube model; the important aspects of Freud's thought are perhaps much closer to what Kohut is proposing then Kohut is able or willing to state.

Kohut is, however, not as involved with a critique of Freud as he is in establishing a theoretical–clinical line that is separate from classical analysis. His main concern is to do away with narcissism acquiring "a slightly pejorative connotation", where narcissistic manifestations are viewed as either "a product of regression or defense" (*ibid.*). He has already implicitly and explicitly tried to illustrate the potential countertransference difficulties that analysts have in treating narcissistic patients, and, here, he is again pointing out the difficulties as well as the lack of acceptance of healthy manifestations of narcissism. In terms of a society, if there are not outlets for manifestations of the grandiose self and the idealized object, there will be cultural disruptions that will be difficult to control. He likens the hypocrisy towards sex in the Victorian era to ongoing hypocritical attitudes towards the manifestations of narcissism.

While the analyst's attitude towards narcissism is a key issue for Kohut, in addition, he looks at a number of other issues that gradually will divide him from the American classical community. He makes a distinction between ego dominance and ego autonomy, which, in some ways, is crucial to an important whole aspect of the paradigm in psychoanalysis. Ego autonomy is analogized (by Kohut) to the rider off the horse as he stands by himself and "reflects coolly and dispassionately [about] . . . the data of his observations" (*ibid.*, p. 365). Ego dominance is the rider on the horse, or a person as he responds to his internal world and to "forces within himself as he shapes his goals and forms his major reactions to the environment" (*ibid.*). The ideal of ego autonomy, an analytic goal of classical analysis, is part of Kohut's attempts at the de-mythologizing of classical ideals. It implies something which Kohut, here, does not overtly focus on, but is an essential point in his discussions about the goals of psychoanalysis. The ideal states that a well analysed person is able to stand alone and be completely self-sufficient. It does not take into account the person's continuing need for another. Embedded in this view is the idea of the capacity to be alone, and it is not clear to what extent Kohut's concept of ego dominance embraces this factor. Ego dominance includes the individual's reactions to, and relations with, the environment. It is part of Kohut's movement towards the concept of self-object (selfobject). In this vein, Kohut asks the question as to whether he is "the Pied Piper who leads the young away from the solid ground of the object-libidinal aspects of the Oedipus complex" (ibid., p. 366). He realizes that he is not simply extending Freudian thought, but, in his view, putting forth an alternative to Freudian theory. It is important to recognize that he is contrasting his theoretical views with an American version of Freudian thought (or, one might say, the theory Freud proposed in his late theoretical papers). He asks the question of whether or not he is providing an impetus for "old resistances against the full acceptance of the emotional reality of the Oedipal drama" (ibid.). The form of this question is interesting, since it is Kohut who brings forth Freud's views on the purified pleasure ego (Freud, 1915c), which pre-dates Freud's Oedipal preoccupations. Why is this concept not considered as Freudian as the Oedipus complex? Kohut must have known that Freud, during this period, was positing fixation points that had nothing to do with the Oedipal drama (see Chapter Three). Yet, in his characterization of Freudian theory, he joins with Arlow and Brenner (1964) in their characterization of a Freudian position. They see the Oedipal stage as the bedrock of the internalization of conflict, or the point at which conflict for all disorders is structuralized. While it is true for Arlow and Brenner and for many classical analysts that all conflict stems from the Oedipal stage, Freud, even in 1926, seemed less certain. He remained open to the idea that perhaps there are other ways of conceptualizing these issues that might be more inclusive and more useful in explaining a wide range of experiences.

As a final point around this issue, Kohut presents the conflict between positions as choosing between a theory that emphasizes narcissistic issues and one that emphasizes issues in the "object-instinctual realm" (1972, p. 366). Interestingly, in his 1966 paper, while he maintained that the idealized object was "cathected with narcissistic libido", he stated that even at this early stage there are aspects of object love. In this early, yet relatively full, statement about narcissistic development, Kohut is able to see more of an admixture between object love and narcissism. This admixture will reappear, but in a different form, in his later publications.

Although he had used the term before (1971), Kohut here begins to more forcefully described early experiences in self-object (selfobject) terms. This usages portends the direction of his theorizing: all phenomena will be considered to occur within a selfobject matrix. A selfobject obviously implies a connection in a person's representational field between self and other. At first, Kohut thought of this as an archaic or early form of representation, but this essay may be considered close to the tipping point in proposing his new theory of development. Here, his theory veers towards the importance of self cohesion above all other factors, as well as the idea that selfobject states occur throughout optimal childhood and adult development. The issue of narcissism in this essay becomes omnipresent, and he writes that "the sensitivity of a child about their genitals is at its peak during the phallic phase of psychosexual development . . . this . . . constitutes the leading zone of the child's (bodily) narcissism" (1972, p. 372). There is a similar narcissistic cathexis of the faeces during the anal stage of development, etc.

He is presaging a later tendency to formulate all psychopathology in terms of narcissistic issues. In this conceptualization, the affect of shame and conflicts over exhibitionistic tendencies are pathognomonic to all, or at least most, psychological conditions. In the 1972 paper, Kohut mentions what he calls pseudo classical patients (pseudotransference neurotics). However, he also posits that there are pseudonarcissistic disorders. He relates that the only reliable way to distinguish these disorders is to observe the transference manifestations in a treatment situation. Here, we can see that there is still a type of complementarity in approach, but the basic fault (a Balint term [Balint, 1968]) is derived during the narcissistic phase of development even if there is a transference neurosis. Kohut, as is frequently the case during this era, cites an obligatory passage from Freud. The passage that is quoted involves a commentary about the biographical novelist Emil Ludwig, who was strongly influenced by Adler. In this novel, Ludwig explained Emperor Wilhelm's willingness to take offence and go to war as a reaction to the Emperor's organ inferiority (the Emperor was born with a withered arm). Freud answered in a direct way by saying, "Not so! It was not the birth injury in itself which resulted in Emperor Wilhelm's sensitivity to narcissistic slights, but the rejection by his proud mother who could not tolerate an imperfect child" (Kohut, 1972. p. 372). Thus, Freud was, in effect, saying that if this mother could have provided the appropriate mirroring or narcissistic supplies to this child, he could have overcome his birth defect. Kohut agrees with this analysis and obviously disagrees with Adler's theory of organ inferiority. Interestingly, while Kohut cites Freud in a confirming manner, he then undoes it somewhat by stating that Freud, in speaking of Adler, praised him by noting the valuable work he had done on organ inferiority. This is a clear sign of Kohut's ambivalence, since the quote that he mentions is one where Freud devastates Adler and virtually calls him incompetent and unable to understand unconscious processes. Freud's praise of Adler is almost sarcastic in tone, and, at the very most, it is an attempt to say something positive about a man to whom Freud is saying is unworthy to be an analyst. That Kohut could write as if Freud were praising Adler, I would interpret as a way of undoing his previous comments about Freud. Clearly, Kohut is both bound to Freud and attempting to achieve some autonomy, or at least some dominance over his selfobject tie to Freudian thought.

Narcissistic rage

After this long detour, Kohut does get to the topic at hand, his views on rage and the differentiation between rage and aggression. Kohut's stance is one where he, in effect, states that narcissistic rage occurs when the person has to maintain a sense of grandiosity which is the equivalent of state of "purified pleasure". This state implies that the enraged person has lost his libidinal cathexis for the object toward which the rage is directed. Here, the term "object" has some utility, for the object can be part of one's body or another person. The emotional state of rage does not reach a sated condition until the object has been destroyed (actually or symbolically). Thus, it is not enough to defeat the other person; the enraged individual must destroy or at least utterly humiliate his/her adversary. Shame or, more accurately, a sense of humiliation is at the heart of narcissistic rage, and here Kohut reminds us of his distinction between tragic man (where shame and humiliation are key affects) *vs.* guilty man (Kohut's version of Freudian thought). The image of guilty man does not lead one to shame or embarrassment, but to a feeling of doing something wrong or having anxiety about the thought or plan to do something that is in conflict with internalized standards (superego standards). Kohut is here subtly contending that manifestations of shame and embarrassment are much more common than we have thought. He gives the example of a slip of the tongue while giving a talk; the speaker might joke about the slip, but the speaker is much more concerned about the loss of omnipotent control than the content of the slip. Taking this point to a clinically relevant realm, Kohut states that "Everybody tends to react to psychoanalysis as a narcissistic injury because it gives the lie to our conviction that we are in full control of our mind" (1972, p. 387). For this point, Kohut references Freud, and, as is well known, Freud thought of psychoanalysis as a narcissistic blow not just to the individual, but to society, since it brought into question the issue of conscious control and the conscious rationale for our actions. Freud likened his "discoveries" to Copernicus placing the sun at the centre of our solar system instead of the earth as the centre of the cosmos. This narcissistic blow to our view of the planets and stars was clearly unsettling to many people, and Copernicus's and Galileo's discoveries were fought against by the church and many other authorities. Kohut shows how these narcissistic blows are central to the individual's feeling of lack of control and an attack against the person's (and society's) sense of perfection and control.

As Kohut discusses these blows to narcissism, he reminds analysts that narcissism should not be "destroyed by analysis", but that it can be transformed with the support of a non-hypocritical attitude toward narcissism and a recognition of "its own line of development and which neither should—nor indeed could—be relinquished" (*ibid.*, p. 388). He also points out that, in analysis, narcissistic rage may occur if the analyst can allow the patient the freedom to express his extreme frustration and humiliation at his failure to live up to his sense of grandiosity. Alternatively, narcissistic rage may occur if the patient experiences the failure of the idealized object to provide enough supplies to keep them whole.

This rage need not doom an analysis, but, in fact, provide a useful therapeutic experience if the analytic pair can survive the rage. Gradually, rage can be transformed into aggression, which implies that the state is under the control of the person's ego. Kohut's ideas about aggression involve not only ego control, but are limited in time and space and therefore instrumental in nature. Aggression is designed to accomplish an environmental task, rage is designed to cure an archaic deficit in the grandiose self or idealized object. This deficit usually demands control over a selfobject tie and the control needs to be absolute. If rage persists, the "aims and goals of the personality, becomes more and more subservient to the pervasive rage" (*ibid.*, p. 396). When this occurs, "We are . . . witnessing the . . . establishment of chronic narcissistic rage, one of the most pernicious afflictions of the human psyche" (*ibid.*). Kohut conceives of this rage as pernicious not only to an individual's psychological development, but also in terms of a society's health. Kohut is naturally occupied with narcissistic concerns of Germany and the rise of Hitler and the Nazi regime. In his analysis, the collective humiliation of Germany after the First World War was a strong factor in understanding the rise of the Nazi party in Germany. Kohut ends this essay on a regretful note; he clearly has wanted to talk to the social implications of his concepts and was not, nor will ever be, fully satisfied with his efforts in this area.

The split becomes more distinct

During the five years after the paper on narcissistic rage (1972), there was a strong movement of analysts, who were frequently called self-psychologists, who adhered to Kohutian theory. Gedo and Goldberg (1973) produced what, in another era, might have been a seminal volume that attempted to comparatively explore psychoanalytic theories that were in existence at the time of publication. They showed the continuities between Kohut and Freud and ego psychology, and tried to evaluate the differences among theoretical positions. This volume had little effect on the psychoanalytic community since, as Bob Dylan had proclaimed in a different context, the times they were a-changing, and positions were beginning to diverge and separate. Self-psychology was now an important movement in the USA. This movement did not see itself as a supplement to Freudian psychoanalysis, but, rather, as a replacement for Freudian psychoanalysis and ego psychology. Authors like Goldberg, Wolf, Stolorow, Atwood, and the Ornsteins came to clarify, explicate, and, at times, extend the concepts that Kohut had put forth. In many ways, Kohut's next work, *The Restoration of the Self* (1977), solidified his movement away from a Freudian orientation. He could not fully move away, and so we will see oscillations in Kohut's positions, but the main impetus of his papers after 1975 is the establishment of a self-psychological theory that is gently (or, in the hands of others, strongly) in opposition to Freudian theory, and covering ground as yet unexplored by authors in the Freudian tradition.

The need for self

Kohut begins *Restoration of the Self* by examining the termination phase of psychoanalysis. In effect, he says that if a patient is able to create a new selfobject pattern, then a termination phase has begun. More specifically, it is possible to achieve analytic success by uncovering an exploration of the primary defect and "via working through and transmuting internalization, sufficiently filled out so that the formerly defective structures of the self have now become functionally reliable" (1977, p. 4). (Internalization is Kohut's term for new selfobject structures that become internalized as part of the self.) It is also possible to achieve analytic success without uncovering the "primary defect", but by developing or encouraging existing compensatory structures that "have now become functionally reliable" (*ibid.*). This second pathway seems remarkably like Sullivan's concept of functional autonomy, and, in a subsequent publication, Kohut (1984) expresses surprise that a friendly colleague would have the impression that Kohut has moved to the position where depth exploration is considered unnecessary. The unidentified colleague had the impression that Kohut advocated breaking off analyses before getting into material that is too disturbing. Kohut is surprised by this reading of the text, and attempts to clarify his position. He says that in only a small number of cases, and not in the majority of cases that he has commented on, is it possible to continue an existing compensatory structure as the main avenue in an analytic treatment. Although a quantitative exploration of cases and the number of cases where compensatory structure criteria are utilized is explored by Kaufmann (1983), it is not the numbers that are germane in this context. Rather, what is more important is the direction of Kohut's writings, and one interpretation is that he is bringing forth a concept that is analogous to Sullivan's functional autonomy. The uncovering of unconscious fantasy, or unconscious ideation, is diminished in the course of the exploration of issues in the *Restoration of the Self*. Instead, Kohut speaks of

> A valid termination of an analysis that has—in terms of structure—*not* dealt with all the layers of the essential pathology of the analysand, that has—in terms of cognition—not led to the undoing of all infantile amnesias, to the expansion of knowledge concerning all those events of childhood that are genetically and dynamically related to the psychopathology from which the patient suffers. [1977, p. 64]

Here, Kohut is not mentioning a small number of cases; he is clearly stating that in analysis of the self one does not have to deal with all layers of structure or fantasy. It does not seem surprising that his otherwise supportive colleague might have the impression that Kohut does not see the need to explore some difficult issues and still be able to conclude a fully successful analysis. Kohut strongly implies that there may be a greater possibility of success if one facilitates the building of compensatory structures. It is surprising that Kohut is startled by his colleague's response. It is probably a sign of his defensiveness, for he could have argued that his technique leads to depth in other senses of the term, particularly in terms of the analysand's deep experience in the selfobject transference. The analyst's experience also will be deeply involving if he/she employs a consistent introspective–empathetic stance. However, certain types of content will be less readily available, and I believe this is borne out in the cases Kohut and his colleagues cite (Kaufmann, 1983).

The key element in treatment is the quality of selfobject transference. An analysis should facilitate creative functioning, and it is through the selfojbect transference that creativity is facilitated.

Kohut, in this vein, states,

> I presented clinical material in support of the thesis that we may consider an analysis completed when by achieving success in the area of compensatory structures it has established a functioning self—a psychological sector in which ambitions, skills, and ideals form an unbroken continuum that permits joyful creative activity. [1977, p. 63]

The idea of joyful creative activity is a key element in Kohut's ideas about analytic success. One might say that, in Kohut's view, tragic man's creativity is unleashed in analysis and becomes joyful, hopeful, and able. It is rare that guilty man is thought to do as well. Kohut, in stating his criteria for analytic success, continuously compares his stance to analysts who believe that the end of an analysis is the full exploration and resolution of Oedipal fantasies. While this is certainly the dominant Freudian view of his time, it was not the only view that was available for comparison.

If the cohesion and continuity of the bipolar or nuclear self is crucial to achieve via the analytic process, Kohut understandably sees an obligation to provide a theoretical structure for the concept of self. His conceptualization of analytic success naturally leads him to a discussion of the need in psychoanalysis for a psychology of the self. Clearly, Kohut, by the time of this volume, has gently left the terminology describing two separate developmental lines and instead conceptualizes development in terms of the "bipolar self". The bipolar self indicates a stronger relationship between two components of the self structure, which still are the grandiose–exhibitionistic self, and the idealized object or parental object. The nuclear self contains this bipolar structure as well as an intermediate area, which deals with the executive functions of the person (self). The "executive functions (talents, skills) are needed for the realization of the patterns of the basic ambitions and basic ideals that were laid down in the two polar areas" (*ibid.*, p. 49). These executive functions take the place of the (Freudian) ego. In addition, Kohut shows how the concept of self is necessary to understand clinical material that in the past was either only partly understood or misunderstood.

What is distinctly new in this volume is Kohut's declaration that the drives are what he terms disintegration products that are produced by the lack of appropriate parental empathy. Thus, a preoccupation with "anal concerns" (dirt, tidiness, compulsions, and oscillations between these traits) signals a break down of parental responsiveness during this period. What needs to be emphasized is that it is the coherence of the self and the selfobject relationship that is crucial in development. If we take the Oedipal child as an example (and this is a frequent example of Kohut's), then we can say that during the Oedipal period there are two forms of anxiety that may be present.

> The primary anxiety of the Oedipal period, which I consider to be the more basic of the two types, arises in response to the defective empathy of the child's parents, that is, in response to the selfobject matrix that does not sustain the child. [1984, p. 16]

The secondary anxiety, which, according to Kohut, is often more apparent, is what Freud and Klein described as anxiety over sexual and destructive drives. This secondary anxiety occurs because of the disintegration of the healthy Oedipal self, which otherwise is "characterized by affectionate and assertive attitudes" (*ibid.*). The first anxiety is seen as disintegration anxiety and "It is the deepest anxiety man can experience" (*ibid.*). The depth of this anxiety is such that the attempt to describe it is likened to the attempt to describe the indescribable. It is more basic than, although not unrelated to, the fear of death. In searching for words, Kohut calls this anxiety a loss of humanness. Kohut provides some dreams and experiences centred around these dreams that he feels provides some sense of disintegration anxiety.

> The first of these dreams, which I have described in some detail before, is Mr. Z's dream of seeing his mother from the back. Briefly stated, Mr. Z's anxiety at the point of his analysis when the dream occurred related to this relinquishment of a selfobject. More specifically, the anxiety related to the relinquishment of the selfobject functions of the mother whose own needs for selfobject had up to that point prevented Mr. Z. from disentangling his personality from hers. By accepting this enslavement, he had, up to this time, retained the hope that his tentative moves toward independent maleness would ultimately elicit an accepting—approving smile from her that would consolidate his self. By rejecting the enslavement, as he was in the process of doing with a father—analyst, Mr. Z. gave up

this hope, confronting for a last time the horrible fear that he could never again elicit his mother's smile. The mother had become faceless. [1977, pp. 16–17]

Clearly, this dream could be interpreted in many ways, but Kohut, with this now somewhat famous patient Mr. Z (one biographer [Strozier, 2001] has suggested that Mr Z is Kohut himself), sees the faceless mother as a loss of the hope of an adequate selfobject experience and consequently a loss of humanness. Kohut reconstructed this experience through the nature of Mr Z's transference and Mr Z's difficulty in engaging in a selfobject transference state. Here, it is important to keep in mind that Kohut sees this transference as important for two related reasons: (a) to understand through an introspective–empathic stance Mr Z's self states; (b) to begin the process of transmuting internalization (Kohut, 1971, 1977, 1984). For this process to continue, there must be optimal frustration in the context of an empathic analyst. In both his 1977 and 1984 volumes, Kohut emphasizes a concept that I alluded to earlier in the chapter (Kohut, 1959); that is, an introspective–empathic stance. Kohut has argued that psychoanalytic data and concepts are only feasible through the utilization of this stance. In this early paper (1959), he argued that Freud's concept of drive is clinically relevant in so far as one can experience it via the patient's transference. He concluded that while sex and aggression were possible to experience in the analytic situation, biological concepts, such as Eros and Thanatos, were not. In retrospect, this essay was one of the forerunners of a number of trends that has moved psychoanalytic clinicians towards more experience-near concepts.

At this point, we can summarize Kohut's positions and ask whether, in fact, at the end of his career he still adheres to the idea of complementary theoretical positions. The concept of complementarity states that it may be that the use of more than one theory is useful to explain experiences or data within a realm of common, or, rather, overlapping, experiences. Thus, one theory might explain Oedipal disorders (classical theory) while another theory might account for pre-Oedipal disorders (self-psychology). Kohut, in his 1977 volume, carefully states that classical theory is an adequate explanation for Oedipal disorders. He states an important prerequisite for this comment: an analysand must come to the Oedipal stage with an intact, cohesive self-structure. Even with this intact nuclear self, if one has "object instinctual" Oedipal conflicts, the same factors are present as would be the case with psychological disruptions at any other point in development. The cause is always related to the lack of parental empathy, where there was not an adequate selfobject present for the child. This will lead to drive disintegration experiences. It may be possible to analyse a person with such a history by utilizing classical technique, but, even here, the person would be better off with an analyst who utilized principles derived from self-psychology. This is a pallid form of complementarity, and, whatever Kohut's ambivalence about giving up his Freudian legacy, it is clear that he thinks that he has supplanted classical theory and, at this point in time, he equates Freudian and classical theory.

If drives are disintegration products, is there a body self in Kohut's theorizing? Is aggression either appropriate assertiveness or some form of narcissistic rage? Is Kohut's theoretical stance primarily one that is tailored for the psychoanalytic situation, and are his developmental theorems mostly a guide to produce an analyst who values the introspective–empathic approach? These are questions to consider, but, for now, we can say that Kohut is clear that the self needs selfobjects during one's entire life span. Kohut distinguishes between archaic selfobjects and selfobjects that are useful in helping an individual to a joyous creative life. Thus, the structure building that goes on in psychoanalysis is the establishment of new selfobject relationships. Some of Kohut's ideas about psychoanalytic treatment will be discussed more fully in the commentary section, but it is clear that he does not favour early interpretations. In fact, Kohut advocates interpreting only when the patient experiences a break in empathy and the pattern of interpretation has a clear formulation. First, there is an empathic comment about the patient's pain (anxiety, anger, rage, etc.) in being, or experiencing being, misunderstood by the analyst. This is followed at some relevant point by a genetic interpretation (genetic meaning one from the patient's past, usually childhood) showing the patient how this feeling occurred as a result of (usually) parental lack of empathy (or parental inability to provide an adequate selfobject for the patient). The goal of the interpretative efforts are both to provide understanding and a demonstration of empathy, and, as importantly, to allow the patient to continue their transference experience on the way to more adaptive selfobject structures. There are two final points to be made about Kohut's theorizing: one involves his view of normal or optimal development, and the other is a comment on the experience of reading his books and essays.

Kohut clearly believes that, with appropriate parenting, joy and creativity are part of ordinary human experience. Kohut is, of course, a sophisticated analyst and scholar, and so I am sure he did not see joy and creativity abound in the highways and byways of Chicago. What he must be stating are his ideals, if one experienced parenting that could provide the appropriate selfobject experiences for the developing child. He is not the pessimist that Freud was, but seems more like Winnicott in this attitude. He tries to make it clear that, in treatment, he does not blame the patient's parents, but, rather, over an analysis, he expects that the patient will be empathic to the difficulties that confronted his or her parents. Moreover, he consistently holds to the idea that the analyst's introspective–empathic stance should not preclude her from being objective. The use of the concept of objectivity is interesting in light of many relational writers positing the impossibility of the analyst being objective in the treatment situation. More accurately, these writers would claim that objectivity is a meaningless concept. Many would say that Kohut's stance on objectivity is simply an unfortunate residue of his Freudian past and not in line with his new positions. We will all have to mull this and similar issues over and over again.

While Kohut's positions can be stated in a relatively simple, straightforward manner, his discussions are always rich and complex. He, in my view, is always thoughtful and, although his solipsistic approach to the literature is troublesome, he is not alone in taking this approach. Clearly, his relationship to Freud in many ways dominated his approach, and his writing rarely reflects other influences. It is clear that, gradually, Kohut felt it important to establish a position independent of Freud and the contemporary followers of a classical position. Whether one agrees or disagrees with Kohut, if you read his discussions you will encounter a supremely thoughtful mind. Given that this is true, and he himself had to endure a good deal of pain in having to flee his native country, one wonders at the sources of the utopian ideals that stayed with Kohut until the end of his life. A classical analyst would, at the very least, invoke the concept of a character formed in part by profound reaction formation. This simplified view of a complex mind, if applied in this manner, would illustrate the limitations of the classical model.

Commentary

Kohut, in my view, is one of the authors who has changed psychoanalysis in a way that truly enlarges or widens the scope of the field (Stone, 1961). Like Stone, he is helping the clinician treat patients who were deemed untreatable by analytic methods. In my experience, psychoanalysis is now the preferred treatment of choice for the patients that Kohut has described. He has, in Bach's (1985, 1994, 2006) terms, shown us how to enter the world of patients who are narcissistically vulnerable. Winnicott, Klein, Balint, and Fairbairn were also opening the treatment doors for similar patients with similar issues. Kohut, however, is the only theorist who systematically presented a method of treatment that could be understood by future clinicians. His developmental theory is, in this regard, less significant than his ideas about treatment. The developmental ideas that he presents are in accord with a treatment method that advocates the importance of empathic resonance as well as the importance of the reparative effects of facilitating the occurrence of narcissistic transference states.

The developmental model he presents does not feature the infant's/child's active tendencies and, instead, sees the child as only having psychological conflicts as a result of parental lack of empathy. If this is your model, then it is reasonable to have a treatment where this empathy is provided to the patient. However, I would posit that it seems unreasonable that Kohut did not allow for some children who were more aggressive than others, some who felt inadequate despite reasonable parental empathy, and some who transcended parental boundaries in secretive ways and experienced guilt for these transgressions. I have described these children without using the concept of drive, for it seems to me that one can advance the idea of an child with active impulses without using drive theory. Children, clearly, differ in terms of activity levels and sensitivity thresholds, and these differences may alter the way the child perceives the world and internalizes object representations as well as prohibitions and ideals. Kohut's theory does not account for tendencies that the child may bring to the world and how these tendencies may affect mother–child and parental–child interactions.

Leaving aside Kohut's developmental ideas, in my view he advocates that the analyst only interprets when the patient experiences a perceived break in empathy. This can happen due to a variety of circumstances: the analyst's lack of empathy, a long weekend, a disturbing thought that begins to emerge and is externalized to the analyst, etc. There are, in my view, two consequences of limiting interpretative interventions in this way.

1. The patient is not left to explore their negative and often hateful feelings.
2. It is difficult for the patient to experience themselves as separate from the analyst in the analytic situation.

Thus, when the patient is in a negative state, the analyst rapidly attempts to facilitate a return to one or another form of positive transference states. There is an implicit (perhaps more than implicit) message that we (the analytic couple) need not or should not explore these types of feelings. Kohut (in 1977) says, in effect, it is the rare analyst who plumbs the depths of a patient's early (unconscious) life. In my view, if the analyst does not do this the patient is never truly liberated from their early conflicts. Kohut would argue that it is rare for a patient ever to be liberated in this manner; rather, what a good treatment does is form a better selfobject bond that enables the patient to better access their abilities and interpersonal capacities. Kohut takes seriously Sullivan's concept of functional autonomy and conceptualizes a treatment situation that builds a new structure that sits atop or alongside early conflicted internalizations. The analytic relationship, in effect, powers the new structure, which is conceptualized as a new selfobject bond. In my view, Kohut is correct that all or most good analytic experiences end with an improved selfobject bond. However, if one proceeds in the way Kohut advances, there is less room for independence and a lowered probability of a patient developing the ability to continue the analysis after the analysis proper is over. In the final chapters, I present clinical ideas in much greater detail. Although I have outlined some disagreements with Kohut, in my view his contributions far outweigh any disagreements that are presented. Many of my ideas about treatment are strongly influenced by Kohut's contributions. His conceptualizations allow a Freudian to enter the patient's world in a way that enriches the analytic situation. His theory has certainly touched a number of analysts who are self-psychologists, as well as others who come from different theoretical perspectives. It is of note that, in self-psychological circles, Kohut's theory is characterized as classical self-psychology and analysts like Anna Ornstein (1994) and Paul Ornstein (2004) are considered classical self-psychologists. Analysts who place intersubjectivity at the centre of their theoretical matrices are viewed as moving away from classical self-psychology.

CHAPTER FOURTEEN

Kernberg: integrating object relations and ego psychology*

Summary

This chapter follows Kernberg's theoretical integrations as well as his clinical observations. There is a long section on the borderline syndrome and Kernberg's use of Kleinian concepts. In addition, we look at some of the criticisms that have been levelled at Kernberg over the decades. We present the view that at least some of the criticisms are based on Kernberg's object relations perspective.

The beginnings of an integrative approach

It is a difficult task to attempt to summarize and critique Otto Kernberg's psychoanalytic contributions, for he has presented

---

*A version of this chapter has been published previously: Carsky, M., & Ellman, S. (1985). Otto Kernberg: psychoanalysis and object relations theory: the beginnings of an integrative approach. In: J. Reppen (Ed.), *Beyond Freud* (pp. 257–296). Hillsdale, NJ: Analytic Press.

systematic and wide-sweeping clinical and theoretical statements. His work touches on many, if not most, of the topics that have been of interest to contemporary analysts. Even reviewers who have been sharply critical of Kernberg, such as Calef and Weinshel (1979), have stated that "no other single colleague has been so instrumental in confronting American psychoanalysts with Kleinian concepts and theories" (1979, p. 470–471). Although there is no question that Kernberg has been strongly influenced by Kleinian concepts, there is also no question that he is attempting to integrate many different parts of what is called the British object relations school, as well as aspects of Freudian thought, ego psychology, and different strands of research in neurophysiology and physiological psychology. This list is by no means complete. Kernberg is strongly interested in affect research as well as research in psychotherapy.

Kernberg has attempted to combine at least four elements from either an ego psychological or object relations perspective. These are as follows.

1. *Structure.* Although Kernberg has moved the concepts such as self-representation, self-image, and so forth into a more central focus, he has retained Freud's tripartite structure of ego, id, and superego. As we will see, with most of these concepts Kernberg utilizes object relations theorizing to a greater extent when dealing with questions of structuralization early in childhood development and utilizes the tripartite model in later childhood development, particularly in the Oedipal period.
2. *Defence.* Although defence is certainly a part of structure, the concept of defence is important enough in Kernberg's writings to warrant special notice. By and large, what Kernberg calls low-level defences are those that have been discussed by object relation theorists (such as splitting and projective identification), whereas most of Kernberg's high-level defences (such as repression and isolation) stem from Freudian and ego psychological theorists (see Chapter Five). In Kernberg's conceptualizations, the main defences utilized are, thus, an important indication of the general state of an individual's psychological structure.
3. *Development.* Kernberg has attempted to integrate the concept of object relations positions (paranoid–schizoid, depressive position) with the concept of psycho-sexual development and

Mahler's (1968; Mahler, Pine, & Bergman, 1975) developmental findings. Here again, one may see the viewpoint of Mahler and object relations being used more extensively in considering pre-Oedipal development, while Kernberg utilizes ego psychological concepts in considering Oedipal development.
4. *Instinct or drive.* This is a concept that Kernberg has inconsistently maintained in his theorizing. Since some object relations theorists, such as Fairbairn or Guntrip, have explicitly rejected Freud's, Hartmann's, or Klein's concept of drive, Kernberg is not combining two points of view, but, rather, including his version of Freudian ego psychological theorizing in his theoretical framework. It should be pointed out that Kernberg's conceptualization of emotion and affect are particularly important in his theorizing, and, for Kernberg (1976, 1980c, 1982d), these concepts replace drive as a motivational concept.

The main focus of Kernberg's theorizing is the type of patients that, in the past, have been described by Fairbairn (Chapter Nine), Winnicott (Chapter Ten), or Balint (1968). Kernberg has grouped these patients, and maintains that many of these other theorists wrote about people who manifest borderline pathology.

In describing Kernberg's work, we will first note the clinical observations which Kernberg's theory seeks to explain. Then we will present summaries of his contributions in four areas: (a) development; (b) psychoanalytic classification of character pathology, including the borderline diagnosis; (c) treatment implications, derived from the developmental theory and diagnostic system, including the rationale for various treatment recommendations as well as Kernberg's view of countertransference and the therapeutic stance; (d) a theory of drives or early affects. Finally, we will comment on Kernberg's critics and will ourselves critically review what we consider to be major elements in Kernberg's contributions to psychoanalytic theory.

Summary of Kernberg's work

The clinical observations

Kernberg's clinical observation of "borderline adults" has been one of the factors that has led him to expand "traditional" psychoanalytic theory. He observes that this type of person can often maintain rapidly fluctuating, contradictory ego states. These ego states can be manifested as rapidly changing, intense transference reactions (from idealization and love to intense hatred and rage) and can also be seen in initial clinical contacts. Kernberg (1967, 1975, 1980c) has inferred that these contradictory ego states are actively separated or split, and that a person who shows splitting cannot reconcile these contradictory states. In fact, if someone else points out the person's contradictory attitudes, states, or actions, the person would always manifest anxiety. A person's reaction to such an intervention is an important diagnostic indicator to Kernberg (1976, 1981d).

Kernberg feels that when analysts and therapists do not recognize that splitting is taking place, they may fail to understand what is happening in a therapeutic situation. He notes a tendency for alternating transference states to remain static when therapy is viewed over a long period of time. The analyst sometimes takes one of the positive states to be the manifestation of a good working alliance or, alternatively, might feel that a patient's rageful attacks may represent an important break-through, in which the patient may become aware of and begin to understand these "primitive impulses". Kernberg believes that often no intrapsychic change is taking place. Instead, the patient simply alternates presentation of these states. Often, the patient uses the tolerant atmosphere of therapy to derive greater gratification of (in particular) his or her aggressive impulses than would be allowed elsewhere. Or, as in the Menninger study of the effects of supportive psychotherapy (where there was little transference interpretation, and signs of latent negative transference, especially, were unacknowledged), the patient–therapist relationship is shallow or mechanical (Kernberg et al., 1972).

Kernberg points out that, according to traditional observations of this patient population (Federn, 1947; Frosch, 1960; Knight, 1954; Schmideberg, 1947; Zetzel, 1971), they tend to lose the ability to test reality adequately in the context of the psychotherapy (tranference psychoses), to act out severely, and to consciously experience primary process material while apparently lacking a capacity for introspection and insight. The primitive, early reactions of borderline patients to their therapists seem to be not only pre-Oedipal in content, but also less organized than neurotic transference.

Kernberg (1976) concludes that the work of various object relations theorists (Klein, Fairbairn, Guntrip, etc.) described these reactions most accurately as recreations of early actual or fantasized object relationships, as "the pathologically fixed remnants of the normal processes of early introjection" (1976, p. 25). These observations and conclusions led Kernberg to propose both a developmental model to account for borderline pathology and technical innovations for the psychotherapy of borderline conditions.

The developmental model

Kernberg's (1966, 1975, 1976) developmental model is organized around the internalization of object relationships, a process he takes to be crucial in the formation of psychic structures. He posits three types of internalization, or, in his terms, three different identification systems. Each process results in a psychic structure, which is named accordingly (introjects, identifications, and ego identity). Thus, the process of introjection results in an introject, and so forth. As Kernberg (1976) described it: "All processes of internalization consist of three basic components: (a) object-images or object-representations; (b) self-images or self-representations; and (c) drive derivatives or dispositions to specific affective states" (*ibid.*, p. 26). Psychic organization takes place at two levels. In the earlier and more basic organization, splitting is the main defence mechanism; during these periods, self–object–affect (S–O–A) units with opposite affective tones are unintegrated, either as a passive consequence of lack of maturity or as active process (splitting). In the more advanced level of organization, repression is the main defence utilized. Ego and superego development and integration can be assessed by the degree to which repression and its associated higher-level defences have succeeded the more primitive condition (Kernberg, 1976).

Kernberg follows Melanie Klein (1946) in taking introjection to play an important role in the early development of the ego. However, he suggests that it is a mechanism based on primary autonomous functions of perception and memory, rejecting Klein's views of the importance of very early oral incorporative *fantasies*. We will, at a later point, describe Kernberg's more detailed account of the relationship between his model and findings in cognition, perception, and neurophysiological processes.

Kernberg (1976) defines introjection as "the reproduction and fixation of an interaction with the environment by means of an organized cluster of memory traces" (*ibid.*, p. 29) with the S–O–A components. For him, those components are

> (i) the image of an object, (ii) the image of the self in interaction with the object, and (iii) the affective coloring of both the object-image and the self-image under the influence of the drive representative present at the time of the interaction. [*ibid.*]

Introjection goes beyond the primary apparatuses because it entails complex organization of the results of perception and of memory traces, in which perception of the external world is linked to perception of subjective experience. Although the earliest introjections do not clearly differentiate self and object images, a dyadic element is present.

The affective tone of the introjection is important because the various S–O–A introjections are gradually sorted and organized by affective valence. Kernberg (1976) writes,

> Introjections taking place under the *positive valence* of libidinal instinctual gratification, as in loving mother–child contact, tend to fuse and become organized in what has been frequently called "the good internal object". Introjections taking place under the *negative valence* of aggressive drive derivatives tend to fuse with similar negative valence introjections and become organized in "the bad internal objects". [*ibid.*, p. 30]

Kernberg sees affect in the first months of life as particularly important. Its "irradiating" effect on introjects (which may include perceived self and object representations) is such that the resulting perceptual constellations differ most according to their associated affective states. Affect states, then, are the manner in which introjects of opposite valence are kept apart, since the immature psyche is unable to integrate different temporal experiences and opposite affective experiences.

Although Kernberg stresses the importance of affect in building up separated S–O–A units, his account of developmental stages parallels that of Mahler (1968; Mahler, Pine, & Bergman, 1975). His stages may be summarized as follows.

Stage 1. This is the stage of normal autism, or primary undifferentiation in the first month of life, before the "good", combined self-object constellation develops through positive experiences. Pathology, at this stage, would mean that this undifferentiated image would not develop, and a normal symbiotic relationship with the mother would not take place, being replaced by autistic psychosis.

Stage 2. This stage, normal "symbiosis", from the third or fourth to the sixth or ninth month, consists of the consolidation of an undifferentiated, "good" self-object representation, and corresponds to the periods of Mahler's symbiotic phase and differentiation subphase. Even when self- and object images begin to be separated, still within the umbrella of libidinally organized S–O–A units, they are weakly delineated, and, Kernberg (1976) says, there is a "persisting tendency for defensive regressive refusion of 'good' self and object images when severe trauma or frustration determine pathological development of this stage" (*ibid.*, p. 60). Fixation at, or regression to, this self-object dedifferentiation and loss of ego boundaries is typical of childhood symbiotic psychosis (Mahler, 1968), most types of adult schizophrenia (Jacobson, 1954b), and depressive psychoses (Jacobson, 1967).

Stage 3. In this stage, self- and object representations are clearly differentiated, within both the core "good" self-object and core "bad" self-object. Self-images from one positively experienced S–O–A unit are linked with those from other positively valenced S–O–A units, with parallel joining of object representations. With the increasing complexity of the resulting representations, this process "contributes to the differentiation of self and other and to definition of ego boundaries" (Kernberg, 1976, p. 30). This stage corresponds to Mahler's separation–individuation phase (excluding the differentiation subphase), and lasts from six to nine months of age through eighteen to thirty-six months. Object constancy (Hartmann, 1964c) and stable ego boundaries should be achieved, but relationships are still with part objects. Integration of self- and object representations occurs only at the close of this stage. Kernberg follows Mahler in suggesting that borderline pathology follows from fixation and/or regression to this phase of internalized object relationships.

This is the stage in which active separation (the defence of splitting) between good self-images and bad self-images and between good object and bad object images occurs. In patients with borderline pathology, the combined S–O–A units of opposing valence persist in an unintegrated fashion, and are not replaced or accompanied by higher-level developments. Kernberg (1976) maintains that, when opposing S–O–A units are initially introjected, they are kept apart to avoid the anxiety associated with the negative valences "from being generalized throughout the ego", and to "protect the integration of positive introjections into a positive ego core" (p. 36). However, defensive splitting represents a later development, in which the opposing S–O–A units are actively separated.

Kernberg suggests that the ego comes into being at the point when introjections are used defensively. This is a state in which the "good internal objects" (mostly undifferentiated self- and object representations with a positive valence), along with the "good external objects" (positively experienced aspects of reality), form the purified pleasure ego, while the negative S–O–A units are viewed as outside. "Good" self-images and "good" object images begin to be separated. Slightly later, all these "units" become more elaborate, and the differentiation between "good internal objects" and "good external objects" occurs. Now, the defence of projection can be utilized across a relatively clear boundary, so that the array of "bad external objects" includes some that are "bad" via projection of introjections that had a negative valence. This clear utilization of projection is an important development of Stage 3. Correspondingly, the defensive use of active splitting decreases over time, and the individual successfully traverses to Stage 4.

Although we have been focusing on the building up of S–O–A units and the unfolding of defensive processes, the second internalization process, identification, also begins to be used in Stage 3. This is a higher-level form of introjection, which includes the role aspects of the interpersonal interactions and hence requires some development of perceptual and cognitive abilities so that socially recognized functions can be conceptualized by the child (Kernberg, 1976, p. 31). The affective components of such internalizations are also more advanced and differentiated than those associated with introjections. The view of the self is, likewise, more differentiated, so that it is possible to view the object taking a role with respect to the self. Identifications, like introjection, contribute to the formation of psychic structure and yet may also be used for defensive purposes. Identification continues as a process throughout life at different levels of ego integration, and its results are more subtle and better integrated when the ego is more integrated and splitting mechanisms are not used (*ibid.*, p. 77). In psychotic identifications, where self- and object images are pathologically refused, identifications are distorted by the projection of primitive superego forerunners or repressed drive derivatives on to the object, so that the internalized object relation is altered in the direction of "all good" or "all bad" introjections. (Kernberg adopts Jacobson's [1954a] definition of refusion as attempts to maintain absolute gratification through fantasies that the self and object are merged, fantasies that ignore realistic differences.) When pathological identifications occur at a more integrated level, they result in pathological character traits.

Stage 4. In Stage 4, contradictory self- and other representations are integrated into percepts of the self and others that more accurately reflect complex experiences of the self and other persons. Failure to achieve this integration results in "identity diffusion". In this stage, repression appears as a defence, and ego, superego, and id are also differentiated. This period begins toward the end of the third year of life and continues through the Oedipal period. Pathology from this stage is that of patients with neuroses or "higher-level" character pathology (hysterical, obsessive–compulsive, and depressive–masochistic characters).

Narcissistic personality disorders may also result from abnormal development during this stage, when, instead of integration of self and object, there is, in Kernberg's words,

(1) a pathological condensation of real self, ideal self, and ideal object structures; (2) repression and/or dissociation of "bad" self-representations; (3) generalized devaluation of object representations; and (4) blurring of normal ego–superego boundaries. [1976, p. 68]

This results in a grandiose self, which is separated from negatively valenced S–O–A experiences in a splitting process more typical of Stage 3.

Kernberg interprets Stage 4 as representing the achievement of what Klein (1948) termed the "depressive position", in which, because of the new, more complex view of others as the objects of both hatred and love, both guilt and concern begin to appear. Representations of an ideal self and ideal object develop as wishes to counteract the increasingly accurate awareness of reality. Repression, which prevents the irruption into consciousness of various drive derivatives, separates id from ego during this stage, and the id becomes more organized. Hence, in neurotic or other higher-level psychopathology, one does not readily see primary process or direct expression of drives.

Integration of the superego as an independent intrapsychic structure takes place in Stage 4. This has two aspects: the condensation of ideal self- and object images into the basis of the ego ideal, and the integration of this with the sadistically determined superego forerunners. These superego forerunners are what Kernberg terms the

> fantastically hostile, highly unrealistic object images reflecting "expelled", projected and reintrojected "bad" self-object representations . . . and reflecting primitive efforts of the infant to protect the good relationship with the idealized mother by turning the aggressively invested images of her (fused with the respective self-images) against himself. [1976, p. 71]

With integration come decreases in projection and in the fantastically hostile and unreal nature of the superego elements.

Ego identity, the third process in the internalization of object relations, begins to occur in Stage 4. Ego identity is "the overall organization of identifications and introjections under the guiding principle of the synthetic function of the ego" (*ibid.*, p. 72). This refers to the organization of a self-concept and of deeper, more realistic concepts of others.

Stage 5. Consolidation of superego and ego integration takes place in Stage 5, and ego identity continues to evolve. The individual is able to learn from experience, and "an integrated self, a stable world of integrated, internalized object representations, and a realistic self-knowledge reinforce one another" (*ibid.*, p. 73). Representations of a social and cultural world are included. The internal world gives increasing meaning to present interactions and provides support for the individual in times of crisis. The individual has the capacity to discriminate subtle aspects of him- or herself and of others, and develops "depersonified" attitudes and values with increasing capacity to communicate views and experiences in a way that others can understand. These capacities are absent in pathological conditions organized at earlier stages; the most striking example is the narcissistic personality, who cannot convey more than a shallow sense of who he or she is or who the other is in an interaction (*ibid.*). Although intimate connections among drives, affects, object relations, and cognitive and other ego functions are implied throughout Kernberg's model, these form a particularly complex and dense matrix in the successful outcome of Stage 5: the healthy personality.

The psychoanalytic classification of character pathology

Kernberg's (1980a) model of psychopathology is primarily a conflict model; constitutional deficits may contribute to the intensity of certain conflicts and, hence, render the development of pathological ego structures or character traits more likely. For example, an infant constitutionally endowed with an intense aggressive drive may project more aggressively tinged S–O–A units on to external figures and may develop pathologically intense fears of castration directed at abnormal images of dangerous parents (Kernberg, 1975). Or, children with organically based perceptual or other learning problems may have introjections and identifications distorted by their faulty apparatuses of primary autonomy. However, when considering adolescent and adult patients, Kernberg's position is that character pathology is best understood and interpreted as the result of dynamic conflicts. Even if a learning disability is present in a borderline patient, only after considerable treatment can its effect be differentiated from the results of pathological splitting and associated primitive defences (Kernberg, personal communication).

Levels of character pathology

The developmental model previously outlined is the basis for a highly specific classification of higher-level, intermediate, and lower-level (borderline) character pathology. This classification is based on determining the level of instinctual development, superego development, defensive operations, and internalized object relations (Kernberg, 1976). Kernberg (1980c, 1981c) has been a vocal critic of the *DSM-III*'s (American Psychiatric Association, 1980) categorization of personality disorders, because it fails to consider these psychoanalytic perspectives and thereby omits certain important diagnostic entities. In Kernberg's system, higher-level character pathology is marked by the achievement of genital primacy in the instinctual sphere; a well-integrated but excessively severe superego; defence mechanisms organized around repression (including intellectualization, rationalization, undoing, and higher forms of projection); and a stable, well-integrated concept of self and others. Most hysterical, obsessive–compulsive, and depressive–masochistic personalities are in this group—the classical neurotic patients.

At the intermediate level, pregenital fixation points are present, the superego is less well integrated than in higher-level pathology, and sadistic superego precursors play an important role. Defences are organized around repression, but some more primitive defences are present, with more infiltration of instinctual impulses than is present in the more sublimatory or reactive traits characteristic of higher-level pathology. Ego identity is established, and there is a stable concept of self and others, but object relations are quite conflicted. Many oral, passive–aggressive, sadomasochistic, and better-functioning infantile personalities and some narcissistic personalities are at this level.

Lower-level character pathology is characterized by borderline personality organization with, in the instinctual realm, "pathological condensation of genital and pregenital instinctual strivings . . . with a predominance of pregenital aggression" (Kernberg, 1976, p. 141). Lack of superego integration and the continuing influence of sadistic superego forerunners are more marked than in the intermediate group. Defences are organized around splitting, with primitive forms of projection, denial, and other mechanisms, which allow partial expression of the rejected impulse to a greater degree than in the other levels of pathology. Object constancy is not firmly established, identity diffusion is present, and object relationships are conceptualized in terms of part objects.

The borderline concept

Kernberg is one of a very small number of investigators who have actually given a detailed definition of the term "borderline personality". He provides a description of the intrapsychic structures and other concepts he considers relevant to this diagnosis, along with a sophisticated phenomenological description of the patients. Kernberg prefers the term "borderline personality organization" to "borderline state" or "borderline personality disorder", underlining his belief that such patients have a specific and stable personality organization characterized by ego pathology, which differs from neuroses and less severe character disorders on the one hand, and the psychoses on the other. These patients suffer from a particular type of psychic organization, which has a certain type of history and resistance to rapid change. They are not in a transitory "state", fluctuating between neurosis and psychosis, nor are they defined solely by their obvious symptoms, as in psychiatric use of the term "disorder". Kernberg (1967, 1975) stresses that similar symptomatology may occur as a result of different intrapsychic configurations and conflicts, so that very detailed diagnostic study is necessary.

Kernberg's delineations of borderline and narcissistic patient groups rely on description of symptoms and complaints presented by these patients, but also, just as important, on inferences about types of psychic structure, defences, and predominant conflicts. In his concern with "internalized object relations", he has devoted considerable work to explicating the method by which one makes inferences about this and other hypothetical constructs, such as defences or structures, on the basis of a patient's interview behaviour, for example.

On a descriptive level, patients suffering from borderline personality organization present symptoms that, if occurring in combination, suggest pathological ego structure: chronic, diffuse anxiety; poly-symptomatic neuroses (severe phobias, rationalized obsessive–compulsive symptoms, multiple, elaborate, or bizarre conversion symptoms, dissociative reactions, hypochondriasis with chronic rituals and withdrawal, and paranoid trends with other symptoms); polymorphous perverse sexual trends; impulse neurosis; and addictions (Kernberg, 1975). Certain lower-level character disorders (infantile, narcissistic, antisocial, and "as-if" personalities) and paranoid, schizoid, hypomanic, or cyclothymic personalities also usually have borderline structure.

Inferences about the patient's psychological organization are based on other observations. "Nonspecific manifestations of ego weakness" are noted by assessing lack of anxiety tolerance, as when additional anxiety results in further symptom formation or regressive behaviour; lack of impulse control, where any increase in anxiety or drive pressure results in unpredictable impulsivity; the lack of developed sublimatory channels (here, the patient's talents and opportunities must be considered). A second sign is the appearance of primary process thinking, particularly in unstructured situations such as projective psychological testing (Carr, Goldstein, Hunt, & Kernberg, 1979; Kernberg, 1975). The presence of the primitive defensive operations of splitting, projective identification, denial, primitive idealization, and devaluation are important signs of borderline pathology. These may require subtle inferences from interview behaviour or interactions with the interviewer over a period of time to establish their presence.

Special diagnostic issues

Several examples exemplify Kernberg's contention that similar symptomatology may stem from different types of underlying pathology and structure.

Hysterical vs. infantile personality. Hysterical patients, while showing superficial similarities to infantile patients, have some conflict-free areas where their functioning is stable and appropriate. They are impulsive or clinging only in certain relationships or areas of conflict. Their need to be loved and admired, although it has oral, dependent components, is closer to an expression of genital needs. Oedipal dynamics contribute to differential relationships with men and women, and the provocativeness of these patients is usually not accompanied by promiscuity. Stable, if neurotic, heterosexual relationships are present.

In contrast, infantile patients are more socially inappropriate and impulsive across all areas of life. Oral, demanding elements are more prominent, so that the need to be loved is "more helpless" in quality, and exhibitionistic trends have a primitive, narcissistic, exploitive quality. Promiscuity may be present in conjunction with unstable, changing relationships (Kernberg, 1975). Such patients frequently are organized at a borderline level (Kernberg, 1981c).

Depression. Kernberg stresses the importance of differentiating depression as a symptom from depressive–masochistic character traits. The higher-level depressive personality, for example, may experience depression in connection with guilt over Oedipal strivings or with true concern for the self and others, because of the presence of superego integration. Depression that represents helpless rage or disappointment in an ideal suggests less superego integration. Severe depression that causes breakdown in ego functioning also suggests the presence of a sadistic superego, probably associated with borderline organization. However, both the quantity and quality of depression must be considered when making a structural diagnosis, as the absence of any depressive concern or guilt for others may also be a sign of borderline organization in narcissistic and antisocial personalities (Kernberg, 1975, 1977a).

Adolescence. The stresses of identity consolidation in adolescence may, in conjunction with environmental pressures (such as gang membership or cultural norms), suggest the presence of severe personality disturbance. Kernberg recommends assessment of the presence or absence of whole-object relationships, ideals, and the capacity for sublimation and work. Adolescents with borderline personality structure will be far less able to describe themselves or their friends in depth and do not show evidence that they can invest themselves in ideals or goals that have meaning to them (Kernberg, 1978, 1979b, 1982b).

Borderline vs, schizophrenic conditions. In the absence of clear signs of formal thought disorder, hallucinations, or delusions, the primitive defences present in both borderline and schizophrenic conditions serve different functions, which can be used in interviewing to make this distinction. In patients with borderline structure, these defences protect the patients from the experience of ambivalence, and "a feared contamination and deterioration of all love relationships by hatred" (Kernberg, 1975, p. 179). Schizophrenic patients use splitting and allied mechanisms to prevent "total loss of ego boundaries and dreaded fusion experiences with others" (*ibid.*), particularly under the stress of strong affects. This is because persons with psychotic structure do not have clearly differentiated self- and object images. Since primitive defence mechanisms cause ego weakness in patients with borderline structure, interpretations should strengthen the ego and lead to better functioning in the interview: more reflectiveness and attempts at integration and better reality testing. Interpretation of the same primitive defences in schizophrenic patients reveals difficulty with self–object differentiation and hence leads to regression: more overt primary process or delusional thought, loosening of associations, or paranoid distortions of the interviewer in response to the interpretations given during the interview. Hence, the interview should be conducted with enquiry into responses which are unusual or subtly inappropriate, to test the patient's defensive functioning.

Transference psychosis, which may be present in both borderline and schizophrenic conditions, is different in each group because of the different mechanisms involved. With borderline patients, the transference psychosis is limited to the treatment hours and responds to Kernberg's recommendations for structuring the treatment. With psychotic patients, their psychotic behaviour and lack of reality testing in treatment is, for a long time, no different from that outside the treatment. Later on, they may feel convinced that they and the therapist are one. This is in contrast to the transference psychosis of borderline patients, who always maintain some sort of boundary, even if they feel themselves to be interchanging aspects of identity with the therapist (Kernberg, 1975, 1980c).

The therapeutic stance: treatment implications

In psychotherapeutic treatment of seriously disturbed patients, Kernberg suggests, non-verbal aspects of the patient's communication play a larger role than they do in the treatment of healthier patients. Patients with borderline or schizophrenic conditions may manifest non-verbal behaviour that is at odds with their remarks as a result of the use of splitting. Or they may express an S–O–A unit through attempts to induce the therapist to play one of the roles in this unit, attempts that may be conveyed through non-verbal means or through the use of words for their emotional effect. Kernberg (1975, 1977b) recommends that the therapist follow Bion's (1965, 1967a,b, 1970) idea of the analyst as a "container" to try to integrate within himself or herself the disparate elements the patient presents, in order to articulate the patient's current experience and defences in the transference. The analyst's willingness to tolerate great confusion, fragmentation, and aggression in the patient, while actively seeking to explore it, thereby conveying an attitude of hope and acceptance, makes possible the treatment of very seriously disturbed patients.

In a similar vein, Kernberg (1976, 1981a) is a major proponent of what he terms the "totalistic" view of countertransference, in which countertransference is defined as "the total emotional reaction of the psychoanalyst to the patient in the treatment situation" (1975, p. 49). While advocating the resolution of countertransference reactions, Kernberg stresses the importance of examining one's reactions for information about the patient, a view characteristic of Kleinian and interpersonalist theories. Kernberg claims that, with more seriously disturbed patients, the therapist's reactions have more to do with his or her general capacity to tolerate stress and anxiety than with the therapist's neurotic needs. Since the patient often presents a very chaotic picture, the therapist's attempt to maintain empathic contact with the patient through partial identifications may lead to some regression in the therapist's ability to function (Kernberg, 1975, 1977b). Kernberg (1977b, 1981a) also describes very meaningfully the experience of a therapist in a stalemated treatment effort, and offers suggestions for the resolution of chronic impasses.

The theory of drives or early affect states

We will conclude this summary of Kernberg's contributions with his theory of drives and affects, which, in many ways, is his most carefully considered theoretical statement. We have already summarized Kernberg's model of the developmental stages of internalized object relations, the final phase of which is the integration of contradictory S–O–A units into complex perceptions of self and other, and the maturation of ego and superego into adaptive structures. We consider Kernberg's theory of drives and affects separately, even though it is intended to fit into the developmental model, because it represents an additional focus in his work in which he interprets neurophysiological data and re-examines the dual instinct theory (Kernberg, 1976, 1980d, 1982a,d).

Kernberg proposes that the units of internalized object relations (the S–O–A units) constitute subsystems on the basis of which both drives and the overall psychic structures of ego, superego, and id are organized as integrating systems. Instincts (represented by psychologically organized drive systems) and the overall psychic structures (id, ego, superego) then become component systems of the personality at large, which constitutes the suprasystem. In turn, the units of internalized object relations themselves constitute an integrating system for subsystems represented by inborn perceptive and behaviour patterns, affect dispositions, neurovegetative discharge patterns, and non-specific arousal mechanisms .

Kernberg (1976) states that by conceptualizing the elements of this theory as subsystems and suprasystems, he avoids proposing "a neurophysiological model of the mind or a mechanical model of body–mind equivalence" (1976, p. 86). Thus, he speaks of hierarchies of organized systems. At some point, however, there is a shift from "neurophysiologically based functions" and "physiological units" (which would refer to changes in electrical patterns or neurotransmitters) to the integration of these units into a "higher system represented by purely intrapsychic structures, namely, the primitive units of internalized object relations (self–object–affect units)" (*ibid.*). These units are themselves eventually integrated into id, ego, and superego.

"Affect dispositions", which are inborn and determined by brain functioning, constitute primary motivational systems, in that they represent dispositions to the subjective experience of pleasure and unpleasure. These affect dispositions

> integrate the perception of (1) central (pleasurable or unpleasurable) states [that is, perception in the central nervous system], (2) physiological discharge phenomena, (3) in-born perceptive and behavior patterns, and (4) environmental responses. [Kernberg, 1976, p. 87]

The Freudian concept of instinct may be included here. Affective patterns communicate the infant's needs to the mother and thereby initiate interactions, which are stored as memory traces with affective and cognitive components. "Affects are the primary motivational system, in the sense that they are at the center of each of the infinite number of gratifying and frustrating events the infant experiences with his environment" (Kernberg, 1982d, p. 907), each of which leads to an internalized object relation, fixed by memory.

Affect and cognition evolve together, at first because their respective memory traces are integrated in affective memory (Kernberg, 1976), but, eventually, differentiation of pleasurable and unpleasurable experiences and of components of self and other takes place. At this point, Kernberg (1982d) asserts, the "good" and "bad" experiences generate the overall organization of motivational systems, which we term love and hate.

Kernberg (1982d) then suggests that love and hate become stable intrapsychic structures, "in genetic continuity through various developmental stages" (p. 908), which can be equated with the psychoanalytic concepts of the two drive systems, libido and aggression. At this stage of organization, affects serve a signal function for the two drives, and increasingly complex subjective, behavioural, and cognitive elaborations of affects and drives develop. Drives will always be manifested by wishes in the context of particular object relations, a phenomenon that is more precisely articulated than an affect state.

Kernberg's (1976) theory deals with economic issues as follows. Variations in the intensity of drives or affects can be attributed to either constitutional variations in the innate components of the system (the hypothalamus, genetically determined behavioural patterns, etc.), or to variations in the environment (the responses of the mother, and so forth). Neutralization (Hartmann, 1955a) takes place when positively and negatively valenced self–object–affect units are combined to form more complex and realistic self- and object representations with the achievement of the depressive position. Kernberg (1976) writes,

> *The synthesis of identification systems neutralizes aggression and possibly provides the most important single energy source for the higher level of repressive mechanisms to come,* and implicitly, for the development of secondary autonomy in general. [pp. 45–46, original italics]

What Hartmann termed "fusion of drives" is also included, according to Kernberg, in the combination or integration of opposing affects as part of the integration of contradictory S–O–A units. Similarly, sublimation is not simply a change in the use of drive derivatives in an economic sense; it, too, has an object relations component: sublimatory activity requires the capacity for some whole, integrated object relationships, some genuine concern for oneself and others (Kernberg, 1975, p. 134). None the less, despite the importance Kernberg assigns object relations in his theory of affects and drives, he also argues for the importance of aggressive drive manifestations and the biologically based changes in drives, which influence object relations (as in the genital strivings of the Oedipal period). Thus, he claims to support the proposition that drives, rather than object relations, constitute the primary motivational system of the organism.

Discussion: going over Bion and containment

At the very least, Kernberg has synthesized a good deal of the clinical observations of the object relations school and helped to develop a nosology that orders these observations. Thus, for example, Guntrip's (1968, 1971) or Fairbairn's (1952) observations of the schizoid person fit nicely into Kernberg's conceptualization of one type of patient with borderline personality structure. Kernberg is able to show how some of the writings of Winnicott (1965, 1971), Melanie Klein (1946), Balint (1968), and even Greenson (1954) can be understood within his concept of the borderline personality. His way of thinking about the levels of severity of character pathology, based, in part, on object relations concepts, may prove to be extremely useful. In addition, he has integrated the British (mostly neo-Kleinian) object relations school's stress on aggression into his clinical and technical writings in a way that helpfully underscores the importance of dealing with aggression, both in clinical situations and in theory development.

We consider it a strength of Kernberg's writings that he frequently relates his theoretical points to observable clinical phenomena. For example, he has not only shown in his attempts at theoretical integration how a variety of authors (Balint, 1968; Fairbairn, 1952; Frosch, 1960; Greenson, 1954; Guntrip, 1968, 1971; Klein, 1946; Winnicott, 1965, 1971) refer to the use of primitive defences such as splitting and projective identification by borderline patients (using Kernberg's definition of borderline, not necessarily those authors' own), but he has also sought to describe how one might infer the use of splitting or projective identification by a patient in a clinical interview. Similarly, he is willing to claim that practical consequences follow from his theoretical assumptions about diagnosis, and particularly from assessment of level of defensive functioning. This willingness to make predictions makes it easier for other investigators to test his inferences and conclusions. As an example, Kernberg is remarkably specific and detailed in relating prognosis and choice of psychological treatment method to diagnosis based on his nosology. A patient suffering from a narcissistic personality disorder, without overt borderline-level functioning, should be treated with unmodified psychoanalysis; a patient with narcissistic personality disorder who functions overtly on a borderline level should be treated with Kernberg's modified psychoanalytic psychotherapy. The same types of patients might require a shift to a supportive type of psychotherapy at some point in the analysis or psychotherapy, but this would not result in the type of change to be expected from psychoanalysis or from Kernberg's modified form of psychoanalytic psychotherapy. Some narcissistic patients present negative prognostic features (severe antisocial features, conscious enjoyment of others' suffering, chronic absence of human involvement, etc.), which indicate a need for supportive psychotherapy from the onset (Kernberg, 1975, 1979a, 1980c, 1982c,e).

To summarize at this point, Kernberg's achievements in the areas of clinical writing and observations seem, at the very least, worthy of note.

He has synthesized the writings of a number of authors, particularly those of the British object relations school, but also including Jacobson and Mahler, and shown how their clinical observations can be conceptualized in the context of his definition of the borderline personality organization. He has added a number of his own clinical observations and worked out a detailed classificatory system, particularly for character pathology and the borderline personality, within a five-level structure for describing the full range of psychopathology. He has specified a method of interviewing with stated criteria derived from the interview, through which one can reach complex diagnostic determinations.

He has related his diagnostic categories to choice of treatment and to prognostic statements about therapy outcomes.

Kernberg has covered a vast territory in his clinical writings, and he covers it in a systematic fashion. We must join other writers (Calef & Weinshel, 1979), however, in wondering how he is able to make so many prognostic statements with such assurance. His level of specificity is rare in our field, and it would be virtually impossible for Kernberg to have personally diagnosed and treated (and treated to the point of termination, in order to substantiate prognostic claims) all the different types and subtypes of patients that are the subjects of his classification system, treatment recommendations, and prognostic statements. Thus, his prognostic statements, for example, must come from a combination of research findings, consultations, supervision, and his experience of being involved in and directing a variety of clinical facilities.

Does Kernberg base his prognostic statements on research findings (Kernberg et al., 1972) from the Menninger outcome studies, or on his impressive clinical experience? It is often difficult to tell, but, most often, he writes with the assurance and precision of someone who has a great deal of empirical research to buttress his points. He, understandably, does not give extensive clinical examples, that is, complete case studies, for, if he did, given the range of categories and subcategories he discusses, he would literally fill our journals with clinical examples. Though it is beyond the scope of our chapter to evaluate the major outcome research with which he has been involved, we believe that Kernberg would acknowledge that his assurance about all his prognostic statements could not reasonably be based on his or other investigators' research. Moreover, although his research is of great interest, it is by no means free from serious methodological criticisms, which affect the types of prognostic statements Kernberg has made. It is our assumption, then, that a number of Kernberg's statements and recommendations are based on his clinical experience. Given that this is the case, it is understandable that Kernberg has been criticized (Calef & Weinshel, 1979) for his tone in his clinical writings. (Although in one recent paper [1982e], Kernberg notes the necessity for caution in such statements and urges further research, the preponderance of his writings imply greater surety about these matters.)

He writes as if he has sound evidence for his assertions, but, at least up to this point, he has not fully indicated the nature and extent of his evidence. We join in the criticism that has been leveled at Kernberg in this area, but we wish to note what we believe are two mitigating considerations. First, one can criticize any number of psychoanalytic authors for writing as if something had been "demonstrated" when they were really stating their views based on, perhaps very interesting, but nevertheless limited, clinical observations. Second, unlike the types of statements made by many other psychoanalytic authors, Kernberg's statements are in a form that makes them potentially testable (although to test his assertions would require a very elaborate and difficult research undertaking). His more recent research with his associates (Kernberg, Yeomans, Clarkin, & Levy, 2008; Lenzenweger et al., 2005) focuses on transference based interpretations and, in Chapter Seventeen, there is strong criticism of this type of approach.

A number of analysts have criticized Kernberg's clinical concepts on other grounds than those we have noted. Although it is beyond the scope of this exposition to enter into the type of detailed criticism levelled by, for example, Calef and Weinshel (1979), or implied by the type of reconciliation between Kohut and Kernberg attempted by Stolorow and Lachman (1980), we will comment briefly on Calef and Weinshel's critique. We believe that Calef and Weinshel have brought up interesting and potentially devastating criticisms. They include the ones we have previously discussed, and, most seriously, they cast doubt on the validity of Kernberg's contention that there are people with *a stable* personality organization which he has labelled borderline. (A related criticism, that Kernberg claims premature diagnostic closure in a very complex area, which still needs further exploration, is offered by Sugarman and Lerner [1980].) Calef and Weinshel also feel that Kernberg's concepts tend to dilute basic psychoanalytic concepts such as regression, and the very idea of intrapsychic conflict. However, a central point in their critique is their attempt to question the borderline concept itself. They criticize Kernberg for discarding the idea of a continuum that would include borderline and psychotic conditions and for maintaining that conventional reality testing is either present or absent. Instead, Calef and Weinshel (1979) conclude that "the relativity of reality testing . . . makes it a difficult area to establish hard and fast, categorical, isolated criteria for the diagnosis of a psychosis" (1979, p. 485) and, by extension, makes it difficult to delineate people with borderline personality organization from people who are psychotic.

With respect to Calef and Weinshel's criticisms, we would comment that many of their points could be framed and tested or could at least be subject to empirical observation. We would hope that, if they are serious critics, they would endeavour to spell out the empirical justification for some of their criticism. It hardly seems enough to doubt Kernberg's observations. We are not asserting that they are necessarily mistaken about some of their points, but that they should attempt, as Stone (1980), for instance, has done, a more clinically and empirically orientated approach to some of their criticism. To criticize Kernberg's categorical formulation of the concept of reality testing, they might offer data that support a continuum approach. Stone (1980) has provided examples of interviews in which assessment of structure according to Kernberg's criteria was extremely problematic, particularly in patients with unusual types of affective illness or in recovering schizophrenic patients, leading him to suggest that reality testing is not dichotomous in all situations. Our criticism of Calef and Weinshel is that, at times, they seem to come close to simply saying Kernberg is wrong because he is not "psychoanalytic".

This brings us to consideration of criticisms of Kernberg's theoretical endeavours. Calef and Weinshel state that Kernberg's theoretical position is close to, if not actually, a paradigm shift from classical Freudian and ego psychoanalytic theories. Within the limits of their article, however, they do not present convincing logical arguments for their assertion.

The question of Kernberg's theoretical position is taken up more centrally in a paper by Klein and Tribich (1981). In this article, Klein and Tribich are not specifically concerned with the idea of a paradigm shift, but they state that, from their point of view, "Kernberg's rapprochement between Freudian instinct theory and object-relations theory obscures the differences between these two competing theories without taking any recognition of their differences" (1981, p. 41). As is the case with Calef and Weinshel (who criticize Kernberg's more clinical positions), Klein and Tribich raise fundamental questions concerning Kernberg's theoretical positions. For example, they maintain that Kernberg's dismissal of "Bowlby, Fairbairn, Guntrip, and Winnicott is not based on any scientific discussion of their theories but on the fact that these theories reject Freudian motivational theory" (*ibid.*). We will not fully explore Klein and Tribich's criticisms here, but we can comment that we find it strange to maintain that Kernberg rejects all these theories. This, in fact, is not the case; Kernberg does attempt to integrate aspects of Fairbairn, Guntrip, and Winnicott into his theoretical and clinical writings.

Before discussing more substantive criticisms of Kernberg's theoretical work, however, we would like to expand our introductory comments on the state of psychoanalytic theory and theoretical criticism. As we implied, we believe that much of the work in both areas leaves something to be desired, when considered from the point of view of philosophy of science. Because the standards for criticism typically seem to be so subjective (Ellman & Moskowitz, 1980), any new psychoanalytic theoretical proposal or integration is vulnerable. We believe this statement applies, as we have noted, to some of Calef and Weinshel's comments, and we would suggest that it applies also to some, although not all, of Klein and Tribich's remarks. It can be useful to discuss how one theorist's use of a concept differs from another theorist's, but this does not constitute a criticism, unless one discovers logical fallacies within the system or data that contradict the theory. To criticize Kernberg for differing with Freud, for example, is not a theoretical criticism, but a value judgement.

However, we must also tender this and some other general criticisms in consideration of some of Kernberg's writings. We think that his points would be clearer if he would place greater emphasis on stating his definitions, assumptions, and positions, and less on cataloguing theorists with whom he agrees or disagrees. The clarity of the presentation of Kernberg's theoretical propositions sometimes suffers from his tendency to give such qualified and complex statements that it becomes difficult to use his theoretical assertions to make definite predictions. In addition, the "catalogues" of theorists give Kernberg's theoretical work somewhat of an arbitrary feeling, and to what we believe is an arbitrariness in the writings of some of his critics, which seems to imply, "If you disagree with so and so, then you are not psychoanalytic and, therefore, you are wrong." This type of comment, although all too prevalent in psychoanalytic writings, is not up to Kernberg's standards. We would, thus, have to agree with Klein and Tribich (1981, p. 39) when they criticize Kernberg's rejection of Guntrip for his "emotionally charged" attacks on instinct theory. Furthermore, we feel that Kernberg does not have a strong position from which to censure another theorist for deviating from classical psychoanalytic instinct theory.

A logical–theoretical approach to the critical review of Kernberg's theoretical contributions would deal with different types of issues. We would wish to examine questions such as the following: how well does Kernberg integrate object relations theory with Freudian theory? Aside from consideration of various psychoanalytic traditions, does Kernberg have a well-integrated theoretical position? In a more general sense, is Kernberg's theory a good theory, according to the requirements of theory-making, such as logical structure, rules of inference, and so forth (Nagel, 1961, 1995; Popper, 1962)? We would submit that no psychoanalytic theorist's work could withstand this type of scrutiny. Hence, again, the harsh tone of some of the criticism directed at Kernberg seems unwarranted.

It would be useful, however, to discuss briefly some of Kernberg's contributions from the standpoint of these questions to suggest directions for further work. We will comment on Kernberg's instinct theory, since he claims that, in this work, he integrates classical drive theory and object relations concepts as well as newer data from neurophysiological studies. It is, thus, appropriate to ask how well he succeeds in this theoretical integration. This question is separate from comments about the validity, elegance, or heuristic value of Kernberg's theory and from questions about whether or not it is "psychoanalytic".

In his discussion of instinct theory, Kernberg (1982d) goes over a familiar but nevertheless important point: Freud's term *trieb*, which is usually rendered as "instinct", may more reasonably be translated as "drive". Kernberg is pointing out, as have others (Hartmann, 1964c; Holder, 1970; Schur, 1966), that by "instinct" Freud did not mean a fixed, pre-wired, behavioural pattern (which is more of an ethological idea). Rather, in his concept of instinct or drive, a variety of behaviours or mental events might emerge as a result of internal stimuli or excitation. Kernberg's substantive attempt is to link or translate Freud's ideas into modern neurophysiological and neurobehavioural concepts. It is, again, beyond the scope of this chapter to discuss fully this aspect of Kernberg's writings, but, in summarizing Kernberg's ideas, we hope to give a sense of his position and our evaluation of this position.

Kernberg (1976) places affect dispositions at the centre of his statements on motivation. He concludes:

> Affect dispositions constitute the primary motivational systems which integrate the perception of (1) central (pleasurable or unpleasurable) states, (2) physiological discharge phenomena, (3) inborn perceptive and behavior patterns, and (4) environmental responses as they impinge on specialized and general extroceptive and introceptive perceptions. The earliest "selfobject–affect" units are, I suggest, constellations of affectively integrated and cognitively stored perceptions of affective, physiological, behavioral, and environmental changes—perceptions within which the "self" and "nonself" components are as yet undifferentiated. [1976, p. 87]

In this passage, Kernberg is attempting to link what he considers to be Freudian psychoanalytic theoretical statements with neurophysiological statements through the use of an object relations perspective. He goes on to specifically include MacLean's (1967, 1972) model of three concentric brains as being relevant to the way he conceives of instinct as developing in the human being gradually out of the assembly of these "building blocks", so that the series of pleasurable affect-determined units and the series of unpleasurable affect-determined units gradually evolve into the libidinally invested and aggressively invested constellations of psychic drive systems; that is, into libido and aggression, respectively, as the two major psychological drives. In other words, affects are, at first, primary organizers of instinctive components such as specialized extroceptive perception and innate behaviour patterns and, later on, constitute the "signal" activator of the organized hierarchy of "instinctually" determined behaviour (1976, pp. 87–88).

These two extracts give a reasonable flavour of the complexity and direction of Kernberg's ideas on instinct. We believe that, in fact, his theoretical compilation places him substantively closer to

Bowlby (1969, 1973, 1980) and perhaps even Fairbairn and Guntrip than to Freud. Central to Freud's (1915) ideas about instinct is the formulation that it is generated internally and that the instincts appear "as a constant force" (Freud,1915c). Nowhere in Kernberg's writings do we see this essential aspect of Freud's concept that instincts provide a form of constant internal stimulation that makes substantial demands on the nervous system. To quote Freud,

> Instinctual stimuli, which originate from within the organism, cannot be dealt with by this mechanism. Thus they make far higher demands on the nervous system and cause it to undertake involved and interconnected activities by which the external world is so changed as to afford satisfaction to the internal source of stimulation. Above all, they oblige the nervous system to renounce its ideal intention of keeping off stimuli, for they maintain an incessant and unavoidable afflux of stimulation. We may therefore well conclude that instincts and not external stimuli are the true motive forces behind the advances that have led the nervous system, with its unlimited capacities, to its present high level of development. There is naturally nothing to prevent our supposing that the instincts themselves are, at least in part, precipitates of the effects of external stimulation, which in the course of phylogenesis have brought about modifications in the living substance. [Freud, 1915c, p. 120]

We have included this long extract from Freud in an attempt to capture what we believe is a subtle but, nevertheless, important difference between Freud and Kernberg's concept of instincts. Certainly, from at least 1915 on, Freud stressed the internal or endogenous nature of the instincts, not only as a motivational concept but also, in higher-level organisms (particularly primates), as a system that stimulated the development of the central nervous system itself. Thus, the infant's and child's task of "mastering" internal or endogenous stimulation is, in fact, a central task. Clearly, environmental factors can make this task easier or harder, and clearly the environment is important in development, but the "constant pressure" of endogenous stimuli will be there regardless of the type of "instinctual building blocks" that are present in the infant's environment. If we take Kernberg seriously in his attempted neurophysiological integration, then he is moving toward more of an environmentalist position than Freud held. By and large, Kernberg does not see endogenous stimulation as a central concern. Hence, in this area of his theorizing, he has not really integrated Freud's position into his own.

We would say that, in general, Kernberg has not fully integrated the various positions he uses; that critics (Calef and Weinshel, Klein and Tribich) appear from both sides of the controversy between Freudian and object relations theories is consistent with this view. At times, Kernberg merely places together different theoretical positions rather than integrating these positions, for example, by showing how a particular definition of a concept adds to the power of the theory. Similarly, he often presents his selections among possible points of view without giving the clinical or logical justification as to why he has chosen certain positions and not others. It is never really clear that additional explanatory power is gained by combining object relations and Freudian (or ego psychological) concepts.

This brings us to a related logical criticism. Given that he has selected and defined certain concepts in the formation of his theory, Kernberg provides little in the way of theoretical or logical structures (rules of inference) to show how his theoretical positions link together in an overall theoretical system. For example, he might begin to provide rules that would predict under what circumstances active splitting replaces passive splitting and develop criteria independent of the theoretical concepts to test the predictions implied by such rules. At this stage, he does not clarify the explanatory power of his theory. To put this in another way, he does not show what the developmental, affect, or instinctual aspects of his theory really add to our understanding of his clinical and nosological observations and conceptions. In a sense, to use Rubinstein's (1967) term, his theory often seems to be "merely descriptive". Although this is not necessarily a criticism, Kernberg obviously aspires to something more. Yet, often he does not show how this theory is more than a plausible restatement of his clinical points.

We have been critical of Kernberg in the latter part of this review, but we reiterate that these criticisms follow from the application of standards that, in our opinion, no psychoanalytic theorists could meet. We have expected Kernberg to present a full-blown theory of the kind that neither Freud nor Klein managed to produce. Moreover, if Kernberg has not carried out the type of theory building or logical analysis that would enable him to present more convincing arguments, neither have his critics. One must sympathize with Kernberg to some extent, since his task is the harder one and since he has, at times, attempted to alter or clarify his positions in response to points raised by critics.

In conclusion, we would say that Kernberg has raised fundamental issues and, more than any other contemporary writer, he has pursued these questions with vigour and insight. The answers he proposes are among the most interesting presented by today's psychoanalytic theorists. He is also one of a relatively small number of psychoanalytic thinkers who devote considerable attention to research issues and findings (Carr, Goldstein, Hunt, & Kernberg, 1979; Kernberg, 1981b; Kernberg et al., 1972). Despite our critique, we are impressed with Kernberg's attempts to develop a comprehensive and systematic theory of development, psychopathology, and treatment, and he must be considered a major psychoanalytic theorist. In many areas, one cannot begin to formulate appropriately a problem without referring to Kernberg's work. That is, by itself, no small achievement.

Author's addendum

The present chapter is a collaborative effort between myself and Dr Monica Carsky, a close friend and colleague. Part of the reason for this collaboration is my sense of her appreciation for Otto Kernberg's contributions. If I were writing the chapter and commentary section without her influence, I would perhaps stress to a greater extent that Kernberg's integration is one that is glued together rather than a true integration. I would perhaps comment that he is neither a Kleinian or someone who is an ego psychologist, and both theories seem a bit off kilter in his theoretical world. However, rather than trudging over covered ground, I will look at Kernberg's recent ideas about psychoanalytic technique with particular reference to the role of interpretation. The role of interpretation is covered in Chapters Seventeen and Eighteen.

CHAPTER FIFTEEN

Bion, Klein, and Freud

"... several things dovetailed in my mind, and at once it struck me, what quality went to form a Man of Achievement ... I mean Negative Capability, that is when man is capable of being in uncertainties, Mysteries, doubts, without any irritable reaching after fact and reason"

(Keats, 1817)

"To put it in a formula: he must turn his own unconscious like a receptive organ towards the transmitting unconscious of the patient"

(Freud, 1912e)

Introduction and summary

A key concept in the work of Wilfred Bion is that of "linking": it is fundamental in his understanding of the development of thinking and the development of the mind; the mechanism for thinking thoughts in the analysand, as well as a crucial element in a mutative interpretation on the part of the analyst. Linking can also be seen as inherent in the development of his own thinking about the work of psychoanalysis, in that he brings important elements from the work of Freud forward and links them to concepts from Melanie Klein, as well as the contemporary Kleinian Hannah Segal, and links all of them to his experience working with groups and psychotic patients.

Bion's work also can be seen as a link between the Freudian and object relations theorists and the more contemporary schools of thought within psychoanalytic theory, such as the relational and intersubjective, for which, in many ways, his work is a forerunner. In addition, there are many important areas of overlap between his theories of development and current theories from developmental neurobiology.

Bion's contribution to psychoanalytic theory and technique has often not been understood, due to his unique and often dense or obscure use of language. His use of terms such as "beta" and "alpha" are chosen precisely due the fact that they are free from the psychoanalytic canon and therefore as free as possible to be unburdened by overloaded or received meanings. His writing, in fact, is in total concert with the ideas he presents in that he forces the reader/clinician to make their own links and is adamantly opposed to theory as dogma. His written work exemplifies a marriage of form and content; while, in the largest sense, he feels that the task of psychoanalytic work is Truth, Truth itself is elusive, ever-evolving and unknowable. The closest we can get to it is to be present in the ever-changing experience of two beings in a vital, tensive relationship in a particular space and time.

This brief overview will review the major concepts that Bion presents in his writing, focusing on how those concepts relate to each other and how they inform the transference in the analytic relationship.

Overview of the development of thinking

Beta and alpha elements

Bion, following Freud, asks what conditions and experiences are necessary for the development of an apparatus for thinking thoughts, which involves linking sense impressions and affects, and linking those linked proto-mental thoughts with concepts that have meaning and language that can be used for thinking and communicating.

He takes as a critical foundation for his exploration of this question the proposition from Freud (1911b) that the development of thinking is coincident with the gap experienced by an infant between an emotional or physical need and the delay of gratification or relief from the tension produced by the need caused by the reality principle. In "Formulations on the two principles of mental functioning" (1911b), Freud says,

> Thinking was endowed with the characteristics which made it possible for the mental apparatus to tolerate an increased tension of stimulus while the process of discharge was postponed ... It is probable that thinking was originally unconscious, in so far as it went beyond mere ideational presentations and was directed to the relation between impressions of objects, and that it did not acquire further qualities perceptible to consciousness, until it became connected with verbal residues. [*ibid.*, p. 215]

The raw mode of early immediate experience is classified or interpreted by the infant in some fashion; that is, by an archaic distinguishing of pleasure from pain or good from bad. There is a parallel here with Kant's anticipatory *a priori* categories to which experience approximates. These raw sensory–emotional elements in the environment Bion refers to as beta-elements, and he says they exist in and of themselves (the thing-in-itself) and prior to thinking. By superimposing the Kantian *Ding-au-sich* on Freudian and Kleinian theory, Bion is able to argue that pure thoughts have an existence of their own, an existence which is older than the mind which thinks those thoughts—they exist independently of any particular individual.

For Bion, as for Freud, consciousness itself, as well as thinking, arises out of the infant's need to free himself from the clutter of direct sensory impressions. That is, thinking may be seen as originating in grasping the meaning of experiences that organize and explain those raw sensory impressions. .

In their original state, however, beta-elements cannot be thought about or interpreted; they can only be experienced directly and reacted to in one way or another. In *Elements of Psycho-analysis*

(Bion, 1963), Bion argues that the most primitive experience is governed by beta elements: they are "thoughts without a thinker". The ability to transform beta elements into elements that can be used for thought is initially dependent upon someone who is able to contain the projected elements: this transformative function he calls "alpha-function". Alpha function is a conversion function that endows the raw affective–sensory beta elements with meaning, thereby enabling them to be utilized in the service of thinking. The beta elements then become "alpha elements" and can be repressed, used for dreaming, and they become part of the unrepressed unconscious as part of implicit and explicit memories.

Alpha elements emerge through a linking process of a pre-existing preconception that creates an anticipation, which then is met with a realization in external reality, thereby producing a conception leading to thoughts that can be used for thinking. The accumulation of alpha elements creates the apparatus for thinking thoughts—in other words, thoughts exist prior to a thinker who thinks the thoughts and the ability to think thoughts actually "creates" the thinker.

This is a clear reversal of Cartesian dualism. In the place of "I think, therefore I am", Bion posits something like the following: "I am, therefore I feel, therefore I have thoughts which need a thinker to think them". Bion's ideas can be seen to clearly adumbrate the experimental work of neurologists like Antonio Damasio (1994), who proposes that

> The lower levels in the neural edifice of reason are the same ones that regulate the processing of emotions and feelings, along with the body functions necessary for the organism's survival. In turn, these lower levels maintain direct and mutual relationships with virtually every body organ, thus placing the body directly within the chain of operations that generate the highest reaches of reasoning, decision-making, and, by extension, social behavior and creativity. Emotion, feeling and biological regulation all play a role in human reason. [*ibid.*, p. xiii]

Alpha function, container–contained, and the thinking couple

For Bion, as with Freud, the infant needs to develop a tolerance of frustration in order to stay in the space or gap between wanting and getting the need met in order to develop the ability to symbolize and think. What Bion adds to this is that this tolerance is provided by a receptive and "metabolizing" mother or "container", who is the "alpha function" for the infant's beta elements.

Bion (1970) posits the "contained" as the infant and the projected beta elements, while the "container" is the "mother" or attuned care-giver. The prototype of container or containing function is the mother in a state of reverie being capable of withstanding the infant's terror and nameless dread of annihilation in the face of absence, physical, emotional, or cognitive. This safe place shares many qualities with Winnicott's "maternal holding environment", but adds the notion of a "thinking couple" with the emphasis on the mother's capacity to withstand raw emotions and transform them into digestible bits of meaning which can be added to other bits.

Beta elements are often projected into whatever container is available, where they may be transformed by someone else's (i.e., the mother's) alpha functions, sensory data, whether internal or external, that have not been transformed into symbols, which are defined as organized and integrated mental representations. These data are experienced as concrete objects in the psyche or as bodily states reacted to in a corporeal fashion. Given that they are unmentalized, such experiences are only "accretions of stimuli" (cf. Freud) and, as such, cannot be stored as memories or used by the individual.

Beta elements are experienced concretely; they might be compared to faeces, which are to be expelled. The beta elements are projected into a breast that is not there (the no-breast); subsequently, the mother (a good object) transforms the no-breast into a breast and adequately contains the infant by virtue of nurturing, feeding, and holding. For the infant, beta elements are experienced as having been transformed by the breast into alpha elements with their own psychic meanings attributed to them. In this case a state of "reverie" may exist, a state in which the mother psychically nourishes the baby's mind. The emergence of alpha-function allows a relationship to be experienced; such a relationship, then, becomes the verb which links objects, leading eventually to such feelings as envy and jealousy.

This process of alternating projection and introjection was refined by Bion (1959, 1962a, 1963) in developing the concept of containing. If this does not happen and there is a failure of containment and attunement, then the infant must expel the undigested terrifying feelings into whatever can serve as a container, and, as a result of this projection, the external world becomes housed and peopled with persecutory objects. Then, through the process of introjection, the infant finds that the internal world is likewise peopled and housed with persecutory objects. The inside is smothering and claustrophobic and the outside is a war zone filled with immanent fragmentation.

With nowhere to go, the infant must try to find a form of containment. Esther Bick called this a "second skin" in autistic children. Bion calls it a "mental skin". The infant, then, is at the mercy of what Bion calls the "ego-destructive super-ego", or "Super-ego", which forbids thinking and forces the evacuation of all thoughts and emotions from the mind. The early failure on the part of the mother leads to splitting and attacks on linking and pathological projective identification as part of a futile attempt to preserve a toxic closed system.

Bion then presents three different forms of the container–contained relationship: the parasitic, the symbiotic, and the commensal. The first two lead to a variety of forms of defensive adaptation and a predominance of psychotic thinking, whereas the third promotes the ability to develop being able to tolerate and transform bodily states and affects into thought, and thoughts into more complex creative thinking.

Psychosis

Bion traced the origins of psychosis to the infant's terror about the mother's failure to contain his or her fear of dying (Grotstein, 1981). These writings, developed during the 1950s, anticipated many of the concepts which were later to be elaborated by Winnicott and Kohut, especially those related to the centrality of empathy in mother–infant bonding. It was in this context that Bion developed the "container" and "contained" concepts. Specifically, he argued that the infant's inability to split-off and project adequately—an inability attributable to the lack of an adequate container to hold the split-off projections—was the root cause of psychosis. Therefore, he postulates (1970) that the origins of psychosis are due to this failure of the mother to provide an adequate "container" for the infant.

The mother must provide certain supports for the baby; specifically, she must have the capability of absorbing baby's anxiety, unwanted parts of his self, as well as part of the baby's mental apparatus—beta elements—that pose (to the infant) a threat to his very existence. Bion states, "Fragmentation occurs because what is expelled is the very means of perceiving and organizing reality—the mechanism for thinking thoughts—the mind" (1962b, p. 90).

Any relationship may be conceptualized as a contact through which one component "becomes jammed into another, with or without violence" (Hinshelwood, 1989, p. 231). A variety of relationships may exist between a container and the contained: the container may explode the contained, the contained may strangle or suffocate the container, or a more positive mutual accommodation may ensue. Bion originated the concept with reference to developmental processes, but broadened its application to virtually all types of human interaction.

Bion used the term "nameless dread", a term first used to describe "a dread of powerlessness in the face of instinct tension in childhood", to refer to the fear that affects the infant whose mother is incapable of "reverie" (one of the functions of the adequate container). Such a mother is unable to contain the terror experienced by the infant and make that terror meaningful; consequently, the object is experienced as rejecting.

An unaccepted projection to the mother is rejected and returned unchanged to the infant. Repetitions of experiences of this type of projective failure lead to the formation of an internal object through introjection. The infant's original meaning of projection is stripped away and reintrojected as nameless dread (Bion, 1962b).

Therefore, the container–contained relationship is crucial for the development of learning and for abstractions to be formed, which begin with the formations of words that are names for certain sensory information that are frequently conjoined. These simple abstractions lead to more and more complex hypotheses and abstractions that eventually can be known as a scientific deductive system.

The key Bionian concept of the alpha function is therefore posited as a transformational capacity to decontaminate the infant's anxieties, which have been projected on to the container (mother). Those anxieties were originally experienced by the infant as threatening; thus, the mother must transform them into another form that is bearable and integratable by the infant: this relationship can be characterized as the "thinking couple". When there is a failure of the alpha function, the mother does not accept the infant's projection of a feeling. Instead, the infant introjects a greedy, devouring breast from this rejection. The infant then experiences the environment as something he cannot gain from, and, therefore, is not able to develop the capacity for symbol formation and to be able to think and learn from experience. Therefore, when alpha function is underdeveloped, the individual has no capability to integrate and defuse the dangerous beta elements; one possible (and perhaps probable) outcome is psychosis (Grotstein, 1981).

Projective identification

Central throughout all of Bion's work is the concept of projective identification; the concept certainly provided the theoretical context within which Bion developed his theory of "container–contained". He expanded Klein's (1946) definition that focused on projective identification as a defensive mechanism that occurs in the paranoid–schizoid position, entailing projecting (in phantasy) parts of the ego into the object as a means of controlling or taking over its envied contents. In Klein's view, this leads to a feeling of depletion or of being robbed of the contents of one's self. Klein's concept of projective identification had already been fruitfully applied, as, for example, by Rosenfeld:

> The patient . . . projected his damaged self containing the destroyed world, not only into all the other patients but into me, and had changed me in this way. But instead of becoming relieved by this projection he became more anxious, because he was afraid of what I was then putting back into him, whereupon his introjective processes became severely disturbed. [Rosenfeld, 1965, pp. 80–81]

Bion (1959) posits a "normal" or "healthy" form of projective identification that involves the earliest form of communication by projecting into the object states of mind, affect, and/or body. In

Bion's view, "normal" projective identification is crucial for the infant's anxieties to be contained and transformed, therefore leading to the capacity of the infant to develop the ability to generate thoughts from experience. In order for projective identification to even occur, there must be a container into which the projection can be sent. To the extent that the maternal response is adequately containing and nurturing, the infant reintrojects the breast/container, a container capable of converting beta elements into alpha elements.

If, however, projective identification is met with an unresponsive or hostile container, this could produce numerous substantial anxieties, including fears that the attacked object will retaliate and that parts of the self may be imprisoned in the external object and thus controlled by it. As Bion states in "Differentiation of the psychotic from the non-psychotic personalities" (1957),

> The differentiation of the psychotic from the non-psychotic personalities depends on a minute splitting of all that part of the personality that is concerned with awareness of internal and external reality, and the expulsion of these fragments so that they enter into or engulf objects. [p. 43]

K and −K, L and H links, and attacks on linking

Klein agrees with Freud regarding the view that all human beings are born with an innate epistemophilic instinct (or innate desire to know) as being part of the libidinal drive. Bion expands this notion of an epistemophilic instinct and posits emotionally charged links that are inherent within this overall drive to make connections between a subject and object. He designates three groups of links: the K link (knowledge), the L link (love) and the H link (hate).

Of these concepts, K is by far the most important to Bion. The K link involves a desire to know the other, which necessarily involves the toleration of frustration and the pain of not-knowing, as well as awareness of the other and the self. Bion highlights the fact that all learning and growth inevitably involve "catastrophic change": catastrophic because, in any new learning, there is an upheaval and disruption of whatever system and order has been in place. Bion states that

The elements of many scientific deductive systems must be capable of recombination ... On the theory put forward here the freedom necessary for these recombinations depends on the emotions suffusing the psyche because these emotions are the connective in which scientific deductive systems and the elements of the contained learning from experience are embedded. Tolerance of doubt and tolerance of a sense of infinity are the essential connective in the contained learning from experience if K is to be possible. [1977, p. 94]

In terms of the development of the ability to think as a way of modifying the pain of experience, tolerating frustration, and being able to withstand and creatively utilize catastrophic change and, therefore, the ability to utilize thinking in the service of learning from experience, the emotional experience inherent in the K link occurs through the integrative function of the container–contained.

The earliest and most primitive manifestation of K occurs in the relationship between the mother and infant. As part object relationship it may be stated as a relationship between mouth and breast ... In K, L and H being factors and therefore subordinate, the contained is projected into the container and abstraction, of a type that I shall use the term commensal to describe, follows. By commensal I mean container and contained are dependent on each other for mutual benefit and without harm to either. In terms of a model the mother derives benefit and mental growth from the experience: the infant likewise abstracts benefit and achieves growth. [*ibid.*, p. 91]

If there is a failure of receptivity and modification of the projected affects on the part of the mother/object, there is an accumulation of beta elements in the infant and the dominance of mechanisms for evacuating the painful affective states. The K links are then overwhelmingly painful, and the attempts to manage them through splitting and projection can lead to an experience of a blank, meaningless world. The result of this kind of situation results in what Bion calls "attacks on linking" and calls this "−K", which stands for anti-knowledge, or hatred of knowing, learning, or awareness, all of which imply emotional connections, change, and the ability to tolerate space/absence and dependence. If −K predominates, there is a reversal and perversion of what is healthy with what is not. As Bion (1967b) says, "it is a short step from hatred of emotions to hatred of life itself" (p. 107). Bion stresses that a hatred of emotions leads to an intensification of them, and, therefore, to the increasing need for ever more powerful defences against them. In "Attacks on linking", he says,

> The internal object which in its origin was an external breast that refused to introject, harbour, and so modify the baneful force of emotion, is felt, paradoxically to intensify, relative to the strength of the ego, the emotions against which it initiates its attacks. These attacks on the linking function of emotion lead to an over prominence in the psychotic part of the personality of links that appear to be logical, almost mathematical, but never emotionally reasonable. Consequently the links surviving are perverse, cruel and sterile. [1959 (1967), pp. 108–109]

What Bion calls −K, then, has as its goal the stripping of meaning, as opposed to the development of meaning in K. −K destroys, as opposed to promoting, knowledge. Bion states that, in K, "particularization and concretization of the abstract and general is possible"; however, in −K, "the particular becomes denuded of any quality it has; denudation not abstraction is the end product" (1967b, p. 99).

It is also possible that the alpha-process may work backwards, essentially "cannibalizing the already formed alpha-elements to produce either the beta-screen or perhaps bizarre objects" (Meltzer, 1981, p. 530). The bizarre object is conceptualized as a beta-element with traces of ego and superego. In this regard, Bion may be seen as having elaborated Klein's original concepts of sadistic and omnipotent attacks on internal objects and the self-structure. Bion broadened this line of thinking to include attacks on individual ego functions and on "linking" in general. That is:

> Instead of sense impressions being changed into alpha elements for use in dream thoughts and unconscious waking thinking, the development of the contact barrier is replaced by its destruction. This is effected by the reversal of alpha function so that the contact barrier and the dream thoughts and the unconscious waking thinking, which are the texture of the contact-barrier, are turned into alpha elements divested of all the characteristics that separate them

from beta elements and are then projected, forming the beta-screen. [1962b, p. 25]

Bion amplified Klein's concept of sadistic and omnipotent attacks on internal objects and on the structure of the self to include attacks on the individual functions of the ego and on "linking" in general as the basic operation of thought. In addition, Bion says that the attacks will be aimed at any kind of mental or emotional coupling (called "Oedipal linking") fuelled by envy of the early prototypes of linking: the nipple and the mouth; the penis and the vagina; and the internal parental couple, all of which are hated.

Ps ↔ D

Another aspect of Kleinian theory that Bion brings forward and then expands upon is the concept of the developmental movement from the paranoid–schizoid position to the depressive position. Bion assumes the anxieties, the alternating and split states of persecution and idealization, envy, the defensive use of splitting and projective identification as an attempt to preserve the developing and unintegrated ego, the phantasies of omnipotence and the experience of the other as "part-objects" that are outlined by Klein (1946) as part of the paranoid–schizoid position. In addition, he also assumes the confusion and concrete thinking that is inherent in this position and brings forward Segal's (1957) important contribution regarding concrete symbolic equations as part of primitive or psychotic thinking.

The movement from part-objects to the recognition of the other as a whole object and the resulting ambivalence, as well as the shift from the total concern for the survival of the developing self to the capacity for concern for the object resulting in feelings of loss, awareness of dependence, guilt, and the desire for reparation, as well as the increased capacities for abstraction and integration that are part of the depressive position as presented by Klein, are also assumed by Bion.

In addition to adding his theory that there is primarily positive and normal projective identification that is crucial for the developing child in order for them to internalize the containing alpha function of the mother and therefore negotiate the anxieties and pain of the depressive position, Bion also expands Klein's concept of the fluctuations of these positions over time to present the notion that, once the depressive position had been "achieved" developmentally, there would continue to be an important dynamic relationship between the kinds of thinking inherent in both positions that continues to be necessary throughout the lifespan for learning, growth, development, and creative thinking. He notates this flux as Ps ↔D.

The dynamic oscillation of Ps ↔ D assumes a tolerance for the catastrophic change that occurs with new learning and for the disintegration of previously held views in the service of new integration without the fear of annihilation, fragmentation, or the need for resorting to primitive defence mechanisms. This is differentiated from the use of manic defences against depression in the movement back to Ps from D in Kleinian theory. Bion postulates this movement as the essence of creative thinking, in that it allows for insight, learning from experience, and an increasing ability to play in an ambiguous state of not-knowing in the service of the truth in experiences as they change in time. This "truth", in Bion, ultimately is signified by "O" (1970), which he calls the absolute Truth, the unknown, ultimate ground of Being that underlies all experience and which is always already present, and yet is unknowable. For Bion, "becoming O" is to be in a state of transformation in which one is always "becoming who one is" (cf. Nietzsche, 1882), in other words, Being = becoming. In healthy development, this oscillation continues throughout life and assumes an internalization of both container and contained within the mind in an ever-moving and changing dialectical relationship that allows for a vital, tensive, and fluid opening of the self to the unknown, or "O".

Technique

In discussing the importance of the mother's acceptance of the infant's projected feelings in the service of normal development, Bion emphasizes the importance of "maternal reverie": "The mother's capacity for reverie is the receptor organ for the infant's harvest of self-sensation gained by its conscious" (1962a, p. 116). This concept of maternal reverie is analogous to the analytic stance in the sense that the analyst must, like the mother, be receptive to the terrors and anxieties of the patient, be capable of containing and modifying the patient's projective identifications through translation in meaningful interpretations, and therefore be part of a "thinking couple".

This state of reverie directly refers to the maintenance of Freud's (1911b) "evenly-suspended attention" and allows the analyst to "make a selection" from the material that is presented that arises *not* from his expectations, but organically, from out of seemingly unconnected elements in a session:

> To put it in a formula: he must turn his own unconscious like a receptive organ towards the transmitting unconscious of the patient. He must adjust himself to the patient as a telephone receiver is adjusted to the transmitting microphone. Just as the receiver converts back into sound waves the electric oscillations in the telephone line which were set up by sound waves, so the doctor's unconscious is able, from the derivatives of the unconscious which are communicated to him, to reconstruct that unconscious, which has determined the patient's free associations. [1911b, pp. 115–116]

Bion, in his paper "Notes on memory and desire" (1967a), takes this further, and states that the analyst must not just suspend his attention, but also his memory and desire in the service of being fully present to what is happening in the moment-to-moment evolution of each session: "Psychoanalytic 'observation' is concerned neither with what has happened nor with what is going to happen but with what *is* happening" (1967a, p. 17).

In order to have the discipline to stay in this state of receptivity and not default to theoretical formulations, memories of the past, or desires for the future, the analyst, in Bion's view, must be able to tolerate not-knowing and the catastrophic changes that allow him to be emotionally present for the unique person who is his patient. In other words, not only is the analyst facilitating the development of thinking in the patient, the analyst must also be able to play in the creative flux of Ps ↔ D. When the analyst can do this, Bion suggests that a nodal point or "selected fact" (a term he brought in from the mathematician Henri Poincaré) will naturally emerge. The selected fact is a coherence that brings together certain elements into an insight, understanding, or discovery that then can be named and communicated as part of an interpretation. The interpretation then performs a linking function that is crucial for the development of thinking and linking in the analysand:

> In any session, evolution takes place. Out of the darkness and formlessness something evolves . . . It shares with dreams the quality of being wholly present or unaccountably and suddenly absent. *This evolution is what the psychoanalyst must be ready to interpret.* [1967a, p. 18, my italics]

and

> His interpretations gain in force and conviction—both for himself and his patient—because they derive from the emotional experience with a unique individual and not from generalized theories imperfectly "remembered". [*ibid.*, p. 19]

This is not to say that Bion is suggesting that there is no past: in fact, for Bion, the transference is certainly always an externalization of unconscious phantasy, but it is always first and foremost in the here-and-now that the projections are happening. Therefore, there is a horizontal or linear understanding in Bion of the early deficits, phantasies, and defences that need to be kept in the back of one's mind regarding the particular patient's experience in transitioning from Ps ↔ D, as this will inform the analyst about the kinds of projections he is receiving and how he is being experienced and "used" by the analysand, but this information becomes linked only in concert with the moment-to-moment experience. Bion talks about the importance of multiple "vertices", from which an analyst needs to look at any given phenomenon; this occurs by holding all of them open and allowing oneself to learn what is going on at a particular point in time, given the constantly shifting process of linking and attacks on linking in the patient, between the patient and analyst, and within the analyst. These vertices include the patient's history, theoretical understanding of development, the history of the analytic treatment, and the analyst's own history and countertransference.

However, for Bion, all of that must be eschewed for each session: "The psychoanalyst should aim at achieving a state of mind so that at every session he feels he has not seen the patient before" (1967b, p. 18). Therefore, the analyst's "understanding" of what is going on regarding the transference, projective identification, thinking, or attacks of linking will only cohere out of the evolution of a selected fact that emerges from experience. As he says, "The only point of importance in any session is the unknown. Nothing must be allowed to distract from intuiting that" (*ibid.*, p. 17).

Bion emphasizes the importance of opening up the space for the analyst's intuition, which is the leading skill that enables the analyst to track the oscillations between linking and attacks on linking from moment-to-moment during a session. As intuition is privileged, and memory and desire are put aside, the analyst can remain open to, and grounded in, "O", thereby facilitating what Bion calls "transformations in O". As Grotstein (2007) states,

> According to Bion, the analyst, in response to and in resonance with the emotional outpourings from the analysand, must allow himself, in a state of reverie, to become induced into a trance-like state in which his (the analyst's) own native, internal reservoir of emotions and repertoire of buried experiences can become selectively recruited to match those he is experiencing resonantly from the analysand's inductions—and then become them (transformation in O).Then the analyst ponders over his experience, thinks about it and then interprets it. [*ibid.*, p. 54]

Therefore, Bion is focused on what can enable the analyst to fully utilize their intuition in the service of facilitating the creative, transformational mental and emotional growth of the patient and to enter into each session with a mind unhindered by expectations so as to allow them to see each patient anew with each session. However, this takes thorough theoretical training, a complete training analysis, and tremendous discipline in order to let that all go and have faith that what is important will emerge eventually. It is apt that Bion quotes from Kant: "Intuition without concept is blind; concept without intuition is empty" (cited in Boris, 1986, p. 171).

The grid

All of the major concepts discussed in the body of this paper are the building blocks that went into Bion's model of thinking called "The

Grid", as shown in Figure 3 (Bion, 1977). The organizing principle of the grid involves the nature of thought: the vertical axis of the grid refers to the development or evolution of thought *per se*, while the horizontal axis refers to "thinking about the thoughts by an apparatus of thinking known as the mind" (Grotstein, 1981, p. 515). The major categories of the grid refer back to Freud's "Formulations on the two principles of mental functioning" (1911b).

	Definitory hypothesis 1	Phi 2	Notation 3	Attention 4	Inquiry 6	Action 6...n
A Beta elements	A1	A2				A6
B Alpha elements	B1	B2	B3	B4	B5	B6
C Dream thoughts, dreams, myths	C1	C2	C3	C4	C5	C6
D Pre-conception	D1	D2	D3	D4	D5	D6
E Conception	E1	E2	E3	E4	E5	E6
F Concept	F1	F2	F3	F4	F5	F6
G Scientific deductive system		G2				
H Algebraic calculus						

Figure 3. Bion's Grid.

The evolution of human thought proceeds along a genetic axis (i.e., the vertical axis of the grid); thoughts emerge out of the sensory impressions (beta elements) being transformed by alpha function to produce alpha elements. After this transformation, those alpha elements become suitable for experiencing, dreaming, and being thought about at a conscious level.

At a fundamental level, Bion's grid attempts to explain how thoughts grow in complexity, sophistication, and abstraction. Levels of complexity are associated with the sophistication of thoughts that can be "grown". Bion also suggests that there is a parallel growth in the mind of something in the service of destruction (an anti-thought). In the positive grid, mother and her mind (represented by the breast) elaborate the elements of feelings, states, and dream-thoughts that permit the baby to think. In the negative grid, experiences are dealt with by turning them into lies. A life poisoned by lies withers into mental illness (a type of mental death).

The vertical (genetic) axis of Bion's grid shows development of thought. Progress should be thought of in terms of increasingly competent reality testing. At the lowest level (Row A), the concern is only with "things"; at this level, there is no distinction between inanimate and psychic objects. Development along the vertical axis gradually moves through alpha elements (Row B), Dream Thoughts and Myths (Row C), Preconception (Row D), Conception (Row E), Concept (Row F), the Scientific Deductive System (Row G), and Algebraic Calculus (Row H).

The horizontal (systematic) axis shows development in the realm of communication. The columns of the horizontal axis refer to development on several dimensions: Definitory Hypotheses (Column 1), Psi/the lie (Column 2), Notation (Column 3), Attention (Column 4), Inquiry (Column 5), and Action (Column 6).

Bion conceived of the Grid as a "psychoanalytic game", an instrument for the developing intuitive system of the analyst, enabling him to track (after a session) what is happening to the patient's and his own thinking during a session.

Conclusion

Bion conceptualizes the unconscious mind as being inherently imaginative, creative, and fluid. The threshold of creativity lies at the barrier between consciousness and unconsciousness; this is represented by the "C" level of Bion's grid. At this level, creative imagery emerges in the context of phantasies, dreams, and myths.

Bion's body of work reflects the evolution of a general theory of thinking that may be seen as constituting "a radical reorientation of psychoanalytic theory in the direction of mainstream Western epistemology" (Grotstein, 1981, p. 15). While he utilized the "standard" starting point of Freud's instinctual drive theory, Bion augmented it substantially, drawing insights from such sources as Plato (e.g., theory of inherent forms and pure thoughts) and Kant (e.g., the *ding au sich*/thing-in-itself). From the general body of Freud's and Klein's writing, Bion synthesized ideas from two particular sources: (a) Freud's "Formulations on the two principles of mental functioning", and (b) Klein's theories about the transition from the paranoid–schizoid to the depressive position, splitting and projective identification, and symbol formation.

His thinking was also informed by philosophical and mathematical concepts as he began to reframe Freudian thinking with insights from both Plato's rational pre-determinism and (perhaps more centrally) Kant's epistemology. Bion's emphasis on inherent preconceptions, for example, can be traced to Plato's Theory of Forms and Kant's *a priori* concepts.

For Bion, pure thoughts exist as inherent preconceptions: "I am, therefore I have thoughts without a thinker which demand a mind to think about them". Consistent with Kant, Bion believed that there was no such thing as nothingness; there is always something. Instead, "nothing" becomes "no-thing"; that is, the presence of an absence or an empty category. In the case of the absence of the breast, that very reality can bring with it a sense of nameless dread. The presence of this not-breast is so overwhelming to the infant that it can only cope by −K (not knowing). Bion (1977) notes that

> ... the human being, like nature, abhors a vacuum, cannot tolerate empty space ... the intolerance of frustration, the dislike of being ignorant, the dislike of having a space which is not filled can stimulate a precocious and premature desire to fill the space. One should therefore always consider that our theories, including the whole of psychoanalysis, psychiatry, and medicine, are a kind of space-filling elaboration ... indistinguishable from paramnesia [1977, p. 3]

Bion's view of the psyche is both cosmic and cosmological in nature; Bion's man is similar, in many respects, to Nietzsche's "Ubermensch", in that he presents a view of vital "mental health" as one that involves a movement toward increasing ability to embrace the unknown, tolerate radical ambiguity, have faith in the unknowable and retain conscious awareness of one's own thinking, the need for the creation of beliefs, and the need for words to express the inexpressible. This view of mental health involves a way of understanding the work of psychoanalysis as the facilitation of the development of the emotional and cognitive abilities necessary to support a way of being that is an ongoing creative and transformational process of "becoming who one is".

For Bion, the letter "O" symbolizes the fundamental article of faith that there is an experience and an experiencer, and that there exists an ultimate or absolute truth which is unknowable (Bion, 1977). This concept may be traced to the Kantian *noumenon*; and, just as in Kant's philosophy, and given the limits of human consciousness, ultimate truth can never quite be comprehended. Bion (1985) states the primary problem explicitly as follows:

> I am. Therefore I question. It is the answer—the "yes I know"—that is the disease which kills. It is the Tree of Knowledge which kills. Conversely, it is not the successful building of the Tower of Babel, but the failure that gives life, initiates and nourishes the energy to live, to grow, to flourish. The songs the Sirens sing and have always sung is that the arrival at the inn—not the journey—is the reward, the prize, the cure. [*ibid.*, p. 52]

Bion continues to inspire us to not heed the Sirens and find our rewards in the ongoing journeys upon which we embark with each patient.

CHAPTER SIXTEEN

From ego psychology to contemporary conflict theory: a historical overview

Arnold D. Richards and Arthur A. Lynch

Summary

This chapter is primarily a review of the movement from Freud's structural theory to modern conflict theory. It covers authors such as Arlow and Brenner in more detail than in any other chapter of the present volume. The chapter also details the controversies that led to some of the formulations that present day conflict theorists have presented. Some of the material overlaps Chapters Four, Five, and Seventeen, but the viewpoint is quite different. In the present chapter, the main perspective is showing how various influences led to contemporary conflict theory. In Chapter Seventeen, the self and object Freudians are featured, and in Chapters Four and Five theorists are discussed without reference to contemporary conceptualizations.

Introduction: brief history

Ego psychology is rooted in the third and final phase of Freud's theorizing (Rapaport's [1959] classification), and takes *The Ego and the Id* (1923b) and *Inhibitions, Symptoms and Anxiety* (1926d) as its foundational works. More specifically, it grows out of Freud's final model of the mind, the structural hypothesis of id, ego, and superego. Levy and Inderbitzen (1996) aptly define ego psychology in terms of the underlying assumptions of Freud's structural hypothesis:

> Ego psychology is: a systematic and coordinated conceptualization of various mental activities grouped together by virtue of their similar aims and behavioral manifestations especially associated with delay or control of instinctual discharge, on the one hand, and adaptation to reality opportunities and danger on the other. [*ibid.*, p. 412]

In *The Ego and the Id*, Freud explained why the structural hypothesis was preferable to the earlier topographic point of view, which used the property of consciousness to characterize mental activity. This model, with its three structural agencies, constituted a balanced approach to psychic functioning that allows for both environmental and biological determinants, for both purpose and drive, and for both the reality principle and the pleasure principle. In *Inhibitions, Symptoms, and Anxiety*, Freud considered the clinical implications of his earlier partitioning of the human mind. He began by identifying an error in the prestructural theory: the formulation that repression causes anxiety. He then shifted from an energetic model to a meaning model, the central idea being that childhood wishes are associated with childhood dangers related to loss. These dangers are loss of the object (a significant person), loss of the object's love, loss of, or injury to, the genitals (castration), and fear of punishment (guilt). On this model, a threatening wish seeking expression in consciousness signals danger to the ego, which occasions anxiety. In Freud's monograph, the ego is at the centre of exploration, but the primary importance of relationships, internal and external, real and fantastic, is also brought into focus. This emphasis on the relational, or interpersonal, was anticipated in *Group Psychology and the Analysis of the Ego* (1921c), where Freud wrote,

> In the individual's mental life, someone else is invariably involved, as a model, as an object, as a helper, as an opponent; and so from

the very first individual psychology, in this extended but entirely justifiable sense of the words, is at the same time social psychology as well. [p. 69]

Arlow noted, in a personal communication, that the clinical material informing the structural hypothesis is to be found in a number of cases Freud published around the same time. These include "Some character types met with in psychoanalytic work" (1916a), "Mourning and melancholia" (1917e), "A child is being beaten" (1919e), "Associations of a four-year-old child" (1920d), "The psychogenesis of a case of homosexuality in a woman" (1920a), and "Some neurotic mechanisms in jealousy, paranoia, and homosexuality" (1922b).

Modern ego psychology begins with the contributions of Richard Sterba, James Strachey, and Anna Freud. It took shape in the 1930s, as analytic theorists probed further the clinical, and especially the technical, implications of the structural hypothesis. Many contributions were made during this era by such theorists as Wilhelm Reich, Hermann Nunberg, Karl Abraham, and Paul Federn, and many more were made in ensuing years by theorists like Edward Glover, Rene Spitz, Erik Erikson, and Annie Reich. The most important contributors, however, were Anna Freud, Heinz Hartmann, Rudolf Loewenstein, Ernst Kris, Phyllis Greenacre, Otto Fenichel, and Edith Jacobson, all of whom extended or modified Freud's theory in varying degree.

Two crucial papers of 1934, Sterba's "The fate of the ego in analytic therapy" and Strachey's "The nature of the therapeutic action of psychoanalysis", laid the groundwork for the technical modifications that arose in the aftermath of the structural hypothesis by offering two contrasting visions of the theory of therapeutic action. On the one hand, Sterba described a therapeutic split in the patient resulting in an experiencing ego and an observing ego. The analyst was to side with the latter, helping patients to incorporate the analyst's observing function in order to strengthen their own. Strachey stressed incorporation from the side of the superego rather than the ego. The analyst was to help the patients diminish the harsh, judgemental character of their conscience by offering for identification and incorporation his greater tolerance for drive expression.

These contrasting viewpoints came to the fore in two pivotal events of 1936. In the Marienbad symposium of that year, Strachey's emphasis on the patient's introjection of the analyst's superego and on the importance of the resulting superego alliance seemed to carry the day, though not without dissent (Friedman, 1988). Nevertheless, Anna Freud's *The Ego and the Mechanisms of Defence*, published that same year, echoed Sterba's concern with the technical importance of strengthening the patient's observing ego in order to achieve mastery over the experiencing ego. Anna Freud's clinical contribution to this task was to single out the ego's unconscious defensive operations as perhaps the most important set of ego activities entering the treatment.

Many later contributions to the theory of pathology, technique, and development owed a debt to Anna Freud's *Ego and the Mechanisms of Defence*. Following its publication, the history of psychoanalytic technique, from an ego psychology standpoint, can be seen to revolve around a single issue: the clinical role of the analysis of conflict and defence opposed to the analysis of unconscious mental content. The position taken on this key issue provides a basis for differentiating among the major contributors to the theory of technique. The issue is central to the differences between Anna Freud and Melanie Klein, and also serves to distinguish the technical recommendations of Sterba, Strachey, Nunberg, Fenichel, and Hartmann, Kris, and Loewenstein.

Levy and Inderbitzen (1996) note how Anna Freud's reframing of the technical issue of the analyst's attitude complemented an attentiveness to the patient's observing ego. This latter emphasis is the ego-psychological tributary flowing from Sterba's influential paper of 1934. As Levy and Inderbitzen remark,

> Her recommendation that the analyst listen from a point equidistant from id, ego and superego emphasized the importance of neutrally observing the influence of all three psychic institutions. However, the analyst's activity (interventions) always begins with and is directed toward the ego and in this sense the analyst is actually nearer to the ego than to the id or superego. The ego wards off not only derivatives of instinctual drives but also affects that are intimately connected with the drives. She advocated that priority be given to the interpretation of defenses against affects as well as defenses against instinctual drives. [p. 414]

Anna Freud's ego-psychological rationale for Freud's technical requirement of analyst neutrality, an issue that has generated controversy to the present day, was influential during this period. Greenacre's (1954) advocacy of the blank screen, with no disclosure or social contact, stood at one extreme, while a middle position was taken by Leo Stone (1961), who recommended benign neutrality and physicianliness. Others staked out a position in the middle by advocating the role of the real relationship as a therapeutic and curative factor. Ralph Greenson (1965) wrote of the working alliance, Elizabeth Zetzel (1956) of the therapeutic alliance, and Hans Loewald (1960, 1971) of the role of the relationship. At the other extreme stood Sandor Ferenczi's (1920) active therapy, Franz Alexander's (1956) corrective emotional experience, and Harry Stack Sullivan's outright disregard of the transference. Theorists at this more active end of the spectrum believed that the analyst's direct involvement in the patient's treatment was necessary for a lasting therapeutic effect.

Within psychoanalytic ego psychology, Sterba's concern with the fate of the ego has been more influential than Strachey's attentiveness to a therapeutic partnership between analyst and analysand superegos. Strachey's position is continued in the Kleinian, object relations, and self-psychological schools, whereas the Sterba–Anna Freud line extends to the development of American ego psychology in the 1940s and 1950s. This was also the period when analysts who had lived and worked in Central Europe in the 1930s, and immigrated to the United States later that decade and in the 1940s, continued Freud's 1920s exploration of the structure and functioning of the ego. Its members were Anna Freud (who immigrated to the UK), David Rapaport, Hermann Nunberg, Robert Waelder, Ernst Simmel, Siegfried Bernfeld, Erik Erikson, Otto Fenichel, Edith Jacobson, Margaret Mahler, and the triumvirate of Heinz Hartmann, Ernst Kris, and Rudolf Loewenstein.

The Hartmann era

What was the ego-psychological paradigm that grew out of the collective efforts of these émigré theorists? Whereas the ego of Freud's topographical theory was conceptualized mainly in opposition to the id, the pioneer ego psychologists took a much larger purview. For them, the ego was a complex structure, emerging, as Freud had noted, out of the perceptual apparatus, and functioning as an executive forging compromises among id, superego, and external reality.

Hartmann, Kris, and Loewenstein (1946), proposed revisions to the Freudian models of mind, development, pathogenesis, and technique. They understood survival as a primary motivating force, and adaptation to the environment as essential to this end. The reality and pleasure principles were reconceptualized in line with this insight. One result of this effort was the transmuting of psychoanalysis into a general psychology of the human condition, ranging from the pathogenic to the normal. Hartmann's 1958 monograph, *The Ego and the Problem of Adaptation*, is in the spirit of Freud's lifelong project of creating a bio/psycho/social model. Hartmann emphasized that the individual is born with innate psychic structures (the primary autonomous ego functions of perception, memory, thought, and motility) into an average expectable environment, and that the individual's personality is moulded by this social surround. The child growing up in a familial and societal world learns to fit in or adapt to the environment. The alternatives are to change the environment (alloplastic adaptation), to change oneself (autoplastic adaptation), or to leave the environment. Hartmann and Kris (1945), like Freud, stressed that "psychoanalysis does not claim to explain human behavior only as a result of drives and fantasies; human behavior is directed toward a world of men and things" (p. 23). They believed that the child, in interaction with the environment, acquires secondary autonomous ego functions, and develops a sense of self and other, while mental equilibrium is promoted by an ego that mediates inner and outer imperatives (fitting them together). The adaptive viewpoint emphasized the role of the environment in the shaping of conflicts and added the interpersonal dimension to the psychoanalytic intrapsychic emphasis. It should be recognized that, during the 1940s and 1950s, both ego psychologists and the interpersonal school were exploring the influence of relationships and the role of the environment on the individual.

A second thrust of Hartmann's theoretical project was to widen the categories of motivation from the more confined aims of libidinal pleasure and destruction, or love and hate, proposed by Freud. Hartmann retained Freud's energic model and language, but offered the concept of neutralization as a way out of Freud's narrow and experience-distant drive/energy/instinct box. Neutralized libido came to include a range of experiences from lust, sensuousness, and intimacy to friendliness, warmth, and affection. Neutralized aggression, likewise, subsumed a spectrum of experience, from self-assertion and competitive strivings to hate and destructiveness. Each had its place in the individual's panoply of affects.

Hartmann's and Loewenstein's work (1946, 1949) provided the rationale and impetus for observational research on infants and children. The thrust was to study how mother–child interactions affected the developing ego and the sense of self and other. Hartmann (1950) wrote that "the development of object relations is co-determined by the ego; object relations are also one of the main factors that determine the development of the ego" (p. 105). Contemporaries of Hartmann joined this object relations conversation: Anna Freud (1965) elaborated the concept of developmental line, Edith Jacobson (1964) investigated the self and object worlds, and Margaret Mahler (1963; Mahler, Pine, & Bergman, 1975) provided the classic formulations of separation and individuation. Attention was directed to the impact of the pre-Oedipal period of childhood on later development, as well as to the ways in which external controls, deriving in part from the child's transactions with the parents, are internalized. These various strands were woven into an ego-psychological/object relations fabric.

Edith Jacobson's contributions deserve special mention. She postulated an undifferentiated instinctual energy at birth, which, *"under the influence of external stimulations"* (1964, p. 13, emphasis added), develops into libidinal and aggressive drives. Frustration and gratification, laid down as memory traces of the ambivalent conflicts of childhood, organize affective experience. Jacobson's work figured in debates over the concept of identity in the 1950s and 1960s. Erikson took one position and Greenacre, Mahler, and Jacobson another. For Erikson (1956), identity was like a beach; it remains the same yet changes with the tide: "The term identity . . . connotes both a persistent sameness within oneself . . . and a persistent sharing of some kind of essential character with others" (p. 57). Erikson acknowledged the importance of childhood development, but maintained that a lasting and stable identity is not formed until the close of adolescence. He placed considerable emphasis on social role, values, and ideals. Jacobson took exception to Erikson's formulations. She felt that his theory overemphasized social–descriptive aspects and lacked a clear metapsychological presentation of identity formation. Further, his focus on processes of late adolescence and early adulthood gave short shrift to the immense influence of early childhood. For Jacobson (1964), identity was equated with self-feeling or self-awareness, qualities that emerged in the process of self and object differentiation:

> I would prefer to understand by identity formation a process that builds up the ability to preserve the whole psychic organization—despite its growing structuralization, differentiation and complexity—as a continuity at any stage of human development. [1964, p. 27]

In regard to psychopathology, ego psychologists did not limit their purview to neurosis. In a paper on schizophrenia, Hartmann (1953) described the failure of the capacity to neutralize aggressive energy and thereby to build adequate defensive structures as the most significant aetiological factor in the development of this psychosis. Arlow and Brenner (1964) presented, in essence, the same thesis, but without the economic/energic language. The ego psychological purview extended also to the investigation of character and personality disorders, including the oral character (Glover, 1925), the anal character (Abraham, 1921a), the phallic–narcissistic character (Reich, 1933), the hysterical character (Marmor, 1953), the masochistic character (Stein, 1956), the as-if personality (Deutsch, 1942), the impostor (Abraham, 1925), and the perverse character (Arlow, 1971). Jacobson (1964), in her work on identity, noted that, from the clinical standpoint, "serious identity problems appear to be limited to neurotics with specific narcissistic conflicts, and to borderline and psychotic patients" (p. 29). This expansion in diagnostic categories eventuated in both a clinical recognition of the widening scope of psychoanalysis (Stone, 1954), and of the need for careful empirical studies, for example the Menninger research project (a long-term follow-up of forty-two patients) and the Hampstead index (an in-depth study of the psychoanalytic case material of a two-year-old child).

Clinical implications of ego psychology

Many of the contributions to the theory of ego psychology had general implications for psychoanalytic technique. Anna Freud (1946) shifted the technical emphasis of observation to the ego. She noted that it was only through the patient's ego that the analyst could observe the presentations of the id, ego, and superego with equal attention. Hence, she concluded that the ego is the agency through which analysis occurs. Hartmann's work broadened the scope of understanding beyond the individual's psychopathology to include the total personality, where both non-conflictual functioning and ego autonomy play important roles. Hartmann described how autonomous functions can facilitate (e.g., through self-observation and verbalization) or inhibit (e.g., through purposive thinking) free association. Loewenstein (1982) noted, "if the main though not exclusive interest of psychoanalysis is the study of conflict in man, the *tools* of this study are the autonomous functions" (pp. 213–214). Nevertheless, these functions may, at times, serve resistance and become objects of the analysis. Hartmann (1958) called this unexpected occurrence a "change of function". Loewenstein (1963) moved the understanding of resistance beyond the basic rule by calling attention to the distinction between resistances mobilized to address core conflicts and those mobilized against the emergence of a particular feeling or thought.

Neutralized energy was regarded as a reservoir by which the ego could support its aims and functions independently of drive pressure. Likewise, neutralized energy fuelled the ego's defences against drive demands. Clinically, Hartmann's theoretical concepts provided the impetus for ego psychology to explore such concepts as reality testing, sublimation, altruism, modes of internalization, ideal formation, and self-esteem regulation. These contributions provided a "shift in emphasis . . . [that led to] significant consequences" (Loewenstein, 1954, p. 189) without changing the basic psychoanalytic technique. These ranged from considering the effects on interpretations of speech, timing, and direction to redefining the main therapeutic goals, from recovering repressed material to modifying the ego's mode of functioning. Nunberg (1955) concisely captured the clinical outcome and goals of ego psychology in noting that the changes which are achieved through treatment in the ideal case involve the entire personality and are as follows: the energies of the id become more mobile, the superego becomes more tolerant, the ego is freer from anxiety and the synthetic function is restored. [p. 360]

Interpretation and clinical process

Ego psychology shifted the emphasis in technique from the recovery of the repressed to the modification of the patient's ego, including the alteration of automatic defensive functions. Interpretation, although not the only mode of intervention, is the major intervention that results in insight (Kris, 1956a), the critical element in lasting personality and behavioural change. Loewenstein (1951, 1957, 1958) saw interpretation as a continuous effort aimed at broadening the patient's understanding of how the past remains dynamically integral to current experiences. Loewenstein (1958) argued for a view of interpretation as a process that respects the unique personalities of analysand and analyst, both as individuals and in the therapeutic interaction. Kris (1951) also noted the analyst's role as "participant–observer", a dynamic presence in the analytic situation. Loewenstein provided a framework to guide the analyst in the work of discovering the unconscious meanings that underlie the patient's communications. The analyst gathers evidence for his conjectures from the patient's verbal and non-verbal communication. This careful approach placed a new emphasis on the role of speech (Hartmann, 1951; Loewenstein, 1956, 1961) that increased the personalized sense of the treatment process. Loewenstein (1951) wrote, "Interpretations deal with the individual experiences of a human being. They aim at widening the conscious knowledge of the individual about himself and should therefore deal with the psychological realities of the individual" (p. 5). This aspect of ego psychology is often missed by critics who view it as impersonal and mechanistic.

Kris (1956b), in his paper "The personal myth", elaborated how a person's unique history infuses the self-image with the important early fantasy. The personal myth is preserved as a "treasured possession" and the person re-enacts the repressed fantasy in various aspects of life. The personal myth serves multiple functions, acting as a defence and as a pattern of life. Its interpretation fosters the analysand's reintegration. A major achievement of the contemporary successors of ego psychology has been to elaborate the place of unconscious fantasy and the behaviour of the individual.

> The unacceptable wishes of childhood are part of the persistent unconscious fantasies that seek resolution in the present through compromise formation. As we develop, these fantasies mature and shape our special interests and character traits, determine our behavior, and produce our neurotic symptoms. The essential plot or narrative of unconscious wishes and fears endures even as their manifestations are transformed. [Bachant, Lynch, & Richards, 1995a, p. 75]

Transference and countertransference

We have also noted (Lynch, Richards, & Bachant, 1997) that Freud's definition of transference in 1905 laid the groundwork for the recognition of the therapeutic value of the interactive aspects of the transference. He characterized transference phenomena as

> new editions or facsimiles of the impulses and phantasies which are aroused and made conscious during the progress of the analysis; ... they replace some earlier person by the person of the physician. To put it in another way: a whole series of psychological experiences are revived, not as belonging to the past, but as *applying to the person of the physician at the present moment*. [1905e, p. 116, emphasis added]

Freud (1912b, 1915a; Ellman, 1991) went on to note that transference is found in every adult relationship, a point emphasized by Loewenstein (1969), Brenner (1982), and Bird (1972). Brenner, for example, notes that what distinguishes the therapeutic relationship from the ordinary adult relationship is not the presence of transference, but its use by the analyst to analyse psychic conflict (Bachant, Lynch, & Richards, 1995b).

The concept of countertransference did not become a subject for close investigation until the 1950s, when discussions of the concept burgeoned in the literature. The most systematic papers of this time were written by Annie Reich (1951, 1960, 1966), who followed in the ego psychological tradition. Like other contemporary contributors, Reich chose a broader definition of countertransference than Freud's, but one that stopped short of embracing the analyst's total response to the analysand.

> Countertransference ... comprises the effects of the analyst's own unconscious needs and conflicts on his understanding or technique. In such instances the patient represents for the analyst an object of the past onto whom past feelings and wishes are projected, just as it happens in the patient's transference situation with the analyst. The provoking factor for such an occurrence may be something in the patient's personality or material or something in the analytic situation as such. [1951, pp. 138–139]

Loewenstein (1957) highlighted the difference between, on the one hand, reactions in the analyst that are induced by the analysand, and, on the other, true countertransferential feelings and responses. The former were to be understood as an expression of activity in the analytic relationship. Regarding the distinction between countertransference and the analyst's total response to the analysand, Reich (1966) noted that the analysand is responded to not only as an object for unconscious strivings, but as an object in reality as well. To achieve empathy, she maintained, the analyst must have some object libidinal investment in the analysand. Countertransference occurs only when unconscious infantile strivings are expressed in intense and inappropriate feelings, responses, or actions. Thus, she wrote,

> If, for private reasons, the analyst ... is too charged with his private problems, too many conflicts will be mobilized, too many inner resistances stirred up, or some instinctual impulses too near to breakthrough will threaten. [1966, p. 352]

It is the intensity of these conflicts that blocks understanding, interferes with technique, and leads to a breakdown of the analytic task. Within contemporary conflict theory, Arlow (1971, 1985), Boesky (1982), Brenner (1976, 1982, 1985), Jacobs (1983, 1986), McLaughlin (1981, 1988), and Silverman (1985) are among those who have contributed to the expansion and modification of the current clinical status of countertransference.

Initiating a different line of thought, Heimann (1950) and Little (1951) advocated broadening countertransference to include the total response of the analyst. Gitelson (1952) and Cohen (1952) identified the place of interactions between analyst and analysand; Heimann (1950) stressed that the analyst's emotional response is important for empathy and that countertransference is a creation of the analysand as well as of the analyst. This body of work by ego psychologists and object relations theorists provided the grounding for contemporary debates about transference actualization and enactment. Contributors to these debates include Abend (1989), Boesky (1982), Chused (1991), Jacobs (1993), McLaughlin (1991), Ogden (1982, 1983), Sandler (1976a,b) Sandler and Sandler (1978), Schwaber (1983), and Ellman (1998a). Various subtexts of these debates, which have galvanized discussion (Lynch, Richards, & Bachant, 1997), include the place of philosophical relativism and social constructivism, the clinical valorization of the here and now, the status of the real relationship, the impact of the analysand on the analyst, and the role of the analyst's self-revelation and self-disclosure.

Contemporary conflict theory

The ego-psychological tradition has also come to fruition in the theoretical viewpoint commonly referred to as modern structural theory, although contemporary conflict theory is perhaps a more apt designation and is one that we prefer. This viewpoint was developed primarily by a group of American analysts who trained in the late 1940s and early 1950s and were analysed and supervised, for the most part, by émigrés from Central Europe. Jacob Arlow, David Beres, Charles Brenner, Martin Wangh, and Leo Rangell were members of this original group; all but Rangell attended the New York Psychoanalytic Institute. After completing their training, Arlow, Beres, Brenner, and Wangh met together and subsequently with their teachers and supervisors (Hartmann, Kris, Lewin, Loewenstein, et al.) to examine critically the received psychoanalytic wisdom of their time. Out of this examination, which focused on the concepts of anxiety, repression, defence, and symptom formation, the modern structural viewpoint emerged.

What precisely is the relationship between ego psychology and contemporary conflict theory? The latter is an outgrowth of the former, in as much as it devotes "considerable attention to the role, function, and characteristics of the ego" (Arlow, 1963, p. 576). Yet, as Boesky (1988) has observed, the two are not synonymous, as contemporary conflict theory focuses on the essential interrelatedness of id, ego, and superego. Indeed, Rangell (1988) has suggested "id/ego/superego/external reality psychology" as a more appropriate designation for the theory that embraces the central presupposition of Freud's structural hypothesis: that psychoanalysis is primarily a psychology of conflict. Contemporary conflict theory approaches mental life and all psychic phenomena as the expression of intrapsychic forces in conflict and the resulting compromises. The thrust of contemporary conflict theory has been to refine and amend Freud's hypothesis in order to achieve a fuller appreciation of the range and scope of conflicts and compromise formations in mental life and to develop a more powerful psychoanalytic treatment approach. Initially, this approach led to the espousal of structural concepts as more useful, clinically, than concepts associated with Freud's topographic model. Even within the structural model, moreover, the dynamic and genetic viewpoints were given precedence over the economic/energic. Arlow and Brenner's *Psychoanalytic Concepts and the Structural Theory* (1964) is an important articulation of this viewpoint. Its verdict has been underscored by Boesky (1988), who observes that Freud's concepts of psychic energy are no longer accepted by those espousing contemporary conflict theory.

Along with this selective use of structural concepts comes a trend toward loosening the dependence of conflict theory on Freud's model of the three psychic agencies. Beres gave voice to this trend in "Structure and function in psycho-analysis" (1965), as did Hartmann (1964c) in "Concept formation in psychoanalysis". Beres argued that Freud always understood the psychic structures as "functional groups", and that his emphasis was always on issues of organization and process. Sharing Arlow and Brenner's belief that theoretical concepts are ways of organizing clinical phenomena, Beres urged analysts to follow the functional direction of Freud's theorizing, an approach that viewed the structural entities of id, ego, and superego as metaphorical rather than concrete.

Beres' cautionary advice has generated a range of theoretical responses. One set of responses, associated with the work of Arlow and Brenner, has been to dissociate contemporary conflict theory from the metapsychological propositions that Freud imported into his structural theory. Arlow, Brenner, Beres, and Boesky all argue for the jettisoning of economic concepts, such as cathexis and decathexis, that are far removed from clinical observation. The modern structural emphasis on unconscious fantasy as an ego function, an emphasis growing out of an influential body of work by Arlow (1969a) and Beres (1962), is consistent with this trend.

The progressive loosening of contemporary conflict theory from Freud's formulations of id, ego, and superego has resulted in a more clinically based focus on the components of psychic conflict, a development accompanied by a widening of the experiential and dynamic realm of conflict. The shift in emphasis is from id, ego, and superego as components of conflict to the dynamic constellations closest to the data of observation. The common frame of reference of modern conflict theorists has not precluded their espousal of different clinical emphases. Two major variations, both legacies of ego psychology, focus on the interpretation of conflict and compromise formation in the context of unconscious fantasy (Arlow, Blum, Brenner, Abend, Boesky, Rangell, Rothstein) and on the patient's resistance to awareness of the operation of defences (Busch, 1995; Gray, 1994). The latter perspective is cautious about interpreting unconscious content, emphasizing instead an analytic partnership that facilitates the patient's self-discovery and emerging capacity for self-analysis. Busch links therapeutic success to the extent to which, during analysis, the patient's unbypassed ego functions have been involved in a consciously and increasingly voluntary partnership with the analyst.

An important controversy among proponents of contemporary conflict theory concerns the technical role of the patient–analyst relationship. At issue is the active use of the relationship as opposed to a greater emphasis on interpretation. This attachment/interpretation dialectic has been a major theme of ego-psychological discourse since the 1930s. It was a subject of dispute at the Marienbad symposium of 1936, where Sterba held that attachment was preliminary to understanding, whereas Strachey contended that it was the vehicle of structural change. The debate was continued at the Edinburgh symposium of 1962, where Gitelson, arguing in the spirit of Strachey, held that attachment was "a restructuring experience in itself, operating on the entire psychic apparatus and not just the ego or the superego" (Friedman, 1988, p. 51).

The next instalment of this debate, occurring in the 1960s and 1970s, revolved around the concept of the therapeutic alliance. The proponents of this concept, Elizabeth Zetzel and Ralph Greenson, saw it as redressing the inadequate attention to the real relationship that typified the reigning ego-psychological approach. Their position was opposed by Brenner (1979), who considered the concept superfluous and even countertherapeutic, and by Martin Stein, whose paper "The unobjectionable part of the transference" (1981) offers the clearest statement of the way in which positive transference can be enlisted by patient and analyst together in the service of resistance. It is fair to say that the ego-psychological tradition, from Sterba through Fenichel and Kris to Arlow and Brenner, has been cautious about using the analytic relationship as a lever of treatment. Yet, contemporary analysts trained in the ego-psychological tradition (e.g., James McLaughlin, Owen Renik, Theodore Jacobs, and Judith Chused) are among those who have alerted us to the importance of the analyst's subjective experience as a guide to understanding the patient. These analysts propound a range of positions regarding the nature and extent of the analyst's participation in the therapeutic process, but they share an appreciation of the analyst's subjectivity and find value in the enactments that occur inevitably in analytic treatment.

Contemporary conflict theory, building on the foundations of ego psychology and a spectrum of psychoanalytic theories, is an evolutionary, as opposed to revolutionary, viewpoint, since it takes Freud's conflict psychology as a conceptually and clinically adequate perspective. To be sure, it is a perspective subject to ongoing emendation (as in the work of Arlow, Brenner, and Rangell) and expansion (as in the work of Renik, Jacobs, McLaughlin, and Chused). It is noteworthy that Brenner, in his most recent writings (1994), has dispensed entirely with Freud's model of id, ego, and superego in expounding conflict and compromise formation. And Arlow, for his part, has long argued against the clinical–explanatory importance of a structural model with reified psychic agencies: "Id, ego, and superego," he has remarked, "exist not in the patient but in psycho-analytic textbooks" (personal communication). Still, other prominent contemporary structuralists continue to believe that the tripartite model remains the most illuminating and clinically useful way to understand conflict and compromise. Clearly there is no "last word" in contemporary conflict theory, and future decades will witness continuing advances in our understanding of, and clinical approaches to, "the mind in conflict" (Brenner, 1982).

Having attempted to elucidate the influences and controversies along specific lines of inquiry in the history of psychoanalytic development, we end with a disclaimer: it is not possible to neatly divide psychoanalysis into independent schools with disparate theories and techniques. Rather, psychoanalytic history bears witness to an ongoing process of accommodation and mutual influence. There is a central core of theory from Freud to the present with many diverse elaborations. Often, seemingly radical differences among theories diminish in their clinical presentation. Like any science, psychoanalysis will continue to generate diverse and conflicting positions; it will continue also to be influenced by contributions from the social and natural sciences. Amid these currents of change, a firm grasp of our collective history and scientific influences will help us to avoid the partisan squabbles and irrational battles that too often have plagued our field.

Author's (Ellman) brief note

This chapter gives an excellent overview of the movement from Freud's and then Hartmann's ego psychology to contemporary conflict theory. There are two pivotal authors that are not mentioned, given the timing of the chapter. Smith (1997, 2003) is a cogent author providing structural theory with more elasticity and scope. Lawrence Friedman (1977, 1992, 2002) is perhaps the most astute writer in this tradition, and he is able to bridge theoretical rivers without losing the theoretical structure that he has helped create. Since Chapter Seventeen is both a review and critique of contemporary relational concepts with respect to conflict or structural theory, the fuller commentary is reserved for that chapter. Although I (Ellman) differ from some of the perspectives offered in this chapter, it is my view that my summary chapter will present the reader with these differences. Despite these differences, I believe that Richards and Lynch have provided an excellent review and critique of the material covered in this chapter.

PART III
CONTEMPORARY ISSUES IN PSYCHOANALYSIS

CHAPTER SEVENTEEN

Structural theory, relational critiques, and integrative attempts

Prefatory statement

Although the chapter begins with a historical note, part of the thrust of the present chapter is viewing clinical theories in terms of a far-reaching critique provided by relational psychoanalysts. Relational analysts have offered clinical, theoretical, and philosophic critiques of the psychoanalytic situation with a main focus of their critiques aimed at the structural model, conflict theory, or classical psychoanalysis (I will frequently use these terms interchangeably). After delineating the relational critique, there will be an effort to provide integrative answers that both incorporate elements of the critique and provide integrations that originate from various theoretical perspectives. A central current in this chapter (and volume) is how each position has dichotomized clinical and theoretical issues. When this has been done, the positive aspects of alternative theories have been overlooked, not been recognized, or have been only narrowly understood.

Summary of chapter

The first part of the chapter gives some material relevant to the theoretical and social history of the contemporary era. This leads to a definition of the Freudian position that is being critiqued, and then a brief foray into some of the philosophic issues that are lurking behind the clinical concepts being proposed. Since Stephen Mitchell is such an important figure in relational psychoanalysis, there is a section that looks at Mitchell's writings up to approximately 2000. The mid-section of the chapter builds on Mitchell's critiques and presents relational critiques of the psychoanalytic situation using the classical position and conflict theory as main referents. There is an attempt to honour the critiques while providing both an analysis of the bifurcations these critiques created and some solutions to the splits that have existed. A good deal of the solutions proposed stem from what I have called the self and object Freudians (Ellman, 1998b). Most of the chapter, while clinical, is implicitly built on the theoretical concepts that have been discussed. The last part of the chapter discusses transference and the analytic third.

The beginning of the era

The beginning of this era may remind the reader of an era covered in other chapters (see Chapters Five and Sixteen). We begin in the 1960s, with Arlow and Brenner's (1964) book on the structural theory. One may consider this the beginning of an era or the end of the previous era, depending on your theoretical predilections. Arlow and Brenner, in many ways, were to replace Hartmann and his colleagues as the most prominent protagonists of the structural model. Their work is the prototype of the psychoanalytic theory that will be the critical target for relational psychoanalysis. Arlow and Brenner's volume spells out clearly some of the implications of the structural theory and places Oedipal dynamics as central to all conflicts in all psychogenic conditions. (Brenner's more recent work is discussed in Chapter Sixteen: in this section I am considering his work up to 1982.) They made this statement as a direct translation of Freud's assertion that when one analysed castration anxiety in

STRUCTURAL THEORY, RELATIONAL CRITIQUES, & INTEGRATIVE ATTEMPTS   563

males and penis envy in women, the analysis had reached the bedrock of conflict (see Chapter Four). Thus, in this formulation, even psychotic disorders were seen as manifestations of oedipal conflicts. The question of dynamics, although a distinguishing factor, is not necessarily the decisive factor, the decisive issues involve a combination of intensity of conflict and posited genetic factors. Understandably, they deemed genetic factors as beyond the expertise of psychoanalysts. Ironically, the form of their explanation is reminiscent of Fairbairn's views of the oral stage (paranoid–schizoid) as the only stage where conflicts are established. Obviously the stage is different with Arlow and Brenner's conceptualization, but the concept of a singular stage where conflict is formed is similar. Clearly, for Arlow and Brenner, the child's pre-Oedipal history can effect the intensity of conflict, but the conflict is formed during the Oedipal stage.

Arlow and Brenner's volume, in many ways, signalled the height of popularity of the structural position in the USA. There were few critics within the American Psychoanalytic Association (APA) and in many ways the APA tried to determine what theories were considered to be psychoanalytic. Professions other than psychiatry were not allowed to be trained in institutes of the APA unless there was special permission (a waiver) for candidates who were termed research candidates. In this atmosphere, psychoanalysis was, seemingly, an established medical profession, and, in many ways, that was the intention of Brill (Richards, 1999) when, in 1911, he started the first psychoanalytic institute (New York Psychoanalytic Institute) in the USA. Psychoanalysis was to be a profession alongside medical professions and, by the 1960s, it was a profession that a number of psychiatrists chose in terms of their advanced training.

I have put this brief historical note in this section for, in many ways, it is hard to understand the modern (1960–1980) to contemporary era (1980 to the present) without understanding the extent to which the APA dominated psychoanalysis in the USA, and politically throughout the world. In New York, this domination was beginning to be challenged when a psychoanalytic training programme began at New York University (started by Professor B. Kalinkowitz). This programme was designed to train psychologists with a PhD in Clinical Psychology. The New York State Psychiatric

Society legally challenged the clinical psychologists' right to provide this type of training and, when the case was won by the psychologists, it was correlated with the beginning of a new era. Although there were other non-medical institutes in the city and the country, this case began a movement among psychologists that gradually spread to other mental health professions (e.g., social workers, psychiatric nurses, etc.). Whether these new institutes were a factor in the development of the criticism of classical theory, or whether they were simply a correlation without any causal links, is a matter that I will leave for another writer to sort out. Suffice to say that, during the late 1960s and moving into the 1970s, there were beginning to be cracks in the monolithic structure of the APA, in terms of both theoretical purity and alternative professions and institutes training mental health workers and other interested professionals as psychoanalysts.

One of the Institutes that had been outside the APA, but had been a psychoanalytic institute for a long period of time, was William Allison White (WAW). In this institute, both psychiatrists and psychologists were trained (without a waiver) and the dominant theory was an interpersonal theory derived from Sullivan. Contemporary interpersonal theorists both published Sullivan's views and continued to develop the implications of the theoretical structure that Sullivan began. Many of the critics of the classical theory came from WAW and the programme at New York University (Postdoctoral Programme in Psychoanalysis and Psychotherapy). Some of these critics were members of both organizations. Again, this correlation may or may not be significant, but it is, I believe, historically accurate. Although I am painting a monolithic picture of the APA, this picture is put forth as a historical dramatization. While there was an attempt by members of this organization to promote a psychoanalytic orthodoxy, it is clear from the publications of this period that many American psychoanalytic analysts were questioning this orthodoxy. Stone (1961), Loewald (1960), Sandler (who was in the UK and, for a brief period, in Israel at the time), and Jacobson (1964), among others, were gently and quietly challenging the orthodoxy of the structural position. Loewald (1966), in a scathing review of Arlow and Brenner's (1964) volume, in effect called it an overly simplified version of psychoanalysis and of the human condition. Interestingly, Loewald was deemed by some members of the establishment as someone who was not really an analyst. In many ways, this designation was considered by many to be the death knell of an analyst's career. Loewald's career and reputation survived this description (see Mitchell, 2000).

Mitchell, in writing about the analyst's authority, gives an interesting historical summary. He states,

> there *has* been a strong authoritarian current to the political management of psychoanalysis, at times almost Stalinist in proportions. From Freud's "secret committee," to the banishment of dissidents, to the kind of control Melanie Klein maintained over the minds and publications of her followers (cf., Grosskurth, 1986), to the medicalization of psychoanalysis in the United States and the sometimes medieval practices of both the American Psychoanalytic Association and the International Psychoanalytical Association, the reigning political powers within psychoanalysis have hardly allowed psychoanalytic theorizing to flourish in an atmosphere of freedom and open exchange. It is true that from Freud's day to ours, psychoanalysis has often been under siege, in one way or another. But like the Bolsheviks, the guardians of psychoanalysis often seemed not to grasp that the greater danger is not the wrong ideas but rigidly held ideas. This has become much clearer to us today, and part of the vitality of postclassical psychoanalysis comes from its emancipation from the constraints of Freudian orthodoxy." [1998, p. 73]

Mitchell, in providing this analysis, covers a long historical period and, essentially, provides a review of the unfortunate tendency towards orthodoxy and reductionist leanings in psychoanalytic thought. He sees this as residing in Freudian orthodoxy, which I see as a true but incomplete analysis. A theme that I have stated, and now restate, is the tendency of each psychoanalytic position to develop a certain type of orthodoxy. It is my view that Mitchell, in many of his writings, was a good example of an orthodox theorist. While his orthodoxy may be a necessary response to the dominant theory, it still is the case that all such attempts cause unfortunate splits.

While I am tempted to write more about the politics of the era (up to approximately 1980), it seems to me that I have made the point that there was a strong attempt by the APA to put forward an approved psychoanalytic position. There were also, of course, many creative analysts (from various traditions) that were not engaged politically. The attempt at enforced orthodoxy was in some ways hidden in the Trojan horse of professional standards, through the Board of Professional Standards, a committee of the APA. The more substantive issues are related to the concepts that various critics began to circle around as the hegemony of the psychoanalytic world began to crumble.

In rereading this description, although I believe in its accuracy, I think that it does not do justice to the changes that occurred in the APA after the 1970s. In the 1980s and beyond, a variety of analysts became more accepting of other professions and other positions. Gill, who previously was one of the orthodox members of the APA, in many ways spearheaded changes in the theory. Although I do not know the internal politics during this period and beyond, the organization clearly was much more receptive to other groups and began actively to include other professions. In recent years, APA analysts such as Owen Renik (1998, 1999), Arnold Rothstein (1995, 2002), and Judy Chused (1991, 1996) showed either the flexibility of the structural (conflict) theory (Chused and Rothstein) or the flexibility of the new profession in tolerating Renik's cogent criticisms and analysis of clinical concepts. In order to avoid the type of dichotomization I am arguing against, I find it necessary to put in this historical emendation before looking at the development of clinical concepts in the contemporary period.

Classical psychoanalysis and different views of the Freudian position

The term Freudian is one that can have a variety of meanings around the world. A number of groups in different countries consider themselves to be Freudian in orientation. For example, some of the Kleinians of London see themselves as the natural inheritors of the Freudian mantle. Certain French psychoanalysts, from Lacan to Green, see (or saw) themselves as strongly aligned with the Freudian tradition. Certainly, Loewald and Jacobson in the USA viewed themselves as extenders of the Freudian opus. Each of these groups (or individuals) have somewhat different views of Freud, or, perhaps more accurately, have emphasized different elements of Freud's writings. In the USA, the group that has been most extensively used in critiques of the Freudian tradition are analysts exemplified by Arlow (1969b, 1979) and Brenner (1994, 1996). This has been called, in the USA, the classical (later conflict theory or the structural) position. Although Arlow and Brenner have been taken by relational analysts as prototypic of the Freudian tradition, we will distinguish several different strains in that tradition. One tradition has already been discussed, and, while Hartmann for a period of time was the cynosure of American psychoanalysis, both the relational movement and adherents of conflict theory have almost totally disregarded him. However, unless otherwise noted, the Freudian tradition that we will discuss as we look at relational critiques is the classical, or, in more contemporary terms, conflict theory or the structural position (Abend, 1979) (see Chapter Sixteen). Before we examine relational concepts, we will pause for a moment on a group of writers who initially began to critique the classical position.

Precursors of the relational critique

One part of our contemporary journey begins in the 1970s, when there was a body of literature whose main thrust was an evaluation and criticism of psychoanalytic metapsychology. The roots of this line of thought can be traced at least to Kubie's (1947) criticism of the psychic energy model. More recently, numerous other authors criticized various aspects of what they have labelled metapsychology. But it was George Klein (1973) who first made an appeal for a complete rejection of metapsychology. Gill (1977), Holt (1974), and Schafer (1976), among others, rapidly joined in this appeal. To understand these past decades one can start with George Klein's seminal papers questioning the nature of psychoanalytic explanations. These papers challenged the idea of psychoanalysis as a general theory and proclaimed that psychoanalysis is a theory of meaning, not of mechanism. To this end, George Klein maintained that metapsychology should be abandoned and psychoanalysis should rely on what he called the clinical theory. Klein, in taking this position, was one of the first authors to argue against what he termed metapsychology and, in particular, those aspects of metapsychology that offer mechanistic explanations. Klein assumed that "psychoanalytic" could be divided into two distinct types of theories, and, in part, this assumption was based on Freud's view of psychoanalytic theory (see Chapter Three).

One interpretation of Klein's suggestion is that analysts should be concerned only with the clinical theory and phenomena that is observable in the clinical situation. He was attempting to focus analysts on events they could observe and away from what he considered to be theoretical explanations that were experience distant. Certainly, Klein and others were critical of the theory of drive and psychic energy. These concepts were judged to have no empirical referent, but, nevertheless, were referred to by classical analysts as providing theoretical explanations that Klein saw as mechanistic and overly laden with theory which was far from the patient's experience. Although Klein's critique was joined by Schafer, Gill, Holt, and Spence (1982), contemporary relational writers, while perhaps inspired by these critiques, have provided a broader evaluation of Freudian or classical psychoanalytic theory. Klein, for example, although critical of certain aspects of Freudian thought, was trying to stay within what he regarded as a Freudian paradigm. Relational writers, starting with Greenberg and Mitchell (Greenberg, at this point, has altered his position) have argued that one had to chose between a relational and what they termed a drive/structural model, originally provided by Freud.

Greenberg and Mitchell (1983), and Mitchell in his individual papers, clearly produced the rallying cry and the beginning of theoretical critique for the relational position. Although Greenberg's individual papers (2001, 2002) have been highly influential, they have been increasingly textured and inclusive, while Mitchell has continued for a longer period of time to sound the clarion call for a distinct relational position. (I had planned to write a good deal about Mitchell's more recent book, *Relationality: From Attachment to Intersubjectivity* [2000]. In my view, Mitchell writes the most insightful two chapters on Loewald that are present in the literature. I think it was the beginning of, or some point in, a new integration for him. For this and other reasons, I mourn his death.) Given Mitchell's central position in relational psychoanalysis, we will review his writings and try to illustrate his powerful influence on relational critiques.

Stephen Mitchell: an introduction and overview

In effect, the critique of relational psychoanalysts begins with, and is largely influenced by, the work of Mitchell. For this reason, I am providing an overview of his work up to the point when he published his volume *Relationality* (2000). For those readers who are unaware of Stephen Mitchell's contributions, I thought it useful to give a sense of his life. The following tribute, after his untimely death, was from the institute that Mitchell graduated from, William Allison White (*New York Times*, 24 December, 2000).

> Dr. Mitchell's reputation as a brilliant teacher was well established prior to his graduation from White in 1977. A seminal book, "Object Relations in Psychoanalytic Theory," written with Dr. Jay Greenberg and published in 1983, was a major contribution to psychoanalytic theorizing and first brought the relational, interpersonal approach to the attention of the psychoanalytic world. In the 17 years following, Steve Mitchell continued to write at an astonishing pace, publishing many important papers and books, all of which are widely read. He also founded and edited the journal 'Psychoanalytic Dialogues.' He had a formidable intellect which he made generously available to students and colleagues. He taught, discussed, and debated with a swiftness and clarity that were both dazzling and daunting to his colleagues. His beauty and elegance of thought and of writing transformed abstruse doctrine into coherent concepts valuable to students and professionals at all levels of sophistication. Stephen Mitchell was eagerly sought as a psychoanalyst, a training analyst, a supervisor, a teacher, and a mentor. He was a deeply humane man: warm, boyishly charming, and truly loved. Those who were fortunate to know him well, were profoundly changed by his influence. Steve left an enduring legacy, yet we shall yearn for his deeply inspiring presence among us, and for his vision of future years at the Institute that bears his indelible stamp.

To give an appreciation of Mitchell's influence, Gill notes that when Freudian critics discuss relational theory, it "is discussed almost entirely according to the views of its foremost proponent, Stephen Mitchell" (1995, p. 89). In many ways, the questions raised by Rapaport's ex-students open the path to critiquing Freudian theory along new philosophic and clinical pathways. Mitchell built on these critiques and, inspired by interpersonal theory and object relations theorists, he played a large part in creating the relational position. His training at William Allison White provided a number of influences: Edgar Levenson was among those interpersonalists who strongly influenced Mitchell (Mitchell, 2004). Gill states that he sees "relational theory as an offshoot of interpersonal theory" (1995, p. 89), and clearly this is true for Mitchell's early version(s) of relational theory.

In his earlier writings, he spearheaded efforts to dethrone Freudian theory as the leading perspective in American psychoanalysis. He was certainly one of the figures who brought interpersonal theory to a larger audience and, with Greenberg, made strong attempts to integrate a number of authors as either relational or important precursors of the relational position. Clearly, at the beginning of his career, he and Greenberg wanted to clarify their position and make both a theoretical and political statement to the psychoanalytic community. Thus, their volume was formulated in dichotomous terms: you can use a drive/structural or relational/ structural model, but not both. It was his view at that time, and for most of his life, that these two models could not be reconciled. Whether this was still his view when he wrote *Relationality* (2000) is hard to tell.

If we begin with his earlier statements, we can see that the comments that seem to catch the attention of Freudian analysts are ones that state that "The relational perspective has positioned itself as offering a "revolutionary" view of how psychoanalysis has evolved (Mitchell, 1993, p. 466), "declaring that its development represents a radical departure from the classical tradition" (*ibid.*). This type of comment was particularly aversive to a number of classical commentators (e.g., Bachant & Richards, 1993, Bachant, Lynch, & Richards, 1995a,b) and served to fuel an ongoing debate between the camps. Bachant and Richards maintained that relational theorists, particularly Mitchell, have

> misrepresented drive theory when they maintained that in classical theory, the individual's personality is formed primarily in response to the pressures of drive. They proposed that both normal and pathological dynamics emerge from the interpersonal field. This is not quite as reasonable as it might first appear. Conceptualizing

development as primarily derived from the interpersonal field mitigates the role in psychic development of the intrapsychic dimension; restricts our understanding of conflict; and substantially redefines the concepts of resistance, transference, and the method of free association. [Bachant, Lynch, & Richards, 1995b, p. 74]

Mitchell's answer to the classical critics has been twofold: he declared that he does not present his work as "a comprehensive alternative to classical thought" (1993, p. 462), but, rather, as a way to "offer a methodology for integrating different conceptual strategies". He then goes on to say that his critics are probably

befuddled and perplexed, looking for comforting landmarks as points of reference. . . . When these critics do not find, the Oedipus complex, the id, no instincts they are at a loss as to how analysis can possibly proceed without these concepts. This leads the critics 'to the conclusion that my perspective is rather empty, less comprehensive, less useful than theirs'. [*ibid*.]

This is an interesting extract from Mitchell, since, a few sentences before in the same article, he reminds the reader that he has made a point "of arguing that one of the great, unfortunate mistakes of most of the major post-Freudian theorists (Fairbairn, Sullivan, Kohut, and so on) is that they presented their work as a comprehensive alternative to Freud" (*ibid*.). Why, then, would he be surprised or comment on the fact that classical critics would find his work less comprehensive than theirs? He has already, seemingly, acknowledged that his work is less comprehensive, but, of course, one might surmise that he has not truly acknowledged this at all. He wants, as do a variety of theorists, to be able to say, I don't have all the answers, but if you look at my conceptual strategy I will have these answers. In many ways, Mitchell's inaugural talk to the New York Univerity Post-Doctoral community (which inaugurated the relational track and for which I was the discussant) was this type of promissory note; he said that if you follow the leads started by Spence and Schafer (two types of narrative positions) and George Klein and Gill, and build from them and from Fairbairn and interpersonalist roots, you will develop a better product (theory). One can sympathize with this strategy, since one way for critics to kill a revolution is to overload it with questions and requests. Often, a revolution of any kind cannot answer questions until it develops and is in "office" for a period of time. Our first task, then, is to see the type of concepts that Mitchell puts forth and look at how his assumptions have been developed (up to 2000) since the publication of *Object Relations in Psychoanalytic Theory* (Greenberg & Mitchell, 1983). We will return to the debate after looking at some of his work.

If we follow Mtichell's work from 1979 through 1995, in almost every article (I am not including most reviews in this summary statement, or articles about editorial policy of the newly created *Psychoanalytic Dialogues*) he mentions either Freud and/or the classical tradition. He is the mirror image of the classical writer who starts off every article showing how Freud, in some manner, presaged the issue they are about to discuss. Mitchell, instead, shows how Freud, or a Freudian acolyte, has inevitably gone in the wrong direction and he will now attempt to correct and redirect the psychoanalytic community. This negative reaction to Freud in part follows from his stated position that

> For reasons I have elaborated elsewhere (Greenberg & Mitchell, 1983; Mitchell, 1988), I do not think it is helpful to simply pick and choose pieces of theories, extracting them from their conceptual context and joining them willy-nilly. The clashes between different theories often point to important conceptual problems that need to be thought through, not skipped over. [Mitchell, 1995, p. 580]

Thus, not only is it Mitchell's view that one must choose between drive/structural and relational theories, but it is a mistake to even extract pieces of competing theories. This casts him in a constant position of trying to show the superior utility of a relational position and the uselessness of a drive/structural position. The lack of possibility of choice or integration of aspects of positions strongly reinforces an adversarial position. It gives one the sense that there is nothing good in the other theory, even though Mitchell clearly has made positive statements about Freud's journey and his creation of the field of psychoanalysis. Despite these occasional statements, it is understandable that when an author starts off virtually all of his articles with a negative critique of a Freudian position, many Freudians will respond in kind. They may respond so strongly that they miss the important points that Mitchell has raised. On the other hand, it seems to me that a relational theorist might say that you are leaving out the crucial historical fact that, for decades, the classical position acted as if it was the only possible psychoanalytic position. If one received this type of treatment, would it not be reasonable to assume that the response would contain adversarial replies? I think it is fair to say that there has not been enough fruitful discussion (until the recent past) between the two camps, or, at the very least, that both relational and classical analysts have felt (and often been) misunderstood by the other.

From Mitchell's early work to the middle years

Mitchell's first publication (1978) is one where he clearly establishes himself as breaking from some of the prejudices of the past. He is stating an important point that most liberals had uttered, but he, in print, voiced his opposition to the inherent prejudice of pathologizing sexual preference. He advocated equal treatment of gay and heterosexual individuals in both analytic treatment and analytic training. This may not seem revolutionary today; it is an issue that was more controversial in 1978, and some analysts, even today, encountered this issue with some difficulty. Mitchell's published career as an incipient relational analyst begins, interestingly enough, with his review of Kohut's 1977 volume, *The Restoration of the Self*. In this review (1979), he places Kohut as moving from classical impulse psychology "to a psychology that is object-relational or interpersonal". He credits Kohut for becoming, in Fairbairn's terms, more object-relational, but, "The transition is not complete" (*ibid.*, p. 179). Mitchell still sees Kohut as using language derived from classical libido theory and concepts that are derived from the theory of narcissism. Mitchell also questions whether Kohut's concepts of grandiosity and parental mirroring and idealization are crucial developmental factors. He wonders "whether the salient, injurious dimension is the break in idealization and the failure to reflect infantile grandiosity, or the lack of any kind of real emotional contact" (*ibid.*, p. 180). This is an interesting and subtle way of bifurcating a relational position. Kohut is describing difficulties with one type of "real" emotional contact: parental failure to give or accept idealizing communications. This, in Kohut's view, is one type of important contact, for example, the parental gleam in the eye. Without it, Kohut maintains that the child may be vulnerable to narcissistic or self-esteem difficulties. It is a strange critical comment to imply that Kohut is not taking into account the absence of real emotional contact when Kohut is trying to describe some elements of parent–child contact where the child is not adequately present in the parent's mind. Obviously, from Mitchell's point of view, Kohut is not describing the important "real" type of emotional contact.

This critique may occur because Mitchell maintains that Kohut, clinically, is trying to preserve ties to the classical community. Mitchell sees Kohut as saying that one can interpret either drive derivatives or relational configurations (self difficulties). This is considered by him to be Kohut's first strategy for staying tied to the classical position.

> Kohut's second major preservative strategy ... is his proposition that there are two classes of pathology, disorders of the self and structural neurosis, and that the drive theory is applicable to the latter. Much of Kohut's argument is directed towards an orthodox audience, defending the clinical reality of the 'disorders of the self' necessitating the development of his new psychology of the self.
> [*ibid.*, p. 182]

Thus, although Kohut has taken a step towards a relational theory, it is, for Mitchell, too small a step. He has not completely left the drive/structural model. In my view, a more accurate portrayal is that Kohut has not left aspects of Freud and still sees value in Freud's writings. Kohut has given up more of the classical canon than Mitchell acknowledges, but Mitchell, at this point in time, does not distinguish the classical position from elements of Freudian theory. Interestingly, Greenberg and Mitchell (1983), several years later, use Kohut as an example of the impossibility of a mixed model.

One can see that Mitchell is already demanding purity from a theory that calls itself relational. Clearly, for Mitchell, Kohut's theorizing does not qualify, and this is true in part because Mitchell overstates Kohut's allegiance to classical theory. It is clear from this article and subsequent publications that Fairbairn is a beacon of light in determining who is relational and who fails to join the anointed group. There is no question that Fairbairn played an important role in Mitchell's development as a relational analyst. One can also see this in Mitchell's article (1981) comparing Fairbairn and Melanie Klein's use of the concept of object.

In the next several years, Mitchell develops his position, integrating aspects of Sullivan and Fairbairn. He joins Fairbairn in stating that human beings are fundamentally object seeking rather than pleasure seeking. Mitchell, like Fairbairn and Sullivan, sees Freudian theory as putting relationships secondary to drive or pleasure seeking. Interestingly, Mitchell accepts Sullivan's interactional model and Fairbairn's concept of internal objects. He later relates that, at first, relational theory was "a bridge concept pointing to an implicit congruence in basic presuppositions about mind inherent in what seemed to be the widely divergent traditions of American interpersonal psychoanalysis and British-school object relations theories" (1999, p. 717). Whether this bridge supports both types of theory is a question that has not been fully explored. For example, one might wonder whether Sullivan's fundamental concept of functional autonomy is compatible with Fairbairn and Guntrip's concept of stage-specific dynamics, as well as their theory of internal structures. What is even more troubling to this relationship is that Sullivan rejects the notion of structure and maintains that interactions should be seen in terms of energy (Chapter Eleven).

What is certainly compatible is their focus on the mother–infant interaction. Sullivan is strongly tied to the idea of the interactional field, and this concept is certainly compatible with Fairbairn's theorizing. Influenced by both Sullivan and Fairbairn, Mitchell advocates a social theory of mind, seeing the individual mind as a product of, as well as an interactive participant with, his/her social context. Mitchell states that for relational

> model theorists ... the individual mind is a product of as well as an interactive participant in the cultural, linguistic matrix within which it comes into being. Meaning is not provided a priori, but derives from the relational matrix. The relational field is constitutive of individual experience. [1988, p. 19]

This extract reflects Mitchell's social field perspective and his attempt to isolate the classical Freudian position. He characterizes Freud as portraying the human being with mental content outside of, and prior to, social experience. Mitchell's Freud, views meaning as mainly inherent in man's physiology, his biological equipment.

Mitchell, in rejecting drive theory, replaces this perspective by viewing sex and aggression within a relational template. More specifically, he maintains that sexuality and aggression are not "preformed instincts with inherent meanings, which impinge upon the mind" (*ibid.*, p. 20). Instead, he regards sexuality and aggression as "powerful responses, mediated physiologically, generated within a biologically mandated relational field and therefore deriving their meaning from that deeper relational matrix" (*ibid.*).

Although he emphasizes the formative impact of the relational field, he cautions that the individual is not a blank slate who is simply shaped by the environment. He notes the physiological tendencies and the cognitive capacities that the individual brings to the interaction, which thus contribute to how the environment is integrated. Mitchell maintains that

> Early relationships, like later relationships . . . are not simply registered, but experienced through physiological response patterns, constitutional features of temperament, sensitivities and talents, and worked over, digested, broken down and recombined and designed into the new, unique patterns which comprise the individual life. [*ibid.*]

In Mitchell's view, the individual evolves personality structure out of this continuous interaction with the environment, which can be best analysed in terms of self-organization, object ties, and transactional patterns. He sees the individual as being inevitably conflicted, because the significant human relationships that are so formative are necessarily conflictual. He asserts, "The strands which make up the complexities of personality derive from the inevitable conflicts centering around and between various points of connection and identification with significant others" (1988, p. 277). From his perspective, individuals are typically torn between desires to connect with a parent and individuate, wishes to connect with contradictory parts of their parent, and/or desires to connect with differing or opposing parents.

To this point in our review of Mitchell, a reader can glean the type of influence that he provided for a variety of authors who followed his lead and continue(d) to develop the relational position.

We have stated some of Mitchell's positions, but we have not looked at how these positions are translated into clinical ideas. In the next section, we will look at how these ideas are translated into relational clinical concepts and a relational critique of the classical positions. Later, we will look at some of Mitchell's theorizing in one of his last publications.

The relational critique of the clinical situation

Mitchell's critique of the clinical situation assumes that a number of Freudian clinical concepts are intimately tied to drive theory. Some relational writers (Ghent, 2002) argue that a Freudian clinical theory cannot be separated from what George Klein called Freud's metapsychology. Alternatively, other relational writers (Aron, 1996) maintain that even if there is a Freudian clinical theory that is separated from drive theory, it is based on a one-person as opposed to a relational perspective, which espouses a two-person model. Here, then, are two of the proclaimed dividing points for relational and classical clinical theory; a one person *vs.* two person model of the clinical situation and the rejection of drive theory, or, more broadly, Freud's metapsychology. In the relational characterization, a one person model implies that the analyst is an objective observer of the patient and not reciprocally affected by, or an active contributor to, the type of events that proceed in the analysis. In this one person model, it is the patient that creates the content, the analyst is the interpreter of this content. There is only one person who is creating the analytic atmosphere (the patient); the other (the analyst) observes, receives, and interprets what the patient produces.

Although Aron might grant the possibility of a Freudian theory without drive, Greenberg and Mitchell saw the drive/structural model of the classical analyst as the basic foundation or postulate for all of the classical position's clinical concepts. Thus, the classical analysts' reliance on free association is seen as assuming that, once a patient is in a recumbent position (on the couch), unconscious ideas (or drive derivatives) will begin to push into consciousness. This technique in classical theory is a way of allowing drive greater access to consciousness. Since drive is a rejected concept, it follows that free association is seen as outmoded aspect of psychoanalytic technique. The Freudian analyst assumes that free association allows the patient to provide the analyst with drive derivatives. Then, the analyst's role is solely or primarily as a decoder of the drive derivatives that are arriving into consciousness. In Hoffman's view (a relational–constructionist position), "the concept of free association denies the patient's agency, denies interpersonal influence and denies the patient's share of co-constructing the analytic relationship" (2002, p. 1). That seems like an overwhelming amount of denial for one concept. We can say that if the concept of free association is dependent on a drive model for its existence, for relational analysts its existence is at least in jeopardy or, perhaps, DOA (dead on arrival). Interestingly, Anna Freud (see Chapter Five) put forth similar objections to the concept of free association.

In the relational critique, the classical model is viewed as asking the analyst to remain anonymous, and anonymity is not viewed as a possibility in the analytic situation. All of the analyst's choices (office décor, clothing, etc.) manifest an aspect of the analyst, and it is impossible to provide anonymity in the analytic situation. Similar arguments are marshalled against analytic neutrality. Any choice of the analyst is not seen as neutral, but as a manifestation of various preferences (e.g., theoretical, personal, etc.). For example, the choice of not speaking is as much a choice as speaking a great deal, and may provide distance, but not anonymity. In this critique, anonymity and neutrality are seen as impossible goals and, in fact, analytic myths. Part of the rationale for anonymity, neutrality, and a reserved or quiet analytic presence is seen as attempting to bolster the authority of the analyst. Relational analysts, understandably, feel the authority of the analyst should not be predicated on the rules of treatment. In other terms, the analytic situation should not be arranged in order to enhance the authority of the analyst. Mitchell, in discussing the issue of analytic authority, states that

> For many, there is a clear analogue between the illegitimate wielding of power in classical psychoanalytic politics and the orthodox analyst's illegitimate claim to a singular scientific knowledge and authority vis-à-vis the patient's mind. In recent years there has been a broad-scale democratization of psychoanalytic institutes that has been constructive and liberating. And there have been attempts to democratize the analytic relationship. Some lines of contemporary psychoanalytic thought, in critiquing classical theory, seem to offer

a kind of relativism or epistemological democracy as the major alternative to what is taken to be classical authoritarianism. [1998, p. 5]

Mitchell's further discussion of analytic authority distinguishes between what may be scientific claims and the religious scientism of Freud and some of his followers. This scientism assumed that all problems were subject to scientific scrutiny and that this line of knowledge would provide both personal and cultural advances. In the lexicon of this volume, it was an example of Freud's metaphysics that was taken as providing the analyst with a sense of increased authority. This line of thinking is apart from the fact that, until recently, there were few attempts to demonstrate the efficacy of analytic treatment.

In various relational critiques, it is not only the rules of treatment that should be rethought, but transference, the main vehicle of the classical tradition, should be reconceptualized. Contemporary relational writers would maintain, for example, that transference is not conceived of by Freud as a relationship "between two people, but rather as the distorted view of the analyst by the analysand" (Gill, quoted in Aron, 1996, p. 48). Aron writes that "It was thought that if the analyst was analyzing correctly, being technically neutral and anonymous, then the transference would spontaneously unfold and would not be distorted by the personality of the analyst" (*ibid.*). The implication of a two-person psychology is that who the analyst is, not only how he or she works but his or her very character, makes a real difference for the analysand. The analyst's personality affects not only the therapeutic alliance or the so-called real relationship, but also "the nature of the transference itself" (*ibid.*, p. 50).

Here, one might ask: is this an all or none concept, or can we conceptualize the extent to which the personality of the analyst affects the manifestation of transference? Perhaps we should ask another question, and wonder not only whether there is some limit to the effect of the analyst's personality, but whether this is true of all personalities or are there some that affect the manifestation of transference less significantly and some to a greater extent? Or, is the statement that the analyst's personality affects the transference not an empirical statement, but a postulate of a relational position?

If it is a postulate, then the questions that were just asked are irrelevant. One might say that transference is created by the analytic pair and not a previous characteristic of the patient or analyst, that transference is not discovered in the analysis, but, rather, created in the interaction between patient and analyst. If that is the position, then transference does not reside in a given person, but is a property of the interaction between (or among) individuals. We have just implicitly outlined three positions: whether one is discussing transference as a characteristic solely of the patient (or analyst), or a tendency that might be affected by the other, or whether there is a new meaning of transference (transference as completely the creation of the analytic pair). This last conceptualization bears little or no relationship to the meaning that Freud put forth. The first conceptualization assumes that there is a structure (or very slowly changing energy formations) that is enduring in an individual that is part of their memory storage and affects their responses to others in a variety of circumstances. The second position makes the same assumption, but emphasizes that the manifestation of transference can be effected by various factors in the analytic situation (e.g., the analyst's personality).

One of the main critiques in contemporary psychoanalysis is the rejection of Freudian thought because of Freud's positivist position. Gill, a prominent relational writer states that "the classical view is certainly a positivist" perspective". (To call Gill a prominent relational analyst is not doing his outstanding career justice. For a long period of time, he was a prominent Freudian and ego psychological analyst, and then one of the creators of the relational position.) The meaning of Gill's critique lies in part in ideas that maintain that the classical position has underestimated the extent that the analyst is part of the interactions that occur in the treatment situation. The idea of an unbiased observer that is seen as part of the Freudian position is strongly rejected on the basis of both philosophic objections and clinical observations. Although Gill is often an acute observer and creative theoretician, it is not clear why he equates a positivist position with the idea of an unbiased observer. One might also be a positivist and maintain that there are interactions and that the observer is affected, but one can specify the operations by which this occurs. What is true is that the way the classical position is characterized is indicative of what we would maintain is a naïve, empiricist position. If we summarize the relational critique, we can note that almost all of the concepts that underlie classical analysis have been brought into question and rejected. Neutrality, free association, evenly hovering attention, the blank screen, the authority of the analyst, and transference all need to be either reintroduced or abandoned. In so far as one is a "Sullivanian" relational analyst, then it may be that the concept of the unconscious also needs to be excluded.

Philosophical aspects of the clinical critique

Lewis Aron sees the impact of postmodernism as being an important influence on the relational writers of the past fifteen years. If we take a soft version of postmodern writings, then we might say that these commentators have brought the social scientific and scientific communities a version of perspective that demands that we include the context of a theory, the biases of an author, and the era that generated the theory in evaluating, or at least in understanding, a theory. Freudian theory is seen as reflecting the prejudices of his era as well as his own personal preconceptions. Certainly, for a period of time, many feminists (Chodorow, 1989) saw Freudian theory as reflecting the prejudices of a male dominated society. (Chodorow's views are a good deal more nuanced as opposed to how she is portrayed in this sentence. Moreover, her views have, in my view, become even deeper over the years.) Phrases such as biology is destiny, and concepts such as penis envy, and the depiction of women as necessarily hysterical and masochistic (not to mention narcissistic) seemed to these feminists to be embedded in the Freudian canon. Even one of Freud's sympathetic biographers (Gay, 1987) did not doubt that, in many ways, Freud was an author of his time and that much of the content of his theory includes the prejudices of the society that he was part of as well as apart from. I also know that surrounding Freud were some of the more astounding women of the era, and that even the psychoanalysis of Freud's generation produced more women analysts than were produced in other professions. Although some feminist theorists have embraced a version of Freudian theory, many Freudians have acknowledged some of the prejudices of the theory and made attempts to change this theory. The question that we will entertain is the extent to which Freud presented the elements of a theory that can tolerate new content while keeping the structure of the theory intact, or, at least, give a semblance of intactness.

A number of relational analysts have maintained that a type of postmodern critique is pertinent to classical views of the psychoanalytic clinical situation. Thus, Aron characterizes a relational version of truth as not an absolute, but, in Aron's terms, "perspectival, plural, fragmentary, discontinuous, kaleidoscopic and everchanging" (1996, p. 24). In contrast to this version of the truth, relational theorists and clinicians have characterized Freudian ideas about technique as involving a one person situation where the analyst claims to be objective, as well as neutral, abstentious, and anonymous. This is somehow linked to Freudian clinicians as embracing a positivist philosophy. Aron (and previously Mitchell) view analysts like Schafer and Spence, although ego-psychologists, as also abandoning what they termed the positivist position of Freudian clinicians. (Schafer [1997], at this point in time, attempts to integrate neo-Kleinian and ego psychological theories. Spence [1982] is a contemporary analyst who had his roots in ego psychological theory. Unfortunately, Donald Spence recently died. He was an analyst who both made significant contributions to the field and quite significant contributions to his friends and colleagues.) Although Schafer and Spence have moved in the relational direction, Hoffman views each of these authors as restrictive constructionists, and Bruner (1993) depicts Spence as a closet positivist. Aron (1996a) sees Hoffman's social constructivism (Hoffman, 1991, 1992) as being a distinctly different rallying cry for relational theory than is present in the work of Spence or Schafer. Hoffman also calls for a paradigm shift from positivism, or what Aron calls objectivism, to a relational-co-constructivist position. An important difference between Hoffman and Schafer is the extent to which the analyst's subjectivity affects the analytic situation. Schafer (1983, 1992) puts forth the view that the analyst can purify themselves of personal factors and be "uncontaminated by the analyst's subjectivity". This can be performed by a continuous exploration of the analyst's reactions or countertransference. Hoffman stresses that "it is the countertransference that is continuous, not its scrutiny" (1992, p. 291). By this, Hoffman is suggesting that the analyst's countertransference is not only continuous, but also part of the construction of the analytic pair. There is no way, in this paradigm, for the analyst to be objective in the sense of knowing that the reactions in the room are a result of the patient's transference (or the patient's reactions). What is constructed is an amalgam of the analytic pair's reactions and sensibilities. Hoffman, in other places (2002), has maintained that he is not an extreme constructionist, but one might ask: what are the guidelines for a moderate constructionist? In the extreme form of the constructionist position, one might say that it is impossible to assess an individual's contributions to the analytic situation; one can only view the patient's or analyst's reactions in terms of the situation that both have jointly constructed. Schafer (1992) argues that if the analyst has an appropriate analytic attitude, it is possible to differentiate the patient's contributions to the analytic situation. If we look at these two different positions on a continuum, then we can say that there is an extreme constructivist position on one end of the continuum and the classical position at the other end. The classical analyst would maintain that it is possible to describe and understand a patient's transference reactions if the analyst is properly trained. Proper training would include the analyst being analysed during their training. The analyst, in this position, is strictly the decoder of the patient's transference. Perhaps this position could be thought of as a classical position in the 1960s. In contemporary psychoanalysis, structural analysts like Brenner (1996) and Rothstein (2002) have distinctly moved away from this extreme position. The extreme on the other end of the continuum would maintain that it is impossible to understand transference from an individual, that transference can only be understood as a creation of the analytic pair. There are few writers who take this extreme position that transference can only be viewed as a creation in the analytic situation. Since the extreme positions have been vacated, perhaps we can look at one type of intermediate position that takes into account, or honours, the relational critique.

Contemporary integrations: redefining some concepts

The task of attempting an integration of theoretical concepts seems daunting at best, particularly since there have been so many critiques that have indicated the impossibility of such an integration. Aron has accused Freudian analysts who have critiqued relational theory of "shabby scholarship and a disdainful tone" (1999). I hope I have somewhat avoided this tone. Aron, on the other hand, praises the scholarship of relational theorists who critique Freudian positions. It is my view that what Aron calls Greenberg and Mitchell's "serious and scholarly study" of the Freudian tradition is overstated. As a case in point, in a previous book (1991), I cited a Greenberg and Mitchell (1983) illustration using the Dora case. They maintained that Dora was a prime example of how Freud utilized what they called the drive/structural model. They stated that the Dora case is useful "because it illustrates the way drives are construed as the sole determinants of an object relationship" (1983, p. 43). They wrote this despite the fact that, in 1900, Freud had neither a drive nor a structural model. One could use the Dora case in exactly the opposite manner, and say that Freud could reach this type of conclusion regardless of the model he had developed during a given era. In my view, although one could find fault with Greenberg and Mitchell's scholarship, it was a book of its time that made an important statement about relational psychoanalysis. My quibbles about their scholarship miss the point of the importance of their theoretical stance. They began a valuable re-examination of both the theoretical and clinical concepts that dominated psychoanalysis before their volume appeared. It is my intention to continue this re-examination. The attempt here is to move past the dichotomous aspects of their re-examination and see what happens when theories touch. In a similar light, I would argue that the Freudian critics are not less (or more) scholarly than Greenberg and Mitchell or other relational analysts.

Although I will take issue with some of the criticisms that relational writers have put forth, let me begin by stating my agreements. These agreements should indicate that my criticisms of the classical tradition are more profound than they are of the relational critique. To begin, I do not think that an analyst can be neutral, a blank screen, anonymous, or objective, at least in the sense of objective that relational writers ascribed to classical theorists. I do not think that all psychopathology (or even most, in my experience) resides in Oedipal conflicts, and to think of conflict solely or mostly in terms of drive and defence, in my view, is a mistake. It seems to me that all analysts owe a debt to Mitchell (and other relational writers) for raising in a systematic way a number of the issues that I have just described. At times, I have heard Freudian analysts maintain that the points that have been raised have always been acknowledged in practice. I have always rejected this kind of comment, since it is my belief that eventually it is the written record that determines theoretical and clinical perspectives. If a given practice was always part of a tradition, why did prominent analysts in that tradition write contrary points of view that were largely uncontested in the literature?

At first it was my intention to look at each critique of Freudian theory and evaluate the critique and give a new contemporary integrative or Freudian version of the concept. Very few critiques encompass the various reasons for the position of a competing theory. In what follows, I will present reasons to retain aspects of certain concepts. Perhaps, for clarity, these concepts should be renamed, but I will not enter this arena. We can revisit the issue of neutrality, free association, truth as an absolute concept, and evenly hovering attention.

In my definition, neutrality can be viewed in a variety of ways, and perhaps should be considered in terms of compromise formation. There is no question in my mind that Freud wanted to stay neutral and objective in terms of his concept of the analyst as detached scientist. (This aspect of the concept should be rejected as providing exactly the wrong analytic attitude.) However, as a clinician, Freud was often compassionate and giving; it may be that the concept of neutrality was an attempt to restrain himself from being too controlling and providing the patient with too much advice. Leaving Freud aside, sometimes the analyst not taking a position on an issue (remaining neutral) is a way of demonstrating their trust in the patient's ability to make their own decisions. It may be that an analyst believes the patient should not make a particular investment, or not choose a particular job, unless the analyst can help the patient understand that this decision is based on conflict or is intentionally a bad (meaning self-destructive) decision, but the analyst should be neutral (in so far as they can be) about the patient's decisions. Perhaps more to the point, the analyst not being neutral assumes that the analyst can make a better decision than the patient. This raises the question about what analysts know (Mitchell, 1997,

1998); it is my view that an analyst (*qua* analyst) knows how to help patients uncover and resolve conflicts. Analysts (at least, the analysts that I have known) are not all-round gurus. Therefore, a certain amount of neutrality indicates trust in both the patient and the analytic process. It also demonstrates the limits of the analyst's knowledge. Winnicott has said that interpretations should show the limits of the analyst's knowledge, and here is another place that it may be wise to demonstrate the limits of the analyst's knowledge. Now, it may be argued that what I have described is not neutrality, but simply a respect for the patient and a realistic assessment of the role of the analyst. It is my view that this is part of what Freud intended in his concept of neutrality. Whether this is the case or not, what is more important is that there is an aspect of the concept of neutrality that should be maintained. It represents both trust in the patient and a certain amount of humility in the analyst.

I would agree with Aron that, for most of an analytic treatment, truth is (and should be) fragmentary, pluralistic, and (my addition) not necessarily the privilege or the possession of either participant. Depending on your view of truth, at some point in a treatment some things seem true. Things that seem true may change or shift in meaning, but here let me use a version of Freud's criteria for a relativistic version of the truth. Freud (1937d) maintained that the function of an interpretation is to lead to new uncovering that helps the analytic pair to understand the past in the present. Here, by "understand", it should be clear that affect is a crucial aspect of understanding. An interpretation, then, is a link that connects aspects of the patient's internal world and, further, connects the patient to aspects of the world that have been previously occluded. Frequently, what is occluded is a capacity for empathy for important figures in one's life, or, in other terms, for the participants in the patient's narrative. Therefore, I would conclude that what is true in a treatment is what is helpful in forming links internally and externally. One must recognize that these links may not be permanent and may be replaced by stronger links that indicate increased understanding and internalization of this understanding. Put in other terms, it seems to me that a better term than fragmentary is probabilistic; one can never be absolute about events in analysis (or most other places), and see their understanding in terms of probabilities rather than an absolute certainty.

In most treatments, free association, for me, is an important ideal. Here, by free association, I mean that the patient can freely talk about whatever comes to mind and not feel inhibited about what they are thinking. In other terms, feelings of guilt or shame should not stop the person from talking about their conflicts. At times in a treatment (as Hoffman described), it may be that a patient feels as if they are passive recipients of their own thoughts. It is to be hoped that this experience is part of their exploration of how their mind works. Some patients (particularly writers and artists) describe this state as similar to a state when they are creating something and they have little conscious idea of what is about to appear. At times, free association is simply meant as a statement that one should feel free to talk. This was part of Freud's original quandary: he wanted patients to talk about their problems and their memories, and he felt the need to invent a quasi scientific rationale for this instruction. It seems that few accept Freud's quasi science, but, in my experience, free association is something that occurs over time and indicates the patient's increasing trust in both the analyst and in the idea of learning about the functioning of his/her mind.

One could make similar statements about each aspect of analysis: yes, the analyst should remain as neutral as possible to allow the treatment to be mostly the patient's treatment even though true absolute neutrality is a myth or, at best, in some limited circumstances, an ideal. In so far as lack of neutrality tilts the treatment away from the patient, neutrality should be re-established. The couch can be used because, for some patients, it facilitates a state where they are freer to talk about things that have been deeply conflict laden. Others might use it to hide conflicts (Goldberger, 1995). Freud's concept of evenly suspended attention is, in my mind, a precursor of Bion's (1962a,b) and later Ogden's (1997a,b) and Ferro's (2009) idea of reverie. It is a state that analysts at times need to enter to understand fantasy at a deeper level, but it is an impossible state to stay in for most of an analytic treatment. Spillius (1988) sees Bion's dictum (see Stevens' chapter on Bion) to be without memory or desire as a restatement of Freud's concept of evenly suspended attention. Therefore, we should take all of these concepts as points on a continuum and try to understand how and why we move along the continuum. The concept of analytic trust is an attempt to understand this movement and look at the ruptures and repairs (Tronick, 2008) that occur in the course of an analysis.

Rather than continue to look at each term in a linear review, I will present a position that tries to take into account recent criticisms while holding on to one version of an integrative Freudian structure. Before entering into this discussion, certain current terms need to be clarified. Analysis, as depicted from an analyst's point of view, is always a two-person event. Whatever the analyst and the analysand do is significant in setting the analytic atmosphere and affects every aspect of the treatment situation. Frequently, at the beginning of a treatment, the patient, however, sees the treatment (if the treatment is going well) as primarily a one-person situation. Even here, we should realize that distinction between a one- and a two-person situation is a dichotomization and does not do justice to the subtleties as well as the oscillating psychological realities of both participants. A pure one-person perception is probably not possible except in certain extreme conditions (some psychoses and some types of dementia). When I describe the patient being in one-person mode, I am not describing a withdrawal, but, rather, at some point in the early phases of treatment, an absorption in imparting the pain of their condition and/or the compelling reasons for their entering treatment. I wrote about a patient who "Before treatment could in some ways proceed she had to fill me and the treatment room with the horror of her life" (1991, p. 316). She could not tolerate me having a separate perspective, even a separate life. (She denied my existence outside of the treatment room.)

As another preliminary point, there will be a question as to under what conditions, if any, interpretative efforts are useful. To answer this question, I must first define what I mean by interpretation. Although there are varied versions of this term, I am restricting the definition to an analyst's efforts to impart meaning to an aspect of the patient functioning that is in some way part of the patient's occluded sense of self. In more common parlance, an interpretation, in this definition, is an intervention by the analyst to a defended aspect of the patient's mental life. Given this restrictive definition of interpretation, it follows (at least from some theoretical perspectives) that when the analyst interprets, she is saying something that the patient does not want to hear or, at least in the patient's history, has not in the past wanted to hear (has defended against). Clearly, a question that is raised from this view of interpretation is whether it is useful ever to interpret in the analytic situation.

Here, it is important to state that, in this framework, if the patient was just about to understand or process the material the analyst is interpreting, by this definition it is not an interpretation. I am highlighting this instance since Kris (1951) has stated this to be an optimal time to interpret. In most instances, I would maintain that the patient is better left to make their own interpretation if the analyst truly believes the material is close at hand.

Analytic trust and the analytic situation: the opening phase

The following are concepts about psychoanalytic therapy that are derived from a number of sources, including Winnicott, Bion, Freud, Kohut, Guntrip, and Klein. It is also conditioned by the important considerations that many relational analysts have brought forth. In this description, I follow the path of patients from the beginning of treatment through the point where the patient can accept transference interpretations.

The first task in analysis is to help the patient begin to create a new object relationship in the therapeutic situation (Bach, 1994, 2006; Ellman, 1991, 1997a, 2005, 2007; Loewald, 1960). For a utilizable analytic relationship, the patient must penetrate the analyst's psychological world and the analyst must facilitate and be receptive to this penetration. The analyst must also gradually allow this penetration to be perceptible to the patient. This process is at the heart of analytic trust and a utilizable analytic relationship. The initial phase of analytic trust, then, can be defined as the patient's realistic view of the analyst understanding and being included in their subjective world. (The patient may have [usually will have] more reactions than simply a realistic view; however, I am emphasizing that it is something that is happening in reality and not simply a fantasy of the patient's.) This understanding is communicated not only in intellectual terms, but also by the analyst feeling the intensity of the patient's responses and being able to communicate this to the patient. The interpenetration is a necessary condition of the patient beginning to feel held (Winnicott, 1956a, 1960a).

This experience, and, often, an experience of containment, are necessary concomitants of trust being built in the analytic situation. Analytic trust is not synonymous with the concept of therapeutic alliance. Therapeutic alliance refers to the patient being allied to the analyst's way of proceeding in the analytic situation. The patient complies with analytic instructions and, as Brenner (1976, 1982) has stated, this compliance is often related to the patient's transference state. Analytic trust may be established whether or not the patient is willing to comply with the analyst's instructions. It involves a penetration of subjective states and a communication of this interpenetration. Undoubtedly, analysts can communicate this understanding in different ways and through different theoretical lenses. Although more will be said later about the analyst's state, it is important that this interpenetration is, in some ways, gratifying to the analyst. What follows are examples of pathways to the establishment of analytic trust.

A patient enters a treatment and complains of not being able to use her mind. As soon as she feels she understands something, it changes. She is anxious if the weather changes or if her employer seems to be looking at her in a different way (positive or negative). This woman has just left a treatment where her analyst terminated the treatment. This occurred after she had left various phone messages over a period of months saying that she felt there was something wrong with the treatment. In a phone message, he finally agreed with her and suggested that she see another therapist who could also provide her with help through medication. After weeks of reflecting her bewilderment about these changes, including the change in her analyst (who was initially confident of being able to help her), we begin to understand that she wants me to remain the same whatever she may say to me or do in our sessions. She wants to be able to change and have me remain the same. The next two years are spent in my remaining relatively consistent and stable while she attempts in various ways to provoke me and destroy my stability. She is constantly testing to see if she can trust my stability. If I attempt to interpret her provocations she becomes irate, and tells me in one form or another that she cannot stand me in this position (an interpretative position). Gradually, she shares her thoughts with me, and at first relates that I hate people and that I am an analyst because I can be secretly contemptuous of her difficulties. It is only when she can consider and feel that there may be more to me than my hatred and the hatred she has put in me that her transference has reached an interpretable form. Before that, I can only reflect her pain at having to "bare her soul" to someone who is secretly contemptuous of her plight.

In this example, there had to be sufficient holding and containment before her transference manifestations were in interpretable form. During the initial periods, I was limited to reflecting her frightening, horrifying, and enraged states. During the period of containment (of course, these periods are largely overlapping) I could first receive her thoughts and not immediately respond to her (Bion, 1962a,b). Then, I might reflect to her how dangerous it must be for her to be in a situation where she was in a constant position of feeling ridiculed and humiliated. I was in a selfobject position until she began gradually to tolerate the other becoming another and she could allow more complicated (a movement towards ambivalence) objects into her representational world. If one conceives of interpretable transference as either a projection (projective identification), or displacement into transitional space, then, in the above example, transitional space had to be created before a projective identification could be interpreted. If there is no transitional space when the analysand projects into the analyst, transference is no longer experienced by the analytic pair as in part an illusory phenomenon, but only as a real occurrence. In the above example, it is not that in fantasy the analyst hates people, but, rather, that the analyst "in fact" hates people, and that is all there is to the analyst. In the absence of transitional space (self-observation as part of this space), interpretations are seen by the analysand as defensive actions by the analyst rather than potentially helpful interventions. Consistent interpretative efforts under these conditions would lead to rounds of mutual enactments (Ellman, 1998a) where patient and analyst would see the other as either unanalysable or unable to helpfully analyse. I will distinguish between analyst induced enactments and patient (analysand) induced enactments. In making this distinction, I am positing that, at times, it is possible to understand the origins of an enactment and to place it mainly within one of the participants of the analysis. However, in this view, an enactment implies an interaction and both parties are affected to some extent by any (or, at least, most) enactments. During an enactment, the capacity, or, at least, the proclivity, to symbolize is impaired or muted. At times, it will not be possible to specify whether an enactment is induced by either the analyst or analysand. Following McLaughlin (1991) and McLaughlin & Johan (1992), this type of enactment will be labelled as a mutual enactment. In this type of enactment, both patient and analyst see the nature of the difficulty residing in the other, and this perception continues for some period of time.

This patient had to feel and experience herself in my mind (a version of Fonagy and Target's [2002] view of mentalization) before she could even tolerate a less toxic rendition of her desperation. Bach has stated that before some patients can hear an interpretation, "fundamentally one must have two parties who view themselves as alive and functional . . . Generally in the transference regression with the narcissistic disorders one or more of these conditions is not met" (Bach, 1985, p. xii). Bach has described clinically what Fonagy (and before Fonagy, Bion and Winnicott, in different ways) has looked at developmentally: many children and patients have to feel themselves alive in the other's mind for them to progress satisfactorily in treatment or in their early development (Benjamin, 1995).

It is important to emphasize that affective interpenetration often is more difficult with patients who have a need to destroy the analytic relationship (as well as other relationships in their life). Some patients, before utilizing a holding environment, frequently have to survive a sense of betrayal, or, in a less dramatic but more continuous manner, the patient has to tolerate a sense of being misunderstood. Bion's ideas about containment are implicitly present in various forms of both Winnicott's and Balint's (1968) formulation about treating the patient who, in Winnicott's terms, is "not well chosen for classical psychoanalysis" (1960b, p. 38). Paraphrasing Winnicott, I would say that surviving rather than sidestepping or avoiding the destructive aspects of the analysand is a necessary condition for a successful analysis to take place. One has to survive the patient's negative affect, but, in the course of survival, it is crucial to be able to return the affect expressed in a manner that is detoxified, to use Bion's term. In more ordinary language, it is important to survive and talk about, for example, the patient's rage without moving away from it or being retaliatory.

My assumption is that there is usually some form of enactment that takes place around negative and destructive tendencies.

With most patients with moderate self-esteem issues, this is not a striking issue in the beginning phases of treatment. However, as vertical splitting becomes more prominent in what many analysts would characterize as borderline experiences, there is a greater chance of containment being a central facet in the beginning phases of treatment. In treatments that I am alluding to, the ruptures are externalized and frequently enacted, and the first rupture that must be endured is one that threatens to break apart the analytic couple.

More dramatic splitting presents at least two different issues that lead to difficulties in the analytic situation. Frequently, affect is quickly disposed of in some form of action or in a rapid negation, projection (for me, the correct term is projective identification), or rapid oscillation (evacuation) to another state or sense of self and other. Here, the interpenetration of affect is even more important, with the analyst not only being able to experience the affect, but gradually present it to a patient who has already left the affective state and clearly wants no part of this experience. Frequently, this type of patient kills the affect with action that, at times, involves substance abuse, and here it is particularly important to re-experience with the patient the affect and experience that had to be evacuated. This has to be done gradually and in successive approximations. Bromberg (2001) has described various types of disassociative states that can occur in the treatment situation. With patients who utilize splitting, these states are common. Gradually, the analyst has to unite these states with reflective comments that show how the patient transitions from one state to another. The following example is of a patient who frequently oscillated between states with the aid of drugs.

This patient wakes up in the morning and snorts cocaine, then, when his agitation becomes too extreme, starts to drink to calm down. He repeats this sequence several times a day. By the time he comes to treatment in the afternoon, he is in a confused, altered state. Gradually, within the treatment, we are able to see how he empties out his mind first with the aid of substances, and then, later in treatment, without their aid. Any topic that alters his self-esteem, brings him into conflict with others, or is embarrassing is immediately negated, minimized, or, if it still exists in his conscious mind, is contradicted in subsequent comments. Our task was, when he passed by an experience, to gradually bring it back and see if he can gradually tolerate the return of the unwanted experience and affect. After several rounds of this type of therapeutic experience, he is more able to endure the ruptures that he experiences in his agitated internal world. His repair had been attempted through substance abuse, but, gradually, we are able to look at the role of substances that fragment his emotional life. It takes two years before he is able to tolerate these states and give up cocaine and alcohol (cigarettes are another matter, and take longer). Experiencing and returning affect to the analytic field is a crucial aspect of the long beginning of this treatment. He must endure some internal ruptures before he is able to begin to repair his psyche. He can only do that if we can tolerate his affect states within the analytic situation.

When this same patient begins to rail about the meaningless of analytic treatment, this, too, must be tolerated and returned to the patient, first directly, and then in synthetic form, so that the patient can see how he attempts to denigrate and demean many situations that threaten to produce aversive states for him. This containment, or the return of affect in general, is not interpretative in that it almost always deals with elements that do not go beyond what, at some point, is consciously available to the patient. Particularly with patients who use vertical splitting as a main defence, it is important not simply to return affect, but to understand and feel how difficult it is for the person to tolerate these states. To summarize, once reflection, echoing, synthetic comments, and containment achieve affective interpenetration, there will be more of a shared analytic field and a strengthening of analytic trust. This development will begin to heal an internal rupture so that subsequent ruptures can be endured in less traumatic form.

This strengthening of trust gradually leads to two interrelated, somewhat "paradoxical" results; at the same time that the analyst is trusted and included in the analysand's world, both members of the dyad are more comfortable in being separate and both are more comfortable in maintaining separate perspectives. If this separation can be tolerated, it is the birth (or a strengthening) of a reflective self-representation within the analytic situation. When the patient begins to include me in their object world, it is then that the possibility opens up to include aspects of the other within what may be the final part of the initial phase of analytic trust.

STRUCTURAL THEORY, RELATIONAL CRITIQUES, & INTEGRATIVE ATTEMPTS 595

Aspects of countertransference: the opening phase

Before discussing interpretive possibilities, what are the difficulties that the analyst faces during this phase of treatment? One could describe this process in a number of ways: surely it is a substantial task to try to feel another's subjective states and gradually attempt to reflect, synthesize, and contain another's feelings in a manner that demonstrates that interpenetration has occurred. The difficulties in these tasks that I will focus on are issues of narcissistic equilibrium. The use of this term is not meant to imply that the analyst is narcissistic, but, rather, issues of self-continuity, self-esteem, and self-expression are continuously present in the analytic situation for the analyst as well as the analysand. Thus, it was not surprising to me that when I presented a version of this approach, an analyst who was attempting to be conciliatory commented that some of us are more active and some of us wait and are willing to do nothing for a period of time. His impression of my approach in building analytic trust was that the analyst did nothing. My view is that the analyst is quite active in listening and in offering the type of interventions that allow the patient to be able to consistently tolerate, disclose, and feel their subjective states. Moreover, my version of containment includes the analyst putting feelings back into the patient that the patient usually wants to get rid of as quickly as possible. Thus, containment, synthesis, and reflection are active processes that allow the patient to utilize the analyst while beginning to explore their subjective world and the intersubjective world that the analytic pair is creating. Frequently, it is difficult for patients to talk about issues that result in feelings of shame, and sometimes disassociated states are hidden if the analyst in some way demands early compliance to the analytic situation. Analytic rules or early interpretations at times demand compliance, or at least a response that is required by the analyst and the analytic situation. During the early period(s) that I have tried to describe, it is not that the analyst does not concern herself with unconscious fantasy, but, rather, it is not the prime focus until the patient can tolerate, or wants to include, another in their concerns. At times, a difficulty in this approach is the analyst wanting to continue early phases of holding. Sometimes the analyst and the patient may have to be awakened by the dominant emergence of unconscious fantasy. Another way of describing this state is provided by Ferro, when he describes the analyst's moving from a normal state to being enmeshed in a dream state, where the patient's and analyst's unconscious fantasies are together in a new field. Using the sleep metaphor, I would say the analyst moves from slow wave sleep to the psychoactive state of rapid eye movement or REM (dreaming) sleep.

For some analysts, this type of beginning phase may be difficult, since they are, in effect, excluding aspects of their analytic selves. It may be that the analyst will feel they are not doing anything, or are not really doing analytic work during this phase of treatment. Thus, an analyst might offer an interpretation that the patient is not able to use, or might confront the patient about aspects of their functioning in a way that the patient does not see as useful. This is the type of analyst-induced enactment that occurs when the analyst feels some narcissistic disequilibrium, when they experience not being included in the analysis as full partners, more importantly, as what they see as real analysts. At times. not being included as an analyst, or. from the analyst's perspective. not being able to be an analyst, can lead to a type of fragmentation or lack of self unity. It may be that these feelings lead the analyst to have to disclose a part of themselves to feel more real in the analytic situation; this is an intervention that may help the analyst feel more like themselves.

There are some analysts who are able to achieve analytic trust even though they begin to interpret from the beginning of a treatment. From my theoretical perspective, there are two possible ways of understanding this different approach. The first is an oft-repeated characterization of treating certain types of non-classical patients; when asked what they remembered about interpretations, the patient mentions the rhythm or the timbre of the analyst's voice, or some other aspect of the physical feature of the analyst's office, or listening to the way the analyst moves in her chair. These patients often immediately rid themselves of the content of the interpretation and hear only a soothing voice or an authoritative stance on the part of the analyst. This helps the patient feel comforted, and indicates that the analyst is there for her/his benefit. In short, it is not the content of the interpretation, but some other characteristic of the analyst that leads to analytic trust.

Alternatively, patients may be able to process interpretations early in the analysis if, in the interpretations, the analyst is able to demonstrate that they are able both to feel the patient's subjective world and, in particular, the interpretation includes the adaptive perspective (Rapaport & Gill, 1959). In other terms, the analyst is capable of not only understanding the patient's conflict or distress, but able to give what Steiner (1994) labels a patient centred interpretation. The analyst could empathize with the patient's point of view that, given their distress, their behaviour or fantasy was the only alternative open to them. Despite these caveats about the development of analytic trust, I would still say that, for most clinicians, interpretative efforts early in the treatment can either serve to disrupt a patient or put the patient into a position of having to comply with the analyst's treatment method and perspectives.

Britton described a patient who could not tolerate any of his interpretative efforts, or even any of his spoken interventions. Britton gradually stopped his interpretative efforts. During one session, when he was thinking of an interpretation, the patient said to him, "stop that fucking thinking" (1997, p. 247). She could not tolerate his independent thoughts at that point in the treatment. (Britton interpreted this in terms of being unable to accept the Oedipal triangle.) One could dwell on this example for awhile since it also raises the question of projection and projective identification, but at this point we might be content to say that the patient could only tolerate one psychoactive person in the therapeutic situation (we will come back to this case later in the chapter). Although it might be the case that various Kleinian analysts experienced what Britton reported (the patient's inability to tolerate independent thought), Britton's paper was, as far as I can tell, the first such report by a Kleinian analyst. Analysts from other perspectives have made similar reports 10–15 years before Britton's paper (Bach, Kohut, Ellman, etc.). It was an interesting paper from a neo-Kleinian perspective, since so much of their technique depends on interpretative efforts. My view is that Britton was using this case illustration because, in my terms, he endured a sense of narcissistic disequilibrium and kept the analysis alive by letting the patient determine how he should intervene. In paraphrasing Steiner's terms, Britton allowed for a patient-induced analytic atmosphere. He endured not feeling like an analyst (who would ordinarily interpret) and allowed the patient to create her own analytic situation.

Transference and interpretative possibilities

To discuss interpreting transference, it seems to me that we have to posit a patient who sees the analyst as another, at least somewhat separate, object (person). As an example, a patient entered treatment with the concern that she had developed a cancerous brain tumour. She had been to a number of specialists (several neurologists) who assured her that this was not the case. Nevertheless, when we began treatment, her concerns focused exclusively on her body and her interpretation of various bodily sensations. Gradually, as the treatment progressed, she begins to recognize and gradually mention aspects of my waiting room, reading material, my tie, etc. Along with that development, she is able to talk about the impact she has on others, and not only the toxins that her family and friends are pouring into her, literally and symbolically. When this interplay begins (between self experience and some consideration of the other) the analyst, it seems to me, naturally sits further back in his chair and elements of unconscious fantasy begin to drift into the analyst's consciousness and are retained. Since I wrote this a while ago, I should restate this and say that elements of her experience start to be looked at in a way that is not exclusively dominated by her conscious experience. In my view, the analyst has started to more acutely perceive unconscious communications that are now less bound up in her symptoms. I have written about this patient (Ellman, 1998a), where, although she was ready to receive interpretative remarks, she was not ready to receive transference interpretations. When I interpreted too quickly, this caused a return of her symptoms and we spent another year developing trust before we moved on to the issues that had troubled her at least since her mother died when she was three years old.

This was not the case with Dr A.

Dr A was a surgical resident when a senior colleague first referred him to me. He came for a consultation because of an "embarrassing incident" that he did not want to relate to me in his first consultation session. He mentioned to me that he had discussed this event with the previous analyst that he had seen (in consultation), but that analyst had a "supercilious" attitude. Since Dr A's first language was not English, I asked him to tell me a bit more about the analyst's attitude, and he mentioned that the analyst began to question him and began to take a history. In short, the first analyst began to treat Dr A like a patient and this was clearly a humiliating experience for Dr A. During our first meeting, he mentioned that he was having some difficulties with his fiancée and with his chief resident. It was important for him to tell me that, despite these difficulties, he was probably going to be chief resident next year and that he already had several excellent job offers. (He told me, in effect, that he was desired.) At the end of our first meeting, he thanked me for my time and told me that I had been of "good value" to him. He said that he would think about the treatment but that he thought that he had cleared up his difficulties. Given this somewhat rapid departure, I was surprised when, a week later, he called and asked if he could meet with me another time. When we met he wondered if I had any questions and I wondered what he would like to talk about. After several moments of awkward silence he began to tell me about the "incident". He knew a famous actor from his homeland, and he, the actor, and his fiancée went out together one night. For the rest of the session Dr A described some of his feelings about the fact that the three of them had sex together. His fiancée was very upset that he had forced (or at least agreed to) this arrangement. Dr A was upset that he had been so influenced by this famous man. He began to tell me that famous people had always fascinated him, and that his father is considered a famous patriot in his country. After he told me this the session was almost over, and I asked him whether he wanted to schedule another session. At that point he again rose and thanked me for my help, and said that he thought that he was feeling better. After several consultations, he agreed to try twice a week psychotherapy. After eight months he began a four times a week analytic treatment. He needed no coaxing to use the couch, since he preferred not to see my face, but rather wanted to fill the room with his feelings, thoughts, fantasies, and projections (see Goldberger, 1995, for a discussion of the use of the couch). Whenever there was a break that was longer than our normal weekend break, Dr A would, at the beginning of the session, thank me and tell me that he had decided to end the treatment. He always included the idea that I had been of help to him. Thus, one might say that, for him, every out of the ordinary variation in schedule was experienced as a difficult separation and tended to produce a feeling of a rupture in our relationship. Why this was true was one of the central questions in our eight-year treatment.

As the treatment progressed, Dr A began an idealizing transference where he considered me not only a good analyst, but also an outstanding neuro-scientist. Most of our sessions had an intermingling of his pain in contemporary relationships and a description of his family life and why he felt that it had been necessary for him to leave his birthplace. It took him a while to begin to tell me about his alcoholism (his alcoholic blackouts) and how, at times, his feelings of humiliation were so strong that he needed to "black" (block) them out. In my mind, although he certainly experienced humiliation, his depressive feelings were much more difficult for him to acknowledge.

At the same time that his idealizing transference was forming, he also began to talk about the alteration of states that would at times overtake him; when he performed a successful operation, for a period of time he fantasized that he was or would be the greatest surgeon in the world. He felt that none of the faculty or attendings had anything to teach him and that soon he would be recognized for his unrivalled talent. Maslow's (1962) description of pique experiences seemed to almost describe the state that would occur at times. If he felt that he made a mistake, he would be extremely worried that he would be demoted to becoming a scrub nurse. It took a period of time for him to talk about why his perceived failures were usually accompanied by the fantasy of his becoming a scrub nurse. His mother had been a scrub nurse, and in his move to the USA he at first worked as a scrub nurse since he "felt" he could not get any job as an MD until he was licensed. In my mind, his move to the USA had some aspect of an identification with his mother, but it was not at all clear as to why I felt this was true. He talked about how his mother had been independent and how both she and his father had affairs. He mentioned a number of things about his past, but none of them seemed to touch his extreme sensitivity to our separations.

Gradually, as the treatment progressed, he began to improve; he broke up with his fiancée and met a woman who eventually became his wife. His alcoholic bouts (and blackouts) were mostly a thing of the past, and his relationships with his peers and supervisors (now partners) had greatly improved. However, he still quit analysis at each separation and this was something that did not seem to be able to be interpreted away.

After our second transference cycle (cycles will soon be described) I began to interpret his selfobject transference where we were both famous in the field of neuroscience. Slowly, we began to understand the roots of his grandiosity and how his grandiosity was used to bolster his oscillating self-esteem. His real accomplishments now seemed more genuine to him, and at times he was genuinely proud of his successes. His ability to endure transference interpretations increased his trust in the process, since he now could feel that he could tolerate something that was distressing that did not accord with his conscious thoughts. Other thoughts could be of value to him, and the therapeutic relationship could survive the crisis of differences. The differences were that, at the time of the interpretations, we had different views about the nature of our interaction. It was previously quite difficult for him to tolerate opinions that were different than his opinions.

After his residency (his third year in treatment) he was offered a professorship at a good medical school, and there he did both clinical work and research. At the end of the fourth year of the analysis, the patient decided to get married. At this same time, he was offered a job in Texas. Accepting the post meant that he would have to stop analysis. It was not clear to him (or to me) that this opportunity was one that would be of benefit to him. Nevertheless, he seemed compelled to take this job with what seem like diminished clinical and research possibilities compared to the position he held in the New York area. I, of course, wondered about my reaction to the idea of what I considered to be his unilateral termination (or premature termination). He seemed determined to go forward on this path until a long separation (two weeks) occurred and he had the following dream:

> You were giving a lecture and it seemed to me—at least I thought that you were doing well—I was in the audience and watching you. For some reason I was watching your face and your expressions seemed vacant [he said a version of vacuous] . . . The audience was enthusiastic but you still seemed not to respond and then suddenly . . . I was in Moscow [his home city] and I thought this is the most beautiful city in the world.

Although, by that time, he was someone who found value in dreams, he began to say how this dream was meaningless and how this time he was serious and that "analysis had gone as far as it could go". I said to him that he talked about analysis as if it was person or a thing separate from us, and he belittled my remark. I could feel that I was annoyed with Dr A. I said that if he wanted to leave it was certainly his right and there was nothing that I could do about it (I said some other things that must have been angrier, because I did not write them down). After this clipped, enacted interchange, things in the session shifted and Dr A began to talk about an operation he had just performed, then he said that it seemed to him that I looked sick. He said that he was not sure why he thought that, but it came to his mind that when he came into the office that I looked sick. It seemed to me that we were back in the dream, and I commented that, in the dream, even though things seemed to be going well for me, I seemed sick or at least non-responsive. He, at that point, became quite sad and said that he really felt that I had helped him a great deal and that he wanted to know in reality, not in the dream, whether or not I was sick. I said to him that dream was very real to him and it was beginning to feel real to both of us. Perhaps he thought that I was ill because he was planning to leave me and we had just separated? He was somewhat disorientated, and the session ended with my feeling that something important had happened, but I was not sure what it was.

In the next session, he began by saying that he was disappointed that I did not answer his question and that he never seems to have my full attention. This seemed odd to me, and again I was reminded of the dream from the session the night before. I said that this time it seems that his reaction to our separation was where he felt that I was unresponsive to him and then excused me by saying that I must be sick. He said that he thought that I was sick even though he knew (sort of) that perhaps I wasn't. I mentioned that he never talked about how he felt when our separations occurred. He began to talk about an event in his life when he said that he had a dream about his mother and she was there but not really moving. He described this dream and some of his thoughts for a long while and then paused. The thought that occurred to me seemed far fetched, but I said to him that I thought that at some point in his life his mother was sick or depressed and that no matter how good an audience he was for her he couldn't please her. Moreover, in the dream about me, he was also the audience and wondered if he could really please me; if he could, perhaps I would never leave him. This led to a string of thoughts (some were memories) about how he remembered and was told how precocious he was as a child. He also remembered how he was unable to tolerate criticism when he went to school. He would begin to cry if he made a mistake. We began to realize that with his (maternal) teachers he needed always to please them, and if he was told that he was wrong, or did not understand something, the fear of (maternal derived) separation surfaced. Over a period of several sessions we put together a reconstruction where his mother was taken away ill (I thought depressed), and that he fantasized that he had not been delightful enough (his word from another language). In my terms, he had not delighted her enough and so she left for others in a despondent state. Later that year, his mother visited him (for the first time in several years) and he asked her about this and she told him that she had been depressed after the birth of his sister and was hospitalized for at first a month, and when that was ineffective, she was hospitalized for several additional months after being home for only two or three weeks between hospitalizations.

This transference–countertransference sequence, which led to a reconstruction, was a turning point in the treatment. A number of issues around sibling and Oedipal rivalry gradually emerged, and, as they emerged in different contexts, they occurred in an increasingly object related manner. His somatic delusion (that he had cronic syphilis from the age of seventeen to the present, a delusion that, even though he knew it was an impossibility, he held on to until 4½ years into the treatment) gradually was understood as a damaged penis unable to really delight his mother or any other woman in a continuous manner. It was also seen as a punishment for his desire to be delighted by or receive pleasure from a woman. His homosexual concerns were, in part, a wish to be willing to tolerate assistance from a man who would help him navigate the difficulties of keeping a woman happy. His idealizing transference had largely homosexual underpinnings, both in the sense of Freud's use of the term in normal narcissistic development, and in his conflict about submitting to the powerful male (the famous male). Repair of the maternal rupture that was continuously reproduced in the treatment situation was, nevertheless, key to allowing other issues to effloresce in the transference.

The two illustrations are used to show first of all that, in my view, early transference interpretations are frequently difficult for patients to utilize. However, once a patient is able to utilize this type of interpretation, it strengthens trust. This is the case because the patient has endured the crisis of differences and found that a different perspective might be useful. The analytic couple surviving a potential crisis of difference also brings forth a different relationship between the two participants, one of increased trust and acceptance of differences. So far, the crisis of differences is expressed in terms of the patient or analysand. As a treatment situation becomes more and more a true two-person situation, it is often difficult for the analyst to see the patient, since the patient, to an extent, is becoming their own analyst. A disequilibrium occurs because the analyst role is shifting and the two voices become more equalized. In addition, the patient knows their internal world in a way that can only be approximated by the analyst. As the treatment progresses, the patient is able to provide increasingly more insights and new directions that cannot be envisioned by the analyst. An analytic task at various points in the treatment is to allow the patient to conduct the treatment with the analyst either as facilitator or, at times, as interpreter, truly in the Winnicottian sense of interpreter. That is, the analyst shows more clearly the limits of his or her knowledge in facilitating the patient's movement to feel and understanding their conflicted thoughts..

A word about cycles of transference, or cycles of transformations. Freedman has described movements in the therapeutic situation that he labels transformation cycles (1994) and O'Shaughnessy (1981) has described cycles of defences where, through the cycles, defences become more stable and less debilitating. In this formulation, there is a similar view of transference cycles, where, once Ms W was able to work through elements of her idealization in the transference, she was able to centre on other affects and fantasies in the transference. Eventually, she came to what I thought was the most important cycle, her anger (rage) and gradual mourning about her lost mother. (During this cycle, when her rage was contained, she could move into the depressive position and mourn the loss of her mother.) Each cycle has a dominant theme and when the dominant theme is worked through often, analytic trust has to be partially regained. This is particularly true with patients who use splitting as a defence, for, in some ways, in the early parts of the treatment, the new transference cycle is like an almost completely new relationship. Thus, even though interpretations within the cycle build trust, at times the end of the cycle calls for a therapeutic realignment before the next cycle begins. For some patients, the cycles will go relatively smoothly and the shifts even undetected, but with other patients there are distinct cycles that mark a new relationship for a period of time.

Transference and countertransference in the total situation

In my view, there are countertransference issues at each point of an analytic cycle; if an analyst is comfortable in reflection, synthesis, and containment it is a task to move to an interpretative stance. I have already described some of the difficulties at the beginning of the treatment, but at different phases of the treatment situation there are two other types of concerns that I believe are common in psychoanalysis. The first is accepting the patient's transference without intervening before the patient has experienced the transference with some (sufficient) intensity. I have hypothesized that every theoretical position (Ellman, 1998a) has a way of reducing the intensity of the transference or interfering with the manifestation of the transference. Pine (1992) has advocated that the analyst should strike while the iron is cold with borderline patients. While I can understand this advice, from my perspective, if one has to strike while the transference is cold, then striking is a bad idea. One should wait until there is sufficient analytic trust and then allow the transference to gain some intensity so that the analytic couple can begin to trust that they can survive intense reactions. Gill and Muslin's (1976) idea of rapid transference interpretations is, in my view, a way of limiting the patient's ability to get to the type of intense reactions that can be authentic in a therapeutic situation. The classical analyst's distance is often a way of keeping the analyst away from the transference intensity, and it becomes difficult for both parties to fully believe in the analysis. I believe that the relational analyst's disclosures may frequently be a way of diverting the analytic couples' attention from the transference. It may also be a way of fragmenting the consistent manifestation of a transference cycle.

Before describing some difficulties in receiving the transference, it is important at least to state a conceptualization of transference. In my view, Klein (1952a) dramatically shifted the concept of transference and Joseph (1985) continued to develop the Kleinian–Bionian concept of transference. Joseph (1985) following Bion (1962a,b) sees transference not as simply a direct (or indirect) reference to the person of the analyst, but, rather, "it must include everything that the patient brings into relationship" (1985, p. 62). She goes on to say,

> Much of our understanding of the transference comes through our understanding of how our patients act on us to feel things for many varied reasons; how they draw us into their defensive systems; how they unconsciously act out in the transference. [*ibid.*].

She relates how what occurs happens in words and non-verbally, and is expressed in terms of the patient's inner world "elaborated in childhood and adulthood experiences". This broader view of transference accomplishes something that Freud had begun to see, but eventually left under various internal and external pressures that made it extremely difficult for him to progress further after his revolutionary understanding of transference. Bion, Sandler (1976b), and Joseph also take up the concept of countertransference, and, rather than see countertransference solely in terms of an obstacle, see it as a unique source or "as an essential tool of the analytic process" (Joseph, 1985, p. 62). Thus, what I have been describing as countertransference obstacles is countertransference in one sense of the term, but, in Joseph's more inclusive concept, one might consider the analyst's reactions that I am describing as something that is a result of the patient drawing us into the dynamics of the patient's inner world. This inclusion in the patient's internal world can be an important source of understanding.

According to Klein (1952a), "transference originates in the same processes which in the earliest stages determine object-relations" (p. 53). The earliest processes involve projective–introjective sequences where feelings, impulses, and beginning representations are put into the other object (usually the mother or her breast). For Klein, the earliest processes involve oscillations of love and hate, and she has maintained that "the analysis of the negative as well as of the positive transference and of their interconnection ... is an indispensable principle for the treatment of all types of patients" (*ibid.*). In fact, Klein has consistently emphasized the negative, or, more accurately, destructive, tendencies in the transference.

Interestingly, an analyst from the USA, Brian Bird (1972), viewed transference in as complete a manner as did Klein. He did not reference Klein, which for American analysts was not unusual. Bird viewed transference as "universal mental function which may well be the basis of all human relationships" (Bird, 1972, p. 267). He also maintained that "analysts themselves regularly develop transference reactions to their patients including periods of transference neurosis, and that these transference reactions play an essential role in the analytic process" (*ibid.*). Bird's view is that the analyst's transference is mobilized by the analysis, but is inherent to the analyst. He does not want to call the analyst's reaction countertransference, because the analyst is not, in his view, just responding to the patient's transference, but all relationships are built on transference and the analyst is not immune from this universal tendency. Thus, Bird, without a social-constructivist theory, maintains that an analysis is constructed through the transference tendencies of both parties. This is as radical a view as any we have encountered, although this did not seem to be Bird's intent. Brenner (1994) has, in his discussion of compromise formation, also conceptualized transference as a universal function. If we combine Joseph's conceptualization with Bird's, we can say that there are projective—introjective transference sequences that occur between analyst and analysand throughout an analytic treatment.

To return to a previous question, what are the elements in the analytic situation that would lead to the analyst not receiving the patient's transference? The phrase "not receiving" is here meant to imply that the analyst in some way defends against utilizing the patient's transference. Clearly, in the position of analytic trust, the analyst may decide not to interpret transference in the belief that the interpretation is not utilizable at a given point in treatment. At times, this theoretical position might be a way of avoiding discussing (interpreting) the transference with the rationale (rationalization) that there is not enough trust in the analytic situation at a given point in time. It may, particularly, be a way of avoiding the unfolding of the negative transference, since this type of transference is particularly stressful for the analytic couple. Without presenting further illustrations, the present thesis is that every theoretical orientation has ways of deflecting and interrupting the interpretable manifestation of transference. While it may still be possible to gain salutary therapeutic results without admitting the transference "as to a playground" (Freud, 1914g), in my view, the most complete analyses allow the transference the type of freedom that Freud alluded to in his transference paper. This paper demonstrated his new ease in the transference. In addition, the analysis of transference allows the type of trust that cannot be attained in any other manner. The analysis of the transference allows the patient to put their most hateful elements into another and have the relationship survive. The immediacy of the transference also allows for the analytic pair to feel the dynamics in an immediate way, which is not available through the discussion of other current relationships or reconstructions. Surviving, feeling, and understanding intense destructive feelings that have been struggled with for most of a person's life is a true analytic triumph.

Intersubjectivity and the analytic third

Earlier in this chapter, we looked at relational challenges to the classical position and I put forth concepts that I maintain are at least as far from the classical position as they are from the relational critique. Bion's concepts take contemporary analysts into the space that relational critiques require of an analytic theory. From Bion, Ogden, Joseph, and Stolorow and Atwood (1992), it is impossible to think of the analytic situation without an intersubjective perspective. Here, it is important to state different definitions of intersubjectivity. Benjamin (2000) describes intersubjectivity as referring "to that zone of experience or theory in which the other is not merely the object of the ego's need/drive or cognition/perception, but has a separate and equivalent center of self" (p. 45). Benjamin's concept leads to the idea of recognition of the other as another separate from the self. I would conclude (Fonagy & Target, 2002) that this can only occur if, developmentally or in analysis, you first experience yourself as present in the parent's or analyst's mind. Intersubjectivity, in this sense of the term, is not simply dependent on the recognition that the analyst is also a person (with transference reactions), but that the analyst is able to find and communicate that there is a continuous place for the patient in the analyst's mind. In my view, this is done through what Gruness and I have termed affective interpenetration (Ellman, 1998a; Gruness, 1984). Affective interpenetration is an important step, but not yet the full explication of intersubjectivity; for this to occur, there then needs to be an appreciation of the patient as a separate person whom, at times, the analyst psychologically separates from, while at other times their psychological world is shared. This separation frequently occurs as a consequence of interpretation, and, in the Freudian opus, this interpretative element typically speaks to a part of the patient's functioning that the analyst views as unconscious fantasy. Thus, in this type of separation, the patient sees that the analyst does not view their world with the same eyes or with the same thoughts. As I have outlined, this separation is much more easily tolerated after the patient has experienced themselves as present affectively in the analyst's mind (part of the development of analytic trust). In Benjamin's conceptualization, intersubjectivity collapses

> when the tension or dialectic between negation and recognition collapses ... we see breakdown. Breakdown means unassimilable difference. It feels impossible to recognize the other because her "interpretation" of our actions and intentions, or even her very existence, is too alien (too negating) to our own sense of self. [2000, p. 47]

Here, she is presenting a view of intersubjectivity that is implicitly a continuous, rather than a dichotomous, concept. The tension between negation and recognition is, in effect, a quantitative concept, and the collapse of the tension between these two processes leads to a breakdown in the person's ability to experience the other as having meaningful actions and experiences or as being a meaningful other. The tension between the acceptance of the other as another subject or self (my preference is to continue to use the term self, although Ogden and others have made a strong argument for the term subject) is an important consideration in development or in the therapeutic process. Before continuing this discussion on intersubjectivity, we should go to another view of the term.

Stolorow and Atwood (1992) talk about intersubjectivity as a "theory . . . or systems theory in that it seeks to comprehend psychological phenomena not as products of isolated intrapyschic mechanisms, but as forming at the interface of reciprocally interacting subjectivities" (p. 1). They are not presenting a specific psychological concept, but a postulate in their theory that says that all phenomena are to be viewed in this particular manner. In this context, I am using this quote to distinguish the use of the term intersubjective as a theoretical postulate (Stolorow and Atwood) as distinguished from the concept where the term refers to a particular psychological process (Benjamin, 2000). It is only in a usage like the one that Benjamin puts forth that we can meaningfully talk about the development of an intersubjective process in the psychoanalytic situation. To declare that all processes are intersubjective is, perhaps, an important historical antidote to maintaining that all processes can only be viewed as intrapsychic events, but it is equally polemical and sterile. The declaration of intersubjectivity as a universal condition, in my view, also clashes with the view of how one comes to know and appreciate the other's mind. To come to appreciate another's unique sense of self implies that there is a time preceding this appreciation when this state did not exist. If intersubjectivity is defined in this way, then there is a point before intersubjectivity, and, therefore, it is not an omnipresent condition. Of course, a theoretical postulate has heuristic utility, but, at this point in psychoanalysis, it may be more prudent for a theorist to state that she/he deems it important to look for the intersubjective or intrapsychic aspects of a situation rather than declare that, of necessity, all psychological events are to be considered in terms of one's postulates.

The analytic third: different conceptualizations

Clearly, I am advocating that the term intersubjectivity should refer to either a developmental or therapeutic process. A further question now arises in distinguishing the concept of intersubjectivity from the overlapping concept of the analytic third. Ogden's idea of the analytic third begins with Winnicott's statement that there is no such thing as an infant without maternal care (Winnicott, 1960a). Ogden extends this idea to the analytic situation, where there is

STRUCTURAL THEORY, RELATIONAL CRITIQUES, & INTEGRATIVE ATTEMPTS   611

no such thing as a patient without an analyst and no analyst without an analysand. It is hard to argue with either statement; clearly, a helpless infant would never survive without some form of maternal care. However, we know that some children (Anthony, 1980) with minimal mothering do well, while most children with minimal mothering do quite poorly. Similarly, what could it mean to picture a patient without an analyst or an analyst without a patient? Perhaps there is such a thing as a true self-analysis, but most commentators have noted that the most famous self-analysis (Freud's) was, in large part, influenced by Freud's transference to Fliess (Gay, 1988). In any event, what Ogden means to impart is an image of the analytic situation that involves dialectical interactions which can occur at every or any level of consciousness. In the way that he has conceptualized this idea, it is a continuous process that always

> reflects the interplay of three subjectivities: that of the analyst, of the analysand, and of the analytic third. The analytic third is a creation of the analyst and analysand, and at the same time the analyst and analysand (*qua* analyst and analysand) are created by the analytic third (there is no analyst, no analysand, and no analysis in the absence of the third). [Ogden, 1997b, p. 8]

One might ask, however, whether there are differences in the types of third that are constructed and how we understand these differences. If one assumes that there is a constant dialectic between different tendencies, then the dialectic between the analytic couple necessarily creates the third subjectivity. Perhaps it is more important to understand that the ideal of the third is that we, as analysts,

> ask of ourselves that we be unconsciously receptive to being made use of in playing a variety of roles in the unconscious life of the analysand. Unconscious receptivity of this sort involves (a partial) giving over of one's separate individuality to a third subject, a subject that is neither analyst nor analysand but a third subjectivity unconsciously generated by the analytic pair. [*ibid.*, p. 9]

Later, we come back to the question of the extent to which both members of the analytic pair give over their individuality. In the present conceptualization, this varies, and the way one loses their individuality changes as the treatment progresses. However, before going into this issue more fully, we can view another related conceptualization of the analytic third.

Aron and Benjamin have put forth several different conceptualizations of the analytic third, including an early discussion that built on Piagetian theory. More recently, Aron, in summarizing Benjamin's work, has related several different meanings of the term. Benjamin distinguishes the one-in-the-third from the third-in-the-one. The one-in-the-third (or the rhythmic third) is based on the two partners "sharing a dance or a pattern together" (Aron, 2006, p. 356). She is relating this sharing to rhythms in the infant's–mother's gaze–gaze aversion sequences, "reciprocal speech, gestures and mutual mirroring". The oneness of the pair is accomplished through mutual accommodation and the way that two people "are continually influenced by the very patterns and rhythms that they have previously established with each other" (*ibid.*, p. 357). The roots of this triangularity are clearly pre-Oedipal, and Aron points out that for many analysts (he cites Green and Ogden), triangularity is part of pre-Oedipal development. He might well have cited Abelin's (1975) research on early triangulation, as well as Jacobson's ideas (1964) about the differing functions of triangulation in terms of the pre-Oedipal rival. Aron distinguishes Benjamin's concept of the one-in-the-third from Ogden's, since Aron states that

> In Ogden's example, it is the mother who contains the third element intrapsychically, while, in the rhythmic third, the thirdness is a new creation emerging with the space of the dyad, rather than in the mind of one or the other participants alone. [Aron, 2006, p. 357]

Here, we will revisit this point and wonder about the creation of pre-Oedipal rhymicity and its analogue in the treatment situation.

The third in-the-one concept is also labelled as the "symbolic or the moral third . . . or the intentional third" (*ibid.*). This concept is based on Gergely's concept (Gergely, 2004; Gergely & Watson, 1996) of the marked response (discussed in Fonagy & Target, 2002). Gergely, in several publications, has shown that parental attunement or mirroring never perfectly matches the infant's initial responses. In effect, the parent knows this, and exaggerates or marks their response to indicate to the infant that it is a mirroring response and related to the infant's previous behaviour. It is to indicate or mark for the infant the mother's understanding of the infant's affective state. The mother, in her responses (with infants and older children), responds in a manner that both shows the child that it is present in the mother's mind and, at the same time, demonstrates her separateness. Aron and Benjamin conclude that "mirroring with its marked component, is a dyadic phenomenon, functioning as a differentiating third point emerging between the infant and the attuned parent" (Aron, 2006, p. 358). Both rhythmicity and markedness are considered to be "found in pre-oedipal mother–infant relations, and that both principles become further differentiated, elaborated and structured during the oedipal and post-oedipal phases. Nevertheless, thirdness itself arises conceptually as independent from oedipal triangulation" (*ibid.*, p. 359). Aron goes on to say that, in agreement with Stern (2004),

> intersubjectivity is best conceptualized as an independent motivational system fostering group formation and group cohesion in a hypersocial species... From an evolutionary perspective, it is likely that as a social species we would be born with some innate competence to deal with multipartite relationships. [*ibid.*]

Aron discusses in some detail the importance of disclosure in the analytic situation. Disclosure, in one sense of the term, is the analyst talking about their internal processes in the creation of an intervention. Aron quotes Bollas (1989) and Bach (2006) in articulating "a rationale for some... sharing of the analyst's inner workings" (Aron, 2006, p. 361). Bach talks about allowing the patient to witness his mind at work and, in effect, to view his free associations in reaching his formulations. Here, a contemporary Freudian can only agree that this form of disclosure is important in the analytic process. It is to be hoped that analysts frequently display how they think and, in Winnicott's terms, show the limitations as well as the usefulness of their interventions. There is another sense of disclosure that seems to run rampant in some psychoanalytic communities, where the analyst displays an aspect of themselves because they can no longer contain the analysand's transference; this form of disclosure is a way of avoiding the patient's inner world.

Britton (1997) details what I will describe as a Kleinian view of the analytic third. He summarizes Klein's positions and her interest in what she and Freud (see Chapter Two) called the epistemophilic impulse. Klein viewed an individual's ability to adapt to reality as correlated with their capacity to tolerate the deprivations and frustrations of the Oedipal situation. Of course, in her theory, the depressive position is coincident with Oedipal dynamics. Thus, in the depressive position, the child has to face the recognition of the parental sexual relationship. This "involves relinquishing the idea of sole and permanent possession of mother and leads to a profound sense of loss, which if not tolerated, may become a sense of persecution" (Britton, 1997, p. 243). Britton describes patients who have endured the Oedipus situation before the individual has "established a securely based maternal object. [Thus] the Oedipus situation appears in analysis only in primitive form and is not immediately recognizable as the classical Oedipus complex" (*ibid.*, p. 244). We have briefly referred to one of the cases Britton cites, a patient who could not, for a period of time, tolerate his interpretative efforts—indeed, could not tolerate his independent thoughts. Britton viewed this woman as lacking the "third position". More concretely, she "could not include within [her] most personal version of me my relationships with others. It was also intolerable for [her] to feel that I was communing with myself about them independently of them" (*ibid.*, p. 246).

For the child to tolerate independent thoughts, the child must acknowledge that, at times, there is a parental relationship that stands apart from either parent's relationship with the child. This relationship, then, is also part of the child's view of the world where different object relationships can meaningfully co-exist. In Britton's terms, "The closure of the Oedipal triangle by the recognition of the link joining the parents provides a limiting boundary for the (child's) internal world" (*ibid.*, p. 245). This triangular space is bounded, and it allows for all the potential relationships within this space. "It includes, therefore, the possibility of being a participant in a relationship and observed by a third person as well as being an observer of a relationship between two people" (*ibid.*). Clearly, Britton's view of the analytic third is based on Oedipal dynamics, which, unless successfully traversed, do not allow one to tolerate a fully differing other. I have previously critiqued the Kleinian position as conflating triangulation with the Oedipal situation. In my view, there are various triangulations that are present pre-Oedipally that do not involve Oedipal dynamics. However, before I present a modification of Britton's point of view, let us return to the Aron and Benjamin formulation of Britton's example.

Aron and Benjamin maintain that

> Britton constructed a relationship with Miss A in which he reflected back her own point of view as it was inevitably filtered through his own thought processes and emotional responsiveness. ... His thought became available as an object for use, facilitating reflecting, each person thinking about the other's thought. [Aron, 2006, p. 360]

They go on to talk about Britton's dyadic relationship with the patient, subtly shifting to his own marked (in Gergely's sense of the term) perspective. Gradually, the analyst, in their view, has to have "some kind of dialogue with him- or herself, something in the form of: 'I am of two minds about this idea, I can hold on to two ideas, two points of view, some conflict or disagreement with myself'?" [Aron, 2006, p. 361]. It is the analyst's internal dialogue that "creates a third point with what was a simple dyad, a triangular space where there was only a line" (Aron, *ibid.*).

I would venture that thirdness, as a continuous function, is not always easily achieved and is certainly not permanently present in most people. Freud attempted to capture this idea when he conceptualized the stage of object choice as coming after the stage of narcissism (see Chapter Three). Listen to what Freud says about his new stage: "In the present stage the component instincts have come together but there is an (object) choice that is extraneous to the subject's own self. In addition the primacy of the genital zones has not yet been established" (Freud, 1913i, p. 321).

What is the struggle that Freud is attempting to capture? It is the child's difficulty in giving up the pleasures of narcissism and anality for the love of an extraneous object (the mother, in Freud's concept, in my view, the joint parent). Freud's theorizing involves the idea that the child, at this point in development, is emerging from narcissism. Narcissism was a time where the child wants the people around her/him to want what he (the child) wants and to think the way he thinks. The child finds it hard in a consistent way to tolerate differences in desire or constraints on desire. But, when the external world begins to put constraints on the child's bodily pleasures, the child experiences this as a powerful attenuation in the mother's gleam in the eye (Kohut, Chapter Thirteen). If we take Freud's interest in narcissism seriously, then, although constraints have come gradually for the toddler, it becomes a narcissistic blow to find out that the mother does not delight in the child's activities and bodily pleasures (including products, odours, play, etc.). The child, in encountering restraints, is, in a vital respect, engaging another mind. This mind has gradually and continuously put constraints on the child, and these constraints have caused adaptive defensive responses on the part of the child. The child begins to recognize that this other mind (the mother's) is different from its mind. Edith Jacobson's theory about this time of life has both the child's sense of self and the mother as split representations. She sees the original split that Freud depicted at the beginning of narcissism (during the purified pleasure ego) continuing during the stage of narcissism. Freud is silent about this, but if we segue into Jacobson's description of this time of life, we see her introducing the concept of the pre-Oedipal rival. In my view, Mahler and Gosliner's (1955) view of the father, as well as Abelin's (1975) observations and ideas about triangulation of the pre-Oedipal father, all have been stated by Jacobson (1964). Mahler, in typical grudging form, acknowledges this in some of her early writings. It is important to realize that, although Jacobson's book *The Self and the Object World* came out in 1964, her views were published in German many years before the English publication.

Here, the rival performs many functions, and some not typically associated with rivalry. The rival is the child's way of easing its aggressive and destructive burdens (towards its internal objects), particularly the object that is becoming (has become) the bad mother. The father and sibling rivals (as well as others) are recipients of the child's projective identification, and so the rivals that are envied and introjected and identified with are also repositories of hatred towards the mother. The toddler may then identify with the rival's hatred of the mother, and this closeness to the rival will oscillate during the time that Mahler calls the end of practising through rapprochement. I could go on about how Jacobson enriches Winnicott's ideas about the environmental and the object mother, but I

STRUCTURAL THEORY, RELATIONAL CRITIQUES, & INTEGRATIVE ATTEMPTS 617

want to reach the idea of thirdness. Jacobson looks at the task of the child reaching the point that Freud calls object choice, which Mahler calls the end of rapprochement, and a point where the child, if things go well, develops object constancy. The child, at this point, consolidates the images of the good and bad mother and begins a new type of triangulation. The previous triangulation served to preserve the image of the good mother through what Kleinians call projective identification. The bad mother was projected into the rival and introjected as a joint object representation. Thus, the rival carried some of the child's hatred and was also an ally against the bad mother. The rival, of course, was also a rival for the good mother. When the good and bad representations of the mother are fused, there is the new triangulation.

The triangulation of the oedipal rival is not what I would regard as the beginning of the third. The third begins when the child starts to understand another's mind as being firmly separate from its own mind. This happens during the period of 3–4 years old, and Jacobson's concepts would lead us to predict that the more severe the split, the more difficult it will be for the child to begin to understand the mind of another. Freud's view of object choice clearly is describing a child who is beginning to understand and accept the mind of another as different from its own. To the extent that this happens, narcissism is put aside for a more mature type of object relationship. The child no longer is linked to the mother in a linear fashion, the mother is now firmly different and, at important times, has different aims and desires.

Object choice allows the child to proceed towards object love (which has its beginnings in the Oedipal stage). The act of choice implies that the child is secure in its love of the mother (joint parent) and, although it does not fully comprehend her reasons for these demands and restrictions (there are many other important restrictions, tasks, and demands, toilet training is but one), it trusts the mother; it has learned to trust its love for the mother and the mother's love for him/her. Thus, the mother and child have survived the anal stage (or age of restriction) without sadism dominating their relationship. This is not object love and there are still strong narcissistic elements present in the child, but a significant barrier has been crossed. The child is moving towards understanding and taking into account another mind that has different aims and desires. The thirdness (or precursor) that has occurred is that there is now transitional space between the child's desires and the child's thinking about the mother's desires with respect to the child. It is a thirdness that can easily collapse. It is dependent on the idea that she is doing this because of her love for me. I know that she loves me even though I do not understand her reasoning. (A position the in love adult male is frequently in.)

As the child advances towards the Oedipal drama, the issue of thirdness indeed becomes highlighted to a greater extent (or perhaps is present fully for the first time). She is now performing actions that have nothing to do with me and with a rival (who is also a loved object), in activities that are separate from me. For the child to understand this and accept it to some extent (without being forced to accept it), thirdness must come into play. The child must be able to begin to see another's perspective that does not prominently include the self. It is the beginning of true empathy mired in the child being able to see itself outside of the parental couple without violently impinging on the parental couple. It is a true object relations thirdness, and it seems to me that Aron and Benjamin confuse the precursors of thirdness with the development of the analytic third. From my perspective, it is a triumph of object love and is dependent on a balanced love of the parental couple (either a realistic or phantasized couple) and a narcissistic investment in the self.

In this formulation, though, what is love? If Benjamin (1988) and Aron and Benjamin "define the quality of relationships by what kind of thinking we do in them" (Aron, 2006, p. 362), I would define the quality of relationships by the type of love present in them. Intersubjectivity, in their definition, "is precisely the mental space to observe and feel in the interaction". Intersubjectivity takes many forms: it can be the love of a parent who has gradually and painfully come to know that their excitable child needs to calm down by himself. The parent, allowing the child the space to be alone, may be an important part of love, and the child, feeling this space, may develop an intersubjective other who cares for him. What of the space that a child needs to lie to a parent to test their omniscience and begin to soften their idealizations of the parent? Interactions where both parties are coming to learn about each other's mind are crucial during development, but sometimes silence and allowing the other to be alone while with you can be equally important. In my model of object love, knowing the other's mind is being able to feel and respect certain endogenous tendencies in the child or in the clinical situation. Thus, for some children, even the active mother must realize that if she is active while the child is active, this will sum up to an aversive experience for both of them (see Chapter Eighteen). Love, then, is not simply what goes on in the interaction, but showing that one cares enough for the other that it is possible to leave them alone without having to interact. It is the total caring and empathic response for the other that, at times, means not knowing and recognizing the limitations of what you can provide.

This, of course, brings me to the clinical situation, where Aron and Benjamin state that "only the emergence of the analyst's feeling in the interpersonal field allows it to become outside, objectified, and so part of his reflection" (Aron, 2006, p. 364). This, it seems to me, is true in some situations, and analysts frequently attempt to suppress their feelings (I doubt that they are truly hidden) instead of owning their responses (feelings and mistakes) in the clinical situation. However, I doubt that this is the only way for a feeling to become part of her/his self reflections. It is one important way, which occurs more often than we had previously acknowledged, but it is not the only way, and, with some patients, I doubt that it is the preferred way. Many patients need to have a one-person field for a long period of time, and they do not want continuously to hear about the analyst's difficulty in decentring. Rather, the patient needs to develop the type of trust that the pre-object choice child needs to have before he can give up a body pleasure for the greater pleasure of enjoying the mother's love. They need to experience what I have called the beginnings of analytic trust. It is with the interpenetration of minds that one comes gradually to know the other. When the analyst can enter the patient's world, there is an interpenetration that allows the patient to know the analyst in a manner that goes beyond considerations of disclosure. From there, it is with the development of the capacity for object love that that the other can be tolerated and loved as another with a separate life and loves. We should not see this capacity as another psychoanalytic variable that is stated in dichotomous terms. Rather, the capacity for object love and thirdness (self reflection) should be seen in continuous terms, with almost all humans having some capacity.

The goal of psychoanalysis is not intersubjectivity, but, rather, to develop the capacity for object love and the ability (free of inhibitions and anxieties) to fulfil that capacity in a variety of human activities. The ability to self reflect, or to know another's mind, can occur in a variety of ways; these conditions can occur in some people who do not have the ability to love another. Tennessee Williams's capacity for thirdness, under some conditions, was truly remarkable, as was James Joyce's, or Robert Solloway (physicist), but their capacity to love in a relationship was or is impoverished. Thirdness is not a goal, it is a requirement to get to the goal, and, with some narcissistic patients who may love in a particular manner, it is a requirement that will be met only fleetingly, even though they may have truly satisfying relationships. I believe that Kohut was correct when he stated that we all have selfobject relationships. I also believe that every analysis ends with elements of a transference cure (selfobject relationship). The question that Kohut did not fully entertain is the extent to which an individual can look beyond the selfobject relationship and care for the other. He argued against the classical view of autonomy, but he did not wrestle with the question of the capacity to be alone and follow one's ideas. These two capacities, to be alone and for object love, are what allow for a meaningful thirdness in object relations and in the nutritive pursuit of one's ideals. The capacity for object love is the requirement for a thirdness that can be used in true and meaningful empathic responses. This is an aspect of Freud's vision that I hope we can hold on to and extend.

CHAPTER EIGHTEEN

A tentative developmental model

Summary

This is one of the few chapters where there is a mention of research. The research is presented to illustrate a developmental model that combines physiological factors with relational factors. The research includes some mention of rapid eye movement (REM) sleep research as well as research in motivational pathways of the brain. The chapter includes a model of mother–infant interactions. It ends with a clinical case to illustrate the model in terms of the clinical situation.

Introduction

In 1995, Freudian and relational psychoanalysts published an article comparing and contrasting the two theoretical positions. Merton Gill, who by that time was clearly a relational analyst, summarized the positions and maintained that both types of theory, to some extent, account for both innate and experiential factors but differ in at least four ways.

> First, it is uncontestable that the classical point of view emphasizes the innate over the experiential, whereas the relational emphasizes the experiential over the innate. Second—and really a correlate of the first—in the classical view, the innate is explanatorily superordinate to the experiential (sometimes reductively so), whereas in the relational, the experiential is explanatorily superordinate to the innate (sometimes reductively so). The issue is a hierarchical one. Mitchell saw the bodily urges—part of intrapsychic structure—as expressed by way of interpersonal relations. Hoffman (personal communication, August 1992) criticized Mitchell's description in that "what seems to be underestimated in this kind of formulation is the importance of sexual interest and desire in itself rather than as a channel for something else which is not intrinsically sexual." Third, the classical point of view emphasizes how the past determines the present, whereas the relational point of view emphasized how the present can be illuminated by the past. On the whole, the classical point of view sees the present as a repetition of the past, whereas the relational point of view sees the present as more independent of the past. Fourth, the relational view stresses new interpersonal experience over insight as mutative, whereas the reverse is true in the classical view. [Gill, 1995, pp. 91–92]

In this extract, Gill summarizes what other authors (Greenberg & Mitchell, 1983; Mitchell, 1995) have seen as the unbridgeable gulf that exists between relational and classical points of view. Although Gill sees more overlap between theoretical perspectives, the gulf is still difficult to bridge in his formulations. One or the other type of formulation must be dominant or superordinate, from Gill's perspective. The contention throughout this volume is that the dichotomous statement of various theorists makes a truly interactional theory difficult to construct. If one is told there is an unbridgeable gulf, one has to choose sides. The question that will preoccupy us in this chapter is whether or not there is, in fact, an unbridgeable gulf, or whether there is a theory, or, at the very leas,t a theoretical outline, that can accommodate both extremes. Are there some people where innate factors predominate and others where experiential factors predominate? A truly dynamic theory would have moving parts that would allow one to account for both types of people. Of course, in this statement, there are two types of people, when in reality there are an infinite variety of human beings, most of whom fall in between the two extremes. In other terms, can we construct a theory that might posit universal genotypic tendencies but that would still provide the possibility that these tendencies might be expressed in a variety of phenotypic ways that might allow for some people, perhaps most people, the relative unimportance of the universal genotypic tendency? We should keep in mind, before we look at a concrete example of this type of conceptualization, that, in our view, Gill is correct; both types of theory account for both innate and experiential factors and yet have differing basic postulates (and differ in more than the four ways he has outlined). In any of the theories that we have gone over, the question will be the extent to which one factor predominates over the other and the extent to which the theory can include a variety of factors that lead to different types of phenotypes. In other terms, can the theory move so that it can accommodate factors that it normally does not accentuate? Can a drive/structural theory be stated in a manner that, under some conditions, the environment is more important than drive in understanding a patient, or in understanding a child's developmental patterns. Can an experiential theory accommodate some individuals where normally occurring (by this, I mean I am excluding biological factors that are known pathological entities) biological or physiological factors are more important than environmental issues? Perhaps more importantly, can a theory be even more flexible than so far outlined and state things in contingency terms that imply or state probabilities? Thus, a certain type of infant might be difficult to soothe under many conditions, but can the theory state some conditions under which this difficulty is minimized? Can a theory comprise postulates that allow for a number of interactional circumstances?

Darwin and Freud: a mismatch

Although, clearly, Freud was impressed with Darwinian theory, his own theoretical efforts at times disregarded the implications of Darwin's concepts. In Chapter Three, I discussed Freud's instinct theory, which posited survival of the self and survival of the species as dual instincts. Survival of the self was the dominant instinct in early development. Survival of the species was thought to be prominently manifested only with the beginning of the stage of narcissism. Despite Freud's reliance on instinct theory as an explanatory postulate, he maintained that the infant's first response to deprivation was to hallucinate the breast. This hallucination (or fantasy) was thought to be pleasurable, but when the unpleasure of hunger exceeded the pleasure of the hallucination, the infant attempts various behaviours (usually crying) and the response that is reinforced replaces the waking hallucination. In this theory, the primary or first process (see Chapter Two) is dictated by the pleasure principle and turns the infant away from reality. Here, it seems there is a contradiction between the assumption of the pleasure principle dictating the first psychological state as opposed to the instinct of survival of the self being the main determinant of the infant's response to deprivation. Therefore, pleasure becomes the primary postulate in Freud's theory. However, instincts in this theory are ostensibly the primary motivators, and nowhere does Freud say there are some behaviours that occur before instincts are operative. Given this analysis of Freud's theorizing, if one wanted to stay within a Freudian paradigm, then at least one aspect of the theory would have to change.

If we were to do a complete retrospective of Freud and Darwin, we would have to trace the various places that Freud puts forth Lamarckian, rather than Darwinian, hypotheses. The last of these formulations was in *Moses and Monotheism* (1939a). However, Freud's Lamarckian explanations are not relevant to the present discussion. What is relevant is how one constructs a psychoanalytic theory that is both psychoanalytic and Darwinian. The following theory is an attempt at making this connection. Clearly, this type of theory blends or combines both innate and experiential factors.

A theory of endogenous stimulation

The presentation of this theory will be followed by an attempt to look briefly at how this type of theory relates to clinical concepts. Although we have amassed a reasonable amount of supportive experimental evidence, I do not think that the theory that will be put forth has been shown to be true or is largely accepted by the scientific community. It is a theory that I believe, but that is my metaphysics; there are alternative concepts, such as affective thresholds, that, to some extent, provide rough theoretical equivalents. In my view, the present theory presents at least greater heuristic value.

Theoretical summary

The present model starts with the dream as the entry into a theory of endogenous stimulation. It is my view that the dream represents a person's attempt to deal with issues of survival (Ellman, 2000) that, in early development, directly involve issues of pleasure and unpleasure. The self, in some manner, is usually represented in the dream, and, even in early infancy, self and object representations are at least vaguely present. In the dreams of children or adults, the self representations may be disguised or occur in symbolic form.

My view of dream formation is closely linked to a theory of the function of rapid eye movement (REM) sleep (Ellman, 1992; Ellman & Weinstein, 1991). In this theory, REM is thought to (some may say has been shown to) activate pleasure pathways that are neural networks which are intimately tied to basic behavioural functioning necessary for a mammal to survive. In the rat, what I have called basic behaviours might include nest building, food seeking, courting, sexual behaviours, and, most fundamentally, aggression. Whenever a mammal goes into REM sleep, the intra cranial self-stimulation (ICSS, a term used when an animal will work [perform a task] to receive electrical stimulation to a part of the brain, a phenomenon discovered in rats by Olds [1958] through stimulation of the hypothalamus) or pleasure pathways are activated and, in turn, are a factor in regulating basic behavioural areas. The memories associated with these areas are simultaneously stimulated. In humans, activation of these areas frequently (virtually always) activates memory systems that involve conflict, and, most typically, the dream (the mentation present in REM sleep) contains material about issues that are most important and/or most threatening to the individual. Under optimal circumstances, the dream provides some way of resolving a conflict, and the dream is forgotten. If the dream is particularly stimulating or anxiety provoking, the dream is more likely to be remembered. Anxiety dreams occur when the system is over-stimulated either psychologically or physiologically.

The concept of over-stimulation, or too much stimulation, will be discussed later in this chapter. In traumatic dreams, the dreamer cannot envision a way in which threat can be resolved. These dreams are frequently repeated until some threat resolution is seen as possible. In traumatized patients, this may not occur, or only occur with good enough psychological treatment.

I have emphasized the survival nature of dream mentation, but I should point out that, in optimal or good enough development, the first dream is hypothesized to be a memory of a satisfying event. The infant in this state envisions satisfaction of a need state that is important to its survival, and this memory is in turn consolidated. In good enough development, the dream state is seen as adaptive rather than regressive. This theory leads to a revision of Freud's concepts of primary and secondary process. In this theory, if development is going well the first images of the infant are adaptive and self-enhancing, thus moving the infant to adaptive attachment behaviours. REM sleep is designed to facilitate a mutually gratifying interplay between infant and mother. However, even if Winnicott is correct (see Chapter Ten) in his view of absolute dependence, there will, of necessity, be conflict early on in the infant's life. No matter how dedicated the parent, optimal gratification will not always take place, and, to some extent, even the healthiest of infants will experience what Winnicott (1962a) called "falling to pieces", or annihilation anxiety. Thus, registration of anxiety-producing survival issues will enter the infant's dream-world early in life. The issues that are brought up in REM sleep mentation are survival issues that usually (virtually always) involve an element of the body–self represented in the dream. (These issues are not always brought up in a painful manner; the infant may dream of successfully eliciting gratifying experiences. Nevertheless, this success, at some level, is perceived as necessary for well-being or, to use Winnicott's language, going on being to continue.) Here, by body–self, I mean that the infant and developing child usually represent the self in terms of their bodily experiences or bodily functions. Are these survival issues wishes?

From my perspective, sometimes a motivating factor for a dream might be a wish that is seen by the dreamer as important for their well being; however, a dream could just as easily be motivated by a fear or some anxiety that is not related to a wish. In this theoretical statement, the adaptive and survival functions of the dream are the central postulates. It is important to recognize that because there was an attempt at an adaptive solution, it is not necessarily the case that the solution continues to prove to be adaptive. It is perceived to be the best solution available to the dreamer at a certain point in their life. Given the repetitive nature of some conflicts, the perceived adaptive solution may come from a period that is early in the dreamer's life and no longer be adaptive. The idea that the solution is no longer adaptive may only be a perspective that comes from outside the dreamer (from another person).

To finish this theoretical summary, in this conceptualization, REM sleep is one form of endogenous stimulation. In addition, the same mechanisms that caused REM to be activated every 70–90 minutes during sleep are also activated during waking hours. (This hypothesis originated with Kripke and Sonnenschein [1973] and Globus [1970].) This endogenous rhythm tends to periodically activate mammals. Thus, whales that have REM sleep every 120 minutes would be activated with this REM periodicity, whereas a human would be activated every 90 minutes (humans' REM periodicity). The difference between REM activation and waking activation is that, during REM sleep, there is an active inhibition that stops the organism from moving. This active inhibition is not present at birth. (The inhibition occurs at the level of the pons, where motor impulses are blocked at this level. If an impulse gets through at the level of the pons, there is a further inhibition at the level of the spinal cord.) At birth and for several months after birth, the infant is moving its limbs and sucking vigorously during REM sleep. Parents frequently mistake early REM for waking.

Before we leave this theoretical summary, we might ask the question: how does this theory differ from Freud's drive or instinct theory? Freud's theory saw instinct as the main determinant of an individual's psychological world. The present theory pictures endogenous stimulation as one factor in an individual's development. For some individuals it may be an important factor, and for others relatively inconsequential. The present theory also sees endogenous stimulation as a factor to facilitate attachment, rather than as a factor that induces regression (in the sense that Freud used the term in *The Interpretation of Dreams*). Freud saw the infant first hallucinating the object and, at least for a short period of time, being satisfied with the hallucination or the visual experience of the object. It is our view that the infant, when activated by need, probably first responds with a genetically pre-programmed response (crying) to elicit a built-in response from its parents. If it is sometimes the case, as Freud posited, that the infant first visualizes the satisfying object, then we would assume it does this to adaptively remember the source of comfort or pleasure. What is primary in this model is the adaptive aspect of endogenous stimulation; this internal stimulus is programmed to obtain a response from the infant's care-givers. The interaction with care-givers is not simply around need, but is present for a range of interactions that allow the infant to begin to cathect, or affectionately represent, the main care-giver (usually the mother).

Freud's view was that pleasure is associated with drive reduction, and he came to that perspective for a variety of theoretical as well as historical reasons. Pleasure can occur in a variety of ways, and we can say unequivocally that there is a good deal of evidence that indicates that drive reduction is not the only pathway for pleasurable experiences. Given these views about endogenous stimulation, it is apparent that we see the primary, or first, process that the infant goes through as one that provides signals to its care-giver(s). It is only if (or when) the care-giver does not respond to the infant's signals that the infant might resort to producing memories of the satisfying event. If this happens in a continuous manner (memory instead of real satisfaction), the memory will become aversive rather than satisfying and, if not responded to, the infant may fail to thrive. Here, the main point is that the primary activities are the infant's signals to its mother; secondarily, the infant may produce memories of satisfying events as a way of soothing or reassuring itself.

What is Freudian?

Since I have implicitly differed with a number of Freud's assertions, what about my theory that endogenous stimulation is Freudian? There is a quick, uncomplicated answer to this question and a long, complicated answer that will require us to retrace some of the ground that Fairbairn and Mitchell have covered. The quick, uncomplicated answer is that this theory is Freudian in three important points of convergence: one, it hypothesizes a periodically activated internal or endogenous source of stimulation. As a second point, the pathways that are activated are pleasure pathways. As a third point, the infant or the developing child is seen as representing itself in part through body functions. Bodily functions are seen as an important aspect of the child's representational network.

Pleasure and object, not pleasure vs. object

The more complicated answer starts with Fairbairn's concepts and ends with some developmental ideas that we have so far not considered. Fairbairn and Mitchell maintain that humans are object seeking as opposed to pleasure seeking. This, in my mind, is a false dichotomy; infants are both object and pleasure seeking. In ideal development these things are co-ordinated so that the main object or mother is also the main pleasure giver. If things are going well the mother also gradually receives a good deal of pleasure from the infant. This reciprocal interaction provides for the infant the greatest probability of survival with a sense of security. Here, what we mean by security is that the infant's sense of "going on being" is a secure feeling and minimally disturbed during development. This is, then, the primary thesis, that survival of the self is the main motivational issue and a feeling of security or trust is a key factor in this sense of survival. Obviously, an infant can physically survive and still be severely disrupted or traumatized, and so, when I say survival of the self, I am not talking only about physical survival; rather, survival with a feeling of intactness and a sense of going on being that is not severely disrupted. In Winnicott's terms, the child does often experience falling to pieces or annihilation anxiety (Hurvich, 2003).

Although one might say that the first modes of communication between infant and mother are through pleasure and unpleasure sequences, I would agree with Fairbairn (Chapter Nine), Mitchell (Chapter Seventeen), and Bowlby (1969, 1973, 1980) that the overall function of these modes of communication is to bind the mother–infant pair into a libidinal unit (which is, of course, a Freudian way of describing the unit). In the present theory, this is in order to insure the survival of the infant. Here, then, we might say that for the health of the infant, both mother and infant eventually have to be object seeking. This is an aspect of early development that Freud barely mentions, and when he does, his most important statement is in a long footnote (see Chapter Three [Freud's third theory] and Chapter Ten, p. 402, where Winnicott uses Freud's footnote). However, if we look at the infant at birth, Fairbairn's dictum that humans are object seeking rather than pleasure seeking seems out of touch with an infant who is mostly sleeping, eating, and needing a variety of biological functions to be monitored. Moreover, in a sense, both object seeking and pleasure seeking seem out of touch with an infant that needs mostly to receive and be held. Although the infant is certainly more active mentally than one might have imagined in 1900, it is still primarily sleeping (10–17 hours a day), eating, and needing to be changed and comforted (held). Winnicott's description of absolute dependence seems to me the most accurate description of the activities between the mother and the infant. Winnicott is not merely describing the interaction, but also picturing the internal state of the infant. He assumes these internal states need to be anticipated (object presenting) by the mother in such a manner that the infant experiences the environment as providing for it when a need arises, or even slightly before a need arises. This is Winnicott's meaning of natural omnipotence, the sense of an infant that its experienced needs (no matter how inchoate the experience) are quickly gratified by the environment. In Winnicott's terms, this is good enough mothering. Although I agree with Winnicott that the infant will be well taken care of with what he calls good enough mothering, I believe good enough mothering is hard to do.

Pleasure or object seeking, or a different vehicle

Let us return to a question that we seemed to have answered: is the infant object seeking, pleasure seeking, or both in its first few days of life? I have intimated that the dichotomy is a false one, but I have also implied that perhaps neither theoretical postulate talks to the infant's primary needs. As Prescott states (2001) what is crucial in mother–infant contact is newborn/infant carrying [which] is another "infra-human primate maternal universal" that has been largely lost to homo sapiens mothers. In [my] view, body movement (vestibular–cerebellar simulation) is the external umbilical cord—the primary sensory stimulation in utero—that conveys continuing basic trust and security to the newborn/infant. [2001, p. 227]

If Prescott is correct, then the prime issue for a newborn infant is not pleasure or object seeking, but a continuing sense of basic trust and security that makes the new environment more manageable and lessens the probability that birth and its immediate after effects are traumatic. It seems that a prime way the mother makes contact with the infant is through comfort first of all. This is object seeking by the mother and undoubtedly pleasurable for the infant. If one wants, this can be called object or pleasure seeking, but, in my view, it is primarily security building.

If one maintains that humans are object seeking and not primarily pleasure seeking, what is the mechanism by which this tendency towards object seeking is maintained? Although this is not discussed by Mitchell or Fairbairn, the assumption is that human beings are genetically programmed as object seeking primates. Hrdy and others have argued for seeing human genetic endowments as more plastic or flexible than there being either an object or pleasure gene. Taking a step back from this, Mary Jane West-Eberhar, a sociobiologist quoted by Hrdy, maintains that

> Nothing is genetically determined in the sense of determined by genes alone. No gene is expressed except under particular circumstances ... It's a kind of biological illiteracy to talk about a gene *for* anything other than a particular protein molecule. [Hrdy, 1999, p. 56]

Obviously, Eberhard is talking about the flexibility of genetic expression given the multiplicities of environments that human beings have established. Hrdy reinforces this point when she states that "No gene or set of genes, or even any one mechanism influencing people to favor kin, has been identified. We do not know even a fraction of the ways that kin selection works" (*ibid.*, p. 63). What is interesting in terms of Homo sapiens being portrayed as object seeking, is that, comparing human beings to other primates,

Homo sapiens has the worst record for violence against infants and children, as well as intra- and inter-species violence. Humans also outdistance other species in terms of child abuse, homicides, abandonment, and neglect statistics, as reviewed by Hrdy (1999). In addition,

> Parents are by far the greatest perpetrators of child abuse and maltreatment (80%), as given by a recent Bureau of Justice Statistics report. In that report, mothers and fathers were equal (31%) in the murder of all children under age five (1976–98). [Prescott, 1996, p. 156]

Prescott, in a number of publications, and Hrdy, in her encyclopaedic book, review some data on our closest living genetic relative, the bonobo chimpanzee. To this point, Prescott presents the data on the genetic similarities between the bonobo chimpanzee and humans. He relates that

> A comparison with homo-sapiens closest living genetic relative—the bonobo chimpanzee—is illustrative. Genetic (DNA) communality between the two species has been given at about 98% but some estimates, derived from the data in Jared Diamond's 'The Third Chimpanzee' (2006), are closer to 99.1% communality. The genetic distance between the bonobo and the common chimpanzee is estimated at 0.7% DNA with a difference from homo-sapiens at about 1.6% of DNA. [Prescott, 2001, p. 227]

While the bonobo is the most peaceful and nurturing primate in studied existence, human beings are clearly the most violent primates that have been researched. The bonobo breast-feeds until its offspring are 3–4 years old. It also carries its offspring to approximately the same age (female) while the male is carried by the mother up to adolescence. Prescott hypothesizes that this may be one of the reasons that bonobo males are not violent towards other offspring, females or males. Prescott asks; "How can 'evolutionary biology' explain this behavioral difference between bonobo and homo sapiens?" (2001, p. 228). His answer is muted but clear: evolutionary theory cannot answer this question. It is the culture of the different species that account for the differences. Whether this is true or not, in my view, is unknown, but it is logically possible that these small genetic differences between the bonobo and humans may account for the increase in violence. Another argument for the importance of cultural differences comes from common chimpanzees that are also only slightly genetically different than the bonobo (0.7% DNA). The common chimpanzees, however, have a markedly different culture and are more violent. There are alpha males in this culture, and a good deal more inter- and intra-species violence. The bonobo has what is described as a matrilineal society, as opposed to the common chimpanzee's patrilineal organization. (Although we will not discuss them, there are three different genetic strains among chimpanzees.)

Arguing against a reductionist view of genetic differences, there is evidence that suggests that carrying has distinct effects in human infants as well as in the bonobo. Canadian researchers (Hunziker & Barr, 1986) looked at the effect of carrying, using amount of infant crying as their dependent measure ($n=99$). They found a significant difference in crying between infants that were carried *vs.* infants that were treated "normally". The difference at six weeks of age, with an increase in carrying time of two hours, was an overall reduction of one hour (43%) in crying and fussing behaviour. This experimental study confirmed anecdotal cross-cultural evidence gathered by Brazelton and his colleagues (Brazelton, 1974, 1981). Although these were not large scale studies, at this point in time it seems reasonable to hypothesize that the differences in child rearing account for many of the differences in crying and feelings of disruption in infants. West-Eberhard's view (see above, p. 631) of genetic influence seems to be at least partly upheld by the differences in species and across cultures. One may ask how this relates to psychoanalytic conceptualizations, particularly how this effects the dichotomization of object as opposed to pleasure seeking. Here, the point is that humans are neither primarily one thing or the other; they are, as a group, flexible, and will adapt to a variety of environments with different phenotypic characteristics.

Some related issues

Can we say that violent societies simply distort human beings' essential tendencies and that violence is a societal aberration that has little to do with our underlying tendencies? What seems to be more likely is the evolutionary research provided in the volume *The Beak of the Finch* (Weiner, 1994). This may provide a model for how humans have adapted to violence. In this study, documented by Weiner and performed by Peter and Rosemary Grant, they found that the beak of the finch changed depending on the environment of the finch. Gradually, the finch (the study was done on the Galapagos) began to adapt to different environments by selective breeding. The survival of the finch was dependent on whose beaks were the most useful for a given environment. Whether the human infant is object seeking or pleasure seeking depends on the environment and how the infant has been selectively bred (not necessarily consciously, but intentionally, nevertheless). Is secure attachment to a maternal figure important?

It depends on the type of individual that you want to turn out; if you want aggressive males who can serve in an armed force and can be ruthless, then the society might gradually adopt different types of attachments. We know from contemporary and historical patterns (the Spartans as opposed to the Athenians) that there are different modes of attachments. Moreover, within a society, there are different matches between mother and infant. We will shortly look at the beginning of a model that tries to describe and explain an aspect of infant–mother interactions. Before we look at these interactions, we can reinforce the idea that the human genotype generally allows for a variety of adaptations and a given society will influence the type of adaptations that at some level it tries to produce.

The good enough mother

In the previous summary, the amount of REM sleep present in the newborn was not mentioned. Infants at birth may spend 10–12 hours a day in REM sleep. To the extent that an infant is premature, then, to that extent, the percentage of REM sleep increases. Therefore, the mother must be able to recognize that the movements of the infant during REM sleep are not waking behaviours, and at times this is difficult to recognize, particularly with infants with large pupils whose eyelids are not completely closed. The recognition of the infant's state is one aspect of good enough mothering. It may seem strange to think that a mother cannot tell when the baby is asleep. However, REM sleep movements look like waking behaviours. This, of course, is not nearly the most difficult discrimination of state that a mother has to make.

For good enough (Winnicott's good enough) mothering to occur, the mother must be object seeking. How can we doubt that a mother is object seeking? While, in western societies, we assume that the mother will be interested in her infant, this is much less certain than most of us believe (see Hrdy, 1999). As Winnicott, Searles (1965), and others have pointed out, the mother needs a good deal of support and gratification to provide what most infants need for mental and even physical health. The chances of survival of the infant will be greatly increased if there is a good deal of maternal support. The main support for the mother is the environment that surrounds her (husband, mother, wise elder, etc.).

Less obviously, one of these sources may be the infant; if the infant is gradually a pleasure giver to its care-giver(s) as well as a receiver of pleasure, the probability of its healthy survival is greatly increased. Thus, in the present picture, if the infant does not make contact with its mother, its survival is in jeopardy. Perhaps one should say that those infants that have a higher probability of surviving in health find pleasure in object seeking. Clearly, the highest probability for infants surviving combines infants and mothers that find pleasure in object seeking and, in addition, are supported by the environment around them.

Brief review of the physiology of pleasure pathways

Before entering a discussion of mother–infant interactions, we again return to the pleasure pathways (ICSS sites) that have been discovered in most mammals. To review, these are sites that Olds first discovered: he found that when he delivered electrical stimulation to the hypothalamus, rats would learn a variety of tasks to obtain this stimulation. When the animal works to obtain this stimulation, this behavioiur has been labelled intra cranial self-stimulation (ICSS). Many areas in the mid-brain have been found to be ICSS or pleasure sites. Our laboratory (Ellman & Steiner, 1971) was the first (or one of the first) to elicit ICSS from the hindbrain or the pons (the area in the pons was the locus coereleus). (Stein's laboratory and Crowe's laboratory would disagree and say they were the first to elicit ICSS from the locus coereleus.)

An aspect of pleasure pathways is that the determination of pleasure (reinforcement) is dependent on at least three factors. The intensity of the stimulation, the rate of delivery of the stimulation, and the extent that the animal is in control of the stimulation. Steiner, Bodnar, Achermann, & Ellman (1973) have shown that stimulation of an ICSS site can produce escape and avoidance behaviour if the stimulation is made intense enough. Thus, as intensity increases, response rate increases up to a point, and then further increases in intensity lead to response rate decreases. When intensity is high enough, stimulation to a positive site turns negative or aversive. One could show similar results varying the rate of stimulation. At some point when rate is increased enough, stimulation to positive sites turns negative. Interestingly, if one allows an animal ICSS at the same time each day, response rates will stabilize. If, on one day, at the same time of day, rather than allowing the animal to respond, the experimenter gives the animal the same intensity and rate of stimulation that the animal chose the day before, the animal will escape from this stimulation (Steiner, Bodnar, Achermann, & Ellman (1973). This is at least some evidence that the animal wants to regulate its own rate of stimulation, even if the rate it receives was identical to the rate it chose the day before (at the same time of day). The assumption is that, in humans, the experience of being in control of the pleasure is as important a factor as it is in other mammals. The range of this experience can be huge, given both behavioural and cognitive responses as well as conscious and unconscious fantasies about control.

We have theorized that the ICSS system fires with REM periodicity in all mammals and we also hypothesize that this endogenous stimulation forms a bell-shaped curve in the human population. Thus, from one end of the curve to the other marks a large difference in the type of internal stimulation a person is self-generating. A neurophysiological implication of the research is that this endogenous system courses through the pons to the mid-brain, through to cortical areas. We have shown in a number of stimulation studies (Bodnar, Ellman, Coons, Achermann, & Steiner, 1979; Bodnar,

Steiner, Frutus, Ippolito, & Ellman, 1978a; Bodnar, Steiner, Healey, Halperin, & Ellman, 1978b; Ellman, Achermann, Bodnar, Jackler, & Steiner, 1973, 1975; Ellman, Achermann, Farber, Mattiace, & Steiner, 1974), and in a lesion study (Farber et al., 1976), that pontine lesions and pontine stimulation affects mid-brain sites. In return, mid-brain sites can effect ICSS behaviour at pontine sites. This continuous interaction can activate the system outside of the normal ICSS (REM) periodicity. Therefore, if there is an attack or there is extreme hunger, the system is mobilized. Given normal mid-brain thresholds, the ICSS system is activated with REM periodicity.

The mother–infant dyad and REM sleep

In what follows, I will simply state our theory with the understanding that it is a theory, not findings that have been demonstrated experimentally. I am, however, using some of our past experiments as a model for this theoretical exploration. To keep within the paradigm of our past experiments, I am using the term stimulation instead of activity or behaviour; therefore, there will be stilted sentences in what follows. These sentences will state that the mother stimulates the infant when, in fact, the mother is playing with, feeding, holding, or changing the infant. In any of these exchanges, the mother, to a certain extent, stimulates the infant, and this will be our focus. To begin this discussion, we will picture an infant with a high level of endogenous stimulation. The hypothesis is that individuals differ in the amount of endogenous stimulation that they produce. (We are using the term "amount", but more intense stimulation is probably produced by the rate of stimulation per unit time.) This stimulation is produced every 70–90 minutes in human beings (REM periodicity). Since we are imagining an infant with a large amount of endogenous stimulation, for this type of infant a small amount of external or exogenous stimulation will be mildly pleasurable and larger amounts or more intense stimulation will be unpleasurable. The summation of internal and external stimulation in this illustration pushes the infant into the negative, or unpleasurable, range of experience. Thus, what other children experience as a normal amount of pleasurable stimulation may be experienced as unpleasurable for the high endogenous infant. This infant will be like the animal that receives too much stimulation; they will want to escape from the situation that is producing unpleasure or pain for them. Since the normal mother wants to bind with her infant, it will be painful for her when her infant responds negatively to a range of her behaviours that she intends as behaviours to entertain or even soothe the infant. It will be the task of this mother to attenuate her responses and try to feel and accept what the infant is experiencing. If she can contain her disappointment and feel the infant's experience, the infant has a greater probability of binding with its mother. It is a difficult task for a mother to be able to feel her infant's painful experiences even though the mother perceives herself to be behaving in a "normal" manner. Of course, there may be the ideal mother who does not take it as a narcissistic blow if the infant responds negatively to her seemingly moderate attempts at engagement. Most mothers will want the infant to respond positively to their ministrations and, when this does not occur, it requires a resilient mother to accept this and learn to titrate (effectively modulate) the level of her activities with the infant. What happens if she feels that she is a failure or feels that there is something wrong with her infant? This may spur her either to provide more stimulation for the infant (to desperately try to attract the infant) or, alternatively, to keep her distance from her child. It can easily be a narcissistic blow (not to mention a depressant) for a mother if a baby fails to respond to what Laplanche (1997) has called the mother's seductions. This might happen actually or metaphorically. The task of dealing with a high endogenous stimulation infant may be quite difficult for a mother who, for one reason or another, wants to be active in producing responses in her infant. For a high endogenous infant, the adaptive internal response may be to begin to develop false self responses. In other terms, the infant learns to respond to a mother who is disappointed and wants the infant to enjoy her active stimulation. False self, in this context, means that the infant is forced to comply with external demands at a time when it requires effort and requires the infant to inhibit its normal responses. In this description of early development (0–5 weeks), the infant should not be overly concerned with external objects. The beginning of a false self development signals the infant's attempts at limiting its spontaneous actions (gestures). Other infants who are unable to falsely comply may turn away and fail to engage with their environment. A mother who is able to feel the infant's displeasure to active or intense stimulation and is able to modulate her responses may gradually be delightfully surprised by the infant's/developing toddler's spontaneous activity. The word "toddler" is put in here because it may take a period of time for the mother to be able to actively enjoy her child. This type of infant/toddler might then be able to seduce and intrigue its mother. If the mothering is facilitating, this may allow the infant to be in touch with their active internal life and eventually enjoy their sense of self. An infant with a mother who is negatively affected by the infant's sensitivity might lead the infant to try to silence or actively inhibit their internal stimulation, or actively evacuate their mind in some manner. Certainly, Klein's concept of projective identification is relevant to the way these infants may evacuate their minds.

What about an infant with low levels of endogenous stimulation? Here, one sees a child that will be less likely to respond to normal amounts of exogenous stimulation. The exogenous stimulation may not be pleasurable or intense enough to entice the child. This mother may be disappointed because of the lack of response of the infant. The disappointment may be less intense than that of the mismatched mother of the high endogenous infant, since the low endogenous infant is not turning away or fretting as actively, it is simply not responding with enough pleasure. Again, the ideal mother feels that the baby either needs more stimulation to engage it, or, at times, the mother deals with her disappointment that the infant is not as reinforcing as she would wish. If the mother cannot contain her disappointment, then she may either turn away herself or try to get the infant to act in a manner that is uncomfortable for the infant. She may, too continuously, try to produce a response in the infant. This type of mismatch also may produce a false self, as may be the case with a number of mismatched mother–infant dyads.

Let us focus for a moment on the mother's tendencies. In a study performed by Alfasi-Siffert (1985), she looked at gaze–gaze aversion in three-month-old infants. Part of the paradigm for this type of experiment was used by Stern (1985). In this study there were two different conditions: one where the mother and infant's gaze–gaze aversion patterns were recorded, while the other involved an experimental confederate who was trained to gaze at the infant only when the infant wanted to initiate gazing. With most mothers, the infant would gaze and meet the mother's gaze, and then the infant would dart away (move its gaze away) and then come back again to gaze. Most mothers would allow the infant to dart away, and then the infant would return to meet the mother's gaze. One mother, however, would follow the infant's gaze when it darted away and she would try to regain contact. When she did this, the infant would again dart away, and, rather than having a period of gazing and a period of darting, this pair engaged in virtually continuous darting. In this study, we could compare the infant's responses to its mother with the infant's responses to the confederate. Since the confederate did not try to stop the infant from darting away, the infant with the confederate looked like other infants in terms of a gaze–gaze aversion, return gaze pattern. This mother could not tolerate the infant being separate from her, even in terms of gaze patterns. She stimulated the infant to such an extent that the infant continuously wanted to avoid her gaze. Here is a case where the infant seemed to have mid-range sensitivities but his mother was so overly stimulating that he found it difficult to tolerate. This example tells us that it is not just the infant's sensitivity, or lack thereof, that determines patterns of interaction. It is always the interaction between mother and infant that determines the effects of stimulation, but, clearly, in some interactions, one party or the other accounts for most of the interaction.

Some other theoretical issues

Although it has taken a while, we can now come back to the differences in theories that Gill outlined and ask whether it useful to conceive of developmental issues in either innate or experiential terms. The way most theories are stated, there is a universal tendency that is crucial and other "less important" influences are also included. Human beings are object seeking, not primarily pleasure seeking, is an example of such a statement. The Freudian view of the primacy of instinct is another example. In the present theoretical matrix, the major influence differs depending on the individual and the stimulating environment the individual encounters. One infant may primarily be affected by experiential circumstances, while another may be primarily affected by innate considerations. Even this statement is misleading, since it is not truly an interactive statement. The high or low endogenous stimulation infant may not be affected by innate factors in some environments. A more precise formulation is to state that there is a higher probability of these infants being affected by innate factors in some societies.

Our prevailing transferences may prevent us from looking at the mother–infant dyad in interactive terms. It is hard to see both sides of the interaction and not focus on the side that our bias moves us towards. That is why, in viewing these types of situations, statistical findings are best forgotten, and it is useful, with dyads as well as individuals, to be as without memory and desire as we can be. Thus, even though I am proposing a theory of endogenous stimulation, this trait of an infant or individual is only one factor in a psychoanalytic model that, in my view, should be a multiple factor model. Sometimes, we will weight a given factor as important, but, in almost all cases, it is the interaction that we should focus on. In my view, in most societies environmental events will be the predominate factors in our understanding the dyad's interactions. However, here, as well, we should be as without memory and desire as we can be. In these few pages I have tried to illustrate how an interaction model will take us closer to understanding developmental experiences. If we attempt to separate out statistically which factors are more important, I believe that we would find that it would vary depending on the sensitivities of the infant and the mothering patterns the infant encountered. (As I am sure some readers have noted, instead of talking about high endogenous stimulation infants, I use the phrase "sensitivities of the infant". Sensitivity is seen as a manifestation of endogenous tendencies.) Moreover, how the infant is evaluated will depend on the society that does the research; thus, one society may measure certain traits while another will be interested in other factors. In this theoretical perspective, it is a mistake to think of development in absolutist terms. It is a mistake to maintain that one factor (either experiential or innate) is, in general, more important than another; it is always the interaction. While some interactions will seem typical, it is a mistake to be trapped mentally in usual occurrences. This is simply a reminder that even the worst environmental conditions can be survived by some people and even the most difficult infants, under some conditions, can develop along healthy lines. As a clinical point, one should not assume that what we see as horrifying or adequate conditions are necessarily experienced by another in the same way. While I have looked at one factor in terms of mother and infant interactions, clearly infant development can be seen in terms of many more factors than considered here. To illustrate the interactive point, we can consider some issues that theorists have posited are important in early development.

Melanie Klein emphasizes the infant's frustration tolerance as important in understanding early development. She writes as if this is a characteristic inherent in the infant, as opposed to one that is the result of interactions between mother and infant. In the high endogenous infant, more of these infants will display lower frustration tolerance, given that these types of infants are more sensitive to a range of stimuli and often harder for mothers to read consistently. However, a mother who can read this type of infant may help develop an infant/child who eventually has greater than normal frustration tolerance. This type of child may experience the mother's mind and caring in a manner that leads to more gratitude than is usually the case. In addition, this type of infant may develop into a person who has access to a greater range of internal states. If one can access and control these states, frustration tolerance may develop along wide and deep lines. Thus, frustration tolerance, while important, should also be seen as almost always a product of environmental–infant interaction.

Winnicott's version of good enough mothering makes it seem as if good enough mothering is a normal state for mothers. While he acknowledges that the mother needs support, nevertheless he writes as if mothering is a state that a woman can easily transition into once the infant is born. Reading Hrdy's book (1999) about mothers, infants, and natural selection, one gets a view of mothering from a number of different perspectives. Hrdy relates how important it is for the infant to seduce the mother into caring, since it is her thesis that motherhood is neither instinctive nor automatic. While puerperal insanity (a term Winnicott uses) may invade some mothers, Hrdy documents higher rates of infanticide and abandonment than would occur if all mothers developed this type of fever. Magurran (2000), in a review, states that Hrdy goes so far as to suggest that the extraordinary plumpness of newborn humans, much fatter than other infant primates, is an attempt to convince their parents that they are worth rearing. Even an infant's smile becomes, in Hrdy's eyes, part of its strategy to seduce its mother.

Even with this seductiveness, many mothers have a hard time attaching to their infant, perhaps because some infants are not that seductive, more likely because some mothers are not ready or able to mother at some points in their lives. In terms of the interaction between mother and infant, Hrdy makes it clear that the seduction by the infant is an important part of most interactions. Winnicott, with all his sensitivity, is still writing largely from the baby's perspective. He accentuates the mother's tasks in providing an auxiliary ego for the infant, but he has a hard time in remembering how the mother needs to be at least somewhat induced (seduced) by the baby. This seduction is particularly important given all that the mother has to provide during what Winnicott describes as the period of absolute dependence.

Primary and secondary processes, aggression, and Ms W: a note about treatment

One of the changes in Freudian theory that is being proposed is his concept of the sequence of primary and secondary processes. Freud theorized that primary process is the first type of thought that occurs in the newborn. I have tried to point out that, even within his own theory (during the era covered in Chapter Three), this sequencing does not make logical sense. Freud, between 1908–1917, thought that the first instinct to be activated is an instinct for survival of the self. If primary process thought occurs first, it does not help the infant survive, since it takes the infant away from reality. If, as Freud conceptualized, all initial thought is originally generated instinctually, then this is a logical contradiction. A genetically programmed instinct for survival should not take the infant away from the environment that can provide it with sustenance. In the present concept of endogenous stimulation, the infant is drawn to those aspects of the environment that provide it pleasure. If the infant is programmed genetically, it is programmed to find pleasure through its mother. It is also adaptive for the infant to be able to find pleasure autoerotically, since this is one way for the infant gradually to be able to develop a firm concept of body self. Freud's version of primary process is seen as a secondary process designed to help the infant at times where its mothering object is not available, or is unavailable longer than the infant can tolerate. Fantasy of the desired object is a way of controlling the pleasure and bringing some pleasure to the infant that is experiencing deprivation. Of course, Freud had both psychic energy assumptions about primary process and a theory of cognition. His original concept of primary process may be a good end point on a cognitive scale that charts different forms of thought. It is hard to imagine that one has seen pure primary process thought in adults.

In schizophrenic patients that I have treated, one can see a number of primary process tendencies. A patient of mine, when feeling conflicted, would condense several sayings and would relate that she felt left out in cold field (a conflation of out in left field and left out in the cold). This type of condensation indicated how left out of the object world she felt. When she felt hopeful, but was still going through an overt psychotic process, she saw me as Saint Hellman, who, she later told me, was a French saint of a previous century. Both of these forms of primary process are by no means pure primary process. Holt (2002) has suggested that a good deal of our everyday thought is somewhere between primary and secondary process, although we have not as yet formed a scale to be able to categorize these forms of thought. Freedman's (1994, Freedman & Lavender, 2002) ideas about forms of symbolization and Bucci's (1985) concepts of different types of symbols are certainly steps towards such a scale.

If one accepts these emendations to Freudian theory, then we can, in some sense, return to a version of Freud's early instinct theory. There, the two instincts were survival of the self and survival of the species, and it is a reasonable hypothesis to imagine that both of those tendencies are hard wired into human beings. We have already looked at the differences between a theory of endogenous stimulation and Freud's instinct theory, but, to this point, we have not presented a theory of aggression. In the present theory, aggression is seen as one aspect of all, or most, survival activities.

A TENTATIVE DEVELOPMENT MODEL   645

For example, if food gathering is an activity that is being primed or lowered, thresholds for aggression are simultaneously lowered. In this theory, aggression is a possible concomitant of all mid-brain regulated activities. Whatever the survival activity, the threshold for aggression is lowered. The organism, then, is always somewhat prepared for threatening circumstances in all survival activities. This may seem like a strange idea; if one is having sex or eating, thresholds for aggression are also lowered. To sharpen this perspective, the threshold is lowered in the active phase of the activity, after consummation, the assumption is that all thresholds are then raised. If consummation occurs, the assumption is that the organism feels safe enough to let this happen. Species with poor judgement about this are no longer with us.

Leaving aside the specifics of consummation, the main point in this hypothesis is that aggression is a behaviour that is more likely to be primed than any other behaviour. This is the preprogrammed part of endogenous stimulation; clearly, there are many things that may, in the development of an individual, specifically inhibit aggression or transform aggressive tendencies so that they are blended with many other behaviours. However, in a theory that places survival as a key concept, aggressive sites are the ones that are most easily triggered. As a final aspect of the concept of aggression, aggression is seen as a pleasurable activity. Sites that trigger aggression (Ellman, Achermann, Bodnar, Jackler, & Steiner, 1973; Olds, Allan, & Briese, 1971; Valenstein, Cox, & Kalkolewski, 1968) are also sites that lead to positive reinforcement. Conversely, all sites that trigger flexible aggressive responses are also ICSS sites. (This is my reading of the literature and experience in the laboratory; if this has not also been tested, then it is a prediction that I would offer.) This concept, then, is very different than the one that Freud offered in the era of the structural theory (see Chapter Four). Freud's concept of Thanatos posited a self-destructive drive that could be projected outward. The projection of Thanatos was the way Freud explained aggression towards other people. Klein's view agreed with Freud, and assumed that a destructive drive was actively present at birth. Clearly, these concepts differ from the one that is being put forth in this chapter. However, let us hypothesize a mismatched infant; for example, a high endogenous infant with a mother who is overly stimulating might look like a Kleinian baby.

The infant might want to get rid of the maternal representation, since the mother is a frustrating, aversive presence. It might need to split the representation of the mother to hold on to something good about the maternal presence. Thus, in this theory then, there may be infants that look like Kleinian infants and other infants that look more Winnicottian (Ellman, 1992). The theory actually would posit a range of infants that might provide support for different theories. That is, some infants might support Winnicott, some Klein, Fairbairn, Stern (1985), etc.

Since the previous chapter mostly discussed clinical concepts, here I will only briefly discuss the clinical implications of the present theoretical endeavour. In the previous chapter, I have accented the development of analytic trust in the therapeutic situation. I also said at the end of the chapter that I would try to show how endogenous factors were important in the analytic process. In my theoretical matrix, a key element in the development of trust is the interpenetration of affect states; that is, feeling in a deep way what the patient is experiencing. In my view, this interpenetration involves gradually understanding the patient's endogenous tendencies. This became clearer to me in the treatment of Ms W.

Ms W was twenty-five years old when I began to see her in first three, and then four, times a week treatment. She was a woman filled with remorse that frequently led to extreme self-loathing and self-criticism. At the beginning of treatment, she was severely depressed and had just signed herself out of a hospital ward where she was being treated for depression. She had a severe eating disorder and, when she entered treatment, she was about seventy-five pounds (5 ft 8in tall) and was so thin that she could barely sit without substantial pain. (Several years ago I saw her for two sessions, and she mentioned that when she started treatment she was seventy-five pounds. I had thought that she was sixty-nine pounds, and reported this at an IPA conference (2000).) Her conscious life was devoted to feelings of regret that at times was disrupted by bouts of rage at those around her. She felt that her ex-boyfriend and her mother had put her in the vulnerable situation that led to her being raped and assaulted. Feelings of rage did not last long, since they not only disrupted any sense of stability she was able to establish, but also threatened to destroy the only object relations that she felt she had retained. Her fleeting anger (at times rage) could mostly safely be directed at Harid, who had decided that he could not marry her because of their religious differences (she is Jewish, he is Turkish and Moslem). This happened about six months before she moved into her own apartment and, while sunbathing on the roof of her apartment house, she was assaulted at knife point, raped, and beaten. This incident was extremely debilitating and traumatic, and amplified her eating difficulties, which began when she and Harid broke up.

When the treatment started, she was awash in regret that she had not converted to the Muslim religion. At times she berated herself for not converting and, when calm, would fantasize about converting and having Harid return. These fantasies were disrupted by thoughts where she depicted herself as a wanton woman, one who would never be accepted by Harid's Turkish parents. Her guilt about her past sexuality was a powerful factor, and she came to understand part of her anorexia as attempting to eliminate the observable feminine parts of her body (her large breasts and her other curves). Her sense of remorse was strongly associated with powerful guilt about her wanting to possess Harid, and we came ultimately to understand her wish to steal Harid (a first son of wealth and fantasized power) away from his parents and his culture. It took a reasonable amount of time for her to begin to talk about her being raped. This surprised me, since I had thought that this would be constantly on her mind. However, I underestimated the amount of shame that she experienced and, fortunately, I allowed her to determine when we would discuss this traumatic event.

I will not go on about Ms W except to say that, during this period, I had seen several women who were anorexic: all of them (four) had severe conflicts with their mothers. They all had strong hatred towards, and yet at the same time could not easily differentiate from, their mothers. I felt that this was the case with Ms W, and, although after four years of treatment her symptoms had abated and she had begun a promising career, very little psychoactive was occurring in her treatment; her analysis, in my view, was at a standstill. She maintained her benevolent view of me and remained quite angry with her mother, with whom she had broken off all relations. Her verbalizations in her analysis were more like discussions with a caring (combined) parent, and my attempts to interpret her use of me were greeted with compliance and a certain bemused acceptance. There was little new that was happening in her treatment and yet she displayed no interest in ending it, and, in fact, seemed quite content as we entered the fifth year of her analysis.

Up to this point in the treatment, although the patient had certainly shown improvement, she still was not able to utilize her transference reactions in a therapeutically meaningful way. If I was idealized, it was "only real"; during the earlier phases of treatment, when she displayed paranoid reactions about my attacking her in one form or another, that, too, was only real for her. I have described this treatment in more detail in another paper (Ellman, 1999, 2006) but, for the purposes of the present discussion, one can say that it was not until she could gradually trust with me certain types of erotic transference reactions that she could utilize the treatment in a manner that led to new pathways and a different form of self-reflection.

In the fifth year of treatment, she had repeated dreams of her father, but he looked somewhat different and frequently he was bald (as I am). It was when she allowed herself to comment on the woman who was in the other office that the treatment substantially shifted. She had known for a while that the woman in the other office was my wife, but now everything that this woman did seemed to bother her. She wondered how I could possibly be married to someone like her, and strong rivalrous feelings began to emerge. As we explored those feelings, she began to remember that she was quite depressed when she was 4–5 years old. She remembered colouring everything black and being angry at her parents, and she was told that she had never been like that before. She suddenly realized something that must have been apparent to her at some point in her life, that her sister's birth was extremely upsetting to her. Her transference became not only erotic in nature, but classically oedipal. She wanted my attention and continued her rivalrous feelings with my wife and with other female patients. She began to envision the two of us having a child together, and, although now she was more self-reflective, the idea that we were apart was painful to her. There always seems to be someone in the way she commented to me, and then she said she wished that I would change offices—she laughed, and said "Perhaps you could move to my building." The dynamics that continued to unfold then were intermingled with her guilt about her wishes to eliminate my wife, who, at times, she reflectively felt "couldn't be as bad as I think she is." I could continue to follow the path of Ms W's Oedipal dynamics, but, rather than do that, I will try to explain how these dynamics influenced her symptoms and why she became depressed during her childhood rather than being a child who suffered disappointment and then gradually adjusted to her new circumstances (which her parents had seemingly tried to prepare her for).

Ms W was your quintessential high energy person. After her depression she talked incredibly quickly, eventually was extremely energetic. and did everything at a breakneck pace. She spoke a little too loudly and laughed enthusiastically, and was in general somewhat boisterous. When she came back to see me (she had finished her analysis several years before the visit), she said to me, "Some people don't like my enthusiasm, the fact that I talk loud and move quickly, and I have come to accept that I can't please everyone. I have also come to accept that this is the way that I am and some like it and some don't." I thought that this was an excellent piece of self-awareness that she had somehow achieved on her own. I agreed with her that once her depression lifted, she was a dynamo and it was not a manic state (at least in one sense of manic, that is, as a defence against depression), it was her true self. What we discussed was a correlate of her high endogenous states, that is, her extreme sensitivity and how powerfully she experienced the world if it entered her internal space. Sometimes, she was so active that she was oblivious to the world around her, but when her environment was perceived by her, it was experienced intensely. When she experienced a sustained conflict situation, the birth of her sister, the dynamics that she experienced was so intense that she became disorganized. What for others might have been a resulting neurotic organization, given the stage of her development, was for her so intense that she developed the capacity for debilitating symptoms. I doubt that she would have been hospitalized for depression if she had not been raped, but before this event, when she and Harid parted, her depression seemingly was quite severe. In her reconstruction of her childhood depression, it took her quite a while to get over the birth of her sister. It has now been fifteen years since the end of her analysis and Ms W has flourished. She has a successful career and a successful marriage. During that time, I have seen her for a two-session consultation when she wanted to discuss her relationship with her husband's daughter. She has called me a few times to tell me about her promotions and a show that her husband has produced. She has not suffered another depression. I think that she has learnt about her intensities and learned to accept and regulate her internal states. In my view, she is an example of a person with a high endogenous motor who had a tendency to experience things quite intensely. At times her internal states and external stimulation summated into intense experiences. Over time, she came to realize this, gain acceptance and then control of her internal life, and then be able to utilize her high level of activity and her rich, active, internal world.

Brief foray into Oedipal dynamics

I realize that, in this brief clinical vignette, one may not be convinced that Ms W's dynamics were really Oedipal. In fact, I am not entirely sure what Oedipal really means at this point in time. Klein has not convinced me about Oedipal dynamics being present at 4–6 months of age, but she and the neo-Kleinians have convinced me of the mixture of stages and of bodily zones that appear in every part of development. Hence, in my view, there is no anal stage where the child is concerned exclusively with anality, but, rather, there are points in development where certain themes predominate, but other themes are also present. Are there aspects of triangulation earlier than 3½–5 years old, when, classically, the Oedipal stage is thought to occur? Clearly, I think that this is the case and Abelin's (1975) work on early triangulation as well as Jacobson's (1964) view of the pre-Oedipal rival are examples of triangulation that occurs earlier than the classical Oedipal period. In my view, what is unique about the Oedipal stage is what Freud implied in what I have called his third era, the beginnings of the capacity for object love and true empathy. By true empathy, I mean not simply experiencing what another is feeling, but being able to consider another as a separate other. This means, for the child, being able to accept the other person as having separate views and predilections and at times not having them (the child) as their main concern. This entails realizing and accepting that the other person has a life outside of their concern for your life. This is a difficult task for the child, and probably, for most people, never completely accomplished. It is hard to recognize the other as having their own concerns and being able to feel, understand, and accept the other as a another that is (in some ways) separate from you. I think Ms W was reaching that point in her development when her sister was born, and she was beginning to realize her mother as another, rather than as just part of her as a narcissistic object. Her intensity made the birth of her sister feel traumatic rather than difficult. It was a betrayal that depressed her and left her internal objects as enemies who could not be trusted.

Clearly, one may have many different views of this clinical illustration. The main point, however, is to try to show that intensity matters and can often change the way an event is perceived or experienced. I have tried to give one view of how different intensities come into being, but, obviously, one may substitute the concept of threshold for frustration or other thresholds without including the concept of endogenous stimulation. I believe this concept might have more explanatory power, but the crucial point is that, in the clinical situations, one of the most important aspects of analytic trust is being able to feel the other's intensity level. This will help the analytic pair to build a facilitating intersubjective environment.

It is unlikely that anyone will doubt that intensity factors are important in development or the clinical situation. In this chapter, I have tried to present a model that looked at one of the underlying factors in determining intensity. I have also tried to look at the plasticity of the human mind and tried to show (or imply) that past dichotomies such as object and pleasure can be meaningfully joined in understanding human experience.

Epilogue

Brief introductory statement

Clearly, I believe that the stipulation by Mitchell that there is a basic incompatibility between the drive/structural and the relational/structural models presents a false dichotomy. In my view, any contemporary theory has to include genetic, object relational, cognitive, and physiological sources (including endogenous ones), in a multiple factor model. Developmental or therapeutic encounters are not reducible to either object relations or endogenous factors. What I have left out in the preceding sentences are cultural factors, which are, in many ways, overriding influences in determining patterns of development and the evaluation of pathology of a given individual. Although I have alluded to the role of culture (in Chapter Eighteen), it has not been a focus of the present volume. In mentioning the flexibility of the transition from genotype to phenotype, I have not tried to theorize or fantasize about the limits of this movement. I have given some indications of the role of adaptation, and the way that the beak of the finch is a beginning model for understanding how traits are groomed and how they evolve. I have tried to indicate how a society can groom traits and that, in many ways, normality or pathology is a result of the society's values. Hartmann's concept of adaptation has been too easily overlooked, in part because of his attempt to rescue aspects of Freudian theory that were not salvagable. All of the factors that I have cited, in my view indicate that any reductionist theory does not do justice to the multiple factors that influence human development and the therapeutic situation.

Influences informing the present volume

If I were to cite one overriding influence for the present volume (excluding Freud), surprisingly, it would be Stephen Mitchell (see Chapter Seventeen). It is surprising to me, and, although I have always appreciated Mitchell's keen intellect, until I systematically reviewed all his writings I did not realize the depth and breadth of his contributions. When I said earlier that I belatedly mourn his passing, it is not that I did not mourn his passing at the time of his untimely death. Rather, the mourning reaction recurred in the writing of some of this volume. In a cogent manner (best described by Aron) he has provided a critique that should stimulate all analysts to consider the points that he has raised. Although I believe implicitly that I have a long history of agreeing with many of his arguments, even where I have felt that I have been in agreement he has caused me to pause and reflect on why I would agree. I have been obliged to ask how the relational critiques alter my theoretical or clinical matrix. For example, if I believe that the analysis of transference is an important aspect of analytic treatment, how do I reconcile this view with the challenge to concepts such as anonymity and abstinence? In fact, what do I mean by transference if I believe that, to some extent, most interactions are co-constructed? If I agree with many relational challenges, how does this change my ideas about transference and the treatment situation? I have tried to answer these questions in Chapter Seventeen, but, clearly, the analysis that Mitchell and others have provided has powerfully touched my theory and my clinical work. Of course, this influence started with Sullivan (for me through Searles) and Fairbairn (for me through Guntrip). Both Guntrip and Searles provided powerful clinical concepts and illustrations that convinced me that the classical theory, or, at least, the version from the USA, was not my theory.

Of course, it should be clear that many of my views have been touched by various classical writers. Arlow's exquisite but limited view of the role of fantasy is, for me, important and illustrative of how one can be influenced by a perspective but not consider oneself part of that theoretical matrix. Arlow's highlighting the role of fantasy is an important reminder, but his emphasis tends towards the monolithic. Moreover, the importance of Oedipal dynamics for him and Brenner is as overstated as is Fairbairn's emphasis on schizoid dynamics, or love made hungry. Yet, both points of view have sensitized me to important dynamics. I still believe that Freud's theoretical base provides the widest support for a new theory, but I also believe that Kleinian and Bionian theory are compatible with that base. Both of these theorists have changed the landscape of therapeutic interactions. I would change the time sequence of Klein's developmental theory, but this is a task for another time. Still, in my view, Klein, Bion and the neo-Kleinians have extended and reshaped the base that Freud provided.

Many self-psychoanalysts find Kleinian theory to be at odds with their theoretical views. I, on the other hand, find a great deal of compatibility between Winnicott, Bion, and Kohut. All focus on the present moment in a manner that allows the past (or the patient's experience consolidated in memory) to be present seamlessly. Clearly, Kohut has strongly influenced my concept of analytic trust. Bach has developed ideas about narcissism and the treatment situation that extend Kohut's concepts and bridge the gap between self and object Freudians and Kohutians. I have tried to indicate in Chapter Seventeen how this bridge is formed, and which conceptual masses are joined by it. Clearly, I believe almost every theorist that I have covered has extended my ideas about development and, more germanely, the therapeutic situation. Certainly, Sullivan and Winnicott provide models for authenticity that I find important and clinically compelling. Although I have not cited her enough, Edith Jacobson is a figure behind most of the developmental and clinical concepts that I have enunciated. The idea of endogenous stimulation being shaped by the environment is a direct paraphrasing of her view of drive.

Issues of development and psychoanalytic developmental theory

Here, I have tried to show how variations in endogenous factors or environmental factors might produce an infant that looks more like the infants that Klein described, and other factors might produce infants that look more like infants that Winnicott has described. Looking at these factors in Chapter Eighteen was clearly not meant as a developmental theory, but, rather, as a part of a theory that has moving pieces and attempts to have multiple factors that are weighted differently, depending on both endogenous and exogenous factors. As I alluded to earlier, one of the most important exogenous factors is the culture of a given family. The culture will set the adaptation conditions for the infant/developing child. These conditions will have to be included more explicitly in all types of psychoanalytic theories. To repeat what I have just stated, Jacobson's concepts have certainly guided this environmental view.

While I have used the term "multiple factor model", I have meant this as an inclusive term. Thus, Lichtenberg's (1992) hierarchical model is, for me, one example of a multiple factor model. Similarly, the writing on gender by Harris (2004) is another multiple factor model. In a separate publication, I plan to write on the uses and limitations of chaos theory as a multiple factor model. This is, unfortunately, not possible in the present volume.

Overall structure

I have included a number of theorists in order both to refer to these theorists and to allow the reader to determine if their view of a given theorist coincides with mine. I have tried to enter the world of each theorist, but, undoubtedly, the world that I have fashioned is not one that every reader has entered. The statement about each theorist allows the reader to challenge my views and fashion their own theoretical vision. It has also seemed important to me to try to show how various theories have developed. It is useful to see what a theorist is opposing as well as what they are embracing. It is my hope that this work encourages more theoretical touching and the constructing of wider and deeper psychoanalytic theories.

REFERENCES

Abelin, E. L. (1975). Some further observations and comments on the earliest role of the father. *International Journal of Psychoanalysis, 56*: 293–301.
Abend, S. (1979). Unconscious fantasy and theories of cure. *Journal of the American Psychoanalytic Association, 27*: 579–596.
Abend, S. (1989). Countertransference and psychoanalytic technique. *Psychoanalytic Quarterly, 58*: 374–395.
Abraham, K. (1921a). Contributions of the theory of anal character. *International Journal of Psychoanalysis, 4*: 400–418.
Abraham, K. (1921b). Psychoanalytic studies on character formation. In: *Selected Papers on Psychoanalysis.* London: Hogarth, 1927.
Abraham, K. (1924). A short study of the development of the libido, viewed in the light of mental disorders. In: *Selected Papers on Psychoanalysis.* London: Hogarth, 1927.
Abraham, K. (1925). The influence of oral erotism on character-formation. *International Journal of Psycho-Analysis, 6*: 247–258.
Akhtar, S. (1994). Object constancy and adult psychopathology. *International Journal of Psycho-Analysis, 75*: 441–455.
Alexander, F. (1956). *Psychoanalysis and Psychotherapy.* New York: Norton.

Alexander, F., French, T. M., Bacon, C. L., Benedek, T., Fuerst, R. A., Wilson, M., Grinker, R. R., Grotjahn, M., McFadyen Johnson, A., Vincent McLean, H., & Weiss, E. (1946). *Psychoanalytic Therapy, Principles and Application*. New York: The Ronald Press Co.

Alfasi-Siffert, G. (1985). Unpublished Doctoral dissertation.

American Psychiatric Association (1980). *Diagnostic and Statistical Manual of Mental Disorders* (3rd edn). Washington, DC: American Psychiatric Association.

Anthony, E. J. (1980). The family and the psychoanalytic process in children. *Psychoanalytic Study of the Child, 35*: 3–34.

Anzieu, D. (1989). *The Skin Ego*, C. Turner (Trans.). New Haven, CT: Yale University Press.

Arlow, J. A. (1963). The supervisory situation. *Journal of the American Psychoanalytic Association, 11*: 576–594.

Arlow, J. A. (1969a). Fantasy, memory, and reality testing. *Psychoanalytic Quarterly, 38*: 28–51.

Arlow, J. A. (1969b). Unconscious fantasy and disturbances of conscious experience. *Psychoanalytic Quarterly, 38*(1): 1–27.

Arlow, J. A. (1970). Heinz Hartmann—1894–1970. *Psychoanalytic Quarterly, 39*: 620–621.

Arlow, J. A. (1971). Character perversion. In: I. M. Marcus (Ed.), *Currents in Psychoanalysis* (pp. 317–336). New York: International Universities Press.

Arlow, J. A. (1979). The genesis of interpretation. *Journal of the American Psychoanalytic Association, 27*: 193–207.

Arlow, J. A. (1985). Some technical problems of countertransference. *Psychoanalytic Quarterly, 54*: 164–174.

Arlow, J. A., & Brenner, C. (1964). *Psychoanalytic Concepts and the Structural Theory*. New York: International Universities Press.

Aron, L. (1996). *A Meeting of the Minds: Mutuality in Psychoanalysis*. Hillsdale, NJ: The Analytic Press.

Aron, L. (1999). Toward a triadic relational theory. *Psychoanalytic Dialogues, 9*: 441–443.

Aron, L. (2006). Analytic impasse and the third: clinical implications of intersubjectivity theory. *International Journal of Psychoanalysis, 87*: 349–368.

Aserinsky, E., & Kleitman, N. (1953). Regularly occurring periods of eye motility and concomitant phenomena during sleep. *Science, 118*: 273–275.

Ayer, A. J. (1956). *The Problem of Knowledge*. London: Macmillan.

Ayer, A. J. (1972). *Probability and Evidence*. London: Macmillan.

Bach, S. (1985). *Narcissistic States and the Therapeutic Process.* Northvale, NJ: Jason Aronson.
Bach, S. (1994). *The Language of Perversion and the Language of Love.* Northvale, NJ: Jason Aronson.
Bach, S. (2006). *Getting From Here to There: Analytic Love, Analytic Process.* Hillsdale, NJ: The Analytic Press.
Bachant, J. L., & Richards, A. D. (1993). Relational concepts in psychoanalysis: an integration, S. A. Mitchell (Ed.). *Psychoanalytic Dialogues,* 3: 431–460.
Bachant, J. L., Lynch, A. A., & Richards, A. D. (1995a). The evolution of drive theory: a response to Merton Gill. *Psychoanalytic Psychology,* 12: 565–573.
Bachant, J. L., Lynch, A. A., & Richards, A. D. (1995b). The evolution of drive theory: a response to Merton Gill. *Psychoanalytic Psychology,* 12: 71–87.
Balint, M. (1958). The three areas of mind—theoretical considerations. *International Journal of Psychoanalysis,* 39: 328–340.
Balint, M. (1968). *The Basic Fault: Therapeutic Aspects of Regression.* New York: Brunner/Mazel.
Benjamin, J. (1995). *Like Subjects, Like Objects: Recognition And Sexual Difference.* New Haven, CT: Yale University Press.
Benjamin, J. (2000). Intersubjective distinctions: subjects and persons, recognitions and breakdowns. *Psychoanalytic Dialogues,* 10: 43–55.
Beres, D. (1962). The unconscious fantasy. *Psychoanalytic Quarterly,* 31: 309–328.
Beres, D. (1965). Structure and function in psycho-analysis. *International Journal of Psychoanalysis,* 46: 53–63.
Bergman, A. (1980). Ours, yours, mine. In: R. F. Lax, S. Bach, & J. A. Bland (Eds.), *Rapprochement: The Critical Subphase of Separation–Individuation* (pp. 199–216). New York: Aronson.
Bergman, A. (1982). Considerations about the development of the girl during the separation–individuation process. In: D. Mendell (Ed.), *Early Female Development: Current Psychoanalytic Views* (pp. 61–80). New York: Spectrum Publications.
Bergman, A. (1999). *Ours, Yours, Mine: Mutuality and the Emergence of the Separate Self.* Northvale, NJ: Jason Aronson.
Bergman, A., & Chernack, M. (1982). From command to request: the development of language in the treatment of symbiotic psychotic child. *International Journal of Psychoanalytic Psychotherapy,* 9: 583–602.

Bergman, A., & Ellman, S. J. (1985). Margaret S. Mahler: symbiosis and separation–individuation. In: J. Reppen (Ed.), *Beyond Freud* (pp. 231–256). Hillsdale, NJ: Analytic Press.
Bergman, P., & Escalona, S. K. (1949). Unusual sensitivities in very young children. *The Psychoanalytic Study of the Child*, 4: 333–352.
Bergmann, M. (Ed.) (2000). *The Hartmann Era*. New York: Other Press.
Berman, E. (1996). Searching for Winnicott. *Contemporary Psychoanalysis*, 32: 158.
Bibring, E. (1941). The development and problems of the theory of instincts. *International Journal of Psychoanalysis*, 22: 102–131.
Bion, W. R. (1957). Differentiation of the psychotic from the non-psychotic personalities. In: *Second Thoughts: Selected Papers on Psychoanalysis* (pp.43–64). London: Heinemann, 1967.
Bion, W. R. (1959). Attacks on linking. *International Journal of Psycho-Analysis*, 40: 308–315. Reprinted in: *Second Thoughts: Selected Papers on Psychoanalysis* (pp. 93–109). London: Heinemann, 1967.
Bion, W. R. (1962a). A theory of thinking. In: *Second Thoughts: Selected Papers on Psychoanalysis* (pp. 110–119). London: Heinemann, 1967.
Bion, W. R. (1962b). *Learning from Experience*. London: Tavistock.
Bion, W. R. (1963). *Elements of Psycho-analysis*. London: Heinemann.
Bion, W. R. (1965). *Transformations*. London: Heinemann.
Bion, W. R. (1967a). Notes on memory and desire. In: *Cogitations* (pp. 380–385). London: Karnac.
Bion, W. R. (1967b). *Second Thoughts: Selected Papers on Psychoanalysis*. New York: Jason Aronson.
Bion, W. R. (1970). *Attention and Interpretation*. London: Heinemann.
Bion, W. R. (1977). *Two Papers: The Grid and Caesura*, J. Salomao (Ed.). Rio de Janeiro: Imago Editora [revised edition London: Karnac, 1989].
Bion W. R. (1985). *All My Sins Remembered: Another Part of a Life*. Oxford: Fleetwood Press.
Bion, W. R., Rosenfeld, H., & Segal, H. (1961). Melanie Klein. *International Journal of Psychoanalysis*, 42: 4–8.
Bird, B. (1972). Notes on transference: universal phenomenon and hardest part of the analysis. *Journal of the American Psychoanalytic Association*, 20: 267–301.
Bodnar, R., Ellman, S. J., Coons, E. E., Achermann, R. R., & Steiner, S. S. (1979). Differential locus coerulues and hypothalamic self-stimulation interactions. *Physiological Psychology*, 7: 269–277.
Bodnar, R., Steiner, S. S., Frutus, M., Ippolito, P., & Ellman, S. J. (1978a). Hypothalamic self-stimulation differs as a function of anodal locus. *Physiological Psychology*, 6: 48–52.

Bodnar, R., Steiner, S. S., Healey, J., Halperin, J., & Ellman, S. J. (1978b). Monophasic pulse pair analysis of intracranial self-stimulation loci. *Physiological Psychology*, 6(2): 48–52.

Boesky, D. (1982). Acting out: a reconsideration of the concept. *International Journal of Psychoanalysis*, 63: 39–55.

Boesky, D. (1988). Comments on the structural theory of technique. *International Journal of Psychoanalysis*, 69: 303–316.

Bollas, C. (1989). *Forces of Destiny: Psychoanalysis and Human Idiom*. London: Free Association.

Boris, H. N. (1986). Bion re-visited. *Contemporary Psychoanalysis*, 22(2): 159–184.

Bowlby, J. (1969). *Attachment and Loss: Vol. 1. Attachment*. New York: Basic Books.

Bowlby, J. (1973). *Attachment and Loss: Vol. 2. Separation*. New York: Basic Books.

Bowlby, J. (1980). *Loss: Sadness and Depression*. London: Hogarth.

Brazelton, T. B. (1974). The origins of reciprocity: the early mother-infant interaction. In: M. Lewis & L. A. Rosenblum (Eds.), *The Effect of the Infant on its Caregiver* (pp. 49–76). New York: Wiley.

Brazelton, T. B. (1981). Neonatal assessment. In: S. I. Greenspan & G. H. Pollock (Eds.), *The Course of Life: Psychoanalytic Contributions Toward Understanding Human Development*, Vol. 1 (pp. 203–233). Washington, DC: U.S. Government Printing Office.

Brenner, C. (1955). *An Elementary Textbook of Psychoanalysis*. New York: International Universities Press.

Brenner, C. (1976). *Psychoanalytic Technique and Psychic Conflict*. New York: International Universities Press.

Brenner, C. (1979). Working alliance, therapeutic alliance, and transference. *Journal of the American Psychoanalytic Association*, 27: 137–158.

Brenner, C. (1982). *The Mind in Conflict*. New York: International Universities Press.

Brenner, C. (1985). Countertransference as compromise formation. *Psychoanalytic Quarterly*, 54: 155–163.

Brenner, C. (1994). Mind as conflict and compromise formation. *Journal of Clinical Psychoanalysis*, 3(4): 473–488.

Brenner, C. (1995). Some remarks on psychoanalytic technique. *Journal of Clinical Psychoanalysis*, 4(4): 413–428.

Brenner, C. (1996). *Beyond the Ego and Id Revisited*. An internet discussion at Clinical Psychoanalysis.org.

Breuer, J., & Freud, S. (1893a). On the psychical mechanism of hysterical phenomena. *S.E.*, 2: 3–17. London: Hogarth.

Breuer, J., & Freud, S. (1895d). *Studies on Hysteria. S.E.*, 2: 1–306. London: Hogarth.
Bridgeman, P. W. (1927). *The Logic of Modern Physics*. New York: MacMillan.
Britton, R. (1997). The missing link: parental sexuality in the Oedipus complex. In: R. Schafer (Ed.), *The London Kleinians* (pp. 242–259). Madison, CT: International Universities Press.
Bromberg, P. (2001). *Standing in the Spaces*. New York: Routledge.
Bruner, J. (1993). Loyal opposition and the clarity of dissent: commentary on Donald P. Spence's "The Hermeneutic Turn". *Psychoanalytic Dialogues*, 3: 11–19.
Bucci, W. (1985). Dualcoding: a cognitive model for psychoanalytic research. *Journal of the American Psychoanalytic Association*, 33: 571–607.
Busch, F. (1995). *The Ego at the Center of Clinical Technique*. Northvale, NJ: Jason Aronson.
Busch, F. (2006). Talking with strangers. *Psychoanalytic Review*, 93: 463–475 [*The Ego at the Center of Clinical Technique*. Northvale, NJ: Jason Aronson].
Busch, F. (2007). The emergence of self-observation in relationship to pathological attractor sites. *International Journal of Psychoanalysis*, 88(2): 423–441.
Calef, V., & Weinshel, E. M. (1979). The new psychoanalysis and psychoanalytic revisionism. *Psychoanalytic Quarterly*, 48: 470–491.
Carnap, R. (1952). *The Continuum of Inductive Methods*. Chicago: University of Chicago Press.
Carr, A. C., Goldstein, E. G., Hunt, H. F., & Kernberg, O. F. (1979). Psychological tests and borderline patients. *Journal of Personality Assessment*, 43: 582–590.
Carsky, M., & Ellman, S. (1985). Otto Kernberg: psychoanalysis and object relations theory: the beginnings of an integrative approach. In: J. Reppen (Ed.), *Beyond Freud* (pp. 257–296). Hillsdale, NJ: Analytic Press.
Chodorow, N. (1989). *Feminism and Psychoanalytic Theory*. New Haven, CT: Yale University Press.
Chused, J. E. (1991). The evocative power of enactments. *Journal of the American Psychoanalytic Association*, 39(3): 615–640.
Chused, J. E. (1996). The therapeutic action of psychoanalysis: abstinence and information. *Journal of the American Psychoanalytic Association*, 44: 1047–1071.

Cohen, M. B. (1952). Countertransference and anxiety. *Psychiatry*, 15: 231–243.
Coles, R. (1992). *Anna Freud: The Dream of Psychoanalysis*. New York: Addison-Wesley.
Damasio, A. (1994). *Descartes' Error*. New York: G. P. Putnam's Sons.
Deutsch, H. (1925). The psychology of women in relation to the functions of reproduction. *International Journal of Psycho-Analysis*, 6: 405–418.
Deutsch, H. (1942). Some forms of emotional disturbance and their relationship to schizophrenia. *Psychoanalytic Quarterly*, 11: 301–321.
Diamond, J. (2006). *The Third Chimpanzee: The Evolution and Future of the Human Animal*. New York: HarperCollins.
Eissler, K. R. (1971). *Talent and Genius*. New York: World Publishing.
Eissler, K. R. (1985). *Three Instances of Injustice*. Madison, CT: International Universities Press.
Ellmann, R. (1987). *Oscar Wilde*. New York: Viking Press.
Ellman, S. J. (1991). *Freud's Technique Papers: A Contemporary Perspective*. Northvale, NJ: Jason Aronson.
Ellman, S. J. (1992). Psychoanalytic theory, dream formation and REM sleep. In: J. Barron, M. Eagle & D. Wolitsky (Eds.), *Interface of Psychoanalysis and Psychology* (pp. 357–374). Washington, DC: American Psychological Association.
Ellman, S. J. (1996). Commentary on the British Schools of psychoanalysis. In: D. Hill & C. Grand (Eds.), *British Schools of Psychoanalysis* (pp. 49–72). Northvale, NJ: Jason Aronson.
Ellman, S. J. (1997a). An analyst at work. In: J. Reppen (Ed.), *More Analysts at Work* (pp. 91–115). Northvale, NJ: Jason Aronson.
Ellman, S. J. (1997b). Termination and long term analysis. *Psychoanalytic Psychology*, 14(2): 197–210.
Ellman, S. J. (1998a). Enactment, transference, and analytic trust. In: S. Ellman & M. Moskowitz (Eds.), *Enactment: Toward a New Approach to the Therapeutic Relationship* (pp. 183–203). Northvale, NJ: Jason Aronson.
Ellman, S. J. (1998b). The unique contribution of the contemporary Freudian position. In: C. Ellman, S. Grand, M. Silvan, & S. Ellman (Eds.), *The Modern Freudians: Contemporary Psychoanalytic Technique*. Northvale, NJ: Jason Aronson.
Ellman, S, J. (1999). The concept of enactment: cutting edge or current fad. *Journal of Clinical Psychoanalysis*, 8(1): 9–61.
Ellman, S. J. (2000). Dreams: commentary of paper by Hazel Ipp. *Psychoanalytic Dialogues*, 10: 143–157.

Ellman, S. J. (2005). Book review: psychoanalysis and research. *Journal of the American Psychoanalytic Association, 53*: 639–643.
Ellman, S. J. (2007). Analytic trust and transference: love, healing ruptures and facilitating repairs. *Psychoanalytic Inquiry, 27*: 246–263.
Ellman, S. J., & Antrobus, J. (1991). *The Mind in Sleep: Psychology and Psychophysiology.* New York: Wiley.
Ellman, S. J., & Moskowitz, M. (1980). An examination of some recent criticisms of psychoanalytic "metapsychology". *Psychoanalytic Quarterly, 49*: 630–662.
Ellman, S. J., & Moskowitz, M. (Eds.) (1998). *Enactment: Toward a New Approach to the Therapeutic Relationship.* Northvale, NJ: Jason Aronson.
Ellman, S. J., & Steiner, S. S. (1971). Relation between REM sleep and intracranial self-stimulation; a reciprocal activating system. *Brain Research, 19*(2): 290–296.
Ellman, S., & Weinstein, L. (1991). REM sleep and dream formation: a theoretical integration. In: *The Mind in Sleep: Psychology and Psychophysiology.* New York & London: Wiley.
Ellman, S. J., Achermann, R. F., Bodnar, R. J., Jackler, F., & Steiner, S. S. (1973). Differential mediation of intracranial self-stimulation in rat dorsal midbrain areas. *Physiology and Behavior, 11*: 592–596.
Ellman, S. J., Achermann, R. F., Bodnar, R. J., Jackler, F., & Steiner, S. S. (1975). Comparison of behaviors elicited by electrical brain stimulation in dorsal brainstem and hypothalamus of rats. *Journal of Comparative Physiological Psychology, 88*, 316–328.
Ellman, S. J., Achermann, R. F., Farber, J., Mattiace, L., & Steiner, S. S. (1974). Relationship between dorsal brain stem sleep sites and intracranial self-stimulation. *Physiology and Behavior, 2*(1): 31–34.
Emde, R., Gaensbauer, T., & Harmon, R. (1976). Emotional expression in infancy: a biobehavioral study. *Psychological Issues, 10*(1) Monograph 37.
Erikson, E. H. (1956). The problem of ego identity. *Journal of the American Psychoanalytic Association, 4*: 56–121.
Fairbairn, W. R. D. (1940). Schizoid factors in the personality. In: *Psychoanalytic Studies of the Personality* (pp. 3–27). London: Routledge & Kegan Paul, 1952.
Fairbairn, W. R. D. (1941). A revised psychopathology of the psychoses and psychoneuroses. In: *Psychoanalytic Studies of the Personality* (pp. 28–58). London: Routledge & Kegan Paul, 1952.
Fairbairn, W. R. D. (1943). The repression and the return of bad objects. In: *Psychoanalytic Studies of the Personality* (pp. 59–81). London: Routledge & Kegan Paul, 1952.

Fairbairn, W. R. D. (1944). Endopsychic structure considered in terms of object-relationships. In: *Psychoanalytic Studies of the Personality* (pp. 82–136). London: Routledge & Kegan Paul, 1952.
Fairbairn, W. R. D. (1946). Object relationships and dynamic structure. In: *Psychoanalytic Studies of the Personality* (pp. 137–151). London: Routledge & Kegan Paul, 1952.
Fairbairn, W. R. D. (1951). A synopsis of the development of the author's views regarding the structure of the personality. In: *Psychoanalytic Studies of the Personality* (pp. 162–179). London, Henley & Boston: Routledge & Kegan Paul, 1952.
Fairbairn, W. R. D. (1952). *An Object-Relations Theory of the Personality*. New York: Basic Books.
Fairbairn, W. R. D. (1956). Reevaluating some basic concepts. In: D. E. Scharff & E. F. Birtles (Eds.), *From Instinct to Self: Selected Papers of W. R. D. Fairbairn, Volume 1: Clinical and Theoretical Papers* (pp. 129–138). Northvale, NJ: Jason Aronson, 1994.
Farber, J., Ellman, S. J., Mattiace, L., Holtzman, A., Ippolito, P., Halperin, R., & Steiner, S. S. (1976). Differential effects of bilateral dorsal hindbrain lesions on hypothalamic self-stimulation in the rat. *Brain Research*, 117: 148–155.
Federn, P. (1947). Principles of psychotherapy in latent schizophrenia. *American Journal of Psychotherapy*, 1: 129–139.
Ferenczi, S. (1909). Introjection and transference. In: *Sex in Psychoanalysis* (pp. 35–57). New York: Basic Books.
Ferenczi, S. (1920). The further development of an active therapy in psychoanalysis. In: *Further Contributions to the Theory and Technique of Psychoanalysis*. New York: Brunner/Mazel.
Ferro, A. (2009). *Mind Works: Technique and Creativity in Psychoanalysis*. London: Routledge.
Fonagy, P., & Target, M. (2002). Early intervention and the development of self-regulation. *Psychoanalytic Inquiry*, 22: 307–335.
Fosshage, J. (1994). Toward reconceptualizing transference: theoretical and clinical considerations. *International Journal of Psycho-Analysis*, 75(2): 265–280.
Foucault, M. (1994). *The Order of Things: An Archeology of the Human Sciences*, A. Sheridan (Trans.). New York: Vintage Books.
Freedman, N. (1994). More on transformation enactments. In: A. K. Richards & A. P. Richards (Eds.), *The Spectrum of Psychoanalysis: Essays in Honor of Martin S. Bergmann* (pp. 93–110). Madison, CT: International Universities Press.

Freedman, N., & Lavender, J. (2002). On desymbolization: the concept and observation. *Psychoanalytic Contemporary Thought, 25*: 165–199.

Freud, A. (1927). *Introduction to the Technique of the Analysis of Children*. London: Image, 1946.

Freud, A. (1946). *The Ego and the Mechanisms of Defense*. New York: International Universities Press.

Freud, A. (1965). *Normality and Pathology in Childhood: Assessment of Development*. New York: International Universities Press.

Freud, S. (1888). Preface to the translation of Bernheim's *Suggestion*. *S.E., 1*: 73–87. London: Hogarth.

Freud, S. (1894). Extracts from the Fliess papers. Draft E: How anxiety originates. *S.E., 1*: 189–194. London: Hogarth.

Freud, S. (1894a). The neuro-psychoses of defence. *S.E., 3*: 43–61. London: Hogarth.

Freud, S. (1895a). *A Project for a Scientific Psychology. S.E., 1*: 283–397. London: Hogarth.

Freud, S. (1895b). On the grounds for detaching a particular syndrome from neurasthenia under the description of anxiety neurosis. *S.E., 3*: 87–114. London: Hogarth.

Freud, S. (1898a). Sexuality in the aetiology of the neuroses. *S.E., 3*: 263–285. London: Hogarth.

Freud, S. (1900a). *The Interpretation of Dreams. S.E., 4–5*. London: Hogarth.

Freud, S. (1901b). *The Psychopathology of Everyday Life. S.E., 6*. London: Hogarth.

Freud, S. (1905c). *Jokes and Their Relation to the Unconscious. S.E., 8*. London: Hogarth.

Freud, S. (1905d). *Three Essays on the Theory of Sexuality. S.E., 7*: 125–245. London: Hogarth.

Freud, S. (1905e). *Fragment of an Analysis of a Case of Hysteria. S.E., 7*: 7–122. London: Hogarth.

Freud, S. (1907b). Obsessive actions and religious practices. *S.E., 9*: 116–127. London: Hogarth.

Freud, S. (1908b). Character and anal erotism. *S.E., 9*: 169–175. London: Hogarth.

Freud, S. (1909b). Analysis of a phobia in a five-year-old boy. *S.E., 10*: 3–149. London: Hogarth.

Freud, S. (1909d). Notes upon a case of obsessional neurosis. *S.E., 10*: 153–249. London: Hogarth.

Freud, S. (1910c). Leonardo da Vinci and a memory of his childhood. *S.E., 11*: 59–137. London: Hogarth.

REFERENCES 667

Freud, S. (1911b). Formulations on the two principles of mental functioning. *S.E., 12*: 213–226. London: Hogarth.
Freud, S. (1911c). *Psycho-analytic Notes on an Autobiographical Account of a Case of Paranoia (dementia paranoides)*. *S.E., 12*: 3–82. London: Hogarth.
Freud, S. (1912b). The dynamics of transference. *S.E., 12*: 97–108. London: Hogarth.
Freud, S. (1912e). Recommendations to physicians practising psychoanalysis. *S.E., 12*: 109–120. London: Hogarth.
Freud, S. (1912–1913). *Totem and Taboo. S.E., 13*: 1–255. London: Hogarth.
Freud, S. (1913). Letter to Ludwig Binswanger of February 20, 1913. In: *Erinnerungen an Sigmund Freud* (p. 65). Bern: Francke Verlag, 1956.
Freud, S. (1913i). The disposition to obsessional neurosis: a contribution to the problem of the choice of neurosis. *S.E., 12*: 313–326. London: Hogarth.
Freud, S. (1913m). On psycho-analysis. *S.E., 12*: 205–212. London: Hogarth.
Freud, S. (1914c). On narcissism. *S.E., 14*: 67–104. London: Hogarth.
Freud, S. (1914g) Remembering, repeating and working-through. *S.E., 12*: 145–156. London: Hogarth. London: Hogarth.
Freud, S. (1914d). On the history of the psycho-analytic movement. *S.E., 14*: 3–66. London: Hogarth.
Freud, S. (1915c). Instincts and their vicissitudes. *S.E., 14*: 111–140. London: Hogarth.
Freud, S. (1915a). Observations on transference-love. *S.E., 12*: 157–171. London: Hogarth.
Freud, S. (1915d). Repression. *S.E., 14*: 143–158. London: Hogarth.
Freud, S. (1915e). The unconscious. *S.E., 14*: 161–215. London: Hogarth.
Freud, S. (1916a). Some character types met with in psychoanalytic work. *S.E., 14*: 309–336. London: Hogarth.
Freud, S. (1916–1917). *Introductory Lectures on Psycho-analysis. S.E., 15/16*: 243–448. London: Hogarth.
Freud, S. (1917d). A metapsychological supplement to the theory of dreams. *S.E., 14*: 222–235. London: Hogarth.
Freud, S. (1917e). Mourning and melancholia. *S.E., 14*: 239–258. London: Hogarth.
Freud, S. (1918b). *From the History of an Infantile Neurosis. S.E., 17*: 7–122. London: Hogarth.
Freud, S. (1919e). "A child is being beaten": a contribution to the study of the origin of sexual perversions. *S.E., 17*: 177–204. London: Hogarth.

Freud, S. (1920a). The psychogenesis of a case of homosexuality in a woman. *S.E., 18*: 146–172. London: Hogarth.
Freud, S. (1920d). Associations of a four-year-old child. *S.E., 18*: 266. London: Hogarth.
Freud, S. (1920g). *Beyond the Pleasure Principle. S.E., 18*: 7–64. London: Hogarth.
Freud, S. (1921c). *Group Psychology and the Analysis of the Ego. S.E., 18*: 67–143. London: Hogarth.
Freud, S. (1922b). Some neurotic mechanisms in jealousy, paranoia, and homosexuality. *S.E., 18*: 221. London: Hogarth.
Freud, S. (1923b). *The Ego and the Id. S.E., 19*: 3–66. London: Hogarth.
Freud, S. (1923c). Remarks on the theory and practice of dream-interpretation. *S.E., 19*: 109–121. London: Hogarth.
Freud, S. (1924d). The dissolution of the Oedipus complex. *S.E., 19*: 172–179. London: Hogarth.
Freud, S. (1925h). Negation. *S.E., 19*: 235–239. London: Hogarth.
Freud, S. (1925j). Some psychical consequences of the anatomical distinction between the sexes. *S.E., 19*: 243–258. London: Hogarth.
Freud, S. (1926d). *Inhibitions, Symptoms and Anxiety. S.E., 20*: 77–174. London: Hogarth.
Freud, S. (1927e). Fetishism. *S.E., 21*: 152–159. London: Hogarth.
Freud, S. (1930a). *Civilization and Its Discontents. S.E., 21*: 59–145. London: Hogarth.
Freud, S. (1933a). *New Introductory Lectures on Psycho-analysis. S.E., 22*: 3–182. London: Hogarth.
Freud, S. (1937c). Analysis terminable and interminable. *S.E., 23*: 211–253. London: Hogarth.
Freud, S. (1937d). Constructions in analysis. *S.E., 23*: 257–269. London: Hogarth.
Freud, S. (1939a). *Moses and Monotheism. S.E., 23*: 3–137. London: Hogarth.
Freud, S. (1940a). *An Outline of Psycho-analysis. S.E., 23*: 141–291. London: Hogarth.
Freud, S. (1987). *A Phylogenetic Fantasy: Overview of the Transference Neuroses*. E. Grubrich-Smitis, A. Hoffer, & P. Hoffer (Eds.). Cambridge, MA: Harvard University Press.
Freud, S., & Bullitt, W. (1967). *Thomas Woodrow Wilson, A Psychological Study*. Boston, MA: Houghton Mifflin.
Friedman, J. A. (1988). The idea of narcissism in Freud's psychoanalysis. *International Review of Psychoanalysis, 15*: 499–514.

Friedman, L. (1977). A view of the background of Freudian theory. *Psychoanalytic Quarterly, 46*: 425–465.
Friedman, L. (1988). *The Anatomy of Psychotherapy*. Hillsdale, NJ: Analytic Press.
Friedman, L. (1992). How and why do patients become more objective? Sterba compared with Strachey. *Psychoanalytic Quarterly, 61*: 1–17.
Friedman, L. (2002). What lies beyond interpretation, and is that the right question? *Psychoanalytic. Psychology, 19*: 540–551.
Frosch, J. (1960). Psychotic character. *Journal of the American Psychoanalytic Association, 8*: 544–551.
Furer, M. (1967). Some developmental aspects of the superego. *International Journal of Psycho-Analysis, 48*: 277–280.
Gay, P. (1988). *Freud: A Life for Our Time*. New York: Norton.
Gedo, J., & Goldberg, A. (1973). *Models of the Mind: A Psychoanalytic Theory*. Chicago, IL: University of Chicago Press.
Gergely, G. (2004). The role of contingency detection in early affect-regulative interactions and in the development of different types of infant attachment. *Social Development, 13*(3): 468–478.
Gergely, G., & Watson, J. S. (1996). The social biofeedback theory of parental affect-mirroring. *International Journal Psycho-Analysis, 77*: 1181–1212.
Ghent, E. (2002). Wish, need, drive: motive in the light of dynamic systems theory and Edelman's selectionist theory. *Psychoanalytic Dialogues, 12*: 763–808.
Gill, M. M. (1976). Metapsychology is not psychology. In: M. M. Gill & P. S. Holzman (Eds.), *Psychology versus Metapsychology* (pp. 71–105). Psychoanalytic Essays in Honor of George S. Klein. New York: International Universities Press.
Gill, M. M. (1977). Psychic energy reconsidered—discussion. *Journal of the American Psychoanalytic Association, 25*: 581–597.
Gill, M. M. (1983). The point of view of psychoanalysis: energy discharge or person? *Psychoanalysis and Contemporary Thought, 6*: 523–551.
Gill, M. M. (1995). Classical and relational psychoanalysis. *Psychoanalytic Psychology, 12*: 89–107.
Gill, M. M., & Muslin, H. L. (1976). Early interpretation of transference. *Journal of the American Psychoanalytic Association, 24*: 779–794.
Gitelson, M. (1952). The emotional position of the analyst in the psychoanalytic situation. *International Journal of Psycho-Analysis, 33*: 1–10.
Globus, G. G. (1970). Rhythmic functions during sleep. In: E. Hartman (Ed.), *Sleep and Dreaming*. Boston: Little, Brown. International Psychiatry Clinics, 7(2).

Glover, E. (1925). Notes on oral character formation. *International Journal of Psycho-Analysis, 6*: 131.
Glover, E. (1955). *The technique of psychoanalysis*. New York International Universities Press.
Goldberger, M. (1995). The couch as defense and as potential for enactment. *Psychoanalytic Quarterly, 64*: 23–42.
Goldman, D. (1993a). *In Search of the Real: The Origins and Originality of D. W. Winnicott*. Northvale, NJ: Jason Aronson.
Goldman, D. (1993b). *In One's Bones: The Clinical Genius of Winnicott*. Northvale, NJ: Jason Aronson.
Good, M. I. (1995). Karl Abraham, Sigmund Freud, and the fate of the seduction theory. *Journal of the American Psychoanalytic Association, 43*: 1137–1167.
Good, M. I. (2006). *The Seduction Theory in its Second Century: Trauma, Fantasy and Reality Today* (pp. 245–263). Madison, CT: International Universities Press.
Gray, P. (1994). *The Ego and the Analysis of Defense*. Northvale, NJ: Jason Aronson.
Greenacre, P. (1954). The role of transference—practical considerations in relation to psychoanalytic therapy. *Journal of the American Psychoanalytic Association, 2*: 671–684.
Greenberg, Joanne (1964). *I Never Promised You a Rose Garden* (as Hannah Green). New York: Holt; London: Pan.
Greenberg, Jay (2001). Thinking, talking, playing: the peculiar goals of psychoanalysis. *Psychoanalytic Quarterly, 70*: 131–147.
Greenberg, Jay (2002). Psychoanalytic goals, therapeutic action, and the analyst's tension. *Psychoanalytic Quarterly, 71*: 651–678
Greenberg, Jay, & Mitchell, S. (1983). *Object Relations in Psychoanalytic Theory*. Cambridge, MA: Harvard University Press.
Greenson, R. R. (1954). The struggle against identification. *Journal of the American Psychoanalytic Association, 2*: 200–217.
Greenson, R. R. (1965). The working alliance and the transference neurosis. *Psychoanalytic Quarterly, 34*: 155–181.
Grosskurth, P. (1986). *Melanie Klein: Her Life and Her Work*. New York: Alfred A. Knopf.
Grotstein, J. (Ed.) (1981). *Do I Dare Disturb the Universe? A Memorial to Wilfred R. Bion*. Beverly Hills, CA: Caesura Press.
Grotstein, J. (1994). Cover note. In: D. E. Scharff & E. F. Birtles (Eds.), *From Instinct to Self: Selected Papers of W. R. D. Fairbairn*. Northvale, NJ: Jason Aronson.
Grotstein, J. (2007). *A Beam of Intense Darkness*. London: Karnac.

Gruness, M. (1984). The therapeutic object relationship. *Psychoanalytic Review, 71*: 123–143.

Guntrip, H. (1968). *Schizoid Phenomena, Object Relations, and the Self.* New York: International Universities Press.

Guntrip, H. (1971). *Psychoanalytic Theory, Therapy, and the Self.* New York: Basic Books.

Guntrip, H. (1975). My experience of analysis with Fairbairn and Winnicott. *International Journal of Psychoanalysis, 2*: 145–156.

Harris, A. (2004). *Gender as Soft Assembly.* New York: Routledge.

Hartmann, H. (1948). Comments on the psychoanalytic theory of instinctual drives. *Psychoanalytic Quarterly, 17*: 368–388.

Hartmann, H. (1950). Psychoanalysis and developmental psychology. In: *Essays on Ego Psychology: Selected Problems in Psychoanalytic Theory* (pp. 108–109). New York: International Universities Press, 1964.

Hartmann, H. (1951). Technical implications of ego psychology. In: *Essays on Ego Psychology: Selected Problems in Psychoanalytic Theory* (pp. 142–154). New York: International Universities Press, 1964.

Hartmann, H. (1953). Contribution to the metapsychology of schizophrenia. In: *Essays on Ego Psychology: Selected Problems in Psychoanalytic Theory* (pp. 182–206). New York: International Universities Press, 1964.

Hartmann, H. (Ed.) (1955a). Notes on the theory of sublimation. In: *Essays on Ego Psychology: Selected Problems in Psychoanalytic Theory* (pp. 215–240). New York: International Universities Press.

Hartmann, H. (Ed.) (1955b). The development of the ego concept in Freud's work. In: *Essays on Ego Psychology: Selected Problems in Psychoanalytic Theory* (pp. 268–296). New York: International Universities Press.

Hartmann, H. (1958). *Ego Psychology and the Problem of Adaptation* (first published in German in 1939). New York: International Universities Press.

Hartmann, H. (1964a). Psychoanalysis and the concept of health. In: *Essays on Ego Psychology: Selected Problems in Psychoanalytic Theory* (pp. 3–18). New York: International Universities Press.

Hartmann, H. (1964b). The development of the ego concept in Freud's work. In: *Essays on Ego Psychology: Selected Problems in Psychoanalytic Theory* (pp. 268–296). New York: International Universities Press.

Hartmann, H. (1964c). Concept formation in psychoanalysis. *Psychoanalytic Study of the Child, 19*: 11–47.

Hartmann, H., & Kris, E. (1945). The genetic approach in psychoanalysis. *Psychoanalytic Study of the Child*, 1: 11–30.
Hartmann, H., & Loewenstein, R. M. (1962). Notes on the superego. *Psychoanalytic Study of the Child*, 17: 42–81.
Hartmann, H., Kris, E., & Loewenstein, R. M. (1946). Comments on the formation of psychic structure. *Psychoanalytic Study of the Child*, 2: 11–38.
Hartmann, H., Kris, E., & Loewenstein, R. M. (1949). Notes on the theory of aggression. *Psychoanalytic Study of the Child*, 3–4: 9–36.
Heimann, P. (1943). Some aspects of the role of introjection and projection in early development. In: P. King & R. Steiner (Eds.), *The Freud–Klein Controversies* (pp. 687–709). London: Routledge, 1991.
Heimann, P. (1950). On countertransference. *International Journal of Psychoanalysis*, 31: 81–84.
Heimann, P. (1952). Certain functions of introjection and projection in early infancy. In: P. Heimann, S. Isaacs & J. Riviere (Eds.), *Developments in Psycho-Analysis*. London: Hogarth.
Heisenberg, W. (1979). *Philosophical Problems of Quantum Physics*. London: Ox Bow.
Hinshelwood, R. D. (1989). *A Dictionary of Kleinian Thought*. London: Free Association Books.
Hoffmann, I. Z. (1991). Discussion: toward a social-constructivist view of the psychoanalytic situation. *Psychoanalytic Dialogues*, 1: 74–105.
Hoffmann, I. Z. (1992). Some practical implications of a social constructionist view. *Psychoanalytic Dialogues*, 2: 287–304.
Hoffman, I. Z. (2002). Paper presented to the PEP CD Conference, Spring, New York.
Holder, A. (1970). Instinct and drive. In: H. Nagera (Ed.), *Basic Concepts of the Theory of Instincts*, Vol. 3 (pp. 19–22). New York: Basic Books.
Holt, R. (1974). Freud's mechanistic and humanistic images of man. *Psychoanalysis and Contemporary Science*, 1: 3–24.
Holt, R. (1989). *Freud Reappraised: A Fresh Look at Psychoanalytic Theory*. New York: Guilford Press.
Holt, R. (2002). Talk at Austin Riggs—Rappaport–Klein Study Group.
Hopkins, L. (2006). *False Self: The Life of Masud Khan*. New York: Other Press.
Hrdy, S. B. (1999). *A History of Mothers, Infants, and Natural Selection*. New York: Pantheon Books.
Hunziker, U. A., & Barr, R. G. (1986). Increased carrying reduces infant crying: a randomized controlled trial. *Pediatrics*, 77(5): 641–648.

Hurvich, M. (2003). The place of annihilation anxieties in psychoanalytic theory. *Journal of the American Psychoanalytic Association, 51*: 579–616.
Isaacs, S. (1943). The nature and function of phantasy. In: P. King & R. Steiner (Eds.), *The Freud–Klein Controversies* (pp. 264–321). London: Routledge, 1991.
Isaacs, S. (1952). The nature and function of phantasy. In: Klein et al. (Eds.), *Developments in Psychoanalysis*. London: Hogarth.
Jacobs, T. (1983). The analyst and the patient's object world: notes on an aspect of countertransference. *Journal of Clinical Psychoanalysis, 31*: 619–642.
Jacobs, T. (1986). On countertransference enactments. *Journal of the American Psychoanalytic Association, 34*: 289–307.
Jacobs, T. (1993). *The Use of the Self*. Madison, CT: International Universities Press.
Jacobson, E. (1954a). The self and the object world—vicissitudes of their infantile cathexes and their influence on ideational and affective development. *Psychoanalytic Study of the Child, 9*: 75–127.
Jacobson, E. (1954b). Contribution to the metapsychology of psychotic identifications. *Journal of the American Psychoanalytic Association, 2*: 239–262.
Jacobson, E. (1964). *The Self and the Object World*. New York: International Universities Press.
Jacobson, E. (1967). *Psychotic Conflict and Reality*. New York: International Universities Press.
Jones, E. (1952). Preface. In: W. R. D. Fairbairn, *An Object-Relations Theory of the Personality*. New York: Basic Books.
Jones, E. (1955). *Sigmund Freud Life and Work, Volume Two: Years of Maturity 1901–1919*. London: Hogarth.
Joseph, B. (1985). Transference: the total situation. *International Journal of Psychoanalysis, 66*: 447–454.
Kaufmann, P. (1983). Exploring the self psychological case book. Unpublished doctoral thesis, City University of New York.
Keats, J. (1817). *Letters of John Keats* (p. 43), R. Gittings (Ed.). London: Oxford University Press, 1970.
Kernberg, O. (1966). Structural derivatives of object relationships. *International Journal of Psychoanalysis, 47*: 236–253.
Kernberg, O. (1967). Borderline personality organization. *Journal of the American Psychoanalytic Association, 15*: 641–685.
Kernberg, O. (1975). *Borderline Conditions and Pathological Narcissism*. Northvale, NJ: Jason Aronson.

Kernberg, O. (1976). *Object Relations and Clinical Psychoanalysis.* New York: Jason Aronson.

Kernberg., O. (1977a). Characterological determinants of depression. Paper presented to the Symposium on Brief Psychotherapy, sponsored by the American Psychiatric Association, Ontario, Canada.

Kernberg, O. (1977b). Structural change and its impediments. In: P. Hartocollis (Ed.), *Borderline Personality Disorders* (pp. 275–306). New York: International Universities Press.

Kernberg, O. (1978). The diagnosis of borderline conditions in adolescence. *Adolescent Psychiatry,* 6: 298–319.

Kernberg, O. (1979a). Character structure and analyzability. Panel presentation for *Character Structure and Analyzability,* Scientific Meeting of the Association for Psycho-Analytic Medicine, New York.

Kernberg, O. (1979b). Psychoanalytic psychotherapy with borderline adolescents. In: S. C. Feinstein & P. L. Giovacchini (Eds.), *Adolescent Psychiatry,* Vol. 7 (pp. 294–321). Chicago: University of Chicago Press.

Kernberg, O. (1980a). *Contemporary Psychoanalytic Theories of Narcissism.* Unpublished manuscript.

Kernberg, O. (1980b). *Internal World and External Reality.* New York: Aronson.

Kernberg, O. (1980c). Neurosis, psychosis and the borderline states. In: H. I. Kaplan, A. M. Freedman & B. J. Sadock (Eds.), *Comprehensive Textbook of Psychiatry,*Vol. 3 (pp. 1079–1092). Baltimore: Williams & Wilkins.

Kernberg, O. (1980d). The place of affects in psychoanalytic theory. In: *New Directions in Affect Theory.* Panel at the Annual Meeting of the American Psychoanalytic Association, San Francisco.

Kernberg, O. (1981a). Countertransference, transference regression, and the incapacity to depend. In: *Current Concepts of Transference and Countertransference,* Symposium organized by the Association for Psychoanalytic Medicine, New York.

Kernberg, O. (1981b). *Dilemmas in research on long-terra psychotherapy.* Paper presented at the Annual Meeting for the Society for Psychotherapy Research, Aspen, Colorado.

Kernberg, O. (1981c). *Problems in the classification of personality disorders.* Presentation at clinical rounds, The New York Hospital-Cornell Medical College, Westchester Division.

Kernberg, O. (1981d). Structural interviewing. *Psychiatric Clinics of North America,* 4: 169–196.

Kernberg, O. (1982a). *An Ego Psychology-Object Relations Model of Psychoanalytic Psychotherapy.* Unpublished manuscript.
Kernberg, O. (1982b). *Identity, Alienation, and Ideology in Adolescence.* Presentation at the Annual Meeting of the American Society for Adolescent Psychiatry, Toronto, Ontario, Canada.
Kernberg, O. (1982c). *The Psychotherapeutic Treatment of Borderline Personalities.* Presentation at the review-update program on narcissistic and borderline personalities at the American Psychiatric Association, Toronto.
Kernberg, O. (1982d). Self, ego, affect, and drives. *Journal of the American Psychoanalytic Association,* 30: 893–918.
Kernberg, O. (1982e). Supportive psychotherapy with borderline conditions. In: J. O. Cavenar & H. K. Brodie (Eds.), *Critical Problems in Psychiatry* (pp. 180–202). Philadelphia, PA: Lippencott.
Kernberg, O., Burstein, E. D., Coyne, L., Appelbaum, A., Horwotz, L., & Voth, H. (1972). Psychotherapy and psychoanalysis: final report of the Menninger Foundation's psychotherapy research project. *Bulletin of the Menninger Clinic,* 36(1&2).
Kernberg, O., Yeomans, F. E., Clarkin, J. F., & Levy, K. N. (2008). Transference focused psychoanalysis. *International Journal of Psychoanalysis,* 89: 601–620.
King, P. (1989). Activities of the British Psychoanalytic Society during the Second World War and the influence of their interdisciplinary collaboration on the development of psychoanalysis in Great Britain. *International Review of Psychoanalysis,* 15: 15–33.
King, P. (1991). Background and development of the Freud–Klein controversies in the British Psychoanalytic Society. In: P. King & R. Steiner (Eds.), *The Freud–Klein Controversies.* London: Routledge.
King, P., & Steiner, R. (Eds.) (1991). *The Freud–Klein Controversies.* London: Routledge.
Klein, G. S. (1973). Is psychoanalysis relevant? *Psychoanalysis and Contemporary Science,* 2: 3–21.
Klein, G. S. (1976). Freud's two theories of sexuality. In: M. M. Gill & P. S. Holzman (Eds.), *Psychology versus Metapsychology: Psychoanalytic Essays in Honor of George S. Klein* (pp. 14–70). New York: International Universities Press.
Klein, M. (1927). Symposium on child analysis. In: *Love, Guilt and Reparation, and Other Works, 1921–1945* (pp. 139–169). New York: The Free Press.

Klein, M. (1928). The early stages of the Oedipus conflict. In: *Love, Guilt and Reparation, and Other Works, 1921–1945* (pp. 186–189). New York: The Free Press.

Klein, M. (1930). The importance of symbol-formation in the development of the ego. In: *Love, Guilt and Reparation, and Other Works, 1921–1945* (pp. 219–232). New York: Free Press.

Klein, M. (1932). *The Psychoanalysis of Children.* The International Psychoanalytic Library, No. 22. London: Hogarth.

Klein, M. (1933). The early development of conscience in the child. In: M. Klein & J. Riviere (Eds.), *Psychoanalysis Today.* New York: Covici-Friede.

Klein, M. (1935). A contribution to the psychogenesis of manic-depressive states. In: *Love, Guilt and Reparation, and Other Works, 1921–1945* (pp. 262–289). New York: Free Press.

Klein, M. (1937). Love, guilt and reparation. In: *Love, Guilt and Reparation, and Other Works, 1921–1945* (pp. 306–343). New York: Free Press.

Klein, M. (1940). Mourning and its relation to manic–depressive states. In: *Love, Guilt and Reparation, and Other Works, 1921–1945* (pp. 344–369). New York: Free Press.

Klein, M. (1945). The Oedipus complex in the light of early anxieties. In: *Love, Guilt and Reparation, and Other Works, 1921–1945* (pp. 370–418) New York: Free Press.

Klein, M. (1946). Notes on some schizoid mechanisms. In: *Envy and Gratitude and Other Works, 1946–1963* (pp. 1–24). New York: Free Press.

Klein, M. (1948). On the theory of anxiety and guilt. In: *Envy and Gratitude and Other Works, 1946–1963* (pp. 25–42). New York: Free Press.

Klein, M. (1952a). The origins of transference. In: *Envy and Gratitude and Other Works, 1946–1963* (pp. 48–56). New York: Free Press.

Klein, M. (1952b). Some theoretical conclusions regarding the emotional life of the infant. In: *Envy and Gratitude and Other Works, 1946–1963* (pp. 61–93). New York: Free Press.

Klein, M. (1952c). On observing the behavior of young infants. In: *Envy and Gratitude and Other Works, 1946–1963* (pp. 94–121). New York: Free Press.

Klein, M. (1955). The psycho-analytic play technique: its history and significance. In: *Envy and Gratitude and Other Works, 1946–1963* (pp. 122–140). New York: Free Press.

Klein, M. (1957). Envy and gratitude. In: *Envy and Gratitude and Other Works, 1946–1963* (pp. 176–234). New York: Free Press.

Klein, M. (1961). *Narrative of a Child Analysis: The Conduct of the Psycho-Analysis of Children as Seen in the Treatment of a Ten-year-old Boy*. New York: Free Press.
Klein, M. (1975). The development of a child. In: *Love, Guilt and Reparation, and Other Works, 1921–1945* (pp. 1–53). New York: The Free Press.
Klein, M., & Tribich, D. (1981). Kernberg's object-relations theory: a critical evaluation. *International Journal of Psycho-Analysis,* 62: 27–43.
Klein, M., Heimann, P., Isaacs, S., & Riviere, J. (1952). *Developments in Psychoanalysis*. London: Hogarth.
Knight, R. P. (1954). Borderline states. In: R. P. Knight & C. R. Friedman (Eds.), *Psycho-analytic Psychiatry and Psychology* (pp. 97–109). New York: International Universities Press.
Kohut, H. (1959). Introspection, empathy, and psychoanalysis—an examination of the relationship between mode of observation and theory. *Journal of the American Psychoanalytic Association*, 7: 459–483.
Kohut, H. (1966). Forms and transformations of narcissism. In: P. Ornstein (Ed.), *The Search for the Self: Selected Writings of Heinz Kohut, 1950–1994*, Vol. I. New York: International Universities Press.
Kohut, H. (1968). The psychoanalytic treatment of narcissistic personality disorders—outline of a systematic approach. *Psychoanalytic Study of the Child*, 23: 86–113.
Kohut, H. (1971). *The Analysis of the Self*. New York: International Universities Press.
Kohut, H. (1972). Thoughts on narcissism and narcissistic rage. *Psychoanalytic Study of the Child*, 27: 360–400.
Kohut, H. (1977). *The Restoration of the Self*. New York: International Universities Press.
Kohut, H. (1979). An addendum to '"The advantages of Freud's technique as shown in the analysis of the rat man". *International Journal of Psychoanalysis*, 60: 215–216.
Kohut, H. (1984). *How Does Analysis Cure?* A. Goldberg & P. E. Stepansky (Eds.). Chicago, IL: University of Chicago Press.
Kripke, D., & Sonnenschein, D. (1973). A 90 minute daydream cycle. *Sleep Research*, 00: 187–189.
Kris, E. (1951). Ego psychology and interpretation in psychoanalytic therapy. *Psychoanalytic Quarterly*, 20: 15–30.
Kris, E. (1956a). On some vicissitudes of insight in psychoanalysis. *International Journal of Psycho-Analysis*, 37: 445–455.
Kris, E. (1956b). The personal myth. *Journal of the American Psychoanalytic Association*, 4: 653–681.

Kubie, L. S. (1947). The fallacious use of quantitative concepts in dynamic psychology. *Psychoanalytic Quarterly, 16*: 507–518.

Laplanche, J. (1997). The theory of seduction and the problem of the Other. *International Journal of Psychoanalysis, 78*: 653–666.

Lenzenweger, M. F., Clarkin, J. F., Kernberg, O. F., Levy, K. N., Meehan, K. B., & Reynoso, J. S. (2005). Abstracts of the 2005 poster session of the American Psychoanalytic Association winter meeting: the relation of reflective function to neurocognitive functioning in patients with borderline personality disorder. *Journal of the American Psychoanalytic Association, 53*: 1305–1308.

Levy, S., & Inderbitzen, L. (1996). Ego psychology and modern structural theory: consolidation of ego psychology. In: A. Tasman, J. Kay & J. Lieberman (Eds.), *Psychiatry*, Vol. 1 (pp. 412–413). Philadelphia, PA: Saunders.

Lichtenberg, J. D. (1982). Reflections on the first year of life. *Psychoanalytic Inquiry, 1*: 695–729.

Lichtenberg, J. D. (1992). *Psychoanalysis and Motivation*. London: Routledge.

Likierman, M. (2001). *Melanie Klein: Her Work in Context*. New York: Continuum.

Little, M. (1951). Countertransference and the patient's response to it. *International Journal of Psychoanalysis, 32*: 32–40.

Loewald, H. (1960). On the therapeutic action of psychoanalysis. *International Journal of Psycho-Analysis, 43*: 16–33.

Loewald, H. (1966). Review of *Psychoanalytic Concepts and the Structural Theory*, by J. A. Arlow & C. Brenner. *Psychoanalytic Quarterly, 35*: 430–436.

Loewald, H. (1971). Some considerations on repetition and repetition compulsion. *International Journal of Psycho-Analysis, 52*: 59–66.

Loewald, H. (1980). *Papers on Psychoanalysis*. New Haven, CT: Yale University Press.

Loewald, H. (1984). Review of the selected papers of Margaret S. Mahler. *Journal of the American Psychoanalytic Association, 32*: 165–175.

Loewenstein, R. M. (1951). The problem of interpretation. *Psychoanalytic Quarterly, 20*: 1–14.

Loewenstein, R. M. (1954). Some remarks on defenses, autonomous ego, and psychoanalytic technique. *International Journal of Psychoanalysis, 35*: 188–193.

Loewenstein, R. M. (1956). Some remarks on the role of speech in psychoanalytic technique. *International Journal of Psychoanalysis, 37*: 460–468.

Loewenstein, R. M. (1957). Some thoughts on interpretation in the theory and practice of psychoanalysis. *Psychoanalytic Study of the Child*, 12: 127–150.
Loewenstein, R. M. (1958). Remarks on some variations in psychoanalytic technique. *International Journal of Psychoanalysis*, 39: 202–210.
Loewenstein, R. M. (1961). Introduction to panel: the silent patient. *Journal of the American Psychoanalytic Association*, 9: 2–6.
Loewenstein, R. M. (1963). Some considerations on free association. *Journal of the American Psychoanalytic Association*, 11: 451–473.
Loewenstein, R. M. (1969). Developments in the theory of transference in the last fifty years. *International Journal of Psychoanalysis*, 50: 583–588.
Loewenstein, R. M. (1982). Ego autonomy and psychoanalytic technique. In: *Practice and Precept in Psychoanalytic Technique: Selected Papers of Rudolph M. Loewenstein* (pp. 211–228). New Haven: Yale University Press.
Lynch, A. A., Richards, A., & Bachant, J. L. (1997). Interaction in the transference/countertransference continuum. Paper presented at the 40th International Psychoanalytic Association Conference, Barcelona, Spain.
MacLean, P. D. (1967). The brain in relation to empathy and medical education. *Journal of Nervous and Mental Disease*, 144: 374–382.
MacLean, P. D. (1972). Cerebral evolution and emotional processes: new findings on the striatal complex. *Annals of the New York Academy of Science*, 193: 137–149.
Magurran, A. (2000). *New York Times* on the Web, 23 January.
Mahler, M. S. (1942). Pseudoimbecility: a magic cap of invisibility. In: *The Selected Papers of Margaret S. Mahler, Vol. 1* (pp. 3–16). New York: Jason Aronson.
Mahler, M. S. (1952). On child psychosis and schizophrenia: autistic and symbiotic infantile psychoses. In: *The Selected Papers of Margaret S. Mahler, Vol. 1* (pp. 131–153). New York: Jason Aronson.
Mahler, M. S. (1963). Thoughts about development and individuation. *Psychoanalytic Study of the Child*, 18: 307–324.
Mahler, M. S. (1966). Notes on the development of basic moods: the depressive affect. In: *The Selected Papers of Margaret S. Mahler, Vol. 2* (pp. 59–75). New York: Jason Aronson.
Mahler, M. S. (1968). *On Human Symbiosis and the Vicissitudes of Individuation: Infantile Psychosis*. New York: International Universities Press.

Mahler, M. S. (1979). *The Selected Papers of Margaret S. Mahler, Vols. 1, 2, & 3*. New York: Jason Aronson.
Mahler, M. S., & Gosliner, B. J. (1955). On symbiotic child psychosis—genetic, dynamic, and restitutive aspects. *Psychoanalytic Study of the Child, 10*: 195–212.
Mahler, M. S., & McDevitt, J. B. (1968). Observations on adaptation and defense in *statu nascendi* development. *Psychoanalytic Quarterly, 37*:1–21.
Mahler, M. S., Pine, F., & Bergman, A. (1975). *The Psychological Birth of the Human Infant: Symbiosis and Individuation*. New York: Basic Books.
Mahler, M. S., Ross, J. R., & DeFries, Z. (1949). Clinical studies in benign and malignant cases of childhood psychosis (schizophrenia-like). *American Journal of Orthopsychiatry, 19*: 295–305.
Marmor, J. (1953). Orality in the hysterical personality. *Journal of the American Psychoanalytic Association, 1*: 656–671.
Maslow, A. H. (1962). *Toward a Psychology of Being*. New York: Van Nostrand.
Masson, J. M. (1984). *The Assault on Truth: Freud's Suppression of the Seduction Theory*. New York: Farrar, Straus and Giroux.
Masson, J. M. (Ed. & Trans.) (1985). *The Complete Letters of Sigmund Freud to Wilhelm Fliess: 1887–1904*. Cambridge, MA: Harvard University Press.
McDevitt, J. B. (1979). The role of internalization in the development of object relations during the separation–individuation phase. *Journal of the American Psychoanalytic Association, 27*: 327–343.
McDevitt, J. B. (1983). The emergence of hostile aggression and its defensive and adaptive modifications during the separation–individuation Process *Journal of the American Psychoanalytic Association, 31S*: 273–298.
McDevitt, J. B., & Mahler, M. S. (1980). Object constancy, individuality and internalization. In: S. I. Greenspan & G. Pollock (Eds.), *The Course of Life: Vol. Infancy and Early Childhood* (pp. 407–424). Washington, DC: US Government Printing Office.
McLaughlin, J. T. (1981). Transference, psychic reality, and countertransference. *Psychoanalytic Quarterly, 50*: 639–664.
McLaughlin, J. T. (1988). The analyst's insights. *Psychoanalytic Quarterly, 57*: 370–388.
McLaughlin, J. T. (1991). Clinical and theoretical aspects of enactment. *Journal of the American Psychoanalytic Association, 39*(3): 595–614.

McLaughlin, J. T., & Johan, M. (1992). Enactments in psychoanalysis. *Journal of the American Psychoanalytic Association, 40*: 827–841.
Meltzer, D. (1981). A note on Bion's concept of "reversal of alpha function". In: J. S. Grotstein (Ed.), *Do I Dare Disturb the Universe? A Memorial to W. R. Bion* (pp. 529–536). Beverly Hills, CA: Caesura Press.
Mitchell, S. (1978). Psychodynamics, homosexuality, and the question of pathology. *Psychiatry, 41*: 254–263.
Mitchell, S. (1979). Twilight of the idols: change and preservation in the writings of Heinz Kohut. *Contemporary Psychoanalysis, 15*: 170–189.
Mitchell, S. (1981). The origin and nature of the "object" in the theories of Klein and Fairbairn. *Contemporary Psychoanalysis, 17*: 374–398.
Mitchell, S. (1988). *Relational Concepts in Psychoanalysis*. Cambridge, MA: Harvard University Press.
Mitchell, S. (1993). Reply to Bachant and Richards. *Psychoanalytic Dialogues, 3*: 462–480.
Mitchell, S. (1995). Commentary on "contemporary structural psychoanalysis and relational psychoanalysis". *Psychoanalytic Psychology, 12*: 575–582.
Mitchell, S. (1997). Psychoanalysis and the degradation of romance. *Psychoanalytic Dialogues, 7*: 23–41.
Mitchell, S. (1998). The analyst's knowledge and authority. *Psychoanalytic Quarterly, 67*: 1–31.
Mitchell, S. (1999). Looking back looking forward. *Psychoanalytic Dialogues, 9*: 717–719.
Mitchell, S. (2000). *Relationality: From Attachment to Intersubjectivity*. Hillsdale, NJ: Analytic Press.
Mitchell, S. (2004). My psychoanalytic journey. *Psychoanalytic Inquiry, 24*: 531–541.
Money-Kyrle, R. (1975a). Introduction. In: M. Klein (Ed.), *Love, Guilt and Reparation* (pp. ix–x). London: Hogarth.
Money-Kyrle, R. (1975b). Explanatory notes. In: M. Klein (Ed.), *Love, Guilt and Reparation* (pp. 431–438). London: Hogarth.
Moore, G. E. (1905). The nature and reality of the objects of perception, *Proceedings of the Aristotelian Society New Series, 6*(6): 69–127 [reprinted by Courtesy of the Editor of the Aristotelian Society].
Nagel, E. (1961). *The Structure of Science*. New York: Harcourt, Brace & World.
Nagel, T. (1995). *Other Minds: Critical Essays, 1969–1994*. Oxford: Oxford University Press.
Nagera, H. (1964). Autoerotism, autoerotic activities, and ego development. *Psychoanalytic Study of the Child, 19*: 240–255.

Nietzsche, F. (1882). *The Gay Science*, W. Kaufmann (Trans.). New York: Random House, 1974.
Nunberg, H. (1931). The synthetic function of the ego. *International Journal of Psycho-Analysis, 12*: 123–140.
Nunberg, H. (1955). *Principles of Psychoanalysis*. New York: International Universities Press.
Nunberg, H., & Federn, E. (Eds.) (1909). *Minutes of the Vienna Psychoanalytic Society, Vol. 2: 1908–1910*. New York: International Universities Press.
Ogden, T. H. (1982). *Projective Identification and Psychoanalytic Technique*. New York: Jason Aronson.
Ogden, T. H. (1983). The concept of internal object relations. *International Journal of sycho-Analysis, 64*: 227–241.
Ogden, T. H. (1997a). Reverie and metaphor . *International Journal of Psycho-Analysis, 78*: 719–732.
Ogden, T. H. (1997b). *Reverie and Interpretation: Sensing Something Human*. Northvale, NJ: Aronson.
Olds, J. (1958). Self stimulation of the brain. *Science, 127*: 315–324.
Olds, J., Allan, W. S., & Briese, E. (1971). Differentiation of hypothalamic drive and reward centers. *American Journal. Physiology, 221*: 368–375.
Ornstein, A. (1994). Trauma, memory, and psychic continuity. *Progress in Self Psychology, 10*: 131–146.
Ornstein, P. H. (2004). The elusive concept of the psychoanalytic process. *Journal of the American Psychoanalytic Association, 52*: 15–41.
O'Shaughnessy, E. (1981). A clinical study of a defensive organization. *International Journal of Psycho-Analysis, 62*: 359–369.
Petot, J. M. (1990). *Melanie Klein: Vol. 1, First Discoveries and First System 1919–1932*, C. Trollope (Trans.). Madison, CT: International Universities Press.
Petot, J. M. (1991). *Melanie Klein: Vol. 2. The Ego and the Good Object 1932–1960*, C. Trollope (Trans.). Madison, CT: International Universities Press.
Pine, F. (1981). In the beginning: contributions to a psychoanalytic developmental psychology. *International Review of Psychoanalysis, 8*: 15–33.
Pine, F. (1992). Response to discussants. *Contemporary Psychoanalysis, 28*: 295–299.
Popper, K. (1962). *Conjectures and Refutations: The Growth of Scientific Knowledge*. New York: Basic Books.

Prescott, J. W. (1996). The origins of human love and violence. *Prenatal and Perinatal Psychology Journal*, 10(3): 143–188.
Prescott, J. W. (2001). Along the evolutionary biological trail. A review and commentary on *Mother Nature: A History of Mothers, Infants, and Natural Selection* by Sarah Blaffer Hrdy. *Journal of Prenatal and Perinatal Psychology and Health*, 15(3): 225–232.
Pribram, K., & Gill, M. (1976). *Freud's "Project" Reassessed*. New York: Basic Books.
Racker, H. (1968). *Transference and Countertransference*. London: Hogarth.
Rangell, L. (1988). The future of psychoanalysis: the scientific crossroads. *Psychoanalytic Quarterly*, 57: 313–340.
Rank, O. (1924). *The Trauma of Birth*. New York: Robert Brunner, 1952.
Rapaport, D. (1959). A historical survey of psychoanalytic ego psychology. In: G. F. Klein (Ed.), *Psychological Issues*, Vol. 1 (pp. 5–17). New York: International Universities Press.
Rapaport, D. (1967). *The Collected Papers of David Rapaport*. New York: Basic Books.
Rapaport, D., & Gill, M. (1959). The points of view and assumptions of metapsychology. In: *The Collected Papers of David Rappaport* (pp. 795–811). New York: Basic Books.
Reich, A. (1951). On countertransference. In: *Annie Reich: Psychoanalytic Contributions* (pp. 136–154). New York: International Universities Press.
Reich, A. (1960). Further remarks on countertransference. In: *Annie Reich: Psychoanalytic Contributions* (pp. 271–287). New York: International Universities Press.
Reich, A. (1966). Empathy and countertransference. In: *Annie Reich: Psychoanalytic Contributions* (pp. 344–360). New York: International Universities Press.
Reich, W. (1933). *Character Analysis*. New York: Orgone Institute Press.
Renik, O. (1998). Getting real in analysis. *Psychoanalytic Quarterly*, 67: 566–593.
Renik, O. (1999). Playing one's cards face up in analysis: an approach to the problem of self-disclosure. *Psychoanalytic Quarterly*, 68: 521–539.
Resch, R. C. (1979). Hatching in the human infant as the beginning of separation–individuation: what it is and what it looks like. *Psychoanalytic Study of the Child*, 34: 421–441.
Richards, A. D. (1999). A. A. Brill and the politics of exclusion. *Journal of the American Psychoanalytic Association*, 47: 9–28.

Riviere, J. (1936). The genesis of psychical conflict in earliest infancy. *International Journal of Psychoanalysis, 17*: 395–422.
Roazen, P. (1995). *How Freud Worked: First Hand Accounts of Patients.* Northvale, NJ: Jason Aronson.
Rodman, F. R. (2003). *Winnicott: Life and Work.* Cambridge, MA: Perseus.
Rosenfeld, H. (1952). Notes on the psychoanalysis of the super-ego conflict of an acute schizophrenic patient. *International Journal of Psychoanalysis, 33*: 111–131.
Rosenfeld, H. (1965). *Psychotic States.* London: Hogarth Press.
Rothstein, A. (1995). Psychoanalytic technique and the creation of analysands: on beginning analysis, *Psychoanalytic Quarterly, 64*: 306–325.
Rothstein, A. (2002). Reflections on creative aspects of psychoanalytic diagnosing. *Psychoanalytic Quarterly, 71*: 301–326.
Rubinstein, B. B. (1967). *Explanation and Mere Description: A Metascientific Examination of Certain Aspects of the Psychoanalytic Theory of Motivation.* New York: International Universities Press.
Sandell, R., Blomberg, J., Lazar, A., Carlsson, J., Broberg, J., & Schubert, J. (2000). Varieties of long-term outcome among patients in psychoanalysis and long-term psychotherapy: a review of findings in the Stockholm Outcome of Psychoanalysis and Psychotherapy Project (Stoppp). *International Journal of Psycho-Analysis, 81*: 921–942.
Sander, L. W. (1976). Issues in early mother–child interactions. In: E. N. Rexford, L. W. Sander & T. Shapiro (Eds.), *Infant Psychiatry: A New Synthesis* (pp. 127–140). New Haven, CT: Yale University Press.
Sandler, J. (1976a). Actualization and object relationships. *Journal of the Philadelphia Association for Psychoanalysis, 3*: 59–70.
Sandler, J. (1976b). Countertransference and role-responsiveness. *Review of Psycho-Analysis, 3*: 43–47.
Sandler, J., & Freud, A. (1983). Discussions in the Hampstead index of The Ego and the Mechanisms of Defense. *Journal of the American Psychoanalytic Association, 31S*: 19–146.
Sandler, J., & Freud, A. (1985). *The Analysis of Defense: The Ego and The Mechanisms of Defense.* New York: International Universities Press.
Sandler, J., & Sandler, A. (1978). On the development of object relationships and affects. *International Journal of Psychoanalysis, 59*: 285–296.
Sandler, J., & Sandler, A. (1994). Comments on the conceptualisation of clinical facts in psychoanalysis. *International Journal of Psychoanalysis, 8*: 15–33.
Sandler, J., & Sandler, A.-M. (1998). *Internal Objects Revisited.* London: Karnac.

Schafer, R. (1968). *Aspects of Internalization*. New York: International Universities Press.
Schafer, R. (1970). An overview of Heinz Hartmann's contribution to psychoanalysis. *International Journal of Psychoanalysis, 51*: 425–446.
Schafer, R. (1976). *A New Language for Psychoanalysis*. New Haven, CT: Yale University Press.
Schafer, R. (1983). Introduction. *Psychoanalysis and Contemporary Thought, 6*: 403–404.
Schafer, R. (1992). *Retelling a Life: Dialogues and Narration in Psychoanalysis*. New York: Basic Books.
Schafer, R. (Ed.) (1997). *The Contemporary Kleinians of London*. Madison, CT: International Universities Press.
Scharff, D. E., & Birtles, E. F. (Eds.) (1994). *From Instinct to Self: Selected Papers of W. R. D. Fairbairn* (Volume 1: *Clinical and Theoretical Papers*) Northvale, NJ: Jason Aronson.
Schmideberg, M. (1947). The treatment of psychopaths and borderline patients. *American Journal of Psychotherapy, 1*: 45–55.
Schur, M. (1966). *The Id and the Principles of Regulatory Functioning*. New York: International Universities Press.
Schwaber, E. (1983). Psychoanalytic listening and psychic reality. *International Review of Psycho-Analysis, 10*: 379–392.
Schwartz, F., & Schiller, P. (1970). A psychoanalytic model of attention and learning. *Psychological Issues, Monograph, 23*. New York: International Universities Press.
Searl, N. (1929). The flight to reality. *International Journal of Psychoanalysis, 10*: 280–291.
Searles, H. F. (1965). *Collected Papers on Schizophrenia and Related Subjects*. New York: International Universities Press.
Segal, H. (1957). Notes on symbol formation. *International Journal of Psychoanalysis, 38*: 391–397.
Silverman, L. H. (1967). An experimental approach to the study of dynamic propositions in psychoanalysis—the relationship between the aggressive drive and ego regression. *Journal of the American Psychoanalytic Association, 15*: 376–403.
Silverman, M. (1985). Countertransference and the myth of the perfectly analyzed analyst. *Psychoanalytic Quarterly, 54*: 175–199.
Simon, B. (1992). "Incest—see under Oedipus complex": the history of an error in psychoanalysis. *Journal of the American Psychoanalytic Association, 40*: 955–988.
Singer, E. (1993). Transference and parataxic distortion. *Journal of Contemporary Psychoanalysis, 29*: 418–440.

Skinner, B. F. (1953). *Science and Human Behavior*. New York: Macmillan.
Smith, H. F. (1997). Resistance, enactment, and interpretation: a self-analytic study. *Psychoanalytic Inquiry, 17*: 13–30.
Smith, H. F. (2003). Analysis of transference: a North American perspective. *International Journal of Psychoanalysis, 84*: 1017–1041.
Solms, M. (1997). *The Neurophysiology of Dreams*. Mahwah, NJ: Lawrence Erlbaum Associates.
Spence, D. P. (1982). *Narrative Truth and Historical Truth: Meaning and Interpretation in Psychoanalysis*. London & New York: Norton and Company.
Spillius, E. B. (Ed.) (1988). *Melanie Klein Today: Development in Theory and Practice*, Vols. 1 & 2. London: Routledge.
Spitz, R. (1945). Hospitalism. *Psychoanalytic Study of the Child, 1*: 53–74, New York: International Universities Press.
Spitz, R. (1957). *No and Yes: On the Genesis of Human Communication*. New York: International Universities Press.
Stein, M. H. (1956). The problem of masochism in the theory and technique of psychoanalysis. *Journal of the American Psychoanalytic Association, 4*: 526–538.
Stein, M. H. (1981). The unobjectionable part of the transference. *Journal of the American Psychoanalytic Association, 29*: 869–892.
Steiner, J. (1994). Patient-centered and analyst-centered interpretations: some implications of containment and countertransference. *Psychoanalytic Inquiry, 14*: 406–422.
Steiner, R. (1989). "It's a new kind of diaspora...". *International Review of Psychoanalysis, 16*: 35–72.
Steiner, R. (1991). Background to the scientific controversies. In: P. King & R. Steiner (Eds.), *The Freud-Klein Controversies* (pp. 227–263). London: Routledge.
Steiner, R. (2001). An essay marking its centenary: some observations on the sources of Freud's *The Psychopathology of Everyday Life*. *Neuro-Psychoanalysis, 3*: 221–241.
Steiner, S. S., Bodnar, R. J., Achermann, R. F., & Ellman S. J. (1973). Escape from rewarding brain stimulation of dorsal brainstem and hypothalamus. *Physiology and Behavior, 11*: 589–591.
Steingart, I. (1983). *Pathological Play in Borderline and Narcissistic Personalities*. New York: Spectrum.
Steingart, I. (1995). *A Thing Apart: Love and Reality in the Therapeutic Relationship*. Northvale, NJ: Jason Aronson.
Sterba, R. (1934). The fate of the ego in analytic therapy. *International Journal of Psychoanalysis, 15*: 117–126.

Stern, D. (1971). A micro-analysis of mother-infant interaction. *Journal of the American Academy of Child Psychiatry, 13*: 501–517.
Stern, D. (1974). The goal and structure of mother-infant play. *Journal of American Academy of Child Psychiatry, 13*: 402–421.
Stern, D. (1982). Implications of infancy research for clinical theory and practice. Paper presented to the 13th Annual Margaret S. Mahler Symposium, Philadelphia.
Stern, D. (1985). *The Interpersonal World of the Infant*. New York: Basic Books.
Stewart, W. A. (1963). An inquiry into the concept of working through. *Journal of the American Psychoanalytic Association, 11*: 474–499.
Stewart, W. A. (1963). *Psychoanalysis: The First Ten Years 1888–1898*. New York: Macmillan.
Stolorow, R. D., & Atwood, G. E. (1992). *Contexts of Being: The Intersubjective Foundations of Psychological Life*. Hillsdale, NJ: Analytic Press.
Stolorow, R. D., & Lachman, F. M. (1980). *Psychoanalysis of Developmental Arrests*. New York: International Universities Press.
Stone, L. (1954). The widening scope of indications for psychoanalysis. *Journal of the American Psychoanalytic Association, 2*: 567–594.
Stone, L. (1961). *The Psychoanalytic Situation: An Examination of its Development and Essential Nature*. New York: International Universities Press.
Stone, M. H. (1980). *The Borderline Syndromes*. New York: McGraw Hill.
Strachey, J. (1934). The nature of the therapeutic action of psychoanalysis. *International Journal of Psychoanalysis, 15*: 127–159.
Strozier, C. (2001). *Heinz Kohut: The Making of a Psychoanalyst*. New York: Farrar, Straus and Giroux.
Sugarman, A., & Lerner, H. (1980). Reflections on the current state of the borderline concept. In: J. Kwawer, H. Lerner, P. Lerner, & A. Sugarman (Eds.), *Borderline Phenomena and the Rorschach* (pp. 11–37). New York: International Universities Press.
Sullivan, H. S. (1931). Review: *The Morbid Personality*, by S. Lorand. *International Journal of Psychoanalysis, 12*: 497–499.
Sullivan, H. S. (1934). Review: *Towards Mental Health*, by C. Macfie Campbell. *International Journal of Psychoanalysis, 15*: 346–347.
Sullivan, H. S. (1940). *Conceptions of Modern Psychiatry*. New York: Norton.
Sullivan, H. S. (1950). The illusion of personal identity. In: *The Future of Psychiatry and Social Science*. New York: Norton, 1962.
Sullivan, H. S. (1953). *The Interpersonal Theory of Psychiatry*. New York: Norton.

Sulloway, F. J. (1979). *Freud: Biologist of the Mind*. New York: Basic Books.
Sutherland, J. (1989). *Fairbairn's Journey into the Interior*: London: Free Association Books.
Tronick, E. (2008). Multilevel meaning making and dyadic expansion of consciousness theory: emotional and other polymorphic meaning making systems. In: D. Fosha, D. Siegel & M. Solomon (Eds.), *The Healing Power of Emotion: Neurobiological Understanding Sand Therapeutic Perspectives*. New York: Norton.
Valenstein, A. F. (1973). On attachment to painful feelings and the negative therapeutic reaction. *Psychoanalytic Study of the Child, 28*: 365–392.
Valenstein, E. S., Cox, V. C., & Kalkolewski, J. W. (1968). Modification of motivated behavior elicited by electrical stimulation of the hypothalamus. *Science, 157*: 552–554.
Vorus, N. (1998). The concept of phantasy in psychoanalysis: an examination of the place of reality in the Freud–Klein controversies. Unpublished dissertation, City University of New York.
Vygotsky, L. (1978). *Mind in Society: The Development of Higher Psychological Processes*. Cambridge, MA: Harvard University Press.
Wälder, R. (1936). The principle of multiple function: observations on over-determination. *Psychoanalytic Quarterly, 5*: 45–62.
Wallerstein, R. S. (1988). One psychoanalysis or many? *International Journal of Psycho Analysis, 69*: 5–21.
Weiner, J. (1994). *The Beak of the Finch: A Story of Evolution in Our Time*. New York: Random House.
White, R. W. (1963). Ego and reality in psychoanalytic theory. *Psychological Issues, 3*(11): 1–196.
White, R. W. (1992). Who was Morton Prince? *Journal of Abnormal Psychology, 101*: 604–606.
Winnicott, D. W. (1931). *Clinical Notes on the Disorders of Childhood*. London: William Heinemann.
Winnicott, D. W. (1935). The manic defense. In: *Collected Papers: Through Pediatrics to Psycho-Analysis* (pp. 129–144). New York: Basic Books.
Winnicott, D. W. (1936). Appetite and emotional disorder. In: *Through Pediatrics to Psychoanalysis: Collected Papers* (pp. 3–21). New York: Basic Books.
Winnicott, D. W. (1941). The observation of infants in a set situation. In: *Through Pediatrics to Psychoanalysis: Collected Papers* (pp. 52–69). New York: Basic Books.

Winnicott, D. W. (1945). Primitive emotional development. In: *Through Pediatrics to Psycho-Analysis: Collected Papers* (pp. 145–156). New York: Basic Books.

Winnicott, D. W. (1951). Transitional objects and transitional phenomena. In: *Through Pediatrics to Psychoanalysis: Collected Papers* (pp. 229–242). New York: Basic Books.

Winnicott, D. W. (1953). Transitional objects and transitional phenomena. *International Journal of Psychoanalysis, 34*: 89–97.

Winnicott, D. W. (1954). The depressive position in normal emotional development. In: *Through Pediatrics to Psychoanalysis: Collected Papers* (pp. 262–277). New York: Basic Books.

Winnicott, D. W. (1956a). Primary maternal preoccupation. In: *Through Pediatrics to Psychoanalysis: Collected Papers* (pp. 300–305). New York: Basic Books.

Winnicott, D. W. (1956b). The antisocial tendency. In: *Through Pediatrics to Psychoanalysis: Collected Papers* (pp. 306–315). New York: Basic Books.

Winnicott, D. W. (1958a). Ernest Jones. *International Journal of Psycho-Analysis, 39*: 298–304.

Winnicott, D. W. (1958b). Psycho-analysis and the sense of guilt. In: *The Maturational Processes and the Facilitating Environment* (pp. 15–28). New York: International Universities Press.

Winnicott, D. W. (1958c). The capacity to be alone. In: *The Maturational Processes and the Facilitating Environment* (pp. 29–36). New York: International Universities Press.

Winnicott, D. W. (1960a). The theory of the parent–infant relationship. In: *The Maturational Processes and the Facilitating Environment* (pp. 37–55). New York: International Universities Press.

Winnicott, D. W. (1960b). Ego distortion in terms of true and false self. In: *The Maturational Processes and the Facilitating Environment* (pp.140–152). New York: International Universities Press.

Winnicott, D. W. (1962a). Ego integration in child development. In: *The Maturational Processes and the Facilitating Environment* (pp. 56–63). New York: International Universities Press.

Winnicott, D. W. (1962b). A personal view of the Kleinian contribution. In: *The Maturational Processes and the Facilitating Environment* (pp. 171–178). New York: International Universities Press.

Winnicott, D. W. (1963a). The development of the capacity for concern. In: *The Maturational Processes and the Facilitating Environment* (pp. 73–82). New York: International Universities Press.

Winnicott, D. W. (1963b). Dependence through independence. In: *The Maturational Processes and the Facilitating Environment* (pp. 83–92). New York: International Universities Press.

Winnicott, D. W. (1965). *The Maturational Processes and the Facilitating Environment.* New York: International Universities Press.

Winnicott, D. W. (1971). *Playing and Reality.* New York: Basic Books.

Wolff, P. (1966). The causes, controls and organization of behavior in the neo-nate. *Psychological Issues, Monograph*, 5: 1–104.

Young-Bruehl, E. (1988). *Anna Freud: A Biography.* New York: Summit.

Zetzel, E. R. (1956). Current concepts of transference. *International Journal of Psychoanalysis*, 37: 369–376.

Zetzel, E. R. (1971). A developmental approach to the borderline patient. *American Journal of Psychiatry*, 4: 149–155.

INDEX

Abelin, E. L., 612, 616, 650, 657
Abend, S., 553, 555, 567, 657
Abraham, K., 106, 217–220, 225, 232, 236, 250–252, 307–308, 310, 324, 327–329, 335–337, 342, 352, 387, 543, 548, 657
abuse
  child, 4, 20, 23, 58, 632
  sexual, 4, 20–24, 58–59, 64–65, 330
  substance, 593–594
Achermann, R. F., 636–637, 645, 664, 686
Achermann, R. R., 636, 660
Adler, A., 100–101, 191, 476–477
affect, 8–10, 14, 18, 21–23, 46, 70, 113–116, 119, 136–137, 139, 158–159, 174, 182, 185, 232, 238, 243, 266, 308–309, 311, 321, 344, 349, 375, 391, 407, 409, 419, 430–432, 435, 450, 478, 492–493, 495–496, 498, 501, 505, 507–510, 514, 517, 519, 522, 524, 526–528, 530, 544, 547, 577, 579–580, 582, 586, 588, 592–594, 604, 609, 613, 624–625, 637, 639, 640–641, 646
  see also: self-object-affect attunement, 211
  valence, 249, 293, 496
aggression, 58, 97, 131–132, 146, 155–156, 178, 183–184, 197–201, 205, 207, 210–211, 220, 223, 232, 240, 242–243, 266, 294, 297, 299–303, 307, 316, 334, 348–349, 380–381, 383–385, 393–394, 400, 404–405, 409–410, 445, 472, 477, 479, 484–485, 487, 494, 496, 500–502, 507, 509–510, 517, 547–548, 576, 616, 625, 634, 643–645
Akhtar, S., 150, 657
Alexander, F., 458, 469, 545, 657–658
Alfasi-Siffert, G., 639, 658
Allan, W. S., 645, 682
alpha *see also*: beta
  elements, 522, 524–525, 529, 531, 538
  function, 524–525, 527–528, 531–532, 538

ambivalence, 69, 106–107, 136, 143, 239, 241, 257, 280, 301, 340, 348, 350–351, 373, 381, 398–399, 436, 442, 449, 477, 485, 505, 532, 547, 591
American Psychiatric Association (APA), 502, 563–566, 658
anal, 29, 64, 68–69, 76, 96, 147, 160–161, 220–223, 236, 240, 242, 244, 300–301, 303–305, 316, 335, 337, 483, 548 *see also*: sadism, zone
   erotism, 324
   fixation, 335
   pleasure(s), 96
   stage, 162, 222, 229, 252, 304, 337, 476, 617, 650
anger, 128, 142, 150, 161, 297, 309, 384, 386, 389, 441, 443, 449, 485, 604, 646–648
Anthony, E. J., 611, 658
Antrobus, J., 30, 81, 664
anxiety
   annihilation, 209, 312–313, 377–379, 626, 629
   birth, 160
   castration, 142, 161–162, 164–165, 223–224, 245, 248, 253, 562
   depressive, 233, 296, 300–302
   neuroses, 23, 124, 158
   objective, 176
   paranoid, 233–234 ,298, 320
   persecutory, 299, 311–312, 314–315, 319–323, 386
   psychotic, 373
   schizoid, 296, 298, 320
   separation, 293, 442
Anzieu, D., 376, 658
Appelbaum, A., 494, 512, 520, 675
Aristotle, 35, 45
Arlow, J. A., 190, 208–210, 475, 541, 543, 548, 552–556, 562–564, 567, 655, 658
Aron, L., 577, 579, 581–582, 584, 586, 612–613, 615, 618–619, 654, 658
arousal, 8, 18, 65–66, 161, 188, 256, 271, 420,422, 437, 508, 551
   instinctual, 395
Aserinsky, E., 81, 658
attachment, 55, 60, 78, 104, 394, 443–444, 459, 555–556, 626–627, 634
   libidinal, 89, 340, 403, 409, 438
Atwood, G. E., 480, 608, 610, 687
autoerotism, 29, 62–63, 68, 70, 74–75, 78, 83, 89–94, 97–99, 101–102, 121–123, 125, 208, 251, 267, 271–278, 282, 287–288, 305, 372, 388, 402–403, 405, 428–429, 451–452, 454, 461, 465, 644
autonomy, 204–207, 395, 441, 443–444, 449, 477, 480–481, 488, 495, 501, 509, 546, 549, 575, 620
   ego, 204, 206, 474, 549
Ayer, A. J., 415, 658

Bach, S., 125–126, 353, 417, 487, 589, 592, 597, 613, 655, 659
Bachant, J. L., 551, 553, 570–571, 659, 679
Bacon, C. L., 469, 658
Balint, M., 360, 365, 390, 396, 476, 487, 493, 510, 592, 659
Barr, R. G., 633, 672
behaviour
   adult, 98, 322
   basic, 334, 625
   human, 546
   patterns, 508, 517
   pleasurable, 274–275
   social, 333, 524
   sexual, 61, 625
   waking, 634–635
Benedek, T., 469, 658
Benjamin, J., 592, 608–610, 612–613, 615, 618–619, 659
Beres, D., 553–555, 659
Bergman, A., xx, 208, 434, 437, 441, 444–445, 454–455, 493, 497, 547, 659–660, 680
Bergman, P., 199, 660

Bergmann, M., 195, 204, 208–209, 211, 660
Berman, E., 400, 401, 660
beta elements, 522–525, 527–532, 538 *see also*: alpha
Bibring, E., 88, 173, 660
Bick, E., 526
Bion, W. R., xix–xx, 18, 216, 325, 328, 360, 396, 506, 510, 521–540, 587, 589, 591–592, 606, 608, 655, 660
Bion's
  Grid, 536–539
  H, 529–530
  K, 529–531
  –K, 529–531, 539
  L, 529–530
  O, 533, 536, 540
Bird, B., 551, 607, 660
Birtles, E. F., 330–332, 335, 342, 685
Blomberg, J., 213, 684
Bodnar, R., 636–637, 645, 660–661, 664, 686
Boesky, D., 552–555, 661
Bollas, C., 613, 661
borderline, 491, 505, 511, 513, 593
  conditions, 373–374, 407, 495, 505–506, 513
  disorders, 5, 103, 323, 503
  organization, 505, 511, 513–514
  pathology, 493, 495, 497–498, 502, 504
  patient(s), 338, 373–374, 414, 465, 493–494, 501, 503, 506, 548, 605
  personality, 502–505, 510–511, 513–514
  structure, 505–506, 510
Boris, H. N., 536, 661
Bowlby, J., 331, 419, 515, 518, 629, 661
Brazelton, T. B., 437, 633, 661
Brenner, C., 29, 74, 208–211, 217, 475, 541, 548, 551–557, 562–564, 567, 583, 590, 607, 655, 658, 661

Breuer, J., 4–8, 10–11, 13, 31, 41, 38, 48, 117, 661–662
Bridgeman, P. W., 191, 415, 662
Briese, E., 645, 682
British Psychoanalytic Association, 218
British Psychoanalytic Institute, 329, 361–363
British Psychoanalytic Society, 169, 256–257, 259, 286, 289, 361, 385, 390
Britton, R., 471, 597, 614–615, 662
Broberg, J., 213, 684
Bromberg, P., 593, 662
Bruner, J., 582, 662
Bucci, W., 644, 662
Bullitt, W., 228, 668
Burlingham, D., 172
Burstein, E. D., 494, 512, 520, 675
Busch, F., 180, 212, 214, 555, 662

Calef, V., 492, 512–515, 519, 662
care-giver(s), 43–44, 55–56, 421, 431, 437–438, 444, 449, 525, 628, 635
  substitute, 448–449
Carlsson, J., 213, 684
Carnap, R., 415, 662
Carr, A. C., 504, 520, 662
Carsky, M., xx, 491, 520, 662
Case studies
  Breuer
    Anna O (Bertha Pappenheim), 4–5, 8
  Ellman
    Dr A, 598–603
    Ms W, 604–605, 643, 646–651
  Freud
    Dora, 19, 584
    Little Hans, 116
    Otto (Oscar Rie), 37–40, 47
    Rat Man, 126, 188
    Wolf Man, 103, 126, 130
  Klein
    Erich, 217, 219–220, 230
    Richard, 241–242
    Rita, 217, 219–220, 241–242

Kohut
  Mr Z, 483–484
castration complex, 100–101, 210
censorship, 28, 31, 36, 41, 49–54, 58,
    79–80, 110–111, 117–118
Charcot, J. M., 4, 8, 10–13, 24
Chernack, M., 437, 659
Chicago Psychoanalytic Institute,
    458
Chodorow, N., 581, 662
Chused, J. E., 553, 556, 566, 662
Clarkin, J. F., 513, 675, 678
clinical experience, xix, 15, 17, 127,
    134, 253, 261, 326, 365, 418, 512
cognitive, 35, 110–111, 165, 194, 248,
    273, 275, 278–279, 302, 344,
    374–375, 391, 409, 438, 441,
    450, 481, 496, 498, 501, 508–509,
    517, 525, 540, 576, 608, 636, 644,
    653
  function, 29, 138, 206, 407
  operation(s), 55
  process, 28, 31–32, 48, 58, 79, 137
  structure(s), 138, 450
Cohen, M. B., 553, 663
Coles, R., 172–173, 663
compromise formation, 28, 41,
    45–46, 80, 116, 141, 174–175,
    184, 208, 354, 551, 554–556, 585,
    607
conscious(ness) (Cs.), 4, 6, 9, 11–13,
    15, 30–32, 35–37, 40, 45–46,
    48–49, 50–56, 58, 80, 86,
    104–105, 110–111, 113–116,
    118–119, 133–139, 149, 156–157,
    159, 163–164, 175–176, 182,
    185–187, 213, 299, 500, 523,
    539–540, 542, 577–578, 598, 611
  see also: preconscious(ness),
    unconscious(ness)
containment, 197, 231, 246, 288, 303,
    314, 323, 345, 348, 350–351,
    373, 381, 395, 400, 404, 482,
    506, 510, 524–530, 532–534,
    590–595, 604–605, 612–613,
    638–639

controversial discussions, xx, 218,
    255–256, 258, 285–286, 289, 298,
    304, 328–329, 361–362
Coons, E. E., 636, 660
countertransference, 331, 466–467,
    470, 474, 493, 507, 535, 551–553,
    582–583, 595, 603, 605–607
  see also: transference
Cox, V. C., 645, 688
Coyne, L., 494, 512, 520, 675

da Vinci, L., 93
Damasio, A., 524, 663
Darwin, C., 77, 147, 623–624
death, 151–152, 156, 293, 302, 345,
    367, 379, 388, 463, 483, 538
  instinct, 152–153, 155–156,
    169–170, 200, 220, 232, 259,
    293, 308, 312, 324, 344, 379,
    383, 388, 410
  Thanatos, 131–132, 151–152,
    154, 158, 169–170, 200–201,
    205, 216, 220, 232, 312, 328,
    334, 344, 379, 410, 484, 645
defence see also: hysteria
  inhibitive, 175–177, 179
  manic, 239, 302, 365, 367, 387, 533
  mechanism(s), 175, 180, 184–185,
    187, 199, 212, 251, 346, 354,
    369, 445, 495, 502, 505, 533
  primary, 197, 319
  primitive, 196–197, 199, 319,
    501–502, 504, 505–506, 510,
    533
  restrictive, 178–180, 199
DeFries, Z., 431–432, 680
depression/depressive see also:
    anxiety
  infantile, 236, 243
  manic, 232, 236–237, 250–251, 324,
    335, 341
  position, 216, 232–241, 243–244,
    249–253, 256–258, 273, 291,
    296–298, 301–303, 313–316,
    319–323, 325–326, 342, 346,
    382, 384–387, 389, 409–410,

INDEX 695

492, 500, 509, 532–533, 539, 604, 614
state(s), 232, 236, 250, 335, 340
Deutsch, H., 223–224, 548, 663
development(al)
  early, 35, 42, 44, 55, 74, 77, 89–91, 107, 125, 138, 140, 160, 194, 202, 204, 213, 217, 219, 226–228, 230–231, 234–236, 239, 250–251, 272, 291–294, 303, 306, 313, 316, 322, 349, 352, 372–375, 380, 390, 399, 402–405, 424, 427, 430, 432, 449, 450–452, 454–455, 458, 495, 592, 623, 625, 630, 638, 642
  ego, 189, 279, 282, 294, 296–297, 399, 432
  infant/child, 64–65, 67, 95, 99, 227, 257, 289, 313, 327, 373, 376, 380, 387, 392, 402, 406, 421, 461, 642, 656
  narcissistic, 106, 108, 140, 461–464, 467, 473, 476, 603
  normal, 62, 76, 96, 178, 201, 295, 314, 408, 431–432, 438, 451, 461, 499, 533
  oedipal, 225–226, 228, 241, 317, 383, 400, 462, 493, 612
  optimal, 99, 122, 154, 162–163, 221–222, 227, 231, 238, 242, 249, 285, 310, 316, 321, 380, 390, 393, 404, 409, 486
  sexual, 29, 72, 75, 143, 476, 492
  superego, 140, 146, 162–163, 198, 206, 215, 220, 225, 231–232, 238–239, 243–244, 247, 249, 464, 495, 502
Diamond, J., 632, 663
dream
  book, 27–31, 37, 39, 41, 51–53, 57, 76, 79–80, 110
  day, 47
  formation, 28–29, 34, 37, 39, 41, 45, 50, 57, 80, 625
  interpretation, 187–188
  "Irma's", 38, 47
  nightmare(s), 27, 30, 79, 369
  process, 28, 33, 53, 80
  wish, 35–37, 39–40, 42
  work, 28, 80

ego *see also*: development, id, superego
  central, 347–350
  dominance, 474–475
  early, 293, 313
  ideal, 108, 132, 140, 145, 147, 155–156, 208, 350, 462–463, 500
  identity, 495, 500, 502
  libido, 80, 88–90, 102, 124–125, 153–154
  original, 94, 347–348
  pleasure, 91, 93–94, 288, 428
  purified (PPE), 91, 93–95, 97, 99, 106, 160, 251, 253, 272, 287–288, 326, 404–405, 409, 428, 451, 461–462, 475, 477, 498, 616
  primitive, 255, 269, 281, 283
  psychology, 169, 171, 177, 190, 192, 195–196, 204–206, 208, 210–214, 285, 453, 479–480, 491–493, 514, 519–520, 541–557, 580, 582
  reality, 91–92, 94, 288, 402, 428, 450
  regressed, 354
  structure, 134, 293, 312, 322, 333, 345–348, 376, 501, 503
Einstein, A., 88, 333, 419
Eissler, K. R., 24–25, 411, 663
Ellman, S. J., xiii–xv, xviii–xix, xx–xxi, 17, 25, 30, 49, 81, 86, 123–124, 126, 129, 171, 208, 256, 286, 326, 373, 455, 470, 491, 515, 551, 553, 557–558, 562, 589, 591, 597–598, 605, 609, 625, 635–637, 645–646, 648, 660–665, 686
Ellmann, R., 61, 75, 663

Emde, R., 439, 664
envy, 142–143, 223–225, 246–247, 252, 289, 291–292, 298, 303, 307–327, 410, 442, 525, 532
  excessive, 315, 318
  penis, 142, 161–162, 165, 224, 226, 246–248, 252, 317, 327, 563, 581
  primary, 303, 309–310
Erikson, E. H., 173, 543, 545, 547–548, 664
Eros, 131–132, 151–155, 158, 197, 200, 205, 216, 232, 312, 328, 410, 484 *see also*: life instinct, sexual instinct
Escalona, S. K., 199, 660

Fairbairn, W. R. D., xiv, xix, 190, 241, 251, 291–293, 296–297, 326–327, 329–359, 413, 419, 424, 487, 493, 495, 510, 515, 518, 563, 571, 573–575, 628–631, 646, 654–655, 664–665
false connection(s), 18–19, 21–22, 39–40
fantasy, 3–4, 18, 25, 31, 57, 60, 67–69, 76, 80, 83, 85, 93, 95, 107, 112, 120, 133, 142, 146, 159, 161, 178, 184, 215, 259, 288, 360, 365–367, 371–374, 379, 381, 386, 400, 404, 409, 412, 416, 463–464, 467–468, 470, 482, 495, 499–500, 542, 546, 550–551, 587, 589, 591, 597, 599–600, 603–604, 624, 644, 647, 653, 655 *see also*: phantasy
  child's, 67, 337, 468
  destruction, 102, 120, 161, 398
  omnipotent, 365–366
  unconscious, 135, 147, 175–176, 186, 191, 211, 410–411, 417, 481, 551, 555, 595–596, 598, 609, 636
Farber, J., 637, 664–665
father *see also*: penis
  complex, 92, 145
  figure, 285, 385

Fechner, G., 47, 148, 158
Federn, E., 93, 682
Federn, P., 93, 494, 543, 665, 682
Ferenczi, S., 84–85, 94–95, 162, 216–217, 219–220, 232, 236, 250–251, 326, 413, 545, 665
Ferro, A., 587, 596, 665
fetish(ist), 62, 164
Fliess, W., 7, 23, 25, 38, 41–42, 47, 59, 99, 158, 611
Fonagy, P., 592, 608, 612, 665
Fosshage, J., 125, 665
Foucault, M., 398, 665
free association, 34, 125, 186–188, 395–396, 435, 534, 549, 571, 577–578, 581, 585, 587, 613
Freedman, N., 604, 644, 665–666
French, T. M., 469, 658
Freud, A., xvii, xix, 132, 162, 169–191, 196, 199, 205, 210, 212–213, 217–218, 257, 261, 267, 272–284, 286, 288–289, 294, 354, 361–363, 385, 414, 543–545, 547, 549, 578, 666, 684
Freud, S., xiii–xiv, xvii, xix, xxi, xxiii–xxv, 3–25, 27–81, 83–166, 169–175, 178, 180–181, 186–194, 196–200, 203–209, 212, 215–226, 228–229, 231–232, 236, 239–243, 245, 247–257, 259–261, 264–268, 270–273, 277, 279, 282–289, 292, 297–298, 304–308, 310, 312, 324, 326–336, 338, 342–347, 349–352, 356–361, 363–366, 368, 374–376, 379, 381–385, 387–388, 398–399, 401–411, 414–416, 418, 427–430, 449–455, 458–462, 470, 473–479, 483–484, 486, 492–493, 515–519, 521–525, 529, 534, 537, 539, 541–543, 545–547, 551–552, 554–557, 562, 565–568, 571–572, 574–577, 579–582, 584–587, 589, 603, 606, 608, 611, 614–617, 620, 623–624, 626–628, 630, 643–645, 650, 654–655, 661–662, 666–668
Friedman, J. A., 544, 556, 668

Friedman, L., 557, 669
Fromm, E., 191–192, 414
Fromm-Reichmann, F., xvii, 414
Frosch, J., 494, 510, 669
frustration tolerance, 227, 242, 299, 524, 539, 642
Frutus, M., 636–637, 660
Fuerst, R. A., 469, 658
Furer, M., 445, 669

Gaensbauer, T., 439, 664
Gay, P., 24–25, 38, 58–59, 164, 581, 611, 669
Gedo, J., 479, 669
genital *see also*: penis, phallic, zone
   desires, 245, 248, 303, 315, 317, 420
   female, 164, 224
   impulse, 315–316
   interest, 75, 96, 99, 101, 116, 338, 476
   male, 73, 142, 245, 248, 542
   orgasm, 75
   pre-, 64, 74–75, 78–79, 225, 243–245, 303, 502
   primacy, 68, 74–76, 90, 242, 245–248, 420, 502, 615
   sex, 72, 78
   stage, 74, 221, 223–225, 229, 248, 253, 303, 335
   stimulation, 64, 68
   trends, 301–302, 304, 315
Gergely, G., 612, 615, 669
Ghent, E., 577, 669
Gill, M. M., xxv, 42, 86, 129, 419, 566–571, 579–580, 597, 605, 621–623, 640, 669, 683
Gitelson, M., 553, 556, 669
Globus, G. G., 627, 669
Glover, E., 170, 236, 255, 258, 261, 263, 267–270, 281–284, 286–288, 362, 543, 548, 670
Goldberg, A., 479, 669
Goldberger, M., 213, 587, 599, 670
Goldman, D., xx, 360, 363, 399, 670
Goldstein, E. G., 504, 520, 662

Good, M. I., 24, 670
Gosliner, B. J., 616, 680
gratitude, 224–225, 289, 291–292, 307, 311–312, 314, 320–322, 642
Gray, P., 180, 212–214, 555, 670
greed, 291, 299–301, 303, 307, 309, 311, 314, 321, 324, 327, 368–369, 528
Green, A., xxi, 566, 612
Greenacre, P., 543, 545, 547, 670
Greenberg, Jay, xxii–xxiii, 195, 201–203, 341–342, 351, 401, 403, 414, 416–423, 425, 568–570, 572, 574, 577, 584, 622, 670
Greenberg, Joanne, 414, 670
Greenson, R. R., 510, 545, 556, 670
Grinker, R. R., 469, 658
Grosskurth, P., 565, 670
Grotjahn, M., 469, 658
Grotstein, J., 330–331, 526, 528, 536–537, 539, 670
Gruness, M., 609, 671
guilt, 135, 166, 220–221, 223, 228–229, 232, 242, 262, 296, 298, 300, 302, 311, 314–316, 320–322, 343–344, 380, 382–385, 389, 398, 405, 409, 478, 482, 487, 500, 505, 532, 542, 587, 647, 649 *see also*: unconscious
Guntrip, H., xvii, 332, 341, 352–358, 414, 493, 495, 510, 515–516, 518, 575, 589, 654, 671

hallucination(s), 5, 42–44, 49–50, 55, 91, 102, 104, 255, 264–268, 271, 288, 297, 352–353, 370–372, 393–394, 433, 505, 624, 627–628
Halperin, J., 637, 661
Halperin, R., 637, 665
Hampstead Clinic, 172, 361
Harmon, R., 439, 664
Harris, A., 656, 671
Hartmann, H., xix, 169–171, 173, 190–213, 288, 351, 414, 429, 453, 471, 493, 497, 509, 516, 544–550, 553–554, 557, 562, 567, 654, 671

hate, 54, 99, 107–108, 115, 181–182, 222–223, 226–227, 230, 238–239, 243, 245, 248–249, 262, 271, 293–294, 296–297, 306, 311, 313, 317–318, 321, 324, 339–340, 355, 365–366, 379, 381–383, 394, 405, 409, 488, 494, 500, 505, 509, 529–532, 547, 590–591, 607–608, 616–617, 647
Healey, J., 637, 661
Heimann, P., 258, 262, 276, 298, 303, 553, 672, 677
Heisenberg, W., 419, 672
Hinshelwood, R. D., 527, 672
Hoffmann, I. Z., 578, 582–583, 587, 622, 672
Holder, A., 516, 672
Holt, R., 148, 567–568, 644, 672
Holtzman, A., 637, 665
Hopkins, L., 361, 411–412, 672
Horney, K., 191, 225, 414
Horwotz, L., 494, 512, 520, 675
Hrdy, S. B., 631–632, 635, 642–643, 672
humiliation, 10, 187, 463, 468, 472, 477–479, 591, 599–600
Hunt, H. F., 504, 520, 662
Hunziker, U. A., 633, 672
Hurvich, M., 629, 673
hypnosis, 4, 7–8, 11–14, 186, 188
 see also: hysteria
hypochondria, 124–126, 467, 470, 503
hysteria/hysterical, 4–13, 15, 18, 20–21, 24, 34, 64, 69, 89, 103, 116, 119, 123–125, 127, 159, 179, 335, 338–339, 345, 499, 502, 504, 548, 581
 attacks, 8
 defence, 6, 12–13, 15
 hypnoid, 12–13
 retention, 12–13

id, 83, 131, 135, 137–141, 145–149, 153–155, 157–158, 165, 174–176, 180, 186–188, 193–194, 196, 204, 207, 209–210, 212, 221, 230–231, 264, 279–283, 288, 333, 345, 347–348, 351, 376, 381–382, 399, 404, 422, 492, 499–500, 508, 542, 544, 546, 549–550, 554–557, 571
 see also: ego, superego
impulses, 180, 188–189, 397, 399
Inderbitzen, L., 542, 544, 678
internal saboteur, 347–350
International Psychoanalytic Association (IPA), 217, 646
intervention(s), xxi, 150, 205, 213, 356, 358, 414, 488, 494, 544, 550, 588, 591, 595–597, 605, 613
intra cranial self-stimulation (ICSS), 625, 635–637, 645
introjection, 94–95, 105, 108, 141, 177, 180–182, 209, 226, 233–235, 243, 246, 249, 251, 255, 258, 261, 270–272, 276, 288, 293–295, 297, 299–300, 302–303, 305–307, 309, 311, 385–387, 392, 423, 428, 433, 442, 449, 462, 495–496, 498–501, 525–528, 531, 544, 616–617
 see also: projective–introjective
 infant, 528–529
 parental, 162
 primary, 272
Ippolito, P., 636–637, 660, 665
Isaacs, S., 258–278, 280–284, 298, 303, 673, 677

Jackler, F., 637, 645, 664
Jacobs, T., 552–553, 556, 673
Jacobson, E., 93, 207–208, 403, 429, 452, 454, 461, 471, 497, 499, 511, 543, 545, 547–548, 564, 566, 612, 616–617, 650, 655–656, 673
Janet, P., 4, 10–11
jealousy, 145, 225, 303, 309–311, 316–318, 321, 525, 543
Johan, M., 592, 681
Jones, E., 85–86, 164, 218, 257, 331–332, 363, 386, 673
Joseph, B., 606–607, 673

Jung, C. G., 90, 100, 146, 191, 251, 411

Kalinkowitz, B., 413, 425, 563
Kalkolewski, J. W., 645, 688
Kaufmann, P., 481, 673
Keats, J., 521, 673
Kernberg, O. F., xix–xx, 236, 338, 429, 491–520, 662, 673–675, 678
King, P., 218, 255, 257–258, 261–262, 264–265, 267–268, 270, 272–277, 280–284, 287, 289, 675
Klein, G. S., xxv, 567–568, 571, 577, 675
Klein, M., xiv, xix, 74, 84, 132, 156, 169–172, 196, 209, 215–254, 256–258, 263–264, 266, 269–270, 273, 278, 281, 286, 289, 291–330, 342, 346, 349, 359–367, 371, 373–374, 376, 379, 383–389, 397–399, 401, 405, 409–410, 419, 424, 471, 483, 487, 493, 495, 500, 510, 514–516, 519, 522, 528–529, 531–533, 539, 544, 565, 575, 589, 606–607, 614, 639, 642, 645–646, 650, 655–656, 675–677
Kleitman, N., 81, 658
Knight, R. P., 494, 677
Kohut, H., xvii, xix, 125, 331, 414, 457–489, 513, 526, 571, 573–574, 589, 597, 616, 620, 655, 677
Kripke, D., 627, 677
Kris, E., 192–194, 200, 205, 210–212, 429, 453, 543–547, 550, 553, 556, 589, 672, 677
Kubie, L. S., 567, 678

Lacan, J., xxi, 566
Lachman, F. M., 513, 687
Lamarckism, 146, 165, 228, 624
Laplanche, J., xxi, 638, 678
Lavender, J., 644, 666
Lazar, A., 213, 684
Lenzenweger, M. F., 513, 678
Lerner, H., 513, 687
Levy, K. N., 513, 675, 678

Levy, S., 542, 544, 678
Lewin, K., 553
libido, 4, 69, 71, 75, 92–95, 101, 104–106, 115, 120, 124, 141, 145, 153, 159, 188–189, 200, 207, 220, 227, 232, 234–235, 242, 244–245, 265, 267, 276–278, 287–288, 293–295, 299–300, 303–304, 311, 327, 334, 336, 339, 343, 345, 347–349, 365, 403–406, 408–409, 432, 434, 459–461, 467, 472–473, 477, 496–497, 509, 517, 529, 547, 573, 629 see also: attachment, ego, narcissistic, object, oral, zones
Lichtenberg, J. D., 452, 656, 678
life
    adult, 60, 62–63, 65, 76–77, 174, 236, 324, 393
    emotional, 292, 298, 471, 594
    fantasy, 67
    infant's, 295, 299, 301, 325, 348, 385, 390, 394, 433, 626
    instinct, 312, 318, 320 see also: Eros
    internal, 295, 312, 359, 397, 639, 650
    mental, 40, 54, 88, 117–118, 208–209, 221, 231, 260, 263–264, 270, 277, 280, 301, 416, 424, 431, 542, 554, 588
    phantasy, 215, 255, 266, 271, 309
    sexual, 23, 62, 65–66, 70, 74–75
Likierman, M., 292, 325–327, 678
Little, M., 553, 678
Loewald, H., xvii–xviii, 430, 461, 545, 564–566, 568, 5809, 678
Loewenstein, R. M., 194, 200, 210–212, 429, 453, 543–547, 549–553, 672, 678–679
Lorenz, K., 334
Lynch, A. A., xx, 551, 553, 558, 570–571, 659, 679

Mach, E., 191
MacLean, P. D., 517, 679
Magurran, A., 642, 679

Mahler, M. S., xix–xx, 208, 427–437, 442, 444–445, 448–455, 493, 511, 545, 547, 616–617, 679–680
Marmor, J., 548, 680
Maslow, A. H., 600, 680
masochism, 62, 70, 98, 132, 135, 177, 338, 463, 468, 499, 502, 505, 548, 581
Masson, J. M., 23–24, 41, 47, 99, 680
masturbation, 3, 22, 64, 73, 224, 400, 409
Mattiace, L., 637, 664–665
McDevitt, J. B., 438, 442, 445, 447–448, 680
McFadyen Johnson, A., 469, 658
McLaughlin, J. T., 552–553, 556, 592, 680–681
Meehan, K. B., 513, 678
melancholia, 102–106, 108–109, 123, 125, 155, 236, 239–240, 345
memory, 4, 8–10, 13–17, 20–22, 31–32, 43, 49–52, 55–56, 62, 64, 67, 94, 110, 137, 157, 179, 186, 189, 268, 273, 281, 283, 287, 343, 396, 452, 467, 471, 495, 509, 524–525, 534, 536, 546, 580, 587, 603, 625–626, 628, 641, 655
  intolerable, 343
  pathogenic, 4, 15–17, 19–20, 67, 186, 326
  trace(s), 14, 43, 48–49, 157, 268, 270, 281, 496, 508–547
metapsychology, 33, 85–87, 118, 128–129, 195, 261, 281, 284, 333, 548, 555, 567–568, 577
  papers, 84–85, 129, 427, 452
Mitchell, S., xxii–xxiii, 195, 201–203, 331, 341–342, 351–352, 401, 403, 414, 416–423, 425, 562, 568–579, 582, 584–585, 622, 628–629, 631, 653–654, 670
model
  classical, 487, 578
  conflict, 209, 501
  developmental, xiv, 407, 487, 495, 501, 507, 621
  drive/structural, xxii, 83, 131, 137, 140, 158, 169–170, 174, 210, 342, 554, 557, 561–562, 568, 570, 574, 577–578, 584, 653
  hydraulic, 78, 147
  multiple factor, xiii–xv, xxii, xxv, 641, 653, 656
  topographic, 85, 109–110, 133, 554
  U-tube, 474
Money-Kyrle, R., 231–233, 236, 239, 289, 327, 681
Moore, G. E., 415, 681
Moskowitz, M., xxi, 86, 129, 515, 664
mother
  bad, 421, 616–617
  body, 222–223, 226, 229, 231, 240, 246–248, 300, 432
  breast(s), 142, 244–245, 277, 293, 299–300, 303, 308, 310, 316–318, 324, 327, 336, 370
  –child pair, 431, 434–436, 446–447, 488, 496, 547
  good, 421, 443, 617
  –enough, 201–202, 288, 295, 352, 377, 388, 403, 408, 630, 634–635, 642
  –infant relationship, xiv, 216, 309, 331, 363–364, 372, 375, 377, 383, 402, 406, 432–433, 526, 575, 613, 621, 629–630, 635, 637, 639, 641
mourning, 103–104, 236–237, 239–240, 289, 302, 323, 604, 654
Muslin, H. L., 605, 669

Nagel, E., 87, 516, 681
Nagel, T., 87, 516, 681
Nagera, H., 465, 681
narcissism, 66, 77, 80, 83–84, 88, 90–97, 99–103, 106–109, 119–127, 132–133, 150–154, 160, 197, 229, 240, 305–307, 339, 383, 404–407, 409, 423, 425, 427, 432, 439, 442, 457–466, 469–479, 487,

503–505, 511, 548, 573–574, 581, 592, 595–597, 615–618, 620, 638, 651, 655 *see also*: development, self, transference
identification, 107–108
libido, 99, 141, 154, 158, 459, 466–467, 475
personality, 499, 501–502, 511
primary, 208, 277, 287, 388, 428, 432, 450–452, 459, 461
rage, 457, 472, 477–479, 485
self, 463–465
stage, 90–91, 93–96, 99, 120, 160, 253, 288, 615–616, 623–624
negative therapeutic reaction (NTR), 148–150, 311
neurophysiology, xxv, 3, 11, 77, 198, 492, 496, 508, 516–518, 636
neuroses/neurotic *see also*: anxiety, transference
actual, 3, 20, 22–23, 124, 159
experience, 10
obsessional, 85, 119, 124–125
psychogenic, 3, 20, 159
symptoms, 3, 16, 45, 103, 551
traumatic, 9, 69, 149–150
neutralization, 197–201, 205, 434, 509, 547–549
New York Psychoanalytic Institute, 553, 563
New York State Psychiatric Society, 563–564
Nietzsche, F., 533, 540, 682
Nunberg, H., 93, 170, 196, 453, 544–545, 549, 682

object *see also*: self-object-affect, splitting
bad, 234, 237, 249, 294, 297, 299–302, 313–314, 317, 322–323, 342–349, 354–356, 366, 388, 404, 498
cathexis, 78, 105–106, 109, 120, 140–144, 153, 158, 459
external, 96, 99, 105, 120, 155–156, 227, 230, 233–234, 236, 243, 268, 272, 274–275, 278, 282, 300, 306, 312, 338–340, 370, 392, 403, 498, 529, 638
good, 234–235, 237–238, 245, 247, 249, 294–295, 299–301, 305, 308, 310–317, 319–323, 325, 343–345, 348, 354–355, 388, 397–398, 400, 496, 498, 525
idealized, 295, 314–315, 318, 320, 322–323, 350, 461–464, 466, 468, 472, 474–475, 478–479, 482
internal, 107, 120, 226–227, 230, 235, 243, 246, 249, 261, 271, 276, 279, 294, 304, 306, 318, 321, 337–338, 388, 392, 394, 400, 496, 498, 527, 531–532, 575, 616, 651
libido, 78, 88–90, 94, 102, 125, 141, 153, 158, 196, 336, 338, 429, 432, 442, 450, 459, 462, 473, 475, 552
lost, 103–104, 119–121, 238, 244, 387
love, 29, 39, 74–75, 77–78, 80, 83–85, 90–91, 93, 96–97, 99–100, 102–103, 106, 109, 114, 121–123, 125–126, 141, 143, 153–154, 158, 162, 223, 225, 240, 311, 314, 317, 338, 340, 405, 429, 433, 442–443, 459–461, 473, 476, 617–620, 650
new, 105, 320, 329, 412, 589
part, 232–234, 262, 278, 294, 299, 307, 327, 336, 381, 404, 433, 497, 502, 530, 532
primary, 242
relations, xvii, xxii, 84–85, 89, 91, 102, 143, 182, 200, 202–203, 235, 240, 243, 259, 267, 271–280, 283, 285, 292–295, 297, 304–307, 329–330, 333, 341, 344–346, 352, 355, 357–358, 377–380, 386, 392, 397, 402–403, 405, 454, 459,

464, 474, 483, 485, 491–493, 495, 497, 499–503, 505, 507–511, 514, 516–517, 519, 522, 530, 545, 547, 553, 570, 573, 575, 584, 589, 603, 606, 614, 617–618, 620, 646, 653
seeking, xiv, 333–334, 351–352, 575, 629–631, 634–635, 640
self, 98, 208, 439, 475–477, 479–481, 483–486, 488, 497, 500, 506, 517, 591, 601, 620
sexual, 60–61, 63, 65, 89, 141, 152
whole, 232–235, 249, 253, 289, 301, 325, 336–337, 369, 379, 381, 388, 505, 532
word, 121
objectivity, 260, 263, 269, 279, 285, 371, 435, 486, 710
obsessive-compulsive, 20–21, 89, 96, 103, 123, 179, 335, 338, 499, 502–503
Oedipus/oedipal, 59, 84, 229, 231, 317, 332, 356, 431, 482, 505, 532
see also: development
child, 143, 146, 253, 383, 409, 483
complex, 74, 100, 131–132, 141–147, 158, 207, 218, 220–221, 226, 240–241, 243–249, 252–253, 302–303, 316, 318, 380, 385, 409, 475, 571, 614
conflict, 99, 127, 143, 207, 220–221, 223, 228, 240, 243, 245, 247, 316, 383, 399, 485, 563, 584
disorders, 484
drama, 127, 133, 162, 221, 231, 253, 475, 618
dynamics, 97, 99–101, 127, 142, 144, 209, 215, 221–222, 226–227, 243, 252–253, 320, 325, 349–350, 504, 562, 614–615, 649–650, 655
negative, 100, 143–144, 245–247
positive, 100, 143–144, 161, 245, 247–248

pre-, 74, 146, 430, 442, 462, 464, 484, 494, 547, 563, 612–613, 615–616, 650
rivalry, 39, 207, 245, 603, 612, 616–617, 650
situation, 222–224, 245–246, 248, 250, 302–303, 321, 346, 349–350, 400, 409, 614–615
stage/period, 74, 97, 142–145, 162, 213, 216, 221, 225, 240, 252–253, 316–317, 325, 346, 349–350, 385, 409–410, 462, 464, 466, 475, 483–485, 492, 499, 510, 547, 563, 613, 617, 650
triangle, 162, 221–222, 226, 239, 253, 597, 613–614
Ogden, T. H., xxiv, 417, 553, 587, 608–612, 682
Olds, J., 625, 635, 645, 682
omnipotence, 126, 237–239, 297, 301, 311, 319, 353, 373, 377–379, 387–388, 390, 393, 395, 403, 431–433, 440–443, 476, 532, 610, 630 *see also*: fantasy, phantasy
attack(s), 531–532
control, 365–367, 387, 393, 412, 443, 478
oral *see also*: sadism, zone(s)
desire(s), 234, 242, 302, 315, 317
excitement, 392
impulse, 271, 299, 324, 327
libido, 224, 233, 248, 282, 299, 308, 327
phase(s), 140, 229, 236, 242, 244, 335, 339–340, 350–351
pleasure, 394, 406
stage, 68, 107, 215, 221–222, 224, 231, 244, 251–252, 304, 308, 336, 386–387, 563
tendencies, 64, 335
orgasm, 23, 42, 75, 77, 148, 158
Ornstein, A., 480, 489, 682
Ornstein, P. H., 480, 489, 682
O'Shaughnessy, E., 604, 62

paranoia, 34, 89, 93, 102, 123, 125, 234–236, 238–239, 241, 244, 246, 249–251, 289, 295, 316, 318, 335, 338–339, 503–504, 506, 543, 648 see also: anxiety
paranoid-schizoid position, 196, 241, 244, 251–252, 291, 295–303, 316, 320–321, 325–326, 388, 424, 454, 492, 528, 532, 539, 563
paraphrenia, 89, 124 see also: schizophrenia
parent(s)/parental
  combined, 230–231, 303, 317, 647
  couple, 532, 618
  figure, 161, 466
  idealized, 367, 461–462, 465, 467, 500
penis, 71, 73, 116, 143, 161, 164, 224–226, 240, 242–243, 246–248, 262, 316–317, 532, 603 see also: envy
  father's, 222–224, 231, 240, 245–249, 303, 310, 317–318
perceptual system (Pcpt.), 48–49, 51, 56, 58, 136–138, 156–157
Petot, J. M., 216–220, 325, 682
phallic stage, 68, 74, 132, 142–143, 161, 221, 223, 252–253, 335
  see also: genital stage
phantasy, 163, 174, 186, 215, 221, 226, 228–230, 237–238, 244, 246–249, 258–261, 263–276, 279, 281–282, 283, 285, 288, 294, 298, 300–305, 308–310, 315–317, 328, 371, 386, 387, 528, 535, 539, 551, 618 see also: fantasy, life
  internal, 268, 275, 278
  omnipotent, 237–238, 312, 387, 532
  related, 273–274
  unconscious, 149, 219, 251, 259–261, 263–265, 270–272, 280, 535
Piaget, J., 195, 450, 612
Pine, F., 208, 434, 437, 444, 493, 497, 547, 605, 680, 682

pleasure see also: anal, ego, oral
  principle, 57, 93, 147–151, 155, 203–204, 266, 272, 279, 334–345, 542, 546, 624
  seeking, xiv, 56, 333, 352, 575, 629–631, 633–634, 640
  –unpleasure, 51, 98, 203
Popper, K., 516, 682
preconscious(ness) (Pcs.), 28, 32, 35–37, 40–41, 45–46, 49–55, 58, 79–80, 111, 113, 115–119, 134, 136–138, 149, 170, 282, 348
  see also: conscious(ness), unconscious(ness)
  system, 32, 45, 51–52, 54, 58, 80, 104
  wish, 35, 45
Prescott, J. W., 630–632, 683
pressure technique, 4, 15, 31, 34, 188
Pribram, K., 42, 683
Prince, M., 34
process
  primary, 17, 28, 31, 44, 52, 54–55, 57, 79, 83, 91, 111, 114, 117, 134–135, 141, 148, 203, 205, 267, 276–277, 279–283, 368, 375, 494, 500, 504, 506, 626, 643–644
  secondary, 28, 31, 44, 52, 79, 83, 91, 111, 114, 117, 134, 141, 148, 205, 267, 280–283, 373, 626, 643–644
projection, 94–95, 108, 138, 147, 156, 177, 180–183, 196–197, 199, 201, 209, 226, 229–230, 234–235, 240, 243, 251, 255, 258, 272, 276, 280, 294–295, 298–300, 302, 305–307, 309, 315–316, 319, 374, 379, 386–387, 392, 428, 498–502, 504, 524–530, 532–533, 535, 552, 591, 593, 597, 599, 617, 645
projective
  identification, 201, 226, 229, 250–251, 291, 294, 300–301, 306, 312, 319, 321–322, 326, 360, 379, 419, 492, 504,

510–511, 526, 528–529, 532, 534, 536, 539, 591, 593, 597, 616–617, 639
–introjective, 216, 226, 250–251, 294, 306, 326, 379, 429, 606–607
mechanisms, 43, 449
Psychoanalytic Institute of New York, 430
psychosis *see also*: transference
autistic, 432–433, 497
childhood, 196, 430–433
symbiotic, 433, 497
psychotic *see also*: anxiety
disorders, 5, 20, 563
patients, 330, 352, 368–369, 373, 413, 423, 425, 465, 506, 522, 548
puberty, 59, 64, 68, 70, 72–75, 99, 133, 177

Racker, H., 417, 683
rage, 9, 280, 472, 477, 479, 485, 494, 505, 592, 604, 646 *see also*: narcissistic
Rangell, L., 553–556, 683
Rank, O., 160, 191, 683
Rapaport, D., 86, 129, 190, 192, 204, 206, 541, 545, 569, 597, 683
rapid eye movement (REM), x, xiv, 30, 49, 81, 316, 395, 596, 621, 625–627, 634–637
reality
external, 260, 266–267, 279, 295, 304, 366–367, 370–371, 395, 524, 529, 546, 554
inner, 281, 365–367, 383, 393, 396
internal, 265–267, 366–367
outer, 334, 339, 345, 393
principle, 203–204, 265, 270, 334, 345, 523, 542
psychic, 67–69, 260–261, 264, 268, 295–296, 381, 385–386, 397
testing, 44, 102, 104, 178–179, 197, 203, 205, 270–271, 276, 280, 283, 296, 374, 393, 407, 433, 506, 513, 514, 538, 549
regression, 28, 31, 34–35, 44, 46–47, 49–50, 52, 58, 79–80, 85, 127, 177, 187, 224, 242, 258, 262, 265, 268–269, 280–281, 283, 296, 302, 337, 354–355, 368, 396, 437, 444, 465–466, 474, 497, 504, 506–507, 513, 592, 626–627
regulation, 158, 202–203, 268, 275, 437, 458, 524, 549, 625, 636, 645, 650
drive, 462
tension, 427, 433
Reich, A., 543, 552, 683
Reich, W., 189, 411, 543, 548, 683
Renik, O., 556, 566, 683
repression, 34, 36, 64, 73, 85, 104, 109–116, 128, 133–134, 136–137, 140, 145, 147, 149, 159, 175, 177, 179, 184–185, 196, 199, 219, 221, 224, 245, 299, 331, 343–350, 354, 356–357, 463–464, 470, 492, 495, 499–500, 502, 509, 524, 542, 549–550, 554
after, 112–113, 115–116, 119
primal, 36. 110, 112–113, 115, 327
secondary, 110, 113, 327
Resch, R. C., 439, 683
Reynoso, J. S., 513, 678
Richards, A. D., xx, 551, 553, 558, 563, 570–571, 659, 679, 683
Riviere, J., 250, 255, 266, 298, 677, 684
Roazen, P., 126, 684
Rodman, F. R., 360–362, 401–402, 410, 684
Rosenfeld, H., 196, 216, 528, 660, 684
Ross, J. R., 431–432, 680
Rothstein, A., 555, 566, 583, 684
Rubinstein, B. B., 519, 684

sadism, 21, 67–68, 70, 97–98, 107, 152, 155, 177, 221, 223, 227, 229, 231–233, 235, 239–240, 242–244,

250, 308, 338, 366, 468, 500, 502, 505, 531–532, 617
anal, 83, 90–91, 96, 101, 103, 122, 125, 220–224, 236, 324, 327, 405
oral, 221, 231, 233, 242, 244, 293, 300, 308, 324
Sandell, R., 213, 684
Sander, L. W., 437–438, 684
Sandler, A., xviii, 417, 553, 684
Sandler, J., xviii, 173, 178–183, 204, 417, 553, 564, 606, 684
Schafer, R., 191–192, 236, 567, 568, 571, 582–583, 685
Scharff, D. E., 330–332, 335, 342, 685
Schiller, P., 206, 685
schizophrenia/schizoid, 89, 102, 109, 119–121, 123–125, 195–199, 201–203, 213, 251, 292–293, 295–298, 307, 326, 335, 339–341, 346, 349, 352, 354–355, 388, 414, 417, 425, 497, 504–506, 510, 514, 548, 644 *see also*: paranoid-schizoid, paraphrenia
dilemma, 339–340, 349
dynamics, 291, 295, 326, 329–330, 342, 346, 655
individual, 339
mechanics, 296, 298–299
personality, 354
Schmideberg, M., 362, 494, 685
Schreber, D. P., 85, 92–93, 120, 180–182, 197, 297–298
Schubert, J., 213, 684
Schur, M., 38, 516, 685
Schwaber, E., 553, 685
Schwartz, F., 206, 685
Searl, N., 365–366, 685
Searles, H. F., xvii, 414, 635,654, 685
seduction hypothesis/theory, 20, 23–25, 28, 58–59
Segal, H., 216, 522, 532, 660, 685
self
analysis, 4, 24–25, 59, 555, 611
bad, 294, 300, 497–500
bipolar, 468, 482

destruction, 196, 345, 585, 645
esteem, 184, 417–418, 424, 441, 458, 464, 466, 469, 473, 549, 574, 593, 595, 601
false, 377–378, 390, 397, 407, 638–639
good, 497–498
grandiose, 208, 464, 465–472, 474, 479, 499
ideal, 499–500
image, 492, 495–498, 550
interest, 77–78, 404
narcissistic, 463–465
object, 98, 208, 439, 475–477, 479–481, 483–486, 488, 497, 500, 506, 517, 591, 601, 620
-object-affect (S-O-A), 495–499, 501, 508–510
organization, 404, 422, 576
preservation, 89, 93–94, 98, 152, 194, 240, 287
psychological, 92, 403, 452
reflection, 157, 619–620, 648
regard, 104
representation, 108, 141, 181, 184, 207–208, 492, 495, 594, 625–626
true, 360, 367, 377, 390, 396, 649
sexual *see also*: abuse, behaviour, development, life, object
activity, 64, 222, 240
discharge, 20, 22–23, 42, 75, 77, 148, 158
drive, 197, 200
experience, 24
instinct, 61, 65, 70, 88–89, 93, 152, 200, 405 *see also*: Eros
practices, 3, 22–23, 62
psycho-, 29, 476
stage(s), 68, 84, 133, 251
sexuality
adult, 60, 62, 64, 72, 74, 142
bi-, 61, 144, 244, 247
childhood, 17, 39, 60, 72, 76, 133, 161, 221
hetero-, 74–75, 177, 504, 573

homo-, 29, 60–62, 75–77, 96,
    99–100, 106, 108, 143, 146,
    177, 181–182, 197, 245,
    317–318, 461, 543, 603
infantile, 62–63, 65, 69–70, 76, 236
Silverman, L. H., 199, 685
Silverman, M., 552, 685
Simon, B., 24, 685
Singer, E., 422, 685
Skinner, B. F., 424, 686
Smith, H. F., 557, 686
Socrates, 27, 30, 50, 79
Solms, M., 81, 686
Sonnenschein, D., 627, 677
Spence, D. P., 568, 571, 582, 686
Spillius, E. B., 328, 587, 686
Spitz, R., 194–195, 429, 445, 543, 686
splitting
    of consciousness, 6, 11–12
    of the object, 244, 293–294, 297,
        388, 442
Stein, M. H., 548, 556, 636, 686
Steiner, J., 597, 686
Steiner, R., 5, 218, 255–256, 258–259,
    261–262, 264–265, 267–268, 270,
    272–277, 280–284, 287, 289, 675,
    686
Steiner, S. S., 635–637, 645, 660–661,
    664–665, 686
Steingart, I., 397, 686
Sterba, R., 543–545, 555–556, 686
Stern, D., 351, 402, 437, 450, 613,
    639, 646, 687
Stevens, V., xx, 587
Stewart, W. A., 3, 5, 687
Stolorow, R. D., 480, 513, 608, 610,
    687
Stone, L., 461, 487, 545, 548, 564, 687
Stone, M. H., 514, 687
Strachey, J., 218, 385, 543–545, 556,
    687
stranger reaction, 445–446
Strozier, C., 458, 484, 687
subjectivity, xxiv, 255, 259–261, 263,
    266, 269, 271, 278–279, 285–286,
    331, 362, 392, 395, 400, 407, 416,
    435, 496, 508–509, 515, 556, 582,
    589–590, 595, 597, 610–611
inter-, xxiv, 128, 489, 522, 568,
    595, 608–610, 613, 618, 620,
    651
Sugarman, A., 513, 687
Sullivan, H. S., xvii, xix, xxi, xxiv,
    191–192, 352–353, 413–426,
    480–481, 488, 545, 564, 571, 575,
    581, 654–655, 687
Sulloway, F. J., 24, 688
superego, 83, 105, 131–132, 135,
    139–141, 145–147, 155–156, 158,
    160, 162–163, 165, 174, 176, 178,
    181, 193, 198–199, 204–207, 216,
    220–222, 228–232, 239, 244, 246,
    249–250, 254, 261, 300–302, 304,
    343–344, 346–347, 350, 383, 385,
    419, 422, 445, 462–463, 466, 478,
    492, 499–500, 502, 505, 507–508,
    531, 542–546, 549–550, 554–557
    see also: development, ego, id
    early, 229, 232, 254, 300
    female, 224–225, 231, 247, 254
    male, 223, 246, 254
    structure, 162–163, 176, 198, 201,
        215, 253–254, 316, 321, 344,
        463
survival
    mechanism(s), 194
    of the self, 70, 77–78, 80, 88–89,
        92, 170, 194, 204, 405,
        623–625, 629–630, 635,
        643–644
    of the species, 70, 74–75, 77–78,
        80, 89, 170, 623, 644
Sutherland, J., 330–331, 688
symbol(-ism), 20, 41, 45–46, 49, 54,
    105, 112, 116, 126, 143, 175,
    187, 228–231, 234, 261, 310,
    318, 325, 337, 394, 423, 425, 449,
    477, 525, 540, 592, 598, 612, 625,
    644
    equation, 532
    formation, 528, 539
    functioning, 441, 443

system
  nervous, 13, 331, 420, 508, 518
  psychical, 31, 91, 118, 156, 375
  primary, 9, 16, 20, 22, 56–57
  secondary, 9, 16–17, 20–21, 31, 57–58
  sensory, 48

talion principle, 161, 223, 229, 247, 388
Target, M., 592, 608, 612, 665
Thanatos *see* death instinct
Tower of Babel, 540, 708
transference, xxiii–xxiv, 3, 7, 17–20, 28, 31, 33, 35, 39–41, 49–50, 55, 80, 105, 109, 111, 123–129, 135, 148, 166, 188–189, 212, 217, 220, 251, 291–292, 304–307, 310–311, 319, 325–326, 344, 357–358, 367, 369, 373, 396, 402, 410–411, 425, 459, 464–471, 476, 481, 484, 488, 494, 507, 513, 522, 535–536, 545, 551–553, 556, 562, 571, 579–581, 583, 589, 591–592, 598, 600–601, 603–609, 611, 613, 620, 641, 648, 654 *see also*: countertransference
  experience, 486
  mirroring, 465, 468–469
  narcissistic, 127, 459, 465, 471, 487
  neurotic/neuroses, 109, 116, 218, 344, 476, 494, 607
  patient's, 188, 470, 484, 583, 590, 605, 607
  psychosis, 506
trauma, 3, 8–9, 11–13, 16, 20, 22, 24, 69, 125, 148–151, 159, 163, 172, 198–199, 209, 222, 293, 330, 337, 340, 344, 348, 353, 355–356, 373–374, 442, 451, 462, 464, 466, 497, 594, 626, 629, 631, 647, 651
Tribich, D., 514–516, 519, 677
Tronick, E., 588, 688

unconscious(ness) (Ucs.), 32, 36–37, 41, 45–46, 49–55, 57–58, 136, 539 *see also*: conscious(ness), fantasy, phantasy, preconscious(ness)
  idea(s), 4, 31, 36, 40, 45, 51–52, 80, 114–115, 136, 187, 416, 481, 577
  impulse, 162, 174–177, 187
  process(es), 10, 33, 128, 296, 416, 424, 477
  sense of guilt, 139, 145, 166
  wish, 27–28, 30–31, 35–36, 42, 44–46, 52, 79, 151, 251, 551
urethral stage, 229, 244

Valenstein, A. F., 150, 688
Valenstein, E. S., 645, 688
Vienna Circle, 191, 415
Vincent McLean, H., 469, 658
Vorus, N., xx, 256, 287, 289, 688
Voth, H., 494, 512, 520, 675

Wälder, R., 177, 688
Wallerstein, R. S., xviii, 688
Wangh, M., 553
Watson, J. S., 612, 669
Weber, M., 191
Weiner, J., 634, 688
Weinshel, E. M., 492, 512–515, 519, 662
Weinstein, L., 625, 664
Weiss, E., 469, 658
White, R. W., 34, 66, 688
Wilde, O., 60, 75
William Allison White (WAW), 564, 569–570
Wilson, M., 469, 658
Winnicott, D. W., xiv, xvii, xix, 201–202, 208, 288, 292–293, 295, 313, 331, 353–354, 356–412, 414, 418, 437–438, 454, 486–487, 493, 510, 515, 525–526, 586, 589, 592, 610, 613, 616, 626, 629–630, 635, 642–643, 646, 655–656, 688–690
wish fulfilment, 34–35, 37–38, 40, 43–44, 264, 266–268, 283
Wolff, P., 316, 690

world
    external, 44, 91, 93–95, 98–99,
        107–108, 124, 133–134, 138,
        145–146, 155–156, 158, 175,
        178–179, 181, 193, 227, 234,
        263, 272, 275–276, 282–283,
        287, 296, 302, 308, 372, 378,
        396–397, 405–406, 427–428,
        437, 451, 496, 518, 526, 616
    internal, xxiv, 95, 145, 165, 181,
        202, 206, 235, 247, 250, 265,
        276, 279, 312, 314, 323, 360,
        364, 372, 375, 402, 474, 500,
        526, 586, 594, 604, 606, 614,
        650
    object, 95, 102, 233, 323, 339, 358,
        442, 547, 594, 644
    outside, 44, 68, 103, 176, 272–273,
        279, 282, 427, 431, 433, 440,
        443–444, 447–448
    psychological, 235, 260, 460, 589,
        609, 627, 713

war
    First, 126, 165, 216, 326, 479
    Second, 172, 292, 330, 347

Yeomans, F. E., 513, 675
Young-Bruehl, E., 171–172, 257,
    690

Zetzel, E. R., 494, 545, 556, 690
zone(s)
    anal, 63–64, 68–69, 420
    erotogenic, 63–65, 68–71, 73, 331,
        392
    genital, 63–64, 70–71, 73, 75, 99,
        317, 420, 615
    libidinal, 336
    of interaction, 420
    oral, 63–64, 68, 316–317, 336, 392,
        420
    pregenital, 72, 74–75, 78
    primary, 70
    psycho-sexual, 244, 315

Made in the USA
Las Vegas, NV
15 April 2024